Gandhi Before India

ALSO BY RAMACHANDRA GUHA

Patriots & Partisans
India After Gandhi: The History of the World's Largest Democracy
How Much Should a Person Consume?
The Last Liberal and Other Essays
A Corner of a Foreign Field: An Indian History of a British Sport
Environmentalism: A Global History
An Anthropologist Among the Marxists and Other Essays
Savaging the Civilized—Verrier Elwin, His Tribals and India
The Use and Abuse of Nature (with Madhav Gadgil)
The Unquiet Woods

EDITED WORKS

Nature's Spokesman: M. Krishnan and Indian Wildlife
Makers of Modern India
The Picador Book of Cricket
Social Ecology

Gandhi Before India

RAMACHANDRA GUHA

ALFRED A. KNOPF   NEW YORK   2014

THIS IS A BORZOI BOOK
PUBLISHED BY ALFRED A. KNOPF

Copyright © 2013 by Ramachandra Guha

All rights reserved. Published in the United States by Alfred A. Knopf,
a division of Random House LLC, New York, and in
Canada by Random House of Canada Limited, Toronto,
Penguin Random House companies.

www.aaknopf.com

Originally published in hardcover in Great Britain
by Allen Lane, an imprint of Penguin Books Ltd., London, in 2013.

Knopf, Borzoi Books, and the colophon are registered trademarks of
Random House LLC.

Library of Congress Cataloging-in-Publication Data
Guha, Ramachandra.
Gandhi before India : how the Mahatma was made / Ramachandra Guha.
pages cm
Includes bibliographical references and index.
ISBN 978-0-385-53229-7 (hardcover)   ISBN 978-0-385-53230-3 (eBook)
1. Gandhi, Mahatma, 1869–1948. 2. East Indians—South
Africa—Politics and government. 3. South Africa—Politics and
government—1836–1909. 4. Statesmen—India—Biography. I. Title.
DS481.G3G824 2014
954.03'5092—dc23
[B]   2013025014

Front-of-jacket photograph © Bettmann/Corbis
Jacket design by Carol Devine Carson
Manufactured in the United States of America
First United States Edition

For E. S. Reddy

Indian patriot, South African democrat, friend and mentor to Gandhi scholars of all nationalities

Contents

Illustrations

All images are reproduced by kind permission of the Sabarmati Ashram Archives, Ahmedabad, apart from the following:

Images 1 and 2 by kind permission of the Nehru Memorial Museum and Library

Image 3 by kind permission of Iravati Guha

Image 17 by kind permission of E. S. Reddy

Image 29 by kind permission of the Tata Central Archives

Image 15 reproduced by permission of Getty Images

Image 16 reproduced by permission of Corbis Images

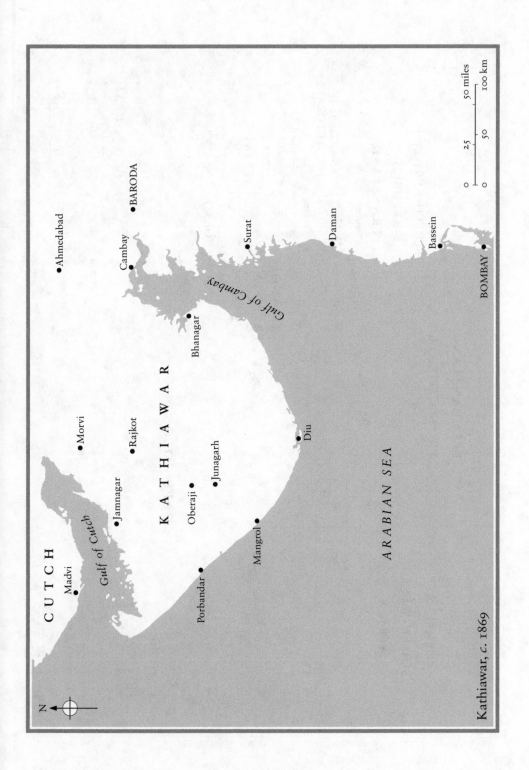

N

CUTCH

Madvi

Gulf of Cutch

Jamnagar

Morvi

Rajkot

KATHIAWAR

Oberaji

Junagarh

Porbandar

Mangrol

Diu

Bhanagar

Cambay

Gulf of Cambay

Ahmedabad

BARODA

Surat

Daman

Bassein

BOMBAY

ARABIAN SEA

Kathiawar, *c.* 1869

0   25   50 miles
0   50   100 km

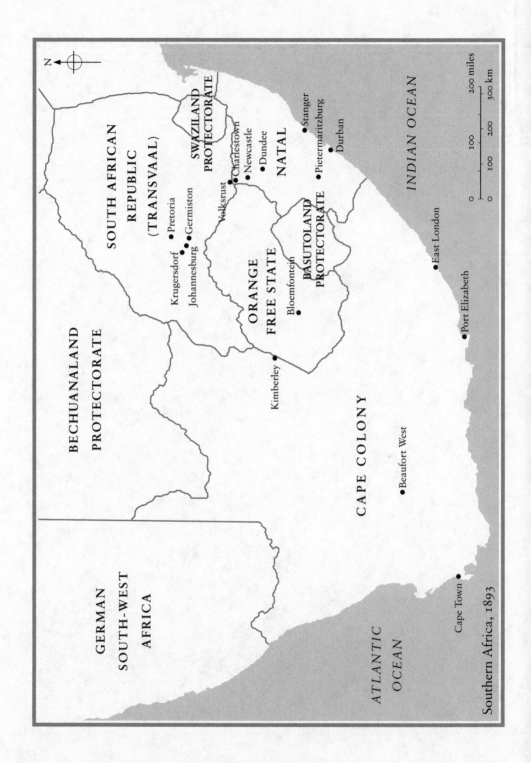

GERMAN
SOUTH-WEST
AFRICA

BECHUANALAND
PROTECTORATE

SOUTH AFRICAN
REPUBLIC
(TRANSVAAL)

• Pretoria
Krugersdorf •• Germiston
Johannesburg

Volksrust •

SWAZILAND
PROTECTORATE

Charlestown •
Newcastle •
Dundee •

NATAL

• Stanger
Pietermaritzburg •
• Durban

ORANGE
FREE STATE

Bloemfontein •

BASUTOLAND
PROTECTORATE

• Kimberley

CAPE COLONY

• Beaufort West

• East London

• Port Elizabeth

INDIAN OCEAN

ATLANTIC
OCEAN

Cape Town •

N

0   100   200 miles
0   100 200 300 km

Southern Africa, 1893

I understand more clearly today what I read long ago about the inadequacy of autobiography as history. I know that I do not set down in this story all that I remember. Who can say how much I must give and how much omit in the interests of truth? ... If some busybody were to cross-examine me on the chapters already written, he could probably shed much more light on them, and if it were a hostile critic's cross-examination, he might even flatter himself for having shown up the 'hollowness of many of my pretensions'.

—M. K. Gandhi, *An Autobiography,*
or the Story of My Experiments with Truth

Prologue: Gandhi from All Angles

I might never have written this book had I not spent the spring term of 1998 at the University of California at Berkeley. The university had asked me to teach a course on the history of environmentalism, till then the chief focus of my research and writing. But I was tired with the subject; I suggested that I instead run a seminar called 'Arguments with Gandhi'.

At the time, Gandhi's vision of an inclusive, tolerant India was being threatened from both ends of the political spectrum. From the right, a coalition of Hindu organizations (known as the Sangh Parivar) aggressively pushed for a theocratic state, a project Gandhi had opposed all his life. On the left, a growing Maoist insurgency rejected non-violent methods of bringing about social change. To show their contempt for the 'Father of the Nation', Maoists demolished statues of Gandhi across eastern India.

Despite these attacks from political extremists, Gandhi's ideas survived. They were given symbolic – but only symbolic – support by the Government of India, and more emphatically asserted by social workers and activists. The course I wished to teach would focus on Gandhi's contentious legacy. However, my hosts in Berkeley were unhappy with my proposal. They knew that my contribution to Gandhian studies was close to nil, whereas a course on environmentalism would always be popular in California, a state populated by energy entrepreneurs and tree-huggers. The university worried that a seminar on Gandhi would attract only a few students of Indian origin in search of their roots, the so-called 'America Born Confused Desis' or ABCDs.

Finally, after many letters back and forth, I was permitted to teach the course on Gandhi. But within me there was a nagging nervousness. What if my counsellors were correct and only a handful of students showed up, all Indian-Americans? On the long flight to the West Coast I could think of little else. I reached San Francisco on a Saturday; my class was due to meet for the first time the following Wednesday. On Sunday I took a walk down Berkeley's celebrated Telegraph Avenue. On a street corner I was handed a free copy of a local weekly. When I returned to my apartment I began to read it. Turning the pages, I came across an advertisement for a photo studio. It said, in large letters: 'ONLY GANDHI KNOWS MORE THAN US ABOUT FAST'. Below, in smaller type, the ad explained that the studio could deliver prints in ten minutes, in those pre-digital days no mean achievement.

I was charmed, and relieved. A Bay Area weekly expected its audience to know enough about Gandhi to pun on the word 'fast'. My fears were assuaged, to be comprehensively put to rest later that week, when a full classroom turned out to meet me. Thirty students stayed the distance. And only four of them were Indian by birth or descent.

Among my students was a Burmese girl who had fled into exile after the crushing of the democracy movement, a Jewish girl whose twin guiding stars were Gandhi and the Zionist philosopher Martin Buber, and an African-American who hoped the course would allow him to finally choose between Malcolm X and Martin Luther King Jr. There was also a Japanese boy, and plenty of Caucasians. In the class and in the papers they wrote, the students took the arguments with Gandhi in all kinds of directions, some of them wholly unanticipated by the instructor.

The course turned out to be the most enjoyable I have ever taught. This, I realized, was almost entirely due to my choice of subject. How many students in Berkeley would have enrolled for a course called 'Arguments with De Gaulle'? And if an American historian came to the University of Delhi and proposed a course entitled 'Arguments with Roosevelt', would there have been any takers at all? Roosevelt, Churchill, De Gaulle – these are all great national leaders, whose appeal steadily diminishes the further one strays from their nations' boundaries. Of all modern politicians and statesmen, only Gandhi is an authentically *global* figure.

What accounts for Gandhi's unique status? He worked in three different countries (and continents): Britain, South Africa and India. Anticolonial agitator, social reformer, religious thinker and prophet, he brought to the most violent of centuries a form of protest that was based on non-violence. In between political campaigns he experimented with the abolition of untouchability and the revival of handicrafts. A devout Hindu himself, he had a strong interest in other religious traditions. His warnings about individual greed and the amorality of modern technology, seemingly reactionary at the time, have come back into fashion as a result of the environmental debate.

Educated in Victorian England, making his name in racialist South Africa, Gandhi's life and work are writ large against the history (and geography) of his time. The years of his most intense political activity witnessed the rise of Bolshevism, the rise (and fall) of fascism, the two World Wars, and the growth of anti-colonial movements in Asia and Africa. While Gandhi was leading a mass movement based on non-violence in India, Mao Zedong was initiating a successful violent revolution in China.

To both scholar and lay person, Gandhi is made the more interesting by his apparent inconsistencies. Sometimes he behaved like an unworldly saint, at other times like a consummate politician. Asked by a British journalist what he thought of modern civilization, he answered: 'I think it would be a good idea.' Yet this foe of the West acknowledged three white men – Henry Salt, John Ruskin and Leo Tolstoy – among his mentors. This rebel who called the British Empire 'satanic' wept when London (a city he knew and loved) was bombed during the Second World War. And this celebrated practitioner of non-violence actually recruited Indians to serve in the First World War.

Gandhi enjoyed a long life and is enjoying a vigorous after-life. His message was communicated – or travestied, depending on one's point of view – in a film made by Richard Attenborough in 1982, a film that won nine Oscars and was a box-office hit. His example has inspired rebels and statesmen of the calibre of Martin Luther King, Nelson Mandela, the Dalai Lama and Aung San Suu Kyi. The techniques of non-violence that he fashioned have endured. A study conducted of some five dozen transitions to democratic rule concluded that in over 70 per cent of cases, authoritarian regimes fell not because of armed resistance but because of boycotts, strikes, fasts and other methods of protest pioneered by this Indian thinker.[1] Most recently, during the so-called 'Arab Spring', activists in Egypt, Yemen and other countries displayed photographs of Gandhi and closely studied his methods of struggle and protest.[2]

More than six decades after his death, Gandhi's life and legacy are discussed, and sometimes acted upon, in countries he barely even knew of. And he continues to loom large in the life of his native land. His ideas are praised as well as attacked; dismissed by some as dangerous or irrelevant, yet celebrated by others as the key to resolving the tension between Hindus and Muslims, low castes and high castes, humans and the natural environment.

Testimony to Gandhi's global significance is provided by the books about him that roll off the world's presses. These have been enabled by the publication by the Indian Government of the *Collected Works of Mahatma Gandhi*. The series runs to a hundred volumes, a colossal effort of editing and collation that includes tens of thousands of letters, speeches, essays, editorials and interviews that can be reliably attributed to Gandhi.

Gandhi wrote well, and he wrote a great deal. From 1903 to 1914, and again from 1919 to 1948, he published weekly newspapers in Gujarati and in English. While his prose was demotic and direct in both languages, his Gujarati writings are more intimate, since he shared a moral and cultural universe with the reader.[3] Because of the quantity of his prose, and perhaps its quality too, one might say that there was actually a fifth calling that Gandhi practised – that of editor and writer. This complemented and enhanced his other callings, with his views on politics and society (and much else) being articulated in periodicals owned or at least controlled by himself.

All (or almost all) of Gandhi's writings are now available in his *Collected Works*. Priced at Rs 4,000, or about £50, the English edition has recently been put on a CD-ROM. The volumes are also available on multiple websites. They have been industriously mined by Gandhi's biographers, and by those who have written studies of his religious thought, his economic thought, his philosophy of non-violence, his attitude towards women, and his views on drink, drugs and gambling.[4]

As a consequence of the easy availability of the *Collected Works*, Gandhi's ideas, campaigns, friendships and rivalries have come to be seen very largely – and sometimes exclusively – through the prism of his own writings. This reliance on Gandhi's words can often narrow the historical landscape against which his life and work were enacted. Sixty-five years after his death, the general public knows a good deal more about what Gandhi thought of the world, but virtually nothing at all of what the world thought of him.

A decade ago, after teaching that course in Berkeley, I decided I would write a many-sided portrait of Gandhi, which would explore his words and actions in the context of the words and actions of his family, friends, followers and adversaries. The *Collected Works* are indispensable, but they are only one source among many. So I began visiting archives that held the private papers of his contemporaries. I studied the papers of his major South African associates. I examined the letters to Gandhi and about Gandhi written by the many remarkable men and women who worked alongside him in the Indian freedom struggle. I examined the writings, published and unpublished, of Gandhi's four children.

I also studied the perceptions of those who opposed Gandhi. The officials of the British Empire had superb intelligence-gathering skills, as well as a fifty-year-long interest in Gandhi. They were obsessed with him in South Africa, where he was a constant irritant in their flesh, and still more obsessed with him in India, where he led millions of his compatriots in protest against the iniquities of British rule. In national and provincial archives in India, England and South Africa, I read the letters, telegrams, reports and dispatches whereby the functionaries of the Empire commented upon their most dangerous (not to say most distinguished) rebel.

Not all those who opposed Gandhi, of course, were British or Afrikaners. Many were Indians, and some, Indians of great distinction. These included two brilliant London-trained lawyers, the Muslim leader Muhammad Ali Jinnah and the leader of the low castes, B. R. Ambedkar; as well as the writer Rabindranath Tagore, the first Asian to win a Nobel Prize. These three are deservedly famous, but Gandhi had other major critics in India, as well as less well-known opponents of his work in South Africa. Their writings (published and unpublished) are vital to a fuller understanding of Gandhi's thought and practice. What Gandhi said and did makes sense only when we know what he was responding to.

Another crucial set of sources are contemporary newspapers. The first reference to Mohandas K. Gandhi in print appears to be in the *Kathiawar Times* in 1888, reporting his imminent departure to study law in London. But it is from his time in South Africa, and his assumption of a public role, that we find Gandhi appearing regularly in the news, at first in decidedly local newspapers such as the *Natal Mercury* and the Johannesburg *Star*, and later in more international and important periodicals such as *The Times* of London and the *New York Times*.

I cannot claim to have read the press all through Gandhi's long life. Still, I have consulted thousands of newspaper reports on the interest and controversy generated by his campaigns, both in South Africa and in India. Like the government intelligence reports, these present a day-to-day narrative of Gandhi, and like them again, they do so from all the places visited by a man always on the move. They give voice to people who are otherwise unknown: the peasants, workers, merchants and clerks who were powerfully affected by Gandhi, and whose views are captured in correspondents' reports and letters to the editor.

Searching for materials on or about Gandhi that are not in the *Collected Works*, I consulted archives in five countries (in four continents). These travels and researches were principally conducted to find material that did not carry my subject's name or signature. Yet I also found, to my pleasure and surprise, dozens of letters written by Gandhi himself that, for one reason or another, had not come to the attention of the compilers of the *Collected Works*.

The diversity and depth of this new – or at least so far unused – material is explained in greater detail in 'A Note on Sources' at the end of this book. Drawing on this research, I plan to write two volumes of biography, in an attempt to create a fuller sense of Gandhi's life, work and contexts. This, the first book, examines his upbringing in his native Gujarat, his two years as a student in London and, most intensively, his two decades as a lawyer, home-maker and community organizer in South Africa. The second book will cover the period from our subject's return to India in January 1915 to his death in January 1948. It will provide a social history of his political campaigns, of his reform movements and of everyday life in his ashram.

These studies of the African Gandhi and the Indian Gandhi each contain many different characters and stories. Some are charming, others tragic, yet others resonant with social or political meaning. The geographical breadth extends over Asia, Africa and Europe, and even, here and there, North America. The narrative flows from desert to mountain, from city to village, from river to sea. The historical breadth extends from the second half of the nineteenth century down to the present day.

In reading (and telling) these stories we meet Hindus, Muslims, Jews, Christians, Buddhists, Parsis, Jains, Sikhs, and even the odd atheist. Many characters come from the labouring classes – they include farmers, craftspeople, shopkeepers, housewives, scavengers and mineworkers. Others come from an elite background, being prosperous businessmen, powerful proconsuls, decorated generals and elected heads of state.

These diverse landscapes and human beings are given meaning by their relation to Mohandas K. Gandhi. It is his journey that we follow, from Gujarat to London to Natal and the Transvaal and then back to Gujarat, and on to a thousand places beyond. It is by tracing his steps and recalling his actions that we encounter these many landscapes and this range of remarkable people.

There are some striking resemblances between the central character in this story and his counterpart in the great Indian epic, the Ramayana. The hero of that story, Lord Ram, also travels long distances, sometimes willingly, at other times unwillingly. He too spends long periods in exile, and has a loyal and very supportive wife, whom (like Gandhi) he does not always treat with the respect and understanding she deserves. He is also a man of high moral character, who occasionally entertains dark and dangerous thoughts. Both Gandhi and Ram have powerful adversaries, who are not without a certain appeal of their own. Both men could not have done what they did, one in myth and the other in reality, without the self-effacing support of very many others. And both have enjoyed a vigorous and contentious after-life.

But one should not push the parallels too far. The morals that the Ramayana seeks to establish are cultural and familial – how to deal with one's wife, for example, or with one's father or step-mother, or how to uphold the *dharma* of caste and community. In the case of our own epic, the morals are more explicitly social and political. We are asked to choose between rule by foreigners and self-rule, between violence and non-violence, between the aggressive proselytizing of one's faith and the loving understanding of another, between a respect for natural systems and an arrogant disregard of them. Sometimes, *pace* the Ramayana, the 'right' choices may in fact involve a reversal of the traditional order, as in the abolition of Untouchability or the granting of equal rights to women.

That said, in both epics the morals are secondary. What really matters are the stories, the richness of the human experience they contain, the fascination of the central character and of those who worked with or fought against him.

The narrative of the current book begins with Gandhi's birth, in October 1869, and ends with his departure from South Africa in July 1914. Much of this time was spent as a lawyer and activist in Natal and the Transvaal. Gandhi's biographers have tended to skip hastily over this phase of his life, treating it as a prelude to his later, apparently more important, work in India. They have chosen to consider his life in teleological terms, with his work in South Africa preparing the way for his more important work in his homeland.[5]

Haste and teleology – these twin temptations – do injustice to both man and place. As social reformer, popular leader, political thinker and family man, Gandhi was fundamentally shaped by his South African experience. In turn, he had a profound impact on the history of that continent, with his ideas and attitudes influencing later struggles against racism.

When Gandhi first landed in Durban in 1893, South Africa was very much a nation-in-the-making. Its separate colonies governed themselves. Some, like Natal, were ruled by British expatriates; others, like the Transvaal, were ruled by Afrikaners of largely Dutch descent (then known as 'Boers'). In the only part of Africa with a European climate, the colonists set about creating a homeland for themselves. There were, of course, very many Africans who had lived there from long before the white man arrived. But through a series of wars and conquests they were being thoroughly subjugated.

Between the dominant Europeans and the subordinated Africans lay the Indians. They had come in as labourers, imported to work in the mines and sugar plantations, and on the railways. There were also a significant number of Indian traders, and a few professionals. By the time of Gandhi's arrival there were about 50,000 Indians in this part of the world, a majority of them in Natal.

Gandhi lived for long periods in both Natal and the Transvaal – roughly a decade in each. Natal was on the coast, dominated by the British, with an economy founded on sugar and coal. Transvaal was inland, ruled by the Boers, and going through a massive boom due to the discovery of gold. The material riches, relative underpopulation and glorious climate of both colonies was attracting settlers from

Europe as well as Asia. Gujaratis, Tamils and Hindi-speakers came across the Indian Ocean; Anglicans, Catholics, Jews and Theosophists via the Atlantic. These were all people in search of more – far more – material prosperity than they could ever find at home.

The great rush to colonize and claim South Africa took place at roughly the same time as the westward expansion of the United States. The attractions of open territory, of fabulous natural wealth (and natural beauty), of escape from an over-populated and class-ridden Old World – these were what the two processes of economic migration had in common. But whereas the European colonists of western America had merely to deal with the natives, their counterparts in southern Africa had this additional complicating factor – the presence of Indians from India, who were not indigenous but emphatically not European either.

It was in this strange scenario that Gandhi came to acquire, and practise, his four major callings – those of freedom fighter, social reformer, religious pluralist and prophet. In fact, an early (and now largely forgotten) associate of his once identified as many as *seventeen* identities that Gandhi bore in the years he spent outside India. 'South Africa is the grave of many reputations,' wrote this man, adding: 'It has certainly been the birth-place of a few, and one such is that of Mohandas Karamchand Gandhi. *Diwan*'s son, barrister, stretcher-bearer, pamphleteer, cultured thinker, courteous gentleman, manual labourer, nurse, teacher, agitator, propagandist, sterling friend, no man's enemy, ex-convict, *sadhu*, chosen leader of his people, and arch passive-resister.'[6]

Of these seventeen identities, the last has had the greatest impact on the history of the world. Gandhi gave the name 'satyagraha' (or truth-force) to the techniques of mass civil disobedience he invented in South Africa and later used in India, and which his followers or admirers used in other countries. Before Gandhi, those discontented with their superiors had either petitioned their rulers for justice or sought to attain justice by means of armed struggle. The distinctiveness of Gandhi's method lay in shaming the rulers by voluntary suffering, with resisters seeking beatings and imprisonment by breaking laws in a non-violent yet utterly determined manner.

In 1916, not long after Gandhi left South Africa, a publisher in a small town in central India brought out a history in Hindi of the satya-grahas Gandhi had led. The book was presented as 'the story of that heroic battle, which was the first of its kind in the history of the world', a battle where 'there were no guns and bombs and cannons' (and 'no shells thrown by aeroplanes' either), a battle which showed that 'strength of character can conquer any other kind of strength'. The publisher hoped the reader would 'swell with pride' as he learnt of how 'coolies and labourers' in the diaspora had 'shamed and shocked educated elites [in India] with their resolution and spirit.'[7]

At this time, Gandhi had been back barely a year in India. The British were solidly in control of the subcontinent. Still, what might have sounded hyperbolic in 1916 may seem more reasonable a century later. For the Indian freedom struggle, the civil rights movement in the United States, the civic resistance to Communism in Eastern Europe and China (including Tibet), the ongoing protests against military dictators in Burma and the Middle East, have all taken some or much inspiration from techniques of protest first forged by Gandhi in the Transvaal. The colossal and still expanding influence of satyagraha mandates a closer attention to the precocious protests of Indians in South Africa, to aid a deeper understanding of Gandhi in his time, and of his still unfolding legacy in ours.

Rather than rely on Gandhi's own recollections (contained in two books published a decade and a half after he left South Africa), I have here examined his early satyagrahas through the prism of contemporary documents. These letters, speeches, newspaper accounts, court cases and government reports give a more immediate sense of how Gandhi formulated his ideas of civil disobedience, of how he designed its methods and techniques, and how he mobilized people to court imprisonment. From these varied sources we can track how the protests unfolded and what forms they took, who followed Gandhi (and why) and who opposed him (and why), and where the funds for sustaining the resistance he led were coming from. The historical reconstruction of these first satyagrahas also throws a sharp light on a crucial period of South African history, as once separate colonies came together in a territorial Union that consolidated white sentiments and prejudices against the hopes and aspirations of the darker races.

The political Gandhi may be illuminated from more angles than his own. So also the personal Gandhi. Here too, the South African experience was fundamental and formative. Most Indians of Gandhi's generation worked and died in the same town or village in which they were born. In their everyday lives, they mostly met and spoke with people who had the same mother tongue and the same ancestral faith as they. By coming to South Africa, Gandhi was taken out of this conservative, static world into a country still in the process of being made. Durban and Johannesburg, the two cities where he lived and worked, were attracting migrants from Europe and Asia, and from other parts of Africa. In this heterogeneous and ever-changing society, Gandhi forged enduring friendships with individuals of ethnic and religious backgrounds very different from his own.

Strikingly, perhaps even tragically, the friends and associates of Gandhi's South African years are largely absent from the historical record. This is due to a combination of factors – an excessive reliance on the *Collected Works*; the tendency to treat the life before India as a prelude to the real story rather than as having an integrity of its own; and the tendency among biographers and hagiographers to magnify the role and personality of their main subject. Most Indians – and, following Attenborough's film, many non-Indians too – are moderately well acquainted with the colleagues and critics of the mature Gandhi. Yet they know very little about those who worked with him in South Africa. Here, his closest friends outside his family were two Hindus (a doctor-turned-jeweller and a liberal politician respectively); two Jews (one a journalist from England, the other an architect originally from Eastern Europe); and two Christian clergymen (one a Baptist, the other an Anglican).

These six men were, so to speak, the South African analogues of Gandhi's famous colleagues in the Indian freedom struggle – Jawaharlal Nehru, Vallabhbhai Patel, Subhas Chandra Bose, Madeleine Slade (Mira Behn), C. Rajagopalachari, Maulana Azad, *et al.* They are much less recognized (in some cases, unrecognized), although their impact on Gandhi's character and conduct may have been even more decisive, for they came into his life when he was not yet a great public figure or 'Mahatma' – as he was in India – but a struggling, searching activist.

The letters to and by these friends of his South African period illuminate Gandhi's anxieties, struggles and relationships in rich and often unexpected ways. Yet these materials have, remarkably, not been consulted by previous biographers. This may only be because they are not printed in the *Collected Works*, but rest in archives in New Delhi and Ahmedabad, in Pretoria and Johannesburg, in London and Oxford, and even, in one case, in the Israeli port town of Haifa.

*

In 1890, in 1900, in 1910, the majority of those who lived in South Africa were Africans. Sometimes, as sharecroppers and labourers, they worked for their white masters. In more remote areas, they lived away from them as herders and hunters. However, in both city and country-side, they rarely came into daily competition with the British or the Boers. There were few African traders, and still fewer African doctors or lawyers.

Because they were better educated and better organized, some Indi-ans could more actively challenge the facts of white domination. The rulers responded by changing the laws: by disallowing Indians from liv-ing in or opening shops in certain locations, from moving from one province to another, from seeking admission to the best schools, from importing brides from India with whom they could raise families and thus bring more Indians into the workforce. In so far as these restric-tions were later extended more thoroughly to the Africans, the Indians should really be considered to be among apartheid's first victims. And in so far as it was Gandhi who led the first protests against the racial laws, he should really be more seriously recognized as being among apart-heid's first opponents.

Gandhi's struggles in Natal and the Transvaal also shaped nationalist politics in India, as well as imperialist agendas in Great Britain. From one vantage point, Gandhi was merely a community organizer. How-ever, since his work had an impact on the politics of three continents, it had much larger consequences. In an age when even the telephone had not come into common use, when the fax and the internet lay many decades in the future, Gandhi's struggles thus carried connotations of what is now known as a 'global social movement'.

Gandhi's South African campaigns were an early example of 'diasporic nationalism', a nationalism later practised assiduously by (among others) Irishmen in Boston, Jews in New York, Palestinians in Tunis and Sikhs in Vancouver, who have likewise struggled both for civil rights in the land they happened now to live in and for freedom for their compatriots in the land they had left behind.

The predicament of Indians in South Africa in Gandhi's day also anticipated the predicament of Muslims in Europe and of Hispanics and Asians in North America today. Should immigrants be allowed to prac-tise their own faith and speak their own language? How can they combat discrimination in school and in the workplace? What forms of political organization are best suited to their needs and hopes? What are the rights and responsibilities of the host community and the migrants respectively, in maintaining social peace and democracy?

These questions are as urgent in our time as they were between 1893 and 1914, the years that Mohandas Gandhi lived in Natal and the Transvaal. Gandhi's African years show how the first phase of globalization, with its willing and sometimes unwilling migration of groups and communities, produced difficulties and discontents not dissimilar to those produced by our own, even more globalized world.

Middle Caste, Middle Rank

Gandhi's caste, the Banias, occupied an ambiguous place in the Hindu social hierarchy.[1] Above them lay the Kshatriyas and the Brahmins, traditionally rulers and priests. These were the 'upper' castes, so called because of the temporal and spiritual power they exercised. Below the Banias lay the Sudras and the Untouchables, who worked as farm labourers, artisans and scavengers. These were the 'lower' castes, so called because of the stigma attached to their traditional occupations, and because of their dependence, for instruction and occasionally for succour, on those above them.

The Banias were placed in the third stratum. They were, in more senses than one, middlemen. Their traditional occupation was trade and moneylending. They lent money to peasants and labourers, but also to kings and priests. They ran shops and stores that catered to all sections of society. The services they provided were indispensable; perhaps for this reason, the Banias were not trusted very much by those they served. In popular folklore, they were cunning and avaricious. They were said to maintain two sets of accounts: one written in a legible script and intended for the tax official; and a second, representing their real transactions, written in code. As one Hindi proverb had it, even God himself could not decipher the Banias' handwriting.

The Bania was a survivor, adept and adaptable, possessing the skills and instincts to see him through periods of adversity and political instability.[2] The Banias of Gujarat, writes their modern historian, were 'renowned for their smooth tongue' (in contrast to the arrogance of the Brahmin and the brashness of the Kshatriya). They cultivated 'a soft and persuasive way of speech' while extolling the quality of the goods they sold. 'They would always try to avoid a confrontation with customers and clients, backing down when necessary'. The code of the caste stressed 'hard work and frugal living'. Thus 'Baniyas were taught never to be idle, and they had in consequence a reputation for being a restless people, irritated when there was no work at hand'. [3]

In the political economy of medieval and early modern India, Banias played a crucial role. Agriculture, the mainstay of subsistence, required them to provide credit to peasants in periods of distress and scarcity. Warfare, the mainstay of politics, required them to advance money to, and hoard jewels for, chiefs seeking to expand or defend their territories.[4]

Gandhi's native region, Kathiawar (also known sometimes as 'Saurashtra'), is an ear-shaped peninsula some 23,000 square miles in area, in the central part of the western Indian state of Gujarat. Kathiawar has a coastline that extends over 600 miles, with many deep harbours. It has a long history of trade, both up and down the west coast of India, and with the Middle East and Africa. By one estimate, the peninsula's sea trade in the late sixteenth century was of the order of Rs 30 million a year. The items bought and sold included agricultural commodities, spices, jewels, arms and, sometimes, slaves. The transport, loading and unloading of these materials was done by labourers of the Sudra castes. However, their purchase, storage and sale was undertaken largely by the Banias.[5]

The peninsula was one of the first centres of urban civilization in the subcontinent. Cities have existed here from Harappan times, more than 3,000 years ago. Through the medieval period, Kathiawar was divided into many small principalities, each requiring a capital city. Dotted with towns small and large, sited on the coast as well as inland, Kathiawar in the late nineteenth century had an urban population of well over 20 per cent. (Elsewhere in the subcontinent, urban settlements accounted for barely 10 per cent of the population.)[6]

The ubiquity of agriculture and of warfare, the importance of coastal trade, a large urban population – these made Kathiawar most attractive to the Bania. Within the towns, merchants were organized in powerful guilds, which pressured kings to grant land and tax concessions for homes and businesses. Here they worked as merchants, shopkeepers and moneylenders. But what made the Banias of Kathiawar distinctive was that they were not confined to their traditional occupations. They also worked for the state, as revenue collectors and civil servants.[7] In Hindu states or kingdoms, the second most important person was the Diwan, or chief minister. This key post was almost always taken by a member of the two highest castes, Brahmin and Kshatriya. Not so in Kathiawar, where members of the merchant caste could aspire to become chief ministers. Among the many Bania Diwans in Kathiawar were Mohandas Gandhi's own father and grandfather.

Porbandar, Gandhi's birthplace, is on the south-west of the Kathiawar peninsula. It has a moderate climate, with sunny but not sweltering days, and evenings cooled by the sea breeze. An English visitor observed that Porbandar 'had received from Nature an unimaginable splendour of sea and sky'. Built entirely of stone and protected by great high gates, the city looked out 'from a jutting headland into the infinite expanse of ocean'. Its air was 'fresh with the salt spray' of the sea, which was 'driven along the beach from great combing breakers as they burst into white foam'.[8] The town gave its name to the state, which in the 1860s covered about 600 square miles, in a broad band along the coast. Closer to the sea the land was marshy, but as one moved inland it became arable. On this drier ground, the peasants of Porbandar grew rice and lentils.

A good quarter of the state's citizens lived in Porbandar town, participating in the commerce of the port, whose ninety-foot lighthouse could be seen from miles out at sea. There had once been 'a brisk trade with the ports of Sind, Baluchistan, the Persian Gulf, Arabia, and the east coast of Africa'. However, the emergence of Bombay had seriously diminished the traffic of ships and goods in and out of Porbandar. At the time of Mohandas Gandhi's birth in 1869, the main imports were timber from Malabar, cotton and tobacco from Bombay and Broach, and grain from Karachi.[9]

The rulers of Porbandar were from the Jethwa clan of Rajputs. They claimed to be the oldest ruling dynasty in Kathiawar, dating back to the ninth century. Their fortunes had ebbed and flowed down the years, as they fought with the neighbouring states of Nawanagar and Junagadh. As a consequence of battles lost or won, their capital had shifted around considerably, but from the late eighteenth century they had been based in the port town of Porbandar.[10]

Porbandar was one of some seventy chiefdoms in Kathiawar. So many states in such a small territory encouraged a proliferation in titles. Many rulers called themselves 'Maharaja' if they were Hindu, and 'Nawab' if they were Muslim. Others used more exotic titles such as 'Rao' and 'Jam Saheb'. The ruler of Porbandar was known as the 'Rana'.

The peninsula of Kathiawar has a stark, somewhat special beauty. Apart from the long coastline, it has several low ranges of hills, on which are perched temples holy to Hindus as well as Jains. In Gandhi's boyhood, the countryside teemed with wildlife: leopards, lions and deer abounded. The bird life remains spectacular: flamingos on the coast, storks and cranes in the fields, doves and warblers and hornbills in the woods.

The first census, conducted in 1872, estimated the peninsula's population at about 2.3 million. While 86 per cent of Kathiawaris were Hindus, they belonged to different castes and sub-castes, each with their distinctive rituals and ways of living. About 13 per cent of the population were Muslim. The bulk were descended from Hindu converts, but some claimed an Arabian or African lineage. Endogamous groups among the Muslims included the Memons, who belonged to the mainstream Sunni tradition of Islam, and the Khojas and Bohras, who were considered more heterodox because they followed a living leader.

The Muslims of Kathiawar were traders, farmers and artisans. However, despite their varying occupations and orientations, they all spoke the language of the land, Gujarati, rather than Persian or Urdu, the languages associated with Muslims in the north of India.[11] Then there were the Jains and the Parsis, more of whom were present here than in other parts of the subcontinent. The Jains were a sect that had broken away from the Hindu fold in about the ninth century BC. The Parsis, also known as Zoroastrians, had fled to India from Persia after the rise to power in that land of the Shia branch of Islam. The Jains and the Parsis, adding to the heterogeneity of Kathiawar, were both admired for their scholarship and business acumen. The Jains were further respected for their austere personal lives; the Parsis, for their easy emulation of Western manners and mores.

Unlike in eastern or southern India, the British did not choose to rule over Kathiawar directly. About 80 per cent of the peninsula remained with Indian rulers. These potentates were tolerated, so long as they recognized the military and political superiority of the British, and allowed them to monitor trade and the movement of people.

The British placed the chiefs of Kathiawar in seven categories. Class I rulers had full jurisdiction over their subjects: they could, provided they followed due process, convict criminals, and even hang them. Those in lower categories were denied the powers of capital punishment and of extended imprisonment. Class VII chiefs, for example, had to obtain the permission of the British to levy fines of more than Rs 15 or to impose sentences longer than fifteen days in jail.

The states of Kathiawar were divided into four geographical divisions, each with a British agent, to whom the chiefs reported. Some towns had British garrisons; others, British railway engineers or Christian missionaries. Detachments of troops led by white officers visited ports and towns at subtle intervals. Sometimes a higher dignitary came calling – the Governor of Bombay perhaps, or even the Viceroy. For them large *darbars* were held and hunting expeditions organized. The pomp and the hospitality was a sign of princely deference to the Raj; it made clear to everyone who, ultimately, was in charge.[12]

Of the seventy-four chiefs in Kathiawar, only fourteen were placed in Class I. The Rana of Porbandar was one of them. This fact was broadcast to his 70,000 subjects, among them the Gandhis, a family that for several generations had been in the service of the state. The first Gandhi in public service, named Lalji, migrated from Junagadh State to work in Porbandar. Lalji Gandhi served under the Diwan, as did his son and grandson. Only in the fourth generation of service did a Gandhi achieve the coveted post of Diwan, or chief minister. This was Uttamchand Gandhi, also known as 'Ota Bapa', 'Ota' being a diminutive of his first name, and 'bapa' the Gujarati word for 'father' or 'respected elder'.

Uttamchand Gandhi's first job was as Collector of Customs in Porbandar port. He was then asked to negotiate the transfer of slivers of land between Porbandar and Junagadh, so that each state could consolidate its territory. Proficiency in both jobs was rewarded with the prize post of first minister to the king.

As Diwan of Porbandar, Uttamchand Gandhi put the state's finances in order. He also secured the trust and good faith of the British overlord. When two Englishmen were murdered by bandits along the Porbandar–Jamnagar border, Uttamchand Gandhi told his ruler to say that the place where the crime was committed lay in the other state. The hills where the murders took place were remote and valueless; better not to claim them, if that disavowal helped bring Porbandar closer to the Raj and its rulers.[13]

Uttamchand Gandhi seemed set for a long tenure as Diwan, when the Rana of Porbandar suddenly died. The male heir was too young to ascend the throne, so the power devolved in the interim to his mother, the Queen Regent. She resented the Diwan's prestige and influence; by one account, she even sent a body of troops to attack his house. Uttamchand Gandhi then left Porbandar and settled in his ancestral village of Kutiyana in Junagadh State.[14]

The Nawab of Junagadh sent for Uttamchand Gandhi to ask if he needed anything from the *darbar*. The visitor, showing up at the palace, saluted the Nawab 'with his left hand in outrage of all convention'. When a courtier chastised him, Uttamchand replied that 'in spite of all that I have suffered I keep my right hand for Porbunder still'.[15]

After the death of the Queen Mother in 1841, Uttamchand Gandhi returned to Porbandar. His property was restored. The family story says that the new rana, Vikmatji, urged him to resume the office of Diwan, which he declined. The records in the archives complicate the tale. There was a British garrison in Porbandar, paid for from the state's funds. The town's merchants complained that the soldiers were often drunk and harassed them for cash. Vikmatji thought that since there was little threat of piracy, the soldiers could be sent back to Bombay. Uttamchand Gandhi disagreed; the British, he said characteristically, had still (if not always) to be humoured.[16]

Vikmatji listened at the time; but remained unhappy with the burden the garrison put on his finances. In 1847 he chose Uttamchand's son Karamchand (known as Kaba) as his Diwan, giving him a silver inkstand and inkpot as the sign of his office. The new Diwan was just twenty-five, closer in age to Vikmatji, and more amenable to the ruler's wishes (and whims) than his tough and overbearing father.

Kaba Gandhi was short and stocky, and wore a moustache. He had little formal education; studying briefly in a Gujarati school before joining the Rana as a letter-writer and clerk. He enjoyed his ruler's trust, became Diwan at a young age, and by 1869 had given more than two decades of service in that post. In that time he had also married three times. His first two wives died early, but not before producing a daughter apiece. The third marriage proved childless. With no heir in sight, he sought his wife's permission to take another consort (permitted under traditional Hindu law).

The request granted, Kaba Gandhi chose a woman twenty-two years younger as his fourth wife. Named Putlibai, she came from a village in Junagadh State. They were married in 1857, and in quick succession she bore him three children. A son, Laxmidas, was born in or around the year 1860. A daughter named Raliat was born two years later, followed, in about 1867, by a second son named Karsandas.[17]

In the spring of 1869 Putlibai was pregnant once more. As she awaited the birth of her fourth child, the state of Porbandar was mired in controversy, caused by the actions of Kaba Gandhi's ruler and pay-master, Rana Vikmatji. In April, a slave named Luckman as well as an Arab soldier were killed on the orders of the king. The former in particular met with a gruesome end. His ears and nose were slit and then he was thrown off the town walls to his death.

Told of the killings, the British agent asked Rana Vikmatji for an explanation. The Rana replied that the slave Luckman was an attendant to his eldest son, whom he had made a 'habitual drunkard'. When the Rana and his wife were out of town, Luckman promoted his prince's 'indulgence in ardent spirits', as a result of which he 'expired in extreme agony'. The Rana had to punish the 'murderer of our son'; he admitted to having ordered the cutting of nose and ears, but claimed the deadly fall was an accident.

As for the Arab soldier, Rana Vikmatji said he had entered the *zenana*, the women's quarters of the palace, where he 'took hold of our late son's widow' and attempted to molest her. The soldier too had to be put to death, for violating 'the fidelity he owed to his master, and like a robber secretly and at night invad[ing] the sanctity of the zenana so jealously guarded by Hindoos, especially Rajputs'.

The British were unpersuaded by the Rana's explanations. In view of these 'serious instances of abuse of power', his status was downgraded – previously a prince of the First Class, he would now be put in the Third Class. He was deprived of the power of capital punishment over his subjects. As a mark of good behaviour he had to establish criminal courts run on modern principles of justice.[18]

The archival record of these incidents in Porbandar does not contain any hint of the feelings of the Rana's Diwan. In a small state with a small court, one suspects that Kaba Gandhi knew of the close relationship between the prince and his slave. What advice did the Diwan give his ruler? Did he counsel against the mutilation of the slave or the execution of the soldier? Did he help in drafting Vikmatji's letter of explanation? To such questions we have no answer. But of the fact that

Kaba Gandhi felt his ruler's demotion most keenly there can be no doubt. News of the king's troubles would have reached the servants, and Kaba's pregnant wife Putlibai too.

It was on 10 September 1869 that the Bombay Government formally downgraded Rana Vikmatji by making him a Ruler of the Third Class. Three weeks later, amidst this background of violence and humiliation, the wife of the Rana's longserving Diwan gave birth to her fourth child. He was a boy, who was named Mohandas Karamchand Gandhi.

Since the year 1777, the Gandhi family had lived in a three-storey house close to one of the old city gates of Porbandar. The rooms – twelve in all – were large but with little light. On the second floor there was a large balcony; this was where the family repaired in the evenings, to refresh themselves with the sea breeze. Below the house was a tank to store water. Since the aquifer under Porbandar was brackish, it was necessary to harvest and husband rainwater. Before the monsoon, the roof of the Gandhi home was cleaned. Then as the rain ran down it was purified by some lime, attached to the mouth of a pipe which linked the roof to the water tank below.[19]

Putlibai's youngest son, Mohandas, was born in a room on the ground floor. A later visitor wrote, 'the room is dark. The corner is darker still. No window opens out [to] the verandah. A small door opens out in another room just behind this one at [the] opposite corner.'[20]

As was customary in Indian households, the baby Mohandas was looked after by the women around him. Apart from his mother and his aunts, his girl cousins and especially his elder sister Raliat took turns holding and playing with him. The sister recalled that, as a little boy, Mohandas was 'restless as mercury'. He could not 'sit still even for a little while. He must be either playing or roaming about. I used to take him out with me to show him the familiar sights in the street – cows, buffaloes and horses, cats and dogs ... One of his favourite pastimes was twisting dogs' ears'.[21]

Gandhi's mother, Putlibai, was born in a village named Dantrana, set amidst hills and on the banks of a river thirty miles inland from Porbandar. Her father was a shopkeeper. The American scholar Stephen Hay points out that Mohandas's mother 'would have had to develop a good deal of patience and forbearance as a young bride, for her husband's other wife, whom she had in a sense displaced, was both ill and barren, and the two lived under the same roof for some years'.[22]

The household that Putlibai ran in Rajkot was vegetarian. Like other members of their caste, the Gandhis never cooked meat or eggs. *Hobson-Jobson*, that compendium of customs and manners prevalent in nineteenth-century India, notes of the Banias of Gujarat that they 'profess[ed] an extravagant respect for animal life'.[23] Their fastidiousness had made the Banias an object of derision. The meat-eating castes disparaged them as '*dhili dal*', soft like lentils. In turn, the merchant castes looked down on 'what they saw as the dirty and degrading eating habits of most non-Baniyas'.[24]

Some Bania households refused to eat vegetables grown 'under the ground', such as onion and garlic. Bania women watched vigilantly over their cooking fires, lest a passing insect enter the pot and pollute the food. Somewhat unusually, Kaba Gandhi would help his wife cut and clean the vegetables in preparation for the evening meal.

The Rajputs of Kathiawar (the Ranas of Porbandar included) liked hunting, smoking and drinking. The peasants of the peninsula enjoyed the same pleasures, albeit at less regular intervals. Banias like the Gandhis rigorously eschewed meat, tobacco and alcohol. Yet their vegetarian cuisine was subtle and wide-ranging. The main cereals were millet and rice. There were also many varieties of lentils. With these staples went an assortment of special snacks, many distinctive chutneys and pickles, several very fine desserts, but also a unique mixing within the meal of spicy and sweet dishes.[25]

Another feature of the Gandhi household was piety. Putlibai was a woman of self-sacrificing discipline and a stoic religiosity, who (as her son remembered) would

> not think of taking her meals without her daily prayers. Going to *Haveli* – the Vaishnava temple – was one of her daily duties . . . She would take the hardest vows and keep them without flinching. Illness was no excuse for relaxing them . . . To keep two or three consecutive fasts was nothing to her. Living on one meal a day during *Chaturmas* was a habit with her. Not content with that she fasted every alternate day during one *Chaturmas*. During another *Chaturmas* she vowed not to have food without seeing the sun. We children on those [rainy] days would stand, staring at the sky, waiting to announce the appearance of the sun to our mother.[26]

The sub-caste the Gandhis belonged to was known as Modh Bania, the prefix apparently referring to the town of Modhera, in southern Gujarat. Their *kul devata*, or family deity, was Ram. There was a Ram temple in Porbandar. (One of the temple's founders was a Gandhi.) The region was steeped in the traditions of Vaishnavism, the worship of Vishnu and especially his avatars Ram and Krishna. Up the coast from Gandhi's place of birth lay the town of Dwarka, where Krishna is believed to have lived in adulthood, and which since the ninth century AD (at least) has been one of the great pilgrim centres of the Hindu tradition.[27]

Mohandas's mother introduced him to the mysteries – and beauties – of faith. Putlibai was devout, but not dogmatic. Born and raised a Vaishnavite, she became attracted to a sect called the Pranamis, who incorporated elements of Islam into their worship. The sect's founder was a Kshatriya named Pran Nath who lived in Kathiawar in the eighteenth century. He was widely travelled, and may even have visited Mecca. The Pranami temple in Porbandar that Putlibai patronized had no icons, no images; only writing on the wall, deriving from the Hindu scriptures and from the Koran. Putlibai's ecumenism extended even further, for among the regular visitors to her home were Jain monks.[28]

In 1874, when Mohandas was five, his father moved from Porbandar to Rajkot, on being appointed an adviser to the Thakore, or king, of that state. Two years later he was promoted to the office of Diwan. Kaba Gandhi now had to supervise the state's finances, the registration of all properties, the working conditions of public officials, and Rajkot's trade with other states. As Diwan of Rajkot, Karamchand also served on the Rajasthanik Court, a body of elders set up to mediate disputes between different chiefdoms in Kathiawar.[29]

We do not know why Kaba Gandhi made the move to Rajkot. Perhaps he left Porbandar because his ruler had been demoted to Third Class status. Or perhaps he calculated the new assignment had more prestige. The Agent to the Kathiawar States lived in Rajkot. Since he had the British Crown and the British Army behind him, the Agent was the most powerful man in the peninsula. Moving to Rajkot enhanced Kaba Gandhi's connection to the paramount power. Notably, the Gandhis retained their links with Porbandar. Shortly after Kaba shifted to Rajkot, his younger brother Tulsidas was appointed by Rana Vikmatji as his Diwan.

As the centre of the British presence in Kathiawar, Rajkot had a stud farm, a mission run by Irish Presbyterians, an Anglican Church and a British garrison. It was an important railway junction, with lines linking it to other towns in the peninsula. Rajkot was also home to the Rajkumar College, modelled on a British public school, where the sons of the Kathiawari chiefs were sent to acquire the elements of an English education. Established in 1870, four years before Kaba Gandhi moved to the town, the College had a 'fine building in the Venetian Gothic style', as well as a gymnasium, racquet courts, a rifle range and a cricket pavilion.[30]

As an important man in the town – and region – Kaba Gandhi may occasionally have entered the portals of Rajkumar College in Rajkot. But the school itself was barred to his children. It was restricted to those of authentically Rajput lineage, who might take over as Ranas or Maharajas of their principalities. Some Muslim boys were allowed in – these being the sons or nephews of Nawabs. However, there was no question of a Bania student being admitted into the College.

Kaba Gandhi moved to Rajkot in 1874; his family joined him two years later, on his confirmation as Diwan. The boy Mohandas may (or may not) have attended a primary school in Porbandar. But of his schooling in Rajkot we have some very firm and reliable evidence. This is contained in two books written in the 1960s by a retired headmaster who, in a spring-cleaning operation, stumbled upon the records of Mohandas's years in school.[31]

On 21 January 1879, Mohandas Karamchand Gandhi was admitted into the Taluk School, a short walk from his home in the district of Darbargadh. The subjects taught to Mohandas were Arithmetic, Gujarati, History and Geography. He was expected to learn 'easy mental arithmetic', read and memorize snatches of poetry, take accurate dictation, and acquaint himself with the main rivers and towns of western India.

To begin with the boy's attendance was spotty: in the calendar year 1879 he went to school for only 110 days out of 238. This showed in the results of the final examination, where Mohandas was placed in the lower half of the class. In one set of tests he scored 41.25 per cent (the highest ranked student got 76.5 per cent, the lowest 37.6 per cent). In a second set of exams he did slightly better – at 53 per cent his performance was twelve percentage points above the dullard of the class, but also twelve points below the class leader.

In October 1880, Mohandas appeared for an examination to gain admission to Kattywar High School.[32] Established in 1853, it was the oldest high school in the Peninsula. Mohandas did well in the entrance test – scoring 64 per cent – and was enrolled in the general register of the school. Now, for the first time, he would learn English along with the other subjects.

Kattywar High School was housed in a handsome two-storey structure built with a grant from the Nawab of Junagadh. Classes ran from 11 a.m. to 5 p.m. on weekdays (with an hour's recess for lunch). On Saturdays, the school closed half an hour early. English teaching was given the maximum time – ten hours a week, devoted to reading, spelling and copying; that is to say, to the nurturing of skills essential to employment in the bureaucracy.

In 1881 the Gandhis moved from rented premises to their own home. Kaba Gandhi had bought a large house built in the Kathiawari style, an arched entrance leading into a courtyard around which the rooms were built. It was less than a mile from the high school, so Mohandas walked to his classes, wearing traditional Kathiawari dress – long, loose pyjamas, a buttoned-up tunic and a close-fitting cap.

The chronicler of Gandhi's schooldays tells us that his performance in his new school was 'discouraging'. In his first year, he passed in Arithmetic and Gujarati, but was 'one of the three pupils who secured no marks at all in Geography'. In the end-of-year examination, he ranked 32nd out of 34 students in his division. The next year, 1882, Mohandas hardly attended school, apparently because his father had fallen ill. He could not appear for the annual examination. However, in 1883 he became more diligent. His attendance was regular, and in tests held at the end of the year he averaged a creditable 68 per cent in four subjects, these being Arithmetic, Gujarati, History and Geography, and English. In the terminal examination held in April 1884, he slipped slightly, ending with an average of 58 per cent.

Decades later, after Gandhi had become famous, an American journalist asked his sister Raliat whether her brother was 'a good pupil in school'. She answered: 'He was considered a clever student in his school. He always kept first rank'. Unfortunately, the historical record is at variance with the recollections of a loving sister.[33]

At home, Mohandas Gandhi mostly met members of his own, Modh Bania, caste. Among his classmates at Kattywar High School were Bania boys of other sub-castes as well as some Brahmins. He was also becoming acquainted, for the first time, with Christians and Christianity. Rajkot had several churches (Porbandar had none), and some very energetic missionaries. An Irish Presbyterian based in Rajkot, noticing that 'the Brahmans and Vaniyas are everywhere looked up to as the intellectual class', thought the conversion of upper-caste men could spark a mass exodus from the Hindu fold. The minister parked himself at street corners, acquainting passers-by with the greatness of Christ and the benefits of coming under His care. Mohandas heard the preacher on his way to school, but hurried on, displeased by the calumnies cast on his family's gods.[34]

There were no Christian boys in Kattywar High School, but there were several Parsis, as well as a few Muslims. It was a Muslim named Sheikh Mehtab who became Mohandas's closest friend. The son of a jailer in the nearby Gondal State, Mehtab was introduced to Mohandas by his elder brother Karsandas. Karsandas Gandhi and his Muslim friend were seriously uninterested in their studies. Both failed their exams repeatedly, so that they came to be in the same class as Mohandas, who was several years younger than them.[35]

As Mohandas later recalled, Mehtab 'could run long distances and extraordinarily fast. He was an adept in high and long jumping'. The school's headmaster, a modernizing Parsi named Dorabji Gimi, was very keen on sports and athletics. Whereas Mohandas was an unwilling and incompetent performer, Mehtab was ready to play, compete, and win. Their friendship was founded on this difference, on this very typical admiration for the tall, strong sportsman on the part of a boy who was both shy and unathletic. They became close, so friendly that on one occasion they went to a studio to have a joint portrait taken. The photograph, which has survived, shows the two of them sitting on adjacent chairs. Mohandas's right hand slips diffidently off an ornate table, while Mehtab's rests with a confident authority. The older boy is several inches taller. He is wearing a turban; Mohandas, a cap. From their postures it seems quite clear that it was not Mohandas who was the dominant partner in the relationship.[36]

Early in their friendship, Mehtab suggested to Mohandas that his lack of stature was due to his not eating meat. Besides, there was this verse, attributed to the Gujarati poet Narmad, which in translation ran:

> Behold the mighty Englishman,
> He rules the Indian small,
> Because being a meat-eater,
> He is five cubits tall.

Mehtab cooked meat for his friend by the river, in a house far away from the Gandhi home. The new food did not agree with Mohandas; besides, he feared the disapproval of his mother. When she asked, as she often did, what he had eaten that day at school, what answer would he give her? He was made more uncomfortable by Mehtab taking him one day to a brothel. His friend had paid the bill beforehand, but the novice was 'almost struck blind and dumb in this den of vice'. Since he did not make any move, the prostitute became angry and showed him the door. The experience was chastening, and Mohandas drew away from the company of Sheikh Mehtab.[37]

Young Mohandas was also distracted from his studies by a new companion at home, his wife Kasturba. The precise date of their marriage is unknown. Even the year is disputed – 1883 by most accounts (since Gandhi remembered being married at the age of thirteen), but 1882 or 1881 by others.[38] It was then common for Indians to marry very early. In fact, Mohandas had been betrothed twice already; both times, the girl had died before the marriage could be finalized. When the alliance with Kasturba was confirmed, the family chose to have a triple wedding – so that Mohandas's brother Karsandas and a cousin would get married at the same time as him.

The ceremony was held in the Gandhis' old home town, Porbandar. All that the bridegroom remembered of the marriage was 'the prospect of good clothes to wear, drum beating, marriage processions, rich dinners, and a strange girl to play with'. Some additional excitement was provided by his father appearing for the ceremony swathed in bandages, as a result of the coach that was bringing him to Porbandar toppling over.[39]

Kasturba was from a Bania family in Porbandar. Her father, Makanji Kapadia, was a prosperous merchant, who traded in cloth and cotton.[40] The family lived in a handsome two-storey house, which had twenty rooms and a large water-tank underneath. The house had wooden staircases, as well as elegantly carved shelves and door frames. The walls of the Gandhi home were bare, but those of the Kapadia residence had paintings displayed on them.[41]

Some months after the marriage, Kasturba moved to Mohandas's home in Rajkot. Our knowledge of how the young couple got along – or did not get along – is based entirely on the recollections of the husband. He was, he says, 'passionately fond' of his wife. 'Even at school I used to think of her, and the thought of nightfall and our subsequent meeting was ever haunting me.' Fondness shaded into possessiveness; thus Mohandas was 'for ever on the look out regarding her movements, and therefore she could not go anywhere without my permission'. Even visits to the temple with girlfriends attracted his jealousy. There was, at least on his part, a strong sexual attraction. Kasturba was illiterate; Mohandas was 'very anxious to teach her', but 'lustful love' left him no time.[42]

In the latter half of 1885 the head of the Gandhi household fell seriously ill. The children took turns nursing him. As Mohandas's hands were 'busy massaging' his father's legs, his 'mind was hovering about the bed-room' – this despite the fact that Kasturba was pregnant, which meant that 'religion, medical science and commonsense alike forbade sexual intercourse'. One night, Mohandas was massaging the old man when an uncle offered to take over his duties. The sixteen-year-old seized the chance and 'went straight to the bed-room'. He woke up his sleeping wife and prepared for a bout of love-making. A few minutes later they were disturbed by a knock on the door. It was a servant, come to inform them that Kaba Gandhi had just died.

Forty years later, Mohandas wrote, with an enduring sense of guilt and shame, that 'if animal passion had not blinded me, I should have been spared the torture of separation from my father during his last moments'. When Kasturba lost their baby to a miscarriage a few weeks later, he blamed himself for that, too. It was his inability to control his consuming 'carnal desire' that had led to this 'double shame'.[43]

From personal history remembered – or misremembered – let us return to the firm grounding provided by Mohandas Gandhi's marks in school. In the summer of 1885, he performed creditably in his fifth grade examinations, averaging 55.75 per cent and coming third in his class. He did unexpectedly well in Mathematics (85 per cent), for which he was awarded a scholarship endowed by two Kathiawari princes. The next year his acquaintance with the English language deepened, when he was subjected to 200 pages from Addison's *Spectator* and made to memorize 750 lines of Milton's *Paradise Lost*. He came fourth in the end-of-year examination – now, in the words of the man who discovered his mark-sheets, Mohandas 'could no longer be described as a mediocre student'.

In the last weeks of December 1886, Mohandas was admitted to Grade VII, the highest class in the school. In preparatory tests conducted by his own school he scored an average of 31.8 per cent in five subjects. This poor performance reflected nervousness, since he was soon to take the school-leaving examination known as Matriculation, conducted by Bombay University. In the third week of November 1887, Mohandas went to Ahmedabad to sit the Matric exam, travelling by train. This was his first journey by that mode of transport, as well as his first visit to the largest city in the Gujarati-speaking world.

The Matriculation of 1887 was, in purely intellectual terms, the sternest test of Mohandas's life. Some of the question papers he confronted have survived. For his English paper he had to 'write an essay of about 40 lines on the advantage of a cheerful disposition'. Among the terms he had to define were 'pleonasm' and 'apposition'. For the Arithmetic exam, he had to calculate some very complicated equations, running into tens of decimal points. The Natural Science paper obliged him to provide the chemical formulae of, among other substances, lime and sulphuric acid. The History and Geography test asked him to 'write a short history of Puritan Rule in England' and to draw a map tracing the course of the Rhine. To display his knowledge of Gujarati, he had to translate into that language a passage in English which suggested that instead of erecting statues to (and of) Queen Victoria, the Golden Jubilee of her reign would be more appropriately marked by raising a fund 'devoted to enabling India to take her place in the new industrial world'.

In January 1888, the Matriculation results were published in the *Kattywar Gazette*. More than 3,000 candidates had sat the test, of whom less than 30 per cent were successful. Mohandas was one of them. He did best in English and Gujarati, averaging about 45 per cent in each, but less well in Mathematics and History/Geography. His overall percentage was a modest 40 per cent. He was ranked 404th in the Province, out of 823 students who had qualified in the examination.[44]

Outside school, Mohandas's education was enriched by his growing exposure to Gujarati literature. In the nineteenth century, the advent of the printing press and the appearance of the first newspapers gave an enormous boost to the languages of India. Gandhi's mother tongue was no exception. The first Gujarati novel appeared in 1866, three years before his birth. In the same decade major works of prose and poetry were published by Narmadasankar Lalshankar (1833–66), 'Narmad', the man who, at one remove, had inspired the young Mohandas to experiment with eating meat. The writings of medieval poets appeared for the first time in printed editions – among them the works of Narsing Mehta, a Vaishnava preacher much beloved in Gujarat, who composed many odes in praise of Krishna, and who observed that God appears only to those who could feel the pain of others. These novels and poems were circulating in households such as Gandhi's, being read by young men of his age who had his familiarity with the printed word.[45]

The writers whom Mohandas read most closely were Narmad and the novelist Govardhanram Tripathi (1855–1907). Both were improving reformers who saw British rule as a challenge to the Gujaratis, alerting them to their own faults and weaknesses. Narmad was against caste, against religious dogmatism, and for the remarriage of widows. He was also sharply critical of the corrupt and nepotistic ways of Indian rulers. Govardhanram Tripathi similarly deplored the tribalism of caste and the oppression of women; like Narmad, he thought British rule would shame Indians into discarding outmoded social practices and institutions.[46]

Narmad and Govardhanram were among the writers the young Gandhi read in Rajkot, their works and words merging or clashing with the words he read in school, exchanged with his friends, or listened to at home.

Gandhi's father and grandfather had become Diwans of Porbandar without any formal education. By the 1880s, however, systems of governance and administration were more structured. No longer would a quick if untrained intelligence suffice. An English education and an acquaintance with modern ideas were obligatory for young Indians seeking high office in British India, or indeed in the native states.

By the standards of the Bombay Matriculation, Mohandas Gandhi's performance was undistinguished. Within his own family his scholastic record shone more brightly. His eldest brother, Laxmidas, had dropped out of school and become a minor official in Porbandar State. His other brother Karsandas had not been sent up to sit the Bombay University examination. As a successful Matriculate, Mohandas was the exception – his family expected him now to acquire more certificates.

In January 1888, Mohandas K. Gandhi enrolled for a BA degree in Samaldas College in Bhavnagar. Named for the state's Diwan, the College was the first degree-granting institution in Kathiawar. Mohandas travelled to Bhavnagar with a school friend, undertaking the first part of the journey by camel cart, the second by railway. He rented a room in a Vaishnavite locality. Here he would stay alone, and cook his own food.

There were thirty-nine students in Mohandas's class – four were Parsis, the rest Hindus of either a Brahmin or Bania background.[47] The subjects offered for the BA were English, Mathematics, Physics, Logic and History. There were five hours of lectures every day. The newcomer had particular difficulty with algebra. Once, when the mathematics teacher asked him to come to the blackboard and solve a sum, Mohandas pretended not to hear.

In Bhavnagar, Mohandas was homesick (for his wife, and also for his mother's food) and suffered from frequent headaches. When the first end-of-term examination was held in April 1888 he appeared for only four papers out of seven. Even these he did not do well: in English, for example, he got a bare 34 per cent.[48]

Mohandas returned home for the summer vacation. A family friend came visiting, a 'shrewd and learned' Brahmin named Mavji Dave. He advised Putlibai to withdraw her son from the Samaldas College and send him to London to qualify as a barrister instead. The BA took four or five years, whereas one could qualify as a lawyer in half that time. With a barrister's certificate from London, said Mavji Dave to Mohandas's mother, 'he could get the Diwanship [of Porbandar] for the asking'.[49]

The idea did not at first appeal to Putlibai, who wanted to keep her son closer to home. But Mohandas found the idea compelling. He was to write that 'the desire to go to England . . . completely possessed me'. One does not know why he took so quickly to the proposal – perhaps he had been reading Gujarati travelogues of journeys to Europe and America, which were then gaining wide currency.[50]

Had Gandhi's father still been alive the idea of going to London might never have occurred to him, for his successful conquest of the Bombay Matriculation had already made Mohandas one of the best educated young men in the Peninsula. 'In point of education,' wrote one British official in disgust, 'Kathiawar ranks very low. Few of the chiefs

To settle the matter, a 'huge meeting' of the Modh Banias was called. Mohandas was seated in the middle, while community leaders 'remonstrated with me very strongly and reminded me of their connection with my father'. The boy answered that he was going overseas to study, and that he had promised his mother not to touch a strange woman, or drink wine, or eat meat. The elders were unmoved. For his transgression, the boy would be treated as an outcaste; anyone who spoke to him or went to see him off would be fined. But, as the transgressor recalled, 'the order had no effect on me'. On 4 September 1888, a month short of his twentieth birthday, Mohandas Karamchand Gandhi sailed for London.[57]

2

Among the Vegetarians

As a boy in Porbandar, Mohandas Gandhi often saw boats sailing in and out of the port. But the first ship he actually stepped on to was the one that took him to London. The experience was exciting enough for the young man to maintain – also for the first time – a diary, twenty pages of which were devoted to the passage across the ocean.[1]

The ship's name was the SS *Clyde*. It left Bombay at five o'clock on the evening of 4 September 1888. An hour later the dinner bell rang. Mohandas was accompanied to his table by Triambakrai Mazumdar, a boy from Junagadh (and a Brahmin from the sound of his name) who was also proceeding to London to study. The young Gandhi wore a black coat and carried his own food – Gujarati sweets and savouries that his family had packed for him. His friend was dressed more casually, and was content to eat the ship's fare.

This arrangement continued for the first forty-eight hours. Fortunately, Mohandas then found a native sailor who was willing to cook him rice and *dal*. The sailor also provided *rotis*, but since the man's hands were dirty, the student – a fastidious Bania – preferred to use the English bread for dipping instead.[2]

During the day, Mohandas watched the sailors at work (their 'dexterity', he found, was 'admirable'), played around with the piano (again, for the first time – there seems to have been no music in the Gandhi household in Rajkot), and took the air on the deck above. One day he stayed on past sunset and saw how, on account of the waves and what they reflected, 'the moon appeared as if she was moving here and there'. Then the stars appeared; their reflection in the water gave him 'the idea of fireworks'.

When they berthed at Aden, the passengers rented a boat to take them ashore. Mohandas was impressed by the Protectorate's buildings, but less so by the landscape. In a whole day in Aden, he 'saw not a single tree or a green plant'. That evening the SS *Clyde* entered the Red Sea. Like many others before and since, Mohandas marvelled at the Suez Canal and the 'genius of a man who invented it'. When they anchored at Port Said, he discovered that he had definitively left his homeland behind him. For 'now the currency was English. Indian money is quite useless here'.

A fellow passenger told Mohandas that once they left the Suez Canal, the weather would change: as they got closer to Europe, the only way to beat the cold would be to eat meat and drink alcohol. Mohandas stuck to his diet of rice and lentils. Three days later they reached Brindisi. It was evening, and as the passengers came ashore the gas lamps were being lit. Everyone was speaking Italian. Mohandas was unimpressed by the railway station – it was not as 'beautiful' as those built back home by the Bombay Berar and Central Indian Railway. However, the railway carriages were bigger and better appointed.

At Brindisi, adding to the list of novel experiences, Mohandas was accosted by a local who (presumably speaking in English) said: 'Sir, there is a beautiful girl of fourteen, follow me, sir, and I will take you there, the charge is not high, sir.' The Indian avoided him. The next stop was Malta. Here Mazumdar and Mohandas hired a carriage to take them around. They saw an old church and the local museum, which displayed weapons of war and a chariot that had once carried Napoleon Bonaparte. Three days later they arrived at another colonial outpost, Gibraltar, where they were impressed by the quality of the roads.

Mohandas Gandhi's diary of his voyage to London is unusually attentive to the landscape. Roads, buildings and vegetation are described with care. Nature had distributed its gifts very differently than in his native Kathiawar. In the towns he had seen en route the hand of man appeared to work very differently too. When the ship reached the port of Plymouth, Mohandas suddenly felt cold. It was eleven at night, and winter was approaching. He reflected that, despite the warning and inducements along the way, he had reached England without betraying the three promises – not to eat meat, drink alcohol or have sex with strangers – that he had made to his mother in Rajkot.

From Plymouth, the ship proceeded to its final destination. On 29 September, three weeks after it had left Bombay, the SS *Clyde* berthed at the newly built Tilbury Docks. Mohandas and Mazumdar disembarked, and boarded a train to travel the twenty miles to London. Their first night in the city was spent in the Victoria Hotel on Northumberland Street, next to Trafalgar Square.[3]

London in 1888 was a great *imperial* city. Queen Victoria had lately observed the Golden Jubilee of her reign. The empire she presided over had planted its flag in the four corners of the world. Even some countries not ruled by Great Britain recognized her superiority. Not long after Mohandas Gandhi arrived in London, the Shah of Persia came visiting. The cover of a popular magazine showed the foreign monarch calling on the Queen in Windsor Castle. Victoria was sketched as small, stout and plain; in fact, as unprepossessing as she really was. With his lissom frame and his stylish clothes, the Shah looked rather grand in comparison. What gave the game away was their respective postures – Victoria sat on her throne, while the foreigner bowed low to kiss her hand.[4]

London in 1888 was also a great *industrial* city. Its factories made lamps and chocolates, shoes and clothes, and a thousand other things besides. The products manufactured in London and the products consumed by Londoners came in and out of the port. The SS *Clyde* was one of a staggering 79,000 vessels that docked in the city in the year Gandhi arrived. Apart from the passengers on board, these ships carried 20 million tonnes of cargo, valued at £200 million.[5]

Finally, London in 1888 was a great *international* city. No city in the world had more people – about 6 million in all, twice the number in Paris – or more nationalities represented in them. There was a large and growing population of Irish Catholics; Germans, Czechs and Italians came looking for work; Ukrainians, Poles and Russians came fleeing persecution. The metropolis was 'perhaps the most cosmopolitan city in Europe', and in its crowded streets, one could hear 'the twanging inflections of Australians, New Zealanders, Canadians . . . [and] the unfamiliar enunciations of Asians and Africans'.[6]

Among these foreigners in London were about 1,000 Indians. Through the seventeenth and eighteenth centuries, the Indians who came to or settled in England were mostly of working-class origin. They were sailors and dockhands, domestic servants and sepoys. There was a 'tom-tom man' named Ram Singh who played the drum in the streets. However, there were also a few aristocrats, drawn from the class of

Maharajas and Nawabs. Then, from the 1850s, an increasing number of Indians came seeking a professional qualification in medicine or, more often, the law.

The two most influential Indians in London at the time of Mohandas Gandhi's arrival were Dadabhai Naoroji and Abdul Karim. Naoroji, a Parsi, moved to London in 1855, as the agent of a trading company. Over time, his interests in business were superseded by his work in politics and social reform. In 1888, he set up a forum to represent Indians in the United Kingdom, which, the next year, was named the British Committee of the Indian National Congress (which had been founded in Bombay in 1885). An Indian whose influence was more discreet was Abdul Karim, a Muslim from Agra who worked on Queen Victoria's staff. Tall and light-skinned, he taught the Queen Hindustani, with digressions into Indian religion. The Queen thought her teacher 'really exemplary and excellent'; under his direction, she had begun greeting Indian visitors in their own language.[7]

The daily round of activities in London reflected the city's capacious internationalism. An Asian potentate would come calling; the zoo would acquire its first hippopotamus. One month there was an exhibition on the abolition of the African slave trade; the next month a different gallery displayed a Javanese village. The local press took a global view of politics – carrying stories on an insurrection in Crete and a revolution in Brazil – and of economics, as in accounts of wine-making in Chile or of the California gold-rush.[8]

En route to London, Mohandas had wired an acquaintance with the date of his arrival. This was Pranjivan Mehta, a doctor from Morbi, a town close to Rajkot, now studying to be a barrister in England. The evening after Gandhi reached London, Dr Mehta came to see him at the Victoria Hotel. As they spoke, Mohandas picked up the visitor's hat and started feeling its felt. A look from Dr Mehta stopped him, and gave Mohandas his first lesson in English etiquette. 'Do not touch other people's things,' Dr Mehta told him. 'Do not ask questions as we usually do in India on first acquaintance; do not talk loudly; never address people as "sir" whilst speaking to them as we do in India; only servants and subordinates address their masters that way.'[9]

The hotel was expensive, so Gandhi and Mazumdar shifted to the home of another man from Morbi, one Dalpatram Shukla. Shukla lived in the suburb of Richmond, eleven miles up the Thames. They boarded with Shukla for a few weeks, before Mohandas found lodgings in West Kensington with a widow whose husband had served in India. She lived in a Victorian terraced house, four storeys high, with a railway line running behind it. The steam trains were distinctly audible from within the home.

The Bania lodger found the food hard to stomach – how long can one survive on bread and milk? Fortunately, while walking around the city, he found some vegetarian restaurants – one on Farringdon Street, another in High Holborn. He also invested in a portable stove, to cook with in his room. Oatmeal boiled in water and eaten with milk or fruit served as a handy breakfast; lunch was eaten out; while for supper Mohandas made himself soup and rice.[10]

On 6 November 1888, Mohandas Gandhi registered himself at the Inner Temple, one of four Inns of Court in London, located just west of the City and close to the river, in 'rather an ill-defined district in which graceful but dingy buildings of diverse pattern and of various degrees of antiquity, are closely grouped together and through [which] wind crooked lanes, mostly closed to traffic, but available for pedestrians'.[11] Three days after joining the Inner Temple, Mohandas wrote to his brother Laxmidas that 'in spite of the cold I have no need of meat or liqour. This fills my heart with joy and thankfulness.'

This is one of only three letters written by Gandhi from London that have survived. The other two, written shortly afterwards, were sent to British administrators in Porbandar, asking them again to finance his education. His brother Laxmidas had budgeted £666 for his time in London; now, after living there for two months, he thought he needed £400 more. 'English life,' wrote Mohandas to the Administrator in Porbandar, 'is very expensive.' The Ranas had shown scant interest in modern learning, but 'we can naturally expect that education must be encouraged under the English Administration. I am one who can take advantage of such encouragement.'[12]

The letters were disregarded. Mohandas, and Laxmidas, would have to find the money themselves.

To qualify as a barrister, Mohandas had to pass two examinations, the first to be taken after he had kept four 'terms', the latter after he had kept nine. The terms were held in the months of January, April, June and

November – the shortest lasting twenty days, the longest thirty-one. Mohandas had to attend a minimum of six dinners each term, and a total of seventy-two dinners in all. This practice allowed apprentice lawyers to meet and speak with their colleagues and superiors. It also made up for an institutional deficiency: the fact that, unlike Oxford and Cambridge universities, the Inns were not residential.

The Inner Temple was so called because, alone among the Inns of Court, it lay just inside the old City walls. It was very English and dominated by public school and university men. Mohandas might have been better off if he had enrolled at the Middle Temple, which (as a lawyer who was there in the 1890s recalled), 'had also English, Scottish, Irish, Welsh, Colonial and others, with hundreds from India's coral strands and Africa's sunny fountains'.[13]

Admittedly, the Inner Temple had the more beautiful garden, 'spacious and sunny and well-turfed', which played host every year to the London Horticultural Society's flower show.[14] This was no use to Mohandas, for as a student he had no chambers in the Temple. He was supposed to spend his days studying, at home. Till he came to sit his exams, he had only to appear at the Inner Temple for dinner, once every ten days or so. A certain amount of ceremony accompanied the meal. The members and students of the Inn, dressed in gowns, entered the hall in procession, standing in silence while the governing body (composed of members who were now Queen's Counsels) sat at the high table located at one end of the room. After the Governors were seated, the members took their places on the low benches assigned to them.[15]

Gandhi's fellow diners were alien to him in class and culture. So was the food. A joint of beef or mutton was set down before a table of four, along with two bottles of wine. The Indian applied for a vegetarian meal, which was usually a mess of boiled potato and cabbage. He made up for this by exchanging his share of wine for his table-mates' fruit.[16]

The Inner Temple followed a very strict dress code. As early as 1546, an internal memorandum had ordered that 'the gentelmen of the company schall reforme them selffes, in their cutt or disguysed apparell, and shall not have long berdes . . .'[17] In the late nineteenth century, this was interpreted to mean that lawyers came to chambers or to court in a dark suit, a dress shirt, and a silk hat. Mohandas took the code very seriously. He dressed well for the dinners at the Temple, and on other days too. A fellow student, bumping into him near Piccadilly Circus, was greatly impressed by the 'fashion, cut and style of Mr Gandhi'. The aspiring lawyer, he recalled years later, was wearing a 'high silk top-hat, brushed, "burnished bright"', a 'stiff and starched collar (known at that time as a Gladstone)', a 'fine striped silk shirt', and dark trousers with a coat to match. On his feet were 'patent leather boots'.[18]

Young Mohandas Gandhi may have worn a Gladstone collar, but he did not take much interest in the man after whom it was named. In 1889 William Ewart Gladstone was one of the towering figures of British and (by extension) world politics. With the death of Benjamin Disraeli, Gladstone's main rival was the new leader of the Conservative Party, Lord Salisbury. They (and their parties) alternated in office, with the Liberals following one set of policies at home and abroad, and the Tories another.

The elite politics of the time was opposed by a growing body of radicals on the left. Karl Marx had died in 1883, but his followers were active in London, planning for world revolution. In 1884 the Fabian Society came into being. This too sought to usher in socialism, albeit by British – that is to say gradualist – methods. In the London chapters of his autobiography, Gandhi does not mention the Liberals or the Tories, the Communists or the Socialists. His interest was taken up instead with a cult of English dissenters possibly even more radical, and certainly very much more obscure.

These were the vegetarians of London. In the window of that restaurant in Farringdon Street Gandhi came across a copy of Henry Salt's *Plea for Vegetarianism*. He read it from cover to cover (it was a slim book). Till then, he had been vegetarian by custom and tradition, but from the moment he read Salt he became 'a vegetarian by choice'. He found that there was a London Vegetarian Society, whose meetings he began to attend. He was so struck by his new creed that he even formed a branch of the Society in the locality where he lived.[19]

The vegetarians whom Gandhi discovered in England had originally taken their inspiration from India. From the Greeks onwards, European travellers in the subcontinent were fascinated by the diet of the Hindus. That a large section subsisted entirely without eating meat repelled some visitors (such as the Portuguese explorer Vasco Da Gama), and deeply impressed others. These Indophiles were particularly struck by the tender care shown to sick or dying animals. Who in Europe could ever conceive of a special hospital for birds? It also came as a surprise that whereas white soldiers could not survive without beer or beef, Indians seemed to fight perfectly well on a diet of rice and lentils.

Through the seventeenth and eighteenth centuries, a series of tracts were published in England and France extolling the virtues of 'Hindu' vegetarianism. Over the decades, however, the Oriental note became more muted and eventually disappeared. When, in the nineteenth century, the first vegetarian anthologies were published in England, and the first vegetarian societies came into existence, the arguments for this very untypical diet were usually made on the grounds of health and, less frequently, on the basis of respect for all of God's creation.[20]

The Indian origins of English vegetarianism were unknown both to Mohandas Gandhi and to the man whose tract so powerfully influenced him. Henry Salt was the son of an army officer who had served in India. Salt himself was born in the subcontinent, but brought back to England as a baby. He was sent to study at Eton and Cambridge, being less than happy in either place. Drifting, he returned to Eton to teach, and married the daughter of one of his former teachers. The marriage lasted, but not the career. Inspired by the ideas of Henry David Thoreau, the couple moved to a village where they lived without servants, while Salt earned money through freelance writing.[21]

In his lifetime Salt published more than forty books. These included lives of Thoreau and Shelley (a fellow vegetarian). By far his most influential works dealt with the reform of diet and the rights of animals. The logic of vegetarianism, he once wrote, 'is not chemical, but moral, social, hygienic'. He rejected the common equation of a meat-free diet with asceticism; to become vegetarian, he argued, was not to deny oneself anything, but simply to share the joy of kinship with the non-human world. The *raison d'être* of vegetarianism was 'the growing sense that flesh-eating is a cruel, disgusting, unwholesome, and wasteful practice'.

A critic charged Salt with inconsistency: milk and eggs also came from animals – if one consumed them, then why not meat? Salt answered by avowing the merits of gradualism. Milk and eggs would in time be abjured by the vegetarians, as meat had already been. But 'surely it is rational to deal with the worst abuses first. To insist on an all-or-nothing policy would be fatal to any reform whatsoever. Improvements never come in the mass, but always by instalment; and it is only reactionaries who deny that half a loaf is better than no bread'.[22]

For Salt, vegetarians were the moral vanguard of the human race. He allowed that 'reform of diet will doubtless be slow'. It would encounter 'difficulties and drawbacks'. Yet as 'the question is more and more discussed, the result will be more and more decisive'. Had not slavery once been practised and defended too? The success of vegetarianism would result in a deepening of democracy. As he eloquently put it, 'it is not human life only that is lovable and sacred, but *all* innocent and beautiful life: the great republic of the future will not confine its beneficence to man.' The 'emancipation of man will bring with it another and still wider emancipation – of animals'.[23]

The regular, beef-eating Englishman saw vegetarians as a small and perhaps even silly cult – their restaurants to be patronized, if at all, when the purse was running empty. The publisher Grant Richards, writing of the London of the 1890s, the London of Mohandas Gandhi and Henry Salt and their Society, mentions 'several vegetarian restaurants dotted about between Liverpool Street and St. Paul's. One in particular I can remember in King Street, Cheapside. One could get a very filling and very horrid meal for sixpence – or was it ninepence? Vegetarianism seems to have made no progress since those days.'[24]

For our visiting Indian, however, the Vegetarian Society was a shelter that saved him. The young Gandhi had little interest in the two great popular passions of late nineteenth-century London, the theatre and sport.[25] Imperial and socialist politics left him cold. However, in the weekly meetings of the vegetarians of London he found a cause, and his first English friends.

At some time – we do not know exactly when, but it must certainly have been into his second year in London – Gandhi came to share rooms with a man named Josiah Oldfield. An Oxford graduate and barrister, now studying to be a doctor, Oldfield was an active member of the London Vegetarian Society. He edited the Society's journal, where (like Salt) he wrote both on diet and on politics, and where (like Salt again), he exuded a heroic optimism, as in an essay where he claimed that 'the one tendency that has pervaded humanity . . . [is] the spirit of progress from bondage towards Liberty.'[26]

Oldfield and Gandhi, the Englishman and the Indian, lived together at 52 St. Stephen's Gardens, Bayswater, in a house overlooking a shady park.[27] This friendship across the racial divide was singular as well as brave. Gandhi and Oldfield threw parties where guests were served lentil soup, boiled rice and large raisins. On other evenings they sallied together into the world, 'lecturing at clubs and any other public meetings where we could obtain a hearing for our gospel of peace and health'.

One evening, Gandhi returned home and told Oldfield of an encounter earlier in the day. An English doctor, on hearing that the law student was a vegetarian, insisted that he make an exception for beef-tea, since, unlike in the tropics, where a diet based on grain and vegetables would do, 'in the cold climate of England the addition of beef or mutton is essential'. They argued, back and forth, till the doctor, in exasperation, exclaimed: 'You must either take beef-tea or die!' Gandhi answered that 'if it were God's will that I should die I must die, but I was sure it could not be God's will that I should break the oath that I made on my mother's knee before I left India'.[28]

Meanwhile, two other friends, an uncle and nephew respectively, asked Gandhi to interpret the Bhagavad-Gita for them. He read the work with the two men, in the then quite recent translation by Edwin Arnold carrying the poetic title *The Song Celestial*. The Englishmen, in turn, introduced him to the work of Madame Blavatsky who, after a life spent wandering around the world (including a spell in India), had settled down in London. The founder of Theosophy sought to reconcile religion with science, and Christianity with Hinduism. That her cult was so manifestly sympathetic to Indian traditions impressed young Gandhi. He met Blavatsky as well as Annie Besant, a firebrand socialist and suffragette who had recently abandoned those creeds to embrace Theosophy.[29]

Moving further outwards from his native Hinduism, Gandhi began reading Christian texts, supplied to him by a vegetarian from Manchester. The Book of Genesis sent him to sleep, but the New Testament he found compelling. The Sermon on the Mount in particular 'went straight to my heart'. The lines about offering one's cloak to the man who had taken away one's coat touched him greatly. Comparing it to the Gita, he concluded that both taught that 'renunciation was the highest form of religion'.[30]

Early in his stay, a friend suggested to Mohandas that, apart from qualifying as a barrister, he could also take the London Matriculation exam. No extra fees were payable, and Indians liked accumulating foreign certificates. After registering for the Matric, Gandhi found that he had to learn Latin – a language utterly foreign to him – and also to take at least one science. The first time he sat the Latin exam he failed. Fortunately he passed the second time around. As for science, he tried Chemistry, but, after finding the experiments too complicated, opted for Heat and Light instead.[31]

Meanwhile, at the Inner Temple, Gandhi had to pass examinations in (among other subjects) Roman Law, Property Law and Common Law. For the first topic he read an English translation of the Justinian code as well as a larger work of interpretation and analysis, William A. Hunter's *Introduction to Roman Law* (third edition, 1885). For the second subject he read Joshua Williams's *Principles of the Law of Property* (sixteenth edition, 1887), as well as several compendia of cases. To understand common law he read two textbooks, new editions of which had appeared in 1888 – John Indermaur's *Principles of the Common Law* and Herbert Brown's *Commentaries on the Common Law*. There was also a special section on Equity, for which he consulted the 1887 edition of a book on the subject by Edmund H. T. Snell.[32]

When he was not reading, or re-reading, these books, Gandhi took long walks through the city. He calculated that he walked an average of eight miles a day. As he told the Indian students who came to London after him, walking was 'a pleasure in the cold climate of England'; besides, for reasons of economy, 'a brisk walk should be preferred to a ride in a train or a bus'. After a walk, Gandhi felt obliged to wash away the sweat and the dirt. Sometimes he went to a public bath (which cost five pence); at other times, he persuaded his landlady to provide him with a little hot water, into which he dipped a towel or sponge that he then ran over his body.[33]

There were excursions in London and some further afield, with Gandhi once travelling to Portsmouth to attend a Vegetarian Conference. Speeches during the day were followed by a relaxing game of bridge in the evenings. Gandhi was partnered by the landlady of the inn where they were staying. She joked and flirted with him. He was attracted by the banter – it was 'the first occasion on which a woman, other than my wife, moved me to lust'. Then, as the flirtation got more intense, the excitement confused and shamed him. Remembering his vow to his mother, he got up from the card table, rushing to his room 'quaking, trembling, and with beating heart, like a quarry escaped from its pursuer'. Although the conference still had some time to run, Gandhi returned the next day to London.

Gandhi also spent some days in Brighton, and went twice to Ventnor, on the Isle of Wight. In 1890 he crossed the Channel to visit the Paris Exhibition, where he saw the newly built Eiffel Tower, but was moved far more by Notre Dame cathedral, with its exquisite sculptures and decorations.[34]

Living in Britain towards the end of the Victorian age, did young Mohandas Gandhi experience discrimination on account of his race or ethnicity? It appears not. The circles Gandhi moved in – those of the vegetarians and the Theosophists – sought affinity of ideas and life-styles, not skin colour. In any case, the Englishman in England was less prejudiced than the Englishman abroad. In India, an Englishman was marked out as a member of the ruling race. Wherever he went, there were a 'large number of dark-skinned men ready and willing to serve him in numerous ways'. At home, however, the Englishman had to post his own letters and carry his own bags. A Tamil journalist visiting London in the 1890s noticed that 'the English are generous by nature and are anxious to please foreigners. I appreciate their hospitality all the more when I find that colour does not influence them a bit in their treatment of Indians.'[35]

In the last week of March, 1890 – a year and a half after he had left India for England – Mohandas sat his first set of law examinations. When the results were announced he found he had done rather better than in the Bombay Matriculation, coming 6th in a set of 46. His name appeared (for the first time) in *The Times*, placed alongside other successful candidates, among them a Parsi named Colah and a Bengali named Sarbadhicary, the Indian syllables sounding (and sitting) oddly alongide impeccably Anglo-Saxon names such as Atkin, Barrett, Clark, Maxwell, Murray, Rose and Smith.[36]

In December of the same year Gandhi sat the final examinations. A month later, on 12 January 1891, he was told that he had passed successfully, coming 34th out of 109.[37]

He had now cleared his exams, but he was still some dinners short of the Temple's prescribed total of seventy-two. He could not return to India until he had attended (albeit not enjoyed) those remaining dinners.

His friend and flatmate, Josiah Oldfield, now persuaded him to spend his last days in London writing for *The Vegetarian*.

It is not uncommon for a writer's first work to appear in a low-circulation niche magazine. But how many can claim that their debut in print took the form of a six-part series? Through February and March 1890, *The Vegetarian* carried the byline of M. K. Gandhi, under the heading, 'Indian Vegetarians – I, II . . .' etc. An introduction to the caste system inaugurated the series. A later essay explained how Asian vegetarianism differed from its European counterpart. 'Unlike the English, the Indians do not take each dish separately, but they mix many things together.' Moreover, 'each dish is elaborately prepared. In fact, they don't believe in plain boiled vegetables, but must have them flavoured with plenty of condiments, e.g., pepper, salt, cloves, turmeric, mustard seed, and various other things for which it would be difficult to find English names unless they be those used in medicine.' The Indian diet was richer and more varied, except in one respect – for 'the fruit, yes, the all-important fruit, is sadly conspicuous by its absence in the above-mentioned specimen dishes'.

Gandhi's essays took apart some common myths and misconceptions. If Hindus 'as a rule are notoriously weak', this was not because of the absence of meat in their diet. The fault was that of the 'wretched custom of infant marriage', which by making girls of twelve have children by boys of sixteen, tended to 'tell on the strongest constitutions'. The writer also had choice words to say about alcohol, which he termed an 'enemy of mankind' and a 'curse of civilization', and incidentally also 'one of the most greatly-felt evils of the British Rule' in India.

Having criticized child marriage – through personal experience – and alcohol – by seeing its effect on other Indians – the writer then turned to a lyrical appreciation of the shepherd, in his view the perfect specimen of *Homo Indicus*. His vegetarian diet, and his daily routine in the fields and forests, made the shepherd's 'an ideal mode of life. He is perforce regular in his habits, is out of doors [with his flocks] during the greater part of his time, while out he breathes the purest air, has his due amount of exercise, has good and nourishing food and last but not least, is free from many cares which are frequently productive of weak constitutions.'

Gandhi allowed that the shepherd had a flaw – one, not more. For 'while a Brahmin would have his bath twice a day, and a Vaisya once a day, a shepherd would have only one bath a week'. Otherwise, it was 'very rare to see any deformity in him . . . Without being fierce as a tiger, he is yet strong and brave and as docile as a lamb. Without being awe-inspiring, his stature is commanding. Altogether, the Indian shepherd is a very fine specimen of a vegetarian, and will compare very favourably with any meat-eater so far as bodily strength goes'.[38]

For someone who never heard English at home, who began learning the language only at the age of eleven, and whose Matriculation marks were so mediocre, Gandhi's prose was surprisingly clear and direct. Noteworthy is his passing chastisement of colonial rule (for promoting the sale and consumption of alcohol) and his praise of the way of life of the shepherd. There were communities of pastoralists in Kathiawar, who came after every monsoon to graze their flocks in the large *gauchar*, or pastureland, that lay outside most towns in the region.[39] Gandhi would have seen them here, and also met them during fairs and festivals, when shepherds came peddling their wares. It may also be that he was influenced by the current of romantic anti-industrialism present in the thought of Henry Salt, and of friends of Salt like Edward Carpenter, who, like William Wordsworth and John Ruskin before them, believed that the farmer and shepherd represented a purer, more natural way of life as compared to the businessman or factory worker.[40]

Now that he was in print, the novice writer wanted more. The series on Indian vegetarians was followed by three articles on Indian festivals.[41] The first series was then reprised for a different journal, in a long essay on 'The Foods of India' which ended with the hope that 'the time will come when the great difference now existing between the food habits of meat-eating in England and grain-eating in India will disappear, and with it some other differences which, in some quarters, mar the unity of sympathy that ought to exist between the two countries'. 'In the future,' thought this Indian visitor to England, 'we shall tend towards unity of custom, and also unity of hearts'.[42]

Gandhi's involvement with the vegetarians of London was far more important to him than is commonly recognized. Had he not joined their Society, he would have kept to his compatriots, as Indian students abroad were wont to do at the time (and sometimes still are). These first, close friendships with English people expanded his mind and his personality. He learnt to relate to people of different races and religious beliefs, to mix, mingle and eat with them, and even to share a home with them.

The London vegetarians provided Mohandas Gandhi with his first exposure to collective social action and with his first public platform. Gandhi's published oeuvre covers dozens of volumes and ranges across many different subjects. It is a striking if little noticed fact that his writing career began with these lucid, informative and surprisingly confident series of essays on the foods and festivals of India. For his Bombay Matric and his Inner Temple barrister's certificate, Gandhi had to cram a mass of facts and bring them out in the order required by the examiners. But in crafting these articles for *The Vegetarian*, he had to apply his mind more intelligently; the facts within him had to be shepherded into a coherent, persuasive argument for an audience with backgrounds very different from his own.

Gandhi the cultivator of friendships across racial and religious boundaries; Gandhi the organizer and mobilizer; Gandhi the writer, thinker and propagandist – all these Gandhis were first displayed in and through his membership of that famously obscure body, the Vegetarian Society of London.

As the readers of *The Vegetarian* were being introduced to the foods of India, a more widely read weekly was presenting a very different picture of the subcontinent. This was the *Illustrated London News*, which regularly ran items on India, on such topics as *shikar* (polo), and the pacification of hill tribes. The issue of 28 February 1891 printed a sketch of a turbaned maharaja in a palanquin, passing supplicants on the street holding out their palms for alms. The portrait carried the headline: 'Riches and Poverty: A Sketch in an Indian Bazaar'.

In truth, the city in which the weekly was printed also had its extremes of riches and destitution. This 'metropolis of wealth and grandeur, culture and sophistication was also a hell of starving, degrading and heart-rending poverty'. London in the nineteenth century was marked by a 'vast extent of misery and distress', which to a contemporary observer was 'evidence of the rotten foundation on which the whole fabric of this gorgeous society rests, for I call that rotten which exhibits thousands upon thousands of human beings reduced to the lowest stage of moral and physical segregation . . .' There was also another side to London, represented most vividly in the parties of the elite, which were distinguished by 'the fact that some of the men and practically all the women [had] made the pursuit of pleasure their main occupation in life'. In these parties, as the novelist William Makepeace Thackeray acidly observed, mothers brought 'their virgin daughters up to battered old rakes . . . ready to sacrifice their innocence for a fortune or a title'.[43]

Mohandas Gandhi had no entrée into high society, into the balls and salons of the great houses in St James's or Grosvenor Square. Nor did he rub shoulders with the labouring poor, whether in their homes in the East End, or in the factories and sweatshops where they worked. Gandhi's encounters with English society were with the people in the middle. The three addresses he is known to have stayed in – Store Street, Tavistock Street and St Stephen's Gardens – were all marked on Charles Booth's 1889 'map of London poverty' as being areas of 'middle-class, well-to-do' housing. Here he met, perforce, with landladies and shopkeepers, and on a more voluntary basis with the dissenters and radicals who came likewise from the middle classes.[44]

In religious terms, Gandhi's London experience was quite varied. He socialized with Hindus and with Theosophists, saw the odd atheist, and even attended service at a Congregational Church in Holborn. His social life was more constrained. The only rich man he met was Arnold F. Hills, owner of the Thames Iron Works, and founder and funder of *The Vegetarian*.[45] Meanwhile, the closest this law student got to the working poor was to listen to their great spokesman in the House of Commons, Charles Bradlaugh.

When he came to London, Gandhi was carrying a letter of introduction to Dadabhai Naoroji, the Parsi liberal who was the 'undisputed leader' of the Indian community in the United Kingdom.[46] It seems he was too shy to seek a private audience, but he often heard Naoroji speak at public meetings. At these meetings he also heard Bradlaugh, a friend of India and Indians, one of the 'most strenuous and picturesque figures' of British politics, a 'self-assertive propagandist of Secularism and Republicanism', a man 'who came from the people and retained to the last some habits of speech which marked him out as a Londoner of the humbler classes'.[47] 'Every Indian [in London] knew Bradlaugh's name', remembered Gandhi in his autobiography. When the radical died in the first week of February 1891, Gandhi took a day off from his studies to attend the funeral at Woking. Bradlaugh was actively irreligious; and many atheists had turned out for the funeral. The Indian was struck more by the fact that 'a few clergymen were also present to do him the last honours'.[48]

On that journey to Bradlaugh's funeral, Gandhi passed the first mosque ever built in England. Modelled on the Moti Masjid in Agra, this had some fine wood-carvings and a body of worshippers who included Queen Victoria's Hindustani teacher. Opening its doors in the autumn of 1889, the mosque lay just outside Woking and was clearly visible to travellers on the train from London.[49]

On the ship to London, and in his first few months in the city, Gandhi was much taken by the need to dress well. He wore his morning coat on visits to friends, brushing and ironing it beforehand. The collars of his shirts were always properly starched. His shoes were immaculately polished.

The longer he stayed in London, however, the more Gandhi came to see the need to live more simply. The austere aesthetic of the Vegetarian Society was one reason; a second, the obligation not to be a burden on his family. While the rupee (or pound) value of their assets has not come down to us, we know that by Indian standards the Gandhis were upper middle-class. Kaba Gandhi was surely paid a handsome salary as Diwan of Porbandar and Rajkot. Over the generations, the family had acquired property and jewels as well. However, Kaba's early death made the Gandhis less secure. Mohandas's brothers had failed even to matriculate. The family's hopes were now invested in the youngest son; hence the taking of a loan and the pawning of jewellery to send him to qualify as a barrister in London.

In Gandhi's first year in England, his living expenses amounted to about £12 a month. In his second year he brought this down to £4 a month. He stopped starching his shirts, inspired by 'some unconventional gentlemen in England who have ceased adoring the fashion as a goddess'. He stopped wearing drawers in summer, thus saving on his washerman's bill. He walked everywhere rather than rely on public transport. To save on stamps, he began sending postcards home rather than placing letters in envelopes. He shaved himself rather than go to a barber. He stopped buying newspapers, and read them in the public library instead.

To aid his experiment in simple living, Gandhi bought a book by a Dr Nichol, called *How to Live on Six Pence a Day*. He set himself a slightly less daunting target: 'to get good, nutritious, healthy and palatable [vegetarian] food for 9s[hillings] per week'. To meet it, he stopped drinking tea and coffee, and resolved only to buy fruits and vegetables that were in season.

He was encouraged by the example of some great Englishmen who had radically cut down on their living costs. Charles Bradlaugh had exchanged a large house for two small rooms, before denying himself further, by lodging above a music shop. Of Cardinal Manning it was said that 'his ordinary meal, in public or private, is a biscuit or a bit of bread and a glass of water'. Despite their frugality, noted Gandhi admiringly, the world knew both men to be 'clever intellectually' as well as 'strong in body'.[50]

On 10 June 1891, with those seventy-two dinners eaten – or half-eaten – Mohandas K. Gandhi was formally called to the bar. The next day he enrolled at the High Court. The same night he gave a farewell dinner to his fellow vegetarians, booking a room for twenty in a restaurant in Holborn. Here, as the Society's journal reported, 'Mr Gandhi, in a very graceful though somewhat nervous speech, welcomed all present, spoke of the pleasure it gave him to see the habit of abstinence from flesh progressing in England, related the manner in which his connection with the London Vegetarian Society arose, and in doing so took occasion to speak in a touching way of what he owed to Mr Oldfield.' Later, in an interview he gave to the journal, Gandhi admitted that he had 'left many things undone' in his years in London. But as he returned home, he carried the 'great consolation with me that I shall go back without having taken meat or wine, and that I know from personal experience that there are so many vegetarians in England'.[51]

The following morning Gandhi took a train from Liverpool Street Station to the London docks. The ship that was to carry him back to India was an Australian steamer, the *Oceana*, a 'vast floating island' weighing 6,000 tons. This took him to Aden, where he transferred to the SS *Assam*, which was bound for Bombay.

Gandhi wrote about the return journey for *The Vegetarian*. Since he was seeing the same things again, the account lacks the enchantment and sense of wonder that characterized his narrative of the voyage out of India. He noted that while the staff on the *Oceana* were polite and neat, the Portuguese waiters on the *Assam* 'murdered the Queen's English', and were 'also sulky and slow'. He was one of only two vegetarians on board; between them, they pressed the steward to provide 'some vegetable curry, rice, stewed and fresh fruit from the first[-class] saloon . . .' The eager Indian convinced the secretary of the ship's committee to allot him 'a quarter of an hour for a short speech on vegetarianism'. The request was granted, and the talk scheduled to preface the next musical evening. In preparation, Gandhi 'thought out and then wrote out and re-wrote' a text aimed at what he anticipated would be a hostile audience. In the end the concert was cancelled, and 'so the speech was never delivered, to my great mortification'.

The SS *Assam* carrying, among other things and persons, M. K. Gandhi, Barrister-at-Law, arrived in Bombay on 5 July 1891. The monsoon had just broken. The passengers disembarked amidst the rain and the wind, soaked to the skin.[52]

3

From Coast to Coast

When Mohandas Gandhi landed at Bombay on his return from England, he was met at the docks by his elder brother, Laxmidas. They proceeded to the home of Dr Pranjivan Mehta, his fellow student in London. Mehta was from a prosperous family of jewellers, who lived in the central Bombay district of Gamdevi, in a large two-storey house with long balconies and carved wooden pillars.[1]

En route to Dr Mehta's house, Gandhi's brother told him that their mother Putlibai had died a few months previously. The family had not wired him in London, lest the news should distract him from his studies. Hearing the news now was a 'severe shock' to Mohandas.[2] Putlibai had been reluctant to allow him to go abroad, and worried he would transgress in matters of morals and diet. He had returned, law degree in hand, and without ever having had meat, alcohol or sex in London. Now he could not tell his mother of these achievements.

In Bombay, at hand to console Mohandas, was a relative of Dr Mehta's, then resident in the family home. Known as Raychand or Rajchandra, he had had a mystical experience when young, and had acquired a reputation as a poet and a student of the Jain scriptures.[3]

As a Jain teacher, Raychand led a simple, even austere, life, although his renunciation was different from and possibly deeper than the norm. While all Jains were vegetarian, the more devout did not even eat onions or garlic, and took great pains not to injure living beings, covering their mouth with a handkerchief lest an insect popped in. There were Jain hospitals for injured birds. Renunciation could take ostentatious forms, as when a wealthy merchant gave away his property in front of an admiring crowd of community members.

Raychand, however, dismissed orthodox Jainism as the 'religion of the mouth-covering (*muh patti*) rather than the soul'. The obsession with formal vows distressed him. He argued that even a householder could practise renunciation, providing for his wife and children while himself cultivating an inner detachment from worldly pleasures.[4]

Raychand was the son-in-law of Pranjivan Mehta's brother. He was a jeweller by profession, combining running a shop with the reading of scriptures and the writing of poetry. Although but a year older than Mohandas Gandhi, he inspired admiration and awe. He was introduced to Gandhi as a *shatavadhani*, one who could remember a hundred things. There was a time when he would demonstrate this skill in public. Lately, however, he had devoted himself to religious pursuits. He knew the Jain and Hindu scriptures intimately, and had also read many texts in Gujarati on Islam and Christianity.[5]

For his first few days in Bombay, Gandhi stayed indoors with Raychand. To amuse him and distract him from his bereavement, Raychand put on a private exhibition of his prowess. The visitor from London was asked to write down paragraphs in several languages and read them out. Raychand reproduced the paragraphs and sentences in exactly the same order. Gandhi was greatly impressed. More than thirty years later, he recalled the impact the Jain scholar made on him:

> His gait was slow, and the observer could mark that even while walking, he was engrossed in thinking. There was a magic in his eyes. They were very sharp; there was no confusion in them. Concentration was engraved in them. His face was round, lips thin, nose neither sharp nor flat, constitution lean, stature medium, complexion not quite fair. His appearance was that of a calm and quiet person. His voice was so sweet that no one would get tired of listening to him. He was always smiling and gay. Inner joy was pictured on his face. He had such a thorough command over language that I do not remember he had ever to search for words while expressing his opinion.

Speaking with (and listening to) Raychand made Gandhi 'realise that school is not the only place where memory can be cultivated, that knowledge also could be had outside schools if one has a desire, an intense desire, to gain it . . .'[6]

After a week spent with Raychand, Mohandas proceeded with his brother to the town of Nasik. His fellow Modh Banias had still not forgiven him for travelling to London. To placate them he took a purificatory swim in the river Godavari and then proceeded to Rajkot, where he hosted a dinner for the leading Banias of the town. It was also in Rajkot that he was reunited with his wife and son, whom he had not seen for three years.

Photographs of Mohandas Gandhi as a young man are scarce; and photographs of his wife as a young lady are practically non-existent. Later pictures, taken when she was in her thirties and forties, show a round-faced woman of undistinguished appearance. One biographer, however, comes up with the enjoyable fantasy that when Mohandas met Kasturba after his return from London he 'was captivated by his wife's beauty'. Apparently, she was

> enchanting . . . to behold. Her smooth skin, her large eyes framed by thick lashes, her tiny figure, shapely and supple as ever under the soft folds of her bright-coloured sari! How beguiling it was to watch her comb her long, gleaming, black hair; to study the simple grace of her movements; to hear, at every step, the musical tinkle of the tiny silver bells that encircled her slender bare ankles.[7]

This is an inspired piece of mind-reading, for which no source is or could be given. Gandhi's account in his autobiography is altogether more prosaic. He writes of their reunion that 'my relations with my wife were still not as I desired. Even my stay in England had not cured me of jealousy. I continued my squeamishness and suspiciousness in respect of every little thing . . .' Other evidence (the fact that Kasturba was soon pregnant) suggests that they did at least resume sexual relations. Meanwhile, encouraged by his experiences in England, Gandhi introduced changes in the household's cuisine, introducing cocoa and oatmeal into the daily diet.[8]

A month after Gandhi's return, his brother Laxmidas was drawn into a controversy in their home town, Porbandar. Laxmidas had attached himself to the heir to the throne, Kumar Bhavsinghji. The Kumar was the son of the prince who, in the year of Gandhi's birth (1869), had 'expired in extreme agony', causing Rana Vikmatji to have the prince's adviser murdered and consequently have his own status reduced to that of a Third Class ruler, and then sent into exile. The Rana's powers had not been fully restored by 1891. He had been allowed back into Porbandar, but he ruled under the supervision of an Administrator appointed by the British. The Rana's grandson, Bhavsinghji, was being groomed for the throne. A British tutor taught him English, History and other subjects; a British engineer took him for excursions into the countryside, identifying sites for bridges to be built; the Administrator had him in his office two or three times a week, so that he could learn to settle disputes among his subjects and lay down state policy himself.

Gandhi writes in his autobiography that 'my brother [Laxmidas] had been secretary and adviser to the late Ranasaheb of Porbandar before he was installed on his *gaddi* [throne] and hanging over his head at this time was the charge of having given wrong advice in that office.'9 Behind that sentence lies a rather complicated story, which had lost its significance in the 1920s – when Gandhi wrote his memoirs – but which may in fact have had a determining impact on his life and career.

Fortunately, a large file of correspondence in the archives allows us to flesh out the tale. We know therefore that in August 1891 Laxmidas was on the staff of the Thakor of Shapur, a *zamindar* in Kathiawar. However, he was often in Porbandar, where (as the Administrator of the State remarked) he 'has been hanging about in some unknown and undefined capacity with Bhavsinghji for the last nine or ten months'.10 By hanging about the young prince, Laxmidas Gandhi may have hoped that when Bhavsinghji became the Rana of Porbandar, he would get a suitable position in his administration. Or perhaps he hoped to exercise influence indirectly, through his brother Mohandas, who, as a London-trained lawyer, was extremely well qualified to be Diwan of Porbandar at a time when the British were modernizing indigenous systems of law and authority. In his memoirs, Gandhi writes that 'my elder brother had built high hopes on me. The desire for wealth and name and fame was great in him.'11 This description allows for either possibility – that Laxmidas hoped he would become Diwan of Porbandar, or (which seems more likely) that his better-qualified younger brother would get the job instead.

Laxmidas Gandhi's patron, young Kumar Bhavsinghji, enjoyed the pleasures of the flesh more than the obligations of kingship. Although married, he maintained a harem. At the time of Gandhi's return from England, the Kumar had just acquired a new mistress. To indulge her he employed new servants, to add to a household staff already in excess of fifty persons. The expenses mounted, and so also the debts. The Administrator wrote despairingly that 'the young Kumar has surrounded himself by some of the worst characters in the state.'[12]

The Kumar and his grandfather had a contentious relationship, the young man choosing to stay in a house away from the palace. On the night of 7/8 August 1891, Bhavsinghji broke into a room on the third floor of the palace. A blacksmith from the town had, at his command, opened the lock to the door as well as the locks to several boxes of jewels that the room contained.

From these boxes, Bhavsinghji helped himself to earrings, nose-rings and bracelets made of gold, rubies and other precious jewels. He also took some expensive dinner services back to his house. However, the blacksmith was stopped and questioned by the palace guards. When he explained why, and under whose instructions, he had intruded into the palace, the Rana alerted the Administrator of the State.

Porbandar's Administrator, a man named S. P. Pundit, now called in Bhavsinghji, who insisted that the jewels belonged to his late parents. Worried that his grandfather would illegally dispose of them, he was pre-emptively claiming his birthright. Rana Vikmatji denied this – he told the Administrator that the jewels were the patrimony of the State, accumulated by several generations of rulers. So long as he was Rana he was in charge of them; when Bhavsinghji ascended the throne, but only then, would the responsibility pass on to him.[13]

That night at the palace, Bhavsinghji and the blacksmith had two other companions. One was the son of a Rajkot merchant to whom the Kumar owed money. The other was Gandhi's ambitious brother Laxmidas. In his testimony to the Administrator, Laxmidas denied he was present at the break-in, claiming he was called in after the blacksmith was detained by the guards. Bhavsinghji, he said, was 'very much perplexed' at being called in to explain the theft. He asked Laxmidas whether he should call in a lawyer from Rajkot to help him. Laxmidas answered that since these were his jewels, that would be an admission of guilt. The prince said, 'All right,' whereupon Gandhi's brother left. Seeking to distance himself from the controversy, Laxmidas told the administrator that he was in the palace 'for five minutes only' before returning home.[14]

The British Political Agent in Rajkot was called in to settle the dispute. The jewels were returned to the treasury, and Kumar Bhavsinghji warned that unless his conduct dramatically improved, he would not be allowed to become Rana when his grandfather passed on. Laxmidas Gandhi was told he could not visit Porbandar without the express permission of the Political Agent in Rajkot.[15]

Barred from his home town, and in disgrace with the authorities, Laxmidas turned to his brother Mohandas for help. Gandhi had briefly met the Political Agent in London. Could he not talk to the man and restore Laxmidas to favour?

Gandhi was hesitant, as he saw it, to 'try to take advantage of a trifling acquaintance in England'. His brother persisted. 'You do not know Kathiawar,' he said, 'and you have yet to know the world. Only influence counts here. It is not proper for you, a brother, to shirk your duty, when you can clearly put in a good word about me to an officer you know.'

Laxmidas was an elder brother; besides, he had come to Mohandas's rescue when he needed money to study law in London. Against his better judgement, Gandhi went to meet the Political Agent. But racial boundaries were far more sharply drawn in British India: in the colony, a casual friendship between an Englishman and an Indian in the metropolis counted for nothing. When Mohandas went to plead his brother's case, the Agent had him thrown out of the office.[16]

By his actions, Laxmidas Gandhi had ruined any chance Mohandas had of early preferment in Porbandar. After the fiasco in the palace the chances of a judgeship or diwanship had receded, if not altogether disappeared.[17] The best option now was for Mohandas to work as a lawyer in British India. In early November 1891 he returned to Bombay, with a view to enrolling in the High Court. He was granted a licence on the basis of a certificate from the Inner Temple and a letter of recommendation from a British barrister.[18]

Bombay in the 1890s had a population of just under 1 million. A British resident called it 'All India in Miniature': anyone walking through its streets could hear forty languages being spoken, while their nostrils were assailed with the 'blending of incenses and spices and garlic, and sugar and goats and dung'.[19] Once a cluster of fishing villages, by the late nineteenth century Bombay was a thriving industrial and commercial centre. There were some fifty cotton mills, employing more than 50,000 people. There was a buzz of economic activity: land reclaimed from the sea, new railway lines laid to link the suburbs to the city, new docks constructed to cope with the increase in shipping. Schools and colleges were being opened all the time. The city was home to all the religions of India (and the world). It was also very diverse in class terms, with a large proletariat, a substantial business community, and a small but growing class of English-speaking lawyers, doctors, clerks and teachers.[20] As the city expanded, wrote one historian, 'all tribes in Western India seemed to have flocked to Bombay, like the Adriatic tribes who took refuge in the city of the Lagoons.'[21] Gandhi's fellow Gujaratis were a key part of this migration, moving down the coast to take advantage of the new opportunities in trade and the professions.

On reaching Bombay, Gandhi rented a set of rooms in Girgaum, not far from the house where he had first met the Jain savant Raychandbhai. The High Court lay some three miles to the south, in the Fort area. One of a series of impressive neo-Gothic buildings, the Court was famed for its gabled roofs, its turrets and its size. The interior area was a colossal 80,000 square feet.[22]

Every morning the young London-trained lawyer walked to the High Court, climbed its long, curving staircase, and went in and out of its rooms. As he recalled, with disarming frankness, 'often I could not follow the cases and dozed off'. The study of Indian law was 'a tedious business'; he found it especially hard to come to grips with the Civil Procedure Code. No briefs came his way, perhaps because he was an indifferent speaker, as well as an outsider to the city. However, he did fight a case in the lower courts, and also made some money drafting a memorial for a farmer whose land had been confiscated.[23]

Mohandas Gandhi was in Bombay, off and on, from November 1891 to about September 1892. (His stay was interrupted by regular trips to Rajkot, which was an overnight journey by train.) Of his impressions of the city he left no record. Did he mix only with his fellow Modh Banias, or did he sample the emerging cosmopolitan culture of Bombay more widely? There was a very active Parsi and Gujarati theatre – did he go to any of its shows? On his way to the High Court he would have seen cricket being played on the Bombay *maidans* – did he ever stop to watch a game?

Only one letter from Gandhi's time in Bombay has survived. Written to a friend, it complains of the lack of work, and also of the fact that 'the caste opposition is as great as ever'. A section of the Modh Banias was holding out, still cross with Gandhi for crossing the *kala pani* to educate himself in London. 'Everything depends', said Mohandas,

> upon one man who will try his best never to allow me to enter the caste. I am not so very sorry for myself as I am for the caste fellows who follow the authority of one man like sheep. They have been passing some meaningless resolutions and betraying their malice clearly in overdoing their part. Religion, of course, finds no place in their arguments. Is it not almost better not to have anything to do with such fellows than to fawn upon them and wheedle their fame so that I might be considered one of them?[24]

Unsuccessful in court, still spurned by his caste, Gandhi found succour in conversations with his new friend Raychandbhai. He visited him in his shop, where he was impressed with the ease with which the poet sat cross-legged on a cushion – so different from the Western way of sitting on a chair or sofa that Gandhi was himself now accustomed to. He was also struck by how indifferent Raychand was to his appearance. The men he met in court paid great attention to every aspect of their dress, yet this jeweller-thinker wore a simple *dhoti* and *kurta*, more often than not unironed. Once, their conversation turned to the subject of compassion towards other beings. Raychand said that while one could not do without leather, one must use it sparingly. Gandhi noticed a leather strip holding up the jeweller's cap. When this was pointed out, Raychand took the piece off. The gesture impressed the disciple – here was a teacher, he thought, open to correction and even refutation.

Raychand told Gandhi that he must look beyond the conventions of his caste. Banias were 'ever punctilious' in small matters, such as not harming insects and not eating certain foods. Yet their compassion was circumscribed. And they were totally lacking in courage. Although the Bania's sphere was business, said Raychand, he must also 'possess the qualities of other castes', learning hard work from the Sudra, fearlessness from the Kshatriya, a love of learning from the Brahmin.[25]

Failing to find regular work in Bombay, Gandhi returned home to Rajkot. He couldn't, it seems, yet argue in court, but as a well-published writer (in the journal of the Vegetarian Society of London) he had the skill to draft memorials. Gandhi set up an office in Rajkot, which began to attract a steady stream of clients. He drafted petitions on their behalf, chiefly to do with land disputes. This brought him an income of Rs 300 a month, adequate to maintain his family, which had now been augmented by the arrival of a second son, who was born on 28 October 1892 and named Manilal.[26]

To do freelance work in a small town rather than (as his London training had led him to expect) build a practice in the great city of Bombay was galling. That, for the first time in his life, he did not have to depend on loans from friends or family was small consolation. Fortunately, as the doors were closing in Kathiawar, an opportunity beckoned in South Africa. A family of Muslim traders from the Gandhis' home town of Porbandar had established a successful business there. Known as Dada Abdulla and Sons, they had branches in Natal, the Transvaal and Portuguese East Africa, trading in a wide range of commodities. The firm's seven shops in the Transvaal were managed by Dada Abdulla's cousin Tayob Haji Khan Mahomed. In July 1890, Tayob's family had purchased these shops for the sum of £42,500, payable in instalments. Early in 1892, the instalments stopped coming. Abdulla was now suing his cousin for the money still owed him, with interest added on. The sum asked for was about £24,700.[27]

British lawyers were appearing for Dada Abdulla in court, but there was a problem – the mechant's own records were in Gujarati. Abdulla was in need of a lawyer who knew both his language and the language of the courts, and wrote to Laxmidas Gandhi asking whether his brother, the London-trained barrister, was prepared to come out and assist him. The firm would provide first-class return fare by boat, board and lodgings, and pay a fee of £105 besides.

Laxmidas discussed the proposal with Mohandas, to whom it greatly appealed. He 'wanted somehow to leave India', and here was 'a tempting opportunity of seeing a new country, and of having new experience'.[28] This statement, from Gandhi's autobiography, may be rephrased in less euphemistic terms. The invitation from South Africa allowed him an escape from the political intrigues at home, and to earn a decent sum of money.

Dada Abdulla's invitation to Mohandas Gandhi was possible, and feasible, only in the late nineteenth century. A Gujarati trader had followed the British Flag into South Africa, where there were modern courts run on modern lines. At the same time, another Gujarati had followed the Flag to its source, qualifying as a barrister in London. In the

1790s there would have been no Indian traders in South Africa; in the
1990s these traders would have been assimilated English-speakers. In
the 1890s, however, the twin processes of globalization and imperialism
brought together a Hindu lawyer from Porbandar and a Muslim merchant from the same town to work together in South Africa. Leaving his
wife and family for the second time in less than five years, Mohandas
Gandhi sailed from Bombay for Durban on 24 April 1893.

The first Indians had sailed for Natal thirty-three years before Gandhi
did. They were a group of indentured labourers brought in to work on
the sugar plantations. When, on 16 November 1860, the SS *Truro*
reached Durban, a reporter from the *Natal Mercury* was at hand to
record its arrival. The passengers who came ashore were

> a queer comical, foreign-looking, very Oriental-like crowd. The men with
> their huge muslim turbans, bare scraggy shin bones, and coloured garments;
> the women with their flashing eyes, long dishevelled pitchy hair, with their
> half-covered, well formed figures, and their keen, inquisitive glances; the
> children with their meagre, intelligent, cute and humorous countenance
> mounted on bodies of unconscionable fragility, were all evidently . . . of a
> different race and kind to any we have yet seen either in Africa or
> England.[29]

The colony of Natal, on the south-east coast of Africa, was controlled
by people of British descent. In the 1840s they had established dominance over the Boers; people of Dutch origin who then retreated to the
interior. The climate and soil of Natal were ideal for growing sugar; the
problem, however, was that Africans were unwilling to spare time from
their fields to work as labourers. A public meeting of whites in October
1851 concluded that 'it is impossible to rely upon the kafir population of this Colony for a permanent effective supply of labour'. So, from
the late 1850s, the Natal Government sought to import labour from
India. Recruiting agents were sent to the ports of Bombay, Calcutta
and Madras; they, in turn, hired sub-agents to scour the countryside.
The men picked up were ferried to the ports and put on ships sailing for
Durban.

The coolies who came to Natal were indentured for five years. They
could re-indenture for a further five years, and then claim a return voyage

home or stay on in Natal as (nominally) free men. On the plantation they were given housing, rations, a modest wage (ten shillings a month) and medical assistance. 'Coolie immigration . . . is deemed more essential to our prosperity than ever. It is the vitalising principle,' wrote the *Natal Mercury* in 1865. So it turned out: whereas the average annual production of sugar in the colony was less than 500 tons in the 1850s, in the 1870s it was close to 10,000 tons, and in the 1890s in excess of 20,000 tons. Sugar exports rose exponentially as a result of the import of Indian labour, increasing fifty-fold in the first decade of their introduction.

A large proportion of the migrants were Tamil and Telugu speakers from south India. Women labourers were also shipped from India, in the ratio of forty women to a hundred men. Brahmins and Muslims were discouraged, because they forbade their women from working outside the house. The recruits came mostly from the low or intermediate castes; at home, they had been agricultural labourers and small peasants. Others had worked as potters, barbers, carpenters and cobblers.

Indian labourers also found work on the Natal Government Railways and in the coal mines. While a steady stream returned home after the expiry of their indenture, others chose to stay on, to work as farmers, market gardeners, fishermen and household servants. By the time of Gandhi's arrival, there were Indians in all parts of Natal, along the coast and inland, in towns and on plantations.

From the 1870s, a rather different class of Indians started entering the colony. These were traders rather than labourers, and came voluntarily. Since they paid their way they came to be known as 'passenger Indians'. They came chiefly from the west coast, and from Gujarat in particular. Many were Muslims; variously of the Bohra, Khoja and Memon castes. Some traders were Hindu, and there were also a few Parsis.

The first Indian merchant in Natal was from Gandhi's home town, Porbandar. A Memon named Aboobaker Amod Jhaveri, he had worked in Calcutta and Mauritius before moving to South Africa. In 1877 he became the first non-white trader listed in the *Business and Residential Directory of the Natal Almanac*. He ran stores in Durban, Tongat and Verulam, and chartered ships to transport commodities to and from India. Jhaveri's success encouraged several of his cousins – among them

Gandhi's future employer Dada Abdulla – to come to Natal and open businesses there.

These passenger Indians came to be known by the Natalians as 'Arabs', an inaccurate description they nonetheless avowed, for it helped distinguish them from their working-class compatriots. Some traders were based in Natal's main city, Durban; others moved into smaller towns in the hinterland, servicing workers in the mines and plantations. Indian merchants worked longer hours and were generally more abstemious than their European counterparts. They also employed their own kinsfolk, cutting down further on costs. Over the years, they came to command an increasing share of the retail trade in the towns of Natal and beyond. In 1870, for example, there were only two shops owned by Indians in Durban; by 1889 there were as many as eighty-five. These merchants also invested in real estate, buying land and buildings which they then leased to tenants.

Some 340 labourers had arrived on the SS *Truro* in 1860. By 1876, there were an estimated 10,626 Indians in Natal. The figure for 1886 was 29,589; for 1891, 35,763. By now, they were almost as numerous as the Europeans, who in 1891 numbered 46,788 (there were an estimated 455,983 Africans). The Indians in this part of Africa were very heavily concentrated in Natal. However, a sprinkling of labourers and merchants had also moved south, to the Cape Colony; and west, to the Boer-controlled region of the Transvaal, where the town of Johannesburg was experiencing a boom based on the discovery of gold.[30]

The Natal Government had appointed a Protector of Indian Immigrants, whose job was to monitor their work and living conditions, and take account of complaints regarding their treatment. The report for 1892–3 noted that, as in earlier years, a large number of labourers had turned to farming and market-gardening on completion of their indenture. The Indians, wrote the Protector, 'have, by industry and sobriety, succeeded in creating a very fair position for themselves in this Colony'. They formed a 'prosperous, orderly, and law-abiding section of the population of the Colony'. Some 150 Indians were on the burgess rolls as taxpayers, and could vote in local elections.[31]

Mohandas Gandhi arrived in Durban on 24 May 1893, exactly a month after he had left Bombay. His ship had called en route at Lamu, Mombasa and Zanzibar. He was met at the quayside by Dada Abdulla, the leading partner in the firm that had hired him, and taken to the merchant's house. Abdulla lived in a small lane off Grey Street in west-central Durban, in the heart of what was an Indian, and more specifically a Gujarati, ghetto. Grey Street ran northwards from the Victoria Embankment and the harbour; whites lived on the stretch closer to the water, giving way to Indians further along the street. The lanes off Grey Street, on either side, harboured shops on the ground floor, with offices and homes above them. The names on the buildings – Jhaveri, Moosa, Mehta, Abdulla, Rustomji – indicated their owners' origins in Western India.[32]

In London, Gandhi had lived with the Christian Josiah Oldfield, in a breach of caste rules kept hidden from the Modh Banias in Bombay and Rajkot. His sharing a home with a Muslim family in South Africa was likewise a transgression of Hindu orthodoxy, made easier by the ocean that lay between where he now was and where those who would pass judgement on him remained.

On the day Gandhi landed, 24 May, Durban's leading newspaper reported the swearing in, for the third time, of Paul Kruger as President of the neighbouring South African Republic (SAR). The paper reproduced his inaugural address, where Kruger said it would be his 'special duty' to see that

> nothing is done by which our independence can be damaged or be brought in danger; that no rights are conceded by which our independence will in any way be endangered, for even the heathen must acknowledge the hand of God in our history, and that it was God that granted us our liberty.[33]

The SAR, also known as the Transvaal, was ruled by the Boers. They were a farming people, devout and dogmatic, convinced that those who were not white and Christian had no claims to citizenship in their land. The British in Natal were interested rather more in trade and commerce, and were less committed to the Book. But they were not without prejudices of their own. In his first week in Durban, Gandhi was taken by Dada Abdulla to the magistrates' court, a short walk from Grey Street. The two men were wearing turbans in the Kathiawari style. Their appearance occasioned some comment, with a report in the *Natal Advertiser* claiming that a 'well dressed' Indian who was an 'English barrister' had entered 'the Court without removing his head-covering or salaaming, and the Magistrate looked at him with disapproval'.

Gandhi immediately wrote to clarify that 'just as it is a mark of respect amongst the Europeans to take off their hats, in like manner it is in India to retain one's head-dress. To appear uncovered before a gentleman is not to respect him.' In the Bombay High Court it was not the custom to bow before the magistrate. Still, he would 'beg His Worship's pardon if he was offended at what he considered to be my rudeness, which was the result of ignorance and quite unintentional'.[34]

The claims case of Dada Abdulla and Company was being heard in Pretoria, the capital of the Boer-controlled South African Republic. After a week in Durban, Gandhi proceeded to Pretoria, by train. He was booked on a first-class coach. Two hours later, when the train was at Pietermaritzburg station, a railway official asked him to move to a third-class compartment. When Gandhi protested that he had a valid ticket, a constable was summoned to take him and his luggage off the train. From the station he sent two telegrams, one to the railway authorities, the other to Dada Abdulla. The latter sent word to the Indian merchants in Pietermaritzburg, who came to the station to comfort Gandhi with their own stories of being discriminated against in the past.

The next evening, Gandhi resumed his journey westwards. He reached the end of the line at Charlestown, and took a stagecoach on to Johannesburg. The white coachman refused to let him sit inside, on the padded seats reserved for paying passengers. When he protested – for he had, again, a valid ticket – the man boxed his ears. Gandhi hung on dangerously to the rails, before getting off, voluntarily, at the first stop, Standerton, where he was – once more – met and consoled by the town's Indian merchants. He reached Johannesburg the following evening, where he had some difficulty getting a hotel room because of his colour. The troubles continued – on the last leg of his journey, by train from Johannesburg to Pretoria, he was asked by the guard to shift from the first-class to the third-class compartment. However, a fellow passenger, himself English, said he was happy to share the cabin with an Indian.

This trip was recounted by Gandhi in his autobiography, written many years after the events it describes. Being a retrospective account, it has a certain moral clarity – as when he writes that even as he was being ejected from one coach to another, he came to the conclusion that 'the hardship to which I was subjected was superficial – only a symptom of the deeper disease of colour prejudice. I should try, if possible, to root out the disease and suffer hardships in the process'.

But it must have been a harrowing experience nevertheless.[35]

The morning after he reached Pretoria, Gandhi called on the lawyer in charge of Dada Abdulla's case. This man, A. W. Baker, turned out to be an active lay preacher. Through him Gandhi met other Christians, with whom he began a lively debate on their respective faiths. Gandhi wore a necklace of beads gifted him by his mother; a Christian friend dismissed this as mere superstition. The Indian gave as good as he got, saying that he could not accept that Jesus was the only son of God, for 'if God could have sons, all of us were his sons'.[36]

A. W. Baker was a colourful character, who had been a carpenter before he became a lawyer. His real passion, however, was taking the Word to the Native. He published a magazine, *Africa's Golden Harvest*, which promoted 'scriptural and missionary enterprise'. Preaching in mines, prisons and hospitals, Baker converted some Africans, who then went out into the north, further spreading the Word. Before accepting Africans into his church, Baker insisted they renounce the amulets used to ward off evil spirits. He vigorously promoted temperance and asked his followers to give up snuff and tobacco.[37]

Baker sent native preachers into the bush, and sometimes travelled into the country himself. On one trip he took Gandhi. They met a Dutch Salvationist, who disapproved of a white man and a brown man travelling together. Baker was undeterred: he was completely free of racial prejudice, if not of religious certitude. His hope for his Hindu friend was that he would soon emerge 'into the full light of the glory of God which is radiant on the face of Christ!'[38]

Gandhi resisted the Word and the Light; at the same time, he could no longer accept that Hinduism was perfect either. For if the Vedas were the inspired Word of God, why could not the Bible and the Koran claim to be likewise? He began to read Christian and Islamic texts, furthering his knowledge, and perhaps also his confusion.

In between his religious studies, Gandhi worked on the legal case that had brought him to South Africa. Dada Abdulla was suing his cousin, Khan Mohammad Tayob, for defaulting on payments previously agreed upon. Gandhi had to translate many letters from Gujarati into English, as he went through the correspondence between the disputants, preparing briefs for the attorneys to present in court.[39]

Living in South Africa, and reading the newspapers, Gandhi could see that the boundaries between different social groups were very clearly marked. In Johannesburg, white traders resentful of competition were seeking to move Indian merchants to locations outside the city.[40] When one newspaper wrote of how European merchants were being driven out of business by 'wily wretched Asiatic traders', Gandhi wrote in to defend his compatriots. 'If one editor edited his paper more ably than his rival, and consequently, drives the latter out of the field,' argued the lawyer, 'how would the former like to be told that he should give place to his crest-fallen rival because he (the successful one) was able?' Should not the European trader, asked Gandhi, 'take a leaf out of the book of the Indian trader, if that be not below his dignity, and learn how to trade cheaply, how to live simply?'[41]

In Natal, the Colonists would soon have 'responsible government', with their own legislature and ministers elected on the basis of a limited franchise. In September 1893 an Anti-Asiatic League was formed to disallow Indians from voting. There were, at this time, a mere 10,729 eligible voters in Natal. All but a handful were European. To maintain white dominance, the vote had to be restricted to the ruling race. As one newspaper wrote: 'It is preposterous that a semi-barbarous horde should be allowed to come here and to claim the franchise on the same terms as it can be claimed by Europeans.'

A few Indian merchants were on the electoral rolls, by virtue of the property they owned. The white League asked judges to disenfranchise them, since 'the Asiatic population of Natal is already larger than the European and if the former are to have access to the franchise, then it will only be a few years until the latter are completely out-voted. Then our children will have cause to curse us for our enormous folly'.[42]

When these newspapers reached Gandhi in Pretoria, he was moved to reply. He reminded white Natalians that Indians were High Court judges in India; and that an Indian, Dadabhai Naoroji, had recently been elected a Member of the British Parliament. Indians in Natal were surely 'civilized' enough for the vote. Nonetheless, he assured the Colonists, his countrymen were 'too much taken up with their spiritual well-being to think of taking an active part in politics . . . They come not to be politicians, but to earn an honest bread . . .'[43]

Through the latter half of 1893, as he worked during the day for Dada Abdulla, Gandhi spent most evenings writing a book he hoped to publish. It was a 'how to' guide, aimed at students who wished to go to London. A man who had successfully and smoothly acquired a barrister's certificate from the Inner Temple would help them 'discover the mystery and lay bare the movements of Indians in England'. The book's first chapter asked: 'Who Should Go to England?' Not those who had 'a weak chest or a tendency to consumption'; nor those who were older than twenty-five. For Indians young enough and fit enough, wrote Gandhi, 'England is the best place for getting an insight into different trades'. To enter the Civil Service, to qualify as a barrister, to study medicine or engineering, a man – any man – would 'learn more during the same time in England as in India'. The quality of education was 'far superior'; and there were less distractions too. Drawing on his own experience, Gandhi wrote of the Indian student that

> while in England, he is alone, no wife to tease or flatter him, no parents to indulge, no children to look after, no company to disturb. He is the master of his time. So, if he has the will, he can do more. Moreover, the invigorating climate in England is by itself a stimulant to work, the enervating climate of India is a stimulant not to work.

Later chapters described, in meticulous and almost wearying detail, the clothes an Indian student in England would need, the furniture and stationery he would have to buy, the food he could or should eat. Against every item its price was listed (thus, for example, mother-of-pearl studs cost a mere eight *annas*, but a morning coat, also indispensable, cost Rs 20).

Several pages of Gandhi's *Guide* outlined the best way to get wholesome and nutritious food at a reasonable price. Those looking for English friends were helpfully told that 'the people of the London Vegetarian Society are always kind and hospitable towards Indians and a more genial man than the editor of *The Vegetarian* it would be difficult to find'. Those with more orthodox, less experimental, tastes were told that contrary to the impression that Englishmen rarely washed, most modern homes had bathrooms – otherwise, too, 'there is nothing to prevent you from leading a purely Hindu life'.

One chapter was addressed to the 'would-be barristers'. The strengths of different Inns were itemized. The books they would read were described, as also the clothes they would wear, the dinners they would attend and the fees they must pay. A monthly visit to the theatre was recommended, as a window into 'the modern habits and customs of England'.[44]

This was Gandhi's first really substantial piece of writing, unpublished in his lifetime, but covering some fifty-five pages of the first volume of his *Collected Works*. His motivations were several. A book under his belt would make him better known in Bombay, where he still hoped to establish himself as a lawyer. The book may also have been an exercise in self-justification, aimed at the Modh Banias who tried to prevent him from going to London. He defied them and went, and now he would encourage others to go there too. From the care with which the book was constructed, and the ease with which the prose flowed, it was evident the young lawyer liked writing, and liked writing in an exhortative vein even more.

In the spring of 1894, the case between Dada Abdulla and his cousin Tayob Khan came up for arbitration. The judge ruled in favour of Gandhi's client. Tayob Khan had now to pay Dada Abdulla £37,000, with costs. Bankruptcy and social humiliation beckoned, until Gandhi suggested a compromise – that he pay the amount on a fresh instalment system.

In the third week of May, Gandhi left Pretoria for Durban. The return journey seems to have been relatively painless, for it is not mentioned in the *Autobiography*. (Perhaps he prudently chose not to travel first-class.) His case successfully concluded, he prepared to return to India. Dada Abdulla threw a farewell dinner, at which the discussion turned to a bill before the Natal Assembly, that would prohibit Indians from enrolling as voters. Abdulla's guests wanted the legislation to be fought, and Gandhi, the lawyer and English-speaker, to stay on and assist them. The 'farewell party was turned into a working committee' to plan the resistance to the bill. So long as Gandhi stayed in Durban, said the merchants, they would pay him an annual retainer.

The chapter on the dinner-party-turned-campaign-committee in Gandhi's autobiography ends with this sentence: 'Thus God laid the foundations of my life in South Africa and sowed the seed of the fight for national self-respect'.[45] The biographer, however, is tempted to invoke the workings of (white) men rather than the ways of (a trans-racial) God. For some time, Indians in Natal had been irked by acts of discrimination. In 1884, they asked the Governor to repeal a law whereby all except Europeans had to carry a pass when out in the streets at night. Traders complained they were not permitted to sell goods on Sunday – the day their main clients, the indentured labourers, were off work – and not allowed to open shops in the city centre.

Before Gandhi arrived, Indian protests against harsh laws were led by a merchant named Hajee Mohammed Hajee Dada, his name denoting a multiple visitor to the holy city of Mecca. In 1890 and 1891, Dada convened meetings urging a more generous treatment of his fellows by the Government of Natal. Dada wanted the Protector of Indian Immigrants to know Tamil and Hindustani, and ideally be an Indian himself. He asked for a ban on the term 'coolies', and for Indians to be allowed to own freehold property and to use the Town Hall in Durban for their gatherings.[46]

In March 1893, months before Gandhi left Bombay, a trader named H. M. H. Wada wrote to the Secretary of State for the Colonies protesting against the handicaps imposed on Indians in Natal. He demanded that they 'be treated upon a footing of equality with all her Majesty's subjects'. As a mark of his irritation – or anger – Wada enclosed two defaced rupee notes with his letter of protest.[47]

The first elections in Natal, held late in 1893, had seen Indians on the rolls exercising their franchise, alongside the more numerous white voters. The elections brought to power a government headed by John Robinson, who came from a family well established in the colony; his father had founded its leading newspaper, the *Mercury*, which the son now owned and ran. The presence of Indians in Natal, claimed Robinson, was 'pernicious on social grounds, commercial, financial, political and especially on sanitary grounds'.[48] He allowed that in 'a subtropical climate indentured labour is indispensable', but thought that Indians who strayed away from the plantations were a threat to the colonists. For the 'frugal and irrepressible "coolie" . . . after his term of service is over, settles on the soil, squats in a small, kennel-like shanty, and lives at a cost which to an Englishman would spell starvation'. The entry of Indians into market gardening and shop-keeping meant that 'the prospects of Natal as a home for white men are being gradually restricted.' Robinson now called for 'a steadfast opposition to an indiscriminate "Asiatic invasion"'.[49]

Robinson's views were echoed by his fellow legislators, his fellow colonists, and the rest of the white-owned press. 'The safety and well-being of the Colony,' said one newspaper, 'depends upon its government being exclusively retained for generations yet to come in the hands of the Europeans.' 'Ramasamy [a pejorative term for an Indian] in or near town is all very well as a grower or purveyor of vegetables,' said another, 'but he is an insanitary nuisance, and in no way can be considered as a desirable citizen.'[50]

In Natal, the franchise was restricted to men over twenty-one years of age who possessed immovable property worth £50 or paid annual rent in excess of £10. There were then less than 200 Indians who met these criteria. Some whites, however, worried that with the economic advancement of the community, Indian voters would soon be counted in the thousands; even, in time, in the tens of thousands. The Indians, warned one Natal official in 1893, were 'becoming a very serious element among us'; they were 'about as prolific as rabbits, and almost as destructive to the welfare of Europeans'.[51]

It was this sentiment, and prejudice, that lay behind the new bill discussed first in the Natal Legislature and then in Dada Abdulla's house. The entrepreneurial skills of the Indians, and their desire for self-improvement, posed a problem for the neat racial order the rulers wished to impose on Natal.

Nothing in Mohandas Gandhi's previous experience had prepared him for the intensity of racial prejudice in South Africa. In Porbandar and Rajkot, it was known that the state's ruler was, in some ultimate sense, subordinate to a white man's Raj, but in those towns and chiefdoms it was Indians who held sway. The British presence was more marked in Bombay, but here, too, in a social and demographic sense the city was essentially Indian. London, where Gandhi had lived as a student, was a great cosmopolitan city, home to people of all races and nationalities. There the Indians were too few to pose a threat to the rulers. Neither his fellow vegetarians nor his fellow law students had ever pointedly drawn attention to the colour of his skin.

In London, Gandhi could share a flat with an Englishman, but in South Africa he could not make a train journey in the company of whites. The newspapers he was reading were making manifest the depth of white animosity towards the Indians. Gandhi had come to South Africa on commercial work; within months of his arrival he had, willy-nilly, been drawn into the maelstrom of racial politics. In June 1894, a petition drafted by him was sent to the Natal Legislature. It quoted various British writers (among them the jurist and political theorist Henry Maine) to show that there existed traditions of self-government in India, from traditional village *panchayats* to a modern legislature in the state of Mysore. In denying Asiatics their rights, argued Gandhi, the new bill would intensify racial feeling in Natal. If passed, it would 'have a tendency to retard, instead of hastening, the process of unification the flower of the British and the Indian nations are earnestly striving for'.[52]

The claim that Indian *panchayats* were an example of representative democracy was rejected by the rulers. Parliamentary democracy in Britain was the product of a thousand years of evolution, whereas *panchayats* were frozen in time – at best, they could be compared to village councils of the Roman era. 'There is not the slightest justification,' wrote the *Natal Mercury*, 'for the contention put forward in the Indian petition that they have the right to be placed on a political equality with the white colonists.'[53]

Through the second half of 1894, Gandhi was busy drafting petitions on behalf of the soon-to-be-disenfranchised Indians of Natal. The Gujarati merchants who paid for these memorials – and who were often their first signatories – usually did not know a word of English themselves. There was no Indian in Durban to whom Gandhi could show his drafts before dispatching them; but it appears he ran them by F. A. Laughton, a European lawyer who occasionally appeared for Dada Abdulla, and whom he had befriended.[54]

Gandhi also sent, under his own name, an 'Open Letter' to all legislators in Natal, pointing out that it was the hard work of Indians that had made this 'the Garden Colony of South Africa'. The letter quoted Schopenhauer, Maine, Bishop Heber, Max Müller and other Western authorities in praise of Indian culture and intellectual traditions.

Individual legislators were asked whether they 'really believe[d] that no Indian British subject can ever acquire sufficient attainments for the purpose of becoming a full citizen of the Colony or of voting'.

A submission of thirty-six paragraphs was also dispatched to Lord Ripon, a former (and moderately liberal) Viceroy of India, now the Secretary of State for the Colonies and thus responsible for overseeing affairs in Natal. This truly was a monster petition, the length of its text matched by the number of people who signed it, more than 8,000 in all.[55] It described the legislation as 'an insult to the whole Indian nation, inasmuch as, if the most distinguished son of India came to Natal and settled, he would not be able to have the right to vote because, presumably, according to the Colonial view, he is unfit for the privilege'.

Gandhi's Open Letter to Natal Legislators noticed the 'fact of an English constituency returning an Indian to the British House of Commons'. This was Dadabhai Naoroji, who in June 1892 had been elected to Parliament for Finsbury in north London, standing as a Liberal. That an Indian was now an MP in England must surely have emboldened the protesters in Natal. At the same time, it acted as a warning to the whites, who were determined not to allow a similar situation in their colony. For if Indians were allowed to vote, how soon would it be before one or even several Indians sat in the Legislature?

Gandhi had begun a correspondence with Dadabhai Naoroji, who was a party and parliamentary colleague of Lord Ripon. He enclosed copies of his petitions, urging Naoroji to intercede on the Indians' behalf. The politicians, he wrote, were merely scaremongering, for 'there is not the slightest probability of the government of the Natives [of Natal] passing from the Europeans to the Indians.' What the proponents of the bill did not want was for 'Indians to elect white members – 2 or 3 – who may look after their interests in the [Natal] Parliament'.

Not yet twenty-five, a Gujarati educated in London who had been but a year in South Africa, Gandhi had now become the leader of the Natal Indians. 'The responsibility undertaken is quite out of proportion to my ability,' he wrote to Naoroji. He was 'inexperienced and young and therefore, quite liable to make mistakes'. He asked the Parsi stalwart for guidance, saying any advice would 'be received as from a father to his child'.[56]

In the second week of July 1894, the Franchise Amendment Bill was discussed in the Natal Legislature. The support for it was overwhelming.

The handful of Asiatics who were on the Voters' List would remain, but no non-whites would in future be allowed to join them. For, as the ministers of the Natal Government noted, if the 8,889 Indians who purported to have signed these petitions had all claimed the right to vote, they would have formed nearly half the electorate. From the European point of view, if 'the Indian vote grew in number and in strength' a 'condition of chronic racial dissension would be unavoidable', as Natalians who were not white sought a greater share of political and administrative power.[57]

The views of his Ministers were conveyed by the Governor of Natal to the Secretary of State for the Colonies. Lord Ripon was told that if Asiatics were not prevented from voting, they would 'soon obtain a controlling voice'. Whereas white opinion was unanimous, 'on the other hand, there are probably not a dozen Asiatics in Natal who really object to the bill. The agitation has been got up by a young Parsee [sic] lawyer, a Mr Gandhi, who arrived here a few months ago. Had it not been for him, the whole thing would probably have passed *sub silentio*.' The Governor thus urged the Secretary of State to advise Her Majesty to approve the bill.[58]

Lord Ripon, in reply, asked for a softening of the legislation. The draft as it stood excluded 'all Asiatics solely upon the grounds of race': this was 'likely to cause discontent' in India, where the first stirrings of a national movement were being heard; as well as in England, where people of colour had the right to vote (provided they met a property criterion) and, as Naoroji's case showed, even to sit in Parliament. 'The great thing is to avoid the naked exclusion in terms of race,' remarked Ripon. Could not the Natal Government think of an alternate solution, such as a higher property qualification or a longer length of residence?

The Governor of Natal consulted his Ministers, who, he found, were committed to the bill as it currently stood. Apparently, the feeling of the Europeans was 'so strong on the matter that no Ministry could exist in Natal for a single week which was not resolutely opposed to the exercise of the electoral franchise by the Indian and other Asiatic immigrants'. If Her Majesty declined to sign it into law, the Colonists said they would have the bill 'passed again and again till it meets with assent'.[59]

The struggle against the new Act prompted the creation of the Natal Indian Congress, founded in August 1894 by a group of merchants living in and around Durban. Abdulla Haji Adam – who was a manager in Dada Abdulla's firm – served as president, and there were as many as twenty-two vice-presidents. A majority were Gujarati Muslims, but there were also a few Tamil-speaking Hindus, as well as a Parsi trader in Durban named Rustomjee. Gandhi served as secretary. The organization listed seven objectives, among them the removal of the hardships of Indians in Natal, the promotion of Indian literature and the promotion of 'concord and harmony among the Indians and the Europeans residing in the Colony'.[60]

The Natal Congress took its name from the Indian National Congress, whose work Gandhi knew of from Dadabhai Naoroji and company. Like that older (and bigger) grouping, it advocated greater rights for Indians, through words rather than action. Neither body was opposed to imperial rule *per se*; they hoped rather to make it more sympathetic to the rights of British subjects who were not white.

In helping found this new Congress, Gandhi was surely inspired by his experiences with vegetarians in London. A body that met regularly, that raised finances and kept minutes, that enrolled new members through conscious campaigning, would, he thought, have more effect than individual letters sent on a more or less ad hoc basis.

A picture of the Natal Indian Congress taken soon after its foundation is revealing. Six men are seated: bearded, clad in long flowing robes, wearing turbans and carrying umbrellas or walking sticks, all are evidently Gujarati Muslims. Seven men are standing: three are bearded, while the others only have moustaches. Among the latter group is Gandhi, clad in an English suit, but with a close-fitting Indian cap. The merchants in the front row paid the bills, whereas the barrister at the back did the work.

In September 1894, Gandhi's application to the Natal Bar came up for consideration. He had submitted copies of his certificates, since the originals lay with the Bombay High Court. The Natal Bar Association sought to bar his candidature on racial grounds. Fortunately, the Natal Supreme Court was unmoved, and Gandhi was granted his lawyer's licence. When he went to court to take an oath, the Chief Justice asked him to remove his headgear. Gandhi complied. When Dada Abdulla complained that he had abandoned his principles, Gandhi said he needed 'to reserve my strength for fighting bigger battles'.[61]

The franchise controversy had made Gandhi a public figure in Natal.

A paper in Durban noted that he 'already exercises considerable influence among his compatriots'.[62] The *Star* of Johannesburg praised the lucidity of Gandhi's style and the 'conspicuous moderation' of his approach. His writings displayed 'a measure of ability which would assuredly surprise many complacent gentlemen who believe that the possession of a white skin is inseparable from a higher average of general intelligence than can be possessed by any one with a darker skin.' The paper nonetheless advised Gandhi not to push the Indian case for the franchise, for 'it may be doubted whether there is a white man on this Continent who would be prepared to see the affairs of any responsibly governed community administered by any other than white men'. Rather than seek to 'achieve the impossible', namely, equal political rights, Gandhi should work for the 'just and humane treatment' of Indians throughout Africa.[63]

Other whites were more critical, accusing Gandhi of a 'lawyer-like' approach which presented only the 'pretty' side of Indian life while leaving out the 'pathetic' side. While Gandhi had focused on the 'character and attainments of the exceptional Indian in India', the average Indian in South Africa was – it was here claimed – a creature of 'bestial habits, given to malingering and dishonest practices'.[64]

One newspaper dismissed the lawyer's petitions in two sharp, short paragraphs:

It is questionable whether Mr Ghandi [*sic*] has done much good to the Indian community by his advocacy. There is such a thing as overproving a case, and when every virtue under the heaven is claimed for the mild Hindoo, the claimant only raises a smile from those who know the facts ... As for the sanitary question, Mr Ghandi cannot persuade us against the testimony of our own eyes and noses.

As for the franchise, despite quibbles as to Indian Village Municipalities, he has not got it in his own country, where the Government is purely autocratic, and no one in his wildest dreams of negrophilism has ever urged that he is fitted for anything else. His claim to vote here, in a country he knows nothing about, and under a constitution he cannot understand, is nothing less than sheer impudence. But if Mr Ghandi really believes the Indian to be persecuted and oppressed in Natal, his line of duty is very clear and simple. Let him try and persuade his countrymen not to come to this accursed country and every true Natalian will do his utmost to second his efforts.[65]

Other attacks were even more intemperate. The *Times of Natal* had written an editorial dismissing Indian claims; in reply, Gandhi said that the title of the editorial, 'Rammysammy', itself displayed a 'studied contempt towards the poor Indian'. He charged the paper with judging people merely by the colour of their skin – 'so long as the skin is white it would not matter to you whether [what] it conceals beneath it is poison or nectar'. Articulated by self-proclaimed Christians, this attitude, said Gandhi, was 'not Christ's'.

To be charged with betraying the founder of their faith was too much for the *Times of Natal* to bear. There was no racist connotation in the epithet 'Rammysammy', said the paper; it often used the term 'Hodge' to describe Englishmen of the labouring classes. As for the critic,

> Mr Gandhi does not meet any of our arguments fairly; he misrepresents the views we expressed, he makes without any call, a parade of Christianity, and so far as lies in his power he does his best to be offensive. His aim, however, is transparent; it is that of introducing himself as a champion of his fellow-countrymen. Should the learned gentleman desire to address us again in a similar strain, with the object of publicity in view, he will save time by communicating directly with the advertising department of this journal.[66]

Gandhi had come to South Africa to help settle a commercial dispute. He had, without expecting or anticipating it, become an activist for a political cause instead. Many Indians in the colony now knew of him; as did many Europeans. How did he respond to this public acclaim and public disparagement? His autobiography is silent on this score. But that he diligently followed the press for every trace of his name seems clear. In a steel almirah in an archive in Ahmedabad lie many volumes of newspaper clippings from the Natal of the 1890s, doubtless collected by Gandhi himself.

In October 1894, Mohandas Gandhi turned twenty-five. No Gandhi before him had travelled outside India. Few had even left Kathiawar. Had his father Karamchand Gandhi not died in 1886, Mohandas might not have left the peninsula either. He would, soon after leaving school, have followed his brother Laxmidas, working for (and intriguing with) a petty prince in the peninsula. Instead, he travelled to London, where

he met Josiah Oldfield, Henry Salt, the Vegetarians and the Theosophists. Then he returned home, where he was deeply influenced by the
Jain savant Raychandbhai. The break-in at the Porbandar Palace forced
him away to South Africa, where his spiritual and political education
was continued by A. W. Baker and Dada Abdulla.

In Kathiawar itself, Mohandas Gandhi could never have met or
befriended these men, who became, as it were, unwitting agents of a
transformative process whereby he moved from orthodoxy to heterodoxy in religion, from lawyering to activism in professional life and
from a conservative inland Indian town (Rajkot) to a growing, bustling
South African port (Durban). Leaving Bombay in 1888 a small-town
Bania with the habits, manners and prejudices of his caste, six years
later Gandhi had become a Hindu who befriended Christians and
worked for Muslims while organizing political campaigns in – of all
places – Natal.

4

A Barrister in Durban

As a London-trained lawyer, Mohandas Gandhi was the only Indian in Durban who bridged the gap between the races. Alone, without his family, he kept a diary, which tells how he passed the time. During the week, he drafted contracts and partnership agreements for his Indian clients, and lobbied for their rights. A lawyer-legislator he came to know well was a man named Harry Escombe. Escombe 'admitted the justice' of their claim for the franchise but said he 'could not help'. By way of compensation, and consolation, he sponsored Gandhi for admittance to the Natal Bar.

Gandhi also befriended a couple named the Askews, Methodists by faith, a 'very kind gentleman' married to 'an extremely kind lady'. The friendship prospered, till the Hindu's earnestness grated on his hosts. A diary entry for Sunday, 16 September 1894 says it all:

> Saw Askews at their house. Mrs A. did not like me to chat on vegetarianism or Buddhism [for] fear that her children may become contaminated. She questioned my sincerity. Said I should not go to their house if I was insincere and not seeking the truth. I said it was not within my power to make her believe that I was sincere and that I had [no] wish to thrust myself on her as a companion. I told her also that I did not go to [her] place as a spy to convert her children.[1]

That Gandhi placed the Buddha on a par with Christ irritated Mrs Askew. His vegetarianism was an even greater problem. The hostess's young son, seeing that Gandhi preferred an apple to a hunk of animal flesh, asked why. The Indian lawyer reproduced the ethical arguments he had first learnt at the feet of Henry Salt. The next day the boy begged his mother not to serve him meat. Convinced (like all good Christians) that

82

eating meat made children strong, she told Gandhi to henceforth speak only to her husband. Gandhi said in that case it was best he stopped visiting them altogether.[2]

In court and out of it, Gandhi was meeting Europeans who were also Christians. They discussed their respective creeds. Gandhi told a friend he wished to attend service at his church. The friend passed on the request to his vicar. To allow Gandhi to sit alongside white worshippers was impossible. The vicar's wife, out of solidarity and sympathy, offered to sit with him in the church's vestibule, from where they heard the service.[3]

Gandhi's religious pluralism was precocious. The late nineteenth century saw the rise, on the one side, of atheistic sentiments among intellectuals, and on the other, of an aggressive proselytizing by missionaries. Even as Gandhi was meeting Christians in Durban, his fellow Kathiawari Dayananda Saraswati was travelling through north India, warning Hindus against the seductions of Christianity.[4]

Like his mother, Gandhi cared deeply about his faith without being dogmatic about it. Pran Nath, the founder of Putlibai's sect, quoted from the Koran; she herself entertained Jain monks. In his open-mindedness, Mohandas was following his mother; yet, as a man, with a freedom to travel denied her, he could take this ecumenism further and deeper, through meeting people of different faiths, and by reading their texts as well.

In his early years in South Africa, Gandhi read two books by heterodox Christians that made a great impression on him. One was *The Perfect Way*, by Anna Kingsford and Edward Maitland. Kingsford was the first Englishwoman to get a medical degree, studying in Paris, where she persuaded her teachers that she could qualify to be a doctor without cutting up a single animal. On returning home, she became active in the Vegetarian Society. Maitland was a religious dissenter: the son of a priest, himself trained to take holy orders, he instead became a Theosophist.

Among Kingsford's other books was *The Perfect Way in Diet*, which argued that the shape of the human face and jaw, and the structure and functioning of the stomach, showed that man was meant to be a herbivore and frugivore, not a meat-eater. She noted that the Hindus, among whom 'a pure vegetarian diet is regarded as the first essential of sanctity', were among 'the first civilised communities', possessing 'a cultus, a literature, and a religious system which many authors deem to be of higher antiquity than those even of Egypt'.

The vegetarian doctor thought that carnivorous tendencies produced many illnesses and disorders. Tuberculosis, gout and epilepsy were a product of eating too much meat. 'In his highest development', she wrote, 'man is not a hunter, but a gardener. The spirit of the Garden is incompatible with that of the Chase, and the inevitable tendency of moral, intellectual, and aesthetic progress is to eradicate in man the desire to kill and to torment'.[5]

After Kingsford died in 1886, Maitland devoted himself to promoting her memory and furthering her ideas. In 1891 he formed an Esoteric Christian Union, which asked humans to renew themselves according to their inner urges rather than follow priests or creeds. The approach was ecumenical. *The Perfect Way*, which was subtitled *Or the Finding of Christ*, spoke appreciatively of Hindu, Buddhist, Sufi and Greek thought. Scorning officials of the Church and authorized (or self-appointed) interpreters, it insisted that 'in the momentous drama of the soul', there were only two people involved, 'the individual himself and God'.[6]

The Kingsford–Maitland view of Christianity appealed to Gandhi because it asked not for exaltation of a personal Saviour, but fidelity to one's conscience. That the principal author was a convinced vegetarian, and that it had nice things to say about his ancestral faith, added to its appeal. The second book that impressed him, Leo Tolstoy's *The Kingdom of God Is Within You* (1893), likewise put salvation in the hands of the individual believer – rather than bishops or Churches – while emphasizing suffering and the simple life.

From the 1880s, Tolstoy had increasingly turned his back on fiction, seeking to express himself via pamphlets and religious tracts. The change in emphasis mirrored a change in lifestyle, whereby a landlord turned to working with his hands, a warmonger converted to pacifism, and a once-devout member of the Russian Orthodox Church began leaning towards other religions.[7] Gandhi was attracted to the moralist rather than the novelist. He does not seem to have read *Anna Karenina* or *War and Peace*, but he read – and reread – *The Kingdom of God Is Within You*. It is a rambling, repetitive book, with one central, powerful message – that a good Christian follows his conscience rather than the laws imposed by tsars, bishops and generals. The book's title comes from a remark made by Jesus, who, when asked how one would recognize the Kingdom of God when it arrived, said that this Kingdom was not something outward and visible, but lay within you.

Tolstoy contrasted the teachings of Christ with the practices of the established Church. Christ abhorred violence, while the Church promoted war and capital punishment. Christ's essence was to be found in the Sermon on the Mount, which exalted the poor, the meek, the righteous and the peace-makers, mandated that 'thou shalt not kill', and urged one to love one's enemies and pray for them. The bishops, on the other hand, followed the Nicene Creed, which represented Christ as judgemental and made the Church infallible, insisting on absolute obedience from its members.

Tolstoy had little time for the Church, or indeed for secular intellectuals who exalted violence. He quoted Émile Zola, 'the most popular novelist in Europe', who had written that 'only an armed nation is powerful and great', that 'the warlike nations have always been strong and flourishing', that 'a general disarmament throughout the world [would] involve something like a moral decadence which would show itself in general debility and would hinder the progress of humanity'. Tolstoy, on the other hand, saluted the conscientious objector, who seeks 'the preservation of his human dignity, the respect of good men and above all the certainty that he is doing God's work'.

Towards the end of the book, Tolstoy saw hope in the redemption of those who held power, in the conscience-stricken official who refused to collect taxes and who released prisoners, in the rich man who built hospitals, schools and homes for the poor. But true liberation would come only when 'each man according to the strength that is in him [will] profess the truth he knows and practise [it] in his own life'.[8]

When he first read *The Kingdom of God Is Within You*, recalled Gandhi years later, he was 'overwhelmed' by the 'independent thinking, profound morality and the truthfulness of this book'.[9] Tolstoy's book reinforced his own heterodoxy, his stubborn insistence on forging a spiritual path for himself regardless of churches and creeds whether Hindu or Christian. Meanwhile, Gandhi was also rereading the Gita, which he saw less as a celebration of a 'just war' and more as a manifesto for ethical conduct, advocating indifference to love and hate, attachment and possession.[10]

*

In November 1894, Mohandas Gandhi placed an advertisement in the Natal newspapers, stating that he was an agent for both the 'Esoteric Christian Union' and the 'London Vegetarian Society', whose literature he stocked and sold. The ad prompted a reader to comment:

> 'Whence come we, what are we, whither go we?' This is not part of an advertisement of Eno's Fruit Salt; they are the three supreme questions which, we are told, humanity has asked itself, and which, Mr Gandhi assures us, find an answer complete and satisfactory in one or two little philosophical works in which he is interested.[11]

Meeting orthodox Christians like the Askews and reading heterodox Christians such as Kingsford and Tolstoy invigorated Gandhi but also perplexed him. Sometime in the late summer of 1894 he wrote a series of letters to his friend and mentor Raychandbhai in India, outlining his confusions. He posed more than two dozen questions, asking, among other things, about the functions of the soul, the existence of God, the antiquity of the Vedas, the divinity of Christ and the treatment of animals.

Raychandbhai answered with patience and at length. Spiritual equanimity was the essence of self-realization. Anger, conceit, deceit and greed were its adversaries. God was not a physical being, he 'had no abode outside the self'. God was emphatically 'not the creator of the universe. All the elements of nature such as atom, space, etc., are eternal and uncreated. They cannot be created from substances other than themselves.' Raychandbhai also believed that 'we may make thousands of combinations and permutations of material objects, but it is impossible to create consciousness.'

The Jain scholar refused to accept the claim of Hindu dogmatists that all religions originated from the Vedas. True, these were very old, older than Buddhist or Jain texts. However, 'there is no logic in saying that whatever is antique is perfect and whatever is new is imperfect and true.' Like the Vedas, the Bible could not be said to contain a perfect or singular truth. 'Allegorically, of course, Jesus can be taken to be a son of God, but rationally such a belief is impossible.'

A question Gandhi asked, emanating from his experiences in Natal, was: 'Will there ever develop an equitable order out of the inequities of today?' The Jain's answer upheld a reformist anti-Utopianism. It was 'most desirable that we should try to adopt equity and give up immoral and unjust ways of life'. At the same time, it was 'inconceivable that all living beings will give up their inequities one day and equity will prevail everywhere'.

Raychandbhai said the 'best thing' would have been for the two of them to 'meet together and have a personal talk about these questions'. Since – with one in India and the other in South Africa – they could not meet, he instructed Gandhi to cultivate 'a detached mind and if you have any doubts please [write again] to me. It is the detached mind which gives strength for abstinence and control and ultimately leads the soul to *Nirvana*'.[12]

Gandhi's theological explorations continued. In April 1895, he visited a Trappist monastery in the Natal highlands, writing about his trip for *The Vegetarian*. The monks ate no fish, flesh or fowl, although an exception was made for the sisters in their midst, who were allowed meat four days a week because they were 'more delicate than the brothers'. The monastery hummed with artisanal activity, its inmates making shoes, tables and kitchen utensils. What really impressed the Indian visitor was the lack of racial feeling. Whereas elsewhere in Natal, there was 'a very strong prejudice against the Indian population', the Trappists 'believe in no colour distinctions. The Natives are accorded the same treatment as the whites ... They get the same food as the brothers, and are dressed as well as they themselves are.' The contrast with other white Christians was stark. 'It proves conclusively,' wrote Gandhi, 'that a religion appears divine or devilish, according as its professors choose to make it appear.'[13]

In June 1895, the non-monastic Christians of Natal brought in a new bill aimed at Gandhi's compatriots. This proposed that labourers who stayed on after the expiry of their contract pay an annual tax of £3, then a substantial sum. The supporters of the tax hoped it would force Indians to re-indenture, or else go back to India.

Over the next few weeks, three memorials were drafted and dispatched by Gandhi. One was to the Natal Legislative Council; a second to the Secretary of State for the Colonies; the third to the Viceroy of India. The Natalians were asked why it was necessary 'to make a man pay heavily for being allowed to remain free in the Colony after he has already lived under bondage for 10 years'. The Secretary of State was reminded that it was 'against the spirit of the British Constitution to countenance measures that tend to keep men under perpetual bondage'. The Viceroy was told that the 'special, obnoxious poll-tax' was designed to ensure that the Indian in Natal

> must for ever remain without freedom, without any prospect of ever bettering his condition, without ever even thinking of changing his hut, his meagre allowance and his ragged clothes, for a better house, enjoyable food and respectable clothing. He must not even think of educating his children according to his own taste or comforting his wife with any pleasure or recreation.[14]

A coalition known as the 'Unionists' was in power in the United Kingdom, which brought together the Conservatives with Liberals who had left their party over the question of Home Rule for Ireland. In the elections of 1895, Dadabhai Naoroji had failed to win re-election, but an Indian standing as a Unionist, Mancherjee Bhownaggree, was successful in his bid to become an MP. The Birmingham businessman and former Liberal, Joseph Chamberlain, was now Secretary of State for the Colonies. In September 1895, Chamberlain wrote to the Natal Government about the Franchise Bill still awaiting approval. The bill, he said, did not distinguish between the 'most ignorant and the most enlightened of the Natives of India'. The 'position and attainments' of the latter class, he thought, 'fully qualify them for all the duties and privileges of citizenship'. The Natalians were surely 'aware that in two cases within the last few years the electors of important constituencies in this country have considered Indian gentlemen worthy not merely to exercise the franchise, but to represent them in the House of Commons'.

Chamberlain accepted that the 'destinies of the Colony of Natal shall continue to be shaped by the Anglo-Saxon race, and that the possibility of any preponderant influx of Asiatic voters should be avoided'. Still, like his predecessor, Lord Ripon, he worried about overtly racist legislation. Like Ripon, he sat on the government benches with an Indian colleague – yet in a colony for which he was responsible, Indians were being denied the vote altogether. A bill which 'involves in a common disability all natives of India without any exception,' he argued, and which 'provides no machinery by which an Indian can free himself from this disability, whatever his intelligence, his education, or his stake in the country . . . would be an affront upon the people of India such as no British Government could be a party to'.

In Britain it was assumed that, with guidance and patronage, a select group of Indians could come to keep the company of white men. The rise of Naoroji and Bhownaggree was proof of the success of this kind of liberal paternalism. Such mobility was harder to imagine or achieve in the Colonies. Especially in South Africa, where it was assumed by the ruling race that *all* coloured people would for *all* time be fixed in a position of cultural and political inferiority.

Seeking a middle way between the hardliners in the colony and the liberals in London, the Governor of Natal had a clause introduced stating that only those who had representative institutions in their own country would be eligible for the franchise. This ruled out Indians, while enfranchising Englishmen and other Europeans from countries with their own parliaments. Thus was a racial bill formally saved from 'the naked disenfranchisement' from which it had previously been marked. The amended draft was sent to Chamberlain in November 1895, and he indicated that if legislation based on this principle was passed by the Natal Legislature, he would advise Her Majesty to assent to it.[15]

While seeking spiritual truths in private, and pursuing racial parity in public, Gandhi had not forgotten his main professional duty, which was to establish a legal practice. Here his clients were all Indians. The judges he appeared before and the lawyers he argued against were all Europeans. Socially or professionally, Gandhi had no dealings with the Africans who constituted the vast majority of the population of Natal.

Gandhi continued to represent his first patron, Dada Abdulla, on whose behalf he sued a ship's captain who, without his employer's knowledge, had transferred passengers from second to first class and pocketed the difference.[16] In another case, he represented 'two well-dressed respectable-looking young Indians, one a clerk and the other a teacher', charged with 'vagrancy' for being out at night without passes. 'Mr Gandhi contended that the men had a perfect right to be out, because they gave a good account of themselves. They were thoroughly respectable lads.' The judge agreed, and dismissed the case against them.[17]

Gandhi defended the rich, the middle-class and the working poor. An indentured labourer was tried for attacking a policeman; the Indian lawyer said his client had been provoked and humiliated. A newspaper now accused Gandhi of violating the codes of the Inns of Court – 'the idea of his having anything to do with defying justice,' it wrote, 'even in the most remote fashion, is simply intolerable.' The 'sooner this gentleman gets the money he wants from the Indian community,' said the paper, 'and clears for his native country, Guam or Britain, the better it will be for himself and the Colony.'[18]

The accusations were unfair. Making money was scarcely Gandhi's sole aim. Consider the case of Balasundaram, an indentured worker beaten up by his master. He spent several days in hospital recovering from his injuries, and then went to Gandhi seeking redress. The local magistrate had issued a summons against the employer. Gandhi, characteristically seeking a compromise, did not press the charges, but arranged for Balasundaram to be transferred to a less brutal employer.[19]

Through 1895 and 1896, Gandhi fought cases on behalf of merchants seeking to recover dues, families seeking a share of a dead ancestor's property, individuals harassed by constables or by plantation owners. One case was particularly resonant: he defended a Muslim who refused to remove his cap when ordered to do so in court by the magistrate. As a barrister Gandhi was obliged to go bare-headed, but he would still uphold the right of an ordinary citizen to dress according to the articles of his faith.[20]

On another occasion, Gandhi was called in by a European colleague to advise on the disposal of the property of a Muslim merchant who had died intestate. The judge hearing the case, Walter Wragg, had previously opposed Gandhi's application to the Natal Bar – ostensibly because Gandhi had produced a self-attested copy rather than an original certificate from the Inner Temple, but more likely because he could not abide the idea of a coloured lawyer. Justice Wragg now insisted that Gandhi was 'as great a stranger to Mohammedan law as a Frenchman . . . Mr Ghandi [sic] is a Hindu and knows his own faith, of course, but he knows nothing of Mohammedan law'. Gandhi answered, spiritedly, that 'were I a Mohammedan, I should be very sorry to be judged by a Mohammedan whose sole qualification is that he is born a Mohammedan. It is a revelation that . . . a non-Mohammedan never dare give an opinion on a point of Mohammedan law'.[21]

A reporter who often covered Gandhi's court appearances remarked that while he did his work well, his

> manner was not aggressive but pleading. He was no orator. When addressing the court he was not eloquent, but rather otherwise; and in his submissions he did not actually stammer, but prefaced his speeches and comments by repeated sibilants, for instance: 'Ess-ess-ess your worship, ess-ess-ess this poor woman was attending an invalid sister and was on her way home after the curfew bell had gone when she was arrested. I ask ess-ess-ess that she should not be sent to gaol, but cautioned ess-ess-ess.'[22]

His speaking deficiencies notwithstanding, Gandhi was soon a prominent member of the Natal Bar. That he had a captive clientele helped: he was the lawyer of all the Indians of Natal, regardless of caste, class, religion or profession. The lawyer who failed in Bombay and Rajkot had spectacularly succeeded in Durban. Gandhi welcomed the financial security, but it appears that he welcomed the social acclaim even more. He was happy to be the lawyer of the Indians, and their spokesman and representative, too.

Durban, Gandhi's fourth port city, was far newer than Porbandar or London or Bombay. In the 1850s it had just two two-storey buildings. As the port grew and the sugar plantations in the hinterland prospered, the city began to expand. A series of impressive stone buildings were constructed between the 1860s and 1880s, among them a court house, a town hall and a Royal Theatre, as well as banks, hotels, churches and a whites-only club. Transport within the city was by horse-drawn trams and hand-pulled rickshaws.[23]

The whites in Durban were, in proportionate terms, more numerous than in Bombay, yet more insecure in their position. Europeans in India knew they were a tiny minority in a well-populated land. They had come to rule but not to settle. On the other hand, like Canada, Australia and New Zealand, Natal was a 'neo-Europe', whose climate, ecology and sparse population allowed the whites to re-create the conditions of life in the mother country. Sensing that this was a country they could make their own, the British set about ensuring their permanent ascendancy.[24]

As Gandhi was making his career in Durban, the Governor of Natal addressed a London audience on the attractions of life in the new colony. Natal had fine scenery and a pleasant climate ('there is no such thing as malaria', noted the Governor), abundant natural resources, and a thriving plantation industry. As for Durban itself,

> its streets are straight, hard, smooth and wide; it possesses a good series of tramways; it is lighted throughout with electric light; it has an ample water supply . . . It possesses a beautiful and well-kept little park; a Town Hall which would be a credit to a town of six times the size and in that Town Hall an organ which costs £3,000. (Cheers.) It has an agricultural showground, cricket and athletic ground, race-course, golf-links, public baths, museum, public library, theatre, an excellent club, and so forth. And an esplanade is being constructed, and is now nearing completion, at a cost, I believe, of about £80,000, along the sea front in the inner harbour, which will add much to the attractiveness of the town.[25]

By this account, Natal was not so much a neo-Europe as a Little England and – happily – without the fog, the smog and the snow. The facilities it provided were, unlike those in England, open to all classes of whites. The settlers in Natal came overwhelmingly from other than aristocratic backgrounds. As missionaries, soldiers, lawyers, mine owners, farmers, sailors and teachers, they made their name in the colony, acquiring a prosperity and social status beyond their reach had they stayed at home.[26]

The Africans in Natal were uneducated and dispersed through the countryside. There was, however, an incipient threat to the political and economic dominance of the Europeans. This came from the Indians, and more particularly the 'passenger' Indians. Indeed, had it not been for the Indian merchants – their number, their wealth and their visibility – Durban could have passed for a European city on an African coastline. Unlike plantation labourers, Indian traders tended to be based in the towns, where they conducted their business and, increasingly, bought land and built houses. In 1870 there were 665 Indians in Durban, who between them ran two shops and owned property worth £500. By the end of the century, there were 15,000 Indians in Durban, who ran more than 400 shops and owned property worth more than £600,000. The British were alleged to be a nation of shopkeepers, but in this place at this time they were being given a run for their money.[27]

The demographic challenge was as real as the economic one: whereas in 1870 there were five Europeans to every Indian living in Durban, by 1890 the ratio was closer to two to one. The pattern was similar in other towns of Natal, where, again, Europeans constituted about 40 per cent of the population and the Indians a threatening 20 per cent. As Robert Huttenback has written, this 'increasing urban concentration of Indians particularly frightened and offended many European settlers to whom it connoted both domestic propinquity and increased commercial competition'.[28]

To social proximity and economic rivalry was now added a third challenge – political competition. In 1891, following the decision to grant 'responsible government', the Governor of Natal had espied a very distant threat from the unenfranchised Africans. 'The danger in the future,' he wrote to the Secretary of State for the Colonies, 'would arise from the awakening of the Native mind – guided as it only too probably might be by unscrupulous political agitators – to the fact that its interests are not directly represented in the Colony: but this, I think, is a contingency that may fairly be left to be grappled with when it arises.'[29] The Governor could scarcely have anticipated that it would be Indian minds that would be awakened first, their aspirations stoked and articulated by a political 'agitator' who – at the time this prediction was made – was a shy and diet-obsessed law student in London.

This student was now the Secretary of the Natal Indian Congress (NIC). In August 1895, the NIC celebrated its first anniversary. Presenting a report on the first year of the organization, Gandhi noted its spread to other towns: apart from Durban, branches had been opened in Pietermaritzburg, Verulam, Newcastle and Charlestown. Subscriptions of £500 had been collected; Gandhi thought at least £2,000 were needed to 'put the Congress on a sure footing'. Cash was supplemented by gifts in kind, with 'Parsee Rustomjee stand[ing] foremost in this respect'. Rustomjee was a spice and dry goods trader in Durban, who had supplied the Congress with lamps, paper, pens, a clock and labour to clean the hall where it met. Other Gujaratis were also active in donations; however, as the Secretary noted, 'the Tamil members have not shown much zeal in the Congress work'.[30]

The energetic Rustomjee was born in Bombay in 1861. He came to Natal in his early twenties, and at first worked in an Indian store in Verulam. He then set up his own business, which expanded rapidly – by

1893 (when Gandhi arrived) he was one of Durban's largest merchants. His full name was Jivanji Gorcoodoo Rustomjee. Although a Zoroastrian by faith, he worshipped often at the shrine in Durban of Datta Peer, a Tamil Muslim who had arrived in the colony as an indentured labourer before becoming a Sufi mystic. A story current in Indian circles claimed that Parsee Rustomjee was once charged with the import of saffron, then a white monopoly. He prayed at the shrine of Datta Peer, whereupon the saffron in his warehouse miraculously turned to cardamom, confounding the customs inspectors.[31]

After Mohandas Gandhi established himself in Durban, Parsee Rustomjee became a devotee of the Hindu lawyer, and hence a steadfast supporter of the Natal Indian Congress. Congress meetings were often held in his shop in Field Street, the audience standing or sitting amidst the sacks of grain and bottles of pickles. On successive Sundays in September 1895, Gandhi – then just short of his twenty-sixth birthday – spoke to a mixed audience of Hindus and Muslims, outlining his plans for their future. A government spy, taking notes, reported Gandhi as saying:

> I may go [to India] for a while, in five or six months, but then there will be four or five advocates like me, who will come here to watch over your interests ... and they will see that Indians are treated on the same footing as Europeans. If you unite and we work together we shall be very strong ... I am sorry that the Indians in Johannesburg have not someone now with them as I am with you, but that will come before long.[32]

Seeking to widen the Congress's circle of patrons, Gandhi toured Natal in the company of other NIC workers. The police asked a plantation owner to monitor his movements. We know thus that in the first week of November, Gandhi and company crossed the Umgeni River, visited a couple of estates and stopped at Verulam for the night. Here the collections were good – in the range of £50 – but the next day they met stiff resistance, when the Indians in the village of Victoria refused – perhaps out of fear of their white masters – to part with any money. Gandhi took out his turban and placed it at their feet. He and his colleagues refused to eat the dinner brought for them. The protests worked: one by one, the Indians reached into their pockets.

Gandhi's final stop was the Tongat plantation, where he addressed the indentured labourers. The verdict of the planter/police informant on the lawyer was less than complimentary. Gandhi 'will cause some trouble I have no doubt,' he wrote: 'But he is not the man to lead a big movement. He has a weak face. He will certainly tamper with any funds he has the handling of. Such at any rate is my impression of the man – judging him by his face.'[33]

With a weak face, hesitant in court, polite in print and courteous in conversation, Mohandas Gandhi yet represented the first challenge to European domination in Natal. By the 1890s, Africans in the Cape had discovered modern forms of political expression. A Native Educational Association was formed in 1879, its members educated by missionaries and proficient in English. A South African Native Association and the Transkei Mutual Improvement Society were started soon afterwards. There were influential African reformers in the Cape, such as the teacher J. T. Jabavu, who edited a newspaper detailing acts of discrimination while urging closer bonds between blacks and whites.

The Cape also had some precociously liberal whites, who allowed people of colour on to the electoral rolls, so long as they passed a property and literacy test. In Natal, however, the whites were more reactionary, and the Africans less educated. When the Natal Indian Congress was formed, there was no comparable Native Association in the colony. In 1894 and 1895, there was no African Gandhi in Natal, no black lawyer who appeared in court or wrote regularly for the newspapers.[34]

Despite their mildness and their moderation, Gandhi and his colleagues thus represented something quite radical in Natal's modern history. The reaction they provoked is proof of this. A columnist in the *Natal Mercury*, signing himself as 'H', published periodic attacks on Gandhi and his work. In October 1895 he said Gandhi was 'a paid agitator' for the Indian merchants. 'H' called upon the Europeans to stand up and 'capsize the little apple cart Messrs. Gandhi and Co. are wheeling along'. The attack prompted a rejoinder from Joseph Royeppen, a young clerk in Gandhi's office. 'Not a penny', said Royeppen, was 'given Mr Gandhi in return for his valuable services to the [Natal Indian] Congress'. 'H' was unabashed. He had been told that 'a list was made out and signed by certain Indian merchants and business men, whereby Mr Gandhi was guaranteed £300 (payable in advance) to remain there'. Noting that Royeppen was less than twenty years of age, the columnist said he 'must decline, in future, to reply to all the Indian boys Mr Gandhi may select to write, the fraternity being too large, and my time too limited.'[35]

In October and November 1895, the white colonists in Natal held many meetings in support of the Government's Franchise Bill. The feeling against the Indians was particularly intense in the plantation and mining districts. At a meeting in Stanger, one speaker said that

> the Indians were of a low caste, and not fit for the vote . . . They did not benefit the country, they did not lay their money out here, but they got as much out of the country as possible, and then left it. He would make a difference between black and white. He would not allow the vote to even such a man as Mr Gandhi.[36]

Some Natalians looked enviously across to the Boer-dominated Transvaal, which had 'set its foot down from the first, and made the position of the Indian that ventured within its territories anything but an enviable one'. There, apart from being denied the franchise, Indians were also forbidden to own property and trade in their own names. In the Transvaal, the 'steady and uncompromising firmness' of the Boers had 'overcome the obstinate fussiness of British negrophilists'. On the other hand, the 'shilly-shally half-hearted action' of the Natal colonists had generated 'strength for the sentimental British faddist, and for the unscrupulous Indian agitator'.[37]

Angry whites now called for the 'complete disenfranchisement of the whole of our Indian population'. If this was not done, they warned, and if the 'monstrous and unjust policy of the Home Government' was forced upon them, then

> the early part of 1900 would probably, nay undoubtedly, see us with a Ministry composed somewhat after this fashion: –
>
> Prime Minister – Ali Bengharee
> Colonial Secretary – Dost Mahomed
> Attorney-General – Said Mahomed
> Treasurer – Ramasamy.
>
> In our Supreme and other courts we would have Chief Justice Ghandi [sic] and the other long and white robed gentry he is about to bring from India, and so on, in all public departments . . . What an attractive, pleasing picture! What an impetus to our European prestige and patriotism! What a reward

for our struggles and ambitions! Why, a kafir Ministry would be infinitely more preferable than an Indian. The native is a gentleman compared to him. He is manly, brave, and straightforward, while the Indian is otherwise.[38]

By the end of 1895, Mohandas Gandhi had been resident in Durban for more than a year. He was living in a house of his own, in the central locality of Beach Grove. The house was quite spacious, extending over two storeys, with a verandah and also a little garden. The furniture in the living room was sparse: a sofa and a few chairs, and a bookcase with pamphlets on vegetarianism mixed with the Koran, the Bible, Hindu texts and the works of Tolstoy.

Living with Gandhi in his house were a Gujarati-speaking cook – whose name has not come down to us – and Vincent Lawrence, a Tamil from Madras who served as his clerk. Every morning, Gandhi and Lawrence walked from Beach Grove to the lawyer's office, which was at the corner of West and Field Streets. The streets they passed through had shops owned by both Indians and Europeans – the former hawking fruits, vegetables and groceries; the latter selling less essential commodities such as medicines and chocolates. Below Gandhi's chambers was a shop selling cigars, owned by a former deputy mayor of Durban.[39]

For a while, Gandhi's home was also shared by his old schoolfriend Sheikh Mehtab, a recent migrant from Rajkot to Durban. Gandhi's trust in Mehtab was, as before, misplaced; once, when he came home for lunch, he found his friend in bed with a prostitute. Angry words ensued; when Gandhi threatened to call the police, Mehtab quietly left the premises.[40]

The clerk and cook, on the other hand, gave no trouble. Vincent Lawrence took dictation, typed letters and, when required, translated materials into Tamil (the mother tongue of many Indian labourers in Natal). As for the cook, by preparing his meals and generally keeping the house in order, he left his employer time to read and write.

In the last weeks of 1895, Gandhi published a long pamphlet on 'The Indian Franchise', framed as 'an appeal to every Briton in South Africa'. Extending over fifty printed pages, it provided a comprehensive overview of the Indian question in Natal. Gandhi argued that the 'Indian's fitness for an equality with the civilized races' was demonstrated by the fact that, in British India, they had served as senior civil servants, High Court judges and vice-chancellors of universities. Indian soldiers had shed their blood for the defence of the realm. His countrymen were loyal and law-abiding; it was unfair to relegate them to second-class status in any part of the British Empire.

Gandhi dismissed the fear, widespread among whites, that if the Indian were allowed to vote he would soon dominate the European. Of nearly 10,000 registered voters in Natal, only 251 were Indians, mostly merchants. Gandhi believed that 'the number of trading Indians in the Colony will remain almost the same for a long time. For, while many come every month, an equal number leaves for India'. If the Government wished, they could introduce a more stringent property qualification. But 'what the Indians do and would protest against is colour distinction – disqualification based on account of racial difference.'

The pamphlet consolidated arguments and evidence presented by Gandhi in other forums and other writings. There was, however, one point that he was making for the first time. It had been said of the agitation led by the Natal Indian Congress that 'a few Indians want political power and that these few are Mahomedan agitators and that the Hindus should learn from past experience that the Mahomedan rule will be ruinous for them.' Gandhi said in response that 'the first statement is without foundation and the last statement is most unfortunate and painful.' This was a 'most mischievous' attempt 'to set the Hindus against the Mahomedans' in Natal, 'where the two sects are living most amicably'.[41]

Gandhi sent his pamphlet to a friend in England, the civil servant and author W. W. Hunter. Hunter, in turn, sought an interview with the Secretary of State for India. The claims of the Natal Indians, reported Hunter to Gandhi, had 'unfortunately got mixed up in English opinion with the monotone of complaint made by the Indian Congress party.' The Congress, founded in 1885, had been canvassing for the greater representation of Indians at all levels of government. The cause of Gandhi and his fellows, found Hunter, 'suffers in England from being too prominently connected with the Congress platform'.[42]

As it happened, Gandhi had also posted copies of his pamphlet to Congress leaders in India. A copy sent to the Poona radical Bal Gangadhar Tilak found its way instead to the office of S. M. Tilak and Company in Bombay. The packet was opened by the firm's manager, who noting its contents, wrote back to the author in admiration. 'I have been watching with the greatest zeal your movements in the foreign land,' the parcel's accidental recipient told Gandhi. Saluting his work 'from heart and soul even at the cost of [your] precious life towards the welfare of [our] countrymen,' he hoped that 'the Almighty [would] crown you with success'. The manager gave Gandhi the correct address of B. G. Tilak ('Editor, Kesari and Maratha, Poona City'), before ending with this apology: 'Please excuse me from plying in trade' (rather than national service).[43]

Whether the original mistake was Gandhi's or the postman's one doesn't know. But one should be grateful for the error. For it gave us this charming letter, written by an unknown Indian, the first unsolicited fan mail that we know Gandhi to have received.

Gandhi's pamphlet on 'The Indian Franchise' was widely distributed in Natal, where – among the whites – it attracted scepticism and, at times, outright hostility. One newspaper admitted that the lawyer's tone had at least 'the great merit of moderation'. But it worried that it would lead to greater demands for representation – for Indians to be judges, civil servants and newspaper editors in South Africa, as they were in India. Another paper dismissed the pamphlet as 'specious'. 'Mr Ghandi [sic] may plead his best,' it said, 'but he will never succeed in convincing South Africans that the immigrant Asiatic is a desirable fellow-citizen . . . He may mend his ways in time it is true, but he usually takes the task of amendment very leisurely.'[44]

A third paper, the *Natal Advertiser*, chose to express its reservations in verse. The versifier was not particularly skilled. However, in so far as this was very likely the first poem about Gandhi ever written, and one which keenly captures the animosity against him among the Europeans of Natal, I think I must reproduce it in full:

Goosie, Goosie, Gandhi, Oh!
(An old song, re-sung with apologies.)

> Oh, I am a man of high degree,
>   And seek a proud position,
> For I must become, what seems to me
>   A proud politician.
> For my constituents I must stand
>   In parliamentary traffic;
> So I sailed away from India's strand
>   In the pay of the Asiatic.

Chorus: I'm a regular goosie Gandhi, oh
    With a talent that's quite handy,
    And a pamphlet bash, that's full
    For this sunny-landy, oh!
    I've a temper sweet as candy, oh
    And a book and pencil handy, oh
    You never saw such a social bore
    As Goosie, Goosie, Gandhi, oh!

When the Press and people out of pique
    Behave like a set of ninnies,
I write a book to show they're weak
    And gather in the guineas.
I'm here to fight for the coolie man,
    As I said in my earliest letter.
They must have liberty on a novel plan,
    And I must have something better.

Chorus: I'm a regular goosie Gandhi, oh
    With a talent that's quite handy,
    And a pamphlet bash, that's full
    For this sunny-landy, oh!
    I've a temper sweet as candy, oh
    And a book and pencil handy, oh
    You never saw such a social bore
    As Goosie, Goosie, Gandhi, oh![45]

Gandhi's early political writings are in the *Collected Works*. The details of his early legal career rest in the Natal archives and in old newspaper records. What we do not have access to are letters written from Durban to his family. How often did he write to his wife in Rajkot, and to his brothers? How often did they write back? We cannot say. What we do know is that in May 1896, Gandhi decided to return to India for a few months. He could see that he was 'in for a long stay' in South Africa, where 'people felt the need of my presence'. So 'I made up my mind to go home, fetch my wife and children, and then return and settle out there.'[46]

'There' was South Africa, or, more specifically, Natal. Unable to establish a toehold in either his native Kathiawar or in Bombay, Gandhi was now the most important and influential Indian in this colony. Gujaratis and Tamils, Hindus and Muslims, all looked to him for legal and political advice. To merchant and labourer alike he was 'Gandhi bhai', Brother Gandhi, a term used with affection and respect. He had made a name in Natal, and now he would make his home here too. Like so many other migrants before and since, he had first come alone, so to say experimentally. His career established, and a cause found, he went back to India to bring Kasturba and the children to live with him in Durban.

5

Travelling Activist

On 4 June 1896 'the Madrasi and Gujarati Indians of Durban' threw a farewell party for Mohandas Gandhi. The lawyer was presented with a shawl and medal, and thanked for his work for the community. In a brief speech, Gandhi said the gathering 'showed that whatever castes the Indians in Natal represented they were all in favour of being cemented in closer union'. His talk was translated into Tamil by his clerk, Vincent Lawrence. 'Several songs and speeches followed the presentation, and the proceedings throughout were of a lively and enthusiastic character.'[1]

The next day, Gandhi sailed for India on the *Clan Mcleod*. Some 500 Indians accompanied him to the port, cheering him as he walked on board.[2] Their affection followed him across the ocean. When the ship stopped at Lourenço Marques, the principal port of Portuguese East Africa, the Indians there gave him a warm reception. They had been sent a telegram by Parsee Rustomjee which read: 'Barrister Gandhi left for India via Delagoa Bay. Please go on board and respect him.'[3]

The lawyer was by now an experienced traveller. This, his fourth inter-continental voyage in eight years, was spent chiefly in self-improvement. He played chess, took Urdu lessons from a fellow passenger, and tried to teach himself Tamil from a book.[4]

After three weeks the *Clan Mcleod* reached Calcutta. Gandhi took a train westwards to join his family in Rajkot. He had not seen them since May 1893. His sons Harilal and Manilal were now eight and three respectively. His impressions of them are unrecorded. We do not know how he responded to their growing up, or what relations he resumed with their mother, his wife. He was preoccupied with printing a pamphlet for an Indian audience on the grievances of their countrymen in

South Africa. This drew on his previous petitions, but added some fresh evidence based on personal experience. 'Just picture a country', he told his compatriots, 'where you never know you are safe from assaults, no matter who you are, where you have a nervous fear as to what would happen to you whenever accommodated in a hotel even for a night and you have a picture of the state we are living in Natal.'

Gandhi complained that a law in Durban specified that natives and indentured labourers required passes to go about at night. This, said Gandhi, 'presupposes that the Indian is a barbarian. There is a very good reason for requiring registration of a native in that he is yet being taught the dignity and necessity of labour. The Indian knows it and he is imported because he knows it'. Adding insult to injury, 'lavatories are marked "natives and Asiatics" at the railway stations'.

Gandhi's struggle in Natal was based on a Tolstoyan interpretation of the Christian credo. 'Our method in South Africa is to conquer this hatred by love,' he said. 'We do not attempt to have individuals punished but as a rule, patiently suffer wrongs at their hands. Generally, our prayers are not to demand compensation for past injuries, but to render a repetition of those injuries impossible and to remove the causes.'[5]

Gandhi printed 10,000 copies of what quickly became known as the 'Green Pamphlet' (on account of the colour of its cover). He posted them to newspaper editors across the country, and carried copies with him to Bombay, where he spent much of August and September 1896 lobbying the leading public men of India. He met a Hindu reformer, M. G. Ranade, a Muslim reformer, Badruddin Tyabji, and a Parsi reformer, Pherozeshah Mehta.[6] Ranade and Tyabji were judges; Mehta, a lawyer and legislator. But he met many lesser known people too, pressing his case and his pamphlet upon them. An entry from the account book he maintained for the Natal Indian Congress is proof of his hectic schedule. Dated 20 August, it reads: 'Carriage – House to Fort; Fort to B. K. Road; House to Appolobunder [sic]; Apollobunder to Market; Market to House'. These five journeys cost him about two rupees. Thereafter he took the more prudent step of renting the same carriage and driver for the whole day.[7]

The lobbying had an effect, the Times of India carrying a long leader based on 'Mr Gandhi's able and striking pamphlet'. The paper provided some examples of the 'gratuitous oppression and persecution' as documented by Gandhi: the exclusion of Indians from trams, the consignment of Indians to third-class railway carriages, the harassment of even 'respectable Indians' under a harsh vagrancy law.[8]

On 26 September, a public meeting was convened at the Framji Cowasji Institute to discuss the Indian question in South Africa. Pherozeshah Mehta presided. Gandhi was too nervous to speak. His text was read out for him by the Parsi politician D. E. Wacha. Gandhi, in Wacha's voice, contrasted the situation in India, where the 'representative institutions ... are slowly, but surely, being liberalized', with that in Natal, where 'such institutions are being gradually closed against us'. The British in India now permitted their subjects – admittedly, selectively – to become judges and municipal councillors; in Natal, however, they 'desire to degrade us to the level of the raw Kaffir whose occupation is hunting, and whose sole ambition is to collect a certain number of cattle to buy a wife with, and then, pass his life in indolence and nakedness ... We are hemmed in on all sides in South Africa.' In Natal they were under the 'yoke of oppression'. 'It is for you, our elder and freer brother, to remove it.'[9]

Gandhi's talk created a stir; many people were heard expressing themselves 'in indignant terms about the treatment which our countrymen were receiving in South Africa'. Their indignation was tempered and put in context by the social reformer M. G. Ranade, who was also present at the Cowasji Institute that day. In a talk he delivered soon afterwards, Ranade asked Hindus to 'turn the searchlight inwards'. Unlike some other nationalists, Ranade was keenly aware of the humiliations that Indians were prepared to heap on their own kind. 'Was this sympathy with the oppressed and down-trodden Indians,' he wondered, 'to be confined to those of our countrymen only who had gone out of India?' Or would it be extended to a condemnation of the shameful manner in which low castes were treated within India? Ranade asked 'whether it was for those who tolerated such disgraceful oppression and injustice in their own country to indulge in all that denunciation of the people of South Africa'.[10]

From Bombay, Gandhi proceeded to Poona. Here he met the two rising stars of nationalist politics, the liberal Gopal Krishna Gokhale and the radical Bal Gangadhar Tilak. Gokhale, a protégé of Ranade's, thought social reform was as important as political emancipation; mindful of the sentiments of Muslims, he stayed away from a Hindu idiom in his speeches. Tilak, on the other hand, militantly opposed British rule; he also promoted festivals in celebration of the Hindu god Ganesh and the medieval Hindu warrior Shivaji.[11] Gandhi met both men; both promised to help set up a public meeting.[12]

From Poona, Gandhi took a train further south, to the city of Madras. He was now corresponding with a Bombay lawyer he wanted to come out to South Africa. The previous September, he had promised the Indians of Natal he would bring some barristers to help them. His first choice was F. S. Taleyarkhan, who had travelled with him on the boat back from London to Bombay in 1891. Gandhi told Taleyarkhan that if he came to Natal they could set up a partnership and divide the profits. He thought that they could earn as much as £150 a month. However, he warned Taleyarkhan that an Indian should not 'go to South Africa with a view to pile money. You should go there with a spirit of self-sacrifice. You should keep riches at an arm's length. They may then woo you. If you bestow your glances on them, they are such a coquette that you are sure to be slighted. That is my experience in South Africa.'

Taleyarkhan was a Parsi who liked meat and fish. Gandhi said that if they lived together in Durban, he could offer him 'most palatable' vegetarian food, 'cooked both in the English as well as the Indian style'. If the Parsi insisted on being carnivorous, he could engage a separate cook. Gandhi hoped Taleyarkhan would 'not allow pecuniary considerations to come in your way. I am sure you will be able to do much in South Africa – more indeed than I may have been instrumental in doing.'[13]

Gandhi arrived in Madras on 14 October. This was his first visit to the city, the capital of the Madras Presidency, and the commercial and political centre of a region to which many of the indentured labourers in Natal belonged. He stayed two weeks in Madras, at the Buckingham Hotel, where his bill came to some Rs 74. His other expenses included the sending of telegrams, carriage and tram fares, and the purchase of paper, pen, ink, envelopes, stamps, and 'sulphur ointment' (we know not what for).[14]

From Madras, Gandhi wrote to Gokhale about the struggle in South Africa. He was encouraged that the older man had taken a 'very warm interest in him when they met in Poona. They now 'very badly need[ed] a committee of active, prominent workers in India for our cause'. Unless 'our great men . . . without delay take up this question', insisted Gandhi, the South African example would be followed by other British colonies, who would likewise disenfranchise Indians and deny them their rights. If that happened, 'within a short time there will be an end to Indian enterprise outside India'.[15]

The highlight of Gandhi's stay in Madras was a public meeting held at the Pachiappa's Hall on the evening of 26 October. The posters advertising the meeting had the signatures of forty-one men, among them some of the city's best-known lawyers, editors and businessmen. Those endorsing Gandhi's cause included a fair sprinkling of Brahmins, but also some Chettiar merchants, a handful of Telugu speakers, two Muslims, and at least one Christian. There was also one Knight of the Realm, Sir S. Ramaswamy Mudaliar.[16]

As in Bombay, Gandhi's speech rehearsed the themes of the 'Green Pamphlet'. He tailored it to the audience, speaking of how a 'very respectable firm of Madras traders' in Durban were disparagingly referred to as 'coolie' shopkeepers, and how 'a Madras gentleman, spotlessly dressed, always avoids the foot-paths of prominent streets in Durban for fear he should be insulted or pushed off'.[17] In its report, the *Madras Mail* observed that the speaker 'described accurately and without exaggeration the position of his fellow countrymen in that part of the world'. Wishing 'speedy success to Mr Gandhi and his friends in bringing the Colonials to a better understanding of India', the paper said the 'British Government will be failing in its duty if it allows the strong racial feeling prevailing in the Colonies to be embodied in any Act of Legislature which concerns a British subject'.[18]

There was such a rush at the meeting to buy pamphlets that the author's stock was exhausted. Not that he minded; as he observed soon afterwards, while ordering a reprint, the clamour for copies in Madras was 'a scene never to be forgotten'.[19]

In the last week of October, Gandhi travelled up the Coromandel coast to Calcutta, this his third long train journey in as many months. He was being exposed to the ecological and social diversity of India. He passed by desert and farmland, coast and plateau, seeing a variety of architectural styles, hearing a variety of languages, and sampling different cuisines. From the train window, he would have seen peasants working in the fields. However, his conversations in the towns and cities he stopped in were with lawyers, editors and other members of a growing middle class.

Gandhi had been well received in the Presidency capitals of Bombay and Madras. Calcutta was the capital of the Bengal Presidency, the capital of Britain's Indian Empire, and in 1896 the most active centre of Indian nationalism. The call for greater representation was heard loudest here. As one who asked for greater rights for Indians overseas, Gandhi expected a sympathetic hearing; instead, he was given the cold shoulder. The editor of a prominent Indian newspaper took him to be 'a wandering Jew'. Another kept him waiting for an hour; when he was finally called in, Gandhi was told that 'there is no end to the number of visitors like you. You had better go. I am not disposed to listen to you'.[20]

This lack of enthusiasm may have been because there were fewer Bengalis in South Africa. Or it may have been a manifestation of arrogance. Gandhi spent two weeks in Calcutta, staying at the Great Eastern Hotel in the heart of the city, across the street from the Viceroy's residence. Judging by his account book, he was less busy than in Madras or Bombay. He had his hair cut, his clothes washed, and sent plenty of letters and telegrams. He also went one evening to the theatre, where he watched a Bengali musical. But he was unable to arrange a public meeting.[21]

On 5 November, Gandhi wrote to F. S. Taleyarkhan, asking whether he would be ready to come back to Natal with him (the Parsi asked for more time). He planned to sail from Bombay before the end of the month. The Natal Legislature was due to reconvene in January, when it would discuss the amended franchise, the £3 tax and other matters of interest – or concern – to Indians.

Gandhi went back now to the west coast, where he attended a public meeting in Poona, lobbied further in Bombay and prepared his family for the journey to South Africa. He was particularly concerned about the dress his wife and children would wear. He decided it was best they emulate the Parsis, then regarded as the most progressive people in India. The boys were thus fitted out in trousers and a long coat, while Kasturba was made to wear her sari the Parsi way, with an embroidered border, and her arms fully covered.[22]

Mohandas, Kasturba, Harilal and Manilal Gandhi left Bombay for Durban on 30 November by the SS *Courland*. With them was Gandhi's sister's son Gokuldas, who had been placed in his care. Their passages were free, since the ship was owned by the patriarch's friend, client and fellow community activist, Dada Abdulla.

While Gandhi was away, the whites of Natal had become further agitated about the Indian question. In August 1896, the Tongat Sugar Company asked the Government's help in importing some thirty bricklayers, carpenters, fitters and blacksmiths from India. The company said they would pay three times the wage of an indentured labourer. 'We are not particular as to whether they are Madras or Calcutta men', said the company, 'but, of course, we want good men.'

Private entrepreneurs, motivated by production and cost efficiencies, wished to import skilled labour from wherever they could find it. This rational, capitalist impulse however fell foul of racial and national prejudices. How dare a Natal entrepreneur transport Asians to do jobs that whites could as well undertake? And so the Tongat Sugar Company's application was leaked to the press, prompting 'an indignation meeting of European artisans' in Durban, worried that Indians would take over trades previously in white hands. The 'room was packed to overflowing, the entire audience standing wedged in close contact'. A speaker joked that 'perhaps after the recent ravages of the locusts they [the plantation owners] were going to employ coolie house painters to tip the canes with emerald green (laughter)'. Shouts of 'Black vermin!', 'We won't have the coolie here!' and 'Put a poll tax of £100 on them; that will stop them!' were heard. The meeting asked the Government to immediately stop the import of Indian artisans into the colony.

Unnerved by the protest, the company withdrew their application. Writing to the Secretary of State for the Colonies, the Governor of Natal said the incident was 'of interest as exemplifying the jealousy with which the competition of Asiatics, except, perhaps in the matter of unskilled labour, is regarded in Natal'.[23]

Such was the mood in August. In September, the *Natal Mercury* published a cable sent by the news agency Reuters that summarized Gandhi's 'Green Pamphlet', then just off the press in Rajkot, in this single sentence: 'A pamphlet published in India declares that the Indians in Natal are robbed and assaulted, and treated like beasts, and are unable to obtain redress'. The newspaper commented that by uttering these 'infamous falsehoods' Gandhi had 'done his countrymen a bad turn'.[24]

This bare and not entirely accurate summary of a forty-page booklet prompted a series of verbal attacks on Indians in general and Gandhi in particular. The 'one great point that the Indians individually and collectively seem to forget,' wrote the *Natal Mercury*, 'is that South Africa was captured from the native inhabitants after long years of fighting, and the expenditure of blood and treasure, not one penny of which was borne by the Indians, nor one drop of Indian blood spilt voluntarily.'[25] An editorial writer wrote angrily of 'the agitator Gandhi, whose slanderous statements made before his fellow-countrymen in Bombay have justly roused the resentment of the European colonist.'[26] The attacks on Gandhi in the Durban press prompted his estranged friend, Sheikh Mehtab, to defend him. Having been thrown out of the lawyer's house, Mehtab now lived by himself in a locality named Stamford Hill. From there he wrote a letter pointing out that Gandhi's 'Green Pamphlet', the subject of outrage in Natal, was merely a reprise of his 'Open Letter' and 'Appeal', previously published and circulated in the Colony. 'If all Indians in Natal are robbed, and assaulted, and treated like beasts, and are unable to obtain redress', remarked Mehtab to the readers of the *Natal Advertiser*, 'you should not be surprised.' He urged a fresh reading of Gandhi's earlier pamphlets. 'If you read those two books again,' said Mehtab to the Europeans in Natal, 'you will be able to understand a few subjects very well. If you concede that those two books are right, you should not be surprised that Indians are "shamefully treated".'[27]

In August and September, several ships from India arrived in Durban. They carried indentured labourers contracted for by plantation owners, residents of the colony returning from a visit to their homeland, and some new immigrants. The ships intensified the paranoia and the panic. These landings appeared to be part of an 'organized effort', one 'of those great waves of emigration which sometimes occur, which relieve one country at the time that other countries are peopled'. On 15 October the members of the Natal Government sent an urgent telegram to their Prime Minister, Sir John Robinson, who was then in England: 'Five hundred free Indians arrived last week. Inrush must be stopped, or all lower branches of trade and farming will pass into Indian hands. Explain to Mr Chamberlain we must follow New South Wales' (the Australian colony that had banned immigration of coloured peoples).[28]

The Ministers were reflecting the sentiments of their electorate. On

26 November a large meeting was held at Durban's Town Hall, which urged the Government to preserve Natal as an English colony and 'to maintain the race pure and undefiled' by putting an end to Indian immigration. The hall was packed, with many ladies also in attendance. One speaker, a Mr O'Hea, said

> It was sad to see the flood-gates opened for the entrance to this Colony of these dark and dismal people, who were absolutely useless to the community. They were useless to the butcher, for they did not eat meat (laughter); they were useless to the baker, for they only ate rice (laughter) – the profits on the growth of which went to India, and the profits on the introduction went to the [Indian ship-owners] Dada Abdoolas and Moosas (loud laughter). They were useless to the shoemaker, for they went bare-footed, and they were useless to the tailor because (saving the presence of the ladies) they did not require any of the niceties of the sartorial art (laughter) to produce their unmentionables.[29]

In the next fortnight, three further meetings were held to oppose Indian immigration. The chairman of the Society of Carpenters and Joiners said that at the time of the next election, members 'should vote straight for the candidate who would do his utmost to stop the invasion of the Asiatics'. To the argument that Indians were British subjects, the speaker said

> he should like to know how long the sentiment of British subjects would stand supposing these Asiatics were brought into Lancashire to weave cotton, or into Yorkshire to weave cloth. The sentiment of British subject would be gone in 24 hours – (applause) – and the Government would very soon be compelled to find a method to exclude these Asiatics from England, and if they had to find a way, surely the Colony of Natal could also find a way to exclude them.[30]

In the third week of December 1896, the SS *Courland* arrived off the coast of Durban. With it was another ship, the SS *Naderi*, also coming from India. Between them, the vessels had some 600 Indians on board, Mohandas Gandhi and his family among them. The ships were asked to wait out at sea while the passengers were examined by doctors. There had been an outbreak of plague in the Bombay Presidency, and the authorities were concerned the migrants might be infected with the disease. The etiology of plague was imperfectly understood; it was not yet established that rats and fleas were the disease's main carriers. Some doctors, and more ordinary folk, feared that it could spread through human contact.[31]

As the ships lay moored off the Natal coast, the twelfth annual meeting of the Indian National Congress convened in Calcutta. Gandhi was an absent presence, with his recent lobbying in India informing its deliberations. Among the twenty-four resolutions passed by the Congress was one recording a 'most solemn protest against the disabilities imposed on Indians in South Africa, and the invidious and humiliating distinctions made between them and European settlers'. Moving the resolution, G. Parameshvaram Pillai of Madras observed that while in India, Indians could become members of the Legislative Council, and in England they could win election to the House of Commons, in Natal

we are driven out of tramcars, we are pushed off footpaths, we are kept out of hotels, we are refused the benefit of the public baths, we are spat upon, we are hissed, we are cursed, we are abused, and we are subjected to a variety of other indignities which no human being can patiently endure.[32]

On the other side of the Indian Ocean, the mood was very different. Gandhi had become a hate-figure among the whites of Natal, on account of what he was supposed to have said in his travels in India. On 23 December, the *Natal Advertiser* printed a plea urging swift action against the 'great Gandhi [who] has arrived at the head of the advanced guard of the Indian army of invasion – the army that is to dispossess us of our country and our homes . . . We must be up and doing, and make our arrangements so as to be able to give the invaders a fitting reception.'[33]

A week later, the same newspaper revealed the plan of action decided upon by the hostile whites of Durban. On the day the Indians disembarked, they would be met at the port by a mass of Europeans, formed in 'human lines three or four deep' which, 'with locked hands and arms', would 'offer a complete bar to the immigrants'.[34]

The anger against Gandhi and company was compounded by a paranoia about the germs they allegedly carried. The doctors who came aboard the two ships said they could not yet allow them to land; in their view, plague germs took three weeks to incubate, and it was better to wait and watch. The ships' captains were instructed to have the decks washed and cleaned daily with a mixture of water and carbolic acid. Sulphur fires were kept burning day and night to cleanse the passengers and their possessions of any remnants of the dreaded germs.[35]

A rumour reached Durban that the Indians on board would sue the Government of Natal for illegal detention. Swallowing the rumour whole, a local newspaper concluded that Gandhi's

> keen legal instincts have scented a splendid brief to occupy himself immediately on his release from the 'durance vile' of the quarantine and purifying effects of the carbolic bath. The large sum of money said to have been subscribed for the purpose would naturally go to Mr Gandhi whether the case was won or lost, and nothing in fact could suit the gentleman better than such an interesting case to devote his attention to immediately he got on shore.[36]

This representation of Gandhi as a malevolent, money-grubbing lawyer further consolidated the anti-Indian sentiments on shore. On 4 January 1897, some 1,500 whites gathered for a meeting in Durban's Market Square. As the chairman, a certain Harry Sparks – the owner of a butcher's shop – moved into his chair, it began to rain. He decided to shift the meeting to the Town Hall nearby. Thereupon

> a unanimous and spontaneous move was made in the direction of the municipal hall, the verandahs and space immediately around the main entrance being quickly thronged with a surging crowd of interested and enthusiastic burgesses. Some little time elapsed before the gates were opened, but in the meantime the lights were switched on, and in a few minutes after the gates were thrown open the central hall was thronged from floor to ceiling. The audience when Mr Sparks resumed the chair must have numbered 2,000 . . . [37]

The meeting called upon the Government to send the two ships back to India, and to disallow all Indians other than indentured labourers from entering Natal. A voice in the crowd shouted: 'Let them take Gandhi with them!' The main speaker, a Dr McKenzie,

> relieved himself freely of his opinion about the mischievous Mr Gandhi . . . [H]e said Mr Gandhi had gone away to drag our reputation in the gutters of India, and he had painted Natal as black and filthy as his own

skin ... Mr Gandhi had come to the colony to take everything that was fair and good, and he had gone out of it to blackguard the hospitality with which he had been indulged. They would teach Mr Gandhi that they read from his actions that he was not satisfied with what they had given him and wanted something more. They would give him something more.

The ships carrying Indians to Durban, alleged Dr McKenzie, were part of a larger conspiracy to overturn the racial order in Natal.

It was the intention of these facile and delicate creatures to make themselves proprietors of the only thing that the rulers of this country had withheld from them – the franchise. It was their intention to put themselves in parliament and legislate for the Europeans; to take over the household management, and put the Europeans in the kitchen.[38]

Three days later the whites of Durban held another meeting. Dr McKenzie was once more the lead speaker. 'The Indian Ocean was the proper place for these Indians (applause),' he began. The whites 'were not going to dispute their right to the water there; but they must be careful that they did not give them the right to the land adjoining that ocean (applause).'[39] This meeting, even bigger and more passionate than the last, demonstrated (according to the *Natal Mercury*) that

Mr Gandhi has made a big mistake in imagining that the Europeans of Natal would sit still while he organised an independent emigration agency in India to land his countrymen here at the rate of from 1,000 to 2,000 per month ... Despite his cleverness, [Gandhi] has made a sorry mistake ... Our forefathers won this country at the point of the sword, and left us the country as our birthright and heritage. That birthright we have to hand down as it was handed down to us.'[40]

A phrase, and headline, much favoured by the Natal papers in the last weeks of 1896 was 'Asiatic invasion'. The colonists feared that the few hundred passengers waiting off the coast were the beginnings of large-scale immigration that would decisively alter the demographic profile of Natal. One man was presumed to be at the head of the horde: the lawyer, Mohandas Karamchand Gandhi.

Gandhi was reading the Natal newspapers, which came aboard daily, courtesy of the supply boats. He also got news of the mood on shore from letters sent by friends. An English lawyer wrote to Gandhi on

8 January that if he decided to come off the boat he would 'be roughly handled'. In fact 'the public feeling against yourself, and the landing of the free Indians ... is so great that I begin to doubt if you will make it ashore.' In Gandhi's absence, the Englishman was assisting his clients, and asked him to send a cheque now to cover his fees. For it seemed quite likely that the *Naderi* and the *Courland* would be forced to return to Bombay with their passengers, who were so unwelcome in Natal.[41]

The ships had been moored offshore for some twenty days. In Durban, a 'European Protection Association' was formed to resist the Asiatic invasion. The Association's first meeting was held on 10 January. When one speaker said that the 'mouthpiece' of the Indians 'was a gentleman of the name of Ghandhi [*sic*]', a voice from the crowd interjected: 'Don't say a gentleman'. A rumour spread that Gandhi was cowed by the protests; one newspaper even claiming that 'some of the officials who visited the vessels this morning report that Mr Gandhi and the Indians on board are in a state of "funk", and several were pleading to be taken back to India direct.'

On 11 January, a reporter of the *Natal Advertiser* went on board the SS *Naderi* to interview the captain. There were, he found, 356 passengers on board, including 'infants in arms'; and contrary to the fears on shore, there were no artisans among them. To the question, 'How do the passengers look upon Gandhi?' the captain answered: 'There is not a man on board these ships who knew Gandhi until they landed here. I never heard of him either, and only read his pamphlet during my quarantine.' [42]

The next day the reporter obtained an interview with Gandhi himself. The lawyer refuted the rumours that there were blacksmiths and carpenters on board, and that he was importing a printing press. Most of the passengers were Natal residents, returning after a holiday in India. The newcomers were traders, shopkeeper's assistants, and hawkers. And he had 'absolutely nothing whatever to do' with bringing these other passengers to Natal.

Gandhi drew attention to the wider Imperial dimensions of the controversy. 'Every Britisher is agreed,' he remarked,

> that the glory of the British Empire depends on the retention of the Indian
> Empire and on the face of this, it looks very unpatriotic of the Colonists

of Natal, whose prosperity depends not a little on the introduction of the Indians, to so vigorously protest against the introduction of free Indians. The policy of exclusion is obsolete, and Colonists should admit Indians to the franchise and, at the same time, in points in which they are not fully civilized, Colonists should help them to become more civilized. That, I certainly think, should be the policy followed throughout the Colonies, if all the parts of the British Empire are to remain in harmony.

'What is your object in coming back?', the reporter asked. Gandhi replied,

I do not return here with the intention of making money, but of acting as a humble interpreter between the two communities [of Europeans and Indians]. There is a great misunderstanding between the two communities, and I shall endeavour to fulfill the office of interpreter so long as both the communities do not object to my presence.[43]

Durban has a superb natural harbour, a stretch of sheltered water nestling between a strip of land known as the 'Point' and a wooded hill known as the 'Bluff'. There was a bar of moving sand at the harbour's entrance; this was an impediment to big ships, but in other ways contributed to the safety of the harbour. When the port was first established, the depth of water over the sandbar was only four feet at low tide. Over the decades, dredging had increased the depth, but in 1897 it was still impossible for ocean liners to enter with ease. So they dropped anchor out at sea, transferring their passengers and cargo on to smaller vessels that then negotiated the bar to enter the harbour.[44]

On 12 January 1897, the authorities finally allowed the ships from India to send their passengers ashore. The captains of the *Naderi* and *Courland* were asked to commence landing operations the next morning. The decision was prompted by appeals by the Viceroy in India and the Secretary of State for the Colonies in London, who warned that the agitation in Natal had put a question mark on imperial harmony in the Diamond Jubilee of Queen Victoria's reign.[45]

Word of the compromise – or capitulation – reached the white protesters in Durban. On the morning of the 13th, they began streaming down from the town to the Point, marching in groups defined by trade – the railwaymen together, then the blacksmiths, the carpenters, the mechanics, the shop assistants, the tailors, the bricklayers and finally a number of unaffiliated whites referred to in the newspaper reports as the 'general public'. More than 5,000 Europeans had responded to the call. There was also a 'native section' of about 500 Africans; a dwarf was appointed to lead them, who (to the whites' delight) 'marched up and down in front of their ranks officering them, while they went through a number of exercises with their sticks, and danced and whooped.'[46]

Hearing of the demonstration, the Attorney-General of Natal, Harry Escombe, rushed down to the Point. Escombe was a little man; to make himself heard, he climbed on top of a heap of logs and sought to pacify an increasingly angry crowd. The passengers on the two ships, he said, were innocent men (and women and children) who did not know of the strong feelings in Natal. He urged the crowd to be 'quiet, manly and resolute', to abjure 'haste and hysterics', and to have trust in their Government. Natal was and would remain a white colony. An early session of Parliament would be convened, to pass legislation keeping out Asiatics. Escombe's pleas were answered with shouts of 'Send the Indians back!' and 'Bring Gandhi ashore, let him come here for all the tar and feathers!'

Escombe again urged the crowd to disperse peacefully. This was the sixtieth year of Queen Victoria's reign and 'in the autumn of her life it should never be said that anything which took place in Natal caused the least sorrow or sadness in the heart of that great Sovereign.' The appeal to Imperial honour had some effect, for the crowd began to quieten down, and slowly, to melt away.[47]

Through the day, boats carrying passengers from the *Naderi* and *Courland* came over the sandbar into the harbour. As a gesture of appeasement, the owners had run the Union Jack up at the head of the ships. The passengers quietly disembarked and made their way into the Indian areas of the city. Kasturba and the children were now safely ashore, but Gandhi was still on the *Naderi*, where he had been joined by his friend, the Durban solicitor F. A. Laughton. The Attorney-General had sent word that it might be better for Gandhi to come ashore after dusk, but Laughton did not like the idea of his 'entering the city like a thief in the night'. In any case, things appeared to have quietened down on the Point; the whites were said to have dispersed, and it seemed safe for them to land.[48]

The boat carrying Gandhi and Laughton came ashore shortly before five in the afternoon. As it crossed the sandbar, the passengers would have seen, on the right, the city of Durban; and on the left, the long, low, wooded hill known as the Bluff. Behind them lay the mighty ocean. This was a striking landscape, which at other times might have been savoured for pleasure. But now, with the Bluff on one side and a hostile city on the other, and the ocean and his homeland receding further into the distance, Gandhi may well have had the feeling of being hemmed in.

As their boat was landing, some white boys loitering about recognized the Indian barrister. They sent word to the remnants of the retreating crowd, who hurried back to the Point. Laughton and Gandhi hailed a rickshaw and were about to step into it, when the boys laid hold of the wheels. The barristers tried to get into another rickshaw, but, sensing the mood, the driver was unwilling to take them. Gandhi and Laughton decided to walk on with their luggage. From the Victoria Embankment they walked northwards on Stanger Street, with a crowd of ever greater numbers following them, hissing and jeering. Then they took a turn towards West Street. When they neared the Ship's Hotel – as its name suggests, a place favoured by seamen – Gandhi and Laughton were surrounded, and the former set upon. The Indian became 'the object of kicks and cuffs, while mud and stale fish were thrown at him. One person also produced a riding-whip, and gave him a stroke, while another plucked away at his peculiar hat.'

Gandhi was beaten, but not bowed. Blood was flowing down his neck, but 'eye-witnesses state that he bore himself stolidly and pluckily through the trying ordeal.' He was rescued from the mob by a white lady, who used her parasol to keep away the attackers. She was the wife of the long-serving Superintendent of Police, R. C. Alexander. Alerted by some Indians, a posse of constables arrived to relieve Gandhi – and Mrs Alexander. Superintendent Alexander himself followed soon after.

The policemen safely conveyed Gandhi to Parsee Rustomjee's store in Field Street, locking the doors from the inside as they entered. Outside, the crowd continued to bay for (more of) Gandhi's blood. Superintendent Alexander, now joined by the deputy mayor, urged them to disperse. But more and more whites began to gather around the store; they constituted 'a compact mass of anti-Gandhites'.

According to a reporter on the spot, the crowd 'told the Superintendent what a fine fellow he was, and also exactly their *modus operandi* of dealing with Gandhi. They had a barrel of treacle quite close, and if the

Superintendent would only confide Gandhi to their care, they would undertake that he should be handed back safe and sound, if treacled and sticky.' Then they began to sing a song beginning with the words, 'We'll hang old Gandhi on a sour apple tree.'

Alexander, thinking on his feet, devised a plan to spirit Gandhi to safety. He went into the store and made Gandhi exchange his clothes for the uniform of a government peon. Gandhi's face was blackened and covered with a muffler. Then, escorted by two detectives, Gandhi took a side door out of the house, which led into Parsee Rustomjee's godown, from which the trio escaped into the street and hopped into a carriage that conveyed them to the police station.

A little later, Alexander himself emerged, to tell the crowd that Gandhi was not inside. He invited a deputation to go in and check. Three members of the mob went into Rustomjee's store, and 'reappeared with the intelligence that wherever Gandhi was he could not be found in that building.'

By now it was late evening. It had begun to rain. As the shower intensified, 'the ardent desire of the crowd to see Mr Gandhi began to wane, and in its place a desire arose to find a more comfortable place to discuss the situation than in the middle of a somewhat sloppy road in front of an Indian store in the rain.' So the crowd finally dispersed. Where they went the reports do not tell us. It was probably a place which served refreshments other than tea.[49]

On 15 January, the *Natal Mercury* carried an editorial entitled 'After the Demonstration'. This accepted that the attack on Gandhi was 'an undignified and unmanly act'. It then proceeded to lay the blame on the victim:

> Mr Gandhi has himself been very largely at fault. He has raised the passions of the people, and knowing this he ought to have been better advised than to attempt to come through the very centre of the town immediately in the rear of a demonstration he had been largely instrumental in creating.[50]

This editorial brought forth a long defence of Gandhi and his motives by F. A. Laughton. When the *Naderi* and the *Courland* lay marooned at sea, noted the barrister, the white press and public of Natal had accused Gandhi of many horrible things. They claimed that 'he had dragged our reputations through the gutters of India, and had painted them as black and filthy as his own face'. They claimed 'he was engaging himself on board the quarantined ships in getting briefs from passengers against the Government'. It was alleged that he was in a funk, too afraid to come ashore; according to one rumour, he was 'sitting on the deck of the *Courland* in a most dejected mood'; according to another, 'he was stowed away in the lowest hold.'

In the time he had known Gandhi, Laughton had 'formed a very high opinion of him'. He found Gandhi to be 'both in legal matters and on the Asiatic question, a fair and honourable opponent'. He was well qualified to 'hold the position of leader in a great political question in which his countrymen take as much interest as we do, and who are as much entitled to ventilate their political views as we are'. Now, when he had been repeatedly represented as a 'cowardly calumniator', Gandhi decided to come ashore, so as to 'vindicate himself before the public', so that 'he should not give his enemies an opportunity of saying that he was "funking it".' Instead of waiting till nightfall, Gandhi chose to 'face the music like a man and like a political leader, and – give me leave to say – right nobly did he do it'. As a fellow barrister, Laughton decided to accompany the Indian, and 'to testify by doing so that Mr Gandhi was a honourable member of a honourable profession'. Laughton acted as he did 'in protest against the way in which he [Gandhi] had been treated, and in the hope that my presence might save him from insult'.

Laughton ended his remarkable letter by asking his city and race to tender an apology. 'Durban has grossly insulted this man', he insisted:

> I say Durban, because Durban raised the storm and is answerable for the result. We are all humiliated at the treatment [of Gandhi]. Our traditions concerning fair play appear to be in the dust. Let us act, like gentlemen, and, however much against the grain it may be, express regret handsomely and generously.'[51]

Laughton was among the few Europeans in Durban whose sympathies lay with Gandhi rather than with the mob that sought to lynch him. Others included the Superintendent of Police, R. C. Alexander, and his wife, Jane. A week after the couple had saved his skin, Gandhi sent them a note of thanks, with a present. The letter is not available, nor do we know what Gandhi's gift was. What survives are the couple's replies.

Mrs Alexander said that her preventing further injury with her parasol 'in no way atone[s] for the gross injustice done you by my countrymen'. She would have liked to return the gift, but felt that 'would be but adding another insult, to the many you have had to endure since your return'.

As for the police chief, he thought that he had not done enough to protect Gandhi. 'I am very sorry indeed,' he wrote, 'that I had not sufficient force at my back, to do that duty without inflicting upon you and yours, further degradation, by compelling you to escape the mob, in the disguise of one so very far beneath you.' He trusted that Gandhi, 'like our own Prophet, when placed under a similar trial, will forgive your accusers, for they know not what they did'.[52]

Gandhi was deeply touched by the support of Laughton and the Alexanders. Meanwhile, another European resident of Durban, whom we know only by his initials ('D. B.'), wrote sympathetically of Gandhi's predicament in an essay for the radical New York weekly, *The Nation*. This used the mob rage in Durban to probe the question – who were more reactionary in racial matters, the British or the Americans?

In the middle of the nineteenth century, said 'D. B.', the British were seen as progressive imperialists, who had abolished slavery and promoted free trade. Their empire was 'free to every nationality, and within its confines was known no distinction, Greek nor Jew, circumcision nor uncircumcision, Barbarian, Scythian, bond nor free'. But soon things changed. 'Under the stress of the Indian mutiny [of 1857] and the Jamaican rebellion [of 1865], we developed a brutality as great as was ever shown by a civilized people, and which men of the highest culture tried to justify'. Colony after colony adopted protectionist policies, suppressing native peoples and keeping out coloured immigrants, erecting racial barriers as sharp as in the American South.

British hypocrisy was manifest most strongly in South Africa, where the treatment of Indians was 'flagrantly in contravention of the theory of an empire guaranteeing equal rights and immunities to all subjects'. 'D. B.' summarized the pamphlets written by 'M. K. Gandhi, a Hindu barrister', which had 'strikingly forced upon public attention' the disabilities of Indian subjects of the Empire. Gandhi was rewarded with mob fury and an attempt on his life. The attack and its wider implications were outlined by 'D. B.' in two resonant paragraphs:

In the treatment meted out to [Gandhi] on his return to Natal, at the hands of the people whose conduct towards his countrymen he had exposed, we are reminded of early abolition days in the United States. When his steamer was signaled a crowd of indignant whites collected, who mobbed him, upon his landing, with stones and beating. At length, rescued and taken to a friend's house, stones and missiles were thrown against it, while several stump speeches were made.

Neither great branch of the English-speaking family can, in truth, plume itself upon its peculiar innate virtues or immunity from failings. At the same time, the Constitution of the United States, with equal laws (broken or outraged, it is true, by sectional prejudices) would appear likely more rapidly to tend towards equal liberty and equal rights than the Constitution of the British Empire, under which imperial prejudices and differences of rights and immunities are sanctioned by unequal laws.

This was almost certainly the first mention of Gandhi in the American press, presaging the extensive coverage of his activities as an iconic nationalist leader in the 1920s and 1930s. Gandhi was accustomed to having his name smeared and muddied in the newspapers of Natal. The occasional positive references in the Indian press provided some consolation. Had he seen this piece in *The Nation* he would surely have been more cheered still.[53]

F. A. Laughton, the Alexanders and 'D. B.' were voices at once lonely and brave. More characteristic of the white mood was a comment in the *Times of Natal*, which thought Gandhi 'showed immense folly in landing during daylight while the town was still boiling with excitement'. The newspaper was of the view that the city of Durban, instead of being chastised or condemned, was rather 'to be congratulated. Her citizens have most effectively demonstrated that they are averse to the big influx of Indians . . . Durban, by her agitation against the invasion, has drawn special attention to the subject, and for doing so deserves the thanks of all colonists.'[54]

On 17 February 1897, four weeks after Gandhi finally landed in Durban, the butcher Harry Sparks (the prime instigator of the mob that attacked the lawyer) convened a fresh meeting of hostile Europeans in the Town Hall. This pressed for a bill prohibiting the immigration of

Indians not under indenture. Sparks said 'he was perfectly willing to lay down his life for his home'. Another speaker demanded the Imperial Government not treat Natal as 'a dumping ground for the refuse of India'. A third speaker said

> a great deal has been made of Mr Gandhi in the matter. They would find that Gandhi was supported by only 50 or 60 people in Durban, and there had been no meeting of more than 150 Asiatics in Durban. For Mr Gandhi and his committee to say they represented the 50,000 Indians in the Colony was utter bosh.[55]

Three and a half years before the attack on him at the Point in Durban, Mohandas Gandhi had been thrown out of a first-class carriage at Pietermaritzburg Railway Station. The latter episode is well known – perhaps too well known. If there is one thing anyone anywhere knows about Gandhi in South Africa, it is this incident. One book and one film largely account for this. In 1951, Louis Fischer published *The Life of Mahatma Gandhi*, which drew on the author's acquaintance with his subject in the last decade of his life. This personal intimacy and the evocative prose make for a compelling narrative, and the book has always been in print since its first publication.

Fischer termed Gandhi's ejection from the first-class carriage the most 'creative' experience in his life; 'that bitter night in Maritzburg,' he claimed, 'the germ of social protest was born in Gandhi.' Gandhi's account, in his own autobiography, was embellished in one intensely charged paragraph, where, imaginatively putting himself in the shoes of the victim, Fischer writes:

> Should he return to India? This episode reflected a much larger situation. Should he address himself to it or merely seek redress of his personal grievance, finish the case, and go home to India? He had encountered the dread disease of colour prejudice. To flee, leaving his countrymen in their predicament, would be cowardice. The frail lawyer began to see himself in the role of a David assailing the Goliath of racial discrimination.[56]

This account was then dramatized for a second time in Richard Attenborough's blockbuster film *Gandhi*, which (for this and other episodes) took Fischer's book as its main source. The film begins with Gandhi's assassination in 1948 and then goes straight back to his ejection from the train in 1893, making it the first major moment in the Mahatma's life and career. Based, therefore, on a popular book and an even more popular film, the standard narrative of Gandhi's life draws a straight, clear line from the incident at the train station on to the mass movements he later led in South Africa and in India.

The facts about the Durban attack and its prelude (till now largely unknown) make the line more jagged, more contingent, and more true. When he was thrown out of the compartment in Pietermaritzburg, Gandhi suffered no physical harm. He soon proceeded on his journey. In Durban he was beaten black and blue. The crucial difference, however, is this: in the train, Gandhi was the victim of one person's racism, expressed at one time alone. Off the coast and when he landed in Durban, he was the target of the collective anger of (virtually) all the whites in Natal, expressed continuously for several weeks at a stretch.

The attack in Durban was far more important than the insult in Pietermaritzburg; more revealing of the racial politics of South Africa and of the challenges faced by Mohandas Gandhi himself.

6

Lawyer-Loyalist

In March 1897 Harry Escombe was elected Prime Minister of Natal, the culmination of a long career in the service of the colony. Born in London in 1838, Escombe arrived in Durban as a young man and soon became the leading light of its legal fraternity. He also made significant contributions outside the law; for instance, as chairman of the Natal Harbour Board, he supervised the removal of the sandbar that impeded the entry of ships into Durban harbour.[1]

As a practising lawyer, Escombe had represented Indians both in Natal and the Transvaal. He had even taken briefs for Dada Abdulla and Company. It was he who recommended Gandhi to the Natal Bar. The two men met in court and on the street, for Escombe lived a stone's throw away from Gandhi's home in Beach Grove.

While friendly enough on an individual level, as a politician representing a white electorate Escombe had ambivalent feelings about Indians. In 1890, just after he had entered Parliament, he was walking home when a white mechanic stopped and warned him that 'if you do not vote for the exclusion of the Indian, out you will go.' The encounter made him more proactive; thus, supporting the £3 tax in May 1895, he said in Parliament that it was necessary to 'put an Indian on his guard'. The tax met the wish of white Natalians 'that the Indians are to come here appreciated as labourers, but not welcomed as settlers and competitors'.[2]

The anti-Indian and anti-Gandhi demonstrations of 1896–7 consolidated Escombe's views. When he became Prime Minister, his government proposed three new Acts. The first allowed the colony to deport passengers coming from places where plague or other epidemics

currently raged. The second declared as a 'prohibited immigrant' anyone who could not sign his name in a European language. The third
gave town boards the liberty to deny or refuse to renew trading
licences to those who did not keep their books in English, or whose
premises were 'unprovided with proper and sufficient sanitary arrangements'.[3]

The words 'Indian' or 'Asiatic' did not appear in the Acts. But there
was no mistaking whom they were aimed at. Introducing the new legislation, the Prime Minister said it was required to maintain Natal, 'as far
as it is possible, as a British Colony', and save it from being 'submerged
under an Asiatic wave of immigration'. Escombe continued:

> We ourselves have brought into this Colony 50,000 Indians, and other
> Indians to-day follow in their train because of the stories which go from
> here to their native villages to the effect that Natal is a paradise for Indi-
> ans. And it is. And if you are to allow them to make it a paradise for
> Indians, you will find that, as far as Europeans are concerned, it is an
> exact antipodes of paradise.[4]

In the first months of 1897, the Parsi lawyer F. S. Taleyarkhan wrote
several letters to Gandhi asking when he should come out to Durban. In
early March, Gandhi wrote back wondering 'whether it would be advis-
able, in the present state of public feeling, for you to land in Natal as a
public man. Such a man's life in Natal is, at present, in danger. I am certainly glad you did not accompany me.'[5] Having just experienced an
attack on his life, he refused to expose his friend to the risk of moving
to Natal.

Two weeks later, Gandhi wrote a long letter to the *Natal Mercury*,
his first public statement after his return. He denied that in India he had
'blackened the character of the Colonists', denied that he wished to
swamp the colony with Indians, denied that he had any political ambition whatsoever. He was in Natal

> not to sow dissensions between the two communities [of Indians and
> Europeans], but to endeavour to bring about a honourable reconciliation
> between them . . . I have been taught to believe that Britain and India can
> remain together for any length of time only if there is a common fellow
> feeling between the two peoples. The greatest minds in the British Isles and

India are striving to meet that ideal. I am but humbly following in their footsteps, and feel that the present action of the Europeans in Natal is calculated to retard, if not altogether to frustrate, its realization.

He went on to deplore the recent introduction of Bills in the Natal Parliament 'prejudically affecting the interests of the Indians'.[6]

This letter to the press was accompanied by a formal petition to the Natal Legislative Assembly (the lower house of the colony's parliament). Despite their apparent neutrality in terms of race, said Gandhi, the new Acts were designed 'to operate against the Indian community alone'. Those refused licences were denied the right to appeal in court. This 'would be deemed an arbitrary measure in any part of the civilized world'.[7]

When the colonists were unmoved, the Natal Indian Congress wrote to the Colonial Secretary Joseph Chamberlain, protesting against the Bills drafted to keep out their compatriots. It pointed out that a man learned in Indian languages would not be allowed to land in the colony, merely because he could not write his name in English.[8]

Chamberlain does not appear to have replied to the letter. He was inclined to recommend to Her Majesty that she grant assent to the bill. Speaking to a gathering of colonial prime ministers in London, Chamberlain said he 'quite sympathize[d] with the determination of the white inhabitants of these Colonies which are in comparatively close proximity to millions and hundreds of millions of Asiatics that there shall not be an influx of people alien in civilization, alien in religion, alien in customs'.

When this speech was reproduced in the Natal papers, Gandhi wrote to Dadabhai Naoroji in alarm. The Colonial Secretary had 'completely given up the Indian cause and yielded to the clamour of the different Colonies'. 'We are powerless,' wrote Gandhi to the acknowledged leader of the Indian community in the UK: 'We leave the case in your hands. Our only hope lies in your again bestirring yourself with redoubled vigour in our favour.'[9]

Naoroji sought an appoinment with Chamberlain but was denied one. He then wrote to him with a certain resignation. 'All I ask,' he said, 'is that we are repeatedly told that we are British subjects, just as much as the Queen's subjects in this country are not slaves, and I always look forward with hope to a fulfilment of these pledges and

Proclamations.'[10] Pre-eminent among these pledges was one made by Queen Victoria when the British Government directly assumed charge of India in 1858. This said the Crown and the Empire were

> bound to the natives of our Indian territories by the same obligations of duty which bind us to all our other subjects, and those obligations, by the blessings of Almighty God, we shall faithfully and conscientiously fulfil . . . And it is our further will that, so far as may be, our subjects, of whatever race or creed, be freely and impartially admitted to offices in our service, the duties of which they may be qualified, by their education, ability, and integrity, duly to discharge.[11]

The Natal Acts were, as Naoroji now reminded Chamberlain, in clear violation of this proclamation.

In September 1897, a rift in his party led to Harry Escombe resigning as Prime Minister. Before leaving office, he wrote to Gandhi asking him 'to convey to the Indians the value I set on their good opinion'. Then he added a personal touch: 'I thank you,' he remarked, 'for in bringing me into closer touch with them, you have allowed us to understand one another and this in itself is a great gain.'[12]

In view of the discriminatory legislation that Escombe had, just a few months previously, passed through the Natal Parliament, this was more than a trifle disingenuous. Could it be that even if he could not abide Indians as fellow citizens, he might yet need them as clients in court? One cannot say for certain, for before the year was out, Escombe was dead.

The house in Beach Grove where Gandhi once lived alone was now also home to his wife and children. This was the first time in the fifteen years of their marriage that Kasturba and he were running a house together. In Rajkot they had lived in a traditional joint family set-up, in a two-storey building known as 'Kaba Gandhi no Delo'. The patriarch after whom it was named died in 1885, but his children had lived on there, now with *their* children. The house had many rooms but a single kitchen. Harilal and Manilal played with their cousins in the courtyard and in the streets, and regarded them, as was the custom, as brothers. At mealtimes and at bedtime, they were looked after by their aunts as well as their mother. Now, in Durban, the Gandhis were learning to live as a nuclear family, with Kasturba in sole charge of the kitchen and of her boys too.

Every morning, Gandhi left his wife and children to go to his law office, which was in a columned arcade known as Mercury Lane. His chambers were opposite the office of the city's major newspaper, the *Natal Mercury*.[13] Some details of Mohandas Gandhi's law practice are contained in a set of files kept in the public archives in the capital of Natal, Pietermaritzburg.[14] Much of his work had to do with getting passes and permits. The travel and residency requirements for Indians in Natal were increasingly onerous; Gandhi's job was to effect a temporary, case-by-case relaxation. A merchant from the Cape wanted to visit his partner in Durban; Gandhi wrote on his behalf asking for a one-month pass. Passengers en route to India were marooned in the harbour; Gandhi asked that they be allowed to see the city and return to their ship at night. A trader wished to return to India for a spell; Gandhi asked for a pass for his brother, who would stand in for him in the business.

The names of Gandhi's clients – Dadabhai, Mutale, Munisamy, Hassanjee, Rustomjee, Appasamy, Naidoo, Edward Nundy, Thakarsi – reveal their varying affiliations. They came from Parsi, Hindu, Muslim and Christian homes, and spoke Gujarati, Urdu, Hindi, Telugu and Tamil. The range of cases was likewise impressive. An Indian who was a good typist wished to enter the Civil Service; Gandhi asked that he be accommodated when a vacancy arose. A qualified Indian doctor asked, via Gandhi, to be registered as a medical practitioner in Natal. An Indian merchant had been attacked and robbed by Europeans; his assailants were arrested and then jumped bail. Gandhi asked that his client be compensated from the amount forfeited.

A particularly interesting case was of Mahomed Hoosen, the brother of an Indian merchant in Ladysmith. Hoosen was born with only one arm and one leg. He lived in Gujarat, while his family prospered in Natal. In September 1899, Gandhi requested permission for Hoosen to join them on compassionate grounds. The family, he said, wanted to 'have him by their side so as not only to save expense but also to afford what consolation Mahomed Hoosen can derive from being with them.' He tellingly added: 'The wish in my humble opinion is natural and reasonable. It does not come into conflict with the intention of the legislature namely to restrict the influx of Asiatic competitors.'

(Unfortunately, the records don't tell us whether Mahomed Hoosen was allowed to join his family.)

The range of Gandhi's professional contacts is also revealed in a log-book of letters sent and received by his office. His European correspondents included a Forbes, a Fairfield and a Fraser, probably all lawyers, as were his old friends A. W. Baker and F. A. Laughton (also listed here). Others were planters, a W. R. Hindson and a D. Vinden among them. Among the letters from overseas were several from Dadabhai Naoroji. The names of Gujarati merchants in Durban are not as plentiful as one might expect – this may be because only letters in English are listed, and Gandhi's dealings with his compatriots were largely in their own language.

There is also some correspondence with the Protector of Immigrants, most likely about the treatment of indentured labourers. An Anglo-Indian supervisor at the Esperanza sugar estate had written to Gandhi about the cruel treatment of the coolies there. They were made to work very long hours, in the cold and in the pouring rain. If they complained they were beaten up. The supervisor had 'never seen animals treated as these unfortunate creatures are'. He asked Gandhi to raise the matter with the Protector, without mentioning his informant's name.[15]

The logbook runs from January 1895 to March 1898. The most intriguing entries are two letters from a certain M. A. Jinnah. This is the man, also a Gujarati lawyer trained in London, who, in the 1930s and 1940s, became Gandhi's most implacable Indian adversary. Historians have demonstrated that Jinnah knew of Gandhi's public work in South Africa from about 1908. But in fact, as this logbook (discreetly tucked away, with all of Gandhi's incoming correspondence, in a cupboard at the Sabarmati Ashram in Ahmedabad) reveals, they had first been in contact a full decade earlier.[16]

These letters are dated 21 January and 24 July 1897. The contents are unknown, but, from what we otherwise know of the two men's lives, some speculation may be in order. Could Jinnah's first letter have been a message of support on hearing of the brutal attack on Gandhi at the Point in Durban? Or might both letters have been explorations of interest in a possible career in South Africa?

In 1896, Jinnah returned from London to his home town, Karachi. Soon afterwards, he moved to Bombay. There, like Gandhi some years previously, he found it hard to establish an independent law practice.

We know that Gandhi was keen to bring some barristers to Natal to help him, hence his invitation to the Parsi lawyer trained in London, F. S. Taleyarkhan. Jinnah may very well have known Taleyarkhan in London and Bombay, and thus have known of the opportunities across the ocean. Did he approach Gandhi to find out how to proceed? Or did Gandhi ask him in the first place? Jinnah was a Gujarati Muslim, in terms of personal and professional background extremely well qualified to work as a lawyer among the Indians of Natal.

That Jinnah wrote to Gandhi to commiserate on his injuries is plausible; that he wrote to ask whether they could forge a legal partnership together in South Africa is not entirely impossible. But we must speculate no more. All we now know is that, a full fifty years before Partition and the independence of India and Pakistan, the respective 'Fathers' of those nations were in correspondence.

Gandhi's skills in court were admired by the Europeans who opposed him. In a case of bankruptcy, he represented one creditor, while a white lawyer named R. H. Tatham represented another. When Gandhi's proposal to sell the debtor's business was accepted over an alternate proposal offered by Tatham, the latter jokingly remarked: 'Gandhi's supreme. The triumph of black over white again.'[17]

The young lawyer's work made an impression on two visitors from overseas. In March 1897, the traveller and soldier Francis Younghusband came to Natal. He met Gandhi, whom he described as 'the spokesman of the Indian community and the butt of the [white] agitators'. He found him a 'particularly intelligent and well-educated man'. Gandhi invited the traveller for dinner at his 'well-furnished English villa', where a group of Indian merchants further impressed him by talking fluently 'on all the current events of the time. Such men as these naturally resent the use of the term "coolie" . . . But while they complain of being classed separately from Europeans they are much offended at Kaffirs being classed with them.'[18]

The following year, when the Gandhis were well established in Durban, they were visited by Pranjivan Mehta. The two had been close from their student days in London, the bond made more solid by the fact that it was in Mehta's home in Bombay that Gandhi met the Jain seer Raychandbhai. Mehta was now based in Rangoon, running a jewellery business. In the summer of 1898 he visited Europe, and on his way back stopped in South Africa to see Gandhi. Disembarking at Cape Town, he found at once that he 'was in a place where the colour of the skin counted for everything and [the] man nothing'. He was denied rooms in several hotels, and also treated discourteously on the long train journey from the Cape eastwards to Durban.[19]

Once he reached Natal, Mehta was much happier – nourished by the company of his friend, and impressed by what he was doing there. Mehta was struck by how, under Gandhi's leadership, 'diverse communities [of Indians] remain united and vigilant about protecting the rights of one another.' He was moved by the diaspora's connection to the motherland, manifest in the £1,200 sent from Natal after the great famine and plague of 1896–7. The 'people of India', Mehta told an audience of Gujaratis in Durban, 'can take great pride in the kind of concern you have shown towards them, even though you are thousands of miles away from India.'[20]

While based in Natal, Gandhi was also drawn into the Indian question in the Transvaal. Here, the ruling race were the Boers, who spoke Afrikaans and were largely of Dutch extraction. When, in the first decades of the nineteenth century, the British took firm control of the Cape, the Boers commenced their 'great trek' inland. They established themselves beyond the Vaal and Orange rivers, displacing the Africans and taking control of vast areas of fertile land. Their economy, and their sense of self, was founded on farming, herding and hunting. While the British coveted the coast – which provided access to their jewel in the east, India – the Boers had possession of these inland territories. In the 1850s they formed two, semi-autonomous, republics, the Orange Free State and the Transvaal (the latter also known, from the 1880s, as the South African Republic).[21]

Racial politics in the Transvaal were more complicated than in Natal. The Boers had come here to carve a space separate and independent from the British. For many decades their Utopia lay safe, until the discovery of gold near Johannesburg in 1886 prompted a massive and mad rush of immigrants. By the time Gandhi first visited the city in 1893, English-speaking migrants outnumbered the Afrikaans-speaking Boers by two to one. The workers in the mines were mostly African, but the managers, supervisors and owners were largely English. And as Johannesburg boomed, it was the English, rather than the Boers, who ran the new hotels, restaurants, hospitals, clubs, theatres and other accoutrements of a bustling modern city.

Known as *Uitlanders* (Afrikaans for 'outsider') the English had the numbers; they had the money; what they wanted was a share of political power. The Boers, however, claimed that the Transvaal was their homeland, whereas the Uitlanders were greedy foreigners. The franchise was therefore restricted to those resident in the Republic for more than fourteen years. This was resented by the Uitlanders, who also had other complaints; for instance, that the state enjoyed a monopoly over the production and sale of dynamite, a commodity of vital importance to the mining industry.

In the 1890s, the main question of Transvaal politics was the conflict between Boer and Briton. But there was a secondary problem, namely the contamination of the Boer dreamland by an even less wanted group of immigrants, the Indians. With the mining boom in the Rand their numbers rapidly increased. They set up shops in the main towns, and also opened stores in the countryside. Hawkers with less capital at their disposal sold goods on the streets.

When Gandhi first visited Johannesburg, there were already more than a hundred Gujarati traders in town. Some firms were very large – with assets in the tens of thousands of pounds and branches in Durban, the Cape and Bombay. There was also an emerging Indian working class, composed of labourers, domestic servants and hawkers. In Johannesburg's leading hotels, Indians were 'much preferred [by their employers] to white waiters, owing to their civility, sobriety, and to their being more amenable to discipline.'[22]

A few Indians entered the Orange Free State as well. Before their numbers could increase, the Volksraad, or parliament, expelled them from the province. With special permission, Indians could work in the Free State in strictly menial jobs, such as servants on farms. But more respectable and profitable trades were closed to them.

Encouraged by the Free Staters, in 1885 the Transvaal's Volksraad passed a law making it impossible for 'so-called Coolies, Arabs, Malays and Mohammedan subjects of the Turkish Empire' to buy property. The law also empowered the Government to specify particular streets and localities where Asians would live and trade.

For a decade after the law was passed it lay sleeping on the statute books. But in 1894 Boer politicians, worried that the numbers of Indians were now in the thousands rather than dozens, sought to implement it. Notices were issued that traders who were not white would be sent to designated areas known as 'Locations', within which they had to conduct their businesses.[23]

In desperation, the Indians sought an interview with the President of the Transvaal, the crusty and dogmatic old general, Paul Kruger. Kruger came out to meet them with a Bible in hand. The Indians set out their grievances. The Christian warrior, consulting his Book, answered that they were descendants of Esau and Ishmael, and hence bound by God to slavery. Kruger and his Bible went back to their house, while the Indians retreated, bewildered.[24]

The Indians now approached the British to intervene. An agreement signed in London in 1884 guaranteed the rights of Her Majesty's subjects to trade and live where they pleased in the South African Republic. Indian traders asked only that this clause be honoured. In 1895, pressed by the British, the SAR appointed an arbitrator, a former Chief Justice of the Free State. He heard the two sides and came out strongly in favour of his fellow Boers, noting that

> the constitution of the South African Republic, the terms of which could not have been unknown to the British Government, lays down that no equality between the white and coloured races shall be tolerated . . . every European nation or nation of European origin has an absolute and indefeasible right to exclude alien elements which it considers to be dangerous to its development and existence, and more especially Asiatic elements, from settling within its territory.'[25]

The arbitrator had left a window open – the Indians, he said, could 'test' their case in the High Court in Pretoria. A Gujarati merchant now appealed against the law under which he was to be sent to a Location. (This was Tayob Khan, whose dispute with Dada Abdulla had brought Gandhi to South Africa in the first place.) Brought in on the case, Gandhi argued that Indians were of 'Indo-Germanic' stock, and hence exempt from the racial laws of the Transvaal Volksraad.

One judge on the bench was persuaded by Gandhi's arguments; the other two were not. In August 1898, the Court finally ruled against Tayob Khan. The threat of eviction loomed large. On 31 December

1898, a group of thirty merchants wrote to the Secretary of State for the Colonies in alarm. If implemented, the court's judgement 'would mean practical ruin to the Indian traders in the Transvaal'. They faced a 'constant dread of having their stores shut up at any moment, and being removed on sufferance tenure to locations unfit for comfortable habitation, devoid of sanitary arrangement, situated in a locality unsuitable for trade, and all this for no fault of theirs'.[26]

By 1898, more than a quarter of the world's supply of gold came from the Transvaal. Uitlander mine-owners made extraordinary profits. But the Boer-controlled state did not do too badly either. In 1886, state revenue was £196,000; ten years later, it had jumped to £400,000. The capitalists whose firms had contributed to the growing coffers wanted a greater say in how to spend the government's revenue. On the other hand, those in charge of the state were loath to cede control.[27]

Egged on by the imperial adventurer Cecil Rhodes – who had vast business interests in South Africa – a group of conspirators planned to overthrow Kruger's regime by force. An officer named Jameson was to cross the border into the Transvaal with a force of 1,000 men; meanwhile, the English residents in Johannesburg would start an insurrection. In the event, Jameson's force was surrounded and made to surrender by the Boers; and the uprising within never happened.

The collapse of the 'Jameson Raid' of 1895 intensified the rift between Boer and Briton. The pro-imperial party was led by the Secretary of State for the Colonies, Joseph Chamberlain, and the High Commissioner in Cape Town, Lord Milner. Both believed that control of the Transvaal was central to Great Britain's mission in Africa and the world. In February 1898, Milner wrote to Chamberlain that 'there is no way out of the political troubles of South Africa except reform in the Transvaal or war. And at present the chances of reform in the Transvaal are worse than ever.' Eighteen months later, Chamberlain wrote a memo to the British Cabinet complaining that the Boers were 'flouting successfully British control and interference', and that what happened next depended on 'whether the supremacy which we have so long claimed and so seldom exerted, is to be finally established and recognised or for ever abandoned'.[28]

By this time, the British were shipping large numbers of troops to

South Africa. Ten thousand soldiers came from India and the Mediterranean; several thousand more from England itself. The bellicosity was unmistakable. In October 1899 the Boers asked that troops sent since July of that year be withdrawn. When the British refused, they crossed into Natal, and the war had begun.

One consequence of the war between Boer and Briton was the flight of Indians from the South African Republic. As British subjects, they were identified with the enemy. The Indians streamed into Natal, seeking refuge among their compatriots in the colony. Gandhi and the Natal Indian Congress helped raise money and find homes for them.

The Indians in Natal were merchants and labourers. Few had any military experience. However, Gandhi thought that as subjects of the British Empire they should show support for their side. He had been volunteering with a hospital in Durban, run by a Reverend Dr Booth. Now, with Dr Booth's encouragement, he offered to raise a corps of Indian ambulance workers to care for the sick and the wounded.

On 17 October 1899, days after the beginning of hostilities, Gandhi convened a meeting in Durban to discuss his proposal. Some Indians were opposed to helping the British. Did they not oppress them as much as the Boers? And what if the other side won? Would not the Boers then wreak vengeance on them? Gandhi answered that they lived in South Africa as subjects of the British Empire. To help the rulers now would refute the charge that Indians were interested only in 'money-grubbing and were merely a deadweight upon the British'. Here was a 'golden opportunity' to prove these charges were baseless.[29]

Gandhi's arguments prevailed. The next day he wrote to the Natal Government, 'unreservedly and unconditionally' offering assistance. The Indians did not know how to handle arms, but they still 'might render some service in connection with the field hospitals or the commissariat', thus showing that, in common with other subjects of the Queen, they were 'ready to do duty for their Sovereign on the battlefield'.[30]

By the first week of January, 1900, 500 Indians had agreed to serve in the ambulance corps. A list of volunteers reveals that the Gujarati merchants had prudently stayed away. A large number of Indian Christians had come forward to serve their Sovereign. Others who joined included working-class Hindus, mostly of Tamil extraction.[31]

The Indians were sent into the field, where they followed the soldiers from camp to camp, taking care of the stragglers. The conditions were hard; they had to march up to twenty-five miles a day, go many hours without food and water and sleep out in the open. They were dangerously close to the action, carrying the wounded to safety as shells fell around them. Some volunteers were asked to dismantle Boer telegraph lines. Others were told to gather up rifles and cartridges abandoned by the enemy.[32]

An English journalist left a vivid account of the ambulance corps at work. Following the reversals at Spion Kop, he saw 'the Indian mule-train move up the slopes of the Kop carrying water to the dis-tressed soldiers who had lain powerless on the plain'. After a night's work which would have 'shattered men with much bigger frames', the reporter 'came across Gandhi in the early morning sitting by the roadside – eating a regulation army biscuit'. While the British soldiers were 'dull and depressed', Gandhi 'was stoical in his bearing, cheerful and confi-dent in his conversation, and had a kindly eye'.[33]

Gandhi had asked an English friend, Herbert Kitchin, an electrician with an interest in Indian philosophy, to help with the raising of the ambulance corps. Gandhi managed one unit, Kitchin another. While the lawyer was in Spion Kop, the Englishman was at Elandsla-agte, from where he sent this account of their 'busy and exciting time' at the front:

> I was away with a party of eight Indians, a corporal and a sapper, taking
> down a portion of the Boer telegraph line around Ladysmith. We passed
> three of the Boer laagers. All of them are filthy, and are noticeable for . . .
> the quantity of cartridges scattered about, and the number of bottles and
> English biscuit tins. We could have picked up a sackful of cartridges.
> A party of our men . . . dropped across a party of Boers who put a shell
> on the midst of them. Luckily no one was hurt. I came across a stray
> horse, which I suppose was left behind by the Boers, but it was too wild
> and I could not catch it. Had I been able to, I could have sold it for a
> decent sum.[34]

Even as a non-combatant, the Englishman was enjoying the battle, tak-ing pleasure in the discomfiture of the hated Boers and the scattering of their possessions. Gandhi had joined the British in their fight out of loy-alty and duty. His reactions to this letter are unrecorded. But one thinks the vegetarian Bania could scarcely have seen the fight as his English friend did, as a thrilling and utterly pleasurable chase after a quarry in flight.

At the start of the war the British suffered serious reverses. The Boers were agile fighters, who knew the terrain well. However, over time the greater numbers and superior firepower of the British began to prevail. By the summer of 1900 the war had been largely won, although bands of Boer guerrilla fighters continued to resist capture for many months afterwards.

The Indian ambulance workers had played a modest part in the British victory. To mark this, a meeting was held in the Congress Hall in Durban. This, wrote a Natal newspaper, was 'the first occasion upon which Europeans and Indians in this Colony have met on a common platform for a common purpose'.[35] In the chair was the former Prime Minister of Natal, Sir John Robinson. In the 'struggle for supremacy between Boer and Briton', said Robinson, the Indians had done 'excellent work'. 'I cannot too warmly compliment your able countryman, Mr Gandhi', the Natal leader told the Indians, 'upon his timely, unselfish, and most useful action in voluntarily organising a corps of bearers for ambulance work.'[36]

The volunteers came out of regard for Gandhi, and he solicited them out of regard for the British Empire, of which he was a loyal subject, his criticisms of the Natal Government notwithstanding. Indeed, those criticisms often made the case that discriminatory laws were at odds with British tradition. His 'Open Letter' of December 1894 contrasted the colonists with their compatriots at home – 'I have ... to remind you', said Gandhi, 'that the English in England have shown by their writings, speeches and deeds that they mean to unify the hearts of the two peoples, that they do not believe in colour distinctions, and that they will raise India with them rather than rise upon its ruins.' A petition protesting against the £3 tax in default of re-indenture insisted it was 'in direct opposition to the fundamental principles upon which the British Constitution is based'. A memorial of 1895 to the Secretary of State for the Colonies said the policies in Natal were 'entirely repugnant to the British notions of justice'. The Governor of Natal was told in July 1899 that the Dealers' Licence Act was 'really bad and un-British'.[37]

That telling term, 'un-British', was to be made famous in a book published by Dadabhai Naoroji in 1901, *Poverty and Un-British Rule in India*. This argued that the spread of famine, the drain of wealth and the stifling of Indian manufactures were the result of policies that departed from the ideals of the rulers. Gandhi knew and respected Naoroji; like the Parsi veteran, he was an admirer of the British liberal tradition and its powers, real or fictive, of self-criticism and ameliorative action.

Another Indian leader Gandhi admired, Gopal Krishna Gokhale, distinguished between a 'narrower imperialism' which regarded 'the world as though it was made for one race only', and a 'nobler imperialism' that enabled 'all who are included in the Empire to share equally in all its blessings'.[38] Gandhi's work during the War was done to evoke or re-activate these 'nobler' instincts of the rulers. As he later wrote, 'I felt that, if I demanded rights as a British citizen, it was also my duty, as such, to participate in the defence of the British Empire. I held then that India could achieve her complete emancipation only within and through the British Empire.'[39]

The Anglo-Boer War of 1899–1902 is usually seen as a 'white man's war'. This is not strictly true. In every major battle of the war, non-Europeans played a part. While a handful of Indians served as ambulance workers, many black Africans – Zulus, Xhosas and others – participated as armed combatants. One historian estimates that perhaps as many as 30,000 blacks fought on the British side. Others worked as scouts, spies, servants and messengers. Like Gandhi, these African volunteers believed – or hoped – that 'a British victory would bring about an extension of political, educational and commercial opportunities for black people'.[40]

What Gandhi wrote in these years is printed in his *Collected Works*; samples of what was written to him lie in cupboards in the Gandhi Museum in Delhi and the Gandhi Ashram in Sabarmati. These writings focus very largely on his career as a lawyer and community organizer. What the biographer lacks are contemporary accounts of his personal, familial situation. We know that in 1898 Kasturba gave birth to a third son, Ramdas; and two years later to a fourth, Devadas. But to sense what life was like in the Gandhi household, we have to rely largely on the patriarch's recollections and our own speculations.

Many years later, while writing of their life in Durban, Gandhi said the central challenge he faced was where and how to educate his children. There were a few schools for children of indentured labourers, run by missionaries. For reasons of class Gandhi would not have wanted his sons admitted there. 'I could have sent them to the schools for European children,' he remarks, 'but only as a matter of favour and exception. No other Indian children were allowed to attend them.'[41] This is confirmed by documents in the Natal archives, which tell us that in the last week of February 1897, Gandhi sent a petition requesting that James Godfrey, the son of one of his (Tamil Christian) clients, be admitted to the whites-only Durban High School. The request was denied, the Superintendent of Schools claiming that if the Godfrey child was allowed in, 'a majority of the parents would remove their boys, and the boys who were left would make the Indian's life unsupportable by practical joking.'[42]

If a Christian boy was subject to racist taunts, a Hindu boy would find it even harder. So Gandhi would have reasoned, which is why he chose to educate his sons Harilal and Manilal and his nephew Gokuldas at home. He taught them the alphabet of their mother tongue, Gujarati, himself. An English governess was engaged to teach other subjects. Meanwhile, their mother acquainted them with the myths and morals of their native Hinduism.[43]

The boys could play with one another, but it is hard to see how or with whom Kasturba found companionship. There were no other women in the household. The shopping was in the hands of a manservant; both social custom and personal inhibition prevented Gandhi's wife from going out alone on the streets of Durban. Most of her husband's clients were Gujarati Muslims. Despite a common language, divergent faiths made it hard for Kasturba to break bread with their wives. Even had she sought friendship with them, she would not – with four sons, a nephew and a husband to look after – have had the time.

As a successful barrister, Gandhi had chosen to live not in the Indian ghetto in central Durban but in Beach Grove, on the city's outskirts. His 'well-furnished English villa' (to use Younghusband's phrase) was one of several in the locality, the others occupied by men who were English by blood as well as in spirit. Gandhi's desire to mark his social status by acquiring a house away from where his compatriots lived posed serious problems for his wife. She did not know English, and tradition forbade her from talking to white people anyway. The social distance separating her from her neighbours was even greater than the physical distance between the suburbs and the city. She could not go to meet the Gujarati women in Grey Street unescorted. Her husband was unavailable (and perhaps also unwilling) to take her there. So she retreated further into her home, where her children provided her with both company and consolation.

It was in this house in Beach Grove that Gandhi and Kasturba had a disagreement that he wrote about in his autobiography. Living with the Gandhis were a Gujarati cook and a Tamil-speaking clerk, Vincent Lawrence. Before their conversion to Christianity, Lawrence's family were regarded as Panchammas, a term, translating as the 'fifth' caste, denoting their Untouchable status. Kasturba refused to clean the clerk's chamber pot, and thought her husband should also not pollute himself by doing so. Gandhi was enraged. 'I will not stand this nonsense in my house,' he remembers telling Kasturba in his autobiography, adding the further recollection that, in his fury, he dragged her down to the gate. His wife, weeping, asked if he had no shame, to push her out in a foreign country, with no parents or relatives to take her in. Gandhi pulled himself back in time, and returned with his wife to the house.[44]

In May 1901, Gandhi learnt that his preceptor Raychandbhai had died, at just thirty-three. Gandhi read about Raychandbhai's passing in his office, from a newspaper that arrived in the post. He set the paper aside and resumed his work, but, as he wrote to a friend, 'I can't put it out of my mind . . . [W]henever there is a little leisure, the mind reverts to it. Rightly or wrongly, I was greatly attracted to him and I loved him deeply too. All that is over now.'[45]

From that first meeting in July 1891, Gandhi had accepted Raychandbhai as his mentor. Gandhi's father died when he was in his teens. His elder brothers were incapable of giving him moral (or intellectual) instruction. It was into this vacuum that the jeweller-thinker stepped. He had helped Gandhi come through the loss of his beloved mother. When he was a briefless barrister in Bombay in 1892, Gandhi would leave the court to go to Raychand's shop and speak with him. In South

Africa some years later, torn between religions, Raychand once more helped sort out his confusions.

What did Raychandbhai mean to Gandhi? What did he *learn* from him? Contemporary accounts or letters are scarce, so we must answer these questions with the aid of later reflections. Speaking at Raychand's birth anniversary in 1915, Gandhi said 'he followed no narrow creed. He was a universalist and had no quarrel with any religion in the world.'[46]

Nine years later, Gandhi wrote a long preface to a Gujarati book on his teacher. This recalled that even when Raychand was in his shop,

> some book on a religious subject would always be lying by his side, and, as soon as he had finished dealing with a customer, he would open it, or would open the note-book in which he used to note down the thoughts which occurred to him. Every day he had men like me, in search of knowledge, coming to him. He would not hesitate to discuss religious matters with them. The Poet did not follow the general . . . rule of doing business and discussing dharma each at its proper time, of attending to one thing at a time.

Gandhi took heart from this plurality of vocations, becoming both a hardworking lawyer and a curious seeker himself. While Raychand could teach Gandhi little about the law, he encouraged him to see his faith in broader terms. *Dharma*, said the seer, did not 'mean reading or learning by rote books known as Shastras or even believing all that they say'. It was a combination of theoretical learning and practical knowledge. After a certain level of religious instruction, the scriptures could help no further; but one's own experience certainly could.

There were, argued Raychand, parallels in the teachings of all great religions. All preached against falsehood and against violence. Human beings, following the texts of their faiths dogmatically, had 'erected veritable prison-houses' in which they were, in a spiritual sense, confined. Gandhi, following Raychand, came to the conclusion that 'every religion is perfect from the point of its followers and imperfect from that of the followers of other faiths. Examined from an independent point of view, every religion is both perfect and imperfect'.

When his Christian friends in Johannesburg and Durban were pressing Gandhi to convert, Raychand advised him to stay within the Hindu fold, yet remain open to the teachings of other religions. The seer liked to say that 'the different faiths were like so many walled enclosures in which men and women were confined'. Gandhi, following Raychand, lived in the enclosure he was born into, but breached its walls by frequently travelling into other similarly well demarcated terrains. He never permanently abandoned his compartment for another, yet by visiting other compartments came to see more clearly what united as well as divided them all.[47]

A few months after Raychand's death, Gandhi decided to return home to India. This, on the face of it, was a puzzling move: his legal practice was well established, and he was a figure of some renown in Natal. In his autobiography he writes that he wished to 'be of more service in India', where the movement for political rights was gathering ground.[48] But surely there were other reasons, among them the desire to give his children a decent education. The eldest child, Harilal, was now entering his teens. There was no suitable school for him or his brothers in Durban. In Rajkot, however, they could attend their father's old school, follow him in taking the Bombay Matriculation, and in time build up professions and careers of their own.

That there was now a second Indian lawyer in Natal made it easier for Gandhi to think of going back. This was Rahim Karim Khan, a barrister from Lincoln's Inn who had come out to South Africa in 1899. He joined Gandhi's office and later established his own network of clients. As a Muslim himself, he was trusted by the mainly Muslim merchants in Durban. With Khan's arrival, Gandhi was free to travel to the Transvaal, to more actively pursue his religious interests, and now, in 1901, to return for good to India.[49]

Kasturba may have been even keener than her husband to return. When she married Mohandas in 1883 she had hoped, like her mother and grandmother before her, to raise a family somewhere in her native Kathiawar. She moved to join her husband in Rajkot; a few years later, he left her and their infant son to go to London. He came back, to make her pregnant once more. In May 1893 he left again, this time for South Africa. Three years later the family was reunited. Kasturba's first exposure to South Africa was by way of the mob that attacked (in word and deed) her husband. After this she could scarcely trust the whites; but, confined to her home in Durban, she had few Indian friends either.

In Rajkot, the language that Kasturba spoke at home was also the language of the bazaar. There she had friends and relatives, who would be her children's friends and relatives too. In Durban, on the other hand, she and they had spent four and a half years feeling alien and out of place in a land they could never call their own.

And so the Gandhis decided to return to their homeland. On 12 October, Parsee Rustomjee threw a farewell party for 'the champion of the Indian cause in Natal'. The party was 'the grandest ever attempted or achieved by any Indian': tapestry on the walls, electric lights specially installed, a profusion of flowers and a band of musicians. The substance matched the show; thus, as one grateful journalist wrote, 'the guests were regaled with the most delicate preparations of an Eastern culinary department.' After the food had been eaten, Rustomjee 'placed a thick gold chain round Mr Gandhi's neck, and presented him with a valuable gold locket and a large gold medal suitably inscribed. He was also given a bouquet of white roses, and was garlanded amid deafening cheers.' The lawyer's children were then given gold medals.[50]

The next week, the Gandhis were chief guests at a party hosted by the Natal Indian Congress at their hall in Grey Street. This was likewise a gay occasion, with the staircase festooned with garlands, and Chinese lanterns everywhere. The merchant Abdul Cadir gave the first speech, saying of Gandhi that 'in every sphere of our life, political, social and moral, he has been our guiding star, and his name will be ever enshrined in every Indian heart.' The English lawyer F. A. Laughton, speaking next, said that 'it was a matter of wonderment to him that Mr Gandhi was going at this time, as he had a prominent position at the Bar, and a great influence over the Indian community. He would always be ready to welcome Mr Gandhi's return.'

At this meeting, too, Gandhi was given an array of jewels. These included a diamond ring presented on behalf of the community as a whole, a gold necklace subscribed for by Gujarati Hindus, a diamond pin from Abdul Cadir and a gold watch offered by Dada Abdulla and Company.[51] Gandhi accepted the presents (and the compliments), but three days later he wrote to Parsee Rustomjee saying he was returning the gifts. He wished to make them over to the Natal Indian Congress, to form an emergency fund for times of crisis.[52]

The decision to return the presents caused a terrific row in the Gandhi household. 'You may not need the [jewels]', said Kasturba. 'Your children may not need them. Cajoled, they will dance to your tune. I can understand your not permitting me to wear them. But what about my daughters-in-law? They will be sure to need them. And who knows what will happen tomorrow? I would be the last person to part with gifts lovingly given.'

Gandhi answered that it was not for her to decide what to do with gifts presented to him. Kasturba offered this telling rebuke: 'But service rendered by you is as good as rendered by me. I have toiled and moiled for you day and night. Is that no service?'

His wife's opposition was neutralized by the support of his two elder sons. Harilal, aged thirteen, and Manilal, aged nine, agreed that the presents must be returned. With the assistance of his sons, Gandhi 'somehow succeeded in extorting a consent' from his wife.[53]

Now Parsee Rustomjee begged Gandhi to reconsider his decision. The presents conveyed the community's love for their 'great and honoured' leader. Gandhi's impulsive gesture might now lead to the 'disorganization of a great achievement' – the building of the Natal Indian Congress – 'the credit of which achievement is primarily due to yourself'. The return of the gifts, said Rustomjee, would lead to the 'misconstruction of motives in the donor as in the recipient'.[54]

Gandhi was unyielding. The presents were sent back to the Congress, while their leader prepared to set sail for his homeland.

The Gandhis left Durban in the third week of October 1901. They took a ship that went via Mauritius; this may have been because it was the first vessel they had bookings on. On the other hand, perhaps Gandhi wanted to make his acquaintance with a colony that had once been French before it was British and which, like Natal, had a substantial population of Indians brought out to work on the sugar plantations.

When Gandhi landed in Mauritius, his reputation had preceded him. A local newspaper spoke of how 'he had brilliantly defended the cause of his compatriots in Natal.' The Muslims, who in this island were from northern India rather than from Gujarat, hosted a garden party for him. Flags and buntings fluttered in the wind, while children and adults gathered to pay their respects. Gandhi 'advised the Muslim community to send its children to college, as it was only through education that they would make a mark in life'. He asked the Indian community to take an increasing part in politics, 'not the politics of fight[ing] against the government, but the fight for its rights and a place in the sun under the pavilion of liberty'. When Gandhi heard that the son of his host was standing for election as a municipal councillor, he praised him for taking up a 'beautiful and good' cause.

Gandhi's remarks sparked an angry response from one of the colony's leading intellectuals, the poet and librarian Leoville L'Homme. The Asian way of life, said the French *colon*, was 'absolutely hostile to ours'. If an Indian became a councillor, the mayor of Port Louis would be shaking hands with men who had 'lice in their hair'. The Europeans who had settled Mauritius were bearers of a great military and political tradition. To share power with Indians would reduce these traditions 'to the proportions of a sale register of bales of tamarind'; and to make of the colonists themselves 'cadavers for the non-Christian communities'.

Gandhi was used to being abused by white colonists in Natal. But this piece of invective he did not see, since it was delivered in French. The memories he carried back from Mauritius were of the generosity of the Indians. At a farewell reception, the main speaker, a Muslim merchant, compared Gandhi to a modern-day Pharaoh who guided his countrymen 'in the rough sea far away from the rock-under-water where there may be every chance of being dashed'.[55]

The Gandhi family reached Bombay in the last week of November 1901. After settling Kasturba and the children in Rajkot, Gandhi took a train across the subcontinent to attend the seventeenth session of the Indian National Congress, held that year in Calcutta.

The 1901 Congress had 896 delegates in all. More than half came from the host province, Bengal. Gandhi was one of forty-three delegates from the Bombay Presidency. He stayed at the India Club, on Strand Road, and commuted by rickshaw to Beadon Square, where the Congress was held in a great open-air pavilion. The meeting began with a song composed by Sarola Devi Ghosal, a niece of the poet Rabindranath Tagore. It was sung by a choir of fifty-eight men and boys, with 'the nearly 400 volunteers joining the chorus for good effect'.

The President of the Calcutta Congress was D. E. Wacha, he who had read Gandhi's speech for him in Bombay in 1896. Wacha's presidential address was temperate in tone: speaking of the slow pace of economic development, he said that 'no doubt we have a good Government, but it is not unmixed with many an evil. The desire is that the evil may be purged away, and in the course of time we may have a better Government.' Other speakers were more forthright. 'Is the life function of the Indian *ryot* [peasant] to live and die merely like a brute?' asked G. Subramania Iyer of Madras: 'Is he not a "human being, endowed with reason, sentiment, and latent capacity"?' Under British rule the standard of living had sunk further, such that there were now some 200 million Indians 'grim and silent in their suffering, without zest in life, without comfort or enjoyment, without hope or ambition, living because they were born into the world, and dying because life could no longer be kept in the body.'[56]

In his own speech, Gandhi pointed out that were the president of the Congress, a civilized Parsi, to visit the Transvaal, he might be classified as belonging to the 'coolie' class. The Indians in South Africa were deeply attached to the homeland; when asked to help famine victims in Bombay, they had raised £2,000. Gandhi urged reciprocity. 'If some of the distinguished Indians I see before me tonight were to go to South Africa, inspired with that noble spirit', he remarked, 'our grievances must be removed.'[57]

When he had visited Calcutta in 1896, Gandhi had been cold-shouldered by the local leaders. Five years later he got a warmer reception. His work in South Africa was now more widely known; besides, he had an influential patron, Gopal Krishna Gokhale, who had taken him under his wing. Gokhale was only three years older than Gandhi, but vastly more experienced in public affairs. Teacher, writer, social reformer and Member of the Viceroy's Council, he was one of the best-known Indians in India.

Born in a village on the west coast of India, the son of a policeman, Gokhale had willed himself out of obscurity by hard work and self-learning. Moving to the ancient Maratha capital, Poona, he joined the faculty of Ferguson College, a pioneering centre of modern education. He taught the works of John Stuart Mill and Adam Smith, yet rooted his liberalism in an Indian context, by promoting Hindu–Muslim harmony and an end to caste discrimination. A featured speaker at the annual meetings of the Indian National Congress, he also visited England often, lobbying the Imperial Government to be more sensitive to Indian needs and aspirations. Hearing him speak at Cambridge, a young John Maynard Keynes was impressed, telling a friend that Gokhale 'has feeling, but feeling guided and controlled by thought, and there is nothing in him which reminds us of the usual type of political agitator'.[58]

When the Congress meeting ended, Gandhi moved into Gokhale's house on Upper Circular Road. Over meals and while taking walks, Gokhale told Gandhi of the debt he owed the social reformer Mahadev Govind Ranade, who had died a few months previously. Gandhi observed that Gokhale's 'reverence for Ranade could be seen every moment. Ranade's authority was final in every matter, and he would cite it at every step.' Gandhi was beginning to view his new mentor in the same light, for, as he observed, 'to see Gokhale at work was as much a joy as an education. He never wasted a minute. His private relations and friendships were all for [the] public good.'

Gandhi's spiritual preceptor, Raychand, had recently died; into the void stepped a scholar who would guide him along the path of public service. There remained reservations. One was Gokhale's lifestyle: why, asked Gandhi, did the Poona man travel in a private carriage rather than in a public tramcar? The Imperial Councillor answered that the choice was not out of a love for comfort, but a need for privacy. 'I envy your liberty to go about in tramcars', Gokhale told Gandhi: 'But I am sorry, I cannot do likewise. When you are the victim of as wide a publicity as I am, it will be difficult, if not impossible, for you to go about in a tramcar.'[59]

On 19 January 1902, Gandhi was the main speaker at a meeting in the Albert Hall, off College Street in north Calcutta. He was introduced by Gokhale, who praised his 'ability, earnestness and tact', and professed a 'profound admiration' for his work in South Africa. He said that 'Mr Gandhi was a man made of the stuff of which heroes are made.' If 'Mr Gandhi settled down in this country, it was the duty of all earnest workers to place him where he deserved to be, namely, at their head'.[60]

Gandhi spoke on successive weeks at the Albert Hall. One talk focused on the handicaps of Indians in South Africa. Another spoke of the Anglo-Boer War and of the Indian contribution to it. In peacetime the colonist was rude and hostile, but while at war, recalled Gandhi, the

British soldier was 'altogether loveable. He mixed with us and the men freely. He often shared with us his luxuries whenever there were any to be had.' From his time on the battlefield Gandhi had arrived at this intriguing, complicated, conclusion: 'As a Hindu, I do not believe in war, but if anything can even partially reconcile me to it, it was the rich experience we gained at the front.'[61]

In the last week of January, Gandhi took a ship from Calcutta to Rangoon. On board he wrote a letter of thanks to Gokhale. 'I cannot easily forget how anxious you were to wipe out the distance that should exist between you and me,' he remarked. Then he apologized for raising the question of Gokhale's mode of transport. He had 'no right to question your taste on Monday evening . . . Had I known that I would cause you thereby the pain I did cause, I should certainly have never taken the liberty.' He added a further healing touch, by saying that 'your great work in the cause of education has admirers even on board this little vessel.'[62]

Gandhi had gone to Rangoon to see his old friend Pranjivan Mehta. His medical degree notwithstanding, Mehta had joined the family jewellery business, opening a profitable branch in Burma and establishing himself as a prominent member of the Indian diaspora. From their London days he had been a confidant of Gandhi's. They corresponded regularly, and Mehta had visited the Gandhis in Durban in 1898. We have no record of their conversations in Rangoon, which must have focused on the lawyer's plan of work in India.

While in Calcutta, Gandhi had written to one of his nephews, Chhaganlal, asking him to supervise his children's education. He wanted the boys to be read stories from the *Kavyadohan*, a Gujarati compilation of Hindu myths and legends, since 'there isn't so much moral to be drawn from the works of the English poets as from our old story-poems.' The nephew, himself in his early twenties, was asked to 'see that no bad habits of any kind are picked up by the boys. Mould them in such a way that they always have deep love for truth.'[63]

Gandhi returned to Rajkot in early February. He chose to send his eldest son, Harilal, to a boarding school in the nearby town of Gondal. Chhaganlal taught the other boys, while Gandhi sought to establish a law practice.[64] He stayed in his parents' old house, which still followed the regimen laid down by his mother, of prayers and hymns in the morning and evening. In between, Gandhi attended to his children, went for walks and looked for clients.

The intrigues in Porbandar were now a distant memory; a decade after the palace break-in in which his brother was an accomplice, there was no lingering shadow of suspicion over this Gandhi from Kathiawar. Even so, he found it hard to establish a legal practice in Rajkot. In several months he acquired only three briefs. One took him to Veraval, where a plague was raging, so the court hearing was held in open fields outside the town. The experience encouraged Gandhi to raise funds for the sick. He got Pranjivan Mehta to write a handbook on the treatment of plague victims and distributed it to volunteers.

Gandhi also busied himself with work related to South Africa. He wrote articles for the papers, and sent copies of petitions to public men around India. The costs were paid by the Natal Indian Congress, which granted him an allowance to engage a clerk who took dictation and helped with packing and posting.[65]

The briefs, however, still would not come. Mohandas Gandhi was now a failed lawyer in Rajkot, where his father had once been, as Diwan, the second most important man in town. In July 1902, he moved to Bombay, to make one more attempt at establishing himself in the High Court. He rented an office, and some rooms in Girgaum for the family. Later, they shifted to a larger house in the northern suburb of Santa Cruz.

Meanwhile, in South Africa, the last roaming bands of Boers had surrendered. On the last day of May 1902 the warring parties had signed a treaty at Vereeniging, by which the Boers recognized the British monarch as their sovereign. In exchange, the British agreed that Dutch would continue as the language of choice in the schools and courts of Transvaal and the Orange Free State. The two former republics would be 'Crown colonies', run directly from London. In time they would be granted their own legislatures. The treaty however noted that 'the question of granting franchises to natives will not be decided until after the introduction of self-government.'[66] With this last clause, it became clear that (in the words of a later historian) Vereeniging was in essence 'a tribal peace, written and subscribed to in European interests alone'.[67]

That all of South Africa was now under British control was a source of gratification to the Secretary of State for the Colonies, Joseph

Chamberlain. He planned a trip to the new dominions in the New Year. Hearing of this, the Natal Indian Congress wrote to Gandhi asking him to return. He was needed to secure their rights under the new dispensation. Gandhi agreed at once.

In early November, Gandhi wrote to a friend that he hadn't decided whether Kasturba would accompany him. Even if she did, he would leave Harilal and Manilal behind in Rajkot, where they would study in his old school, while 'a trustworthy, paid man ... would look after their education'. The friend, a former fellow student in London who was now a successful barrister in Rajkot, was asked to allow the boys the use of his tennis court.[68]

In the event, Kasturba and the boys decided to stay in Bombay. Harilal was in boarding school in Gondal, while the other boys were in the care of their mother and their elder cousin Chhaganlal.[69] As in 1893, this time too Gandhi would travel alone in search of better prospects in South Africa.

In his autobiography, Gandhi is enigmatic about why he chose to go back a year after he had left Durban, as he thought (and hoped) at the time, for good. He writes that he was 'settling down as I had intended' in Bombay, and 'felt that before long I should secure work in the High Court'. But 'God has never allowed any of my own plans to stand. He has disposed of them in His own way.'[70]

Memoirs are notoriously misleading, not least because memories are notoriously fallible. When he wrote his autobiography in the 1920s, Gandhi was a great Indian nationalist, the symbol of a country struggling for political freedom. How to explain to himself or to his readers why, back in 1902, he had left the motherland once more? In truth, the decision to leave for South Africa was mandated not by the mysterious ways of fate, but by the mundane facts of failure. Writing to a friend in August 1902, Gandhi noted that he was 'free to lounge about the High Court letting the Solicitors know of an addition to the ranks of the briefless ones'. The response from the political class was likewise dispiriting; when he went to Pherozeshah Mehta for advice, the statesman 'gave me a curse which as he said might prove a blessing. He thought, contrary to my expectations, that I would be foolishly wasting away in Bombay my small savings from Natal.'[71]

Gandhi was unable to break into the ranks of well-established lawyers in the High Court. Those his age, who had been called to the Bar in the early 1890s, had a decade of experience behind them. The man from Rajkot via Durban was, in professional and social terms, an outsider. In any case, the wire from Natal was not a summons but an invitation. If the offer attracted Gandhi, it may have been because in Bombay he was a still unsuccessful lawyer, whereas in South Africa he had loyal and admiring clients.

7

White Against Brown

Gandhi sailed from Bombay in the last week of November 1902. With him were his nephews Maganlal and Anandlal, who had decided to try their luck in South Africa. Their ship reached Durban in the third week of December. The boys proceeded to the village of Tongat, where they planned to open a shop. Their uncle, meanwhile, placed himself at the service of the community. The Mayor of Durban had fixed an appointment for an Indian delegation to meet Joseph Chamberlain – the visiting Secretary of State for the Colonies – on the afternoon of 26 December. Gandhi asked for, and received, a day's postponement, on the grounds that the 26th was a Friday, 'the very time for prayer which most of the [Muslim] gentlemen, who are to form the deputation, would be quite unable to forgo'.[1]

At the meeting on the 27th, Chamberlain was presented with a petition asking for, among other things, the relaxation of the licensing laws in Natal and the provision of schools for Indian children. Chamberlain then took a train inland to Johannesburg, with Gandhi following some days later. The Indians in the Transvaal had asked that, since they had for some years past been 'guided by the advice of Advocate M. K. Gandhi', he also come along with them to meet the dignitary. The government wrote back stiffly that 'the deputation will consist of not more than 15 people, of whom Mr Gandhi cannot be one as he is not a resident of the Transvaal.'[2]

The merchants could not take their man along, but they could at least present to Chamberlain the petition he had drafted on their behalf. This asked that Indians be allowed to own property and trade anywhere, instead of being restricted to specific locations. It claimed that Indians in the Transvaal were 'worse [off] than before' the Anglo-Boer

War. The next week, Gandhi posted a petition to his Indian friends in Cape Town, which *they* would present to Chamberlain when he visited *that* city.Thus, within two weeks of his return to South Africa, Gandhi had written three different petitions on behalf of his countrymen, dealing with their predicament in three different provinces. However, he was less than hopeful of their impact, writing to Dadabhai Naoroji in the last week of January 1903 that he found Chamberlain had been swayed by the colonists' claim that unless stringent measures were put in place, 'this sub-continent would be swamped by the Indians'.[3]

With his family in India, Gandhi corresponded mainly with his nephew Chhaganlal. It was through him that he communicated with Kasturba and the children. Kasturba could read Gujarati, but not, it appears, write it with any fluency. She, in turn, passed on her news by using their nephew as a scribe.

In the first week of February, Gandhi told Chhaganlal that it was not right to have withdrawn Manilal from music lessons, adding: 'The blame is not yours, but your aunt's.' He then turned to his own predicament. There was 'great uncertainty' about his future; life as a lawyer-activist was 'no bed of roses'. The next month was crucial – if he found that it was not possible for him to continue in South Africa, he would return to India and rejoin the family. On the other hand, if he chose to stay on, 'it will be possible to bring you all after six months.'[4]

For the moment, Gandhi chose to base himself in Johannesburg. After the war, the Transvaal had been constituted as a 'Crown Colony'. The Governor, Lord Milner, was the head of its administration. In time, the colony would, on the model of Natal, have its own elected government, run by white legislators elected by white males alone. In this transitional period, it was crucial that Gandhi was at hand to lobby for the Indians.

In the last week of March 1903, Gandhi asked to be enrolled as a practising attorney in the Supreme Court of the Transvaal. He attached a certificate from the Inner Temple and proof that he had practised both at the High Court of Bombay and the Supreme Court of Natal. On 14 April his application was approved.[5] A few months later, he found office space at the corner of Rissik and Anderson Streets, and a room to live in the same block.[6]

Johannesburg in the early 1900s was very much a work-in-progress.

The journalist Flora Shaw captured its mood well, remarking that the city was 'much too busy with material problems. It is hideous and detestable, luxury without order, sensual enjoyment without art, riches without refinement, display without dignity.'[7] Another British journalist observed that everyday life in Johannesburg partook of an 'inborn restlessness. Everybody seems to be always shifting his place of abode. At the end of each month waggonloads of miscellaneous furniture jolt slowly to some new suburb.'[8]

There was an overwhelming preponderance of men in Johannesburg, the gender ratio being two males to each female among the white population, and close to ten males for each female among the black population. The social diversity was enormous – with almost every nation in Europe represented in the city, and almost every tribe in southern Africa too. Fortune seekers and job hunters descended on Johannesburg 'from the ends of the earth: miners from Mozambique, Nyasaland, Cornwall, and Australia; artisans and engineers from Scotland; shopkeepers from Lithuania and Gujarat; financiers from England and Germany'. This was a city where 'everybody came from somewhere else, social arrangements had to be constructed from scratch and everything was up for grabs'.[9]

A census conducted shortly after Gandhi moved there estimated Johannesburg's population to be a little over 150,000. It was growing at almost 10 per cent a year. The city's residents seemed to be in 'a state of perpetual haste'. New roads were being dug, new homes and offices constructed. Wood and other building materials lay piled up on the ground, and a cloud of dust hung in the air. To moderate private enterprise and manage its excesses, the elements of a municipal administration were being put in place. In 1903, as Gandhi made his home in Johannesburg, the first sewage pipes were laid under the ground, and the first storm-water drains constructed above them. In this decade, gas and electricity also made their first appearance in the city.[10]

The year Gandhi moved to Johannesburg, the writer John Buchan published a short, sharp portrait of the city. Buchan was then working on the staff of the Governor, Lord Milner. He saw Johannesburg as 'a city still on trial, sensitive, ambitious, profoundly ignorant of her own mind'. It had a 'short and checkered past'; once a mining camp, then a mining city, would it ever become a cosmopolitan centre of culture and the arts? Would Johannesburg, asked Buchan, 'go the way of many

colonial cities, and become vigorous, dogmatic, proud, remotely English
in sentiment, consistently material in her outlook, and narrow with the
intense narrowness of those to whom politics mean local interests spiced
with rhetoric'; or, as she was 'already richer, more enlightened, and
more famous than her older sisters' (such as Melbourne in Australia or
Wellington in New Zealand), would Johannesburg 'advance on a higher
plane, and become in the true sense an imperial city, with a closer kinship [to the mother country] and a more liberal culture'?[11]

The Indians in Johannesburg lived chiefly in two suburbs – Fordsburg,
to the west, and Vrededorp, to the north-west. Mohandas Gandhi, however, worked and slept in the very heart of the city, within a stone's
throw of its stock exchange, its main post office and its law courts.
Records of Gandhi's law practice in Johannesburg, preserved in the
National Archives of South Africa, tell us his clients were almost all
Indian. Some had lived in Transvaal before the war and wanted to
re-enter the province. Others were already based in Transvaal but
wanted a relaxation of the trading laws. Yet others wanted permits
facilitating travel between the different provinces of South Africa. Their
appeals were drafted and put before the authorities by Gandhi.[12]

As in Natal, Gandhi's law practice was conducted side-by-side with
his public work. The first was necessary to make a living; the second (so
to speak) to live. There was a British Indian Association in Transvaal. Its
chairman was a Muslim merchant, Abdul Gani, whose firm, Messrs
Mahomed Cassim Camrooden and Co., had offices in both Durban and
Johannesburg. The organization's name was noteworthy: these were
not just Indians, but 'British Indians', appealing to His Majesty for their
rights as subjects of the Empire.

In the third week of May 1903, the Association sought an appointment with Lord Milner. Milner's ambivalent attitude towards the
coloured races is manifest in two letters sent in quick succession to his
superiors in London. On 11 May he had proposed making Indians and
Chinese live (and work) in designated areas, because of their 'very
insanitary habits', and because it would 'mitigate the intense hostility
felt towards them by the European element, a hostility which, in view of
the possible introduction of self-government, is the greatest danger by
which they are confronted'.[13]

The next day, Milner wrote that he was in favour of importing Chinese and Indian workers for the railways and the mines. The 'enormous resources' of South Africa could not be exploited because of a shortage of labour, which was 'beginning to assume a really alarming aspect'. 'At present,' complained Milner, 'we are in the absurd position of being flooded by petty Indian traders and hawkers, who are no benefit whatever to the community, and not allowed to have Indian labourers, whom we greatly need.'[14]

When he met Milner, on 22 May, Gandhi told the proconsul that his people 'needed rest from the constant changes of passes and permits'. Milner answered that it was 'no use forcing the position here against the overwhelming body of white opinion'. He defended the policy of creating Asian-only bazaars, arguing that 'it would be a distinct advantage to the Indian community to occupy them instead of causing general opposition to themselves by settling down here, there, and everywhere, among people who do not want them.'[15]

Ten days later, Milner met with members of an organization named the 'White League'. They told the Governor they were opposed to Asians whether as merchants or labourers. The 'Chinese are most immoral', they claimed; as for the Indians, 'coolies are traders, not producers'. One White Leaguer angrily asked Milner: 'How is it that in Canada we do not hear of this sort of thing? There, when they want labour they get white labour from home.'[16]

The Indians held a meeting to counteract the White Leaguers. They gathered in a hall in Johannesburg's Fox Street to hear the BIA chairman, Abdul Gani, complain that the Crown had betrayed them. If the soil of the Transvaal was 'watered with the blood of Englishmen, have not the Indians, too, done their share?' They had hoped that a British victory would bring justice, that their handicaps would 'vanish, as if by magic, as soon as the Union Jack waved over the capital'. This was not to be. For

someone in authority soon discovered that, though British subjects, we were Asiatics after all, so the yoke of the Asiatic Office was placed on our necks. The Asiatic officers naturally, to justify their existence, unearthed the Asiatic laws for us. And now here we are faced with total social destruction ... We are to be branded as a class apart, cooped up in locations, euphemistically to be called bazaars, and probably prevented from owing a patch of land, except in bazaars, and compelled to pay a registration tax of £3. In short, if we would live in the Transvaal we would be content to live as social lepers.[17]

In 1897–8, when he was based in Natal, Gandhi had thought of starting a newspaper focusing on the Indian question in South Africa. Now, in the summer of 1903, he reactivated the idea, and found two men willing to help him. The first, Mansukhal Hiralal Nazar, was a widely travelled Gujarati who had studied medicine in Bombay and run a business in London before migrating to South Africa. The second, Madanjit Vyavaharik, was a former school teacher who owned a printing press in Grey Street in Durban. The press printed wedding cards, business cards, menus, account forms, memoranda, circulars, receipt books, and so on, in 'Gujarati, Tamil, Hindi, Urdoo, Hebrew, Marathi, Sanscrit, French, Dutch, Zulu, &c. &c.'[18] To this already extensive list would now be added a weekly journal of opinion.

Both Vyavaharik and Nazar were active members of the Natal Indian Congress. In 1895 and 1896, Vyavaharik had been asked by Gandhi to go from door to door in Grey Street and around, collecting money for the Congress. Since he had a beautiful hand and Gandhi an illegible one, he had also put the lawyer's words on paper in petitions sent to the government. Nazar, meanwhile, had travelled to London in 1897, sent by Gandhi to counter the colonists' propaganda against the Indians and their ways.[19]

Gandhi's collaborators were based in Durban, the centre of Indian life in South Africa. Vyavaharik's task now was to raise money from merchants and acquire type in the four languages the weekly would print in – English, Gujarati, Hindi and Tamil. Nazar's job was to plan each issue, arrange for articles and translations, edit copy, and see the magazine through the press. From Johannesburg, Gandhi would provide intellectual and moral direction, which included writing many articles himself.[20]

In 1903 there were fourteen printing presses in Durban. All were owned and staffed by whites – with the exception of the press run by Vyavaharik. The new, multilingual journal stood out against a monochromatic background of periodicals written, printed and read in English alone. The staff was suitably diverse – including a Cape Coloured, a man from Mauritius, several Gujaratis and at least two Tamils.[21]

The journal was named *Indian Opinion*. The first issue, appearing on

4 June 1903, announced itself as the voice of the Indian community, now 'a recognized factor in the body politic' of South Africa. The 'prejudice' against them in 'the minds of the Colonists' was based on an 'unhappy forgetfulness of the great services India has always rendered to the Mother Country ever since Providence brought loyal Hind under the flag of Britannia'. An article in the same issue qualified this loyalism, noting that in South Africa, 'if an European commits a crime or a moral delinquency, it is the individual: if it is an Indian, it is the nation.'[22]

In starting *Indian Opinion*, Gandhi was setting himself up as a knowledge-broker and bridge-builder. The journal would carry news of Indians in South Africa, of Indians in India, and general articles on 'all subjects – Social, Moral, and Intellectual'. It would 'advocate' the Indian cause, while giving Europeans 'an idea of Indian thought and aspiration'. Missing from this statement of the journal's aims was any mention of the largest section of the population of South Africa – the Africans themselves.[23]

Each issue of *Indian Opinion* ran to eight pages. A cover page listed the journal's title and the languages it was printed in. A series of advertisements followed. A shop in Durban drew attention to its Raleigh cycles of 'the rigid, rapid, reliable kind'; another shop alerted readers to its stocks of 'Oriental Jewellery'. General merchants in the towns of Natal placed insertions, as did specialized shops selling cigarettes and clothing. Other ads were issued by the paper itself; these asked for a 'good machine boy', for 'a first class Tamil compositor', and for someone who could read both Hindi and English.

Such was the first page; news and commentary in English followed. Later pages carried material in Gujarati and, at the end, in Hindi and Tamil. The annual subscription was twelve shillings and sixpence in Natal and seventeen shillings elsewhere (payable in advance). Single copies sold at threepence each.

New laws in Natal or the Transvaal that affected Indians, news from the Motherland about protests, plagues and great patriots – these were reproduced in *Indian Opinion* in all the languages it printed in. Other articles were tailored to individual communities. The Tamil section covered festivals observed only in South India. It also focused rather more on schools for girls, since – at this stage – Tamils were more keen to educate their women than the Gujaratis.[24]

The English and Gujarati sections of *Indian Opinion* both depended heavily on Gandhi's contributions (often printed without a byline). He wrote short notes and leaders on a variety of topics. The statements of Mayors and Governors were reproduced. Government dispatches and documents were summarized. Cases of harassment and discrimination were analysed.

The post between Durban and Johannesburg was kept busy by a ceaseless flow of letters, articles and proofs between the editor of *Indian Opinion* and the lawyer who, from several hundred miles away, directed its operations. M. H. Nazar worked ferociously hard, planning issues a week in advance, soliciting and editing articles and supervising translations. Funds ran low, as did stocks of type – a compositor told Nazar that he had better go slow on the Gujarati equivalent of the letter 'a' since they had not enough in stock. Nazar wrote to Gandhi that he was 'quite done up' and 'too fagged to think of anything'. The editor worked well past midnight on press days, which meant that he often missed the last tram and had to walk home through the unlit streets of Durban.[25]

As for Gandhi, his writings for this period are very heavily dominated by his public activities. Amidst hundreds of pages of editorials and reports for *Indian Opinion*, petitions to officials and legislators, legal notes and letters to sympathizers in the United Kingdom and India, there are rare, brief, glimpses into his personal life. These include two letters written on the same day, 30 June 1903, six months after his return to South Africa.

The first letter was addressed to his friend Haridas Vora, a fellow lawyer based in Rajkot. Gandhi's eldest son Harilal, now fourteen, had been unwell. Vora had helped him through his recovery. Gandhi thanked his friend for having 'supplied my place to Harilal . . . I can only wish that he was here to be attended by me and regret that he should have been a source of anxiety and worry . . .' He then turned to his own life in Johannesburg. He had 'built up a decent practice', but his public work was causing him 'very great anxiety.' It kept him busy from nine in the morning until ten at night, with intervals only for meals and a short walk.

Gandhi saw no chance of the pace slackening, as the Transvaal Government was planning new legislation aimed at the Indians. Before he left Bombay, he had told his wife that 'either I should return to

India at the end of the year or that she should come here by that time.'
He did not think he could fulfil the promise. Kasturba could join
him, but, he warned, 'she had very little of my company in Natal; probably, she would have less in Johannesburg.' If the family came to South
Africa, the time spent with them, away from work, might mean it
would take up to ten years to meet his obligations. On the other hand,
if they stayed on in India, that 'would enable me to give undivided
attention to public work', and he could return more quickly, say in
'three or four years'. Would Kasturba 'consent to remaining there all
that time?' Having posed the question, he told his friend that 'I wish to
be guided entirely by her sentiments and I place myself absolutely in her
hands.'

Also on 30 June 1903, Gandhi wrote to his nephew Chhaganlal
enclosing a copy of his letter to Haridas Vora. Chhagan was told to

> read it out and explain the situation here to your aunt. It is highly desirable
> that she should decide to stay on there as life here is rather expensive. If
> she remains there, savings made in this place will enable her and the chil-
> dren to lead a comparatively easy life in India. In that case, I may be able
> to return home in two or three years time . . . If, however, she decides to
> leave, make all requisite preparations by October and take the first avail-
> able boat in November. But do try to convince her that it will be best for
> her to remain in India.[26]

From his earliest days in South Africa, Gandhi had collected news
clippings on relations between the races. Now, these were raided for
publication in *Indian Opinion*. A report from the *Transvaal Leader*
featured a white Labour League which opposed Asiatic immigration.
The League believed that 'this nation, occupying the strongest geographical position in the Southern hemisphere, will hold in the event of any
great European war, the key to the South and the East, and that its future
must never depend on a race of helots.'[27] A liberal paper, the *Standard*,
remarked that 'the Hindus appear to have been treated throughout South
Africa much as the Jews were in Europe during the Middle Ages, and as
they are, to a considerable extent, in Russia at this very day.'[28]

In September 1903, an official in the Transvaal Government named
W. H. Moor prepared a report on the Indian question. There were, he

estimated, about 13,000 Indians at the time of the war. When hostilities broke out most left for Natal, the Cape, or Portuguese territory. From September 1901 they had begun returning, with a 'committee of influential Asiatics' consulted on whom to award permits. In September 1902 this committee was disbanded, and a Department of Asiatic Affairs formed to regulate re-entry into the Transvaal. From the end of war to March 1903, some 4,900 permits were issued.

The report was reproduced in full by *Indian Opinion*. Moor had summarized the 'popular feeling' of the whites in the Transvaal and the counter arguments of the British Indians. He did so sequentially, but I have clubbed them together in a chart, so that they can be read side by side. Interestingly, if not unexpectedly, the official spelt out the European position at greater length than the Indian one.[29]

Popular Feeling about Indians	Arguments of British Indians
That their mode of life is mean and dirty.	They deny that they are worse citizens than their fellow subjects; they are ready to submit to sanitary and municipal regulations.
That their low standard of living enables them to accept wages on which a white man cannot thrive and live.	They are anxious for education and capable of benefiting by it.
That they are not good colonists inasmuch as they do not bring money with them, and send their savings to their own countries.	They are industrious, temperate, frugal, law-abiding, and are prepared to settle in the country.
That South Africa is a country where white people can live and make their homes and establish their race; that the Oriental races have ample opportunity for exclusive colonization where the climate suits them, and where white people cannot settle.	As British subjects, they are entitled to equal treatment with others, regardless of colour, caste or creed.

(continued)

Popular Feeling about Indians	Arguments of British Indians
That the invincible hostility and repugnance felt towards the indigenous black races has produced so marked a line of cleavage on the basis of colour that the Asiatic races cannot ever be treated on a basis of equality with the white races; so that the introduction of the Asiatic races adds unnecessarily a third element which cannot be refused and an additional complication in the settlement of the disturbances in South Africa.	They have proved themselves to be public spirited, liberal and charitable, and they maintain their poor.[30]

An editorial in an early issue of *Indian Opinion* sought to see 'The Bright Side of the Picture'. The situation now looked bleak, but the hope, in the long-term, was that

> as the European community grows older, the awkward corners would be rubbed out, and that the different members of the Imperial family in South Africa would be able to live in perfect peace in the near future. The time may not come within the present generation; we may not live to see it, but that it will come no sane man will deny; and that being so, let us all strain our every nerve to hasten its coming . . . by trying to step into the shoes of our opponents and endeavouring to find out what may be running in their minds – to find out, that is to say, not merely the points of difference, but also points of agreement.[31]

It was barely five years since Gandhi had been attacked by a mob that spoke for the white population of Durban, a handful of liberals excepted. Even as he wrote, there was a regular flow of derisive remarks against him in the white press, and of course his compatriots were subject to racial prejudice on a daily basis. And yet, here was the leader of the Indians seeking to live in 'perfect peace' with their oppressors.

Surely, this optimism was a product of the friendships that he had forged. Josiah Oldfield and members of the Vegetarian Society in London; the lawyer F. A. Laughton and the policeman R. C. Alexander in Durban; lay preachers like A. W. Baker in Pretoria – to this list were now added white men in Johannesburg with whom Gandhi took walks, shared meals and debated the rights of the different races in South Africa.

In his first year in Johannesburg, Gandhi befriended four Europeans with whom, for reasons of class and education, he was more temperamentally akin than the Indians whom he represented in court. Of this quartet, the first to enter his life was a man named L. W. Ritch. He was Jewish and originally from London, in which city he (like Gandhi) had sought to broaden his faith with an infusion of Theosophy. He moved to Johannesburg in 1894, and helped found a Theosophical Lodge. This met every Thursday to discuss the works of Madame Blavatsky and Annie Besant.

In a letter to *The Theosophist*, Ritch described the Transvaal

as a republic in name only. Racial hatred, directed most strongly against any nationality of sable exterior, is its most marked feature. This is so even in Natal, where only recently an attempt was made to prevent a number of Indians landing, an attempt however which proved abortive, chiefly to the pluck and persistence of my Indian friend, Mr Gandhi, Barrister-at-Law, a gentleman who has for a long time past been fighting the Indian battle in Natal, almost single-handed.

L. W. Ritch first met Gandhi before the Anglo-Boer War, on one of the lawyer's visits from Durban to Johannesburg. During the war, Ritch left the city. He returned after the peace treaty was signed, and set about re-establishing the Theosophical Lodge. This new, syncretic, cosmopolitan creed was at odds with the prevailing ethos of a city displaying 'the concentrated essence of selfishness, individualism, greed and mammon worship'. Gandhi, who had now moved to Johannesburg – to almost single-handedly fight the Indian battle there – began visiting the Lodge regularly. In and apart from these meetings, he and Ritch found they had much to talk about.[32]

Two other friends came to Gandhi as a consequence of his tastes in food. The lawyer often ate his meals at Johannesburg's only vegetarian restaurant, the Alexandra Tea Room. Another regular visitor to the eatery was an Englishman named Albert West. He has left behind a vivid portrait of the place and its milieu, *c.* 1903:

Around a large table sat a mixed company of men comprising a stockbroker from the United States who operated on the Exchange in gold and diamond shares, an accountant from Natal, a machinery agent, a young Jewish member of the Theosophical Society [this must have been L. W. Ritch], a working tailor from Russia, Gandhi the lawyer, and me a printer. Everybody in Johannesburg talked about the share market, but these men were food reformers interested in vegetarian diet, Khune [sic] baths, earth poultices, fasting, etc. I was specially attracted by this man from India, and Gandhi and I soon became close friends.[33]

It was at the same restaurant that Gandhi met Henry Solomon Leon Polak, a thin, lean, intellectually-minded Jew who had lately arrived from Britain. He, like West, was in his early twenties, a full decade younger than the lawyer he was to befriend. His family were originally from the Continent – one grandparent spoke Dutch, another German. They had moved to England, where Polak's father worked as the advertising manager of a newspaper. Henry himself had studied at a school in Neuchâtel, in the French-speaking part of Switzerland, and then at London University.

While a student, Henry Polak began writing for a Jewish weekly on political matters. He fell in love with a girl named Millie Graham, who was both a Christian and, as an 'ardent social reformer', a supporter of women's suffrage. His family were distressed by the romance, so – in an attempt to break it – they dispatched Henry to join an uncle in South Africa. However, before he left he insisted on formalizing his engagement to Millie.[34]

Polak worked at first in his uncle's business in Cape Town. He soon moved to Johannesburg, where he joined the staff of a local weekly, the *Transvaal Critic*. He had begun reading the works of Leo Tolstoy, and it was a fellow Tolstoyan, a painter and stage actor, who took him to the vegetarian restaurant patronized by an Indian who also admired the Russian writer. As they entered the eatery one day in 1904, the painter pointed Gandhi out to his friend. Polak then took

a swift glance at the quiet, slender, pleasant-looking man sitting at a table alone. Apart from his black professional turban and his dark complexion, there was nothing specially to mark out the already well-known East Indian leader. I was disappointed. I suppose I had expected to see a big, aggressive fellow, who had been the sergeant-major of an East Indian Ambulance Corps during the Boer War . . . I could not guess that, at the moment, I was gazing at the man who was to become the greatest Asiatic of his time.

The two men were introduced, and found that they shared an admiration not just of Tolstoy, but of more obscure authors, such as Adolf Just, author of *Return to Nature*. Polak visited Gandhi at his law chambers, and as the friendship developed, 'we met almost daily and discussed vigorously every problem and subject which interested either of us.' These conversations usually took place over dinner at the vegetarian restaurant, where they ate salads so dominated by a particular pungent bulb that Polak joked that they should start an 'Amalgamated Society of Onion–Eaters'.[35]

Just before or after he met Polak, Gandhi came into contact with Hermann Kallenbach, also a Jew, albeit of a different background and temperament. Born two years after Gandhi, and originally from Lithuania, Kallenbach grew up in Prussia and qualified as an architect. Wiry, strong and extremely athletic, he enjoyed the outdoors, spending his winters skating and his summers swimming and fishing. Body-building was another passion. In about 1896 he moved to South Africa. He was a beneficiary of the construction boom in Johannesburg, designing large buildings that went up in the heart of the city. Like Ritch and Polak, he was part of a substantial wave of Jewish emigration to South Africa, with the population of Jews multiplying tenfold between 1880 and 1904. Many came, like Kallenbach himself, from towns in Russia and Eastern Europe that were home to a rising tide of anti-Semitism.[36]

Kallenbach's office was very close to Gandhi's law chambers. They first met through an Indian merchant who was a client of both lawyer and architect. The friendship with Kallenbach was an inversion of Gandhi's earlier friendship with Sheikh Mehtab. As an athlete who was deft with his hands, Kallenbach was a sort of mature Sheikh Mehtab; except that rather than being looked up to, it was he who admired Gandhi – whose interest in matters of the spirit and steadiness of purpose were in contrast to the architect's restlessness and conflicted sexual desires (he was a bachelor, and at this stage apparently a virgin).[37]

It is striking that of Gandhi's four closest friends in Johannesburg, three were Jews. White-skinned, but not Boer or Briton, and certainly not Christian, the Jews came from families that had been subject to prejudice and persecution. They were quicker than other Europeans to deplore the unreasoning racism of rulers in the Transvaal; quicker, too, to warm to an Indian who was alive, intelligent and less than orthodox in his own religious (or dietary) beliefs.[38]

It is also striking that none of these friends were Gujarati or even Indian. In London, there had been Indian students with whom Gandhi could converse. In Johannesburg, however, he was the only professional in the community. There were no other Indian lawyers, nor any Indian doctors, teachers, editors, or managers in the Transvaal. To be sure, Gandhi was connected to his compatriots by ties of sentiment and culture, but books and ideas were not part of their diet; nor, really, were fruit and vegetables. The Gujaratis in Johannesburg were, as Muslims, hard-core meat-eaters, as were the working-class Tamils and Telugu-speakers who represented, so to speak, the 'other half' of the community. These people were his clients and also his compatriots. He identified with their sufferings. His working day was spent advancing their individual and collective causes. However, for conversation and cuisine he looked elsewhere.

In his 'Guide to London', written in Pretoria in 1893, Gandhi had said that the Indian student abroad was 'master of his time', with 'no wife to tease or flatter him, no parents to indulge, no children to look after'. Ten years later, living alone once more, Gandhi used his freedom from family obligations to explore the dissenting sub-cultures of Johannesburg. Most professionals in the town were likewise single or living apart from their wife and children. They used their time outside work to play and party. Rugby, cricket and horse-racing held no attractions for Gandhi; nor did club life and hunting expeditions. But experiments in diet and inter-faith living did. These interests or obsessions, first visible in London, were now more vigorously pursued amidst Jews, Theosophists, Nonconformists and vegetarians in this new city on a reef.

Outside South Africa, Gandhi's most steadfast supporters were two Parsis in London: the former MP Dadabhai Naoroji and the serving MP M. M. Bhownaggree. He sent them a regular stream of letters on Indian problems in South Africa; they, in turn, passed on his concerns to His Majesty's Government. In 1903 alone, Naoroji sent as many as nineteen letters to the India Office on Gandhi's behalf – this a mark both of the younger man's persistence and the older man's patriotism.[39]

Bhownaggree was scarcely less energetic. He asked many questions in Parliament, where he termed the anti-Indian legislation in India a 'scandal', and in September 1903 posted a letter of twenty printed pages to the Secretary of State for the Colonies, Joseph Chamberlain. Drawing on memoranda sent by Gandhi, this detailed the 'disabilities and indignities' suffered by British Indians in the Transvaal. Bhownaggree warned that 'the affection of the Indian people for King and Empire is undermined by the continuance of the state of affairs in South Africa.'

Soon afterwards, Chamberlain resigned. Bhownaggree now sent the letter to his successor, Alfred Lyttelton, who passed it on to the Governor of the Transvaal, Lord Milner, noting that he could 'not but feel much sympathy for the views expressed in it, and I fear it will be difficult to meet his representations with a fully satisfactory answer.'

When Lyttelton forwarded Bhownaggree's note to him, Lord Milner asked his Lieutenant-Governor, Alfred Lawley, to prepare a rebuttal. On 13 April 1904, Lawley sent his boss a closely argued defence of the policy towards Indians. 'There is not in this country one man in a hundred,' he remarked, 'who would agree to recognise the coloured man as capable of admission to the same social standard as the white.' Then he added: 'I do not seek to justify the prejudices which exist; I merely desire to set them forth. They cannot be ignored. They have got to be reckoned with.'

Like Milner, Lawley thought that while Indians were acceptable as labourers, as traders they posed a serious threat to European interests in the Transvaal. There was a further danger, that if their children educated themselves they might seek a foothold in the professional class. The Asiatic question in South Africa thus drew one 'face to face with a most difficult problem of modern civilisation'. The British Empire included territories of all climatic and vegetative types. Tropical regions like India and arid areas like central Africa were both incapable of 'becoming the permanent home of a white nation'. On the other hand,

South Africa is one of the countries inhabitable alike by Europeans and Asiatics, and it is difficult to conceive any question at the present moment more momentous than the struggle between East and West for the inheritance of these semi-vacant territories. Promises have been made without knowledge or perception of the consequence involved in their fulfilment.

If the redemption of the pledges upon which Sir M. Bhownaggree depends both in letter and spirit means that in fifty or a hundred years this country will have fallen to the inheritance of the Eastern instead of Western populations, then from the point of view of civilisation they must be numbered among promises which it is a greater crime to keep than to break.

Lawley therefore concluded that 'the first duty of statesmen in this country is to multiply homes for white men.'

On 18 April, Milner wrote to the Imperial Government endorsing Lawley's views. The challenge, on the one side, was to prevent 'an indiscriminate influx of Asiatics', and on the other, to facilitate 'a great increase in the white population'. As for Indians already in the territory, Milner thought that 'the attempt to place coloured people on an equality with whites in South Africa is wholly impracticable, and that, moreover, it is in principle wrong.'[40]

Faced with Milner's intransigence, M. M. Bhownaggree turned once more to the British Parliament. Between February and August 1904, he asked as many as twelve questions about the treatment of Indians in South Africa.[41] He also took the debate to the press, telling the *Daily Graphic* that in the Transvaal, 'the Indian subjects of the King are being actually worse treated than they were under Boer rule.' When asked 'why this reactionary course has been taken', Bhownaggree replied: 'I can only put it down to the influence of the White League, a militant body that . . . seems to have obtained a commanding influence over the Transvaal Government.'[42]

Gandhi, meanwhile, was busy writing for *Indian Opinion*, shoring up the sagging spirit of his countrymen. In November 1903 he saluted Dadabhai Naoroji on his seventy-eighth birthday; the Parsi veteran, he said, was 'loved from the Hindukush to Cape Comorin and from Karachi to Calcutta as no other living man in India is loved'. Two months later, he wrote that the lives of Christ and Joan of Arc demonstrated that 'individuals have to sacrifice so that the community may gain a great deal'. Gandhi thought the situation did not call for 'heroic sacrifice' by Indians; rather, 'well-sustained, continuous and temperate constitutional effort is the main thing needed.' For 'if the British machinery is slow to move, the genius of the nation being conservative, it is also quick to perceive and recognise earnestness and unity.'[43]

In February 1904, seeking to get the machinery to move, Gandhi wrote several letters to the Chief Medical Officer complaining that the Indian Location in north-west Johannesburg was 'over-crowded beyond description'. Since Indians had only tenancy rights, they had no incentive to keep the place clean. Gandhi warned that 'if the present state of things is continued, the outbreak of some epidemic disease is merely a question of time.'[44]

Sure enough, bubonic plague broke out in the bazaar in March. Gandhi led the attempts to nurse the victims. A temporary hospital was formed in an abandoned warehouse, where the sick were treated with wet-earth poultices. Many were saved, but at least twenty-one died.[45]

Having failed to provide proper sanitation, the municipality now decided to raze the bazaar to the ground. A contingent of troops evacuated the area and set fire to six whole blocks, containing at least 1,600 buildings. The residents watched in stony silence. The next day, the Indians were taken to a new location, in Klipstruit, ten miles outside the city. The site had previously served as a camp for Boer prisoners-of-war: with tents as houses and no sewage, the place was unfit to live in and to trade – who, whether white, coloured or black, would come and shop there? The Indians who had been dumped at Klipstruit made their way back to Johannesburg in dribs and drabs, living and working at the margins of the city itself.[46]

In May, a trader named Habib Motan appealed to the Supreme Court against the Government's decision to deny him a general licence. He had traded freely before the Anglo-Boer War, and questioned why he had now to be confined to a location. The judge, bravely and perhaps surprisingly, concurred. Gandhi congratulated the merchant for winning his case, but warned 'against being too much elated by this success. Probably it means only the beginning of another struggle. Opposition will be raised up against them throughout the country, and the Government may bring in a bill to counteract the effects of the Supreme Court.' He also drew attention to the problems of Chinese traders, who, in small towns across the province, were being harassed by whites who wanted the custom of Chinese mine workers for themselves. This reminded him 'very much of similar agitation in Durban in 1896' (conducted against the Indians, and against himself).[47]

As Gandhi had predicted, sections of the white public were outraged by the Motan judgement. A deputation of white traders met the Colonial Secretary to complain that 'the Asiatics are getting hold of the native trade, which represents a very large part of the country's wealth'. A hardline group, the East Rand Vigilance Association, urged the Government to 'formulate a new and comprehensive Ordinance, with all possible despatch, such Ordinance to be retrospective and to provide that no Asiatic trading or residence of any kind be allowed in the Transvaal save in bazaars set aside for the exclusive use of Asiatics'.[48]

The East Rand Vigilantes were led by an Anglican clergyman named C. E. Greenfield, of whom Gandhi's weekly wrote that he 'believed justice to be absent from Heaven itself if it contained a British Indian'.[49] The priest represented a wide spectrum of white opinion. At a meeting of European farmers in Pietersburg, one speaker described Indians as

> an evil-smelling race, and an eyesore on this, one of the most beautiful countries in the world. Are we to allow them here? (no). Are we to allow these human parasites to overrun a land which is the heritage of white people and for which they have fought and bled? (no). Then let us take measures before it is too late or they will gain such a foothold as they have already secured in Natal (loud applause).[50]

At another meeting, in Pretoria, a speaker named A. H. Green drew upon thirty years spent as a tea-planter in South India to warn the audience against any 'sentimentalism'. The Hindu was 'a very wily fellow'. If 'you have the Indian with you and do not confine him to living and trading in bazaars', warned Green, then 'he will enter upon the various spheres of work throughout the Transvaal'. He spoke of an Indian he knew, who married an English lady while studying in England, and then took her home, where she had to cover her head and eat separately from him. Who was to say that if more Indians were allowed into the Transvaal, they would not first take their land, then their jobs, and, finally, their women? 'Have you a daughter, Sir?' asked the rabble-rouser of his excited and fearful audience: 'Would you like to see your daughter wedded to an Indian?'[51]

The Transvaal Government now sought to annul the judgement in favour of Habib Motan. Lord Milner was worried that if the verdict was not reversed, 'some thousands of British Indians will be able to demand as of right a privilege from which they had been excluded prior to the recent finding of the Supreme Court.'[52]

Sensing a hardening of the white attitude, Gandhi sought a compromise. He outlined its terms in a proposal sent to Lord Milner in September 1904; this has disappeared from the records, but a letter that accompanied it exists. It throws new light on Gandhi's motivations at this point in time. The letter's tone and contents are extremely conciliatory. Gandhi said his proposals

> meet every reasonable objection of the Colonists in that:
>
> (1) They are intended entirely to prohibit the immigration of all but the fewest Indians of education such as may be allowed to enter the Colony for the assistance of those who are already settled in the country.
>
> (2) They place the issue of new dealers' licences absolutely under the control of the Government or the local bodies if thereto authorised subject to review by the Supreme Court in extreme cases.
>
> (3) Under them compulsory segregation would not be necessary because in Johannesburg and Pretoria, which contain the largest population, there are already locations existing, and in the other places they are totally unnecessary as the present Indian population is too small. There would be very little addition in future and few, if any, new licences would be issued.

Gandhi said of his proposals that they do 'give the right to the Indians of owning fixed property, but, if necessary, certain portions – for instance, farms – may be reserved for exclusive European ownership. In towns it is submitted that there should be no opposition to Indian ownership.' He ended his letter with a plea:

> Throughout my eleven years' connection with the question, my earnest endeavour has been to look at the question from the European standpoint also and to advise my countrymen so far as possible to avoid an appeal to the Home Government. It is the same desire that prompts me to approach His Excellency in the present instance. Should my attendance be required, I would wait on His Excellency.
>
> I beg to repeat that this is written in my private capacity but should His Excellency be pleased to approve of my suggestions, I do not anticipate any difficulty in securing the acceptance of the proposals by my countrymen in so far as such may be deemed necessary.[53]

Even without access to Gandhi's original proposal, we can, with the aid of this fascinating and forgotten letter, divine its contents. The lawyer asked that Indians be permitted to own property and reside in towns alongside white populations *where they already did so*. This would allow them to protect their livelihoods, and their dignity. What he did not ask for was the upholding of their right, as British Indians, to migrate freely to any part of the Empire. Hence the call to limit further immigration to a few educated Indians. The concession re farm ownership was perhaps due to the fact that Boers disliked Indians even more than the British. A new party named 'Het Volk' was campaigning in the Transvaal countryside against 'the free influx of Asiatics', its leaders making what the white press was obliged to refer to as 'violent speeches'.[54]

Gandhi's proposal represented a significant softening of his views. Back in 1894 and 1895, he had asked that educated Indians be granted the franchise in Natal. He now saw more clearly that whites in South Africa (as distinct from whites in England) would not concede the right to vote. So he asked for something more modest – namely, confirmation of their rights of residence, work, travel and trade. Indians could not become equal citizens, but they might yet be treated as honourable subjects, allowed to live at peace and with dignity under the British flag in South Africa.

One motivation for Gandhi's proposal was certainly political. He understood that, in the context of the profound asymmetry of power (and of numbers), Indians could not overcome white prejudice in the Transvaal. However, with the help of sympathetic British administrators, they might moderate or placate it. Hence the compromise suggested by him – virtually no fresh immigration, but no seizures of property or forced relocations either.

Another motivation was very likely personal. Although, as he reminded Milner, he had first come to South Africa eleven years ago, this country was no more 'home' to him than London had been. Gandhi had gone to one place to study, to the other to help fight a legal battle. For all his commitment to the Indians living there, South Africa (like the United Kingdom) remained for him a foreign land. In October 1901 he had sailed from Durban for India, in his eyes for good. In November 1902 he sailed back to Durban, but – in a sign of how temporary he saw this stay would be – left Kasturba and the children behind in Bombay.

For some sixteen years now, Mohandas Gandhi had been a journeyman between continents. Born and raised in Kathiawar, he had braved convention and community to study in England. When he boarded the SS *Clyde* in September 1888, he saw the voyage as his first, but also his last, journey overseas. Having burnished his credentials, he would return to make a career and name in his native Kathiawar; as his mother's spiritual guide had advised her, with a barrister's certificate from London a diwanship should be her son's for the asking. His brother Laxmidas's misdeeds rendered that plan unfruitful, and life became more complicated. Having tried, and failed, to establish himself in Rajkot and Bombay, on his third try Gandhi became a successful lawyer in Durban. Three years there alone; three more years with his family; and then, to educate his children and overcome his wife's loneliness, in 1901 Gandhi returned to India.

A year later he was back in South Africa. This time, the community desired that he be based in Johannesburg. Here he lived the life of an expatriate: working with his Indian clients during the day, and spending the evenings with (white) professionals likewise single or separated from their families. Life in Johannesburg was interesting and intriguing, for a while. But once the Indian question in the Transvaal was settled, he would make one final transcontinental journey and go back home.

Kasturba very much wanted her husband to return to India. And he wished to go back himself. There may have been a lingering ambition to try – for the third time – to establish a practice in the Bombay High Court. There were also options outside the law, in the sphere of politics and social work. For an ambitious patriot, the motherland offered a far larger theatre of action than the diaspora. The experience and credibility that he had acquired in South Africa could be parleyed to great effect back home in India.

There were thus compelling reasons for Gandhi to return finally – after sixteen years on the move, shuttling between three continents – to establish himself as a lawyer and/or social activist in his homeland. Hence the compromise offered to Milner. If Gandhi could secure a settlement which struck a middle ground between the desires of the colonists (the wholesale expulsion of Indians) and the hopes of the more radical of his countrymen (the right of free entry and settlement), he could leave South Africa with his honour intact.

Gandhi's note and letter were passed on to the Governor. Milner does not appear to have called Gandhi for a meeting, or indeed to have taken his proposals very seriously. Gandhi was now losing faith in the intentions of this particular Englishman. As he wrote to Gokhale:

> Contrary to all expectations, Lord Milner, who on the eve of the war, was the champion of the oppressed including the British Indians, has completely

turned round and . . . is quite prepared to deprive the Indians of even what little rights they possessed in the Transvaal before [the] war.[55]

An Englishwoman who got to know Lord Milner during the Anglo-Boer War found him 'clear-headed and narrow', adding, 'Everyone says he has no heart, but I think I hit on the atrophied remains of one.'[56] To his compatriots Milner might sometimes show emotion, but to everyone (and for everything) else he was always hard-headed. As Saul Dubow has written, notwithstanding Milner's own low opinion of Boer culture, the proconsul now understood that 'securing a prosperous and loyal Transvaal was key to establishing and maintaining British political supremacy in South Africa'.[57] In rejecting Gandhi's proposals, Milner was merely recognizing that European sentiment, Boer as well as Briton, was overwhelmingly against the Indians.

Mohandas Gandhi was city-born and city-bred. Born in Porbandar, raised in Rajkot, educated in London; a practising professional in Bombay, Durban and Johannesburg – he had spent all his years in urban centres small, large and massive. In 1904, now thirty-five, he had not spent a night in a village, nor perhaps an entire day either. And yet he had long had a yearning for the rustic life. It was first expressed in London, in the meetings of the Vegetarian Society, where he met Henry Salt and read his friend Edward Carpenter, a Cambridge scholar who had settled in the Yorkshire hills, from where he sermonized against the ills of industrialism. In his own first writings, Gandhi had spoken admiringly of the simple life of the shepherds of Kathiawar. Later he had read Tolstoy, and learnt of the Russian's experiments on the land.

In the latter half of 1904, Gandhi travelled to Durban for work, being seen off at Johannesburg's Park Station by Henry Polak. As the train pulled out, his friend gave him a copy of John Ruskin's *Unto This Last*. This was a polemic against the then very influential science of political economy. Ruskin deplored the tendency of Ricardo, Mill, *et al.* to make money the unit of all exchange and value. A science that regarded air, light and cleanliness, or peace, trust and love as worthless, was in conflict with the teachings of the great religions, and antithetical to the deeper interests of humanity itself. Whereas Ricardo and company rigorously separated economics from morality, Ruskin thought that affection and trust must govern relations between master and servant,

capitalist and worker. A moral economics would be one 'which nour-
ishes the greatest number of noble and happy human beings', not which
promoted the greatest monetary wealth or produced the greatest number of rich people.[58]

The lawyer read *Unto This Last* at once, right through, and was so
moved that he could not sleep that night. The impact was so immense
that, as Gandhi later recalled, 'I determined to change my life in accordance with the ideals of the book.' The core teaching of *Unto This Last*,
as understood by him, was that the work of farmers and labourers was
as valuable as the work of lawyers and factory managers. To work with
one's hands, and on the land, was more honourable than working with
one's brains or with the aid of machines.[59]

Reading Ruskin on the train from Johannesburg to Durban consolidated Gandhi's romantically rural orientation. It prompted him to move
Indian Opinion from Durban's Grey Street to a new home in the countryside. He bought a farm near the station of Phoenix, on the North
Coast Line, some fourteen miles from town. In its issue of 24 December
1904 the journal announced the shift in location. Both printing press
and operating staff would be housed in the farm, where 'the workers
could live a more simple and natural life, and the ideas of Ruskin and
Tolstoy combined with strict business principles'. Those who worked
on the press, whether Englishman or Indian – or neither – would be
paid a modest monthly allowance (of £3) and allotted plots of land to
grow their food. The scheme's promoter described it as 'a bold experiment and fraught with momentous consequences. We know of no
non-religious organisation that is or has been managed on the principles
above laid down.'[60]

One of the first recruits to the new experiment was Albert West. Gandhi had persuaded him to leave his job in Johannesburg and take charge
of the press. When West reached the farm he found it to be a pleasant
enough place, with fruit trees and date-palms, and a river running
through the property. A plot of twenty acres was bought in the first
instance; with another eighty acres added on soon afterwards. On this
land the workers built homes of wood and corrugated iron. Meanwhile,
the press was dismantled and transported from Durban to Phoenix in
four large wagons, each pulled by sixteen bullocks. The machinery was
then reassembled. Gandhi wanted to work the press by hand, but West
insisted on the purchase of a petrol engine (there was no electricity in

the neighbourhood). As a concession to his friend, the Englishman designed a hand-operated machine with a wheel mounted on a wooden frame, which could be used when the oil ran out.[61]

The land, the building materials and the workers' stipends were paid for principally by two men. Gandhi supplied the substantial sum of £3,500 from his own savings. (Clearly, the 'decent practice' he had spoken of to his Rajkot friend was very decent indeed.) The Durban merchant Parsee Rustomjee contributed in cash and in kind – apart from writing cheques, he also donated a large number of sheets of corrugated iron.

By the first week of January 1905, issues printed on the farm had begun reaching the journal's subscribers. Gandhi wrote to Gokhale that he now hoped to establish a school at Phoenix 'which would be second to none in South Africa'. He asked his mentor to recommend an Indian teacher with 'a blameless character', and to send a letter of encouragement for printing in *Indian Opinion*.[62]

Back in 1899, when the two sets of white colonists in South Africa went to war, Gandhi was an Empire loyalist, a believer in Imperial citizenship who thought that flattery and persuasion would end discrimination against Indians in South Africa. Thus he signed up to support the British in their campaign against the Boers. Thus, too, his repeated petititions to London, made in the belief that even if the colonists were sometimes bigoted and narrow-minded, they would be brought around by sagacious Imperial statesmen.

Gandhi took heart from the fact that British officials in India tended to side with his people in South Africa. A leading member of the Indian Civil Service had chastised the Transvaal Government for placing members of an 'ancient and orderly civilization' on a par with 'uncivilized African labourers'.[63] A second ICS man told a delegation from Natal that 'the Indian is not on a level with the kafir; he belongs to a higher class. The Indian trader is almost as advanced as ourselves.'[64]

These views on the hierarchy of civilizations were conventional – Gandhi shared them too (at the time). They placed Indians almost adjacent to Europeans, from which perspective the discriminatory laws in South Africa were clearly misguided, if not actively malevolent. The Viceroy of India, Lord Curzon, thus criticized Lord Milner for 'justifying the vexatious regulations' on Indians in the Transvaal. Curzon thought it 'much more important to conciliate the unanimous sentiment of 300,000,000 of our subjects in Asia than to defer to the prejudices of a small colony of white men in South Africa.'[65]

When Gandhi sailed for Durban in November 1902, his hopes in British justice were largely intact. Two years later he was less naïve. He had once hoped to unite the Indians with the British against the Boers; now, after the war, the British were uniting with the Boers against them. South Africa was not England, where brown men could be elected to Parliament; or even India, where they could become judges and Imperial Councillors. Here, the bonds of race would always trump Imperial loyalties and obligations. The Indian situation in the Transvaal was now uncertain, fraught with difficulties. When, in September 1904, Lord Milner rejected the compromise Gandhi offered him, Gandhi felt he had to stay on. So he asked his wife and children to join him in Johannesburg.

Kasturba arrived in South Africa towards the end of 1904. The eldest son, Harilal, now sixteen, had stayed back in India. He was keen to sit the Bombay Matriculation that his father had taken back in 1887. However, the other sons came out with their mother, as did two nephews, Gokuldas and Chhaganlal.

8

Pluralist and Puritan

Gandhi rented a house in Albemarle Street, in the east Johannesburg district of Troyeville, to accommodate the whole family. As in Durban, theirs was the only Indian home in a white neighbourhood. The two-storey house was spacious, with eight rooms, balconies and a garden.[1]

Gandhi had warned Kasturba that he would spend little time with her in Johannesburg, and so it turned out. He rose early, helped his wife grind flour for the day's meals, then walked the five miles to his office in Rissik Street, carrying a packed lunch of wholemeal bread with peanut butter and a selection of seasonal fruits. His days were spent taking cases, drafting petitions to government and writing for and supervising, long-distance, the production of *Indian Opinion*. He walked home in the evenings, where, after dinner, he taught his sons the elements of Gujarati grammar and composition.[2]

Hermann Kallenbach was a frequent visitor to the Gandhi household. The boys liked him, not least because he brought gifts of chocolates and toys. They were also impressed by stories of his elegant lifestyle; apparently he had a barber come in every morning to shave him in bed.[3]

While the children were being home-schooled, the adult nephew, Chhaganlal, was sent to join the community at Phoenix. His younger brother Maganlal was already working there as a compositor. Chhagan and Magan served as Gandhi's eyes and ears in a community he had founded and funded, but at this stage rarely visited. The uncle wrote to his nephews at least once a week, asking for reports on the staff and the state of the finances. The young men were advised on how to set Gujarati type and where to look for subscribers.

Indian Opinion had now expanded from eight pages to thirty-six. The text was printed in three columns instead of six. The end pages were taken up with advertisements – of, for instance, a 'German East African Fortnightly Steamer for BOMBAY, Direct'. A Calcutta bookseller took space to publicize his wares, which included a volume entitled *Helps to the Study of English*, and another containing *Select Speeches of the Great Orators*. Most advertisements, however, were (as before) for shops and enterprises in Natal selling cloth, cigars, sweets, rice, *ghee* and real estate.

The reports in the expanded *Indian Opinion* covered a wide range of topics. The rise of other Asian nations was noted and appreciated. After the fall of Port Arthur during the Russo-Japanese War, the journal wrote that 'the Japanese, by sheer force of character, have brought themselves into the forefront of the nations of the world. They have shown unity, self-sacrifice, fixity of purpose, nobility of character, steel[y] courage, and generosity to the enemy.' An article in Hindi spoke of a national renewal in China, with moves to create officer corps and military academies on Japanese and Western models. The journal recalled General Gordon's old prediction that when China awoke, the world would watch with fear and admiration.[4]

Indian difficulties in Natal and the Transvaal were written about, but so also was the situation of the other communities in South Africa. A report of April 1905 spoke of a 'monster native petition' signed by 33,000 people, addressed to the Imperial Government in London, which asked that when full autonomy was granted to Transvaal, the interests of Africans be kept in mind, and no class legislation introduced which would 'degrade and suppress all coloured races'. The petition urged the abolition of the death penalty, an end to the practice of whipping Africans, and the granting of permission to 'respectable natives' to travel in 'superior classes' on railways and to vote in municipal elections.[5]

Gandhi's weekly also carried reports on society and politics in India. A report from early January 1905 summarized the presidential address at the Bombay Congress of the liberal imperialist Sir Henry Cotton. Despite their promises, said Cotton, the British had been harsher on Indians than the Boers. 'Their little finger had been thicker than Mr Kruger's loins. Where he chastised with whips, they chastised with scorpions.'[6]

Gandhi's newspaper ran several reports on the opening of an 'India House' in London, promoted by a Gujarati radical named Shyamaji Krishnavarma. The chief guest at the opening was the British Marxist H. M. Hyndman. As *Indian Opinion* reported, Krishnavarma said it 'gave him much pleasure to see his veteran friend Dadabhai Naoroji who, tied down as he was by certain political views, had the catholicity and generosity of mind to give encouragement by his presence that afternoon.' In a later speech, Krishnavarma remarked 'that while under the Mahommedan rule they were hit on the back, under the English rule they were hit in the stomach'.[7]

Mohandas Gandhi's own contributions to *Indian Opinion* included a series of sketches of famous men. In the first week of July 1905 the paper printed a tribute to the Russian writer Maxim Gorky, singling out his criticisms of tyranny and his spirit of public service. In the last week of July it saluted Mazzini, the unifier of Italy, who was yet 'so broad-minded that he could be regarded a citizen of every country'. In August it carried a homage to Abraham Lincoln which stressed his humble origins, his commitment to the poor, his selflessness and his patriotism. September saw the spotlight being turned on Tolstoy, who, born into a rich family, voluntarily embraced poverty, and bravely criticized the Tsar and his policies. The next week a woman was profiled for the first time. This was Florence Nightingale, whose life's story prompted the moral: 'No wonder that a country where such women are born is prosperous. That England rules over a wide empire is due not to the country's military strength, but to the meritorious deeds of such men and women.'[8]

This global-minded Gujarati also wrote of Indians he admired. On the first anniversary of the death of industrialist J. N. Tata, Gandhi observed that Tata 'never looked to self-interest . . . nor did he ever take distinctions of caste or race into consideration . . . [T]he Parsis, the Muslims, the Hindus – all were equal to him.' An assessment of the Bengali social reformer Ishwarchandra Vidyasagar emphasized his work for the education of girls and the emancipation of widows. Vidyasagar's career, wrote Gandhi, made clear 'how Bengal provides an example for the other parts of India to follow.'[9]

With these sketches Gandhi was providing role models for his compatriots. As noteworthy, perhaps, was his appreciation of the African reformer John Dube, who, Gandhi informed his readers, had acquired 300 acres of land quite close to Phoenix, where he 'imparts education to his brethren, teaching them various trades and crafts and preparing them for the battle of life'. When a progressive planter took Dube to meet a group of visiting British scientists, the African told them that the contempt with which his people were regarded was unjustified, since 'they worked hard and without them the whites could not carry on for a moment.'

The praise of Dube revealed a certain broadening of the mind, for Africans – or 'Kaffirs', as Gandhi called them, following contemporary usage – had previously been treated with condescension by the Indian leader. Further evidence of this evolution is provided by an essay attacking the Johannesburg Town Council for compelling African cyclists to wear a large badge on their left arm, so that whites could avoid them. 'May not a Native ask the question,' wrote Gandhi: 'has he no feelings?'[10]

Indian Opinion featured Gandhi the social reformer and community activist, but also Gandhi the seeker and spiritualist, printing a series of talks by him to the Theosophical Society. He had been invited to speak by L. W. Ritch, who was by now not just Gandhi's friend, but a clerk working in his law office. The lectures were on religion, a subject that had long fascinated Gandhi. Born a Hindu and mentored by a Jain, encounters with Christians, Jews, Muslims and Parsis had encouraged him to see his faith in broader, more comparative terms.

These public talks reported the progress of his religious education. Gandhi began with Hinduism, which, he argued, rested on three pillars: the importance of caste in social matters; the importance of pantheism in religious matters; and the importance of self-denial in ethical matters. Gandhi referred in passing to the rise and fall of Buddhism in India, and also mentioned Jainism, whose 'most remarkable characteristic was its scrupulous regard for all things that lived'.

Gandhi's second lecture was on Islam, whose keynote was 'its levelling spirit'. Its 'doctrine of equality could not but appeal to the masses, who were caste-ridden. To this inherent strength was also added the power of the sword.' It thus won many converts in India. However, 'in keeping with the spirit of Hinduism', attempts were made to 'bring about reconciliation between the two faiths'. Among these reconcilers in medieval India were the poet Kabir and the emperor Akbar.

The third lecture dealt with the advent of Christianity in India. European missionaries, admitted Gandhi, had 'pointed out some of the glaring defects in Hinduism', such as caste discrimination and the subordination of women. The last talk observed that 'there have been three assaults on Hinduism', in the form of Buddhism, Islam and Christianity, yet 'on the whole it came out of it unscathed. It has tried to imbibe whatever was good in each of these religions.'

The reaction of the white Theosophists in the audience is unrecorded. However, when the talks were printed, they provoked a torrent of criticism by Muslims, who said Gandhi had insulted Islam by suggesting its converts were of low caste origin. One critic claimed that the ancestors of the Bohras, a prominent community of Muslim traders in Gujarat, had been Brahmin priests. Another observed that 'the statement that the lower classes of Hindus had been converted to Islam is not supported by any Urdu or Gujarati books on Indian history' and are 'figments of Hindu imagination'. A third charged Gandhi with laying excessive stress on the 'bad deeds' of Islam. His writings had 'hurt the feelings of Muslims'; they were 'unbecoming of a worthy person'.

At Gandhi's initiative, the critics had their views aired in *Indian Opinion*. He pointed out in reply that 'no stigma attaches to Islam if the Hindus of the lower castes became Muslims. On the contrary, it shows its excellence, of which the Muslims should be proud.' He insisted that 'to me, personally, there is no distinction between a Brahmin and a *bhangi* [low-caste scavenger]. And I consider it a merit of Islam that those who were dissatisfied with the social distinctions in Hinduism were able to better their condition by embracing Islam.'

The debate carried on for weeks, in public and in private. As the editor of *Indian Opinion*, Gandhi would have the last word. He had come across a piece in a journal called the *Christian World*, which argued that 'religion, by a hundred different names and forms, has been dropping the one seed into the human heart, opening the one truth as the mind was able to receive it.' Gandhi commented that this 'growing spirit of toleration of all religions is a happy augury of the future'. To this spirit of ecumenism,

India, with its ancient religions, has much to give, and the bond of unity between us can best be fostered by a whole-hearted sympathy and appreciation of each other's form of religion. A greater toleration on this important question would mean a wider charity in our everyday relations, and the existing misunderstandings would be swept away. Is it not also a fact that between Mahomedan and Hindu there is a great need for this toleration? Sometimes one is inclined to think it even greater than between East and West. Let not strife and tumult destroy the harmony between

Indians themselves. A house divided against itself must fall, so let me urge the necessity for perfect unity and brotherliness between all sections of the Indian community.[11]

In India, too, the question of Hindu–Muslim unity was in the forefront of political debate. In October 1905, the Bengal Presidency was divided. The eastern part of Bengal was predominantly Muslim; by making it a separate province, the British hoped to wean Muslims away from the Hindu-dominated Indian National Congress. The partition provoked a great outcry – especially among the middle classes in Calcutta, angry that their province was cut in half. Protests to undo the partition took on an increasingly anti-British cast. A movement known as *Swadeshi*, meaning 'of and for one's land', urged the boycott of foreign goods.

Watching from South Africa, Gandhi gave the protests his support. The movement against the partition, he said, 'has in it the germs of the unification of the different communities'. As for the economic boycott: 'What can be more natural than for the people to wish to clothe themselves, to feed themselves, and to supply their luxuries out of home-grown products and home manufactures?' The events in Bengal were compared to the democratic upsurge under way in Russia. 'The movement in Bengal for the use of *swadeshi* goods is much like the Russian movement,' remarked Gandhi. 'Our shackles will break this very day, if the people of India become united and patient, love their country, and think of the well-being of their motherland, disregarding their self-interest.'[12]

In between work and writing, Gandhi snatched time away for the family. In July 1905 he wrote to a friend in Bombay suggesting that he send Harilal to South Africa. The funding of *Indian Opinion* had cut into his savings; besides, with Kasturba and the other children now in South Africa, it made little sense for one son to stay back in India. 'The burden on me here is so heavy that it is difficult for me to meet the expenses there,' wrote Gandhi. 'Nor do I see that Harilal's interests are served thereby.'[13] But Harilal did not want to leave India. Unbeknownst to his parents, the boy had fallen in love with the daughter of the Rajkot lawyer Haridas Vora.[14] With Harilal out of reach, Gandhi turned his attention to his second son, Manilal. In September the thirteen-year-old was sent for a spell to Phoenix, where he was supervised by his cousins.

Gandhi told Chhaganlal to put Manilal to work with his hands. 'The main thing is to clear the big plot of land and water the plants. He will get to know more by himself if he looks after the trees.'[15]

Two sons were temporarily away from the Gandhi household; meanwhile, two friends were welcomed in. Henry Polak had persuaded his family to permit him to marry Millie Graham. Gandhi played a hand here: when Polak's father claimed that the girl was not robust enough for marriage, Gandhi wrote that if Millie was indeed fragile, 'in South Africa, amidst loving care, a beautiful climate and a simple life, she could gain the physical strength she evidently needed.'[16]

To Millie herself, Gandhi offered some advice and instruction. In the time left to her in London, she should pay her 'respects to the Honourable Mr Dadabhai Naoroji, who is the G. O. M. [grand old man] of India. He represents the highest ideals of the Indian patriot.' Then she should go to the Lady Margaret Hospital in Bromley, where Gandhi's former flatmate and fellow vegetarian, Dr Josiah Oldfield, treated the patients to – or with – a 'strictly fruitarian diet'. She should study the conditions of patient care in the hospital, as 'in Phoenix, we are going to have a Sanatorium and any experience you may gain there in such matters will be most valuable.' He had heard of a Tolstoy Farm somewhere near London; perhaps she should visit it and study the principles on which it was based. 'I have,' said Gandhi, 'given you enough hints already as to what might be usefully studied there before you come out to South Africa.'[17]

Millie Graham arrived in Johannesburg in the last week of December 1905. The next day, Henry and Millie went with Gandhi to be married by the Registrar of European Marriages. The Hindu hoped to bear witness to this union of Jew and Christian; the Registrar thought this was not permitted by law. He asked them to come back the next working day. But the next day was Sunday, and the day after that, New Year's Day. And Millie and Henry had waited long enough already. So Gandhi went across to the office of the Chief Magistrate, to whom the Registrar reported. He convinced him that nothing in the law debarred a brown man from witnessing a European marriage. The Magistrate, remembered Gandhi, merely 'laughed and gave me a note to the Registrar and the marriage was duly registered'.[18]

The deed done, the couple moved into the lawyer's home on Albemarle Street. Millie began teaching the boys English grammar and composition, and helped Kasturba in the kitchen. The two women became friends, with the newcomer's buoyant nature overcoming the matriarch's natural reserve and her lack of familiarity with the English language.

For the Gandhis and the Polaks, the day began early. At six-thirty, the men and boys assembled to grind wheat. Before breakfast, Gandhi would do some skipping, a form of exercise at which he was apparently quite adept. After the men went off to work, the children were set to their lessons, supervised by the women. In the evening the family sat down for dinner, an extended meal where the day's happenings were discussed. Afterwards, if there were no guests, passages from religious texts (the Bhagavad-Gita being an especial favourite) were read out loud.

Living with the Gandhis, Millie concluded that with regard to marital relations at least there was a fundamental difference between East and West. Indian husbands were allowed periods of rest and contemplation, but their wives had to work, work, work. 'The East has made [woman] the subject of man,' Millie told Gandhi. 'She seems to possess no individual life.' He answered that she was mistaken: 'The East has given her a position of worship.' As proof, he mentioned the legend of Satyavan and Savitri. When Satyavan died, Savitri wrestled with the God of Death for the return of her beloved. 'She had a hard battle to fight', said Gandhi, but after showing 'the highest courage, fortitude, love and wisdom', eventually won her husband back to her side.

Millie answered that this story actually proved her point. In Indian mythology, it appeared 'woman is made to serve man, even to wrestling with the God of Death for him'. In myth and in reality (seeing how Gandhi treated Kasturba), Millie found Indian women 'always waiting on the pleasure of some man'.[19]

There were also arguments between Polak and Gandhi. The Englishman thought the Indian too even-tempered – when he was slandered in the press, he should write back polemically rather than ignore the matter. Polak, an ardent socialist, found Gandhi to be wholly without interest in economic theories; and far too absorbed in questions of religion. Polak also thought that rather than spend so much time teaching his children Gujarati, Gandhi should make them proficient in English, the language of the world.[20]

Once, after a particularly intense debate between Polak and Gandhi, Kasturba drew Millie aside and asked what the fuss was about. The

Englishwoman tried to explain, as best she could, the intricacies of the political problem that so exercised the men. Millie remembered that as she outlined the argument to Kasturba, 'a suspicion flitted through my mind that she was not altogether cross that Mr Polak was cross with Bapu [as Gandhi was known to his family]. She was vexed with him sometimes, and the anger of another person who, she knew, cared very much for him seemed to justify her own.'[21]

Polak was now working part-time on *Indian Opinion*. His involvement increased when, in January 1906, the editor, M. H. Nazar, died in his sleep at Phoenix, a copy of the Gita by his side.[22] The next month the Hindi and Tamil sections of the journal were dropped. While Chhaganlal saw to the production of the Gujarati pages, Polak took charge of the English columns, editing and reading proofs, and regularly contributing articles himself. He was an enthusiast for the Swadeshi movement, seeing echoes of the search for dignity in Ireland, Poland and other oppressed nations. Polak had not yet visited Gandhi's homeland; even so, reading the reports in the Indian press, he saw – or thought he saw – how

> a new Indian literature is springing up, hot with the fervour of a new national aspiration; new leaders are coming to the fore, earnest with the mystic idea of a united India before their eyes. 'India for the Indians' is the watch-word, and the Motherland is now hailed by those whose minds but yesterday refused to contemplate the union of warring sects, exclusive castes, and striving peoples. To-day, however, an immense fillip is being given to every national hope. National industries are springing up on all sides, and the demand is all for indigenous products and home-manufactured goods.[23]

The fervour was also Henry Polak's. In so wholeheartedly embracing the Indian cause, Polak was acting as a 'non-Jewish Jew', who fought not for the equality of Jew and Gentile, but for an end to all varieties of 'dogmatic narrow-mindedness and fanaticism'. Like Heinrich Heine and Karl Marx, Rosa Luxemburg and Sigmund Freud, Henry Polak believed not in the emancipation of his own race or tribe or sect but in 'the ultimate solidarity of mankind'.[24]

One route for Jews in the South Africa of the late nineteenth and early twentieth centuries had been laid out by the entrepreneur Sammy Marks. Fabulously wealthy owing to his investments in diamond and coal, Marks worked energetically to become part of the ruling elite. He patronized scientific societies and Christian causes, and sought membership in gentlemen's clubs, all 'part of a personal drive towards assimilation into the dominant Anglo-Saxon culture'. In wishing to become – so to speak – an honorary Englishman in South Africa, he simultaneously distanced himself from immigrants from Asia. When a new law considered placing Jews on a par with Indians, Marks successfully petititioned his friends in Government to avoid administering to 'my people' the 'same treatment as is meted out to Coolies'.[25]

The assimilationist path of Sammy Marks was followed, with varying degrees of success, by most Jews in South Africa. But there were significant exceptions, among them Henry Polak. Polak's identification with the Indians was part philosophical, part personal – the latter owing to his admiration for Mohandas Gandhi. Still, his deference was slight compared to that of Gandhi's other Jewish friend, the architect Hermann Kallenbach. Living alone, and removed – in all senses – from his family in Europe, Kallenbach looked to Gandhi for succour and support. A letter written by Gandhi in about 1904 or 1905 bears testimony to the closeness of their relationship. Kallenbach had been beset by nightmares, and asked his Indian friend to help him cope with them.

> You must not [on] any account despond [counselled Gandhi]. By degrees you would get out of the horrible dreams. Just now your mind being in a state of ferment these dreams come to warn you of the secret enemy who may attack you without notice and when you are least prepared to meet him . . . [Y]ou may turn these dreams to good account by keeping an ever present watch on yourself.

This gloss on Kallenbach's nightmares was Gandhi's own; it owed nothing to Freud's *The Interpretation of Dreams*, which was then available only in German. From matters of the mind the letter then turned to matters of the body. 'My diet yesterday,' wrote Gandhi to his fellow food faddist, 'was 4 bananas, 3 oranges, 1 lemon, ½ lb tomatoes, dates, 2 ½ oz. p[ea]nuts, 12 almonds and a paw paw. Two motions in the day. Retired last night after 11, woke up at 4 & left the bed at 5. Eyes have begun to cause a little trouble.'[26]

The Gandhis of Porbandar had stayed away from meat and fish for generations. But this particular Gandhi was now moving towards an extreme elaboration of a vegetarian diet. One of his favourite authors, the anti-vivisectionist doctor Anna Kingsford, claimed that a fruit-based diet was man's genetic inheritance. It also helped cultivate kindness towards others. Her Indian disciple seems to have been taking her theories very seriously indeed.

In 1905, for a coloured couple and a white couple to live together would have been unusual in an English city like London, or in an Indian city like Bombay. In the context of South Africa it was revolutionary. The prejudice against the mixing of the races was perhaps greater there than anywhere else in the world. For Gandhi to befriend Polak, Kallenbach, West and company was an act of bravery; for them to befriend Gandhi was an act of defiance.

How very singular this mixed-race household was is revealed by the diary of Chhaganlal Gandhi. In January 1906, Chhagan travelled to Johannesburg to brief his uncle about Phoenix and *Indian Opinion*. This is how he saw the next few days:

> January 4, 1906: Arrived at Johannesburg station. Rama [Ramdas], Deva [Devadas], Bhai [Gandhi] and Mrs. Polak were there to receive me. Reached home at 7 o'clock with them. After a wash went to the table for dinner. Found the westernized style very odd. I began to wonder, but could not decide whether our ways were better or theirs ... Before the meal Bhai recited a few verses from the Gita and explained their meaning in Gujarati ...
>
> January 5, 1906: Getting up at 5 a.m. was ready by 6.30 ... Everyone went out to work without any breakfast. I walked with Bhai to his office, about two miles [*sic*] away. Talked about the *Indian Opinion* on the way. Bhai started work in his office exactly at 9.30 a.m. Seeing a girl working in the office made me wonder. In the afternoon Bhai and others had a meagre meal of bananas and groundnuts. The accounts of the press were then carefully gone through. Returned home with Bhai at 5.30 p.m. I began to wonder again when I found the English friends, the Polaks, mixing freely with everyone.
>
> January 6, 1906: A few people were invited to dinner at Bhai's house in connection with Mr Polak's marriage. Among the guests were English people, Muslims and Hindus. I felt that they had crossed the limits in their jokes at dinner.
>
> January 11, 1906: Smith, Polak and Mrs. Polak, who are staying at Bhai's house, behave very freely, which makes me think.[27]

Chhagan was puzzled and confused by what he saw – the white lady secretary in his uncle's office, the jokes and the banter and the displays of physical affection (between Henry and Millie) in his uncle's home, the eating at the same table of Hindus, Muslims and Europeans. To his conventional Bania eyes, the household was eccentric. To the conventional white Christian in Johannesburg, the household was positively heretical.

In his first years in Johannesburg, Gandhi deepened his interest in other religions, while befriending several European men (and at least one European woman). Meanwhile, his horizons were being further extended by encounters with mixed-race Africans. Gandhi occasionally visited Cape Town, where there was a small but active Indian community, and where the British administrators he dealt with maintained residences. On these visits he came to know a coloured politician named Dr Abdullah Abdurahman. A Cape Malay, like Gandhi Abdurahman had been professionally trained in the United Kingdom (he studied medicine in Glasgow). Back home in Cape Town, he (like Gandhi again) combined professional work with public service.

Dr Abdurahman was the moving spirit behind the African Political Organization (APO), which pressed for housing rights and the franchise for coloured people. In 1905 and 1906, Gandhi attended some APO meetings and occasionally wrote for its journal. For Abdurahman himself he had considerable respect. But ultimately he felt that their causes must stay separate and distinct. In a fascinating piece in *Indian Opinion* he spelt out his reasons for this:

> This Association of Coloured People does not include Indians who have always kept aloof from that body. We believe that the Indian community has been wise in doing so. For, though the hardships suffered by those people and the Indians is almost of the same kind, the remedies are not identical. It is therefore proper that the two should fight out their cases, each in their own appropriate way. We can cite the Proclamation of 1857 in our favour, which the Coloured people cannot. They can use the powerful argument that they are the children of the soil. They can also argue that their way of life is entirely European. We can petition the Secretary of State for India, whereas they cannot. They belong largely to the Christian community and can therefore avail themselves of the help of their priests. Such help is not available to us.[28]

The statement represented a distinct evolution of Gandhi's views – he now quite clearly recognized that all races other than Europeans suffered from structural discrimination in South Africa. The Indians were not alone. Yet each community had to work out its own path in overcoming the disadvantages peculiar to it.

An Englishman who moved to Johannesburg soon after Gandhi found it 'the most perplexing, and perhaps the most fascinating' place in the world. This city on the make and on the move became more diverse every month (if not every minute). Migrants arrived from at least four continents, seeking a slice of the wealth the gold underneath had spawned. It was 'this cosmopolitan character of the population which forms at once the attractiveness and perplexity of the place. There is no cohesion, there is no monotony.'[29]

This lack of cohesion was a matter of much concern to the ruling race. The Boers had moved to the hinterland of South Africa to escape British domination. There, they had established a simple social order, with two, unequal, divisions: Boer and black. The Uitlanders and the Indians then came to complicate it. A compromise (following a bitter war) was forged with the Uitlanders. The Indians, however, were not European; but nor were they African. They were a perplexing element that complicated the black-and-white social order the whites had hoped to construct in South Africa.

In England and the Netherlands, the countries where the majority of the colonists came from, whites were demographically dominant. In India and Indonesia, countries over which they had political control, the Dutch and the English did not wish to make a permanent home. In this respect South Africa was peculiar and even unique. The Europeans wanted to claim it as their own, an objective to which – at the time – the Indians, and the Indians alone, posed a serious challenge. Hence the enormous hostility towards them. An Englishman visiting the Transvaal in 1905 noticed that, whether as labourers, servants, hawkers or traders, the Indians 'did their work well'. They were 'deft [and] quiet'. The trouble was that 'an Asiatic who competes with a white man is resented; that the man who sells or rents land to him for gain is looked upon as a traitor; and that his competition with white men is regarded as unequal'.[30]

In 1905–6 the Transvaal was in a period of transition. After the end of the Anglo-Boer war it had been constituted as a Crown Colony; now, however, it prepared to be granted 'responsible government'. A new spirit of 'white South Africanism' was abroad, seeking a rapprochement, cultural as well as political, between Dutch and English colonists. These two groups, so recently at war, now forged a common front against blacks and coloureds.[31]

The new constitution of the Transvaal allowed the franchise only to those of European descent. However, for the ruling race that was not enough: they wished to put in place laws and procedures that would steadily reduce the number of Indians. Here, the colonists in the Transvaal found a strong ally in the new Governor, Lord Selborne. Selborne vigorously promoted the agenda of his predecessor, Lord Milner. In secret letters to the Secretary of State for the Colonies, he advanced a novel argument for keeping out coloured immigrants: that the Indians were not wanted because they did not know how to use arms. Whereas 'the white man must always be a fighter', Indians 'are not of any martial race'. What if the Dutch and the British fell out again in the future? It was then likely that the Transvaal would fall 'again under Boer domination, owing largely to the absence of Englishmen, Scotchmen, and Irishmen, ousted by their pressure into other lands'.[32]

Selborne held out the example of Mauritius, a once uninhabited island, discovered by Europeans, that now supported a large population of which 70 per cent was Indian and less than 3 per cent white. If Asians were not kept out of the Transvaal, he warned, then they would likewise come to form a majority of the province. 'Under these conditions,' wrote the Governor, 'South Africa will, for all time, require to be occupied by troops imported from Europe, not only for its protection against foreign invasion but even for the enforcement of order among its native population.'[33]

Gandhi, unaware of these letters, hoped to persuade the new Governor of the Indian case. On 29 November 1905, a delegation led by the lawyer, whose other members were four Gujarati Muslims and a Tamil, met Selborne in his office. They urged him to allow *bona fide* refugees to return to the Transvaal, and also allow merchants to import qualified assistants to work with them. The delegation asked for Indians to have 'perfect freedom of owning landed property and of living where we like under the general municipal regulations as to sanitation and appearance of buildings'. They added a reassuring caveat: 'What we want is not political power; but we do wish to live side by side with other British subjects in peace and amity and with dignity and self-respect.'

Three months later, another delegation led by Gandhi met the Assistant Colonial Secretary in Pretoria. They presented a list of sixteen complaints, among them the delays in getting permits, the insistence that applicants produce witnesses, the refusal to exempt women (even though 'they at any rate do not compete with whites'), the difficulties that children faced in re-entering the Transvaal and the continuing discrimination on trains and trams.[34]

The complaints were disregarded. Some Indians, with Gandhi's encouragement, now sought to overturn the convention whereby Europeans and coloured people did not – or could not – travel together in public. Electric trams had just been introduced in Johannesburg. In March 1906, a Gujarati merchant named E. S. Coovadia took a tram in the company of an English lawyer who worked with Gandhi. Then Henry Polak accompanied the President of the British Indian Association, Abdul Gani, on a similarly transgressive journey. In both cases, the Indians were asked to get off, but appealed against their ejection in court, with Gandhi appearing for them.

The Anglo-Boer regime in Johannesburg was new, and trams were newer still. There was no clear law regulating their use. But custom, or prejudice rather, mandated that they be reserved for whites only. The all-white Town Council debated the matter. One member argued that by allowing coloured people to buy tickets the operations would be made profitable. Other members disagreed, saying that if Indians came aboard, whites would boycott the trams, forcing the company to close. Eventually, regulations were drafted reserving trams for Europeans and their pets alone.[35]

In his dealings with government, the official with whom Gandhi was most frequently in contact was Montford Chamney, who bore the title of Protector of Asiatics. Chamney had previously worked in the tea plantations of eastern India, and had a smattering of Hindustani. He was peppered with requests from Gandhi to grant permits for those hoping to join their families or business partners in the Transvaal. He was impressed with the lawyer's analytical skills, as in 'the facility of fruitful scanning of legal documents and statutes for any blemishes contained'. The appreciation did not extend to the Indian's lifestyle:

'Mr Ghandi's [*sic*] strong predilection for seclusion and the simple life,' complained Chamney, 'made his town residence insipid or even nauseous.' That is to say, dinners in the Gandhi home were – unlike parties on tea plantations in upper Assam – bereft of meat, drink or music, in keeping with the fact that the patriarch 'took no pleasure in sports, games, or general pastimes'.[36]

The relationship between Chamney and Gandhi mixed respect with irritation. When the Protector of Asiatics rejected what seemed a straightforward case, Gandhi wrote saying the decision had come 'as a disagreeable surprise'. He assumed that 'the refusal is more a symptom of the official mind than of your own conviction.' Another time, Gandhi wrote an extended complaint against one of Chamney's subordinates, a 'young man, rather impetuous', prone to 'roughly handle' permit-seekers by kicking them on their shins as they stood to have their height taken.

For his part, Chamney was exasperated with the lawyer's persistence, complaining to a colleague that 'one of the Agents most affected [by the refusal of Permits] is Mr Gandhi himself, who has, I am informed, been accustomed to pledge himself to clients that after they have paid him his fees he will guarantee the issue of permits in their favour.' This was very nearly libellous, but another charge laid by him at Gandhi's door was largely true. Commenting on the spate of letters received by the Government from 'Abdul Gani, Chairman of the British Indian Association', Chamney pointed out that Mr Gani was 'an illiterate man and little more than a figure-head, and that the Secretary of the Association, namely, Mr Gandhi, is the individual with whom we are invariably dealing, no matter who signs these letters.'[37]

In April 1906, a Zulu revolt broke out in Natal. The Government had imposed a poll tax of £1 per head on every male African, aimed at raising revenues and at forcing Zulus into paid employment. The tax caused widespread resentment. Several chiefs sent word to the Natal Government that villagers could not afford to pay the tax. The complaints were disregarded. When the police came to collect the tax by force, the Zulus exchanged non-compliance for armed resistance. The uprising (known as the 'Bambatha Rebellion' after its main leader) quickly gathered momentum, and spread throughout Natal.[38]

The question before the Indians of Natal now was – what position, if any, should they take on the revolt? Gandhi, mindful of making a good impression on the rulers while the Indian community's fate in the Transvaal hung in the balance, told the readers of *Indian Opinion* that 'it is not for me to say whether the revolt of the Kaffirs is justified or not. We are in Natal by virtue of British power. Our very existence depends upon it. It is therefore our duty to render whatever help we can . . . That is, if the Government so desires, we should raise an ambulance corps.' The 'nursing of the wounded,' said Gandhi, was 'just as honourable and necessary as the shouldering of a rifle'.[39]

In the first week of June, twenty Indians were recruited as volunteers. Gandhi's was the first name; the others included several Tamils and a few people from North India. The Gujarati merchants provided goods in kind, such as flour and plates, as well as money, which went to buy overcoats, caps and socks. Thirteen of the twenty volunteers had previously been under indenture. Their tasks were to disinfect camps, dress wounds and carry men on stretchers. The work was hard, with marches sometimes commencing at 3 a.m. The men were often very close to the firing line.[40]

After six weeks at the front, the ambulance corps was disbanded. When they reached Durban, the Natal Indian Congress gave them a reception, at which Gandhi suggested the Government set up an Indian Corps, and 'if for any reason, the traders could not enlist, other educated Indians as well as the servants and clerks of traders could easily do so.' On the battlefield, 'the whites [had] treated the Indians very cordially'; if this fellow-feeling was consolidated in the form of a permanent corps, 'it was likely that in the process white prejudice against Indians might altogether disappear.'[41]

It had cost the state nearly £1 million to suppress the rebellion. Thirty-one combatants on the Government side lost their lives, as against nearly 4,000 Africans, in a war 'carried out with machine guns against spears and shields'. While loyal to the British flag, the Indian ambulance corps tended to the wounded regardless of colour. As an early historian of the rebellion pointed out, 'the whites had no desire to minister to wounded Zulus; without the Indian stretcher-bearers these would possibly have been left to die. There were also hundreds of Africans who had been sentenced to flogging. The Indians ministered to their festering sores.'[42]

*

There, were, *circa* 1906, six separate strands in the life of Mohandas K. Gandhi. First, there was his legal career, his paid work on behalf of his clients in Johannesburg and Durban. Second, there was his work as a political campaigner, his efforts to safeguard the rights of Indians in the Transvaal and Natal. This work was unpaid, but perhaps not without other rewards, as in the esteem it acquired for him within and beyond his community. Third, there was Gandhi the propagandist, who ran a weekly newspaper and wrote much of it, and who, going by the tenor of his writing, seems to have taken great pleasure in the craft of composing an article or a series. His fourth preoccupation, linked to the second and expressed through the third, was to help heal divisions within the Indian community, whether between South Indians and Gujaratis or Hindus and Muslims. Fifth, there were his obligations to his family, which involved not merely earning enough money to keep the household going, but also being a companion to his wife – lonely in a foreign land where she did not speak the language – and a mentor to his sons, whose upbringing had been disturbed by the many moves made as a result of their father's peripatetic career. Finally, there was Gandhi's own process of self-discovery, as manifest in his interest in inter-religious dialogue and in what constituted an appropriate diet. Those two interests, in spirituality and health, were of long standing; to these was now added a third, a concern – soon to become an obsession – with the maintenance of celibacy.

It was in the late (South African) summer of 1906 that Gandhi took the vow of *brahmacharya*. He would now eschew all sexual relations with his wife. By his recollection, the idea had been brewing in his head for some time. Perhaps its roots lay in a conversation he once had with the Jain sage Raychandbhai. When Gandhi praised the conjugal love between Gladstone and his wife – as illustrated by her making tea for him even in the House of Commons – his teacher asked,

> Which of the two do you prize more? The love of Mrs Gladstone for her husband as his wife, or her devoted service irrespective of her relations to Mr Gladstone? Supposing she had been his sister, or his devoted servant, and ministered to him the same attention . . . would you have been pleased in the same way? Just examine the viewpoint suggested by me.

By reflecting on Raychandbhai's question, Gandhi came to the conclusion that he had to make his relations with his wife purely disinterested.

She had, in particular, to stop being the 'instrument' of his lust. The attachment to her had to be other than sexual. So Kasturba and he began to sleep in separate beds. The decision was helped by the fact that both agreed that they did not want any more children.

In the Jain tradition, celibacy occupied an exalted place. Sexual activity involved passion, and was hence injurious to the soul. Jains also thought that sexual intercourse destroyed a number of animate objects dwelling in the female body. Celibacy was thus part of the pursuit of pure *ahimsa*, or non-violence. A gradualist approach was recommended – the practitioner was first told to not have sex during the day, preparing himself in stages for the achievement of complete abstinence. The aspiring *brahmachari* had to stop wearing expensively tailored clothes, and stay away from soap, scents, jewellery and other means of enhancing his attractiveness.[43]

Raychandbhai had, in his early thirties, taken a vow of *brahmacharya* himself. In a discourse entitled 'Views about Woman' he explained its reason and logic. He rejected the common male view that 'a woman has been imagined and taken as a source of worldly happiness.' The pleasure from sexual intercourse was 'only momentary and a cause of exhaustion and repeated excitements'. The organ used 'for the enjoyment of conjugal bliss', commented the Jain sage, 'when looked at through the piercing eyes of discrimination, does not stand fit even for a worthy receptacle for vomiting'.[44]

From 1891, when Raychandbhai and Gandhi first met, until 1901, when he died, the Jain scholar had been a moral compass for the lawyer. His memory became more sacred after his death, as is sometimes the case with a teacher who dies young. (When the person you most revere is no longer around, you tend to strive even harder to live up to what you think he may have expected or hoped from you.) So it was with Gandhi and Raychandbhai. His detachment from worldly ambition, his non-attachment to possession or physical pleasure, impressed Gandhi more and more with every passing year. In a verse Raychand composed when he was eighteen, and which Gandhi liked to quote, we may see the origins of the latter's decision to embrace celibacy in 1906:

> When shall I know that state supreme,
> When will the knots, outer and inner, snap?
> When shall I, breaking the bonds that bind us fast,

Tread the path trodden by the wise and the great?
Withdrawing the mind from all interests,
Using this body solely for self-control,
He desires nothing to serve any ulterior end of his own,
Seeing nothing in the body to bring on a trace of the
    darkness of ignorance.[45]

His teacher's example lay before Gandhi. And there were others. In the Hindu as well as the Jain tradition, renouncers were respected, admired, even venerated. The forgoing of the pleasures of the flesh – both sexual and culinary – was seen as a step towards a purer, more morally meaningful life.[46]

The decision to stop having sex led to a wider reconsideration of his respective callings. When the Bambatha Rebellion broke out, Gandhi had to rush to Natal to raise the ambulance corps. He decided that in his absence Kasturba and the children would be better off at Phoenix, where they would have friends and relations around them, than in the anonymity of an ever larger city. This meant the dismantling of a spacious, well-furnished, smoothly functioning home in Johannesburg. The patriarch who was the architect of the break-up saw it as necessary and inevitable. As he later recalled, 'it became my conviction that procreation and the consequent care of children were inconsistent with public service . . . [I]f I wanted to devote myself to the service of the community in this manner I must relinquish the desire for children and wealth and live the life of a *vanaprastha* – of one retired from household service.'[47]

In its classical, so to say Brahmanical version, a man's raising of a family was followed by a stage where he retreated from social life altogether, by moving to a forest, or *vana*, where he contemplated the meanings and mysteries of life. In Gandhi's case, however, he detached himself from the family in order to more actively engage in society. One wonders if he was at all influenced by the mythical warrior Bhishma, who renounced his kingdom and refused to marry to mark his disregard for power and pleasure. Bhishma's celibacy was widely regarded as a mark of his moral uprightness and commitment to *dharma*. Unlike the Brahmanical monks, the warrior-ascetic did not withdraw from society; rather, he worked (and fought) within it, while serving as a touchstone and model for his fellows. That seems to have been Gandhi's aim, too.

In taking the vow of *brahmacharya* in 1906, Gandhi may also have been influenced by Tolstoy's prescriptive essay, 'The First Step', which had recently become available in English translation. Here, the Russian sage whom the Indian lawyer so greatly admired wrote, 'No good life is thinkable without abstinence. Every attainment of a good life must begin through it' – and then continued:

> Abstinence is a man's liberations from the lusts ... But there are many various lusts in man, and for the struggle with them to be successful he must begin with the basal ones, those on which other, more complex ones have grown up ... There are complex passions, as the passion for adorning the body, games, amusements, gossiping, curiosity, and many others; and there are basal passions, such as gluttony, idleness, carnal love. In the struggle with the passions it is impossible to begin at the end, with the struggle with the complex passions; we must begin with the basal ones, and that, too, in a definite order. This order is determined both by the essence of the thing and by the tradition of human wisdom.[48]

By tradition and upbringing Gandhi was not a 'glutton' – by which Tolstoy meant a man who feasts largely or exclusively on animal flesh – nor consumed by idleness. As a lifelong vegetarian, and a disciplined, hardworking professional, the one basal passion he had to confront and overcome was that of 'carnal love'. And so he decided to take the vow of *brahmacharya*.

9

Trouble in the Transvaal

Once Gandhi had settled Kasturba and the children at Phoenix, he returned to Johannesburg, moving into a smaller house, which he shared with Millie and Henry Polak. This house, in Bellevue East, was half the size of the villa in Troyeville: four rooms rather than eight, each large (or small) enough to accommodate only a double bed.[1]

With Gandhi scaling back on his law practice, they had to cut back on their expenses, and this modest abode was a beginning. In their new house, noted Millie Polak grimly,

> there was no proper plumbing, and a make-shift bath-room had been fixed by previous tenants under the stairs; the waste water from the bath ran down the wall outside into a kind of gutter, which ran along a dark passage, and thus the walls were always damp. These conditions helped to produce big slimy slugs that got into the house.[2]

Millie wished to make the place more pleasant, but her austere Indian housemate got in the way. Gandhi was content with a bare floor and bare walls, whereas Millie wished to adorn them with nice rugs and pretty pictures. When Millie said a painting would hide the wall's ugliness, Gandhi asked her to look out of the window and admire the sunset, more beautiful than anything conceived by the hand of man. She persisted, bringing Henry on to her side. Gandhi eventually conceded that a charming interior was not in competition with the glories of nature without.

The next argument was about food. Gandhi asked that the household's diet exclude sugar, since it was made through the exploitation of indentured labourers. He wanted raw onions and milk banned on the grounds that they excited the passions. Millie was fine with giving up sugar and onions, but not milk. If that liquid stimulated the passions, she asked, why was it considered the best food for babies? Gandhi answered that mother's milk was good for children, but no kind of milk was suitable for adults. Millie commented acidly that one would think they were gourmands; no house in Johannesburg was so concerned with what to eat and especially with what not to eat. 'A man shall be judged by what comes out of his mouth,' she told Gandhi, 'not what by what he puts in it'.

In making a home, Millie Polak had come up against the two stereotypical characteristics of his caste that her Indian housemate, after all these years, still retained. Born a Bania, Gandhi had in most ways radically departed from the conventions and habits of his caste. Banias were notoriously conservative in religious matters; and had a particular dislike of Muslims. Gandhi mixed freely with Muslims and Christians, and even shared homes with them. The dharma of the Bania was making and saving money, but Gandhi exchanged a lucrative profession for social service and had no desire to leave money or property for his children. Banias were averse to political movements – they had stayed away from the Indian National Congress (where Brahmins and Kshatriyas were over-represented). Gandhi, on the other hand, actively sought political engagement. Heterodox in most matters, there were yet two areas in which Gandhi was still, so to speak, of his caste – in his comparative lack of interest in aesthetics and in his thoroughgoing obsession with food taboos.[3]

For all their disagreements, Millie retained a healthy respect for her Indian friend. She was particularly struck by how hard he worked. He attended to his clients all day, including Sunday. The Polaks became accustomed to Indians coming in at all hours, seeking the counsel of their lawyer and leader. As Millie remembered, 'it was not an unusual thing to have four or more men return at midnight with Mr Gandhi, and when all were too worn out to continue to talk, rugs would be thrown down the passage or anywhere else for the visitors to get a few hours' sleep ere they started to tramp back to town.'[4]

In discussing Gandhi's vow of celibacy in the West, one often finds a sense of outrage at his not having consulted his wife. How could he end sexual relations so abruptly? What if she still wanted to continue them? This reaction is very modern (and very Western). It is unlikely that Kasturba was greatly disturbed by Gandhi's vow of celibacy. What worried her far more was its extension, by which Gandhi sought not just to distance himself from her physically, but also from his children, emotionally.

Kasturba was unhappy at the fraught relations between her husband and their eldest son, Harilal. Gandhi had left home (for London) shortly after Harilal was born. In 1892–3, when he was in Bombay, the children were in Rajkot. Not long after they joined him, Gandhi decided to go to South Africa. The family were reunited in 1896, and travelled together to Durban; but they were separated again in 1902.

Harilal was a poor student, and failed to settle down in any of the several schools he studied in. This concerned Gandhi – perhaps because he had once been an indifferent student himself. He had asked Kasturba to bring all their sons to South Africa. However, Harilal stayed behind, ostensibly to appear for his Matriculation. It appears that by now relations between father and first-born were frosty. That, at any rate, is the impression conveyed by a letter written by Gandhi on 28 December 1905, where he told Harilal that he was 'dissatisfied' with him for not writing regularly. Whenever he received news from others, he continued, 'they contain criticism regarding your conduct.' 'Your general conduct towards your parents betrays no love for them,' complained Gandhi.[5]

The relationship between father and son deteriorated further when Gandhi learned of Harilal's love for Chanchal,[6] the daughter of his friend Haridas Vora. Gandhi thought the couple too young to get married, but his brother Laxmidas, who was in Rajkot, sanctioned the wedding, and the marriage took place on 2 May 1906. When the news reached Gandhi, he wrote to his brother saying that 'it is well if Harilal is married; it is also well if he is not. For the present at any rate I have ceased to think of him as a son.'[7]

The harshness of the tone is only partially extenuated by the fact that Harilal was guilty of, as it were, serial disobedience: of not studying properly, of not joining the family in Johannesburg, of not writing letters regularly, and worst of all, of not listening to his father's advice not to get married. Kasturba was deeply worried about the estrangement between father and son. As an (Indian) mother she was perhaps more forgiving of Harilal's transgressions. She also saw that Gandhi's behaviour was not above reproach: that he had alternated between being grossly neglectful and somewhat overbearing. Seeking a rapprochement, she persuaded Harilal to come to South Africa. When he agreed,

Gandhi wrote Montford Chamney, the Protector of Asiatics, a long letter, which reveals the three-way tension between husband, wife and first-born. The letter is dated 13 August 1906:

Dear Mr Chamney,

I have to approach you again on another personal matter. My eldest son, Harilal, has left India. He sent a wire to Phoenix from Mombasa of which my nephew has given me information . . . My boy is to-day over age, that is, he is nearly eighteen. His permit, however, was granted by Captain Fowle when Mrs Gandhi arrived here [in 1904]. On receipt of a cable from Mrs Gandhi I asked for a permit but Mrs Gandhi arrived without my eldest boy and my nephew. My nephew [Chhaganlal] has since come, but my son, Harilal, was not able to do so as he wished to go up for his matriculation examination, and then, unfortunately, he had to be married. He is now on his way. I kept the telegram by me for three days as I was not certain whether I should have my son with me or whether I should send him to Phoenix. I have now come to the conclusion that if you would be good enough to let him come on the strength of the permit having been previously granted or otherwise I should like to keep him under my observation. I have been separated from him now for nearly three years. If you think that you would let him come to me I should thank you to let me have his permit now. His full name is: Harilal Mohandas Gandhi. The permit that was granted by Captain Fowle to Mrs Gandhi was returned to him after her arrival. There was only one document issued for the whole family. I am not certain whether, in the event of your complying with my request, I should have Harilal through from Delagoa Bay or Durban. I should therefore like to have his permit myself so that I can make use of it wherever he has landed. His landing will depend on Mrs Gandhi's intentions and my movements. The steamer is due at Durban on the 26th inst. It is likely that I shall have to be there at that time. In that event, I should meet my boy there and bring him with me. Otherwise, in order that I may see him earlier I should like him to land at Delagoa Bay and come straight to me.

I am
Yours truly
M. K. Gandhi.[8]

Gandhi's writings, whether public or private, were usually lucid and precise – traits that reflected a decade of practice in publishing essays for different journals. This particular letter, however, betrays an uncharacteristic disorder and sentimentalism. It was hardly appropriate that he would reveal to the Protector of Asiatics his disapproval of Harilal's marriage – or that he would speak so frequently and so possessively of 'my boy'. This perhaps reveals his own uncertainty about both matters – he needed to reassure himself that he was right to oppose the marriage, and that he really cared about his son.

The confusion about where Harilal would or should land is also revealing. At this point Kasturba was living, with her other sons, at Phoenix. Ships from India came first to the Portuguese-held port of Delagoa Bay before Durban. From Delagoa Bay, Johannesburg was a few hours away by train. It seems that Gandhi and Kasturba were unsure as to which parent the boy should meet first. If he got off the ship at Delagoa Bay, he could go to his father, with whom he wished to be reconciled. On the other hand, if he carried on to Durban he would first meet his mother, who was both his preferred parent and could advise him on how best to mend fences with his father. There was yet a third possibility, hinted at in the letter, which was that Gandhi himself would go to Durban, in which case Harilal would meet both parents at the same time. Where he would finally land would depend largely on what Gandhi delicately referred to as his wife's 'intentions'.

The day after he wrote to Chamney, Gandhi phoned to urge him to grant the request. (Telephones were then relatively new, and rare, in South Africa; that the father resorted to its use shows how keen he was to have his son join him.) The appeal was successful, for the official replied promptly and with an untypical softness of tone. Within twenty-four hours he had posted Gandhi a letter of authorization, which noted that, as a special exception, 'it will not be necessary for him [Harilal] to report himself at this office. I will have his form of application filled in at Johannesburg after his arrival.' Chamney added that 'of course you will understand that the granting of this permit is not in any sense a precedent.'

There was a further request to be made. According to the rules, Harilal had to enter the Transvaal within two weeks of obtaining the permit. On 17 August, Gandhi wrote to Chamney asking that this period be extended to a month, 'as Mr Harilal is at present in Durban and might be there for some time'. It seems that Kasturba had decided that she would keep her boy for a while at Phoenix before sending him on to confront his father.[9] The reunion, when it did finally take place, was without acrimony. After they met, Gandhi wrote to Chhaganlal that 'I am really delighted with Harilal's taking a deck passage and managing everything himself.'[10] One trusts the praise was passed on to the boy himself.

Now in his mid-thirties, Mohandas Gandhi was no longer interested in becoming a successful, prosperous or famous lawyer. He would work to earn a living, and to subsidize his other, to him more significant, activities. Obligations to his family were likewise undertaken more out of duty than conviction. He could not entirely and permanently separate himself from his children; however, in times of political tension or controversy they took second place.

In August 1906, even as Gandhi was seeking to reconcile with Harilal, the Transvaal Government introduced a new 'Asiatic Ordinance'. This required every Indian resident in Transvaal to register afresh, regardless of age or gender. The certificates of registration had to be carried at all times, and produced on demand. Those not carrying them were liable for arrest, imprisonment and even expulsion from the province.[11]

In Natal, too, Indians could not vote and could not own property in some places. They were subjects rather than full-fledged citizens. However, Indians in Natal did not have to carry identification papers at all times and in all places. The Transvaal Government argued that this new measure was necessary to forestall impersonation and fraud, and to remove the fear among 'the [white] people of the Colony' that 'a general influx of Asiatics would displace many of the Europeans at present employed in trade and commerce, and would end in converting the Colony into an Asiatic, rather than an European, community.'[12]

The Ordinance had been drafted by the Assistant Colonial Secretary of the Transvaal, Lionel Curtis, a protégé of Lord Milner's, educated at Oxford. Curtis's views on race relations, writes his (generally sympathetic) biographer, were 'a conventional amalgam of prejudice, bad history, half-baked Darwinism, and spurious geography producing an elementary blueprint for a system of residential segregation and economic integration'. Curtis argued that 'if the temperate zones are reserved for the white so should the tropical zones be reserved for the Asiatic'. Self-government by and for Indians he dismissed as 'no more in the nature of the people, than it is in the nature of a billiard cue to stand on end without support'.[13]

The Ordinance was intended by Curtis to 'shut the gate against the influx of an Asiatic population', and thereby 'guard the Transvaal as a white reserve'.[14] He was proud of the legislation. It was, he told an admiring audience in Johannesburg, the most important thing he had done. He believed the Ordinance would 'if temperately, cautiously and continually worked . . . keep the Transvaal a white man's country, so far as the circumstances of the country allow. It would save the country from the fate which has overtaken Mauritius and Jamaica.' Then he added a note of self-congratulation: 'A debt of gratitude, the fulness of which the people of this country will never know, is due to [my] office.'[15]

The Ordinance was viewed differently by those subject to its workings. In a letter of 25 August, the British Indian Association said that to make all Asians aged eight and over, of either sex, undergo fresh registration would 'needlessly violate female modesty, as it is understood by millions of British Indians'. An editorial in *Indian Opinion* characterized the new bill as 'abominable'. It threatened to 'invade the sanctity of home life', and appeared to have been drafted 'with the deliberate intention of injuring the Indian community'.

On 1 September, a delegation led by Gandhi travelled to Pretoria to meet the Colonial Secretary, Patrick Duncan. They told him 'that the Asiatic Act would be unacceptable to the Indian community under any circumstances and that re-registration would simply not take place'. The Secretary refused to consider the withdrawal of the legislation. *Indian Opinion* now compared British rule in the Transvaal to the regime of the autocratic Tsar of Russia. While the Russian state 'murder[s] people openly and directly', it said sarcastically, the British in Transvaal 'kill[s] them by inches'.[16]

At their meeting, Gandhi told Duncan that if the legislation went through, the Indians would refuse to abide by its regulations, even if it meant courting arrest. He said he was prepared to be the first to go to jail. That Gandhi was seriously thinking of courting arrest is confirmed by a letter written to him by his friend the Pretoria lawyer R. Gregorowski. Gregorowski told Gandhi that the penalties for failing to

register were severe – imprisonment with hard labour and perhaps a stiff
fine too. He advised the Indians to send a deputation to London, to lay
their case before the new Liberal Government. Gregorowski argued that

> any other form of resistance than by constitutional means is ... to be
> deprecated. It would be an offence to invite people to disobey the law and
> not to re-register. I think such agitation is also bound to fail as not a great
> number of people are made of the stuff that seek martyrdom and Asiatics
> are no exception to the rule. The same result could, I think, be attained by
> constitutional agitation.[17]

Gandhi accepted the advice – for the moment. The British Indian Association would send a deputation to London, whose members would be
'Mr Gandhi and a member from the trading classes'. A thousand pounds
was sanctioned for their expenses. However, to assess the mood of the
community, a public meeting was proposed prior to their departure. To
plan the meeting, a group of Indians met daily in the hall of the Hamidia
Islamic Society, a body funded and patronized by Gujarati Muslims.
Letters were sent to every small town in the Transvaal, urging Indians to
attend. Handbills and posters were discussed and drafted. A list of possible speakers was drawn up and debated.

The meeting, scheduled for Sunday 11 September, was held at the
Empire Theatre, a large hall with balconies that seated close to
2,000 people. On the big day, Indian shopkeepers and hawkers in
Johannesburg stopped work at 10 a.m. The doors of the Empire Theatre opened at noon, to accommodate the people coming in from the
countryside. By 1.30 the theatre was packed to overflowing. Describing
the scene within, the *Rand Daily Mail* wrote that

> even in its palmiest days, the old variety theatre could never have boasted
> of a larger audience than that which assembled yesterday. From the back
> row of the gallery to the front row of the stalls there was not a vacant seat,
> the boxes were crowded as surely they had never been crowded before,
> and even the stage was invaded. Wherever the eye lighted was fez and
> turban, and it needed but little stretch of the imagination to fancy that one
> was thousands of miles from Johannesburg and in the heart of India's
> teeming millions.[18]

Gandhi had invited Patrick Duncan to attend the meeting. The Colonial
Secretary chose to send Montford Chamney as his representative. The

Protector of the Asiatics sat on the dais, silent and uncomprehending, as a series of speakers inveighed against the new ordinance.

Chairing the meeting was Abdul Gani, a Johannesburg merchant who served as the President of the British Indian Association. He sat on a sofa covered with a yellow silk cloth, the person and his background illuminated by electric light. Gani spoke in Hindustani. Whatever his inadequacies as a petition writer, he was clearly a practised orator. His main point was that they should defy the law and go to prison rather than subject themselves to a fresh process of registration. When 'Mr Gani spoke of gaol-going', reported *Indian Opinion*, 'the audience shouted in one voice, "We shall go to gaol, but will not register ourselves again."'

Other speeches were made in Gujarati and English. One speaker, Nanalal Shah, flourished his existing registration certificate before the crowd. This had his name, his profession, his wife's name, his caste, his height, his age and even his thumb impression. 'Is all this not enough?' demanded Mr Shah. 'How can anyone else use this register? Does the Government want now to brand us on our foreheads? I will never return my registration certificate. Neither will I be registered again. I prefer going to gaol, and I will go there.'

Five resolutions were presented to and passed by the meeting. The first outlined what in the ordinance was repugnant; the second asked the Transvaal Government to withdraw it. The third gave formal approval to the delegation being sent to London. The fifth authorized the meeting's Chairman, Abdul Gani, to forward the resolutions to the Transvaal administration and to the Imperial Government in London.

The crucial resolution was the fourth, which said that

> In the event of the Legislative Council, the local Government, and the Imperial Authorities rejecting the humble prayer of the British Indian community of the Transvaal in connection with the Draft Asiatic Law Amendment Ordinance, this mass meeting of British Indians here assembled solemnly and regretfully resolves that, rather than submit to the galling, tyrannous, and un-British requirements laid down in the above Draft Ordinance, every British Indian in the Transvaal shall submit himself to imprisonment and shall continue to do so until it shall please His Gracious Majesty the King-Emperor to grant relief.

Moving the resolution, the Pretoria merchant Hajee Habib said, 'Everything depends upon it. There is no disgrace in going to gaol; rather it is an honour. Only a few people knew of [the Indian patriot] Mr [Bal Gangadhar] Tilak before he went to gaol; today the whole world knows him.' Gandhi spoke after Habib, in (as a reporter on the spot noted) 'clear, low tones, in earnest, serious, and carefully-chosen language'. He said that the responsibility for advising them to go to prison was his. 'The step was grave, but unavoidable. In doing so, they did not hold a threat, but showed that the time for action – over and above making speeches and submitting petitions – had arrived.' Gandhi added that he had 'full confidence in his countrymen'. He 'knew he could trust them, and he knew also that, when occasion required an heroic step to be taken, he knew that every man among them would take it.'

One of the last speakers was a Tamil named Thambi Naidoo. Born in Mauritius in 1875, he had come to the Transvaal as a young man, and set up as a carrier. He probably got to know Gandhi during the plague epidemic of 1904. He was stocky, strongly built, and of firm convictions. Now he stood up to persuade his fellow Tamils to commit to a path of action drawn up by the Gujaratis.

The meeting ended with a vote of thanks, proposed by an M. Lichtenstein and seconded by an I. Israelstam. They (and Gandhi) had been put up to it by Henry Polak. For these were 'both sons of Israel, both, therefore, representative of a people that have, for centuries, suffered persecution and oppression, by reason of the ignorance, prejudice, superstition, and jealousy of their opponents, even as the British Indians in South Africa to-day.'[19]

Thus far, the movement to get the Indians a fair deal in South Africa had followed a strictly legalistic route. Letters, petitions, court cases, delegations – these were the means by which Gandhi and his fellows had challenged laws which bore down unfairly on them. Now, however, they were threatening to defy this new Ordinance and go to jail.[20]

It has been sometimes assumed that this resolution of 11 September 1906, mandating a move from petition to protest, was influenced by Henry David Thoreau's classic tract on civil disobedience, first published in 1849. There is no evidence to support this conjecture. At this time, Gandhi had *not* read Thoreau. Another speculation, offered by the respected Gandhi scholar James D. Hunt, is that he was influenced by protests by Nonconformists against the Education Act in England, which forced Anglican instruction on state-aided schools. Baptists,

Wesleyans and Congregationalists had courted arrest rather than allow their children to be indoctrinated in the official faith of the state.[21]

Gandhi did know some Baptist and Methodist priests in Johannesburg. He did read the British press. The term 'passive resistance', used by him, was one made popular by Nonconformists, although it also had a more distant origin in the term 'non-resistance to evil', made famous in a book Gandhi knew well, Tolstoy's *The Kingdom of God Is Within You*.[22]

These influences may be inferred but they cannot, alas, be demonstrated. Prior to the 11 September meeting, there are no references in Gandhi's writings and speeches to Nonconformist protests against the Education Act in England. On the other hand, Gandhi had conveyed in *Indian Opinion* his admiration for the Swadeshi movement in British India. This admiration was shared by his colleagues – hence the appreciative reference in Hajee Habib's speech to the incarceration of the militant nationalist Bal Gangadhar Tilak.

The idea of protest and sacrifice was more directly influenced by the events in India in 1905–6. But, as Gandhi pointed out, even the defiance of a specific law had indigenous precedents. Writing in Gujarati in *Indian Opinion*, he said of the resolution threatening mass resistance that it

> is, and at the same time is not, unique. We consider it unique, because nowhere else in the world have Indians so far resolved, as they have done now, to go to gaol rather than submit to a law. On the other hand, we do not consider it unique because a number of similar instances are found [in history]. When we are dissatisfied with anything, we resort to *hartal*. In India we often consider it our duty to do so, in order to obtain redress of our grievances, particularly in the Native States. The *hartal* only means that we do not approve of a certain measure taken by the ruler. This tradition of resisting a law has been in vogue among us from very early days, when the English people were in a barbarous state. Thus, really speaking, the Resolution passed by the Transvaal Indians is nothing extraordinary and there is no reason why we should feel nervous.[23]

The editors of the *Collected Works* do not translate the word '*hartal*'. A *hartal* refers to the withdrawal of support and services from the state, or from one's employers. Among the various forms it took, and takes, were workers laying down tools to demand larger wages, peasants migrating from a kingdom to protest high taxes and shopkeepers closing their shutters to protest a new tax. A cognate word is *dharna*. A *hartal* is a collective act of protest; a *dharna* more often an individual act of resistance. A servant who refuses to wait on his master after being abused by him is on *dharna*. When, back in 1894, Gandhi would not eat in an Indian home until his hosts contributed their mite to the Natal Indian Congress, he was invoking this old (and well-regarded) tradition of moral-persuasion-shading-into-coercion. Now, twelve years later, he was redirecting that tradition in a collective protest against a racially biased law.

The Ordinance that sparked the Resolution of 11 September was peculiar to the Transvaal. Residents of British India were *not* required to take out registration certificates. However, Indians in India had protested oppressive laws in similar fashion in the past. In Gandhi's native Kathiawar, a distinction had long been made between two ways of protesting the arbitrary actions of a state. The first was to resort to violence, a method preferred by bandits who roamed the countryside. This was called *baharvatiya* – literally, going outside the law. On the other hand, a grievance could also be expressed without the use of force, as for example by sitting outside the home of the official responsible for the law or measure one was opposed to. By refusing to move, and perhaps combining this with refusing to eat, the protester hoped the state or its representative would be shamed into withdrawing the offending statute. This second, peaceful, form of protest was known as *risaamanu*, which meant the temporary severing of relations between people who were otherwise closely and even intimately connected.[24]

Indian precedents to the Resolution of 11 September existed; and Gandhi knew of some of them. Even so, his appeal to ancient Indian custom legitimized rather than explained the threat to court arrest. For the meeting at the Empire Theatre was carried along by its own momentum. Encouraged by the large crowd, the speakers competed with one another to raise the temperature. The speeches and resolutions represented a specific response to a specific situation. The new Ordinance had consolidated the grievances of the Indians in the Transvaal, who now sought means of protest more direct, and more radical, than any they had resorted to before.

Notably, the Indians were supported by the Chinese in the Transvaal, who, as fellow Asians, were also affected by the Ordinance. The gathering at the Empire Theatre included several Chinese leaders. Two days later, the Chinese Consul-General in Johannesburg wrote to Lord Selborne urging him not to sanction 'an offensive measure' that was in breach of international law and which, if implemented, would harm friendly relations between China and Great Britain. By calling for the compulsory registration of all Asiatics, he said, the Ordinance would subject his countrymen to 'the degrading exposure of all their bodily infirmities which to our Oriental minds is most repulsive, as such a system of identification, is only resorted to in cases of criminals in China.'[25]

The sentiments of those present at the Empire Theatre were endorsed by their long-time supporter in London, Dadabhai Naoroji. As a Gladstonian liberal, Naoroji believed in the politics of gradual and incremental reform. His communications were generally couched in the most understated language. But this new Ordinance in the Transvaal prompted a scathing letter to the Secretary of State for the Colonies. Calling it a 'wanton insult' to his countrymen, a man who had been a rare brown Member of the Mother of Parliaments remarked that

> it is most galling to think that in British territories if [the great England cricketer of Indian extraction] Prince Rangitsinhjee [sic] wanted to enter the Transvaal he should have to apply for a permit and then in order that he might have a glass of beer he should have to apply cringingly to the Government for exemption from the Liquor ordinance [under which Indians were not allowed to buy alcohol] . . . Is this the way in which the most Liberal Government that the Empire has seen for years will protect weak and helpless members thereof?[26]

Back in South Africa, the threat of passive resistance was being held in reserve. For the moment, Gandhi would follow his friend Gregorowski's advice and make a personal appeal to the authorities in London. With him would come Haji Ojer Ally, a businessman active in social work in Johannesburg. They were booked to leave for the United Kingdom in early October. A few days before they departed, the Empire Theatre, the venue of the great meeting of 11 September, was gutted in a fire.

10

A Lobbyist in London

On 2 October 1906, Mohandas Gandhi entered his thirty-eighth year. He spent his birthday in a train travelling across the veld, from Johannesburg to Cape Town. On the evening of the 3rd, he boarded the SS *Armsdale* for the voyage to the United Kingdom.

Gandhi's companion aboard train and ship, Haji Ojer Ally, was a Gujarati born in 1853 in Mauritius. He studied and worked on that island before migrating to South Africa, where he ran a water bottling plant in Cape Town, later shifting base to Johannesburg. Here he branched out from business into community work, opening a 'Hamidia Islamic Society' whose special focus was the education of Muslim youth. He was married to a Malay lady, with whom he had eleven children.[1]

In Cape Town, under the more liberal franchise of that province, H. O. Ally had been both a municipal and parliamentary voter. (Gandhi, arriving in Natal after the reforms leading to Responsible Government, was neither.) 'Though not a finished speaker or an accomplished scholar,' wrote Henry Polak, '[Ally] had a very good command of the English language, as well as of Urdu, a powerful voice, and was possessed of a considerable degree of rough eloquence'. He was also partial to the dramatic gesture – while speaking on the jail-going resolution of 11 September, he did so with a Union Jack draped around his shoulders.[2]

In all respects Gandhi and Ally were a study in contrast. The Hindu was dressed in sober Western clothes, while the Muslim wore flowing Oriental robes and a colourful turban. Gandhi was thin and small-made, Ally tall and grossly overweight. Unlike the lawyer, the merchant was not believed to have taken a vow of celibacy.

These differences emerge quite starkly in Gandhi's account of their voyage together. On board, Ally ate fish for lunch, and fish and sometimes meat for dinner. He also drank tea and ginger ale, and smoked continuously. Gandhi, on the other hand, fed himself on milk, bread, potatoes, stewed fruit and fresh air. The Muslim merchant was reading Amir Ali's *Spirit of Islam* and Washington Irving's *Mahomet and His Successors*. The Hindu lawyer was brushing up on his Tamil, reading a history of Gujarat and a report on 'alien immigration', and composing his dispatches for *Indian Opinion*.

The SS *Armsdale* docked at Southampton on 20 October. The same day, Gandhi gave two interviews to the press. Speaking to the London correspondent of an Indian newspaper, he said the act proposed by the Transvaal Government was 'much more rigorous and severe' than earlier legislation. Speaking to a British journalist, Gandhi said restrictions on Indian immigration into the Transvaal must be 'on such terms as are not humiliating, and do not interfere with the liberty of those already settled in the country.' 'Mr Gandhi states that the Indians are greatly stirred over the matter,' noted the reporter, 'and are prepared to go to gaol rather than submit.'[3]

The day after Gandhi landed, he visited the family of his friend Henry Polak. They lived on Grosvenor Road, in Canonbury, North London. 'Nothing surprised me, as you had prepared me for everything,' wrote Mohandas to Henry, adding. 'Otherwise to meet your sisters and your brilliant father would have been a most agreeable surprise. Both the sisters are really most lovable, and if I was unmarried, or young, or believed in mixed marriage, you know what I would have done!'[4]

The same day, Gandhi wrote to his nephew Chhaganlal making a more neutral case for interracial living. Albert West's sister had chosen to join him in South Africa. Gandhi thought this 'a wise step'. 'We do want some English ladies there [at Phoenix]', he told his nephew. 'Do please make the best use possible of her. Let your wife and other ladies mix freely with her, and let her feel that there is no distance between her and us, and make her as comfortable as possible ... Each party has very strong points for the other to imbibe.'[5]

While Miss West prepared for an austere life among abstemious Indians, Gandhi himself was billeted at the Cecil, one of London's most luxurious hotels. For a visiting delegation, the hotel afforded respectability and a London address that was credible as well as convenient, within walking distance of Whitehall and Charing Cross railway station.[6] Gandhi's first few days in London were spent writing letters on the Cecil's notepaper, addressed to Members of Parliament and newspaper editors whom he hoped to win over to the Indian case. The letters were typed by a Miss Lawson, who had been sent by Polak's father to act as Gandhi's assistant. They referred to H. O. Ally and himself rather grandly in the third person, as in 'I shall be obliged if you would kindly grant the Deputation an interview ...'

Meanwhile, unknown to Gandhi – and Ally – their claims to represent the Transvaal Indians were being challenged. 'It appears that there are two sections among the British Indians in the Transvaal,' wrote the Colony's Governor to the Secretary of State. One group was represented by Gandhi and Ally, while the other 'denies that these two gentlemen have any mandate to represent them.' The Governor himself was 'unable to determine [the] relative strength of the two sections.'[7]

The opposition to the deputation was led by a man named C. M. Pillay, a Tamil who had lived in Johannesburg from before the Anglo-Boer War. In November 1902 – when Gandhi was still in India – Pillay helped draft a petition which daringly asked that the Indians in the Transvaal be

> allowed to come and go freely; that they may trade, buy and sell unhindered and unmolested; that they may acquire, own, and dispose of landed property, without limit, clog, or undue obstacle; that they may, by interposition of their rulers, be preserved from any differentiation in laws, or restriction of person in government, or in treatment; that they may in no way be curtailed of their liberty or freedom ...

The petition went on to demand Indian representation in legislatures and municipal boards. It was signed by twenty-two people, a majority of whom were Tamils.[8]

Two months after this, Gandhi had arrived back in South Africa. Now based in Johannesburg, he quickly became the main channel through which Indian demands were articulated. This irritated C. M. Pillay, who saw the lawyer's rise as a consequence of the support, financial and moral, of Gujarati merchants. When, in March 1904, the white press carried reports on the unsanitary habits of Indian shopkeepers, Pillay wrote to say that whereas the Tamils from the Madras Presidency were 'immune from infectious diseases of all kinds', the 'Bombay Bunnias ... are the most filthiest classes imaginable.' Until about 1890, the Indians in the Transvaal were largely Tamils, but then merchants from Bombay and Gujarat arrived to spoil the show. Because of these Gujaratis, claimed Pillay, the

> Indian community in general . . . are made to suffer for the criminal per-
> versity of a section whose chronic antipathy to cleanliness, fanatical
> adherence to superstition in its grossest form, and mammon worship is a
> most prolific source of contagious disease of the most virulent form.[9]

Pillay signed his letter 'late Secretary, Indian Congress, Pretoria and Johannesburg'. One does not know how many members his branch of the Congress had. At any rate, by 1906 Gandhi's British Indian Association was clearly in the lead when it came to advancing the community's cause. The rivalry was personal, but also communal. As a Tamil, Pillay spoke a different language from Gandhi and the Gujarati merchants. He may also have been originally from a different class, for his name suggests that his forefathers came to South Africa as indentured labourers.

When the 'deputation' proceeded to London, Pillay made common cause with his fellow Tamil William Godfrey, a doctor from Natal now based in Johannesburg. The doctor's rift with Gandhi was of more recent origin. Active in the British Indian Association, Dr Godfrey had been a featured speaker in the mass meeting held in the Empire Theatre on 11 September. He had hoped to be on the ship to London; however, when the BIA thought it wise to send a merchant as well, this left room for only one English-speaking professional, who, of course, had to be Gandhi.

On 15 October, as the SS *Armsdale* made its way across the ocean, William Godfrey and C. M. Pillay sent a letter to the Secretary of State for the Colonies. This claimed that Gandhi and Ally had no mandate to represent the Indians; and added for good measure that the lawyer was a 'well known professional agitator who has made money out of his work'. Gandhi was accused of having 'caused an estrangement between Europeans and Indians'; and Ally of being a pan-Islamist whose allegiances were to the Sultan of Turkey rather than the British Crown.[10]

The petition sent by Pillay and Godfrey had more than a hundred names attached to it. Gandhi's alert (and loyal) friend Henry Polak sought out its signatories. What he found was not edifying. A Tamil owner of an Indian laundry, persuaded by Godfrey that his omission from the delegation represented an affront to the Tamils, had placed a blank sheet of paper in front of forty-five of his workers, and got them to affix signatures and thumb-impressions. Told by Polak that his action had undermined Indian unity, the laundry-owner now disavowed the petition.[11] Two of Godfrey's brothers, who had been Gandhi's friends and clients in Natal, wrote to *The Times* disassociating themselves from their sibling. The British Indian Association wired the Secretary of State to say that Gandhi and Ally were their authorized representatives, and that the 'entire Indian community indignantly repudiate[d]' a campaign based on Godfrey's 'personal animus'.[12]

In London, the man who was at once the larger and lesser member of the deputation had fallen ill. The exact symptoms are unknown; but over-indulgence seems to have been the cause. Ally was rushed from the Hotel Cecil to Lady Margaret Hospital in the town of Bromley, ten miles south-east of Charing Cross. The hospital had been founded in 1903 by Josiah Oldfield, Gandhi's old friend and flatmate from his student days. It was run on strict vegetarian principles, with treatment by diet replacing treatment by drugs. No meat or fish was permitted, nor any alcohol either. The food was cooked with coconut oil, then rather scarce in Britain.[13]

Gandhi wrote to Oldfield urging him to see Ally every day – 'Your presence alone would be inspiring and cheering.' He added that 'expense is of no consideration'. To Ally himself Gandhi offered this explanation of his ill-health: 'I am superstitious enough to say it was due to the cigar.' His recovery might be 'retarded by even one puff of the deadly cigar – such is my strong conviction regarding nicotine'. The next day Gandhi wrote to his compatriot in similar vein: 'I beseech you to keep yourself religiously away from cigars. Certainly, have as much as you like of the hubble-bubble' (which, with its tobacco diluted through water, presumably was less harmful). 'Follow Dr Oldfield's instructions implicitly,' urged Gandhi. 'I am certain that no other doctor could restore you to health with the same amount of despatch as Mr Oldfield.'

The last was said with some conviction, for Gandhi was consulting the same doctor himself. Back in the days when he was practising law in Bombay, Gandhi told Oldfield, he had lost his sense of smell; now he had chronic catarrh. He asked whether his friend could treat him, or instead recommend a throat specialist. Another ailment was related to their shared passion and lifestyle choices. 'I think it was when I was carrying on a fruit-and-nut diet experiment,' wrote Gandhi, 'that I damaged my teeth. I believe that I had permanently damaged two molars and I thought that I was going to lose one of them on board. I certainly tried hard to pull one out but I did not succeed. Would you see them or do you want me to go to a dentist?' Although they were old friends, if Oldfield was to attend to either complaint Gandhi insisted on paying his professional fees.[14]

On 31 October, Gandhi wrote to the Secretary of State for the Colonies, Lord Elgin, requesting an appointment for a delegation consisting of himself, Ally and some well-placed Englishmen; a statement of the Indian case was attached. The meeting was scheduled for 8 November. Since Elgin was a former Viceroy, Gandhi asked some members of the Indian Civil Service to join the delegation. Since he was also a senior British politician, the former MP Dadabhai Naoroji and the serving MP M. M. Bhownaggree were asked to come too. Gandhi went three times to the House of Commons to meet the Liberal MP Harold Cox, who eventually also agreed to come.

In the first week of November, Gandhi had several meetings with a radical and somewhat raffish Indian he knew would never fit into any formal delegation. His name was Shyamaji Krishnavarma. Twelve years older than Gandhi and also from Kathiawar, Krishnavarma had studied at Oxford and been called to the London Bar. Back in India, he held a series of jobs in the Kathiawari principalities before returning to England in 1905.

Krishnavarma thought the Indian National Congress too loyalist by far; what he stood for was complete emancipation from British rule. He established an 'India House' at Highgate in London (not far from the cemetery where Karl Marx was buried), which served as a hostel for students and a forum for debate. Students who lived here took a pledge that they would not work for the colonial bureaucracy when they returned home. Krishnavarma also published a journal called *The Indian Sociologist*, which argued the case for freedom for subject peoples. His greatest English supporter was the socialist and anti-imperialist H. M. Hyndman.[15]

Gandhi knew of Krishnavarma's work, for it had been written about in *Indian Opinion*. Now they met in London, where, to begin with at any rate, the younger man was intrigued by the older man. He was impressed by his learning – Krishnavarma knew Latin, Greek and Sanskrit – and somewhat intimidated by his passion. On successive Sundays, Gandhi passed up invitations to the Polak household in order to debate Indian issues with him. As he wrote to Polak *père*, 'the Pandit of whom I spoke to you and I have not finished the whole of our discussion, and as it is rather important I am afraid I must deprive myself of the pleasure' (of meeting the father and his charming daughters).[16] Later, in a report to *Indian Opinion*, Gandhi summarized the character and credo of his new friend in these words:

> Though he can afford to live in comfort, he lives in poverty. He dresses simply and lives like an ascetic. His mission is service to his country. The idea underlying his service is that there should be complete *swaraj* [freedom] for India and that the British should quit the country, handing over power to Indians. If they do not do so, the Indians should refuse them all help so that they become unable to carry on the administration and are forced to leave. He holds that unless this is done the people of India will never be happy. Everything else will follow *swaraj*.[17]

After a week in hospital, H. O. Ally moved back to the Hotel Cecil. However, on Oldfield's advice, he had hour-long massages every evening, to make him fit for the meeting with the Secretary of State for the Colonies.

Two days before meeting the deputation, Lord Elgin received a joint letter from five Indians from South Africa studying in London – three Christian, one Muslim and one Hindu. The letter was clearly prompted and very likely drafted by Gandhi. It detailed the disabilities under the laws being proposed in the Transvaal, noting that the signatories would not be able to gain entry into the colony on their return. It tellingly added: 'We are here being nurtured in the teachings of Bentham, Austin, and other English writers whose names are a watchword for liberty and independence, and we could hardly believe that anything of the kind referred to above would possibly be applicable to us.'[18]

On the afternoon of 8 November, Gandhi, Ally and ten others were at the Colonial Office to meet Lord Elgin. The first to speak was Sir Lepel Griffin, former Chief Secretary of the Punjab and current chairman of the East India Association. Here is the official transcript of part of what Griffin said:

And against whom is this [offending] legislation directed? Against the most orderly, honourable, industrious, temperate race in the world, people of our own stock and blood, with whom our own language has as a sister-language been connected . . .

And by whom is this legislation instigated? I am told, and I believe it, that it is not by the best part of the British community in the Transvaal, who are, I believe, in favour of giving all reasonable privileges to British Indian subjects; it is by the alien foreign population in the Transvaal who are perhaps to some extent inconvenienced by Indian traders who are so very much more temperate and industrious than themselves. It does not come from the English. The legislation is prompted, and the prejudice against the Indians is encouraged, by the aliens, by Russian Jews, by Syrians, by German Jews, by every class of aliens, the very off-scourings of the international sewers of Europe.

The two questions were pertinent, but Griffin's answer to the second was extraordinary. From where and whence did this diatribe come? Was it a product of Sir Lepel Griffin's own prejudices, or a more general pandering to the anti-Semitism then common among the British ruling class? In fact, it was Boers and Britons, Christians both, who had been in the forefront of the anti-Indian legislation. To be sure, some recent Jewish immigrants to the Transvaal were hostile to Indian traders who competed with them. Even so, Gandhi's closest supporters were, as often as not, Jews such as Henry Polak, Hermann Kallenbach and Lewis Ritch. What did Gandhi think of Sir Lepel's diatribe, as he heard it? Alas, the records are silent on the matter.[19]

Gandhi spoke next, and with sobriety. He explained how the new Ordinance violated the 'fundamental maxim of the British law' that everyone was presumed innocent unless proven otherwise; it 'brands every Indian as guilty'. It originally applied to women too, but as a result of their protests at least this had been withdrawn. The larger worry was that it would be applied elsewhere, that 'what the Transvaal thinks today the other Colonies think tomorrow.'

H. O. Ally spoke briefly, endorsing Gandhi's stand and emphasizing that they were 'loyal British subjects' who did not demand political parity. 'We are content that the white man should be predominant in the Transvaal,' said Ally, 'but we do feel that we are entitled to all the other ordinary rights that a British subject should enjoy.'

The Indian MP M. M. Bhownaggree also spoke. He invoked the duty Elgin owed India and Indians, as the 'custodian and guardian of Indian interests and the protector of their rights, during a memorable and distinguished viceroyalty'. Dadabhai Naoroji drew attention to the political traditions of the party of which he, like the Colonial Secretary, was a member. 'If there is one principle more important than another,' remarked Naoroji, 'it is that of the freedom of British subjects under the British flag, and I do hope that the British Government, especially a Liberal Government, will stand upon that basis.' (It was characteristic that the Indian Tory stressed the official's duty, whereas the Indian Liberal emphasized a broader principle.)

Having heard everybody out, Elgin then responded. He did not think 'that the impression of thumb mark in itself should be a very debasing operation'. Gandhi interjected that it was a ten-finger mark that was required, which in India was asked for only in the case of criminals. Elgin replied, 'I do not want to argue it, but I think that there is just that much to be said.' He then turned to the forces behind the new legislation. He had received many telegrams from different (white) municipalities in the Transvaal urging him to pass the Ordinance. 'I cannot, therefore, entirely subscribe to what Sir Lepel Griffin said about the opposition [of whites to Indians].' He admitted that had he been in the India Office rather than the Colonial Office, he might have himself signed dispatches 'protesting, in as strong language as has been used here, against the restrictions on British citizens'. However, placed where he was, he had

> to recognize the fact that all over the world there are difficulties arising on the part of white communities, and we have to reckon with them. I do not say that they ought always to succeed; they certainly ought not to succeed in points of detail which would, in any way, involve oppression. But the fact of there being that sentiment has to be borne in mind when we have to deal with matters of this description.

He ended with a carefully worded equivocation: 'I have now heard what Mr Gandhi had to say . . . I have heard the other gentlemen who have accompanied him. I will give the best consideration to their representations, and I shall think it my duty to make up my mind with the full responsibility which I have to assume.'[20]

Writing to Henry Polak, Gandhi, ever the optimist, described his meeting with Elgin as 'exceedingly good'.[21] For his part, the Secretary of State for the Colonies was now persuaded that Gandhi and Ally were 'really representative of the majority of their compatriots'. Elgin wrote to the Transvaal Government that while he appreciated the force of white sentiment, he would not want to advise Royal Assent to the new legislation just yet. He asked them 'to favour me with a further expression of your own opinion on the question, in view of the strong, and, as I gather, somewhat unexpected, opposition with which the Ordinance has been met by the majority of the Indian community.'[22]

Two days after Gandhi's delegation met Lord Elgin, *The Times* printed a long article on its mission. Before the Anglo-Boer War, perhaps the Imperial Government could have intervened in favour of the Indians, but it would 'be injudicious, and indeed impracticable, to attempt to settle such a question from Downing Street now, when the colony will enjoy within a few months all the rights of responsible government.' The paper explained why the Indians' claims and demands could not, or rather would not, be conceded:

> No young democratic community of white men can be expected to deal out even-handed justice to formidable rivals in their trade and business who come from another race, with other traditions, other creeds, and other complexions than their own. The fact that the interlopers are subjects of the same Sovereign, and can claim to be treated as members of the same Empire, will probably never, in our time, outweigh these considerations with them. The lapse of years, and perhaps of generations, may be needed to create, if indeed it can ever be created, such a spirit of common Imperial citizenship as will greatly mitigate the combined force of race prejudice and of self-interest.[23]

As a student, Mohandas Gandhi had proved impervious to the delights and distractions of London. Plays, parties and cricket matches did not interest him then. Now he had neither the interest nor the time. He worked from nine in the morning until midnight, lobbying editors, politicians and other men of influence. They, and others like them, were besieged by a torrent of letters. Apparently, as many as 5,000 penny stamps were used by the delegation.

Among the men Gandhi met in pursuit of his case was the campaigning journalist W. T. Stead. Stead had famously – or perhaps notoriously – been sympathetic to the Boer cause during the War, abandoning his earlier support for the imperialism of Cecil Rhodes. Gandhi asked him now to write an article on the Indian question in 'your own graphic style'; he had 'no doubt that some at least of the Boer leaders would listen to you and give effect to your suggestions'.[24] Stead did not write the article requested, but other grandees were more amenable to Gandhi's lobbying. The doctor and naturalist George Birdwood, an old India hand, was deeply impressed with Gandhi's petition to Elgin. He read it 'with the greatest personal delight for the evidence it affords of the ability and wisdom with which young Hindoos like you can handle such intricate and trying [questions of] Imperial policy'. The rejection of the Indian plea, thought Birdwood, would be an 'irretrievable blow to the consolidation of the [British] Empire'. In his view, there was

> no historical people on earth – not even the Scots – who have a better conceit of themselves or better deserve [it] than the Hindoos, who have given India her immemorial name and fame, and a wanton outrage against their racial pride such as that by which they are affronted in South Africa, will strike a deadly blow to their loyalty towards the British 'Raj' which is the mightiest corner-stone of our world-wide Empire.[25]

Meanwhile, pressed by Gandhi, the liberal MPs Harold Cox and Henry Cotton raised a series of questions in Parliament on the harassment of Indians in the Transvaal. They were answered by the Under-Secretary of State, Winston Churchill, a man noticeably sympathetic to the idea that white and brown could never mix. One question related to an eviction notice issued to about a hundred Indian traders in the Johannesburg locality of Vrededorp. The traders had been there for years, and their vested property was valued at £20,000. When Cotton asked why the Indians were made to vacate their stands, Churchill said that there were also Boer traders operating in the market, and 'it is very desirable to keep the white and coloured quarters apart, as the practice of allowing European, Asiatic, and native families to live side by side in [a] mixed community is fraught with many evils, and, in Lord Selborne's opinion, is injurious to the social well-being of all three.'[26]

Gandhi immediately wrote to Lord Elgin, taking issue with Churchill's claims. He said, first, that the Indians in the suburb had legally acquired rights of residence; second, that Indian shops, described by Churchill as 'tin shanties', were in fact 'superior to many of the buildings in Vrededorp'; and third, and most tellingly,

> that if the doctrine of the desirability of keeping the white and the Coloured quarters apart is sound, I fear that there will be an end to British Indian residence in the Transvaal with any degree of self-respect. The logical conclusion of such a doctrine will be a system of locations which can only result in ruination to hundreds of law-abiding and respectable Indians.[27]

On 27 November, Gandhi and Ally met the Under-Secretary of State in his rooms in the Colonial Office. Churchill asked them to send him a short note, no longer than one foolscap page, of what they 'had to say on this Ordinance, on the Vrededorp Stands Ordinance and on the question as a whole'. Ally then reminded him that

> he was the same person who had been present at the Point [in Durban] to receive Mr Churchill on his return from the [Boer] war. And it was the same Mr Churchill that he now pleaded for redress on behalf of the Indian community. Mr Churchill smiled, patted Mr Ally on the back and said he would do all he could. This answer added to our hopes.[28]

His experiences in the imperial capital, meeting doors open, closed and ajar, convinced Gandhi that the Indians needed an organized body to represent them in London. Working via the mail and the telephone, he established a South Africa British Indian Committee (SABIC), which was supported by, among others, Griffin, Naoroji and Bhownaggree. L. W. Ritch, his friend from Johannesburg who had now qualified as a lawyer in London, would serve as secretary. 'I have not told you all about Mr Ritch's capabilities', wrote Gandhi to Bhownaggree.

> He has handled many a meeting and has been secretary of more than one organization. He was twenty years ago perhaps what people may call a rabid Socialist. His has been a most chequered career. Today, I do not own a friend who knows me more than he does. He is one of those men who believe in dying for a cause that he holds dear.[29]

It was Bhownaggree who chaired a farewell meeting for the deputation. This was held on 29 November, in the Richelieu Room of the Hotel Cecil. In attendance were an array of pro-Indian members of the British Establishment, among them the former Governor of Bombay,

Lord Reay; the former Principal of the Mohammedan Anglo-Oriental College, Theodore Morrison; sundry ex-I.C.S. officials and serving Members of Parliament. Those with more personal connections to Gandhi included J. H. L. Polak (father of Henry) and Dr Josiah Oldfield.[30]

Speaking to the gathering, Gandhi singled out the Indian students in the room, whose predicament highlighted the trouble in the Transvaal. These young men contemplated their return to South Africa 'with considerable anxiety and apprehension'; they worried they would share the fate of the dispossessed Indians in the colony. For, as Gandhi observed, 'here, in England, they will become barristers or doctors, but there, in South Africa, they may not even be able to cross the border of the Transvaal.'[31]

Gandhi's energetic lobbying in London alarmed the Transvaal Government. As the deputation sailed back to South Africa, the colony's Lieutenant-Governor wrote to his boss grumbling that 'His Majesty's Government have evidently been greatly impressed by the representation of Messrs. Gandhi and Ally.'[32] The Governor of the Transvaal, Lord Selborne, then wrote a letter to *his* superior, the Secretary of State for the Colonies, pointing out that the Ordinance was 'regarded almost unanimously by the European community as being vital to the best interests of the Colony'. He defended the proposal to make registration compulsory, and warned that the provision of appeal to the Supreme Court (which the Indians were agitating for) would defeat the legislation's purpose, since 'experience has shown how difficult it is when once an Asiatic has entered the country to find him again'. The Governor remarked that

> Mr Gandhi must know better than most people that there is an extensive traffic in permits and registration certificates, and he has had unique experience of the ease with which the Courts can be moved (and rightly so while the law remains as it is) to upset any administrative action which is intended to carry out an effective control over immigration.

The parenthetical comment scarcely served to soften what was a direct insinuation against Gandhi's motives: namely, that he had a vested interest in the old law, and in profitably fighting court cases under it. Selborne then explained the larger project of which the Ordinance was part. 'Every patriotic South African,' he wrote, looks forward to the establishment of a large and vigorous European population here ... The immigration of an Asiatic population on a large scale he regards as a menace to the realisation of this ideal. He sees already in Natal a picture which impresses even the casual observer of the rapidity with which the Asiatic is filling a place in trade, and now even in agriculture, which otherwise would have afforded scope for a growing European population. He sees the same process at work in the Transvaal, more slowly at present, but, capable, as he believes, of rapid acceleration. He is quite willing to recognise the claims which British Indians naturally have on His Majesty's Government, but he protests against, and is prepared to resist, those claims when they involve the peopling of his country which he believes to be fitted to be the home of a strong European nation with a people who can never be to him anything but an alien race.[33]

This defence of the white case begged a crucial question – why were the Indians more 'alien' than the Europeans? Unlike the Africans, neither had originated in the continent. Both groups had come from across the oceans, the Europeans from the West, the Indians from the East, each seeking better prospects for themselves and their families. The Europeans now claimed that South Africa was their home. But why couldn't the Indians be likewise 'patriotic' about a land where they too lived and worked? Evidently, the Indians were seen as the main, perhaps only, threat to the creation of a settler state to be ruled and dominated by whites, with a submissive native population alongside. For South Africa to become more like Australia, Canada and New Zealand, it was imperative that no more Indians were allowed into the territory.

The intensity and passion, even paranoia, that characterized the presentation of the colonists' case was an indirect tribute to Gandhi. The opposition led by him had unnerved and unsettled them. To the Governor's private warnings were now added a book published in London with the alarmist title *The Asiatic Danger to the Colonies*. Written by the Johannesburg journalist L. E. Neame, this aimed at influencing 'home' opinion against the Indians, and thus smoothing the path for the new policies in the Transvaal. Neame was particularly worried by the rise of nationalism in India, as manifest in the Swadeshi movement. He warned that 'the idea is gaining ground that a weak spot has been found in the armour of Europe.' This activist spirit would not just be aimed at British rule in India; it 'may be used for the forcing of many a closed door'. Like

Europe, Asia 'too needs room for its surplus population'; hence the demand, led by Gandhi, to allow Indians the freedom to move to South Africa on the grounds that it was also part of the British Empire.

It was not, however, merely a question of competing numbers. As Neame acutely observed, 'the Asiatic has another fault – from the white man's standpoint. He is ambitious. The plantation coolie may die a coolie; his son may become a landowner, or a small trader or store-keeper, even a merchant on a considerable scale.' As successive generations of Indians graduated to more sophisticated occupations, they took away jobs and trades previously monopolized by the whites. And so this European in Johannesburg plaintively asked: 'What is to be their future if the Indian works in the farm, owns the store, and per-forms skilled labour in the factory?'

Gandhi and company, complained Neame, had mobilized the sup-port of 'Members of Parliament who know India but not the Colonies'. To counteract this, the colonist appealed to the baser instincts of the mother country, by arguing that

> in the end the colony with the largest Asiatic population where white men should dwell will be of least value to the Empire. It is an economic axiom that the white man consumes more than the Asiatic. The trade of a colony with a big white population must be more remunerative to England than that of a colony where a decreasing white population is struggling hard against the competition of the Eastern peoples.[34]

L. E. Neame was answered by Henry Polak, a European who had crossed the racial divide to stand up for the underdog. In a four-part review in *Indian Opinion*, Polak (writing as 'The Editor'), accused Neame of a 'Caucasian bias', as one 'who does not question the ultimate and inherent superiority of the white race' while relegating 'the disturb-ing Asiatic to the limbo of permanent inferiority'. By dividing the world into Asiatic and non-Asiatic, Neame had shown that he 'does not, evi-dently, believe in the brotherhood of man and his unity with Nature. He cannot conceive that men are moulded, all the world over, in the same general way by the same series of circumstances.'

Of Neame's argument that Asiatic traders would swamp white com-petition, Polak archly noted that 'his plea is not that the white man should make a living, but that the Asiatic should not.' For if the Cauca-sians were indeed 'inherently superior', then what is the added advantage to be derived from Registration Laws, Immigration Acts, commercial barriers, protective walls [and other such methods] . . . betokening, not a calm self-assurance, not a strong sense of breathing a purer atmosphere than that breathed by any other, but a mortal fear lest the phantom of an alleged superiority should be discovered and exposed to public derision – a terror lest the windy dummy of inflated self-importance be pricked.[35]

Gandhi and company did not really want to challenge, still less overthrow, European rule in the Transvaal. What they asked for was the safeguarding of existing and previously guaranteed rights of residence, trade and travel. They had said time and again that the political superiority of the whites was not in question, but the ruling race was not reassured. Unlike the Africans, the Indians were adept at trade and (as Gandhi's own example had shown) at the professions. Here they directly competed with Europeans. The danger in admitting more Indians was that the economic challenge would intensify, leading to claims for political representation as well. Hence, as L. E. Neame put it, the door had to be firmly shut to the Indians.

11

From Conciliation to Confrontation

Gandhi returned to South Africa in the third week of December 1906. Landing at Cape Town, he and his colleague H. O. Ally took the train to Johannesburg. Arriving on the morning of the 22nd, they were met at Park Station by a large crowd of Indians. The next day an even larger gathering welcomed the duo at the hall of the Hamidia Islamic Society.[1]

The next week Gandhi and Ally were in Natal, speaking at Verulam and then at Durban, where so many gathered to hear them that the meeting was shifted from the Congress Hall to the covered market at Pine Street. Afterwards, Parsee Rustomjee hosted a dinner in their honour. The next day, Gandhi took Ally and a few others on a tour of Phoenix, where 'the various departments were inspected with interest and the visitors expressed pleasure at what they saw.' That, at any rate, was the claim of *Indian Opinion*; perhaps the epicurean Ally, unused to and disenchanted by the ascetic life, saw things rather differently.[2]

Gandhi had come to Natal not merely to garner praise. The Natal Government was planning fresh curbs on merchants who were not white. On board the RMS *Briton* he had written a note urging that Indian traders be allowed to import clerks and assistants; that when denied a licence they be permitted to appeal to the courts; and that educated or propertied Indians be granted the municipal franchise. Gandhi insisted that 'Natal cannot be allowed to draw upon India for a supply of indentured labour when she refuses to treat the resident Indian population with justice and decency.'[3]

Sent the note by the Imperial Government, the Natal Ministers refuted Gandhi's points one by one. There were already more Indians than whites in Natal; now, 'if permission were accorded to Indian clerks or domestic servants to enter the Colony temporarily, as proposed by

Mr Gandhi, insuperable difficulties would be opposed to returning them at the end of their time.' As for greater leeway in the granting or renewal of dealers' licences, 'the Indian Merchant has already a very strong footing in the Colony' and his European rivals were 'determined that Natal shall be a white-man's colony and that they shall not be ousted by those who are incapable of governing the Colony and whose only object is to make money'. Since the Indians were said to be more loyal to India than to Natal, they could not be trusted with the vote either: 'The European Colonists intend to reserve the franchise, political and municipal, for those who will exercise it for the best interests of Natal.'[4]

Fourteen years of representative government had made the Natal colonists more truculent, more willing to disregard the Imperial interest and treat their coloured subjects as they pleased. Inspectors of the Natal Government would not renew Indian traders' licences, citing unsanitary conditions or unconventional book-keeping. These were the professed reasons; often, it was prejudice or fear of competition that lay behind the refusal.[5]

In the Cape, traditionally the most liberal of the South African provinces, feelings against Indians likewise hardened. When, in 1907, the councillors of Cape Town considered nine applications by Indian traders, they rejected seven outright, referring the other two for more information. The report of the meeting contained the forceful yet representative views of a councillor named Gibbs:

> 'Indians', said Mr Gibbs with great scorn, 'I want none of them – none of that nationality! I'm not in favour of these Indians coming here at all, and I would like to see as many of them as possible getting out of this country . . .
> I really think a good deal of the depression existing at this time is due to them. Why, they live on the smell of an oil-rag, and sleep on the butter! (laughter) I'll do everything possible in my power, whatever Council I'm on, to drive them out. Look at the Post Office returns, and you'll see that all their money gets sent out of the country.'[6]

Soon afterwards, the Cape Assembly constituted a committee to look into the question. The Indians who gave testimony complained about harassment by immigration officials, and insisted that their premises were clean and their accounts up-to-date. European merchants, on the other hand, complained that the Indians 'eat curry and rice without any spoons'. A trader named Philips said 'the Indians come here merely as blood suckers, it is a vulgar term, but true'. Claiming that many Europeans had to 'close their doors' because of competition, the committee concluded that 'it is impossible to view the extinction of the European storekeeper without the gravest fears for the future of the Colony'.[7]

Faced with renewed hostility to his compatriots, Gandhi characteristically did not give up hope. Perhaps if the Indians presented a better face they might be treated more kindly? In two striking articles in *Indian Opinion*, he asked shopkeepers in Natal to maintain proper accounts, keep their premises clean and dress well in order to make sure their licences were renewed. And he urged them not to spit, belch or break wind in public. 'It is sheer stupidity to believe that all these things will not prejudice the Europeans,' he wrote. 'While we live in this country, we should so behave that the whites' prejudices against us are weakened.'[8]

Gandhi also proposed that some Indians from Natal be sent to the United Kingdom to qualify for the Bar. His former assistant Joseph Royeppen was in London, qualifying at Lincoln's Inn. Royeppen had gone under his own steam; Gandhi's friend Pranjivan Mehta – now a prosperous jeweller in Burma – offered to fund another student to follow him. Gandhi's choice fell on Chhaganlal. 'You seem to be the only person who can be depended upon to carry forward the heritage of my thought and words,' he told his nephew. 'Our ultimate capital is not the money we have, but our courage, our faith, our truthfulness and our ability. If therefore you go to England, your intellect remains unspoiled and you return with your physical and mental powers strengthened, our capital will have appreciated to that extent.'[9]

Chhaganlal was the son of Gandhi's first cousin Khushalchand. He was a nephew once removed, yet far closer to him than this relationship might suggest. Twelve years younger than his mentor, he was devoted to Gandhi's example and his ideas. He had acquired his trust by the manner in which he supervised the composing, printing and distribution of *Indian Opinion*. In their father's absence he had to supervise the education of Gandhi's children as well. Gandhi's letters to Chhaganlal thus run seamlessly from matters of politics to the upbringing of his sons. A letter of 7 February 1907 says: 'I know that Manilal is weak in his arithmetic. Please give him adequate attention'; and further – 'Though

Harilal has agreed to stay [in South Africa], I find some uncertainty in what he writes. Therefore, I wrote to you to treat him in such a manner as to have a steadying influence on his mind.'[10] Soon afterwards, Chhaganlal had a child of his own, whereupon Gandhi instructed him on how best to raise *his* baby. He suggested that Chhagan invest in an English cradle, and make sure that the mother's bed was 'kept neat and tidy'. The father should do the cleaning himself, even though this particular form of labour was not consistent with his caste. In the rearing of the child, said Gandhi, 'please do not allow our old customs about untouchability, which are useless and wicked, to come in the way'.[11]

In the third week of February 1907 the white males of Transvaal voted to elect their first government. The party of the Boers, Het Volk, won a majority. General Louis Botha was sworn in as Prime Minister. Another former General, J. C. Smuts, was appointed Colonial Secretary.

Louis Botha was a quintessential Afrikaner – of farming stock, brought up on a large estate in wide open country in a family which read the Bible out loud several times a day. He had been a brave commander during the war, his resistance delaying the British victory by more than a year. Now, however, Botha 'stood for the magic cause of reconciliation between the [Boer and British] races'. The war had ravaged the economy of the Transvaal. To restore it to health the one-time rivals had to work together. Botha himself recognized that there was, after all, 'a great deal in common between the Boer and the English country gentleman – in their joy in country sports, their suspicion of change, their habit of command'.[12]

More than a love of hunting, what compelled Boer and Briton to now stand together was the need to deny people of colour the elementary rights of citizenship. One of the new Government's first acts was to have the Asiatic Ordinance of 1906 made into law. A bill embodying its provisions was introduced in the Transvaal Assembly on 20 March. It went through three readings in a single day, before being sent for approval to the Legislative Council. On the 22nd its passage was announced in the government gazette. Lord Selborne wrote to London urging that the King grant his assent as soon as possible. The 'illicit and unauthorized influx of Asiatics,' he claimed, was 'proceeding at an alarming rate'; the bill, which aimed to check this, represented 'the unanimous demand of all sections of the white community in the Transvaal.'[13]

On 29 March, the British Indian Association convened a meeting to protest the haste with which the bill was passed. More than a dozen people spoke, in at least four languages. Abdul Gani, Chairman of the BIA, said the bill showed that 'our legislators [are] the custodians of the whites alone'. Else 'how could the members become familiar in a night with a bill, which was admittedly very important and complicated?' Another merchant, Essop Mia, extended the charge of racial prejudice to the Governor, noting that 'Lord Selborne has been ill-disposed towards us from the outset. He has always regarded us all as coolies and no better than locusts.' A Hindu priest from Germiston, Ram Sundar Pandit, remarked that 'the mother gives her child milk, but a step-mother eats him up. The Government is like a step-mother.'

The meeting passed a resolution offering 'to submit to voluntary registration' in order to 'satisfy the Government and popular prejudice'. If this offer was rejected, the Indians requested 'full Imperial protection by reason of the fact that British Indians have no voice in the choice of the legislators, and represent a very small and weak minority.' Speaking last, Gandhi said the procedure of voluntary registration would 'be based on mutual understanding ... If gaol-going – which we have been contemplating – comes after this proposal, it will appear more graceful.'[14]

The Chinese of the Transvaal had joined the Indians in their protest. About 1,100 in all, they worked as merchants, gardeners and laundrymen. The new Act would bear down hard on them too. Their leader, Leung Quinn, decided to make common cause with Gandhi. Originally from Canton, Quinn was a partner in a firm of mineral-water manufacturers in Johannesburg. He had 'no intention of registering under any circumstances'. The Chinese Association wrote to the Transvaal Government that it endorsed the resolutions passed by the Indian meeting of 29 March. Thus, as the *Rand Daily Mail* observed, 'the Asiatic communities of the Transvaal are now as unanimously against the act, as perhaps, the white communities are in favour of it.'[15]

The protests were amplified in London, where L. W. Ritch was now based. Ritch sent the Colonial Office a series of letters detailing Indian handicaps in the Transvaal. He asked that Royal Assent to the new Ordinance be withheld.[16] A more pointed petition came from Joseph Royeppen, once a clerk in Gandhi's law office in Durban, now a Cambridge graduate and qualified lawyer himself. After a decade studying in the best colleges in England, Royeppen wished to return to South Africa and practise as a lawyer in the Transvaal. But, as he told Lord Elgin, while he was 'entitled to follow my calling anywhere in His Majesty's Dominions, I shall not be able to do so in a British Colony neighbouring my own home.' The liberties that he had enjoyed in England would be denied Royeppen in the country of his birth, ruled as it was by 'obnoxious restrictions emanating from unreasoning prejudice'.

It is likely that Gandhi put Royeppen up to this challenge; for his case highlighted the hypocrisies of the rulers like no other. Royeppen was a Christian, a Cambridge man, and a barrister of Lincoln's Inn. However, he was not white. If a man with his qualifications was debarred from entering the Transvaal, then 'Indians as a whole will have just reasons for losing much of their faith in the Briton's sense of justice in the colonies.'[17]

Back in the Transvaal, Gandhi asked for and was granted an appointment with the new Colonial Secretary, Jan Christian Smuts, a man who – in the decades to follow – was also to have a most profound impact on the history of the British Empire. Born a few months after Gandhi – on 24 May 1870 – Smuts was, unlike the Indian, 'an expert examination hurdler'. Of proud Boer stock (his family had been in South Africa since the 1690s), Smuts got a first-class in his matriculation, a double first in his BA (from Victoria College, Stellenbosch), and then another first in his Law Tripos at Cambridge.[18]

A lover of poetry (particularly that of Walt Whitman, on whom he wrote an unpublished book), and a keen student of philosophy and science (especially ecology and botany), Smuts returned to his homeland in 1895 and sought to enter public life. In an early speech at Kimberley, he argued that the Boers and the Britons had to close ranks, or else their position would 'become untenable in the face of that overwhelming majority of prolific barbarism'. However, the Jameson Raid made him suspicious of British intentions. In 1897 he shifted from Cape Town to the South African Republic, in an expression of solidarity with his fellow Boers. In June 1898 he was appointed State Attorney there. He became a protégé of President Kruger, their relationship akin to, and sometimes described as, that between father and son.

When war broke out Smuts went at once to the front. Put in charge of a unit of commandos, he led them in a series of marches, attacks and retreats. He gave his troops a sense of discipline and direction, thereby acquiring the rank of General. When hostilities ceased he played a key role in the Treaty of Vereeniging. His command of English, his education in England, his love of American poetry and his knowledge of European philosophy all made Smuts – in the eyes of his erstwhile enemies – an exception. An English friend wrote to him that 'you are the *only* Afrikander . . . who has the power of expressing on paper the sentiments, moral and political, of your people.' Smuts stood out, as 'for the most part the Afrikander people are still dumb, only able to express themselves in deeds.'[19]

Smuts's cosmopolitanism, however, did not cross the boundaries of race. The treaty as drafted by Lord Milner had a clause that read: 'The Franchise will not be given to Natives until after the introduction of self-government.' Smuts had this changed to: 'The question of granting the Franchise to Natives will not be decided until after the introduction of self-government.' The British hoped to delay the granting of citizenship rights to those who were not white; Smuts and company wanted to deny those rights for ever.

After the war Smuts built a successful practice at the Bar, and raised a brood of children. Then he re-entered politics, helping his neighbour and former Commander-in-Chief, Louis Botha, to form a party, known as Het Volk, representing the Afrikaner interest. When their party won the first elections by a whites-only franchise, Botha asked Smuts to serve as Colonial Secretary.

Like Botha, Smuts realized that Boer and Briton had to mend fences to keep out the (coloured) hordes. In August 1902, he wrote to a prominent British politician in the Cape that the 'only hope for the future is that the two parts of the [white] population will be sensible enough to work together on a common basis and leave alone the old rivalries and feuds'. At the end of the year, when Joseph Chamberlain came out to South Africa, Smuts wrote to him on behalf of the Transvaal Afrikaners that the new political arrangements must 'make it plain to the Natives that the war altered the relations between the two white races but not between the white and coloured population of the country'. A memorandum of September 1903, also written by Smuts, opposed the entry of Asians into the Transvaal. The Government, still run by British administrators, was warned of the example of Natal, where 'the Coolie and the Kaffir are gradually encroaching on ground which formerly belonged to whites, and in many of the towns and villages the Coolies are becoming a permanent, if not predominant factor.' It would 'be disastrous to the interests of the white population of South Africa', said Smuts, if Transvaal were to follow 'the desperate and ruinous example of Natal'.[20]

Now, with the passing of the Asiatic acts, Smuts came face to face with his fellow lawyer, fellow family man and fellow belletrist Mohandas K. Gandhi. On Thursday 4 April, 1907, Gandhi, along with five others (including Abdul Gani and H. O. Ally) set off from Johannesburg to Pretoria to meet Smuts. They boarded the 8.35 a.m. express train, normally reserved for whites, but here allowed to carry a few Indians courtesy of a one-time exemption granted by the General Manager of the South African Railways. At the meeting,

> Mr Gandhi narrated all the facts to Mr Smuts. He reminded Mr Smuts that the Indian community had itself registered several times. He . . . showed in other ways also that the Indians were trustworthy. It was with the help of the Indian community that officials of the Asiatic Office who took bribes had been arrested. Taking all this into consideration, Mr Gandhi said, the Government should, on this occasion, agree to the proposal of voluntary registration.

The others spoke in support of Gandhi's proposal. Smuts listened patiently, and after the Indians had been at it for close to an hour, said he had heard several things for the first time, and would make enquiries and send them a written reply. This, when it came some days later, was deeply disappointing. Smuts said that compulsory registration was required because of the 'strong evidence' of 'unlawful infiltration' of Asiatics into the Transvaal. He hoped the Indians 'would co-operate with the Government in every way by registering themselves lawfully, gracefully and expeditiously'. The BIA replied to Smuts, pointing out again 'that the new law gravely offends against [the community's] feelings', and urging once more that 'the Indian proposal be given a trial before the law is enforced.'[21]

This exchange of letters with Jan Smuts on questions of public policy was immediately followed by another exchange on family matters. In early April, Gandhi's brother Laxmidas had written to him with a long list of complaints. The letter is unavailable, but from Mohandas's reply one gets a clear sense of its contents. The brother in South Africa began by outlining the roots of their growing estrangement: 'I am afraid our outlooks differ widely and I see no possibility, for the present, of their being reconciled. You seek peace and happiness through money. I don't depend on money for my peace . . .'

Fifteen years after the palace break-in at Porbandar had destroyed his chances of preferment, Laxmidas remained a bitter and frustrated man. His desire for wealth and fame remained unfulfilled. Now, he chastised his younger brother for not caring enough about the family. Mohandas answered:

> I fail to understand what you mean by the word "family". To me, the family includes not only the two brothers but the sister as well. It also includes our cousins. Indeed, if I could say so without arrogance, I would say that my family comprises all living beings: the only difference being that those who are more dependent on me, because of blood relationship or other circumstances, get more help from me.

He then came to the question of money.

> As for your demand for a hundred rupees a month, I must say that I see neither the means at present nor the need of meeting it. I run the Phoenix Press with borrowed money. Moreover, I may have to go to gaol in the struggle against the new Ordinance. In that case I may become poorer still . . . If, however, the condition here improves during the next few months and I am free from trouble, I shall try to send you the money you have asked for by money order with the sole intention of pleasing you.

Gandhi accepted that, as brothers, 'you and Karsandas have [a right to] a share in my earnings'. He admitted that, by raising the money for him to study in London, Laxmidas had placed him in his debt. However, he pointed out that, while his legal education had cost Rs 13,000, he had since sent his brothers more than Rs 60,000 from South Africa (equivalent to perhaps £320,000 today). 'I do not consider that I have obliged [you] by doing this', he remarked. 'Even if nothing was done for me, whatever I have to do for my blood-brother I would do as a matter of duty.' Then he censoriously added, 'I must say with deep sorrow that, on account of your extravagant and thoughtless way of life, you have squandered a lot of money on pleasures and on pomp and show. You kept a horse and carriage, gave parties, and spent money on selfish

friends; and some money was spent in what I consider immoral ways'
(presumably on prostitutes or on a mistress).[22]

The Gandhi brothers had once been very close – it was Laxmidas
who had stood with Mohandas against their parochial fellow Banias
when he wished to go to England, and who then raised the money for
his fees and living expenses. But over the years they had drifted apart.
Proximity to hedonistic princes in Kathiawar had made Laxmidas less
inclined to follow the austere ways of his forebears. His brother, meanwhile, had taken Bania austerity to ever greater extremes in South
Africa – simplifying his diet, working with his hands, placing himself in
the service of his fellows. Hence the harsh, even savage, letter, in which
a once deferential younger brother chastises his elder for his wasteful-
ness and sinfulness.

The brother put in his place, Gandhi returned to the struggle in the
Transvaal. With the local and Imperial governments unyielding,
the pledge first made in the Empire Theatre in September 1906 would
be honoured. To recall Gandhi's words in that meeting, the time had
come for 'a heroic step to be taken'.

As a lawyer in Natal, Gandhi had sometimes saved clients – rebellious indentured labourers or Indians out at night without a pass – from
a prison sentence. He was the son and grandson of Diwans, among
whose responsibilities had been the management of prisons and prisoners. His forefathers had sent people to jail, whereas as a lawyer he
worked to keep them out. The voluntary courting of arrest was foreign
to his class and profession, as it was to the class and profession of the
people he now hoped to mobilize. Gandhi knew that merchants, whether
Gujarati or otherwise, were not the likeliest of volunteers for jail terms.
Back in September 1906, carried along by the popular mood in the
Empire Theatre, the traders had pledged to court arrest; now, several
months later, were they really prepared to abandon their shops, their
homes, their families, their businesses?

In an article for *Indian Opinion*, Gandhi clarified the future course of
action. Anyone charged or arrested for not taking out a permit would
be defended by him free of charge. In court, he would say that the client
had acted on his advice, in which case it was likely that 'Mr Gandhi will
be arrested and his client let off.' Even if protesters were prosecuted and
sent to jail, 'the chances are that they will soon be released and the law

amended suitably.' The wife and children of anyone in jail would be maintained by public subscription. 'There is no disgrace attached to going to gaol on this occasion,' said Gandhi. 'On the contrary, it will positively add to one's prestige.'[23]

Indian Opinion's leader for 11 May 1907 was headlined 'To the Gaol!' Now that the Asiatic Act had been sent for royal sanction, 'the goal for British Indians in Transvaal is the Transvaal gaol.' The previous September, they had pledged to court imprisonment if the ordinance became law, with their resolution 'flashed across the cable to the world. In the sight of God as well as man, they now stand pledged to the resolve, and by their deed they shall be judged by ever after.'[24]

This editorial, though unsigned, was probably written by Henry Polak. Through May and June, Gandhi published a series of articles under his own name, aimed at strengthening the resolve of the Indians. He quoted a poem by Narmadashanker on the achievements of Columbus, Napoleon, Martin Luther and Alexander. 'With such examples before them,' commented Gandhi, 'how can the Transvaal Indians lose heart even in the smallest degree?' Another essay invoked the Prophet Mohammed, who was in a cave with two disciples when a hostile army came by. The disciples were overcome by fear and terror, until the Prophet told them: 'We are not three. God, Who is a match for all, is also with us.' In the end the army passed the cave without even looking in. A third essay referred the reader to the ongoing protests in the Punjab against oppressive land policies. The leader of the movement, Lala Lajpat Rai, was an uncompromising opponent of Western colonialism. Gandhi admired the method without endorsing the end. The Transvaal Indians should 'show the same courage ourselves, but instead of desiring the end of British rule, let us aspire to be as able and spirited as the Colonists are, and demand and secure the rights we want'. A fourth essay rehearsed the struggles and sacrifices of Cromwell, Mazzini and George Washington, which showed 'that one must pass through suffering before tasting happiness. For [the] public good, men have to suffer hardships even to the point of death.'[25]

The exhortations had their effect. In late May, it was reported that Indians in the Transvaal 'are quietly and persistently making all arrangements for carrying out the historic gaol resolution'. *Indian Opinion* began printing the names of those who had pledged to court arrest. They included Hindus and Muslims, Tamils and Gujaratis.[26]

On 1 June, Gandhi wrote to the Prime Minister, General Botha, seeking an interview. The request was declined. The General and his Government were in no mood to compromise. They had received a reassuring letter from Lord Elgin, which said that since the bill represented 'the general will of the Colony, clearly expressed by its first elected representatives', he would advise the King not to disallow its passing.[27] Later that month the Royal Assent was received. The Act would come into force from 1 July, when Permit Offices would open in various towns, to allow Indians to register. In his 'Johannesburg Letter' of 29 June, Gandhi observed that 'The *Government Gazette* announces that Mr Chamney has been appointed Registrar under the new law. I hope the Indian community will see that he only sits and yawns. This correspondent's name will never be arrested in the register. It is my constant prayer to God that the same may be true of every Indian.'[28]

His overtures to the Government spurned, Gandhi was now in a combative mood. In a letter to the white-owned *Rand Daily Mail* he adopted an unusual, or at any rate untypical, tone of sarcasm. The Secretary of State had apparently stated that thumb and finger impressions were all the same; and that their intent was not to offend or degrade the Indians. 'Lord Elgin may certainly, sitting in his cushioned chair,' remarked Gandhi,

> see no distinction between making a mark with the thumb instead of a pen, but I know that he belongs to that nation which would rise in rebellion from end to end to resent an attack on personal liberty, and that he would be the first person to cry out against even a forcible tracing of his signature. It is the compulsion that stings, not the digit-impression . . . That in the mind of the Government there is no desire to degrade is true only on the assumption that my countrymen are already sufficiently degraded [not] to feel any further degradation in this land of freedom for people other than Asiatics.[29]

A week later, Gandhi wrote once more to the *Rand Daily Mail*, to correct the newspaper's claim that the passive resistance now being planned by the Indians was a 'new way' of protest. Gandhi clarified that

> picketing is by no means a new thing to the Indian mind. The network of castes in India simply illustrates the use and value of that weapon, provided it is rightly used. Ostracism and excommunication are the most powerful instruments resorted to today in India, in unfortunately trivial matters,

and, if the Registration Act now enables my countrymen to realize the use of that terrible weapon for a higher purpose, both Lord Elgin and the Transvaal Government will have deserved their gratitude.[30]

In writing this, Gandhi had in mind his own boycott at the hands of his fellow Modh Banias when, as a young man, he had chosen to study in London. On his return to India he had to dip into rivers and throw feasts to gain readmittance. His caste mates had boycotted him for a 'trivial' matter; whereas he and his fellows were now boycotting the Permit Offices for a decidedly higher purpose.

Pretoria was the first town designated for the registration of Indians. A white newspaper praised the Government's decision to issue permits district by district. If the Ordinance had been introduced simultaneously in the whole colony, 'there might have been a movement to ignore the Act upon something like the large scale hinted at by Mr Gandhi.' 'Pretoria is notoriously the weakest spot in the organisation of the Indians,' said the paper, 'and we do not think that the resistance movement there will make any headway.'[31]

The Permit Office was to open in Pretoria on 1 July. The previous day, 30 June, several hundred Indians met in the town's mosque. The meeting lasted for four hours. The mood was defiant. Gandhi spoke, but the star turn was an imam, Maulvi Mukhtiar, who 'created a sensation' by producing a letter from the South African Railways to the effect that Christian and Jewish ministers were allowed concessionary travel. The privilege was not extended to holy men of other faiths. 'This information added fuel to the fire and showed Indians that a death struggle underlay the Act.'[32]

The Permit Office opened the next morning as scheduled, but no certificates were issued. Encouraged by Gandhi, groups of Indians converged outside the office, 'courteously' persuading those who wished to go in to return home instead. The town was plastered by posters in Gujarati and English, reading: 'BOYCOTT, BOYCOTT PERMIT OFFICE! BY GOING TO GAOL WE DO NOT RESIST, BUT SUFFER FOR OUR COMMON GOOD AND SELF-RESPECT. LOYALTY TO THE KING DEMANDS LOYALTY TO THE KING OF KINGS [namely, God].' In its issue of 20 July, *Indian Opinion* reported with glee that the Permit Officer, a Mr Cody, had in effect enjoyed a fortnight's paid holiday.[33]

The reports of the protests in the Transvaal reached Natal. In an inspired show of support, the Durban Indians staged a play in eight acts to raise money for the struggle. In Act I, a Parsi gentleman, two Muslim merchants and several hawkers expressed their readiness to defy the law and court arrest. In Act II, the women were seen supporting them; in Act III, the Permit Office in Pretoria was shown, with its officials 'sitting yawning and smoking cigarettes'. In Act IV, native policemen came and arrested the resisters. In Act V, the Indians trooped into gaol in batches, 'greeted with loud cheers' by those already inside. In Act VI the prisoners were released by the Colonial Secretary and given fifteen days to register, to no avail, as the Permit Office was shown deserted once more.

Act VII presented, so to speak, a counterfactual alternative – a depiction of events as if the Indians had been so foolish or so weak as to have submitted to the Act. 'All the miserable details of finger-impressions and the giving of names were gone through in the presence of the registration staff, an interpreter and the Kaffir police. Cries of "shame!" greeted this realistic performance.'

The final act, an anti-climax perhaps, showed an Indian charged in court with having a false permit, actually a legal document with some trifling defect, for which he was sent to jail.

After the performance, Parsee Rustomjee came on stage and thanked the actors. A sum of £50 was raised for the passive resisters.[34]

The play was staged in the Indian Theatre on Victoria Street on 13 July. A week later Gandhi visited Durban himself. Speaking to the Natal Indian Congress, he observed with some pride that in India, 'the Government succeeds by setting the two cats – Hindus and Muslims – against each other. Here it is not so. Both the communities are united, hence our courage will bear fruit.' He asked his friends in Natal to 'join us in our sufferings ... When all Indians in the Transvaal are prepared to suffer any loss in the struggle, you should not lag behind in giving monetary help.'[35]

As the end of July approached, the rumour gained ground that the Government would begin arresting the resisters. To those worried by the prospect, Gandhi offered this spine-stiffening advice:

I recommend that, on and from August 1, no Indian whatever should carry any money with him and certainly not gold in any case. Temptation is a very bad thing. Not being used to the idea of gaol, on hearing the sentence of fine, the accused may find his hands unconsciously straying into his pocket or he may cast an imploring glance at his friends. When this happens, he should mentally ask for God's forgiveness, remove his hand [from his pocket], stand erect and, clearing his throat, declare that he will not pay the fine but go to gaol.[36]

On the evening of 24 July, Gandhi was in Pretoria for work. He was met at the train station by a group of merchants, who told him that one of their fellows, named Khamisa, had broken ranks and decided to register. He was coercing his customers to do likewise. Gandhi and his companions went at once to Khamisa's shop, where they ran into a detective. Sharp words were exchanged, the policeman telling the lawyer, 'you know the law, do what is proper'. They were told to leave the premises at once. That same night, at Khamisa's shop, some twenty men registered, and thus 'blackened their hands and faces, and brought a slur on the good name of the Indian community'. Gandhi termed it a 'ghastly betrayal'; the culprits knew they were doing a 'shameful thing', which is why they had taken out permits secretly, at midnight.[37]

Meanwhile, a betrayal of another kind had been committed by Gandhi's colleague H. O. Ally. He had written to Justice Ameer Ali in London, insinuating that the struggle in the Transvaal was motivated by the interests of Hindu hawkers rather than Muslim merchants. The Justice was an important member of the South Africa British Indian Committee. 'We take it as a disgrace to the Indian community that Mr Ally should have penned such words,' wrote Gandhi. 'The Transvaal struggle affects Hindus and Muslims alike.'[38]

To mark a month of continuous protest, some 2,000 Indians met in the grounds of the Pretoria Mosque on 31 July. A special train was chartered to ferry protesters from Johannesburg. Others came from the smaller towns of the colony. A reporter from the *Pretoria News* found the scene one of 'intense interest'; 'in the background, the Mosque with its deep verandahs, its suggestion of solemn worship', and 'in the grounds outside, the great concourse of Indians of all castes and religions, very much in earnest'. Their leader, Mohandas Gandhi, was described as a 'learned Doctor of Laws, scholar and philosopher, to whom the Municipality of Pretoria deny the right to use the footpath, and who may not occupy a seat in the Municipal trams.'

The meeting passed three resolutions. The first chastised the Indians

1 and 2. The home in Porbandar where Mohandas Gandhi was born.

3. The school in Rajkot, where Mohandas Gandhi did not distinguish himself as a student.

4 and 5. Mohandas's parents,
Karamchand (Kaba) Gandhi
(*above*) and Putlibai (*right*).

6. A photograph of the young Mohandas, in traditional Kathiawari dress.

7. Gandhi's preceptor,
the Jain scholar
Raychandbhai.

8. The successful lawyer in Durban, *c.* 1898

9. Kasturba Gandhi and children, *c.* 1899. The infant in her arms is Ramdas, the boy on the stool Manilal, the one to the right Harilal. The eldest of the boys in the picture, on the left, is Gandhi's sister's son Gokuldas. The Gandhis' youngest son, Devadas, was born the following year.

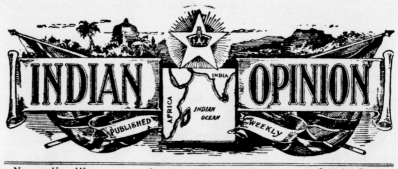

INDIAN OPINION

PUBLISHED — WEEKLY

No. 23—Vol. IX   SATURDAY, JUNE 10th, 1911.   *Registered as a Newspaper*
PRICE THREEPENCE

TRANSVAAL DRAFT MUNICIPAL ORDINANCE

BRITISH INDIAN ASSOCIATION'S PETITION

MR. A. M. Cachalia, Chairman of the Transvaal British Indian Association, has forwarded the following Petition to the Honourable, the Administrator and the Members of the Provincial Council of the Transvaal :—

The Petition of A. M. Cachalia, in his capacity as Chairman of the British Indian Association,

HUMBLY SHEWETH THAT :

1. Your Petitioner has read the Draft Local Government Ordinance 1911, published in the Government *Gazette* of the 17th May, and observes with grave misgivings that several of its clauses threaten the lawfully resident British Indians with further serious disabilities.

2. Your Petitioner remarks that Sections 66 and 67 of the Ordinance empower the Council "to set apart, maintain and carry on bazaars or other areas exclusively for occupation by Asiatics, and control same in accordance with bye-laws to be made from time to time by the Council, and that by sub-section (3) of Section 66 the Council may (subject to the approval and consent of the Governor-General) close such "bazaar" after posting up a notice of their intention to do so, in a conspicuous place. As to this, your Petitioner would observe that, apart from the general question of segregation to which, on principle, your Petitioner takes exception, the powers conferred are capable of being employed most detrimentally to British Indians, especially those of the shop-keeping class who may establish themselves in such bazaars. The expansion of the towns has been followed almost invariably by the closing of the "bazaar" previously established and the consequent removal of its occupants to another bazaar located still further away from the town centres and routes. This uncertainty of tenure militates against business enterprise and prosperity, and constitutes a grave hardship to the British Indians who take up their abode and callings in such "bazaar."

3. Section 75 (12), (13) and (14) and Section 88 (6) especially touch Asiatic interests. Councils will, under these sections continue to control eating houses, butcher's, Asiatic- and Kaffir-eating-houses, pedlar's, hawker's, laundrymen's and laundry licences ; and your Petitioner observes that, while provision is made for appeal to a Resident Magistrate against the refusal of Councils to grant other business licences referred to in the measure, Section 91 expressly provides that "no appeal shall lie against the refusal of the Council to grant any of the above licences." The experiences of British Indians in other Provices of the Union where similar uncontrolled power is or was invested in licensing boards or Councils prompts your Petitioner to protest most earnestly against the express exclusion of the right of appeal against arbitrary refusals to a properly constituted judicial tribunal, apart from the fact that such a provision constitutes an infringement of the liberty of the subject.

4. Your Petitioner further draws the attention of this Honourable House to the fact that there is now no occasion to provide for licensing Asiatic tea-rooms or eating-houses as none such have existed after the withdrawal of the Chinese indentured labourers. The wants of the small Asiatic community residing in this Province are supplied by private boarding houses.

5. Section 92 may, by penalising the employment of Asiatic labour, work serious hardship upon British Indians employed in useful industries, and in some cases may result in the deprivation of their means of livelihood. In the humble opinion of your Petitioner, the discrimination against Asiatics expressed in this Section should be deleted.

6. Your Petitioner further submits that the discretion vested in the Council in regard to the granting or withholding of drivers' licences (Section 93) should be subject to a right of appeal to a judicial tribunal.

7. While your Petitioner's community, bowing to the unhappy prejudice against Asiatics existing in this Province, have not sought the political franchise, they feel keenly the specific disability imposed upon their people by section 114, whereby they are precluded from being placed upon the Municipal Voters' roll, a disability shared by them with such white persons only as have been convicted of serious criminal offences.

Your Petitioner would venture to remind this Honourable House that the Indians are large contributors of municipal rates, and as statistics abundantly prove, are among the most law-abiding sections of the population, and, therefore, ventures to except to their being classed with white convicts.

8. Your Petitioner observes that, Section 171 (b) empowers the prohibition or restriction of the use of tram-cars by "Natives, Asiatics and all persons who are not respectably dressed or well conducted. This restriction is at once humiliating and inconvenient for the Asiatic communities, and, in your Petitioner's humble opinion, totally unwarranted.

9. In conclusion, your Petitioner earnestly calls the attention of this Honourable House to the grievances above indicated, and prays that the Draft Ordinance will be amended so as to grant relief in the premises. And for this act of justice and mercy your Petitioner shall, as in duty bound, for ever pray.

Dated at Johannesburg, this 5th day of June, 1911.

10. A front page of *Indian Opinion*, the journal Gandhi founded in 1903. Note the map on the masthead, linking the motherland to the diaspora. The petition that this issue reproduces, although sent in the name of A. M. Cachalia, was almost certainly written by Gandhi.

11 and 12. Gandhi's closest advisers: the Jewish radical Henry Polak (*left*), and the Gujarati patriot Pranjivan Mehta (*below*).

13 and 14. Gandhi's most devoted assistants: his secretary Sonja Schlesin (*left*), and his fellow Tolstoyan Hermann Kallenbach (*below*).

who had applied for certificates of registration. The second congratulated those who had refused to succumb. The third urged the Government to accept, even now, the offer of voluntary registration. Afterwards, the liberal white politician William Hosken spoke. Originally from Cornwall, a Methodist by faith, Hosken had migrated to the Transvaal to work as a manager in the mines. He was a friend of Gandhi and sympathethic to the Indians, frequently lobbying for them in the Johannesburg Town Council and the Transvaal Assembly. But now he urged the protesters to recognize that there was, as he termed it, 'a dead wall of opposition against them'. He considered the new law 'inevitable', and saw no difference between voluntary and compulsory registration. Hosken called the decision to defy the law a 'mistake', and hoped they would recant. He recognized the spirit behind their opposition – that they did it to retain their dignity as free men, because they believed it to be their duty. But, said Hosken, 'he considered it even a greater call of duty to submit to the inevitable.'

Hosken's speech was translated by Gandhi, who then added some comments of his own. He 'thought and felt most deeply that neither Mr Hosken nor any member of a Western race . . . was capable of understanding what an Eastern mind understood by the inevitable'. Himself 'one of the most peaceable men in South Africa', Gandhi had 'not embark[ed] upon this crusade without mature thought and deliberation'. The Act was 'most despicable', and had to be opposed. For the policy of passive resistance now in place, the lawyer 'personally took full responsibility'. The man from the *Pretoria News* thought Gandhi's gloss had the effect of 'cleverly discounting and weakening the effect which [Hosken's speech] might have had on the less resolute brethren.'[39]

On 8 August, Gandhi wrote to Smuts's secretary disputing the Government's contention that he alone was 'responsible for the agitation against the Asiatic Law Amendment Act'. If the imputation meant 'that my countrymen do not resent the Act at all but that I unnecessarily inflame them,' he remarked, 'I venture to repudiate it altogether. On the other hand, if it means that I have voiced their sentiments and that I have endeavoured, to the best of my ability, to place before them accurately what the Law means, I beg to accept the entire responsibility.' After this combative opening, Gandhi softened his tone, saying, 'I am as anxious to serve the Government as I am to serve my countrymen and I feel that the question is one of very serious and Imperial importance.'

He suggested an amendment to the Act, making registration voluntary, exempting children under sixteen years of age from registering and deleting the clause asking that the certificate be produced whenever required. This would meet the requirements of the Government while removing the stigma attached to the law in the eyes of the Indians. Smuts, however, rejected the compromise; he and his Government were determined to 'carry out in full the provisions of the Asiatic Law Amendment Act and if the resistance of the Indians residing in this country leads to results which they do not seriously face at present, they will have only themselves and their leaders to blame.'[40]

The struggle continued. In Pietersburg, where the Permit Office had now moved, Indian sources claimed the boycott was 100 per cent successful. Even the white papers admitted that fewer than 10 out of 200 residents had registered.[41] The high rate of success may have been influenced by the fact that *Indian Opinion* had printed the names of the renegades in Pretoria who had 'applied for the title-deed of slavery'. The terrible weapon of communal ostracism had also brought poor H. O. Ally to his knees. In the second week of August he sent a statement to the press clarifying that he supported passive resistance in the Transvaal. At the same time, he announced that he was shifting back to Cape Town. *Indian Opinion* commented that the harm done by his earlier letter had been 'partly undone'; it asked Ally to 'render patriotic service' and 'infuse vigour' into community organizations in the Cape.[42]

The conflict was now escalating. In August 1907, the *Star* of Johannesburg wrote of Gandhi that 'he has certainly marshalled his forces well, and the Indians as a rule are prepared to follow him to the extreme.' The lawyer was 'now the recognised leader of the Indian community in South Africa'. He had 'an attractive personality,' said the *Star*, 'and infuses his utterances with that dynamic force that carries conviction. In conversation he has a forcible manner. His eyes brighten with enthusiasm when discussing the subjects uppermost in his mind, and one cannot wonder at the hold he has over the Indians.'[43]

Back in 1895, a reporter in Natal had stressed the stammer in Gandhi's speech, his slow, hesitant delivery when making submissions in court. The next year Gandhi was too shy to read out a text before an audience in Bombay. Now, a decade later, he had clearly matured as a public speaker. His voice was still soft, but the conviction (and courage) it carried was manifest both to dogged follower and to impartial observer. The lawyer had become a leader, indeed, the *recognized* leader of the Indian community in South Africa.

The Transvaal Government had now introduced a new bill, making it mandatory for immigrants or returning residents to fill in a form in a European language. Yiddish was classified as a European language under the Act, whereas Indian languages of greater antiquity and literary sophistication (such as Tamil) were excluded. The insult was compounded by the company the Indians were being made to keep. For the bill had specified various categories of 'prohibited immigrants', which included prostitutes, indigents, lunatics, lepers, spies and convicted criminals.[44]

The *Rand Daily Mail* had claimed that the Asiatics were 'unanimously' against the Act, and the whites just as unanimously in favour of it. There were, in fact, some exceptions – Indians who secretly signed on for permits; Europeans who openly crossed racial boundaries and identified with the protesters. Hermann Kallenbach sent a letter to the *Star* deploring the depiction of men 'who are unselfishly and strenuously' working for their compatriots as 'aggressive agitators'. 'I shall consider it a privilege to visit my Indian friends in gaol,' said Kallenbach, 'and to do my utmost to reduce the hardships of prison life which they are prepared to undergo.'[45]

Similar letters were sent to the press by other white sympathizers, among them a jeweller named Isaac and a draper named Vogl (both also Jewish). But the European who most explicitly identified with the Indians was Henry Polak. Polak published a series of sharp and occasionally savage essays in *Indian Opinion*. One article made fun of the paranoia in the white press about the leader of the passive resisters:

> That remarkable man Mr Gandhi will go down to posterity as a miracle-worker. In the first place, he is supposed to be the *fons et origo* of the opposition to the Law; then he is supposed to have actively incited every Indian in the Transvaal not to obey its provisions; and, lastly, he is supposed to be here, there, and everywhere at the same time urging a policy of non-submission.

These remarks were prompted by reports in one paper that Gandhi had addressed a meeting in Pietersburg; in another paper that he had done the same in Potchefstroom. In fact he had been in neither place recently. 'What feeble creatures Indians are supposed to be!', commented Polak. 'They must always have their nurse with them before they can be trusted to trot along alone.' No one from Johannesburg visited Pietersburg when the Permit Office was opened, nor would anyone go to Potchefstroom or Klerksdorp when the Office shifted there, for 'the local Indians don't require any pin-pricks to make them jump.'[46]

Polak was prophetic. The Permit Office moved on, and the Indians moved away. In early September he wrote mockingly of how 'that ramshackle machine, the Government "perambulator", is still squeaking from town to town, unoiled for lack of registration.' Two weeks later he wrote that 'the "perambulator" is at last to find a resting place for a whole month at a time, after which, no doubt, it will be relegated to the Pretoria Museum, to be kept there until the next Asiatic invasion arrives.' When the Permit Office did reopen, as planned, in Johannesburg, 'the tobacconists of this town shall rejoice greatly at the prospects of all the cigarettes that will be smoked' as the Registration Officials 'while away the weary hours waiting for the unregenerate to reform'.[47]

Some of Polak's pieces were signed, others unsigned. Yet others used the nom de plume 'A. Chessell Piquet'.[48] An essay under this name presented a series of satirical 'silhouettes' of how whites saw the conflict. For the 'Small White Storekeeper' the new law was 'a splendid thing', keeping the coolies in their place. The 'European Wholesale Merchant' thought both the Government and Indians were fools. (Complaining that he hadn't had an order from an Indian merchant for months, he said he would meet Smuts and 'ask him to administer the Law mildly'.) The 'Consumer' admitted the Indians charged far less than the white shopkeepers who lived in style, with 'their plate-glass and stained ceilings'. As for the 'Registration Official', while pleased that 'accommodation up country is much better than it was three or four years ago', he complained that the Indians were 'absolutely misled by their leaders'. He could not bear anyone to mention 'G[andhi]', whose name made him 'quite nervous'. There was, finally, the 'Common-Sense Individual', who thought the passive resistance movement 'splendid', and the 'only way to make an impression on these colour-blind fanatics.'[49]

Henry Polak may have been exceeded in energy and commitment by Gandhi, and by some other Indian passive resisters. But no one *enjoyed* the struggle as much as he did, the joy – and the passion – expressed in the stream of polemics and satires that poured out from his pen.

In September 1907 the name of Henry David Thoreau appeared in the columns of *Indian Opinion* for the first time. Gandhi had only recently become acquainted with his tract on civil disobedience. The jail-going resolution of 11 September 1906 had been invented on the spot; in later weeks and months, Gandhi sought precedents in Indian traditions of boycott and protest. Then he began using the term 'passive resistance', whose origins lay rather in the boycott by Nonconformists of schools that indoctrinated their pupils in the teachings of the Church of England. Now, a full year after the technique of protest was first proposed, the teachings of an American radical were invoked to support it. In Gandhi's paraphrase, Thoreau said that 'we should be men before we are subjects, and that there is no obligation imposed upon us by our conscience to give blind submission to any law, no matter what force or majority backs it.' The American's 'example and writings,' thought Gandhi, 'are at present exactly applicable to the Indians in the Transvaal.'

This was unexceptionable. But Gandhi also wrote that 'historians say that the chief cause of the abolition of slavery in America was Thoreau's imprisonment and the publication by him of the above-mentioned book [*On the Duty of Civil Disobedience*] after his release.' No historians were named, perhaps because they could not be. That Thoreau's tract helped end slavery was, of course, outrageous hyperbole. Was Gandhi writing out of ignorance, or did the claim need to be made to boost his people's morale?[50]

The answer, very likely, is the latter. In a letter written many years later, Henry Polak disputed, as I have here, the view that Gandhi derived his ideas from Thoreau's tract on civil disobedience. Passive resistance had been going on for some time in South Africa before Gandhi became acquainted with the American thinker. However, once he read Thoreau, Gandhi seized upon his ideas as proof of the power of his own approach. In this sense, noted Polak, what Thoreau provided Gandhi with was 'encouragement, not inspiration'.[51]

As passive resistance in the Transvaal gathered momentum, Gandhi was engaged in an intense exchange of letters with a Christian priest who wished to become his disciple. Of German extraction, John Cordes had once been a missionary in Rhodesia. At some stage he acquired and divorced (or abandoned) an African wife. His readings and journeys had turned him away from conventional Christianity and towards Theosophy, the hybrid, occultist religion then gathering a rush of new converts across the world.

Cordes contacted Gandhi in early 1907. He felt constrained by the company of his fellow whites, and thought a spell with Indians in general, and this Indian in particular, would free him more fully from the prejudices of his upbringing. He had heard of Gandhi's work from mutual friends, and had also been reading *Indian Opinion*. He wanted now to cut himself loose, to 'throw the race goggles on the dust heap, to better enjoy the mountain air of freedom from social trammels and acquire a sight fitted for wider truths'.[52]

In Johannesburg, immersed in the protests against the Asiatic Act, Gandhi could not supervise Cordes directly. So he suggested the priest move to Phoenix, where he would be part of a living community. The settlement was now in its third year. It had eight homes, built of corrugated iron supported by wooden planks. Each had two small bedrooms, a living-and-dining room, a kitchen and a bathroom. The fittings in the last were ingenious: with water dripping down from the roof into a watering can, held up by a rope, which served as a shower. The more adventurous could bathe in the stream running through the property. Drinking water came from the heavens; rainwater being collected and stored for future use.

Each house had a vegetable plot attached to it; some settlers maintained these energetically, while others left them to the elements. There were no domesticated animals; no cows and sheep, nor any dogs (but plenty of snakes and jackals). The nearest shops were in Durban, fourteen miles away. During the day the press hummed with activity, compositors setting type and working it through the machines. After dusk, the only noises one heard were the chirping of birds; the only lights one saw flickered in Zulu homes in the valley.[53]

In the first week of July 1907, John Cordes took a train from Rhodesia to Natal. He told his new mentor (whom he had not yet met) that he 'had no breakfast, managing my pursestrings on strictly Gandhian lines'. Within a few days of his arrival at Phoenix he was exulting in the surroundings. 'What a blessing it is,' he told Gandhi, 'to get away from town & its noise & smell, how pleasant to be rid of cuffs & collars, braces and the trappings of towns' war-paint. The wind is nothing, being the mere equinoctial night & morning breeze, to which I am accustomed from Bulawayo.'

Cordes was equally impressed by the human material at Phoenix. 'Dev[a]das will make a splendid lawyer,' he told the (mostly) absent father, 'fancy him cross questioning his elder brother Ramdas the way he does. Manilal will not bless many visitors like me I reckon, he had to work like a horse, & did so like a Trojan, betw[een] his lessons, & his composting job.'[54] Gandhi, in reply, shifted the conversation from his sons to his wife. 'How were you received by Mrs. Gandhi?' he asked Cordes. 'She tells me she feels too shy to sit at the same table with you . . . [S]he is terrified ever having to attend to a guest who is a perfect stranger, and, what is more, wearing a white skin . . . What changes you may have wrought in her mental condition after presenting yourself and your credentials I do not know.'[55]

Gandhi approved of Cordes's desire to 'reach the ladies through the kiddies. I have no doubt that you will succeed. It is the best point of attack.' He was keen to have the visitor's opinion about a community he had founded but could rarely be part of. 'I want to know everything about you and your view of the surroundings,' said Gandhi. 'Are you in tune with them?'[56]

Manilal and Ramdas reported to Gandhi how Cordes was getting along. They told him the priest was doing odd jobs in and around the house. Gandhi wrote to Cordes approvingly; he had, it seems, 'won Mrs. Gandhi entirely to your side. She now says you can remain with her for as long as you like.' To make himself even more at home, Cordes should learn Gujarati, so that 'you may understand the people around you and for whom you are working'.[57]

By October, Cordes was well settled at Phoenix, with a plot of land to call his own, and a modest house under construction. 'Mrs. Gandhi tells me that your palace is visibly growing,' wrote Gandhi in encouragement. 'I only hope that it will be perfectly satisfactory when it is finished, that is to say simple, artistic, hygienic, rain-proof, rat-proof, and a temple of peace.'[58]

These letters between a Christ-loving Hindu and a Hindu-loving Christian escaped the attention of the editors of the *Collected Works*, for they lay in a private home in the town of Haifa, in Israel, a country with which India had no diplomatic relations for decades. The correspondence provides a fascinating window into Gandhi's gift for friendship and his penchant for attracting disciples. Six months after John Cordes moved to Phoenix, he received a letter from Henry Polak agreeing that

> it is very difficult to develop a spirit such as that which moves Mr Gandhi. You are perfectly right in calling it a privilege to be invited to assist him in the task that he has set before himself, and it is in that light that I have always regarded the matter. Whilst I have the ordinary human sympathy for the people down there being kept up all hours of the day and night towards the end of the week [when *Indian Opinion* went to press], I will admit to you quite frankly and privately that I think that no one at Phoenix should raise his voice against it, even though it means death to him. I consider this is a splendid cause to die for, if it is not possible to live for it. The difficulty is, as always, to develop the faculties of imagination and sympathy. It is rarely that his purpose so possessed a man as to make him forget his own comfort, his own health, his own interests, and the happiness of those who serve him. I am more and more coming round to the Ibsen idea that truth must be sought at any cost, and to realise day by day more vividly that, in the words of Dr. Staubman, the greatest man is he who stands most alone. All this, of course, is for your private consumption.[59]

These remarks beautifully capture the ideals and eccentricities of the Gujarati lawyer whom these two Europeans now acknowledged as their mentor and master.

12

To Jail

On 1 October 1907, the Permit Office – which *Indian Opinion* had taken to calling the 'Plague Office' – opened in Johannesburg, which was the Transvaal's largest and richest city and had the largest (and richest) concentration of Indians as well. The fate of the Asiatic Law Amendment Act would be determined by what happened here. Gandhi warned picketers against any intimidation or violence. 'A watchman's duty is to watch, not to assault . . . Our whole struggle is based on our submitting ourselves to hardships, not inflicting them on anyone else, be he an Indian or European.'[1]

A meeting of Indians was held every Sunday in the premises of the Hamidia Islamic Society, in the Johannesburg district of Pageview. When Gandhi was in town, he was always the main speaker. Prominent Gujarati merchants such as Essop Mia and Abdul Gani often spoke. The Tamils were represented by Thambi Naidoo, the carrier who was rapidly emerging as a leading activist in the struggle. To show that the movement was not racist, Henry Polak sometimes added his voice to the chorus. The leader of the Chinese Association, Leung Quinn, was an occasional guest speaker.

Speeches were also being made elsewhere, and by other people. In the first week of October, Jan Smuts told his constituents that the Indians were 'detrimental to the everlasting prosperity of South Africa'. Smuts claimed that their frugal ways were a cause of the current economic depression. He charged that certificates of residence were bought and sold not just in Johannesburg, but also in Durban and as far afield as Bombay. 'I have no quarrel with the Indians,' said Smuts: 'the object is not persecution, but a stoppage of the influx of Indians. We have made up our mind to make this a white man's country, and, however difficult the task before us is in this matter, we have put our foot down, and shall keep it there.' His remarks were greeted with 'loud applause'.[2]

Meanwhile, a white-owned newspaper warned Indians not to listen to Gandhi, a 'mischief-monger' who, after the current conflict was over, would 'pick up his briefcase and go elsewhere'. The warning was disregarded. The picketing in Johannesburg was largely successful. The tactics of Gandhi's own newspaper certainly helped here, for it now published two lists each week, one of new subscribers, the other of Indians who had taken out permits – lists of loyalists and traitors respectively. Among the traitors was a certain S. Haloo, who went to Gandhi's office to explain why he had applied for a permit. Some militants wrote to the lawyer saying that if he entertained this blackleg again, he too would be boycotted. Gandhi endorsed the threat – he wanted, he said, 'all Indians to have the same burning enthusiasm always'.[3]

Through September and October, a petition against the Act, drafted by Gandhi, was circulated among the towns and villages of the Transvaal, and 4,522 signatures were obtained. The document was then posted to General Smuts, along with a breakdown of signatories by religious and provincial affiliations – namely, Surtis (1,476), Konkanis (141), Memons (140), Gujarati Hindus (1,600), Madrassis (991), Northerners (157) and Parsis (17). Of perhaps 8,000 Indians resident in the Transvaal, only about 350 had applied for permits. Ninety-five per cent of these came from a single community, the Memons, a cautious, conservative caste of traders and merchants.[4]

The petition was evidence of Gandhi's wish to show the depth of his support, and a last attempt to get Smuts to withdraw the Ordinance. He was not, it seems, absolutely certain the 'burning enthusiasm' of the Indians would translate itself into courting arrest. For his part, Smuts extended the deadline for Indians to register for a month, from 31 October to 30 November. The two lawyers, placed on opposite sides, each hoped the other would blink first. Gandhi thought the weight of numbers carried by the petition would convince Smuts to repeal the Act. Smuts hoped the passage of time would lead the Indians to reconsider their opposition.[5]

A very large proportion of Indians in the Transvaal were now solidly behind Gandhi. There was a surge in subscriptions to *Indian Opinion* – now up to 3,000, more than twice as many as when the passive resistance movement started.[6] An Indian in Europe was less impressed with Gandhi's movement; this was his former friend and sparring partner, Shyamaji Krishnavarma. In the summer of 1907, Krishnavarma had fled London – after charges were brought against him for preaching disaffection against the Empire – to the relative safety of Paris. From there he followed, with interest and increasing dismay, the progress of the passive resistance movement in the Transvaal.

Krishnavarma's hatred for the British Empire compelled him to make common cause with the Boers. Like the Indians in India, he argued, they were a beleaguered community, fighting for freedom. Recalling Gandhi's support for the British during the war of 1899–1902, he asked, 'What right have the Indians to claim good treatment from the people whom they once injured both morally and politically out of selfish motives?' Under 'such provoking circumstances', he thought the Boers would 'be justified in expelling from the Transvaal, nay extirpating every Indian who had any claim in depriving them of their national political individuality'.

He prefaced his broadside by speaking of Gandhi as 'an amiable person', whose 'gentility and suavity of manner endear him to all with whom he comes in contact'. Despite his 'personal regard' for the lawyer, the radical felt obliged to expose 'him for the mischief he is doing by his public acts and utterances to the cause of political freedom'. It is not clear whether Gandhi read this article, which was published in an émigré journal printed in Paris.[7]

The British Indian Association now had a new chairman – Essop Mia, who had replaced Abdul Gani. On 4 November, Mia posted a letter (written, naturally, by Gandhi) to the President of the Indian National Congress. The annual session of the Congress was to meet the next month in the Gujarati port town of Surat. Mia/Gandhi urged that their struggle be 'in the forefront of the subjects to be dealt with by the Congress'. For, in opposing the Asiatic Ordinance in the Transvaal, they regarded themselves as 'the representatives, in this country, of our Motherland, and it is impossible for us, as patriotic Indians, to keep silence under an insult that is levied against our race and our national honour.'

This was heartfelt, and also true. But then Mia/Gandhi went on to make a larger claim.

We hold that our movement of passive resistance merits the approval of all religious men, of all true patriots, of all men of commonsense and integrity. It is a movement so potent as to compel the respect of our adversaries by virtue of our very non-resistance, of our willingness to suffer; and we are the more firm in our determination to offer this opposition, because we consider that our example, on a small scale in this Colony, whether successful or unsuccessful, may well be adopted by every oppressed people [and] by every oppressed individual, as being a more reliable and more honourable instrument for securing the redress of wrongs than any which has heretofore been adopted.[8]

'A more reliable and more honourable method of fighting injustice *than any which has heretofore been adopted*.' This was a daring, even reckless claim. Not a single Indian had yet courted arrest in the Transvaal. On the other hand, Indians in several provinces (Bombay, Bengal, Madras, Punjab) had been jailed during the Swadeshi movement. Gandhi had attended a solitary Congress (in Calcutta in 1901), giving one of the minor speeches. But here he was, telling Gokhale, Tilak and other nationalist stalwarts that, among a small group of expatriates in South Africa, he had forged a patriotic spirit that equalled theirs, and invented a political technique that they would do well to emulate.

In the second week of November 1907, the case of the first Indian to be prosecuted under the Asiatic Law came up in court. This pioneering offender was a Hindu priest based in Germiston, a railway town some ten miles from Johannesburg. Named Ram Sundar, he was born and raised in the holy city of Banaras, where he learnt Sanskrit, and in time became a priest (and hence acquired the title 'Pandit'). He migrated to Natal in about 1898, married a local Indian girl, and they had two children. In 1905 he moved to the Transvaal to take charge of a temple run by a Hindu trust, the Sanatana Dharma Sabha.

Ram Sundar stayed in Germiston on a temporary permit, which was extended two months at a time. On 30 September 1907 his request for renewal was refused. Asked to leave the colony, the priest said he would not obey the order, 'as he had to remain [in Germiston] to perform his religious duties, there being no one to take his place, and he was quite prepared to suffer the consequences of his disobedience'.

October was the grace period granted by Smuts to the Indians. At the beginning of the next month, the Government decided to act. The recalcitrant Ram Sundar was its first target. On 8 November he was placed under arrest. One of his first visitors in Germiston jail was Henry Polak. As a token of support for Ram Sundar, Indian stores throughout the Transvaal were closed for a day. Indian hawkers went off the roads, and Indian newspaper boys did not do their rounds.

On the 11th, the priest was produced in court, and Gandhi had him released on bail. As he came out of the building, Ram Sundar was received by a shower of flowers. A congratulatory meeting was then convened in the premises of the Sanatana Dharma Sabha. It was chaired by a Muslim priest, Moulvi Saheb Ahmed Mukhtiar, who said it was the duty of holy men of all faiths 'to take the lead in such times of difficulty'. The Tamil activist Thambi Naidoo added 'that the fight would become more exciting only when Punditji went to gaol'.

Ram Sundar's case came up for hearing on 14 November. The first witness for the defence was a Muslim, Imam Abdul Kadir. Prodded by Gandhi, he said that 'the whole of the [Indian] community – both Hindus and Mahomedans – felt very bitterly about the prosecution of the accused.' The next witness was a Hindu from Germiston, Lala Bahadur Singh. He said the Pandit 'had preached against the Asiatic Act purely on religious grounds, because it was against their religious scruples'. The priest observed in his own testimony that their religion prohibited their giving their wives' names, and he objected to giving impressions of his ten fingers.

The courtroom was packed, with a mixed audience of Indians and Europeans (some 300 others were turned away at the door). They heard Gandhi subject Montford Chamney to an intense cross-examination. The Protector of Asiatics said that he had received complaints from white and coloured people that the Pandit was inciting people against the Government. Addressing the court, Gandhi insisted his client was arrested not because he did not hold a permit but 'because he had dared to hold strong views about the Asiatic Act and had not hesitated to place them before his countrymen.' If 'that was a crime,' Gandhi went on, 'then the majority of Indians were guilty equally with the accused'. At this stage, the magistrate, C. C. Gillfillian, interjected to express the 'hope that Mr Gandhi would not burden the records with too much evidence'.

Summing up, the magistrate congratulated Gandhi on his 'very able' handling of the case. He himself felt a 'great deal of sympathy' with 'persons who had to suffer from acts performed from a purely religious point of view'. However, he had to administer the law as it stood. It was not for him to judge whether it was right or wrong. As an act of leniency (or compassion), he would inflict the 'minimum punishment' possible, which in this case was one month's imprisonment without hard labour. This magnanimous speech from the Bench added to the lustre around Ram Sundar. As he left the court, the priest shook hands individually with all present. When he came outside, escorted by policemen, 'he was greeted with loud cheers by the Indians who had assembled.'[9]

Gandhi was greatly encouraged by the cross-class and cross-religious support for Ram Sundar Pandit. A week after the priest was consigned to jail, three delegates left Transvaal to attend the forthcoming Surat session of the Indian National Congress. They were carrying, among other things, a letter from Gandhi to his mentor, Gopal Krishna Gokhale. This stated that

> the struggle we are undergoing here has resulted in making us feel that we are Indians first and Hindus, Mahomedans, Tamils, Parsees, etc. afterwards. You will notice, too, that all our delegates are Mahomedans. I am person-ally proud of the fact . . . May I ask you to interest yourself in them and make them feel perfectly at home? A Hindu–Mahomedan compact may even become a special feature of the Congress.[10]

Once more, a lowly lawyer in South Africa was lecturing his more exalted compatriots in India. Gandhi had already told Gokhale about the worldwide relevance of a small passive resistance movement then still unfolding; now he was suggesting that the religious harmony forged in the diaspora might serve as a model for the overcoming of sectarian differences at home.

With the protests continuing, General Smuts wrote to the Transvaal Governor, Lord Selborne, complaining that 'the Indians, headed by the lawyer Gandhi and certain other agitators, seem to think any conces-sion made to be a symptom of weakness.'[11] The Governor now asked two liberal-minded whites, William Hosken and a Justice of the Peace named David Pollock, to try and reconcile the warring parties. Gandhi once more suggested that the Government withdraw the Act and allow Indians to voluntarily take out certificates of domicile, which would contain 'full identification particulars'. The issue of fingerprints could be left in abeyance, but Gandhi insisted that Montford Chamney be replaced, since he 'is entirely incompetent for the office he holds, in having no legal ability to sift evidence'. Pollock and Hosken took this proposal back to Smuts, who met it with a 'blunt refusal'.[12]

On Sunday 24 November, some 2,000 Indians converged on the Fordsburg Mosque to discuss their future course of action. 'There were men everywhere, on the verandah of the mosque, its terrace and roof.' A dozen men spoke, but the star turn was Gandhi. He claimed that a growing number of whites sympathized with their cause; in any case, their 'petition no longer lay with an earthly ruler; it was to be addressed to the Creator'. Answering questions about what to do when they were arrested, Gandhi said that if asked to provide fingerprints in prison, they should give them. 'This was a struggle for freedom from slavery, not against digit-impressions.' In case Gandhi himself was jailed, then 'Mr Polak would be able to attend to all work, such as sending telegrams, etc.'[13]

In the last week of November, the Governor, Lord Selborne, had a further meeting with whites seeking to mediate between the State and the Indians. A Congregational minister named Charles Phillips told Lord Selborne that 'the coloured people and the educated natives are watching this struggle closely, and that for the first time they recognise that they have an instrument in their hands – that is, combination and passive resistance – of which they had not previously thought.' Selborne himself believed that Africans were incapable of 'combination and organized action'. He worried however that the 'manufacture of martyrs' by the jailing of Indian protesters had undermined the credibility of the Government.

Selborne now wrote to Smuts asking whether it was not possible to 'build a bridge' to the Indians. Perhaps the General could allow them to register voluntarily. Smuts wrote back saying that while he was prepared to meet Gandhi and company in a 'friendly spirit', among his colleagues there was a 'strong popular feeling' against any concessions to them.[14]

Writing to a Cape politician, Smuts admitted that 'the Indian question is a very difficult one here – under the influence of their leaders they have made a very successful resistance to the finger-print registration.' If the protests continued, the Government would be 'forced to resort to drastic steps such as the deportation of the leaders'.[15]

With the Government unyielding, the protests continued. On Sunday, 1 December, another large meeting was held in Fordsburg Mosque. All those present, wrote a reporter on the spot, 'regarded themselves, Hindoos and Mohammedans alike, as attending a religious ceremony'. They 'were all prepared to go to gaol, and even to close their stores'.[16]

Watching these developments from Phoenix was John Cordes. Reading Gandhi in *Indian Opinion*, and reading about the struggle in the white-owned press, prompted him to write a letter of admiration and support. The letter is lost, but we can guess its contents from the answer it elicited. 'You talk of my generalship', wrote Gandhi to Cordes:

> This shows how little you understand me. I do not think that there is any generalship in me at all, but, if my action has been hitherto serviceable to the Indian cause, it simply means to that extent a triumph of truth. My faith in God and truth (two convertible terms) is almost invincible, and if appropriate things come from my pen on appropriate occasions, you may take it that I am not to be credited.[17]

The resolve of the Indians had, by now, impressed some Europeans less in thrall to Gandhi himself. In late November, an article in praise of the resisters appeared in a newspaper published in the Afrikaner stronghold of Bloemfontein. Compulsory registration, it said, had led to 'suffering to the Asiatic community of a kind and to an extent which we are certain the governing race never intended. It is a martyrdom that the Asiatics are now undergoing. No other word would be exact, because their suffering is voluntary, and marks their refusal to comply with what they consider a degrading law.' The paper urged a 'reasonable compromise' on both parties, namely, a return to the offer of voluntary registration that the British Indians had originally made. To continue enforcing the Ordinance as it stood would 'drive the self-respecting class of Indians out of the colony [through deportation] and retain only the moral rabble [i.e., those who register] within it. A law which ... expels the best and keeps the worst stands self-condemned.'[18]

Two weeks later, the *Transvaal Leader* printed a long letter from David Pollock. As of 1 December, noted Pollock, 95 per cent of all Indians in the colony were unregistered, and hence liable to arrest and possible deportation. This was now 'not merely a question of local economics', but 'a matter of grave Imperial concern'. For, said this open-minded white, 'we cannot send thousands of agitators (and agitators for conscience sake, remember!) to complicate still further the problem with which the Government of India is struggling' (namely, the growing movement against colonial rule within India itself). Pollock urged the Government to 'scorn the petty role of persecution', repeal the Asiatic Act and issue certificates of domicile to all lawfully resident Asiatics. It was time, he said, to recognize that a mistake had been made, and to set it right.[19]

On 9 December, Gandhi appeared in court in the town of Volksrust, close to the Transvaal–Natal border. He was defending thirty-seven Indians who had deliberately entered the province without valid permits. Of the protesters only four were Muslims, the others being Hindu. This revealed an interesting lopsidedness, which may have had several causes – among them the example of the Hindu priest Ram Sundar and the charisma of the Hindu lawyer Gandhi; and, on the other side, the reluctance of many Muslim merchants actually to test their commitment by courting arrest.

On 13 December, Ram Sundar Pandit was discharged from prison. He was 'enthusiastically received with garlands and bouquets'. As advised by Gandhi, the priest now wrote to General Smuts that although he had been ordered to leave the colony in seven days, he would stay on to serve his flock in Germiston.[20]

Two weeks later, arrest warrants were issued against twenty-three resisters in the Transvaal. They included Gandhi, Thambi Naidoo (described as 'chief picket, Johannesburg'), the Chinese leader Leung Quinn and Ram Sundar Pandit. Five Muslim merchants also came forward to court arrest. However, the most surprising name was that of C. M. Pillay. Sometime during the course of the year and the struggle, this Tamil rival of Gandhi had become reconciled to his leadership.

Gandhi heard of the arrest warrant against him on the morning of 27 December. The Police Commissioner told him that he was at liberty for twenty-four hours, but had to appear in court the next day. The same evening, a meeting was hurriedly convened in the Hamidia Hall. Here Gandhi termed the legislation under which he faced imprisonment as 'the savage Act of a . . . Government that dares to call itself Christian. If Jesus Christ came to Johannesburg and Pretoria and examined the hearts of General Botha, General Smuts and the others, he thought he would notice something strange, something quite strange to the Christian spirit.'[21]

Back in 1894, on visiting a Trappist monastery in highland Natal, Gandhi had said 'a religion appears divine or devilish, according as its professors choose to make it appear.' In later years he had sometimes lectured Natal colonists on how their acts or actions departed from the spirit of Christ. His remarks here were in character: Gandhi asked Hindus and Muslims as much as Christians to recall the nobler values and practices of their own moral or religious tradition. Had they read these remarks, however, Generals Botha and Smuts would scarcely have appreciated them. Not even the most broad-minded Afrikaner would abide being preached to by a Hindu lawyer with a brown skin.

The case of M. K. Gandhi versus the Transvaal Government came up for hearing in Johannesburg's B Court on the morning of 28 December 1907. Many friends of the accused were present, mostly Indians but also Henry Polak. When Gandhi asked to make a statement, the judge, H. H. Jordan, refused permission, saying, 'I don't want any political speeches made.' Gandhi said he 'simply asked the indulgence of the Court for five minutes'. The judge answered, 'I don't think this is a case in which the Court should grant any indulgence. You have defied the law.' He then gave his order, which was that if Gandhi did not leave the colony within seven days, he would be sentenced to a month in prison for not possessing a valid permit. If he stayed on in the colony for more than a week after *that* sentence expired, he would be sentenced next time to six months in prison. The newspaper report on the case continues:

> Mr Gandhi, interrupting the Magistrate, asked him to make the order for 48 hours. If they could get it shorter even than that, they would be more satisfied.
>
> MR JORDAN: If that is the case, I should be the last person in the world to disappoint you. Leave the Colony within 48 hours is my order.

Immediately after he was sentenced, Gandhi defended the others accused of violating the law. C. M. Pillay, asked why he did not register, said he believed 'that any self-respecting man would not comply with the provisions of the Act, as it simply places our liberty in the hands of the Registrar of Asiatics who, in my humble opinion, is not [a] fit and proper person to hold this post'. This irritated the magistrate, who said 'he would not listen to nonsense of this kind. He thought it was a piece of gross impertinence for a person to come there and abuse an official of the Government in that way.' Gandhi agreed that the remarks were improper, and then asked Pillay: 'Do you object to the officer or the Act?' to get the answer he wanted, namely, 'Mainly to the Act.'

Thambi Naidoo, for his part, told the judge that he 'objected to registration as it placed him lower than a Kaffir, and it was against his religion.' Then it was the turn of two Chinese resisters to speak. One, a Mr Easton, said 'he was not permitted by his religion – Taoism – to give any impressions'; the other, Leung Quinn, said 'he did not take out a permit because it was a law disgraceful to himself and his nation.'

The judge, in sentencing the accused to prison, said they

> had deliberately defied the Government and had taken up a very serious position – one which he was sorry to see any resident in this country adopt. It had been a mistake, he had no doubt, which had been copied from the [Nonconformist] passive resisters at Home in connection with the Education Bill, and that was an attitude which had never appealed to him in any shape at all. The laws of a country must be complied with by the people resident there, and if they could not do that, there was but one alternative – such people must go somewhere else.[22]

One of the accused had in fact already decided to go somewhere else. On the 27th, Ram Sundar Pandit was present in Gandhi's chambers when the Police Commissioner's notice came. He promised to attend court the next day, but when he reached Germiston that evening, he 'called one or two of his disciples and told them that he was thinking of running away, since he could not face a second term of imprisonment. His disciples expostulated with him but he was overcome with fear.' On the morning of the 28th, the Pandit picked up his belongings and took a train to Natal. Gandhi dryly commented that Ram Sundar's fall

> was as sudden as his rise. I have written at great length about him in this paper. All this has turned out to be mistaken. The poems about him have been meaningless. A bad coin will always remain a bad coin. This is a struggle such as will expose everyone in his true colours. So far as the community is concerned, Ram Sundar is dead henceforth. We are to forget him.[23]

Meanwhile, as news of Gandhi's own conviction spread, messages of support began pouring into the offices of the British Indian Association. They came from (among other places) Durban, Pietermaritzburg, the Cape, Bombay and Madras. 'Mr Gandhi will not leave [the Transvaal]', ran one news headline in Natal, continuing, 'Widespread Sympathy'.[24]

The day that Gandhi was tried and convicted, the year's last issue of *Indian Opinion* was printed in Durban. Copies reached Johannesburg by the evening. Readers would have noticed a call urging them to send in Indian equivalents for the terms 'passive resistance' and 'civil disobedience', which had been coined by British Nonconformists and an American writer respectively. Gandhi wanted indigenous replacements, since 'to respect our own language, speak it well and use in it as few foreign words as possible – this is also a part of patriotism.' The prize for the best entry was ten copies of a booklet on the Asiatic Act, which the winner could circulate among his friends.

On 28 December Gandhi had been ordered to leave the colony within forty-eight hours. A week passed, but the summons did not come, perhaps because magistrates and policemen alike were occupied with the New Year's festivities. Telegrams protesting the charges were flying thick and fast between the three continents with which the accused had connections. The British Indian Association in Transvaal wired the South Africa British India Committee in London that the impending arrest of Gandhi and his colleagues placed an 'undue strain [on] Indian loyalty'. The Government of India in Calcutta wired the Imperial Government in London that a meeting of more than 7,000 Gujaratis in Surat had asked the Viceroy to intervene in having the charges against Gandhi and company dropped, and the Act itself withdrawn.[25]

On New Year's Day, 1908, a Baptist minister named Joseph J. Doke walked into Gandhi's chambers at the corner of Anderson and Rissik Street. From a family of Cornish tin miners, Doke had followed his father into the ministry. As a young man he travelled extensively through India, concluding from his experiences of Banaras, Calcutta and Bombay, and Hindus, Muslims and Parsis, that the land was a 'perfect mixture of opposites: I don't understand it.' In later years, he served as a minister in Devon and in New Zealand, before moving to a church in Grahamstown, in the Cape, in 1903. In November 1907, he took charge of the Central Baptist Church in Johannesburg.

Gandhi's campaign appealed to Doke because of its obvious reson-
ances with the passive resistance of his fellow Baptists against the
Education Act in England, which discriminated against children (and
families) who were not of the dominant Anglican faith. That this Hindu
lawyer regularly and approvingly quoted Christ was an added point in
his favour. Doke, writes his biographer, was distressed by the fact that
'the leaders of Christian thought and energy on the Rand were either
apathetic or antagonistic' to Indian aspirations. He, on the other hand,
could not remain 'untouched and indifferent to the cry of a people
where a question of conscience, even religion, was involved'.[26]

When he walked into Gandhi's chambers on New Year's Day, Doke
found a crowd of Indians already there. Later, he sketched the scene
from memory: men in turbans, standing; women in saris, squatting,
some with children in their arms. In the ante-room a flaxen-haired
woman could be seen taking down a client's particulars.[27] This was
Gandhi's young secretary, Sonja Schlesin, a Lithuanian Jew who had
arrived in Johannesburg via Moscow and Cape Town. Hermann Kallenbach had recommended her to Gandhi, who became greatly dependent
on her shorthand and typing skills.[28] By his own admission, Gandhi
knew 'very few whose writing is worse than mine';[29] it fell now to Miss
Schlesin to decipher his drafts and render them in legible English.

Doke went past the secretary's room into the lawyer's office, which, he
found, was 'meagrely furnished and dusty'. As for the man himself, the
minister had expected to find 'a tall and stately figure, and a bold, masterful
face, in harmony with the influence he seemed to exert in Johannesburg.'
To his surprise, Gandhi turned out to be 'small, lithe, spare', with a dark
skin and dark eyes. His hair was black, with a sprinkling of grey.

Seeing the white minister enter, the Indians who were already there
silently left the room. Doke immediately asked Gandhi a direct question: 'How far are you prepared to make a martyr of yourself for the
good of the cause?' and received an equally direct answer: 'It is a matter
with me of complete surrender . . . I am willing to die at any time, or to
do anything for the cause.'[30]

Gandhi met the Reverend Joseph Doke on the morning of 1 January
1908; the same afternoon, he participated in a meeting held in the
Fordsburg Mosque. He spoke for himself, but also for his secretary,
Sonja Schlesin, who had written a speech but was too shy to read it

herself. Gandhi, stepping in, conveyed the European lady's advice that the Indians should 'continue steadfast in your heroic resolve to give up all, aye life itself, for the noble cause of country and religion'. She, and he, reminded them of the struggle of suffragettes in England, who, 'for the sake of a principle', had 'to brave innumerable trials', including imprisonment.[31]

On 3 January, Gandhi defended two passive resisters in court. They were former soldiers of the Indian Army, both Pathans, who had seen action and suffered wounds in the Anglo–Boer War. These facts their lawyer successfully impressed on the magistrate sentencing them. A few days later, Gandhi told the *Star* newspaper that Indians were actually worse off now than under the Boer regime. In another interview, with the *Transvaal Leader*, he complained that Smuts had referred to Indians as 'coolies'. So long as the General 'holds British Indians so cheap and denies them the full status of British subjects', he insisted, 'so long must Indians rest content with imprisonment or deportation'. However, he was still open to a compromise, telling a correspondent from Reuters that if the Act was suspended, he would undertake that every Indian in Transvaal would register himself within a month, 'in accordance with a form to be mutually agreed upon'.[32]

Composing that week's 'Johannesburg Letter' for *Indian Opinion*, Gandhi noted that of the several suggestions for an Indian equivalent to 'passive resistance', one was described as 'not bad'. This was *sadagraha*, which roughly translated as 'firmness in a good cause'. The suggestion came from Maganlal Gandhi. His uncle, and leader, took the liberty of refining it further, to *satyagraha*, or the 'force of truth in a good cause'. 'Though the phrase does not exhaust the connotations of the word "passive"', remarked Gandhi, 'we shall use *satyagraha* till a word is available which deserves the prize.'[33]

On 10 January, this particular passive resister – or *satyagrahi* – was called to appear before a judge for not complying with the sentence to leave the colony. Gandhi reached the court by 10 a.m., with many supporters in tow. The hearing had however been postponed to the afternoon. The Indians then repaired to the Fordsburg Mosque, where, in an impromptu meeting, their leader told them to refute Smuts's claim that 'the whole of this agitation depended upon a few Indians.' If they now demonstrated to the General that 'the majority of Indians were not going to accept the Act, but would rather suffer imprisonment and degradation, [and] forfeiture of all their goods', then Smuts would come to appreciate their qualities and himself say, 'these are the people whom I shall prize as fellow-citizens'.

After lunch, the accused and his associates proceeded to court. It had begun to rain, so an admirer held an umbrella for Gandhi to walk under. A rush of Indians entered the courtroom, before the police barred the rest. Inside, Gandhi pleaded guilty to the charge of disobeying the order to leave the Colony within forty-eight hours. He asked for the 'heaviest penalty' under the law, which was six months in prison with hard labour and a fine of £500. The judge, the same H. H. Jordan, declined to meet his request, instead sentencing him to two months without hard labour.[34]

Gandhi was taken to the Fort Prison, sited on Hospital Hill, a great mound of earth overlooking the cricket and rugby grounds known as 'The Wanderers'. Built in the 1890s, the prison had separate quarters for whites and natives. As an Indian, Gandhi could not be placed with the former, so he had perforce to be put in with the latter. As a free man, he had lived pretty austerely. Although his forefathers had served kings, his own homes were modest. Even so, his new place of residence must have seemed confining, a narrow, dark, 'native block' that contained some seventy-two prisoners.[35]

The arrest of Gandhi, and the course of the passive resistance movement in the Transvaal generally, attracted attention in the neighbouring colony of Natal. Militant whites thought Natal should emulate Transvaal by framing laws 'that will force the Asiatic to leave with disgust'.[36] Less short-sighted whites were not so sanguine; a 'perplexing inter-Colonial situation' might develop should, as some suspected, General Smuts attempt to push the offenders out of the Transvaal. The 'deportation of recalcitrants' would result in an 'unseemly state of things upon the Natal border'. As the *Natal Mercury* put it, 'in this Colony we have our own Asiatic problem, and we do not wish it to be aggravated by the conversion of Natal into a dumping ground for the people of whom the Transvaal wants to rid itself.'

Natal was smaller in size than the Transvaal, yet already had ten times as many Asians. Besides, unlike the Boers, the British had a sentimental and imperial connection to India. The growing movement for national independence there worried them. These fears underlay the somewhat critical coverage given by the *Mercury* to the speeches of

General Smuts. It warned that his tactics of intimidation would only make martyrs of Gandhi and his colleagues, and 'produce quite unforeseen results, both here and in India.'[37]

The Natal Indians, for their part, threw their numbers and their funds behind the passive resistance movement. Hindu and Muslim merchants competed with one another to offer support for the wives and children of those sent to prison in the Transvaal. The ever-generous Parsee Rustomjee pledged to 'stake every penny I had in the world to free South African Indians from the degradation of the Asiatic Act'. Pietermaritzburg alone contributed £3,700 to a fund for the resisters.[38]

The day after Gandhi was incarcerated, a large meeting was convened by the Natal Indian Congress, held in the market adjoining the mosque off West Street in Durban. Here Parsee Rustomjee said the arrests would further test India's loyalty to the Empire, already under strain due to food scarcity and the drain of wealth to England. A second speaker, Hassim Jooma, was reported as saying that all

> Mr Gandhi asked was that no odious class legislation be inflicted indiscriminately upon high and low, educated and illiterate, bonafide pre-war residents and unauthorised entrants into the country. Their blood boiled when they remembered that the Indian ex-soldiers, who, after the war, had made the Transvaal their home, had been given rigorous imprisonment . . . although they fought for the land on behalf of Britain, suffered all the horrors of war, sustained physical wounds and indescribable misery, and now, after the conquest, they were not allowed a peaceful residence in the very land they fought to acquire.

A third speaker, a Dr Nanji, said that there was no need to pity Gandhi, for by his sacrifice 'he had made a name for himself and was known all over the world. But it was Mrs. Gandhi who was grieving over her loss, and they must sympathise with her (Applause).'[39] The meeting sent a collective telegram to Phoenix offering 'their sincere sympathy to Mrs. Gandhi and family during their trouble for the splendid self-sacrifice made by Mr Gandhi in the Indian cause. May India produce many more Gandhis.' This was one of forty-eight telegrams received by Kasturba in the first day after Gandhi's arrest, in which (as *Indian Opinion* reported) 'the prevailing tone was one of congratulation rather than commiseration.'[40]

That the whites of Natal would be ambivalent about the struggle in the Transvaal, and that the Indians of the colony would be supportive, was to be expected. More surprising was the endorsement of Gandhi's movement by the African educator John L. Dube. Writing anonymously in his newspaper *Ilanga lase Natal*, Dube praised 'the courageous manner in which the Indians are acting in the Transvaal.' 'It is common for the Bantu to admire "pluck",' said the reformer, 'especially when the plucky contender has a fair claim for justice.' He sagaciously added that 'slaves never yet made a nation or an Empire; meanness and hopelessness of life are the factors that weaken the Empire, no matter how strong it may have been at first.' In Dube's view, the conflict in the Transvaal was 'the outcome of vanity and inability to guide the differing influences into their respective and proper channels'.[41]

The assessment was wise, and the sentiments uncommonly generous. Dube's own Inanda settlement lay in close proximity to Gandhi's Phoenix Farm. This, and his own big-heartedness, may have led him to forgive or forget the Indians' characteristic tendency to distinguish their cause from that of the 'Kaffirs', whom they thought less civilized than themselves.

13

A Tolstoyan in Johannesburg

In going to jail for a political principle, Gandhi chose to follow people he had previously praised in the pages of *Indian Opinion* – such as the Indian nationalist Bal Gangadhar Tilak, the American radical Henry David Thoreau, the Russian pacifists and the British suffragettes. Even so, the experience was novel for the London-trained barrister, a venture into the unfamiliar, and the unknown.

When, on 10 January 1908, Gandhi reached Johannesburg's Fort Prison, he was undressed and weighed, and his fingerprints were taken. He was given a set of prison clothes, consisting of trousers, shirt, jumper, cap, socks and sandals. Then, since it was already evening, he was sent off to his cell with 8 ounces of bread for his evening meal. The cell was labelled 'For Coloured Debtors', and Gandhi had to share it with a dozen others. They slept on wooden planks, with 'an apology for a pillow'. The meals were dominated by what was known locally as 'mealie pap', a porridge made of maize, which he found difficult to digest. When he protested (in writing), he was given an extra helping of vegetables.

The next morning, the prisoners were taken to a small yard, where they could walk about. The latrines and bathing area were also located here. Gandhi was relieved to see that the cells were washed and disinfected daily. However, with no combs or towels to hand, he worried that he might get scabies. He got permission to call in a barber and have his moustache shaved, and also his head.

At half-past five in the evening the prisoners were taken back to their cells. There was a single light bulb, by which one could read until eight, when this too was switched off. On 14 January, Gandhi was happy to welcome into jail his friends Thambi Naidoo and Leung Quinn, president of the Chinese Association. During the course of the week more passive resisters joined them. They included Tamils, Gujarati Hindus and Muslims. They had now been permitted to receive rice rations, and to prepare their own meals. Thambi Naidoo took charge of the cooking, while Gandhi supervised the serving and washing-up. They found the jail staff quite helpful, except for a stern warder who was nicknamed, inevitably, 'General Smuts'.

The prison authorities had agreed to place a table in Gandhi's cell, and to provide pens and an ink-pot. Gandhi alternated between reading and writing. He had brought the Bhagavad-Gita with him, as well as some books by or about Tolstoy, Socrates and Ruskin. From the prison library he borrowed the works of Thomas Carlyle and a copy of the Bible, whose contents he discussed with a Chinese prisoner.

As more Indians came pouring in, the warders were compelled to erect tents in the yard. Gandhi, out of solidarity, joined his compatriots in sleeping in the open, but worried that their habit of spitting everywhere would lead to the place becoming dirty and infected. Another complaint was directed at the authorities – whereas the prison had a chapel for the Christian inmates, why did they not allow Hindu priests or Muslim imams to visit their co-religionists?[1]

The day after Gandhi's arrest, many Indian stores in Natal and the Transvaal closed in honour of their leader. The lawyer's European friends were also speaking out in support of his movement. Addressing his congregation on 12 January, the Reverend Joseph Doke called Gandhi's campaign 'a heroic struggle for conscience's sake'. He marvelled that 'a little handful of Indians and Chinese should have so imbibed the teaching of Christ in regard to the inherent nobility of man that they should become teachers of a mercenary age, while Christians stand by and smile or are silent as they suffer'. Two days later, Henry Polak told a crowded and enthusiastic meeting of the Chinese residents of Johannesburg that 'the 15,000 Asiatics in the Transvaal were fighting a race fight which was of the utmost importance for the whole world, and that struggle was whether the Asiatic peoples were eternally to be kept in subjection or treated on terms of equality, regarded as fellow-men, as fellow human beings, to be treated as men to men, and not as men to slaves.'[2]

Doke and Polak stressed the principle, while Hermann Kallenbach, just as characteristically, spoke of the personality. Protesting the 'insinuating remarks' in the press attributing 'material and dishonourable motives' to Gandhi's conduct, the architect said that he had not met 'a more conscientious, more honourable or better man'. For 'if Mr Gandhi, after the most thorough test and self-investigation, considers the course to be adopted by him to be the right one, he will not be hindered by any results, however disastrous they may be to himself from a material point of view, or, as we have seen now, from the point of view of his personal freedom.' Kallenbach appealed to his 'fellow-colonists not to be unjust to a man whose motives are of the highest, and who has proved this to us by action'.[3]

Doke, Polak and Kallenbach were all friends of Gandhi. More striking was the support that came from the other side of the colour bar, from Africans whom Gandhi did not know at all. In an article entitled 'A Lesson in True Manliness', the *Basutoland Star* marvelled that the Transvaal Government, 'known all over the world as being very harsh and inconsiderate in its treatment of all persons of colour', was 'almost driven to climb down from its high pedestal by the exhibition of manly qualities by the Indians'. The paper approved of the movement's ends and, as crucially, of the means. 'Man has two ways of resenting or resisting', said the *Basutoland Star*:

> The one is by active resistance, and the other is by passive resistance. The former is not commendable, as it leads to bloodshed, which should be avoided, and the latter is commendable, as it avoids bloodshed and usually ends in a bloodless and amicable settlement of the point at issue. It is the latter mode of resistance, which the Asiatics have adopted, which we commend our people the natives of South Africa to emulate. Gandhi and his compatriots are truly martyrs, and, come what may, true martyrs have before today never suffered in vain ... Our sympathies go out to our oppressed fellow-subjects, who are made to suffer for the same cause that we suffer – viz., our slight pigment of the skin. Truly, the Transvaal has tarnished the fair name of our mighty Empire by its blind colour prejudice.[4]

This statement of solidarity is made more remarkable by the fact that it was unprompted, unsolicited and – so far as we can tell – unrequited.

In the third week of January, Gandhi was visited by Albert Cartwright, editor of the *Transvaal Leader*, a liberal-minded Englishman who had experienced terms of imprisonment himself (for opposing the way the

war against the Boers had been conducted). Cartwright was in touch
with Smuts about a negotiated settlement between the Government and
the Indians. The General was now worried about the pressure on the
jails. As he told a meeting of whites, he had 'sent every leader to prison,
and hundreds more, and it had had no impression.' There were not
enough jails to house all the Indians in the Transvaal. To 'take 10,000 men
by the collar' and put them in prison was 'not only physically but morally impossible'.[5]

Pressure was also being exerted on the Colonial Office by the India
Office, who had been alerted by the Viceroy of 'the existence of a very
strong and bitter sentiment amongst the educated and articulate sections of the native community throughout India on the subject of the
disabilities imposed on their countrymen resident in South Africa.'[6] The
Viceroy had been forwarded an anguished, breathless telegram received
by the Anglican Church in India, which read:

> Barrister merchants traders hawkers agents clerks interpreters government
> officials colonial born married South African children born here [all]
> arrested . . . many families left mercy community some merchants twenty
> years standing including greybeards others gaoled include youths tender
> years 2 old soldiers bearing medals several campaigns also leaders ambu-
> lance corps boer war stretcher corps Natal rebellion . . . [7]

With his ambivalent feelings about British imperialists, Smuts might not
have been swayed by these protests had they not been endorsed by his
old friend, the Cape liberal J. X. Merriman. The treatment of educated
Asiatics like Gandhi, said Merriman to Smuts, 'savour[ed] of the yellow
cap of the Jew, or the harrying of the Moriscoes of Spain'. He urged
Smuts to follow the principle: *Parcere subjectis et debellare superbos* (to
spare the humble and subdue the proud).[8]

Gandhi was likewise amenable to a compromise. Before starting the
satyagraha he had worked hard to avoid it. He was now prepared once
more to try the path of dialogue and reconciliation. The resisters were
all first-time satyagrahis, and doubtless keen to get out of jail as early as
possible.

Cartwright and Gandhi had two meetings, after which the editor
drafted a document wherein the resisters offered voluntary registration
in exchange for the dropping of cases, the release of prisoners, the rein-
statement of Government employees who had become satyagrahis, and

a discussion about the repeal of the Asiatic act. The paper was signed by Gandhi, Thambi Naidoo (on behalf of the Tamils) and Leung Quinn (representing the Chinese).[9]

On 30 January, Gandhi was taken by a posse of policemen to meet Smuts in Pretoria. They discussed the terms of the compromise, with Smuts asking that those Indians who had been loyal to the Government not be harassed. Later, Gandhi wrote to a friend that he and the General

> met as though we had been old chums. He spoke most familiarly and allowed me to do likewise. He began by saying that he had no ill-feeling against me or the Asiatics, that his best friends were Indians at the time he was studying for the Bar, and that he wanted to give every assistance . . . He then said that I should see that the Indians did not crow over their victory and that demonstration was avoided. This was, of course, in our interests, because the Law was yet to be repealed, which he has promised to do, and the repeal of the Law will cost him a great deal of anxiety and trouble . . . [He] came to the door to receive me and we shook hands. There was heartiness on his part in the handshake.[10]

That same evening Gandhi was released. A reporter who met him at Johannesburg station said he 'seemed keenly pleased that a settlement had been come to by which neither side had suffered in honour, integrity or prestige'.[11] The next day, the other passive resisters (about 220 in all) were also set at liberty. Those freed went at once to Gandhi's law chambers. The first to arrive was an ex-soldier named Nawab Khan, 'conspicuous in the uniform of the Bengal Lancers'. Gandhi came soon afterwards, riding a bicycle. A large crowd of Indians had assembled to greet the satyagrahis. A reporter on the spot noted that

> a certain amount of mutual gratification seemed to be going on, but the perfect orderliness which has marked the agitation was maintained . . . [I]n deference to Mr Gandhi's understood wish – that there was to be no demonstration of any kind – they departed quietly after hearing news and exchanging their views.[12]

Gandhi's political style was oriented towards reconciliation and compromise. Petitions, letters, meetings – it was only when these methods had not proven successful that he had chosen to court arrest. But how long could he, and the Indians, sustain the path of struggle and sacrifice? Sensible of the compulsions of his followers, their need to earn a livelihood and not be separated from their families, Gandhi was now amenable to a settlement with Government.

The more militant Pathans, however, were not. They had played their part, as soldiers on the British side, in the war against the Boers. That they were now subjected to humiliating laws by those they had once militarily defeated enraged them. Gandhi had mobilized them for the struggle; now, they would rather fight to the finish. They believed the lawyer had backed down too easily. At a meeting in Johannesburg, they raised objections to the giving of fingerprints, which Pathans such as Nawab Khan thought was humiliating. Back in India, only criminals were asked to provide them, and to submit one's body to such (symbolic) subjection was anathema to their sense of masculinity and tribal pride.

The Pathans were not persuaded by Gandhi's claim that he had himself had his fingerprints taken in prison. Seeking a compromise within the compromise, Gandhi wrote to Smuts asking if thumb impressions alone were acceptable. While to him, 'personally, it is immaterial whether thumb-prints or digit-impressions be given, there are many among the Asiatics to whom the latter presents an impassable difficulty'.[13] Gandhi suggested that educated Indians waive the right to give signatures and offer fingerprints instead.[14]

Extremists on the European side were also unhappy with the compromise. Gandhi should have been exiled from the province, they argued. A meeting of the White League, held in Johannesburg on 1 February, asked its members to 'passively resist the Asiatics by securing pledges from the white people not to deal with the Orientals'. A co-operative society of whites to replace the trade of Indian hawkers was proposed. These colonists 'want[ed] the Asiatics out of the country, and will have nothing to do with them.'[15]

As mandated by the agreement, voluntary registration was scheduled to begin at ten a.m. on Monday 10 February 1908. An office was opened at Von Brandis Square, in the heart of Johannesburg. Hoping to be the first to register, Gandhi left his chambers at a quarter to ten, accompanied by Thambi Naidoo and Essop Mia. The subsequent events are described in a contemporary newspaper report:

On the way, a party of Indians stopped the party [led by Gandhi] and asked what they were going to do.

Mr Gandhi replied that they were going to register, and others endeavoured to explain that, if finger impressions were objected to, the registration officers would not insist.

One of the party raised a stick and hit Mr Gandhi on the back of the head, knocking him to the ground. One of Mr Gandhi's party tried to save their leader, but he also was knocked down with a severe blow on the side of the head.

Mr Mia, the chairman of the British Indian Association, also interfered, and he was put out of action with a blow to the head.

The assailants hit Mr Gandhi several blows with sticks on the head.

The police on point duty saw the disturbance, and their appearance caused the assailants to decamp. Two, however, were arrested. The assailants are Punjabis and Pathans, and they allege that Mr Gandhi has not, in coming to the agreement, guarded their interests.

Considerable excitement prevails, judging by the number of Indians waiting to be registered. The great majority are on Mr Gandhi's side.[16]

This report, from the *Natal Mercury*, needs to be supplemented by one from *Indian Opinion*, from which it appears that Thambi Naidoo may have saved Gandhi's life. The Tamil was carrying an umbrella, and used it to engage the main attacker, Meer Allam Khan, pitting his instrument against the iron rod used by the Pathan. The umbrella finally broke, but by then the commotion had attracted the police as well as the employees of Arnott and Gibson, a law firm which had its offices nearby.[17]

When Gandhi recovered consciousness, he was taken to the private office of J. C. Gibson, a partner in the firm that bore his name. He was bleeding from the lips and the forehead, and two of his front teeth were loose. A doctor was called in to treat the wounds. The Baptist minister Joseph Doke, hearing of the attack, had reached the scene. When someone suggested that Gandhi be removed to hospital, the clergyman offered to take him to his house in Smith Street instead. Doke's son Clement vacated his room for the unexpected guest. Clement's sister Olive watched as the patient was patched up. In her vivid recollection, 'he would not have any chloroform or anything, he just sat on the bed while Mother held him up and the doctors stitched up his wounds. Two stitches were put in his cheek and two on his lip and two on his eye-brow. The last one was almost too much for him; he nearly fainted.'[18]

During the day, Mrs Doke made tea for the stream of Indians who came in to visit their wounded leader. At night, Doke sat by Gandhi's bedside and prayed. For two days after the attack, Gandhi ran a high fever. This, and the injuries to his face and lips, made it very hard for him to eat or drink. Slowly, he began taking liquids and also fruit, and, in time, bread dipped in milk. The wounds were healing, thanks to earth poultices, applied despite the doctor's objection.[19]

Telegrams of support for Gandhi and of thanks to the Dokes began pouring in from all parts of Transvaal and Natal. The Christian couple received money and jewels from individuals and community groups, thanking them 'for their kindly and charitable assistance to our fellow-countryman and leader Mr Gandhi in his time of physical need'. Joseph Doke said he would create a trust fund from the gifts, to fund the education of Indian boys.[20]

Back in 1897, when Gandhi had been attacked by a white mob in Durban, it was a European superintendent of police who, with Parsee Rustomjee, had helped spirit him to safety. Now, when savaged by a group of angry Indians, it was a family of British Baptists who nursed him back to health. In the course of his convalescence, Gandhi became very attached to the Dokes, to the father and daughter in particular. After he had left their household, he would, from time to time, send Olive playful notes, enclosing Indian women's magazines for her to read and demanding that she send chocolates to his law office in exchange. These letters reveal an unexpected tenderness in a man whose missives to his own sons were far more censorious and prescriptive.[21]

For Gandhi, the support given by Albert Cartwright, and then by the Dokes, confirmed that this conflict should not be seen through a purely racial lens. The Indian community, he wrote, should 'give up its anger against the whites. We are often thoughtless enough to say that the whites can have nothing good in them. But this is patent folly. Mankind is one, and even if a few whites make the mistake of considering them-selves different from us, we must not follow them in that error.'[22]

Two days after the attack on Gandhi, a group of Pathans met in a hall in Vrededorp. The principal speaker was Nawab Khan, ex–Bengal Lancers, dressed, as ever, in military uniform. He 'urged on his audience that, now Mr Gandhi had forsaken the right path, they should follow him no longer, and refuse to submit to the indignity of having impressions of their 10 digits taken'. Khan 'worked the audience up to such a pitch' that they followed him in taking an oath not to register.[23]

The Pathans were in a minority. When one newspaper sought to represent it as a Hindu versus Muslim question, a group of leading merchants pointed out that 'the very first men to register on Monday were Mahomedans. So far as South Africa is concerned, happily, on non-religious matters there are no differences between the two communities.'[24] The 'general opinion among the Asiatics', commented one reporter, 'is that the assault on Mr Gandhi was a cowardly one. It is remarkable how true the Asiatics are to their leader.'[25]

The events of recent weeks and months had enormously enhanced Gandhi's standing in the community. Once, he was admired for his professional qualifications and skills – for being the only British-educated English-speaking Indian lawyer in Natal and the Transvaal. His arrest, and the attack on him, gave him an altogether different glow. He was now admired not so much for his education and privilege, as for his courage and conviction. The dignity with which he bore imprisonment, and with which he faced his tormentors, greatly impressed Tamils and Gujaratis, Hindus as well as Muslims.

In the week after the assault on Gandhi, a steady stream of merchants and hawkers got themselves registered. There was now 'a crowd of excited Indians outside the Registration Office', registering under the guidance of Thambi Naidoo, who was sporting a bandaged hand. Those who could sign their names were not asked to provide fingerprints. Gandhi himself registered from his sick-bed, the papers and other equipment being brought to him by the Registrar of Asiatics, Montford Chamney.[26]

In its issue of 15 February, *Indian Opinion* carried an essay of more than 4,000 words, the longest single piece it had published thus far. Written while Gandhi was recovering at the Dokes', it sought to still the unease among some Indians about the settlement. The essay was couched as a dialogue between a 'Reader' asking questions and the 'Editor' seeking to answer them.

The issue that most concerned the Reader was the giving of fingerprints. He wondered how these, so 'objectionable before, have suddenly become acceptable'. Could it be that 'the educated and the rich have had their interests protected at the expense of the poor?' The Editor (Gandhi) answered by saying that now that the law was to be repealed, Indians should not stand on 'false pride'. Even whites who entered Transvaal under the new immigration law had to give fingerprints. If Indians gave them out of 'our own free choice' there should be no objection. Besides, these prints were required only on the application, not on the certificate. To further calm the waters, Gandhi proposed that despite the exemption for those who could sign, men of learning and standing must not avail themselves of it. The 'important thing' was that 'well-educated persons should regard themselves as trustees of the poor.' 'A person like Mr Essop Mia will rise in stature by giving his ten finger-impressions.'[27]

Gandhi's attackers were tried on 19 February. They pleaded not guilty. The victim was not present, but Essop Mia and Thambi Naidoo gave evidence as to the nature of the attack. The defence claimed that when the Pathans stopped to talk with Gandhi, the lawyer abused them in English (this is represented in the court record by a series of dashes), while Thambi Naidoo prodded the Pathans with a stick. It was then that they retaliated. One attacker, Meer Allam Khan, said he 'was sorry when he found that he had hurt [Gandhi]. It was all done in hot blood.'

In his summing up, the magistrate, H. H. Jordan, said that he was

perfectly sure that Mr Gandhi did not use the words alleged against him. He did not think that anyone could be brought forward to say that Mr Gandhi had used bad language. It was from his personal knowledge of the man that he could say that he (Mr Gandhi) was not a man to use words of that description.

The verdict was of an unprovoked assault, and the sentence was three months in jail with hard labour.[28]

Having lost the argument in the Transvaal, Gandhi's critics now sought to renew it in Natal. On 5 March, while he was addressing a large gathering in Durban, some men with sticks rushed towards the platform. The crowd surrounded Gandhi and guarded him. The chairman declared the meeting closed, and Gandhi was taken in a carriage to Parsee Rustomjee's house.[29]

These attacks spoke of a certain desperation. The majority of Indians were solidly behind Gandhi, and the pace of registration steadily picked up. In its issue of 7 March, *Indian Opinion* observed that 'the Permit Office does not have a moment's respite' (in striking contrast to the situation a bare six months previously, when, as the same paper had reported, it was desolate and lifeless). By now, more than 4,000 Indians had already registered, among them some previously recalcitrant Pathans.[30]

On 14 March the British Indian Association gave a dinner for the Europeans who had stood by them. The event was held in the Masonic Lodge, the reservation being made on Gandhi's behalf by Hermann Kallenbach. Forty Indians, paying two guineas each, entertained some twenty-five whites, these being journalists, legislators and lawyers sympathetic to their struggle. The dinner consisted of twenty-four vegetarian items, washed down with lime juice and soda water. The menu card carried the line: 'This dinner is arranged as an expression of gratitude to those whites who fought for truth and justice during the satyagraha campaign.'

Furthering this spirit of inter-racial solidarity, the Chinese gave a dinner on 20 March for their Indian *and* European friends. Our source does not tell us what food was served, but we may presume that it did not exclude fish and meat (nor whisky and wine either). We do know that a Chinese band was in attendance. The band fell silent to allow an oak desk to be presented to Joseph Doke for looking after Gandhi, and a gold watch to be given to Albert Cartwright for his part in arranging the compromise. Henry and Millie Polak also received gifts. Gandhi was presented with an address which praised his 'political acumen'. In a report for his newspaper, Gandhi admitted the Chinese had surpassed the Indians in 'culture and generosity'.[31]

Absent from these dinners was one very early, and very steadfast, European supporter of the Indians – L. W. Ritch. He was now based in London, lobbying the Imperial Government. When a Jewish newspaper took notice of his contribution, Ritch wrote in to say that 'it cannot, of course, be a matter of surprise that the Jew should figure prominently in any movement directed against persecution and intolerance, whether of race or religion.' Speaking of the work in the Transvaal of 'my friends Polak and others', Ritch asked: 'What Jew dare coquette with the demons of racial prejudice, religious intolerance, or the jealousies engendered by superior business acumen, thrift, sobriety and general self-discipline?'[32]

*

In the first week of April 1908, Henry Polak enrolled as an attorney of the Supreme Court of Transvaal. He had completed three years as a clerk in Gandhi's office, and also passed the necessary examinations. As for Gandhi himself, he continued to draft petitions on behalf of clients travelling to India, who wished to have the paperwork in place to allow them re-entry. His clients included Muslims, Hindus, Parsis, Christians and – significantly – some Chinese. Gandhi complained to Montford Chamney of excessive delays in granting exit permits, and of the 'latent feeling of suspicion' in the minds of many Indians that they were being singled out for special harassment.[33]

In the last week of April, three new bills were introduced in the Natal Legislature. The first sought to stop the import of indentured Indian labour after June 1911; the second to suspend the issuing of new trading licences to Indians after August 1908; the third to terminate existing Indian licences after ten years, subject to the payment of compensation equivalent to three years' profit. The bills were clearly meant to protect the interests of European traders against their hardworking Indian counterparts. Even so, they were extremely severe. As a liberal white newspaper pointedly asked:

> Is an Indian not to be allowed to keep a barber's shop to shave and cut the hair of his own countrymen? Is he not to be allowed to hawk the vegetables he grows on the little garden he has, or to sell the fish he may have caught in the Bay or on the open sea? Is he not to be allowed to supply the special wants of his own countrymen in the peculiar articles, some of them connected with religious observances, which no European could very well deal in?[34]

Gandhi welcomed the first bill, for he too wished to see the ending of the harsh, dehumanizing system of indentured labour. But, he wrote, 'the other two Bills are as ignorant as they are tyrannical.' If not rescinded, they might have to be fought 'with the sword of satyagraha'.[35]

In the Transvaal, the compromise between the Indians and the Government was coming under strain. In early May, Smuts decided that the window of voluntary registration would be open for three months altogether. Former residents coming back to the colony after 9 August would have their cases examined under the notorious (and still unrepealed) act of 1907. Gandhi wrote to the Government to reconsider. He had very nearly lost his life as a result of the compromise on the fingerprint question. Now, if he was seen as having acquiesced in closing the door to late-comers, he would be 'totally unworthy of the trust reposed in me by my countrymen'.[36]

On 17 May, the President of the British Indian Association, Essop Mia, was set upon by a Pathan in the street, and badly injured. He was targeted because of his closeness to Gandhi. Gandhi wrote to Smuts, warning that 'many more may be assaulted in [the] near future'. He 'daily receive[d] indignant letters saying that I have entirely misled the people as to the compromise and that the law is not going to be repealed at all'. He asked the Colonial Secretary, 'for the sake of those who have helped the Government', to announce that the Asiatic Act of 1907 would be rescinded, and that new arrivals could register themselves voluntarily.[37]

The Government was unyielding. Voluntary registration would not be permitted beyond 9 August. Smuts's secretary told Gandhi, somewhat gratuitously, that 'if you think that your person is in any way in danger, you will immediately avail yourself of the protection of the police, which the Government will be only too glad to supply.'[38]

The insensitivity of the Government was answered by a hardening of the Indian position. In the last week of May, Gandhi wrote to Montford Chamney asking him to return the papers submitted with his application for registration. He wanted the papers back, he said, because of the Government's 'breach of spirit of the compromise'. Leung Quinn and Thambi Naidoo, his fellow signatories to the pact with Smuts, likewise wrote asking for their papers. Both insisted that 'the only reason we accepted the compromise was in order to bring about the repeal of the Act'. Hundreds of Indians and Chinese followed their leaders in demanding the return of their papers. They were all 'once more prepared . . . to submit to the punishments involved in non-submission to the Asiatic Act'.[39]

Smuts now summoned Gandhi to Pretoria. They met on 6 June, with Gandhi reminding the General of his promise, made in January, that 'if the Asiatics carried out their part of the compromise, you will repeal the Act'. Smuts remembered their conversation differently; he had, he claimed, given no such assurance. The lawyer returned to Johannesburg 'without a definite assurance of repeal'. In despair, Gandhi wrote to Albert Cartwright asking him to resume his role as an 'Angel of Peace' and change the Government's mind in 'favour of Justice and Righteousness'.

Gandhi and Smuts met again the following week. The conversation was less than courteous. The Colonial Secretary said new legislation to govern Indian immigration was under consideration. Gandhi asked that it allow pre-(Boer)war residents and possessors of Boer-issued certificates to voluntarily register, and that educated Indians be allowed to enter on the same terms as Europeans, namely, after passing a test. Smuts would not commit to these terms; what was worse, he insinuated that Gandhi did not really represent the Indians of the Transvaal.

On 22 June, Gandhi met Smuts for the third time in as many weeks. The discussions proved fruitless. In a statement issued to the press, Gandhi charged the General with having 'wrecked a whole compromise to avoid the possible accession to the Asiatic population of the Colony of two thousand Asiatics as an outside figure'. He recalled that when, back in January, he had commenced talks with the Government, some colleagues had warned that the rulers were not to be trusted. They argued that the repeal of the 1907 Act should have preceded voluntary registration. Gandhi had told them 'that was not a dignified position to take up'; now, it seemed, his critics had been vindicated.[40]

Smuts expressed his own frustrations to the businessman William Hosken. While other concessions were possible, said the General, 'the repeal out and out of the Asiatic Act' was out of the question. The 'white population is becoming daily more exasperated and demanding even more stringent legislation'. By making fresh demands, Gandhi had 'thrown away' a 'golden chance for a final settlement'.[41]

The battle lines had once more been drawn. A meeting of Indians was convened on the afternoon of Wednesday 24 June 1908. The venue was the Fordsburg Mosque in Johannesburg, and delegates from all over the Transvaal were in attendance. The meeting resolved that, since the Gandhi–Smuts compromise had been breached by the Government, the Indians would withdraw all applications for licences, reaffirming 'the solemn declaration made on the 11th day of September, 1906, not to submit to the Asiatic Law Amendment Act, but to suffer, as loyal citizens and conscientious men, all the penalties consequent upon non-submission thereto.'[42]

The next issue of *Indian Opinion*, out that same Saturday, warned that in view of the impasse, satyagraha might now have to resume. Gandhi reminded his readers that 'in any great war, more than one battle has to be fought'. In the past decade, the Boers had fought the British and Japan had fought Russia, each war lasting for several years and involving several famous battles. The Indian struggle, though waged with satyagraha rather than gunpowder, was 'no whit less of a war' than the others. The example most relevant to them was that of Japan, for when that nation's 'brave heroes forced the Russians to bite the dust of the battle-field, the sun rose in the east. And it now shines on all the nations of Asia. The people of the East will never, never again submit to insult from the insolent whites.'[43]

In 1903, when Lord Milner first sanctioned specific locations for Indians, a British journalist warned that 'the controversy it will arouse will not be confined to the Transvaal, but will extend to England and India.'[44] And so it did. The facts of the satyagraha in the Transvaal were becoming known in Gandhi's homeland. Copies of *Indian Opinion* were read in Bombay and Madras, and further afield. Letters by Gandhi to Gokhale were circulated within and beyond Congress circles. From the last months of 1907 through the first half of 1908, the satyagraha in South Africa was the subject of reports and editorials in (among other journals) the *Sasilekha* of Madras, the *Vokkaliga Patrike* of Bangalore, the *Indu Prakash* of Bombay, the *Kesari* of Poona, the *West Coast Spectator* of Calicut and the *Desamata* from Rajahmundry – these published in English, Urdu, Gujarati, Hindi, Kannada, Telugu, Malayalam, Tamil and other languages.

The Indian reports on the Transvaal protests argued that discrimination abroad was a consequence of oppression at home. Once India became a free country, it would be difficult for foreigners to treat its citizens with impunity. An Urdu weekly from Madras said racial distinctions in the Transvaal were particularly invidious because the Boers were 'not educated and cultured like the Indians'. They were, in fact, quite 'wild', their wildness evidenced by the fact that there was not a single university in their country. A Tamil weekly printed in the same city called the satyagrahis 'true Aryaputras', who had chosen to go to jail to uphold national honour and self-respect. The *Shakti* of Surat interpreted the struggle more broadly still: the protests of Indians in South Africa, it said, reflected Asia's awakening after centuries of deep slumber. It was a microcosm of a wider 'struggle for existence between the white and the black races'.

The Gujarati press wrote appreciatively of the man leading the resistance, their native son, Mohandas K. Gandhi, born in Porbandar and educated in Rajkot. *Vartaman*, a Gujarati paper published out of Bombay, said the 'whole of India was proud' of 'Mr Gandhi and his gallant band'. The *Mahi Kantha Gazette* of Surat invoked the epics: 'The success of Mr Gandhi', it claimed, 'has proved to the world that in spite of her poverty, Mother India is not yet bankrupt of men of the type of Bhishma, Arjuna, Drona and others.'[45]

This widespread coverage in the press was consolidated by public meetings held in solidarity with the resisters. A meeting in Karachi on 28 January 1908 conveyed its support to 'the relations of Mr Gandhi'. The next day, the Aga Khan chaired a meeting in Bombay, at which some 7,000 people were present. Here, 'references to Mr Gandhi's imprisonment were received with prolonged cries of "Shame".' The repression in the Transvaal, said one speaker, had 'produced a growing sense of wrong and universal indignation among all creeds and castes in India'. Another speaker warned of the dangers to the Raj if the methods practised in South Africa were extended to the subcontinent. 'How will British statesmen carry on the Empire', he asked, 'if 300,000,000 [Indians] are degraded today, disaffected tomorrow, and rebellious in the end?'

At a meeting in Madras, the social reformer and campaigning journalist G. Subramania Aiyar commended the 'manful struggle against oppression and persecution' of Gandhi and company. A meeting in Patna proclaimed that 'India cannot pray to have truer sons than Mr Gandhi and his compatriots.' Other meetings of solidarity and support were held in Surat, Ahmedabad, Kathiar, Lahore, Aligarh, Coimbatore and Jullundur.

The name of Mohandas K. Gandhi was now becoming reasonably well-known in India. A meeting which may have given him great cheer was held in his home town, Porbandar, on 18 January 1908. The venue was an historic building known as the Satsvarup Haveli. A Muslim was in the chair; a Hindu made the main speech. Four resolutions were passed. The last three chastised, in different ways, the Imperial Government for not honouring its obligations to its Indian subjects. These were cast in general terms; the first resolution, on the other hand, expressed a more intimate, local pride and patriotism. It said that

the people of Porbandar have learnt with great sorrow that Mr M. K. Gandhi, who was born at Porbandar, as also other respectable Indians, have been imprisoned by the Transvaal Government. This meeting emphatically declares that they are proud of Mr Gandhi, and that they highly appreciate the services that he is rendering to the Mother-country.

The resolutions were sent to the Secretary of State for India, Lord Morley, urging him to 'view this question from a point considering yourself to be an Indian for the time being. The fate and future of India is involved.'[46]

The support for Gandhi's movement disgusted a visitor to the subcontinent – a globetrotting British preacher named G. N. Thompson. Thompson had spent time in South Africa, where he was persuaded of the need to keep out Asiatics. In the summer and autumn of 1908, he toured the districts of the Madras Presidency, telling audiences that it was 'quite unreasonable for the Sedition mongers here to talk that the Indians in the Transvaal are being ill-treated by the British and consequently loyalty in India is being strained.' For 'the Boers are no subject race and will never be dictated to'. 'Boer law will prevail in the Transvaal'; and 'Mr Gandhi is most perverted in his agitation.'[47]

Back in Johannesburg, Gandhi was cultivating new friendships with white people. A jeweller named Gabriel I. Isaac had become increasingly attracted to the Indian lawyer and his cause. An English Jew, and a practising vegetarian, Isaac raised money for *Indian Opinion* and lived for a time at Phoenix. In a more emphatic expression of support, he offered to temporarily take over the running of shops owned by satyagrahis in jail.[48]

In May 1908, Gandhi spent several days in the company of a visiting English clergyman named F. B. Meyer. Meyer was the pastor of Regent's Park Chapel in London, and a past president of the Baptist Union and of the National Federation of Free Churches. He was well known as a campaigner against prize-fighting. (When asked whether he had ever seen a boxing match, Meyer answered that he would rather undergo a surgical operation than watch one.)[49]

Meyer and his wife had come on a tour of South Africa. They arrived in Johannesburg by way of Cape Town, Kimberley and Bloemfontein. His main contact in the city was his fellow Baptist Joseph Doke, who put him on to Gandhi. After 'prolonged walks and talks' with the lawyer, Meyer 'was led to form a high estimate of his personal character.' Among the topics they discussed were the Hindu view of life (and death), and the use of water in prayer. The priest was impressed to find that 'whilst tenacious of his Hindoo religious views', Gandhi had 'a great reverence for Jesus Christ'.

Meyer expressed a cautious sympathy with Gandhi's movement of passive resistance. On the one hand he seemed persuaded that the Asiatic Act was, in his new friend's words, 'class legislation of a degrading type'. On the other, the whites in the Transvaal had complained to him of the trade practices of the Indians. That prisoners of conscience were put to hard labour made him slightly less than even-handed. 'Obviously I cannot take sides', remarked the minister, 'and I can have no sympathy with any unfair cutting of prices, but it seems barbarous to put Hindoo gentlemen to menial work, generally given to Kaffirs.'[50]

Gandhi was also having regular walks and talks with a European resident in Johannesburg, his friend the architect Hermann Kallenbach. In March 1908, with his family still at Phoenix, Gandhi moved out of the house he shared with the Polaks into Kallenbach's home in the suburb of Orchards. The house combined European elements, such as large bay windows, with African ones, such as a thatched roof. In deference to the latter the owner had called it 'The Kraal'.[51]

The change of residence was prompted by two things. Henry and Millie now had children of their own, and needed the space. And Gandhi wished to pursue his own self-improvement more seriously, a project in which Kallenbach was a far more congenial partner than the Polaks. Before he met Gandhi, Kallenbach had lived luxuriously. After coming under his influence, he had reduced his expenses by some 90 per cent, a fact reported with some satisfaction by Gandhi. Rising at five a.m., they did all their own cooking and cleaning; theirs must have been the only house in this white neighbourhood without a servant. By Gandhi's admission the bulk of the work fell on his Jewish friend. Carpentry was Kallenbach's particular passion, here manifest in the making of new tables and chairs and in continuing modifications to windows and doors.

After breakfast (usually milk and fruits) the friends walked some five miles into the city, to attend to their respective sets of clients. If they had an early meeting they cycled instead, Gandhi getting off his bike on the steeper slopes. Once the day's work was done they walked or cycled back to The Kraal. Gandhi wrote to John Cordes that Kallenbach and he lived a 'reasonable' if not a 'popular' life. They had learnt to be tolerant of one another, and to give each other the benefit of the doubt.[52]

Among the things that brought Gandhi and Kallenbach together was a shared admiration for the works of Leo Tolstoy, who at this time was certainly the most famous writer in the world. Tolstoy was admired for his novels and stories, and in some quarters, even more for his attempts at simplifying his life. In his early fifties he had a conversion experience, following which he gave up alcohol, tobacco and meat. His vegetarianism became so well-known that he was asked to write an introduction to a book of Henry Salt's. He took up working in the fields, and splitting wood and making shoes in a bid to empathize with his serfs. From a martial background, he now began to preach the virtues of pacifism. Although born and raised in the Russian Orthodox Church, he developed a deep interest in Hinduism and Buddhism.

Of Tolstoy's many transitions, the most painful was his embrace of celibacy. In his youth he had been (in his own words), 'a radical chaser after women'. His wife went through more than a dozen pregnancies. He had affairs with peasant women on his estate. A man of 'wild passion', he sought in middle age to give up sex along with the other pleasures he had forsaken.[53]

Tolstoy's embrace of the simple life was widely spoken of, and often emulated. Across Europe, Asia and North America, his followers refused to enrol for military service, established craft and farming co-operatives, practised vegetarianism and preached religious tolerance. Reading and venerating their master, these Tolstoyans sought to do in their homelands what Tolstoy was believed to have done in his.[54]

The experiments of Gandhi and Kallenbach in Johannesburg were of a piece with this worldwide trend. Both were from middle-class backgrounds; both practised professions that brought them close to circles of wealth and power. Reading Tolstoy was for each an educative and even epiphanic experience. For the lawyer, it consolidated the non-attachment to worldly possessions so exalted in the Hindu and Jain traditions; for the architect, it provided an encouragement to embrace a life of austerity and abstinence that his own, Jewish, tradition did not mandate and (at least with regard to celibacy) perhaps did not comprehend.

Gandhi and Tolstoy were akin in good ways and bad. Both were indifferent fathers and less than solicitous husbands. There were also differences. Gandhi's prose style was more restrained, less polemical. Whereas Tolstoy loved nature, and took his family for holidays in the hills, Gandhi did not much care for beaches, parks or forests. Although he often visited Cape Town, there is no record of his ever having climbed Table Mountain. Once, when the Gandhis were in Cape Town and Manilal wanted to stay an extra day to climb it, his father told him that there was no need, since 'when you go home to India you can go up to the Himalayas which contain thousands of Table Mountains'.[55]

Where Gandhi more closely emulated his Russian idol was in his increasing disenchantment with his profession. Despite constantly being urged to do so, Tolstoy turned away from writing the sort of novels which had made him famous. Likewise, Gandhi had come to see his legal practice more as an obligation than as a career. He would attend to cases of discrimination, but his heart lay (as Tolstoy's did) in personal improvement and social reform.

Tolstoy had once written to an English disciple rejecting formal, institutional Christianity, and instead exalting 'the sincere effort made by each individual person to coordinate one's life and actions with those moral foundations one considers to be true, regardless of the demands of family, society, and government'.[56] This, precisely, was the goal that Gandhi and Kallenbach had set themselves. Thus it came to be that, in a South African town in 1908, a lawyer from western India and an architect from eastern Europe set out to run their Tolstoyan experiment. The contours of their life together emerge clearly in a letter written in June 1908 by Kallenbach to his brother Simon. This went into details about their domestic labours – 'we cook, bake, scrub and are cleaning the house and the yard; we are polishing our shoes, and are working in the flower and vegetable garden.'

These activities were foreign to the traditions and habits of the social class to which Kallenbach's family had aspired. As he told Simon, he had now radically departed from the lifestyle of the modernizing Jewish bourgeoisie of Europe. The stimulus for these departures was his Hindu housemate, who was 'a vegetarian according to his religious convictions', and yet 'an extraordinarily good and capable person'. Under his influence Kallenbach had given up meat; even more dramatically, as he informed his brother, 'for the last 18 months I have given up my sex life.' By these changes and choices, Hermann had 'gained in character – strength – mental vitality and physical development; my bodily well-being had become bigger and better.'

In London, twenty years previously, Gandhi had shared a home with

Josiah Oldfield. The flatmates organized parties and visited homes to convert meat-eaters to vegetarianism. Now, living with Kallenbach in Johannesburg, Gandhi sought rather to convert himself (and his house-mate), by practising the austerity and detachment from worldly pleasures advocated by his old preceptor Raychandbhai and his new preceptor Leo Tolstoy.

By this time, there were two distinct groups among Gandhi's follow-ers and friends. One group endorsed his political programme: they were prepared to go to jail for him, and to give speeches and write articles in favour of lifting restrictions against the Indians. Many Gujarati mer-chants and Tamil hawkers fell into this category; as did European friends such as Henry and Millie Polak.

A second, smaller group endorsed Gandhi's moral and spiritual pro-gramme as well. They simplified their diet and their needs, they worked with their hands at home and at the press, they sought to promote inter-faith understanding, they sought (not always successfully) to prac-tise *brahmacharya*. In this group were Gandhi's nephews Chhaganlal and Maganlal, Albert West and the new resident of Phoenix, John Cordes. And now Hermann Kallenbach, too.

Gandhi had already taken a vow of celibacy; Kallenbach, under his influence, joined him. To keep the vow was hard enough for the Indian; but even harder for the Jew. For one thing, Gandhi was older, and had already begotten four children. For another, Indian religious traditions placed a very high value on abstinence from sexual pleasure. However, Kallenbach was younger and highly sexed. Besides, celibacy was utterly foreign to the Jewish tradition, where religious fulfilment was compat-ible with family life and sexual relations.[57]

Gandhi had failed to convert his own eldest son, Harilal, to *brahma-charya*. The boy had married against his wishes, and was planning a family, too. Like Harilal, Kallenbach was deeply attracted to women. That he still chose to be celibate was proof of his admiration, even awe, for Gandhi. Having described, to his brother Simon, his life with his new mentor, Kallenbach spoke of how it might turn out in the future. In three months, he told his brother, payments for work in progress would make him financially independent. Then, with an annual income of £250, he would be free to leave, as he hoped, to study in London. But he would not go alone. For 'probably Mr Gandhi, who is a barrister-at-law, plans to go with me in order to study medicine in London; there he plans to acquaint himself with Hydrotherapy (a branch of Naturopathy). For years, Mr Gandhi had been deeply interested in the study and methods of all natural healing methods.'

Kallenbach himself was undecided what to study, whether 'languages, architecture or even medicine'. He relished the prospect of Gandhi and he being students together, when they would 'naturally, live together in London and continue our life in a similar fashion as we live here'. The plans were firm but not yet final, Kallenbach telling his brother that 'if, for some reason or other, Mr Gandhi will be prevented from leaving South Africa within 3 or 4 months, I intend waiting for him till the end of the year. However, thereafter I intend going on my own.'[58]

The fact that Gandhi was contemplating leaving South Africa in 1908 to study medicine in London seems to have escaped the attention of historians and biographers. But there is a contemporary verification of Kallenbach's claim, in the book of his South African travels written by the Baptist preacher F. B. Meyer. 'He practises as a barrister', wrote Meyer of Gandhi in the summer of 1908, 'but, not content with one profession, is hoping to visit London again shortly, to study medicine, and give his sons wider opportunities for realising the ideals with which he has inspired them.'[59]

Gandhi had long been keen on natural methods of healing – applying mud poultices to wounds, for example, and taking the so-called Kuhne bath, where one cleansed oneself with water in which salt and baking soda were mixed. Hydropathy and naturopathy were attracting increasing attention in the early twentieth century, with influential schools and practitioners across Western Europe and North America. Hot water, cold water and steam were being used to treat fever, pains and other symptoms of ill-health (including alcoholism).[60]

Gandhi's interest in naturopathy was of a piece with his admiration for Tolstoy and Ruskin, whose writings stressed the need to shed possessions and to adopt a sceptical if not critical attitude to the fast pace and material orientation of modern industrial civilization. Still, that he would wish to pursue the study of this unorthodox branch of medicine *full-time* speaks of an interest rather deeper than that suggested by his own writings. He was now almost thirty-nine; established as a lawyer, acclaimed as a community leader, with obligations to his wife and children. What would motivate him now to seek a different career on a different continent? And how serious was this ambition? There is no hint of it in his autobiographical writings; and no hint of course in the exhortative articles for public consumption that he wrote for *Indian Opinion*.

Gandhi had studied law in one city, London, and practised it in four other cities – Rajkot, Bombay, Durban and Johannesburg. His life thus far had been marked by multiple dislocations – as an adult he had lived in a dozen different houses. But at least his career had been the same. And in this career he had steadily become more successful. In recent years, he had increasingly subordinated his legal practice to his social activism. The reasons for this are clear – it was due to the compelling need to secure Indians in South Africa their rights. The reason for his wanting to qualify as a doctor are less apparent. Why now would he want to exchange one profession for another? Perhaps he was bored with the law. The range of cases for an Indian representing other Indians was rather limited in South Africa. The issuing of new permits and licences, the renewal of lapsed permits and licences – these more or less exhausted what he could do for his clients.

Gandhi seems to have thought, or hoped, that the pressure of the protests he led would persuade General Smuts to honour his promise and repeal the obnoxious Asiatic Act of 1907. If that happened, Indians in South Africa would have their rights protected. And he would be free to leave for London to study medicine.

Perhaps, in now contemplating a career in medicine, Gandhi was inspired by the example of others. A woman he greatly admired, Anna Kingsford, had acquired a medical degree despite refusing to dissect animals. She combined medicine with vegetarianism and heterodox Christianity. Two of Gandhi's closest friends, Josiah Oldfield and Pranjivan Mehta, had qualified as barristers and doctors both. Mehta had in fact gone on to take up a third profession altogether, the buying and selling of jewellery. It may be that their successful (and fulfilling) changes of profession now encouraged Gandhi to do likewise. But what did Gandhi mean when he told Meyer that by going to England he would give his sons 'wider opportunities'? Harilal had now worked for almost two years on *Indian Opinion*; and Manilal had begun assisting in the journal's operations as well. Did their father think that by removing himself from the scene, the boys would become more responsible and mature?

*

On the evidence – published as well as unpublished – Hermann Kallenbach was deeply devoted to Gandhi. The Indian was to him a combination of elder brother and moral preceptor. He greatly looked forward to their life together in London. The possible barriers he alluded to – the 'some reason or another' – were, one supposes, personal constraints – would Kasturba and their sons have approved of Gandhi going? – and political compulsions – how would the Indians of the Transvaal and Natal have reacted to the emigration of their leader?

In the event, it was the Government's intransigence that put paid to the plans of the two friends. When General Smuts refused to repeal the Act and, to make matters worse, introduced fresh laws aimed at the Indians, Gandhi and his colleagues were compelled to start a new round of satyagraha. Kallenbach's letter to his brother Simon was posted on 14 June; two weeks later, Gandhi announced to his colleagues that his talks with Smuts had failed. The Indians had now to follow the example of the Japanese and, albeit non-violently, make their European opponents 'bite the dust'.

In early July, writing his weekly 'Johannesburg Letter' for *Indian Opinion*, Gandhi explained what the coming satyagraha was about. It was for the rights of those Indians who held Boer certificates of residence, for those past residents of the Transvaal who were presently outside the colony, and for educated Indians. The methods it would follow were the burning of registration certificates, and the refusal to give signatures or fingerprints if asked to by the police. If traders or hawkers were denied licences because they would not sign or provide fingerprints, they would continue trading. Imprisonment on account of any of these breaches of the law would be immediately accepted. To the resisters, Gandhi would provide legal assistance 'free of charge as usual'.[61]

The British Indian Association now scheduled a mass burning of certificates for Sunday 12 July 1908, but then agreed to a postponement at the request of Albert Cartwright and William Hosken. These white liberals still hoped a settlement would be struck. They carried Gandhi's views to Smuts, and vice versa. In the event, the angels of peace found both sides to be unyielding. Smuts accused Gandhi of exploiting Indian permit-seekers for his professional gain; he even claimed that the lawyer charged his Muslim clients more than his Hindu ones. Gandhi dismissed this as a 'damnable lie'.

The differences between the two men were of perception and of policy. Smuts thought that as many as 15,000 Indians had Boer certificates and hence claims to re-enter the Transvaal; Gandhi insisted that the number did not exceed 1,000. Of 'paramount importance', however, were the rights of educated Indians. Gandhi told Cartwright that he

> should deserve severest condemnation even from General Smuts and all my European friends, if I, a barrister having received a liberal education, were to say that my fellow-barristers should not enter the Transvaal or any other Colony, because they were Indians. Let the education test be as severe as General Smuts chooses to make it . . . [B]ut a racial test I shall never accept.

The result of these differences, said Gandhi, would 'be a petition to [the Transvaal] Parliament against the clause [prohibiting the entry of educated Indians], a petition to the Imperial Government, and, if I can carry my countrymen with me, undoubtedly passive resistance.'[62]

Gandhi's position was consistent with his broader view of the past and future of race relations in South Africa. He was, so to speak, a 'non-racial incrementalist'. While recognizing the technological, political, economic and social superiority of Europeans, he saw no reason why it must necessarily be maintained into the future. Individuals from other cultures were capable, under the right conditions and in the fullness of time, of achieving parity (in all senses) with the ruling race.

These views find expression in a fascinating (and neglected) speech delivered by Gandhi at the Johannesburg YMCA in May 1908. With the recent satyagraha in mind, the Association had organized a debate on the topic: 'Are Asiatics and the Coloured races a menace to the Empire?'

Gandhi may have been the only non-white present; he was certainly the only non-white speaker. Opposing the motion, he pointed out that the labour of Africans and Asians had made the Empire what it was. 'Who can think of the British Empire without India?' he asked, adding, 'South Africa would probably be a howling wilderness without the Africans.'

Gandhi then contrasted western civilization, which was restless, energetic and centrifugal, with eastern civilization, which was contemplative and centripetal. These tended at present to be opposing tendencies, 'but perhaps in the economy of nature both are necessary.' He welcomed their meeting, whereby eastern civilization would be 'quickened with the western spirit', and the latter, presently directionless, would be infused with a purpose. Gandhi believed – or hoped – that as the encounter proceeded, 'the eastern civilization will become predominant, because it has a goal.'

Some Europeans wanted the Indians to be thrown out of South Africa. Gandhi answered these extremists by contrasting different parts of the imperial capital, London.

> There are many complaints against the people living in the East End of London by the people living in the West End, but no one has suggested that, therefore, the people in the East End should be swept away. Sweep away the rack-rent and the conditions prevailing in the East End, and its inhabitants shall be as good as those in the West End.

Gandhi used this comparison to urge the colonists to raise the standing and status of the Indians, their fellow immigrants; allowing them to 'live freely without being restricted, move freely without being restricted, own land, and trade honestly.' He acknowledged that to speak of political rights for Indians and Africans was premature, but insisted these too would come, that, in fact, it was 'the mission of the English race, even when there are subject races, to raise them, to equality with themselves, to give them absolutely free institutions and make them absolutely free men.' If 'we look into the future', he daringly asked, 'is it not a heritage we had to leave to posterity that all the different races commingle and produce a civilisation that perhaps the world has not yet seen?'[63]

Gandhi was now the leading coloured resident of Johannesburg. His speech bore marks of his elevated status, and the responsibilities that went with it. For perhaps the first time in public, he used the neutral 'Africans' instead of the pejorative 'Kaffirs'. The change in language reflected a deeper change in his way of thinking about the world. When he first came to South Africa, Gandhi had pleaded for Indians to be distinguished from Africans, whom he then considered 'uncivilized'. Now, fifteen years later, he brought all races within a single ambit. They all had similar hopes, and would one day have the same rights. In the future, Indians and Africans would be absolutely free men, mingling with Boers and Britons in a nation where one's citizenship did not depend on the colour of one's skin.

With no possibility of a settlement, the protests resumed. From July 1908, Indians began courting arrest by hawking without a licence. They carried baskets of fruit on their heads, went from door to door, and waited for the police to arrest them. Gandhi defended these resisters in court. He asked the accused to make it clear that this was not their normal profession, and that they had taken to hawking to protest against the Government's policies. If Gandhi was busy elsewhere, his colleague Henry Polak defended the violators.[64]

The sentence for hawking without a licence was normally one week in prison. Some satyagrahis became serial offenders, among them Thambi Naidoo. Back in July 1907, when the Indians were resisting registration, the Tamil activist had led the picketing of the Permit Office. When they decided to court arrest, he was one of the first to enter jail. When Gandhi forged a compromise with Smuts, he threw the weight of his fellow Tamils behind the settlement. When Smuts dishonoured the pact, he led the satyagrahis into jail once more.

Thambi Naidoo was born and raised in Mauritius, a British colony where Indians were free to live and trade as they wished. He chafed at the restrictions in the Transvaal, which brought to the fore his natural combativeness and militancy. A carrier by profession, when the satyagraha began he was happy to do any task assigned to him. Posting letters, carrying loads, arranging seats or chairing a meeting himself – all these he did till the time came to go to jail. With the Gujaratis wavering, Gandhi had come to depend on Thambi more and more. He was now Gandhi's chief lieutenant, his position consolidated by the fact that he had, with the adroit use of that umbrella, warded off the lawyer's potential assassins.

Gandhi was suitably grateful to Thambi Naidoo for his support. He called him a satyagrahi 'with few equals', and 'perhaps the bravest and staunchest' of all the Indians in prison. Although he had never been to India, 'his love for the homeland knew no bounds'. Meanwhile, *Indian Opinion* wrote that

> before the movement commenced Mr Thambi Naidoo was a self-satisfied trolley contractor earning a fat living, and was a happy family man. Today, he is a proud pauper, a true patriot, and one of the most desirable of citizens of the Transvaal, indeed of South Africa. His one concern, whether in jail or outside it, is to behave like a true passive resister, and that is to suffer unmurmuringly.

With Thambi in prison, his wife Veerammal had to take care of their brood of children. She had neither the time nor the expertise to manage his business, and so to keep the debtors away she began to sell off his horses and carts, one by one, living from week to week on the proceeds.[65]

In the last week of July 1908, after Thambi Naidoo had been sentenced for the third time within a month, Gandhi, accompanied by Polak, Doke and Maulvi Ahmed Mukhtiar of the Hamidia Islamia Society, called on Mrs Naidoo to 'express their sympathy with her in her difficult position, and the admiration that they feel for her husband's courage and fortitude'. Gandhi and Polak, Hindu and Jew, stood with the family while Doke, the Christian minister, 'offered up a brief prayer asking for help, and Maulvi Sahib told Mrs. Naidoo that his co-religionists were all praying for her husband's welfare.'[66]

Mrs Naidoo was heavily pregnant; the following week, when the child was delivered, it was still-born. Polak accompanied the grieving mother to the cemetery. Later, he composed an editorial suggesting that, in the court of Indian public opinion, 'the murder of Mr Naidoo's child has been attributed to General Smuts.'[67]

To further test the Government, the British Indian Association asked a literate Parsi named Sorabjee Shapurjee Adajania to enter the Transvaal. Adajania, who spoke fluent English, had matriculated from the Surat High School and now worked as a manager of a shop in the Natal town of Charleston. He was as well educated as most Europeans who wished to make a home in the colony. However, his qualifications were, in the eyes of the law, nullified by the fact that he was an 'Asiatic'. He entered the Transvaal in the last week of June, claiming the right to reside as an educated immigrant. He was charged with violating the law, and defended in court by Gandhi. Told to leave the colony within a week, he refused to do so, and was summoned once more to court. The magistrate hearing the case was constrained to admit that Gandhi's arguments were 'very subtle and very able'. The law's racial underpinnings stood nakedly exposed. But the judge was paid to adminster it, which meant that Adajania was sentenced to one month in jail with hard labour.[68]

On 28 July, Gandhi defended six Indians charged with hawking without a licence. Gandhi was now appearing in court two or three times a week for the same purpose. This case was somewhat different, however, for among the accused was Harilal, his eldest son. Harilal, who had just turned twenty, was living at Phoenix, with his mother, his brothers and his wife Chanchal, who had recently joined him from India. He had been persuaded by his father to join the satyagraha. Entering Transvaal from Natal, he was detained at the town of Volks-rust for not having a valid certificate, and told to apply for one in Pretoria. Instead, he proceeded to Johannesburg and immediately began to hawk fruit. Harilal was fined one pound or seven days hard labour; like the others, he opted for imprisonment.

The day Harilal was released, Gandhi wrote a letter to his old adversary Montford Chamney. The tone mixed truculence with triumph. The judge had given Harilal Gandhi another chance to register for a permit. 'I have the honour to inform you,' wrote Gandhi to Chamney, 'that my son has no desire to do so, and that he will be prepared to answer any proceedings that might be instituted against him for breach of the Asiatic Act.'[69]

Shortly after 11 a.m. on 10 August, Harilal Gandhi was asked to produce a registration certificate by a policeman in Johannesburg. When he refused, he was arrested and his fingerprints forcibly taken. (These still exist in a file preserved in the National Archives of South Africa – black smudges of the right and left thumbs, and 'the plain impressions of the Four Fingers [of each hand] taken simultaneously'.) His particulars were taken down – he was, said the record, five feet, four inches in height, of 'stout' build and 'light' complexion, with black hair and two scars on his forehead.[70]

The same afternoon, Harilal appeared in court before Mr Jordan, with 'Gandhi, sen.' appearing for the defence. The father asked that the accused be ordered to leave the colony within twenty-four hours, 'as he wished to go to prison with his friends'. The judge refused to comply, instead giving Harilal a week to leave, or face the consequences. On the morning of the 18th, the grace period having elapsed, Harilal was arrested for refusing to comply with the court order. He appeared once more before Mr Jordan, who sentenced him to a month's imprisonment with hard labour.

The conviction and incarceration of the younger Gandhi generated a wave of sympathy among the Indians of the Transvaal. The Hamidia Islamia Society met and passed several resolutions, the first of which 'congratulate[d] Mr Harilal Gandhi for his courage in suffering for his community at any cost'; the second of which 'sincerely sympathise[d] with and congratulate[d] Mr and Mrs Gandhi on account of the sentence passed upon their son Harilal through the injustice of the Transvaal Government'.[71]

The imprisonment of his son provoked a complex set of emotions in Gandhi. 'I want every Indian to do what Harilal has done,' said Gandhi *père* in a letter to *Indian Opinion*. 'It will be a part of Harilal's education to go to gaol for the sake of the country.' By going to prison the boy had, in a sense, substituted for the father. As Gandhi explained,

> I have advised every Indian to take up hawking. I am afraid I cannot join myself since I am enrolled as an attorney. I therefore thought it right to advise my son to make his rounds as a hawker. I hesitate to ask others to do things which I cannot do myself. I think whatever my son does at my instance can be taken to have been done by me.[72]

There was, then, a sense of pride, and of vindication. But there appears also to have been a residual sense of guilt. 'Harilal is only a child,' said Gandhi in that same letter. 'He may have deferred to his father's wishes in acting in this manner. It is essential that every Indian should act on his own . . .' Might it have been that while the boy was willing and the father willing him on, his mother and wife were not so keen on Harilal's courting arrest?

14

Prisoner of Conscience

The escalation of passive resistance in the second half of 1908 was viewed with some dismay by the white press. A paper in Pretoria thought General Smuts had 'lowered the prestige of the Colony by his handling of the Asiatic question'. It chastised him for having 'started another controversy with Mr Gandhi'. A paper in Johannesburg was less even-handed. It argued that Gandhi's testimony that Smuts had promised the repeal of the 1907 Act was 'certainly not conclusive'; in any case, the General would have had to ratify the promise in the legislature. The paper concluded that 'whatever hardships the Asiatics have suffered they owe entirely to the recalcitrancy and folly of their leader.'[1]

Whether sympathetic to Gandhi or hostile, such comments represented a huge leap in the Indian's standing in the Transvaal. Before the satyagraha of 1907–8, his opposite number on the white side was Montford Chamney. In fact and in fancy, the lawyer was opposed to the bureaucrat, the permit-seeker to the permit-giver. Now, however, he was being equated with the scholar and war hero General Smuts in the popular imagination. They were the leaders of their respective communities, engaged in an argument about the rights and claims of those they represented. This new equivalence is reflected in the cartoons of the time, which, for example, showed the Asiatics led by Gandhi as akin to an elephant, barring the passage of a steamroller driven by the General himself.[2]

On 14 August 1908, Gandhi wrote to Smuts announcing that the Indians would meet soon to burn their registration certificates. Then, characteristically, he tempered his militancy, asking the General to recognize that 'the difference between you, as representing the Government, and the British Indians is very small indeed.' The discrepancy could be removed by the Government accepting the admission of educated Indians and pre-war residents of the Transvaal.[3]

On the afternoon of Sunday 16 August, some 3,000 Asians congregated outside the Fordsburg Mosque. On a raised plaform sat Gandhi, Essop Mia of the British Indian Association, Dawad Mahomed and Parsee Rustomjee of the Natal Indian Congress, the Cape Indian leader Adam Mahomed, and Leung Quinn to represent the Chinese. Below the podium was 'the Press table, and beyond that, a sea of upturned and expectant faces, with determination and a bitter merriment stamped deep upon each of them.'[4]

The main speaker, inevitably, was Gandhi. Once too shy to read from a prepared text, he was now, a decade later, very willing to directly address a large (and mostly captive) audience. Claiming the country to be 'as much the Indians' as the Europeans'', he said the recent laws sought to treat them as cattle and not men. 'I would far rather pass the whole of my lifetime in gaol and be perfectly happy than see my fellow-countrymen subjected to indignity and I should come out of gaol.' The lesson of their struggle was that

> unenfranchised though we are, unrepresented though we are in the Transvaal, it is open to us to clothe ourselves with an undying franchise, and this consists in recognizing our humanity, in recognizing that we are part and parcel of the great universal whole, that there is the Maker of us all ruling over the destinies of mankind and that our trust should be in Him rather than in earthly kings, and if my countrymen recognize that position I say that no matter what legislation is passed over our heads, if that legislation is in conflict with our ideas of right and wrong, if it is in conflict with our conscience, if it is in conflict with our religion, then we can say that we will not submit to the legislation.

This flight into the Empyrean was followed by a direct attack on an earthly being – the Protector of Asiatics, whom Gandhi charged with 'hopeless incompetence and ignorance'. Unless Montford Chamney was removed from his job, claimed the lawyer, 'there will be no peace'.[5]

After Gandhi had spoken, the Indians came up to place their individual certificates in a large three-legged pot previously saturated with wax.

> Paraffin was then poured in, and the certificates set on fire, amid a scene of the wildest enthusiasm. The crowd hurrahed and shouted themselves

hoarse; hats were thrown in the air, and whistles blown. One Indian, said to be a leading blackleg, walked on to the platform, and, setting alight his certificate, held it aloft. The Chinese then mounted the platform, and put in their certificates with the others.[6]

The day after this conflagration, Gandhi was summoned to Pretoria to meet General Smuts. Also present were the Prime Minister (General Botha), the leading Opposition politician Sir Percy Fitzpatrick (representing the British interest), William Hosken, Albert Cartwright and Leung Quinn. They talked for three hours; eventually, the Government agreed to allow prewar residents to return and register; not to register children under sixteen; and to allow thumb impressions or signatures when issuing trading licences. Having yielded on many points, the Government remained adamant that it could not allow the admittance of educated Indians. As for the 1907 Act, it would not be repealed but remain a 'dead letter'.[7]

Three days after this meeting, Smuts introduced a new bill in the Transvaal Legislature, which contained the concessions regarding Boer certificates and minors, but still barred educated Indians. Moving this 'Asiatic Registration Amendment Bill', the Colonial Secretary admitted the depth of the popular opposition he had faced from the Indians. There was, he said,

> no more awkward position for a Government than a movement of passive resistance . . . In more primitive times one would have met it by simply issuing a declaration of war. But in these times it is impossible to do that, and therefore the situation became a very difficult one for us to handle. I did my best . . . to carry out the law and apply the penalties which have been fixed under the law, and as a result early this year many Asiatics were languishing in prisons from one end of the country to the other. This was an undesirable state of affairs.[8]

With outright repression having failed, said Smuts, he had decided to release Gandhi and his colleagues, and draft a bill less onerous than its predecessor, providing for the voluntary registration of all Asiatics legally resident in the Transvaal. Smuts assured his colleagues that compromise certainly did not mean capitulation. Thus,

> Mr Gandhi has referred to Indians being in partnership with the white population of this country. I have nothing to say against that. It is a claim

which may appeal strongly to the Indians and those who are interested in them, but it is a claim that the white population will never allow (sustained cheers). It will be impossible to meet them on that ground.[9]

The former Jameson Raider Percy Fitzpatrick spoke next. Before the War, Smuts and he were on opposite sides; now, with Boer and Briton reconciled, he endorsed the closed-door policy against the Indians. The House had to 'be absolutely firm on the policy that this Colony was not going to be the home for immigrant Asiatics (Cheers)'. South Africa, thundered Fitzpatrick, 'was redeemed from barbarism by the white people'; and it was 'the white people who will have to carry it on, and defend it if needs be.'[10]

The bill was passed by the House within twenty-four hours of its first reading. Writing to the Governor of the Transvaal, Prime Minister Botha claimed it met 'every reasonable claim' put forward by the Indians. The Governor, in turn, wrote to the Colonial Office asking it to recommend that His Majesty assent to it immediately, otherwise 'the Indians will continue their campaign of resistance against the laws in force in the hope that by so doing they may influence the judgement of the Imperial authorities for the purpose of obtaining concessions they are not entitled to in law, in justice, or in reason.'[11]

The questions that immediately come to mind when reading this are, of course: Whose Justice? Which Rationality?[12]

The concessions offered by the Government did not satisfy the Indians. For the notorious Asiatic Act had not been formally repealed, while educated Indians were still barred from entering the Transvaal. So, on 23 August, another bonfire of certificates was organized outside the Fordsburg Mosque. This time, some Pathans also joined in after having 'admitted their previous errors'. The next day, Gandhi wrote to Smuts about this meeting and the strong sentiments expressed therein. He hoped that 'colonial statesmanship will still find a way out of the difficulty, and close the struggle that has now gone on for nearly two years'.[13]

The General chose not to answer. Gandhi now asked four Indians from Natal, among them his old friend and patron Parsee Rustomjee, to come and show their support (the others included the president and secretary of the Natal Indian Congress). The Natalians toured the towns of the Transvaal, collecting certificates to burn. After a week on the road, they were arrested and deported. They re-entered the colony and recommenced their propaganda activities, going around Indian homes in Johannesburg and raising £200 for the campaign; then, hat in hand, going to Heidelberg and Standerton. In early September they were arrested once more; this time, their sentence was three months in jail with hard labour.[14]

The Natalians were all men of property, and they were all Gujaratis. Gandhi's hope was that their example would inspire Gujarati merchants in the Transvaal to more actively court arrest. At the moment, the Tamils were more ready to take the plunge. Gandhi found them to be 'most enthusiastic' for the struggle; by the end of August, fully one-fourth of the Tamil community had been to prison at least once. They included hawkers, artisans, cooks and waiters, all risking their livelihoods for the larger cause of community self-respect.[15]

Gandhi had now made a new suggestion to the Transvaal Government – that a certain number of educated Indians (say six) be allowed into the colony each year. The suggestion was prompted in part by personal considerations – the sense that as a lawyer himself he should not bar the way to other qualified Indians – and in part by national pride, the sense that given the chance, Indians were fully the equal of Europeans in the modern, high-status professions.[16]

Gandhi's demand, said one Johannesburg paper, was very reasonable, for 'even if the full number of six came every year, we doubt if that formidable invasion would ruin the Transvaal.' Other colonies such as Australia and Canada permitted a certain number of Asians to enter each year. By instituting a colour bar, the Transvaal Legislature had 'enacted, for the first time in the history of the Empire, so far as we know, that in no circumstances, under no conditions, shall the people from another of the Imperial states set foot here'.[17]

General Smuts and his fellow ministers saw it differently. One Gandhi was trouble enough. If six such lawyers were allowed in every year, would they not mobilize the Indians for more and greater rights? The problem with educated Indians was that they might instil in their working-class compatriots the dangerous idea that the avowal or denial of equal citizenship should have nothing to do with the colour of one's skin.

Joseph Doke was in London on holiday. Reading the news from the Transvaal and regularly meeting the members of the South African British

Indian Committee, he was itching to get back to where his friend was. On 11 September he wrote to Gandhi that 'you may be sure that my whole heart goes out to you and the Indians in their great affliction ... So go on; the cause is righteous and it *must* prevail. It's only a matter of some time and suffering. We *shall* be the victors. It's a fight not for South African Indians only but for the dumb millions of India!'[18]

In the second week of September, the British Indian Association announced that its chairman, Essop Mia, was resigning in order to go on pilgrimage to Mecca. He was replaced by Ahmed Mahomed Cachalia, also a prominent merchant, who had already proved his credentials by going to jail. On the other side, the Transvaal Government began toughening its stand. The shops of merchants who had courted arrest were boarded up, and their goods confiscated and auctioned.[19]

In the last week of September, Gandhi went to Phoenix for a spell. A small school had been established there, with a Gujarati, Purushottamdas Desai, as principal, and Albert West and John Cordes among the teachers. On this visit, Gandhi hoped to open the school to boarders from elsewhere in Natal. The curriculum was in both Gujarati and English, and included instruction in the religion of the boy's choice. Desai would teach Hindu boys the elements of their faith, West would take care of the Christians, a visiting *maulvi* the Muslims, while (in a typically Gandhian touch) the Theosophist Cordes would instruct those with more unorthodox, experimental leanings.

Just as characteristically, Gandhi paid close attention to what the boys would eat. They were encouraged to consume green vegetables, fresh fruit and pulses. On the other hand, tea, cocoa and coffee were forbidden, as these 'are produced through the labour of men who work more or less in conditions of slavery'.[20]

In Natal, Gandhi was interviewed by a correspondent of the colony's most influential newspaper. He was described as 'the doughty champion of the Indians' cause in the Transvaal' (this said with some relief, since he was no longer the doughty champion of the Indians' cause in Natal). Gandhi told the paper that whites in the Transvaal were 'frightened with the bogey of an invasion of half-educated youths from Natal'. The passive resisters were fighting for something larger, namely 'the honour of India, and for a principle ... viz. that restriction should be based on sensible [criteria] and not on grounds of colour or race'. The education test was not the issue; it could be made as severe as they wanted. It was the exclusion on racial grounds that they opposed. The paper was reminded of the larger Imperial consequences of the controversy. Englishmen 'could not have India as the brightest jewel in the British Crown, and yet use the jewel as a target from every point.'[21]

Joseph Doke, now back in South Africa, had resolved to write a life of his friend, and thus to tell a story of struggle and sacrifice that must and would triumph, a story based in part on what Doke had seen and in part on what the subject could or would tell him. On the last day of September he wrote to Gandhi begging him to

> try and not get confiscated and deported or any thing of that kind – if you can help it just now. I have a thousand questions to ask – on any one of which of course the welfare of the British Empire depends. I want to know why the Indians recalled you from India by cable [in 1902]. I want to know whether the Durban people gave the Indian stretcher-bearers a good send off when they went to Colenso and Spion Kop, and did the work done on the battle fields make them more friendly to you? I want to know all that happened since, and especially I want a good cabinet photograph of yourself – without your hat. So don't get caught![22]

In contrast to Doke's wishes, Gandhi had now decided that he must more actively challenge the Government to arrest him. Gathering a group of Natal Indians, he crossed the Transvaal border on 6 October, and was detained at Volksrust. When asked to produce his registration certificate he said he had none. He was remanded to Volksrust prison, from where he sent a written message to *Indian Opinion*, reminding its readers that 'this campaign knows no distinctions of Hindus, Muslims, Parsis, Christians, Bengalis, Madrasis, Gujaratis, Punjabis and others. All of us are Indians, and are fighting for India.'[23]

On the 14th, Gandhi and those who had crossed the border with him were brought before a magistrate in Volksrust. Gandhi told the judge that 'he took sole responsibility for having advised them to enter the Colony.' He added that 'he was quite prepared to suffer the consequences of his action, as he always had been.' He was convicted and fined £25, or, in default of payment, sentenced to two months imprisonment with hard labour.[24]

The news of Gandhi's arrest was communicated by word of mouth across the Transvaal. The telegraph carried it to London, where, a mere two days after he was convicted, a protest meeting was held in Caxton Hall. Present in London at this time were some celebrated Indian nationalists. One, Lajpat Rai, said that 'Mr Gandhi, in his gaol, had the satisfaction of knowing that he was making history.' Another, Bipan Chandra Pal, said that 'every stroke of Mr Gandhi's hammer on the stones meant a stroke on the shackles which bound their country; every piece of stone severed from another piece by that hammer was a link that removed [Indians] from the chain that bound them to the Mother Country' [i.e., England]. To a great burst of cheering, the Bengali radical continued: 'Go on, brother Gandhi.'

Rai and Pal were two of the three main leaders of the Swadeshi movement; the third was Bal Gangadhar Tilak. The trio were known with affection and admiration as 'Lal, Bal and Pal'. That Gandhi was so extravagantly praised by Lal and Pal in London (Bal was then in jail in India) testified to his rising stature in the national consciousness. His actions in the Transvaal were appreciated both by the established and the emergent nationalists. Thus one of the resolutions at the Caxton Hall meeting was seconded by the radical student leader V. D. Savarkar; another by the young art critic and historian Ananda Coomaraswamy.[25]

Back in the Transvaal, a meeting was held on 18 October to condemn Gandhi's arrest. Some 1,500 people from all over the colony came to the Hamidia Hall. Two black flags were flown at half-mast, to mark the sacrifices of the compatriots in jail. The main speech was by A. M. Cachalia. The Government hoped that by arresting their leader the movement would collapse. Cachalia dismissed this as a 'fallacy of the first order'. With Gandhi in prison, he said, 'each one of us must be prepared to play the leader.'

Harilal Gandhi also spoke at this meeting. 'The day his father was arrested was a festival day for him,' said the son, 'but he could not help feeling how ridiculously the latter had been charged and punished. Asking a man who has been practising in South Africa for 13 years to give his identification particulars was nothing short of cowardice.'[26]

Naturally, the white press in the Rand viewed Gandhi's arrest somewhat differently. In giving Gandhi only two months in jail, said the *Star* of Johannesburg, 'the Transvaal Government has been unduly lenient towards the malicious activities of the leader of the Asiatic movement'. 'Far better it is that the gaols should be crowded,' remarked the paper, 'than that the native population – already somewhat unsettled on the Rand – should be tempted to emulate the tactics of their coloured brethren from the Far East'.[27]

Gandhi was sent to Volksrust Prison, to join (among others) his old Durban friend Parsee Rustomjee. It was the month of Ramadan, so the Muslim prisoners were fasting. In any case, with the preponderance of mealie pap at meals there 'was incessant grumbling about food'. These grumbles reached the ears of Joseph Doke. The good Christian called on the Director of Prisons, telling him that mealie pap was abhorrent to Hindu prisoners, who were mostly vegetarian; as well as to Muslims, since the animals from whom the fat was extracted were not killed in the prescribed fashion.[28]

To fulfil the sentence of 'hard labour', the prisoners were taken every morning to a field with stony soil which they had to dig with spades. The work was new to Gandhi, and he found his hands were soon covered in blisters. 'It was difficult to bend down, and the spade seemed to weigh a *maund*.'[29]

After ten days, Gandhi was moved to Johannesburg, where he was to appear as a witness in a court case. He was taken by train in a third-class compartment. When he disembarked, with his escort, at the city's Park Station, he was noticed by a group of Tamil hawkers. They watched, with fascination and not a little dismay, as their leader – clad in convict's garb of jacket with a numbered badge, short trousers and leather sandals – was marched out of the station and into the road outside. The warder accompanying Gandhi offered him the option of taking a cab to the prison (for which he would have to pay) or walking. The prisoner chose to walk, climbing up the hill with his bags. He was followed, at a respectful distance, by the Tamils, until he disappeared into a prison on whose entrance was carved the motto, 'Union Makes Strength'.[30]

The Tamil hawkers conveyed what they had seen to Henry Polak. Polak issued a statement claiming that the treatment of Gandhi was reminiscent of the Spanish Inquisition, which likewise marched its victims 'clothed in bag-shaped yellow garb' through the town before disposing of them.[31] He also sent an angry telegram to L. W. Ritch in London, who passed on the complaint to the Colonial Office. They, in turn, wrote to the Transvaal Government asking if it was correct that

15 and 16. Two great Europeans who loomed large in Gandhi's life in South Africa: his principal adversary, the Boer general Jan Christian Smuts (*left*), and his principal mentor, the Russian writer Leo Tolstoy (*below*).

ЛЕВЪ ТОЛСТОЙ

17. A photograph of Gandhi, taken in 1909. This was presented by Hermann Kallenbach to Thambi Naidoo, with the inscription (clearly visible): 'If we are true to him we will be true to ourselves.'

18, 19, 20 and 21. Four of Gandhi's staunchest supporters (*clockwise from left*): the Johannesburg merchant A. M. Cachalia, the English vegetarian Albert West, the Tamil radical Thambi Naidoo and the Durban merchant Parsee Rustomjee.

22, 23, 24 and 25. Four more key supporters (*clockwise from left*): Gandhi's argumentative housemate Millie Graham Polak, his son Harilal (as a satyagrahi), and his nephews Maganlal and Chhaganlal, who together kept Phoenix and *Indian Opinion* going.

"The Steam Roller v. The Elephant. (The Elephant 'sat tight'; the Steam Roller exploded.")—*Sunday Times.* [Reproduced by kind permission]

26. A contemporary cartoon of the satyagraha in the Transvaal, with Gandhi on the elephant and Smuts in the steam roller. The elephant is saying, 'Stop yer ticklin', Jan'.

27. The Baptist Minister Joseph Doke, Gandhi's friend, host and first biographer.

28. Leung Quinn, the leader of the Chinese satyagrahis.

29. Two Indians Gandhi greatly looked up to: the liberal politician Gopal Krishna Gokhale (*left*) and the Parsi philanthrophist Ratan Tata (*right*). The photograph was taken in or about 1914, probably in the garden of Tata's house in Twickenham.

30. Gandhi's key lieutenant, Thambi Naidoo, addressing a crowd in or near Durban during the 1913 satyagraha.

31. Gandhi, early 1914, wearing white to mourn the deaths of Indian strikers killed in police firing.

'Gandhi was marched through the streets in convict dress'. The charge was admitted, but qualified by the claim that when conducted from the station to the prison, Gandhi did not have to wear handcuffs, and 'when in Court as a witness he did not appear in prison clothes.'[32]

In Johannesburg Prison, Gandhi was put with convicts serving time for murder and larceny. He felt 'extremely uneasy', more so when an African and a Chinese 'exchanged obscene jokes, uncovering each other's genitals'. For comfort he read the copy of the Bhagavad-Gita he had brought with him. His mood improved when Polak came to visit, and when Kallenbach sent a supply of bread and cheese.

On 4 November Gandhi was taken back to Volksrust. Seeing him enter the train in prison uniform, the hawkers on the platform 'were filled with tears'. Word of his journey got around, so that en route, at Heidelberg and at Standerton, Indians met him with supplies of food, which his escort allowed him to accept.

Shortly after moving back to Volksrust Prison, Gandhi heard from Albert West at Phoenix that Kasturba had suffered a haemorrhage. The doctor attending her was not sure she would survive. West suggested that Gandhi pay his fine and join her. He answered that this would be 'impossible', since 'when I embarked upon the struggle I counted the cost. If Mrs. Gandhi must leave me without even the consolation a devoted husband could afford, so be it.'

Kasturba's illness had once more brought to the fore the competing claims on Gandhi's life. The obligations of family clashed with the demands of the struggle. Kasturba and he had now been married for more than twenty-five years. They had, in the emotional as well as sexual sense, always been true to one another. Perhaps because of their periodic, extended separations, Kasturba deeply cherished their time together. Rajkot, Bombay, Durban, Johannesburg, Phoenix – in all of these places she had lived with him and for him, but never really felt at home. Not fluent in English, reserved by nature, forbidden by custom and tradition to seek out strangers on her own, Kasturba was comfortable in, and comforted by, the company of her children and her husband. The children were with her, mostly, while her husband was mostly absent. And so, all through their time in South Africa, it was her husband's company and attention that she craved most.

Her love was reciprocated. Yet unlike Kasturba, Gandhi had more than his family to look out for or answer to. Asked to choose – as he was here – Gandhi would place the interests of the community above those of his own wife. He explained both the dilemma and his choice in a letter that Manilal could read to her. He told Kasturba that since he had 'offered my all to the satyagraha struggle', he could not cut short his sentence by paying the fine. He asked however for a daily bulletin on her health, and then added these words of encouragement and consolation:

> If you keep courage and take the necessary nutrition, you will recover. If, however, my ill luck so has it that you pass away, I should only say that there would be nothing wrong in your doing so in your separation from me while I am still alive. I love you so dearly that even if you are dead, you will be alive to me. Your soul is deathless. I repeat what I have frequently told you and assure you that if you do succumb to your illness, I will not marry again.[33]

This is a letter of an unusual and perhaps unexpected tenderness. According to custom and tradition, part of the duties of a Hindu wife was to make sure that she did not predecease her husband. This prospect must have worried Kasturba; so too, perhaps, the prospect of Gandhi taking a second wife. His own father had done so, and while his first wife was still alive. Hence Gandhi's assurances, here made (as he notes) not for the first time.

Gandhi was released from Volksrust on 12 December, having completed his term. Before he left the prison, he presented a kindly warder with an inscribed copy of Tolstoy's *The Kingdom of God Is Within You*.[34] When he reached Johannesburg, he was met at the station by a crowd of 300, mostly Indians, but also including Henry and Millie Polak, Joseph Doke and Sonja Schlesin. As 'he jumped from the train, Mr Gandhi was garlanded amidst terrific cheers'. He was then carried shoulder high to the mosque in Fordsburg, where he spoke briefly to a 'most orderly' crowd of some 1,500 people.[35]

While Gandhi was in prison, meetings in solidarity were regularly held at the Hamidia Mosque in Johannesburg. In the last week of November, 'practically the whole Indian community in Johannesburg' turned up for a meeting outside the mosque. The Chinese leader Leung Quinn spoke first. The star turn, however, was A. M. Cachalia, the Gujarati trader who was now chairman of the British Indian Association. Cachalia first quoted Booker T. Washington, who said the black man had to do better than the white man to get any recognition. He then provided a robust defence of satyagraha. Some Europeans feared that the Indians' avowal of passive resistance would provoke the Africans to adopt similar methods, and proceed from there to violent protest. Cachalia thought this preposterous – 'surely passive resistance,' he said sarcastically, 'was not the spark that set ablaze the Natal rebellion of 1906. Rightly or wrongly, it was their sense of injustice that caused that outbreak.'

In Cachalia's opinion,

Men do not proceed from passive to active resistance. The passive resister is higher in the moral scale, and in that of human development than the active resister . . . Passive resistance is a matter of heart, of conscience, of trained understanding. The natives of South Africa need many generations of culture and development before they can hope to be passive resisters in the true sense of the term. Meanwhile, they will be what robust men are – grateful for justice done them, resentful of injustice, and in the latter case they will probably seek their remedy irrespective of example, until the difficult lesson of non-resistance to evil is learnt. But surely our critics would be better advised to urge the natives to substitute for the rifle and the assegai the peaceful methods of the passive resister, and better advised still if they removed the need of any resistance whatsoever . . . by doing justice though the heavens fall.[36]

Cachalia saw, much more clearly than Gandhi, that the roots of native discontent lay in discrimination and expropriation by Europeans. His speech manifested a sure grasp of the thought of Gandhi's own mentor, Tolstoy. And it provided a compelling defence of non-violence as the most moral means of challenging injustice.

As the Indians went in and out of jail in the Transvaal, there was a significant development among their compatriots in Natal. They now had a second weekly newspaper, complementing Gandhi's *Indian Opinion*. Named *African Chronicle*, this was edited by a Tamil named P. S. Aiyar, who had come out to Durban in 1898 and married a local girl. Despite its name the new paper, like Gandhi's own, gave little coverage to 'African' issues. Rather, it was a vehicle for the Tamils of Natal, who did not feel wholly represented in or by *Indian Opinion*, which now carried articles in English and Gujarati only.

African Chronicle made its first appearance in June 1908. It ran to sixteen pages: four in English, eight in Tamil, with a final four pages containing advertisements taken out by Tamil traders and shopkeepers. It carried news of indentured labourers on plantations, and of merchants in towns. Sport was a passion, with football and boxing matches being extensively reported. The editor was particularly preoccupied with the £3 tax on freed labourers, and regularly wrote asking for its abolition. The paper also keenly followed developments in the Transvaal. Early issues praised Gandhi for his 'steadfastness of purpose' and 'deadly earnestness'. His arrest in October 1908 had 'cast a gloom over the Indian community'. Gandhi was 'our esteemed leader' – esteemed for, among other things, his 'characteristic plain and straightforward manner'. The 'meritorious struggle' he led was 'fighting for the honour and freedom of the nation'. The paper endorsed 'Mr M. K. Gandhi's known intense desire to effect a union between these great sections of the Indian population' (namely, Hindus and Muslims). *African Chronicle* shared Gandhi's dislike of Montford Chamney – whom it called 'a little tin-god' – as well as his admiration of Thambi Naidoo. When Naidoo was arrested for the third time, the paper 'congratulate[d] the Indians in South Africa for possessing such a man'.[37]

The conflict between the Indians and the Transvaal Government was played out against the backdrop of a growing movement for the union of the South African colonies. The architects of the war against the Boers, Joseph Chamberlain and Alfred Milner, had always hoped that victory would be followed by a creation of a single integrated state, forming part of the British Empire. In his farewell speech in February 1903, Chamberlain told his audience to 'make preparation for the ultimate federation of South Africa which is destined, I hope in the near future, to establish a new nation under the British flag, who shall be "daughter in her mother's house and mistress in her own".'[38]

In 1906 Transvaal became a 'self-governing colony' on the model of Natal and the Cape. Orange Free State followed two years later. In May 1908, white politicians from the four territories met in an 'intercolonial' conference to discuss the prospects of a united federation. This was followed by a full-fledged 'National Convention', which first met in

Durban in October 1908, followed by meetings in other towns of South Africa.

The motivations of those seeking union were partly economic. The standardization of customs duties, taxes and railway lines would make business much easier. Whites in South Africa were impressed by the example of Canada and Australia, where once discrete territories had come together as single federations. However, they faced a problem largely absent in those other British dominions – a very large native population. Some Africans and some Indians were voters in the Cape. While a few liberals sought an extension of the Cape franchise, most people at the Convention thought that people of colour should not be granted the vote. The Transvaal politician Percy Fitzpatrick insisted that the 'black man was incapable of civilization'. Abraham Fischer of the Orange Free State remarked that since 'self-preservation was the first law of nature', whites should keep the vote to themselves. Another Free Stater, C. R. De Wet, said that 'Providence had drawn the line between black and white and we must make that clear to the Natives [and] not instil into their minds false ideas of equality.'

The delegates from the Afrikaner-controlled colonies prevailed. The Transvaal Prime Minister, Louis Botha, persuaded his Cape colleagues that their priority must be to bring about a 'union of the white races in South Africa'. Complications about the native franchise would imperil this union. It was agreed that while the coloured voters in the Cape would not immediately be disenfranchised, in other colonies only whites would vote; and whites alone would sit in the Union Parliament.[39]

In December 1908, as Gandhi was leaving jail, the Governor of the Transvaal, Lord Selborne, circulated to the members of the Convention some 'informal suggestions on the question of the Native Franchise'. This proposed a 'civilization qualification', whereby to be eligible for the franchise, a man had to (a) commit to monogamy; (b) speak a European language; (c) meet a certain property or income qualification; and (d) be 'habitually wearing clothes and living in a house as distinct from a hut'.

European males who fulfilled these criteria would each have a full vote. On the other hand, 'every non-European who proves the possession of the civilisation qualification before an impartial tribunal' would be given 'a vote equal in value to one tenth the vote of a European'. The son of this civilized native voter, if he likewise met those four criteria, would be awarded one ninth of a vote, his son one eighth, and so on. Selborne's scheme allowed for the possibility of miscegenation. The son of a European father and a non-European mother would – provided he enjoyed the 'civilizational qualification' – have one-fifth of a vote, his son a quarter of a vote, and so on. Finally, there was also an age stipulation. Whereas qualified European males voted at the age of twenty-one, a civilized native or Asian would be allowed to vote only at thirty-one, his son at thirty, his grandson at twenty-nine. The offspring of mixed unions would be granted the franchise at twenty-six.

Selborne's proposals were surely influenced by the ongoing protests of the Indians in the Transvaal. As an Englishman, he knew also of precedents in the home country, where some Indians had been granted the vote and two of them had even entered Parliament. Gandhi himself believed that, given the chance and the freedom, all Indians could prove themselves to be as worthy as all Europeans. To be sure, he thought this might take some time. But his incrementalism was positively radical in comparison to the ideas of colonialists like Lord Selborne. Unlike Gandhi, the Governor thought that only individuals, and not whole communities, could ever ascend upwards on the civilizational ladder. His horizons were also far more extended. Whereas Gandhi hoped for racial parity in his own lifetime, the Governor thought that in ten generations, or perhaps two hundred years' time, a particular man of colour might – always assuming he or his forebears did not slip backwards into polygamy, ignorance of a European language, etc. – come to enjoy the same political rights as a white man.

To be fair to Selborne, his mind at least admitted the odd shade of grey. Most members of the National Convention, on the other hand, thought only in black and white. They wished to deny the vote, any vote, even a fraction of a vote, to non-whites altogether. His Lordship's proposals were rejected immediately.[40]

To this chorus in favour of white supremacy in South Africa, there were two dissenting voices – the brother and sister duo of W. P. Schreiner and Olive Schreiner. W. P. Schreiner was a former Prime Minister of Cape Colony, a liberal by instinct and a humanist by conviction. At the National Convention he urged that members of non-European descent be allowed at least to sit in the Senate, or upper house, of the Union

Parliament. Writing to General Smuts, he said that 'to my mind *the* fundamental question is that of our policy regarding "colour".' To embody in the Union Constitution 'a vertical line or barrier separating its people upon the grounds of colour into a privileged class or caste and an unprivileged, inferior proletariat is, as I see the problem, as imprudent as it would be to build a grand building upon unsound and sinking foundations'.[41]

When he failed to move his colleagues in South Africa, Schreiner travelled to England, to lobby British opinion. The Act of Union being prepared, said Schreiner, was better viewed as 'an Act of Separation between the minority and the majority of the people of South Africa'. Under it, 'the coloured inhabitants are barred from the opportunity to rise and evolve naturally, which is the right of every free man in a free country'.[42]

On this question, the writer Olive Schreiner was even more radical than her brother. Raised in the Cape countryside, she was an autodidact, who read Herbert Spencer, John Stuart Mill and Darwin, while also (like Gandhi) being inspired by the Sermon on the Mount. Writing stories from an early age, Olive was best known for *The Story of an African Farm* (1883), a novel set in the Karoo featuring a brutal overseer named Bonaparte and, to counter him, a woman who sought freedom outside marriage, later described as 'the first wholly feminist' character in the English novel. Olive had lived in London for several years in the 1880s, where she befriended left-wing thinkers such as George Bernard Shaw and Eleanor Marx. This experience informed her book *Dreams*, published in 1890, which presented a series of allegories excoriating the rich and advocating an ethical socialism.[43]

In December 1908, Olive Schreiner was asked this question by a Transvaal newspaper: 'What form of Closer Union do you favour – Federation or Unification; and for what reasons?' She answered that 'all persons born in the country or permanently resident here should be one in the eye of the State', and all should enjoy the franchise, regardless of race or colour. She then offered this arresting vision of the future:

> The problems of the twentieth century will not be a repetition of those of the nineteenth or those which went before it. The walls dividing continents are breaking down: everywhere European, Asiatic and African will inter-lard. The world on which the twenty-first century will open its eyes,

will be one widely different from that which the twentieth sees at its awakening. And the problem which this century will have to solve, is the accomplishment of this interaction of distinct human varieties on the largest and most beneficent lines, making for the development of humanity as a whole, and carried out in a manner consonant with modern ideals and modern social wants. It will not always be the European who forms the upper layer.

The South Africa that Olive Schreiner strove for would draw democratically on all its constituent elements. She spoke thus of the special characteristics of the Europeans – who, 'at least for themselves, have always loved freedom and justice'; of the natives of the country, the Bantu as she called them following contemporary usage – 'one of the finest breeds of the African stock'; and of the Asiatics – 'a section of people sober, industrious, and intelligent'. She argued that 'it is out of this great, heterogeneous mass of humans that the South African nation will be built'. Mindful of the divisions within, she pointedly and prophetically asked: 'As long as nine-tenths of our community have no permanent stake in the land, and no right or share in our government, can we ever feel safe? Can we ever know peace?'[44]

The previous May, speaking to the YMCA in Johannesburg, Gandhi put forward the idea that South Africa should be a nation for more than whites alone. Olive Schreiner now provided a sharper, more passionate statement of that point of view. One does not know whether she had read Gandhi's speech, but her own reflections were reprinted in *Indian Opinion*, where the editor (Henry Polak) said the journal agreed 'entirely' that 'a people kept in a state of political helotage are a source of danger to the State, sooner or later'. Women such as Olive Schreiner, wrote Polak, 'are of greater permanent value to the world than a continent of Napoleons'.[45]

Within a week of his release, Gandhi was back in court defending passive resisters. Once the new, amended Act came into force, some Indians had begun queueing up for certificates. They were picketed by a group of satyagrahis led by Thambi Naidoo. On 18 December, appearing for a group charged with 'causing trouble among Asiatics who are desirous of complying with the law', Gandhi told the judge that his clients 'only want to let those who forget their manhood know that there is such a thing as ostracism'. (The judge answered that it was not ostracism but 'a wholesale fear of incurring grievous bodily harm'.)[46]

The fact that picketing had to be recommended spoke of a real rift in the community. Exhausted by the struggle, hoping to get on with their lives, many Indians were reluctant to go to jail again or to live without certificates of residence. Noting the rush to register under the new Act, Gandhi said 'this need not depress us'. For 'the great Thoreau said that one sincere man is [worth] more than a hundred thousand insincere men.'

The cleavages within the movement were of class and of ethnicity. Hawkers, and Tamils, were now more likely to become satyagrahis than traders or Gujaratis. 'The Tamils have surpassed all expectations', wrote Gandhi in *Indian Opinion*: 'All their leaders are now in gaol.' Also worthy of praise were the Parsees who, despite their small numbers, had made a huge contribution to the political field in India. In South Africa too, 'we do not find a Parsee who has complied with the Government's senseless law.' Gandhi thought that 'Muslims and Gujarati Hindus should hang their heads in shame before the Tamils and the Parsees.'[47]

In the last week of December, Gandhi went to Durban to be with Kasturba. He stayed three weeks in all, with one eye on the health of his wife, and the other on the future of the struggle. On 5 January he wrote to Olive Doke that he had 'not come to Natal to rest and am having none. You wish you were in Phoenix. So do I. You would then have assisted me in nursing Mrs. Gandhi. Now that you may say is very selfish. But self plays a very important part in our lives.'[48]

Gandhi moved Kasturba from Phoenix to Durban, where she stayed with and was attended by a Dr Nanji. He was the best Indian doctor in Natal, and also a close friend who had supported the satyagraha struggle and spoken out in public on its behalf.

On 16 January Gandhi left for the Transvaal. That night he wrote a letter to Chanchal Gandhi asking her to 'give up the idea of staying with Harilal for the present'. 'It will do good for both of you', said the patriarch. 'Harilal will grow by staying apart and will perform his other duties. Love for you does not consist only in staying with you.'

As the letter suggests, it appeared that Gandhi's son Harilal was facing a conflict between the needs of his self and the claims of his society. By January 1909, the twenty-year-old had been to jail twice already. He now prepared to court arrest for a third time. In between jail terms he was based in Johannesburg, assisting in the campaign. His wife Chanchal, at Phoenix, missed him terribly. They now had a baby girl who – if things went on the same way – would grow up with an absent father, much as Harilal himself had done.

In a vivid memoir, Harilal's youngest brother recalled the competing claims on the first of Gandhi's sons. Devadas was some thirteen years younger than Harilal, and just a little older than his brother's child. He adored Harilal, with his cheery manner and his handsome face, his hair parted in the middle 'with beautiful curls over the forehead'. Before one of his departures from Phoenix to court arrest, Harilal told the boy, 'Yes, Devadas, I will send you your top from Durban.' 'I forget the top', wrote the boy, decades later. 'But I remember sharing sweets with my niece the next day, while my sister-in-law shed tears over a letter.'[49]

Harilal was torn between his wife, whom he loved dearly, and with whom he had (by all accounts) a companionable marriage, and his obligations to his father and the movement he led. At this time, Harilal was briefly back at Phoenix with Chanchal. How long he would stay there was not certain, since he might at any moment be asked to re-enter the Transvaal and seek arrest. He communicated his confusions to his father, who answered that he could

> see that you are unhappy. I have got to accept your opinion as to whether you would be unhappy or not on account of separation. However, I see that you will have to undergo imprisonment for a long period ... The struggle is likely to be a prolonged one. There are some indications of its being a short one also. There is a likelihood of Lord Curzon interceding. Let me know what arrangement should be made in regard to Chanchal during your absence.

The letter ends with this intriguing line: 'I have not been able to follow what you say about taking a stone in exchange for a pie. In what context have you written that?' It seems reasonable to assume that Harilal was contrasting the pie of marital bliss with the stone of physical separation.[50]

In the first week of the New Year, *The Times* printed a letter signed by twenty-six Europeans living in the Transvaal. The first signatory was W. Hosken. The others included seven clergymen (among them Joseph

Doke and Charles Phillips), several accountants, the jeweller Gabriel Isaacs, the draper W. M. Vogl, and the missionary-turned-advocate A. W. Baker, all old friends of Gandhi. The letter reminded the British public that 'there is an important body of sympathizers in the European section of the community who are grieved and hurt at the treatment being meted out to the Asiatics [in the Transvaal] for no apparent purpose at all.' The signatories saluted the 'courage and self-sacrifice' of a movement in which 'all faiths and castes are represented'. Morality and the Imperial interest mandated that their demands be conceded. For passive resisters deported to India from the Transvaal would 'not be slow to ventilate [their grievances] amidst the sympathetic surroundings of their native land'.[51]

At this time, Gandhi himself was unsure as to whether the struggle would be long or short. He had, as he indicated to Harilal, some hope that the former Viceroy of India, Lord Curzon, would help bring about a settlement. As Viceroy, Curzon had written with feeling about the 'invidious' and 'odious' handicaps facing Indians in the Transvaal.[52] He was now in South Africa, on a private visit. Gandhi asked to meet him when he passed through Johannesburg; Curzon said this would not be possible since he had 'so short a time here'. However, he asked the Indians to 'give me as full a statement of their case as they can'; he would read this on the train to Cape Town, where he was due to meet Generals Botha and Smuts.[53]

On 29 January, Gandhi wrote a remarkable letter to his nephew Maganlal. Some Gujarati merchants were turning away from the struggle, and the Pathans had been sceptical of Gandhi in any case. With earlier attempts on his life in mind, he told Maganlal that

> I may have to meet death in South Africa at the hands of my countrymen. If that happens you should rejoice. It will unite the Hindus and Mussalmans ... The enemies of the community are constantly making efforts against such a unity. In such a great endeavour, someone will have to sacrifice his life. If I make that sacrifice, I shall regard myself, as well as you, my colleagues, fortunate.[54]

The letter was posted from Natal, where Gandhi had come again to spend time with his wife. Dr Nanji had diagnosed her as suffering from pernicious anaemia, for which the textbook treatment included a healthy dose of beef extract. When Gandhi discovered what Kasturba had been given, he decided to take her back to Phoenix and treat her by his own, naturopathic methods. The doctor remonstrated; he was a man of science, as well as a Parsi, for whom there were no taboos as regards beef. He argued that Kasturba was too sick to be moved. Besides, it was raining heavily. Gandhi was unmoved; he sent a message to Phoenix to make preparations for their arrival. Albert West met them at the station with hot milk, umbrellas and six men to carry Kasturba home in a hammock.[55]

'Dr and Mrs Nanji were much grieved' by his removing Kasturba from their care, wrote Gandhi to Kallenbach. 'They do not believe in water treatment. They consider me to be a brutal husband and Dr Nanji certainly considers me to be either mad or over conceited. I have risked friendships for the sake of a principle.'

At Phoenix, Gandhi gave Kasturba a series of cold baths. He also put her on a diet of fruit. 'She appears to be none the worse for it', he reported to Kallenbach:

> She is probably better. But she has lost heart. She cannot bear the idea of my leaving her bedside for a single minute. Like a baby she clings to me and hugs me. I fear that my departure next week will send her to her grave. It is a great conflict of duty for me. Yet there is no doubt in my mind that I must leave her next week and accept the King's hospitality.

It was a curious sequence of phrases and sentiments: recognizing that he faced, yet again, a serious conflict between family duties and societal obligations, Gandhi had 'no doubt' that (yet again) he would choose to go to prison rather than stay with his ailing wife.[56]

On 2 February, Curzon wrote to Gandhi reporting on his meeting with the Boer soldier-politicians. Botha and Smuts had promised 'to treat the British Indians in the Transvaal in a spirit of liberality and justice'. But no specific promises were made with regard to, for example, the repeal of the 1907 Act or the admittance of educated Indians. Curzon's own view was that 'a final and satisfactory settlement of the vexed problem' would have to await the creation of a single, unified government of all the South African colonies.[57]

The letter was posted to the Johannesburg address of the British Indian Association, who sent it on to Phoenix. Its non-committal, even unhelpful, contents made Gandhi decide to renew the struggle. He may also have been provoked by derisive comments in the Transvaal press, suggesting that passive resistance was on its last legs. 'Mr Gandhi has been beaten', wrote one paper, 'and the sooner he admits it and tells his deluded fellow-countrymen frankly that they have not the ghost of a chance of altering the opinions of the people of this Colony, so much the better for all concerned.'[58]

In the second week of February, Gandhi dispatched Harilal across the border from Natal, to seek (and obtain) his third term of imprisonment. The father followed ten days later. Like his eldest son, he was arrested for refusing to produce a valid registration certificate, and remanded in police custody.

On 25 February Gandhi was brought to trial before a magistrate in Volksrust. He told the court that he would 'continue to incur the penalties so long as justice, as I conceive it, has not been rendered by the State to a portion of its citizens'. Sentenced to pay a £50 fine or accept three months in prison with hard labour, he opted for the latter. Afterwards, he released two letters that he had composed before going to court. The first, in Gujarati, was addressed to the weak-kneed who had succumbed to the Government's demands. It reflected a certain resignation; where once the blacklegs were fiercely chastised, now they were asked to do what they could. 'Those who are fallen can rise again,' said Gandhi. 'They can still go to gaol . . . Even if they cannot, they can offer monetary help, and send statements to newspapers to say that, though they have surrendered, they are in favour of the fight and wish it success.' The second letter, in English, was addressed to his 'Tamil brethren', whom he praised for having discharged their duties 'brilliantly' and borne 'the brunt of the battle'.[59]

To his 'great pleasure', in Volksrust prison Gandhi was placed in the company of some fifty fellow satyagrahis. They included Harilal, and his old and valued friend Parsee Rustomjee. The food this time was 'nice and clean' and included large helpings of ghee. The 'hard labour' they were put to involved repairing roads and weeding fields.

A day after he was sentenced, Gandhi wrote to Chanchal asking her to read 'good writing and poems' to Kasturba, to take care of her own health and to breastfeed her child for some more time. Then he added: 'Harilal and I are quite well [in Volksrust jail]. Be sure that we are happier here than you.' (He spoke for himself, but perhaps not for Harilal.)[60]

After a week in Volksrust, Gandhi was shifted to Pretoria. He travelled with an escort, and at night, shivered under a blanket. His cell in this jail was marked 'isolated'; the bed was hard, there was no pillow, and ghee was served only twice a week (but the dreadful mealie pap every day). The other prisoners were all Africans; one asked Gandhi whether his crime was theft, another if it was the illegal sale of alcohol.

The work he was put to in Pretoria was dreary, namely, polishing the floor of his cell and the corridor. He was also denied permission to write letters in Gujarati. He pleaded that his wife was recovering from a serious illness, and that his letters 'served as medicine to her', but the authorities were unyielding.[61]

Since he could not communicate directly with his wife, Gandhi sent her a message via Albert West. 'Please tell Mrs G. that I am all right', he wrote to West.

> She knows that my happiness depends more upon my mental state than upon physical surroundings. Let her cherish this thought and not worry about me. For the sake of the children, she should help herself get better. She should have the bandages regularly and add hip-baths if necessary. She should adhere to the diet I used to give. She ought not to start walking till she is quite restored.[62]

It was brave and unselfish of Gandhi not to draw attention to his own condition. For this, without question, was his harshest prison term yet. He could write only one letter a month, and there were strict curbs on visitors. Henry Polak applied three times to see him, but was refused permission. However, Gandhi's agent in Pretoria was allowed to visit. This was M. Lichtenstein, the man who, back in September 1906, had offered the vote of thanks at the Empire Theatre meeting which first proposed passive resistance. Now, visiting the leader of the satyagraha in jail, he was dismayed to find him in solitary confinement, where his warders 'regularly abuse and humiliate him', while giving him 'a worse diet than that of a Kaffir prisoner'.

Lichtenstein communicated what he saw to Polak, adding as his own view that he thought Gandhi 'was very near a break-down'. Polak then wrote an anguished letter of complaint to David Pollock, a Justice of the Peace and a well respected resident of Johannesburg. He found it 'heart-breaking' that 'this high-minded gentleman, who has all along conducted a campaign with clean hands and a lofty spirit, is being tortured in this way'. Knowing the prisoner as he did, Polak was certain that

> what is in Mr Gandhi's mind today, in the midst of these degrading circumstances by which he finds himself surrounded, is no thought for himself and his own personal sufferings, but the feeling that, if this treatment is meted out to him, a cultured man, a barrister, a member of a noble Indian family, a man who has refused the Chief Justiceship of his native State, what must be the attitude of the Authorities to his less highly-equipped brethren in the Transvaal who are voiceless ...

In a postscript whose tone matched that of the letter itself, Polak said he dared not communicate these things to Gandhi's wife Kasturba. For 'the poor lady's life is sufficient of a tragedy as it is, with her husband in gaol and her eldest son in gaol ... She is now just managing to drag herself about after a long and painful illness, and it will almost certainly mean a relapse for her, if I so much as whisper what is going on.'[63]

David Pollock passed on this letter to the Governor of the Transvaal, with a note marking his own dismay that Gandhi, 'of all people in South Africa', was marched in handcuffs 'like a common felon through the streets of the Capital' when conveyed from the prison to the courts to testify in a case. He urged Lord Selborne to institute an enquiry 'into the specific allegation that the considerate treatment accorded to political prisoners in civilized territories has not been extended to Mr Gandhi'. Pollock received a brusque reply, stating that 'Mr Gandhi, when he voluntarily sought imprisonment, did [so] of course knowing that he could not expect treatment in any way different from other prisoners.'[64]

This suggests that whereas the Transvaal Government thought Gandhi to be a common criminal, in the eyes of his friends and supporters he was (as Henry Polak put it) 'a political prisoner, fighting for conscience's sake and the self-respect of his people.' Their complaints reached London, and from London were re-directed to Pretoria. This had some effect, for the Transvaal Prime Minister sent David Pollock a terse note saying that 'Prisoner M. K. Gandhi is confined at Pretoria Gaol, where he has been shown special consideration. He was offered ghee but declined. He has however accepted the sleeping outfit reserved for Europeans and is well supplied with books.'[65]

That conditions markedly improved after the interventions of Polak and Pollock is confirmed by Gandhi's own account. The prison director now allowed him the use of a notebook and pencil, and substituted the stitching and mending of clothes for the scrubbing of floors. As a gesture of goodwill, General Smuts also sent him two books on religion.[66] Gandhi answered in kind, asking the boys at Phoenix to make his adversary what the General's son described as a 'stout pair of leather sandals'.[67]

Smuts's gesture, and the more lenient treatment Gandhi was now getting in jail, may have been influenced by the fact that he had recently been issued with a glowing testimonial in the House of Lords. Speaking on 24 March, a former Governor of Madras, Lord Ampthill, drew the attention of his fellow peers to the plight of Indians in the Transvaal. A previous speaker had spoken of Gandhi as a mere 'agitator' and of the protests as 'simply sentimental'. Ampthill vigorously disagreed. The laws the Indians had opposed were, he said, 'humiliating and offensive and unnecessary'. Their leader, 'the son of an Indian gentleman of good birth and high position', and a London-trained barrister himself, had undergone three terms of imprisonment with hard labour 'for the sake of his opinions and because he is defending what he regards as the honour of his community'. Despite his privileged birth and professional qualifications, Gandhi

> devotes all his means and most of his time and energy to public service and to the purest philanthrophy ... This is the man who is leading this movement, and with him there are several hundreds of others who, I can assure your Lordships from the knowledge I possess, will protest to the bitter end, whatever be the extremity of ruin or misery it brings upon them. In these circumstances it is simply fatuous to say that they have no good reason for undergoing sufferings of this kind.[68]

This was an impressive speech; even more impressive, perhaps, was a private letter that Smuts received from his Cambridge friend H. J. Wolstenholme, a don at Christ's College described (by Smuts's biographer) as 'a lapsed Christian who retained his Christian conscience'.[69] The two had been close from their days at university – exchanging notes on works of philosophy and literature, and commenting on each other's manuscripts. Now, reading about the protests by, and the arrests of, Indians in the Transvaal, Wolstenholme reminded Smuts that those he had jailed belong to a race, or complex of races, with an ancient civilization behind them, and a mental capacity not inferior to that of the highest Western people, who are developing rapidly a feeling of nationality and a capacity for the more active and practical life of the more materialized West . . . [The] Indians with whom you have to deal may have little share in this civilization of their race, through lack of education, and this through national poverty, but they are championed by leaders who identify themselves with them, and resent keenly what they regard as unjust and insulting treatment of their people, the more keenly because it is directed against them as a race, a race marked out as 'inferior', like the 'niggers' of America and the 'heathen Chinese', as coloured.

The Cambridge scholar saw an 'epoch-making' change taking place in relations between East and West, whereby the Japanese, the Chinese and the Indians would no longer accept exclusion and disability on the grounds of race. It was increasingly clear that those whom Europeans had dismissed as 'inferior peoples' were not inferior in capacity; they claimed, demanded and deserved equal rights. Wolstenholme told Smuts that 'it would surely be wise statesmanship, as well as good human fellowship, to concede in time and with a good grace what is sure eventually to be won by struggle.'[70]

These were radical ideas, even by the standards of the Cambridge of the 1900s. In the Transvaal of the day they were completely heretical. Smuts's answer to this letter is unavailable; perhaps he had none.

In the last months of 1908, as a steady stream of satyagrahis entered prison, *Indian Opinion* began carrying poems written in Gujarati paying tribute to them. A prolific writer of these salutary verses was Sheikh Mehtab, Gandhi's former schoolfriend and housemate. A poem of January 1909 said Parsee Rustomjee was as brave as (the sixth-century) Arab poet Hatem and (the eleventh-century) Hindu monarch Raja Bhoja. M. C. Anglia and Sorabji Shapoorji were also praised, while Thambi Naidoo was described as 'the lamp of India, the real fighter!' 'If you remain united like this', Mehtab urged the satyagrahis, 'you will see Smuts' resignation.'

In another poem, he said 'we lost India [to the British] due to disunity and quarrels'. He recalled an older and more hallowed epoch, when, 'with unity Ram and Laxman got Sita back'. In yet another, he wrote,

If the whole community is brave
Eid and Diwali can be celebrated
Otherwise [the] Union Jack will tear us apart
And fire will be ablaze.

Here the Muslim poet invoked a Hindu idiom; meanwhile, from the other side, a versifier named Jayshanker Govindji saluted the heroism of the trader A. M. Cachalia, who had seen his business tumble by going to jail. Cachalia was 'the light of his family', 'a true gem of India'. His sacrifice had 'drenched [him] in many colours'.[71]

Gandhi's own stoicism in jail is manifest in the monthly letter he was permitted to write. In the last week of March he wrote to his son Manilal enquiring about Kasturba's health. 'Does she now walk about freely?' he asked: 'I hope she and all of you would continue to take sago and milk in the morning.'

A Hindu swami, Shankeranand, was then touring Natal. The swami was from the Arya Samaj, a brand of militant, adversarial Hinduism which was at odds with Gandhi's more plural and accommodating faith. When he first heard of Shankeranand's militant proselytizing, Gandhi wrote to Maganlal, 'it is very regrettable. It is because of such results that the venerable Kavi [Raychand] used to say that in modern times we should beware of religious teachers.'[72]

The *Natal Mercury* thought that Shankeranand was 'flattening out Mr Gandhi' in the colony, winning the lawyer's followers over to his side. The *African Chronicle* disagreed: 'The responsible section of the Tamil and Hindoostani people', it insisted, 'stand by Mr Gandhi to one man despite what Swami Shankeranand may say.'[73]

The Swami now decided to carry the battle into the enemy camp. Visiting Phoenix while Gandhi was in jail, he told Manilal that, as a boy of high caste, he should wear a sacred thread. Gandhi wrote to his son that he 'respectfully disagree[d] with the Swamiji in his propaganda . . . As it is, we have too much of the false division between the *shudras* [lower castes] and others. The sacred thread is therefore today rather a hindrance than a help.'[74]

The next month it was Polak's turn to receive the one sanctioned letter. Gandhi was worried about their financial situation: 'I hate the idea about Phoenix being in debt,' he wrote. He suggested the debt be cleared by selling jewellery and their law books. Turning to the education of the children at Phoenix, he advised them to read Tolstoy's *Life and Confessions* and the works of Raychandbhai. 'The more I consider his life and his writings, the more I consider him to be the best Indian of his times', remarked Gandhi of his late mentor. 'Indeed, I put him much higher than Tolstoy in religious perception.' Then, turning to personal matters, he asked: 'Is Chanchi cheerful? Or does she brood over her separation from Harilal? Does Mrs. G now take part in household work?'[75]

In February 1909, when Gandhi was in between prison terms, his secretary Sonja Schlesin had articled herself as a clerk in his office. Miss Schlesin's application was witnessed by Gandhi, Polak and her father. Normally, after three years as a clerk one could qualify for the Bar. This Miss Schlesin was very keen to do – she wished to become the first woman lawyer in South Africa, just as her employer had been the first coloured lawyer. She was extremely intelligent and well read, and after five years in Gandhi's office had become closely acquainted with the law, especially as it applied to Indians.

Meeting Gandhi's wide range of clients, and observing lawyers and judges at work, had turned the once-shy girl into an assured (and occasionally combative) young woman. Miss Schlesin, wrote her employer, 'would not hesitate even to the point of insulting a man and telling him to his face what she thought of him. Her impetuosity often landed me in difficulties, but her open and guileless temperament removed them as soon as they were created.' Gandhi indulged Miss Schlesin's idiosyncrasies because of her competence and her commitment. 'Colour prejudice was foreign to her', he recalled, adding, 'I have often signed without revision letters typed by her, as I considered her English to be better than mine, and had fullest confidence in her loyalty'.[76]

The woman who contributed most to Gandhi's work and career was his wife Kasturba. Next, albeit by some distance, was his secretary Sonja Schlesin. She had a natural sympathy with the Indians and great respect for their leader. Yet despite her admiration for Gandhi, Miss Schlesin was keen to do more than draft and type letters. Her intelligence and passion needed more challenging outlets, which qualifying for the Bar could provide her with. In preparation for her change in profession, Miss Schlesin cut her hair short and began wearing a shirt and tie. In April 1909, the Transvaal Law Society wrote back rejecting her application. 'The articling of women', they said, 'is entirely without precedent in South Africa and was never contemplated by the Law.' Miss Schlesin suppressed her disappointment and returned to her regular duties in Gandhi's office.[77]

Gandhi was released from Pretoria Prison on 24 May 1909. The authorities set him free early in the morning, in the hope 'of preventing a demonstration'. However, when he came out at 7.30 a.m. several hundred Indians were waiting at the prison gate, with bouquets and garlands. They conveyed him to the home of G. P. Vyas (a prominent local resister), where he had breakfast.[78]

Gandhi proceeded to the Indian mosque in Pretoria, where he made a plea for donations. 'While in gaol, I learnt from Mr Polak's letter that the British Indian Association has become bankrupt . . . Therefore, those who have been carrying on their business [while others have been in jail] must lighten their pockets.' He carried on to Johannesburg, where he was received at Park Station by a large crowd – mostly Indians, with a few Chinese and European friends such as Joseph Doke. He was garlanded and taken in a procession to the Hamidia Mosque. Gandhi expressed his displeasure at being called the 'King of Hindus and Muslims' by the crowd. He was merely a servant of the community. Urging more people to volunteer for the movement, he said that 'a task that needs a thousand men cannot be accomplished by ten, as it were. The struggle is being prolonged because not enough men join it.'[79]

Two weeks after coming out of prison, Gandhi spoke on 'The Ethics of Passive Resistance' to the Germiston Literary and Debating Society. The Society was run for and by liberal-minded whites. Here, the practitioner-turned-theorist of satyagraha argued that his method of protesting injustice, based on 'soul-force', was superior to rival methods based on physical force; not least because it 'never caused suffering to others'. Therefore, argued Gandhi, the colonists should not take exception to Indians 'making use of this [soul] force in order to obtain a redress of their grievances. Nor could such a weapon, if used by the Natives, do the slightest harm. On the contrary, if the Natives could rise so high as to understand and utilize this force, there would probably be no native question left to be solved.'[80]

On 16 June 1909, a meeting of about 1,500 Indians was held outside the Fordsburg Mosque. It resolved to send a deputation to London to present their views to the Imperial Government. There was a heated discussion on the composition of the delegation. Some argued that a knowledge of English was essential. Others insisted that those who had not been to jail be excluded.

The British Indian Association nominated five men: its chairman, Ahmed Mahommed Cachalia; V. A. Chettiar, chairman of the Tamil Benefit Society; the English- and Gujarati-speaking lawyer, Gandhi; the Parsi, Nadeshir Cama, who had left his job as a postmaster to court arrest; and the Pretoria merchant Hajee Habib, who had previously stayed away from the movement but now declared himself a 'passive resister'. Cachalia, Chettiar and Cama were all in prison, so only Gandhi and Habib were free to go. The meeting also decided that Henry Polak would travel to India to drum up support for their cause.[81]

Before leaving for London, Gandhi spoke to a journalist in Johannesburg, who sent a report on to the *Daily Republican*, published out of Springfield, Massachussets. The article described the sufferings of the Indians, and their satyagrahas against harsh laws, in sympathetic terms. Of Gandhi – whom he had met 'a number of times' – the journalist wrote:

> The struggle has reduced him to poverty, but this he does not regret, nor is he discouraged. Ultimate success he regards as sure. Passive resistance he considers more potent than the exercise of any physical force. Its strength is spiritual and must prevail. 'I am absolutely convinced', he says, 'of the invincibility of passive resistance. It will be the deliverance of Indians in South Africa and India as well.'[82]

In 1909, as in 1906, Gandhi had as his companion to London a representative of the merchant community. The two men left Johannesburg for Cape Town on 21 June. On the train, Gandhi scribbled a series of letters to Henry Polak. The plan was to send Polak to India, to lobby the Government and to raise funds. The letters provided specific instructions on what to say in the press and whom to contact for support.

Articles written by Polak 'should be translated in all the principal languages and widely circulated in India'. Polak was at Phoenix; he was advised that 'unless you find complete encouragement from the people [in Durban] do not go to India.' In an intriguing postscript, Gandhi asked him, in case he did go to India, to come back with a copy of a book on *Saddarshan Samuccaya*, the six schools of Indian philosophy.[83]

On reaching Cape Town, Gandhi was interviewed by a local newspaper. The Indians, he said, hoped the Imperial Government would act before the union of the four colonies was finalized. Their 'great fear' was 'that under the Constitution, it will be a union of white races against British Indians and the Coloured races'.[84]

Boarding ship on the 23rd, Gandhi and Habib were seen off by a group of Cape Indians. The novelist Olive Schreiner had come to bid goodbye to a relative; seeing Gandhi, she insisted on coming on board ship to shake his hand, her gesture watched by many whites. Gandhi, who knew of her work, and who had certainly read her meditations on race reprinted in *Indian Opinion*, was immensely flattered. As he wrote to Polak, 'Fancy the author of "Dreams" paying a tribute to passive resistance'.[85]

Meanwhile, a tribute of a different kind was being conveyed to Gandhi by means of a letter sent from India. The writer was Meer Allam Khan, the man who had assaulted Gandhi back in February 1908. The Pathan and the Gujarati had since mended fences, so much so that Khan had joined the satyagraha. He was arrested, and along with several dozen other resisters, deported to India. Arriving in the motherland in the middle of June, he wrote Gandhi a letter, in English, whose errors of grammar and construction cannot mask its manifest sincerity:

I arrived in Bombay and hoping you are well. I have published all news of Transvaal's operations in Bombay Gujarati newspapers, and I shall publish also in Punjab when I will go there. Please, sir, let me know about the Government law settlement and I hoping you will let me all the news of the case. Besides I shall attend to Lahore Anjumani Islam meeting and I shall speak at the meeting in Lahore all the above operation at Transvaal and shall see to Mr Lala Lajpatrai at Lahore and I shall take his opinion on the above matter and publish in all the Anglo-Indian newspapers. And when I shall approach to frontier then also I shall publish to all of our friend, and I shall try my best and daresay that you may not fear and don't afraid I shall take much effect in this case and I shall go to Afghanistan and will inform each and everyone.

The letter reached Johannesburg just after Gandhi left for London. It was read by Henry Polak, who immediately printed it in *Indian Opinion*. He sent on a copy to Gandhi, who would have read it with interest, pleasure and, one thinks, a certain sense of vindication.[86]

15

Big Little Chief

When Gandhi travelled to London in 1906, his companion was the larger-than-life H. O. Ally. His partner this time, Hajee Habib, was also a Muslim merchant; there the parallels ended. Habib did not smoke or drink, and said his prayers five times a day. He was happy to share Gandhi's diet of fruit and vegetables, although he occasionally indulged himself with fish, and (again unlike the abstemious lawyer) drank tea and coffee.

The British Indian Association had sent their delegates by first class, where Gandhi found himself 'looked after by servants as though they were so many babies. There is something to eat every two hours. We cannot even lift a glass of water with our own hands.' The passengers, he wrote to a friend, are 'too much pampered'. On ship, he had 'to live hedged in on all sides. My prayers here lack the depth, the serenity and concentration they had when I was in gaol.' He wrote this not 'in a frivolous mood, but after deep reflection . . . [W]e would all profit from the kind of simplicity and solitude we find in gaol.'[1]

Gandhi and Habib disembarked in Southampton on the morning of 10 July. They proceeded to London, where they left their bags at their hotel and went to see L. W. Ritch. After lunch, they got to work, or at least Gandhi did. In 1906, a lady sent by Polak's father had served as his secretary; this time, Henry's unmarried sister, Maud, had agreed to take dictation and type his letters. On this, the first day, appointments were sought with Lord Ampthill, the former Governor of Madras who now served as the Chairman of the South Africa British Indian Committee, and with other friends and sympathizers in London and around.[2]

On the 14th, Gandhi wrote to Polak that he was 'very pleased' to have Maud working with him; she had come quite willingly, as she was jobless at home and 'does not like her own company'. Polak himself was now in Gandhi's homeland, promoting his friend's cause, which was also his own. He was instructed 'to see most of the leading Anglo-Indians and Indians ... You will require all the patience and tact you can command.'

Gandhi gave Polak the London news. Mrs Ritch was ill, after his oldest English friend had 'bungled' an operation on her. 'Dr [Josiah] Oldfield', he complained, 'has entirely fallen – even his supposed surgical skill is now no more ... It hurts me to have to write of a man I have held in high estimation, but we have often to break our idols.' On the other hand, other friends were gaining in esteem – such as Lord Ampthill, who, when he met him, had 'transparent honesty, courtesy and genuine humility written on his face'. Gandhi's compatriot Pranjivan Mehta was also in London, where he had come from Rangoon to admit his son to school. Fortunately, and probably not by accident, he was staying at the same hotel, the Westminster Palace.[3]

Gandhi found the Indians in London in a fever pitch of excitement. On 1 July 1909, shortly before he arrived, a student named Madanlal Dhingra had shot Sir Curzon Wyllie, who had been a senior army officer and civil servant in India. The incident occurred at a party at the Imperial Institute, where a large number of Indian students and British guests had gathered. Shortly before 11 p.m., as the guests were leaving, Dhingra went up to Wyllie and fired four shots at him at close range. He died instantly.

At the time, Dhingra was studying engineering at University College, London. A native of Amritsar, he had matriculated from the Punjab University. He told his fellow students he hoped to qualify for the Indian Civil Service. That was a red herring; but of his intelligence there was no question. The doctor called to examine him after the murder found him 'well educated, and of an intellectual type', if 'somewhat reticent in conversation'. He showed 'no signs nor symptoms of insanity'.[4]

At his trial, on 23 July, Dhingra said he did 'not think that any English Law Court has any authority to arrest me or detain me in prison'. He held the English responsible for hanging, deporting and starving to death millions of his countrymen, and for draining wealth out of India estimated at £100 million a year. It was thus 'perfectly justifiable on our part to kill an Englishman who is polluting our sacred land'. He offered this telling analogy:

In case this country is occupied by Germans, and an Englishman not bearing to see the Germans walking with the insolence of conquerors in the streets of London, goes and kills one or two Germans, then if that Englishman is to be held as a patriot by the people of this country, then certainly I am a patriot, too, working for the emancipation of my motherland.

Dhingra hoped to be sentenced to death, 'for in that case, the vengeance of my countrymen will be all the more keener'.[5]

Among the Indians most moved by Dhingra's act was a student from Maharashtra named Vinayak Damodar Savarkar. Deeply committed to the freedom of India – by any means possible – Savarkar, wrote an English friend of his, was imbued with 'a curious and single-minded recklessness'.[6] The judge did not allow Dhingra's statement to be part of the official record, but Savarkar got hold of a copy and leaked it to the press, but not before embellishing it. Here Indian patriotism was given a religious colouring, with Dhingra invoking those divine slayers of evil, Rama and Krishna, in support of his own act. His one prayer, he added, was that he 'may be reborn of the same mother [Goddess, India,] and may I re-die in the same cause till the cause is successful'.[7]

Savarkar and Dhingra were both associated with India House, the institution founded and funded by Shyamaji Krishnavarma, who was now in exile in France. *The Times* noted that Dhingra had 'imbibed with disastrous effect the teaching of Mr Krishnavarma and others who more or less directly favour and commend political assassination.'[8] When he met Krishnavarma in London in 1906, Gandhi had found him both interesting and intriguing. However, the satyagrahas he led in South Africa in 1907–8 had convinced him of the moral superiority of non-violent resistance. Now, back in London, Gandhi was horrified by the outcome of Krishnavarma's preachings. Dhingra's violent and vengeful act, he wrote, 'has done India much harm; the deputation's efforts have also received a setback . . . Mr Dhingra's defence is inadmissible. In my view, he has acted like a coward. All the same, one can only pity the man. He was egged on to do this by ill-digested reading of worthless writings.'

Wyllie, noted Gandhi, had come as a guest among the Indian students. 'No act of treachery can ever profit a nation', he insisted:

Even should the British leave in consequence of such murderous acts, who will rule in their place? The only answer is: the murderers. Who will then be happy? Is the Englishman bad because he is an Englishman? Is it that everyone with an Indian skin is good? . . . India can gain nothing from the rule of murderers – no matter whether they are black or white.[9]

The fall-out of the Dhingra case was the topic of daily discussion between Gandhi and his friend, the doctor-jeweller from Rangoon, Pranjivan Mehta. A sharp critic of British colonial rule, Mehta was at first predisposed to the methods of armed struggle. However, after long arguments in their hotel, he came round to Gandhi's point of view.

These shifts are captured in a series of letters Gandhi wrote Henry Polak. On 20 August, Gandhi told Polak that Dr Mehta now 'understands the struggle much better . . . [H]e has begun to see that passive resistance is a sovereign remedy for most of the ills of life.' A week later, he reported 'further important chats with Dr. Mehta. I think he is convinced now that ours is the right plan.' In another week, Dr Mehta had agreed to fund a scholarship to England for one of the boys being schooled at Phoenix. He wanted this to be one of Gandhi's own sons, but the latter, mindful of propriety, said he would send his nephew Chhaganlal instead. Chhagan would enrol himself at an Inns of Court, take a vow of poverty, stay with a vegetarian family in London, and during his stay 'seek contact with every Indian student, in fact, force himself on their attention and, after insinuating himself in their favour, should present both in his life and by conversations, the Phoenix ideals to them'.[10] The idea, evidently, was to use a convinced follower of non-violence to convert young Indians away from the path laid down by Madanlal Dhingra.

Meanwhile, a student he was talking to in London had cleared up one of Gandhi's old confusions. Gandhi had once toyed with the idea of coming to the United Kingdom to study medicine. Now, a young Indian from Cape Town, studying to be a doctor, told him that in two years he had had to kill fifty frogs. 'If this is so', wrote Gandhi to Polak, 'I have absolutely no desire to go in for medical studies. I would neither kill a frog, nor use one for dissecting, if it has been specially killed for the purpose of dissection.'[11]

From London, Gandhi also wrote regularly to his other Jewish friend, Hermann Kallenbach. We don't, alas, have Kallenbach's letters, but Gandhi's mix affection with instruction. Kallenbach was asked to read a book on the morals of diet, and told to 'count your pennies' and 'hold your possessions in trust for humanity'.

With Gandhi far away, Kallenbach sought consolation by visiting his family at Phoenix. Kasturba and he got on famously. He passed on an account of his visit to Gandhi, who wrote back:

That you should describe Mrs. Gandhi as your mother, shows your ultra-regard for me ... That you can make yourself comfortable in my home (have I one?) without me and with all the awkward ways of Mrs. Gandhi and the children shows the height you have attained. You remind me of friendships of bygone ages of which one reads in histories and novels.[12]

While Dhingra was being tried, and then executed, Gandhi turned his attention to his own cause and his own methods. He had come to London to lobby, peacefully, for the rights of Indians in the Transvaal. 'The best part of the day', he wrote to Olive Doke, 'has to be devoted to interviewing people and explaining the same thing to them over and over and writing to them. At times one has to enter into elaborate explanations of things which may appear to one to be perfectly simple.' Then he added: 'I have done no sightseeing. I seem to have lost all desire for it.'[13]

The lawyer's main adviser in London was Lord Ampthill. Born the same year as Gandhi, 1869, Ampthill was – as described in the *Dictionary of National Biography* – an 'instinctive liberal', descended on both sides from famous Whig politicians. He had hoped to succeed Curzon as Viceroy of India; but the Secretary of State, Lord Morley, found him too pro-Indian for his taste.[14] He certainly displayed much vigour in taking up Gandhi's case. The two men wrote each other almost daily, the Indian sending typed missives (since he had 'a very indifferent and illegible hand'), the Englishman writing by pen, in an elegant, cursive hand.

The Parsi grandee, Sir Mancherjee Bhownaggree, had advised Gandhi to issue a statement to the newspapers about their mission. Ampthill demurred, saying that 'no public pressure would be opportune or wise at the moment'; it might merely 'make the authorities again harden their hearts'.[15] The choice, for Gandhi and the Indians, lay 'between the "diplomatic" and the "political" method'. If they chose the former, then they must leave the conduct of the negotiations entirely to Lord Ampthill and not go to the press, since 'diplomacy is only possible through individual agency and by private action'. He told Gandhi 'not to *publish* or *circulate* anything without first consulting me. It would be fatal if any of the responsible statesmen were offended or put out at the present juncture.' Only if Ampthill's negotiations failed should Gandhi try the public route advocated by Bhownaggree.

Ampthill asked Gandhi two questions. If the Asiatic Act was repealed and six educated Indians admitted annually, would that 'finally remove the sense of injustice and indignity under which the Indian community in the Transvaal is suffering'? He added that there was 'much prejudice in high quarters on account of a belief that "Passive Resistance" in the Transvaal is being fomented and financed by the party of sedition in India who do not desire that the question should be settled. Please tell me how I am to meet this charge.'

Gandhi replied that if the two concessions were granted, 'I would certainly be contented.' To the charge of being a pawn or tool in the hands of revolutionaries in India, he answered,

> I know of no Indian whether here, in South Africa or in India, who has so steadily, even defiantly, set his face against sedition – as I understand it – as I have. It is part of my faith not to have anything to do with it, even at the risk of my life . . . The movement in the Transvaal, with which I have identified myself, is an eloquent and standing protest in action against such methods. The test of passive resistance is self-suffering and not infliction of suffering on others. We have, therefore, not only never received a single farthing from the 'party of sedition' in India or elsewhere, but even if there was any offer, we should, if we were true to our principles, decline to receive it.[16]

The Cape politician J. X. Merriman was also in London at this time. So was General Smuts. Knowing the friendship between the two men, Gandhi asked the liberal Briton to press the hardline Boer into making the necessary concessions. He had, he told Merriman, just received a cable from South Africa 'saying that the struggle has taken its first victim. A young Indian who was serving imprisonment as a passive resister, was discharged in a dying condition and died six days after his discharge. There are at present about 100 Indians in the Transvaal gaols and during the struggle, over 2,500 Indians have passed through them.'

The situation was dire, yet the solution, said Gandhi to Merriman, was 'exceedingly simple'. All General Smuts had to do was repeal the Asiatic Act, while 'placing highly educated Indians on a footing of equality under the Immigration Act'. The Government could make the education test as severe as it wished; and restrict the number of Indians who came in every year. But 'what we resent', said Gandhi, 'is the racial bar, involving as it does a national insult.'[17]

Merriman declined to intervene, so Gandhi now met Lord Morley, who was Secretary of State for India, as well as Lord Crewe, Secretary of State for the Colonies. Both gave him a 'sympathetic hearing', but without any specific assurances. Crewe had spoken with General Smuts, who said he was prepared to allow six educated Indians a year into the Transvaal, but as an administrative concession, not a legal right. If 'equality is conceded in principle,' said Smuts, then 'the practice would ultimately have to conform to the principle, and in the end the Asiatic immigrant would be on the same footing as the European' – a denouement which was, of course, quite unacceptable to the colonists, whether Boer or British.[18]

Smuts also met Ampthill, who told him that Gandhi was 'as clear, convincing, and unyielding from his point of view as you are from yours'. Before the Transvaal Acts of 1907, Indians had enjoyed the theoretical right of entry to any part of the British Empire. Gandhi, wrote Ampthill to Smuts,

> is contending for a principle which he regards as essential and, so far as I can judge, he is no more likely to abandon a cause which he considers vital and just than any of us are likely to abandon our life-long principles of politics or religion . . . It is impossible not to admire the man, for it is evident that he recognises no court of appeal except that of his own conscience.

Smuts answered that he was willing to repeal Act 2 of 1907 – the original legislation aimed at Asiatics, that had so offended Gandhi and his colleagues – and to admit a certain number of educated Indians, but without conceding the principle of theoretical equality. Ampthill now advised Gandhi to accept these concessions. 'I am anxious', he said,

> for the sake of your community, that the struggle should cease, because I think you have already done enough for the sake of honour. You will be gaining something very substantial in the repeal of Act 2 of 1907 and you can make it quite clear that your opinions on the question of right remain unaltered even though you feel justified in giving up a quixotic struggle.[19]

As the word 'quixotic' suggests, after six weeks of intense lobbying on his behalf, Ampthill was a little exasperated with Gandhi. The Indian was getting increasingly impatient too. Joseph Doke reported to Kallenbach that he had received a letter from their mutual friend written in a 'resigned-hopeless strain'.[20] Soon, Gandhi made his sentiments public in a dispatch to *Indian Opinion*. 'The more experience I have of meeting so-called big men or even men who are really great', he wrote,

the more disgusted I feel after every such meeting. All such efforts are no better than pounding chaff. Everyone appears preoccupied with his own affairs. Those who occupy positions of power show little inclination to do justice. Their only concern is to hold on to their positions. We have to spend a whole day in arranging for an interview with one or two persons. Write a letter to the person concerned, wait for his reply, acknowledge it and then go to his place. One may be living in the north and another in the south [of London]. Even after all this fuss, one cannot be very hopeful about this outcome. If considerations of justice had any appeal, we would have got [what we wanted] long before now. The only possibility is that some concessions may be gained through fear. It can give no pleasure to a satyagrahi to have to work in such conditions.[21]

Gandhi spent most Sundays with Millie Polak, who was now living in London with her young children. He renewed contacts with 'Esoteric Christians' he had first befriended in the 1880s.[22] He sought an appointment with, and may even have met, Tolstoy's British biographer Aylmer Maude. He took Pranjivan Mehta and Maud Polak to a farm outside London, run by a Tolstoyan named George Allen. They all enjoyed the visit; however, when Gandhi suggested they walk back to London in the spirit of the occasion, Maud protested, and they had to take the train instead.[23]

These encounters emboldened Gandhi to write directly to Tolstoy. He had, of course, been reading his work for many years now. He was an eager consumer of books and pamphlets written by Tolstoy and published by his acolytes in English translation. He also read books about the Russian master: among the volumes in his library were Ernest Howard Crosby's *Tolstoy as a Schoolmaster* (1904) and Percy Redfern's *Tolstoy – A Study* (1907).[24]

Gandhi was not the first Indian to write to Tolstoy. This was most likely a Madras journalist called A. Ramaseshan, who in 1901 wrote to the novelist describing the pitiful condition of India under British rule. Tolstoy answered that these sufferings would continue 'as long as your people agree to serve [the rulers] as sepoys ... [Y]ou must not help the English in their rule by violence and you must not participate in any way in the government based on violence.' In the following years, Tolstoy was sent letters by Indian Muslims and Indian Hindus, each urging him to study *their* scriptures. Most recently, in June 1908, a Bengali radical named Taraknath Das (then in exile in America) asked Tolstoy to support them in their fight against the British. Das had asked for an endorsement of armed struggle; in reply, Tolstoy wrote despairingly of 'the amazing stupidity indoctrinated in you by the advocates of the use of violence'. He asked the Indian to resist the ruler not by arms, but by non-violent non-cooperation. If Indians took no part 'either in the violent deeds of the administration, in the law courts, in the collection of taxes, or above all in soldiering, no one in the world will be able to enslave you'.[25]

Some of these letters had been reproduced in the Indian press, where Gandhi may have read them. In any case, he had his own reasons for writing to Tolstoy. In a letter posted from London on 1 October 1909, Gandhi said the Russian's life and work had 'left a deep impression on his mind'. He explained the genesis of the satyagraha in South Africa. He now planned an essay competition on the ethics and efficacy of passive resistance, and wanted to know whether Tolstoy thought this consistent with his idea of morality. Gandhi also asked for permission to reprint, in *Indian Opinion*, the letter written to Taraknath Das deploring the use of violence in political movements. If Tolstoy agreed, he wished to delete the slighting reference to re-incarnation, which the Russian did not believe in, but which 'is a cherished belief with millions in India, indeed, in China also ... It explains reasonably the many mysteries of life. With some of the passive resisters who have gone through the gaols of the Transvaal, it has been their solace.'

Tolstoy wrote back immediately. He was pleased to hear of the struggle of 'our dear brothers and co-workers in the Transvaal'. In Russia, 'the same struggle of the tender against the harsh, of meekness and love against pride and violence, is every year making itself more and more felt among us also', as in the growing refusals to undertake military service. However, he thought that 'a competition, i.e., an offer of a monetary inducement in connection with a religious matter would, I think, be out of place.' He agreed to the reprinting of his letter to Taraknath Das. Left to himself, he would not delete the sentence Gandhi disagreed with, 'for, in my opinion, belief in reincarnation can never be as firm as belief in the soul's immortality and in God's justice and love. You may, however, do as you like about omitting it.'[26]

Gandhi reproduced the modified 'Letter to a Hindu' in *Indian Opinion*. He introduced it as the work of 'one of the clearest thinkers in the western world, one of the greatest writers, one who as a soldier has known what violence is and what it can do'. To those Indians at home (and abroad) who saw armed struggle as the necessary route to national salvation, Gandhi pointed out that 'the assassination of Sir Curzon Wyllie was an illustration of that method in its worst and most detestable form. Tolstoy's life has been devoted to replacing the method of violence for removing tyranny or securing reform by the method of non-resistance to evil. He would meet hatred expressed in violence by love expressed in suffering'.[27]

Joseph Doke's biography of Gandhi had just been published in London. This covered the main events of his life thus far – the upbringing in Kathiawar, the student years in London, the insult in the train and the attack on the Point, the racial laws in Natal and the Transvaal and Gandhi's opposition to them – while interpreting his mission in a Christian idiom. In Doke's eyes, the simplicity of Gandhi's life and the truthfulness of his conduct, his readiness to court death in pursuit of justice, made him come closer to 'the Jew of Nazareth' than most practising Christians. Gandhi had himself told Doke that the New Testament, and the Sermon on the Mount in particular, had awakened him 'to the rightness and value of Passive Resistance'.

For all this, if Gandhi was not 'a Christian in any orthodox sense', then 'orthodox Christianity has itself to blame'. Christians in the colonies denied the faith in their laws and their practice. This 'discrepancy between a beautiful creed and our treatment of the Indian at the door,' wrote Doke, 'repels the man who thinks'. To recognize the justice of Gandhi's struggle, to salute the suffering of the satyagrahis, would be the proper Christian thing to do. Doke asked thus for a repeal of the racial laws, a prelude to the construction of 'a new Jerusalem, whose beautiful gates are ever open to all nations; where no "colour-bar" is permitted to challenge the Indian, and no racial prejudice to daunt the Chinese; into whose walls even an Asiatic may build those precious stones which, one day, will startle us with their glory.'[28]

Tolstoy was mentioned in Doke's biography, as a significant influence on its subject. Gandhi now sent the book to the Russian writer, with this gloss on its contents:

> This struggle of the Indians in the Transvaal is the greatest of modern times, inasmuch as it has been idealised both as to the goal as also the methods adopted to reach the goal. I am not aware of a struggle in which the participators are not to derive any personal advantage at the end of it, and in which 50 per cent. of the persons affected have undergone great suffering and trial for the sake of a principle. It has not been possible for me to advertise the struggle as much as I should like. You command, possibly, the widest public today. If you are satisfied as to the facts you will find set forth in Mr Doke's book, and if you consider that the conclusions I have arrived at are justified by the facts, may I ask you to use your influence in any manner you think fit to popularise the movement?

This letter is somewhat self-promoting. Yet it speaks of an extraordinary self-confidence. The struggle in the Transvaal involved a few thousand Indians in a single colony of a single country, and yet Gandhi was already seeing it in world-historic terms – as, indeed, 'the greatest of modern times'.[29]

Even as Gandhi asked Tolstoy to publicize his struggle, he used Tolstoy's name to legitimize the movement in South Africa itself. He published their correspondence in *Indian Opinion*, saying, 'it is a matter of deep satisfaction that we have the support of such a great and holy man. His letters show us convincingly that soul-force – satyagraha – is our only resort. Deputations and the like are all vain efforts.' He spoke of Tolstoy's fearlessness at the age of eighty, as manifest in his continuing criticisms of the Russian state. He quoted passages from Tolstoy's writings chastising 'those who oppress, imprison or hang thousands of men', and which dared 'the tyrannical officers' to arrest him.

> A man who can write this, who has such thoughts and can act up to them has mastered the world, has conquered suffering and achieved his life's end. True freedom is to be found only in such a life. That is the kind of freedom we want to achieve in the Transvaal. If India were to achieve such freedom, that indeed would be *swarajya*.[30]

*

The production of Joseph Doke's book on Gandhi had been underwritten by Pranjivan Mehta. Mehta now offered to fund the printing and circulation of Tolstoy's 'Letter to a Hindoo' as well. He would pay for its publication as a pamphlet in Gujarati and English, and for its distribution in England and South Africa. Mehta thought that Gandhi's nephew Chhaganlal should travel through India promoting these books and booklets. He would pay for that, too. Further, he suggested that Gandhi have a friend (perhaps a British Tolstoyan) write an independent essay 'following Tolstoy's thoughts' and outlining the European writer's interest in India. 'It will be great', wrote Mehta to Gandhi, 'if the essay reaches those [English people] who believe that India is harmful for people of England (except for the rich and those who make their living in India). If we find a person with such thoughts to write the essay, it would be good.'[31]

Mehta's generosity was prompted by his patriotism, and by his affection for Gandhi. From very early in their relationship he had seen in his friend a future leader of India and Indians. In this London autumn of 1909, Mehta and Gandhi spent many evenings at the Westminster Palace Hotel, discussing India's future and Gandhi's place in it. The jeweller was certain that the lawyer would play a central role in the emancipation of their motherland. He wanted Gandhi to come back to India sooner rather than later. If this mission to London was successful, and the constitution of the new Union of South Africa adequately safeguarded Indian rights, the lawyer would be free to return home, to act as a political leader (and moral exemplar) in a much larger territory and among many more of his own people.

That Mehta could in some way aid in the elevation of Gandhi was a matter of pride. A letter written as he was leaving London indicates how he viewed the relationship. 'I forgot to return to you 6 pence I borrowed from you from the hotel stairs', wrote Mehta to Gandhi. 'I will send a check for it and other expenses tomorrow.' Mehta would look to Gandhi for moral and political guidance, so long as financial transactions ran strictly and always in the other direction.[32]

In the middle of September, after ten fruitless weeks in London, Gandhi wrote asking for a further interview with Lord Morley, the celebrated liberal thinker who was now serving as Secretary of State for India. 'We cannot believe', wrote Gandhi, 'that Lord Morley, who is regarded all over the world as the type of British Liberalism would regard with indifference so reactionary and illiberal a policy as that which has been adopted by the Transvaal Government.' Having appealed to Morley's reputation, he now appealed to the duties of his office, by speaking of the support that Henry Polak was receiving on his tour through the subcontinent, which showed that 'India is deeply hurt by the insult that is put upon her by the racial disqualification imported for the first time into colonial legislation, and is much moved by the sufferings that have been gone through by hundreds of British Indians in the Transvaal.'

The letter received an arch reply, which noted that 'the point which you wish to press upon Lord Morley is not new to him'. Morley would not grant another interview. Gandhi and Habib were told to meet the Secretary of State for the Colonies, Lord Crewe, instead. When they did, Crewe asked: 'Can you not accept the substantial thing that General Smuts is willing to give?' Gandhi answered that Smuts's proposal to admit educated Indians by administrative discretion 'still leaves the racial taint on the Statute-book'. Crewe responded, 'What you say is just and proper, but General Smuts is not an Englishman and, therefore, does not like the idea even of theoretical equality.'

At this stage, Hajee Habib played the Imperial card, noting that 'the matter was exciting a very great deal of commotion in India.' Gandhi added that 'the racial question is being very keenly resented in India.' Crewe said he had already spoken to Smuts of the wider repercussions, but the General felt that 'if theoretical equality were kept up, it might be used for fresh agitation in order to increase the demands.' Gandhi clarified that if the principle of right was conceded, 'we should not raise any further agitation.' Crewe said, in closing, that he would discuss the question again with Smuts.[33]

Henry Polak's campaign in India – mentioned meaningfully to Lords Morley and Crewe – had indeed been bearing fruit. Landing in Bombay in the first week of August, he met newspaper editors, leading industrialists (such as the Parsi, Jehangir Petit), rising lawyers (among them the London-educated Gujarati Muslim, Mohammed Ali Jinnah) and veteran nationalists, notably Dadabhai Naoroji, who, despite being very old and very frail, read *Indian Opinion* regularly and said he admired Gandhi's 'persistence and perseverence'. 'All my time has been occupied', wrote Polak to Gandhi, 'in seeing people [and] being interviewed.' His friend's mentor, Gopal Krishna Gokhale, had placed 'the whole of his organisation [the Servants of India Society] at my disposal'. Although Gokhale was 'killing himself with overwork', and had just received 'a most depressing report' from his doctor, he had found time to read a draft of a pamphlet Polak had written on the situation in South Africa. The Professor 'thinks it good, has read it, and whilst he thinks it much too strong in parts (I have since toned it down somewhat), has passed it.' Polak was now in search of a publisher, armed with an assurance from Jehangir Petit that he would underwrite the cost of printing 20,000 copies.[34]

Having acquired a smattering of Hindustani, Polak had taken to addressing Gandhi as 'Bhai', or brother (he later amended this to 'Bada Bhai', elder brother). Hearing of the stonewalling by the big men in London, Polak wrote that 'yours is splendid patience. I envy you. I see more and more the beauty of the Gita teaching – act, and don't worry about results. But I see more and more how difficult it is to do this and admire the man who can.'

Three weeks talking to Indians in India had only consolidated Polak's respect for Gandhi. 'The conclusion I have [come] to after all these conversations and interviews,' he wrote,

> is that India, even at its most intelligent, is many miles behind us in the Transvaal. The people here admit the value of passive resistance, but say that you wouldn't get anyone to go to gaol. I don't know what my country- men are worrying about India for. It seems a harmless enough country. Provided they don't send another Curzon or anyone ... approaching one here, the country is safe for apparently hundreds of years. They want a couple of hundred Gandhis here. Do you know, I haven't met a man here who approaches you spiritually or in intensity of devotion. Mr G[opal] K[rishna] G[okhale] is the nearest, and though he is probably ahead of you intellectu- ally, in public experience, and in administrative power, he is not in the running so far as pure religion is concerned and he himself admits it.[35]

On 14 September, a large public meeting in support of the Transvaal Indians was held in Bombay's Town Hall. Polak and sundry Servants of India did the organizing. An array of knights were in attendance, of dif- ferent faiths – Sir J. B. Petit, Sir V. D. Thackersey, Sir Currimbhoy

Ibrahim. Among the untitled grandees were the lawyer M. A. Jinnah and the editor K. Natarajan. The main speaker was Gokhale, who, after rehearing the facts of discrimination and the course of the struggle, saluted the leadership of 'the indomitable Gandhi, a man of tremendous spiritual power, one who is made of the stuff of which great heroes and martyrs are made'. Gandhi and his colleagues were 'fighting not for themselves but for the honour and future interests of our motherland'. 'I am sure', said Gokhale, that 'if any of us had been in the Transvaal during these days we should have been proud to range ourselves under Mr Gandhi's banner and work with him and suffer in the cause.' This was extraordinary praise, from a man who was perhaps the pre-eminent Indian statesman of his day. Polak, speaking after Gokhale, stressed the unity that had been forged by the struggle. The Indians in the Transvaal had thrown aside 'all ancient misunderstandings. Hindu, Mahomedan, Parsi, Christian, and Sikh have ... stood in the same prisoner's dock and starved in the same gaol.' Class as well as community differences were transcended, as 'the merchant and the hawker, the lawyer and the priest, the Brahmin and the man of low caste, have all drunk the same bitter sweet draught, have all eaten from the same dish of bitter experience.' Polak then named some stalwarts, such as the Tamil Thambi Naidoo, 'who goes to jail with a smile on his face'; the Muslim A. M. Cachalia, who 'lost his whole fortune rather than break his solemn oath' (to go to jail); the Parsi, Rustamjee, who would 'give all he could himself, in the cause of his country'; and, not least, 'Mohandas Karamchand Gandhi, saint and patriot, who would gladly allow his body to be torn asunder by wild horses rather than compromise his honour and that of his country.'[36]

The press reports of this meeting reached Gandhi in London, to cheer and console him after the failure to get the Imperial Government to see his point of view. Later letters from Polak, who had been to stay with the Indian leader in Poona, passed on confirmation of Gokhale's admiration. He held Gandhi up 'as an example of patriotism, moderation, endurance, self-sacrifice and practical endeavour'. 'His profoundest regret', continued Polak, 'is that you are not here to join him and inspire him in his work. Were you two together, it would be a rare combination of soul forces.'[37]

From Bombay, Polak proceeded to Gandhi's homeland, Gujarat, where meetings were held in Surat, Kathore and Ahmedabad, all passing resolutions condemning the 'unjust and degrading legislation' in Transvaal and saluting the sacrifice of those who opposed it.[38]

Polak now moved south to Madras, to the land of the Tamils who had been in the vanguard of the satyagraha in the Transvaal. His host there was G. A. Natesan, an energetic editor, printer and publisher known to his friends as an 'American hustler'. Polak spoke at a public meeting, where, as he told Gandhi, 'I had a fine ovation, and people told me it drew tears. Isn't it wonderful! And yet, the Transvaal story is enough to bring tears.' The people he met in Madras were, like Gokhale, impressed above all by the inter-religious harmony that underlay the struggle in South Africa. 'Everybody to whom I have spoken', he reported, 'Hindu, Mahomedan and Parsi alike, feels that we are far advanced politically over the majority of Indians here. They all feel that we have sent a lesson which they ought to follow but that they will have the greatest possible difficulty in following.'

Polak travelled from Madras to the *mofussil*, to the interior of the Tamil country where so many of the indentured labourers in Natal had their roots. Among the towns Polak visited and spoke in were Madurai, Tirunelveli, Trichy and Tuticorin, drawing the comment from Gandhi that he had seen 'practically the whole of India – a privilege I have myself not yet been able to enjoy'.[39] Not the 'whole of India', actually, for, as Polak cheekily told his friend, he still hoped to 'go over to Malabar before I leave here, in order to see the Nair women, who I am told, take one husband after another. That beats you all, who take one wife after another. I am inclined to think the women are right!'[40]

In the last week of October, G. A. Natesan brought out Henry Polak's pamphlet *The Indians of South Africa: Helots Within the Empire and How They Are Treated*. This was divided into two parts, the first providing an overview of Indian migration into South Africa, the migrants' work as labourers and traders, and the restrictions they faced in different provinces; the second focusing on the Transvaal and the resistance movement there. Written with passion and clarity, it described indenture as a system of 'heartlessness and cruelty', and the free Indian as always living 'in peril of having his feelings outraged and his sense of decency offended in a number of ways'. The anti-Asiatic prejudices of colonial statesmen like Lord Milner and General Smuts were exposed and documented. The struggle of the Indians, who had 'deliberately pitted soul-force against brute-strength', was narrated and celebrated.

While Polak spoke at length of the heroism of ordinary folk, he did not fail to draw attention to Gandhi's own sufferings. He mentioned a protest by him which led to better food being served to the prisoners. He wrote in vivid, even lurid, detail of how a Chinese prisoner attempted a 'bestial act' on an African, with Gandhi, in the same cell, 'dread[ing] every moment that the Chinese, foiled of his horrible purpose with the powerful Kaffir, would direct his attentions to himself (Mr Gandhi)'. On another occasion, Gandhi, reaching for a closet to answer nature's call, 'was seized by a burly Kaffir, lifted high in the air, and dashed violently to the ground. Had he not seized hold of a door-post as he fell he would undoubtedly have had his skull split open!'

Polak ended his pamphlet with a pointed, passionate wake-up call to India and Indians:

Do the names of Gandhi, Dawood Mahomed, Rustomjee Jeevanjee, Cachalia, Aswat, Thambi Naidoo, Vyas, Imam Abdul Kadir Bawazeer, and a host of others, not call forth the flush of shame and indignation upon the cheek of the leaders of Indian thought and life, that these men should have done so much for India, and they so little for their humble suffering brethren in the Transvaal? Mahomedan, Hindu, Parsee, Christian, Sikh, lawyer, priest, merchant, trader, hawker, servant, soldier, waiter, poor man, rich man, grey-beard, child, man, and woman have suffered alike in this gigantic struggle to maintain the national honour unsullied. The Transvaal Indians have understood that upon their efforts depended whether or not this race-virus should infect the rest of South Africa and the rest of the Empire, whether India herself would not have to suffer and drink deep of the cup of humiliation. What of all this has India realized? Have the bitter cries from the Transvaal Indians penetrated to the ears of their brethren in the Motherland?

What patriotic Indians should do, said Polak, was to form a national body with branches in every major city, which would make 'powerful representations' to the Government on the condition of their compatriots in South Africa. Simultaneously, 'the press should agitate the question in season and out of season.' Surely it was not 'beyond the powers of the accumulated intelligence of India ... to keep the ship of State off the rocks of racialism'.[41]

Polak's pamphlet was deemed dangerous enough for the South

African authorities to publicly denounce it.[42] On the other hand, his publisher, G. A. Natesan, was so impressed that he now asked Polak to write a short life of Gandhi, in a series that had previously seen profiles of Dadabhai Naoroji, M. G. Ranade, G. K. Gokhale, Lajpat Rai and other leaders of the Indian national movement.

Modestly titled *M. K. Gandhi: A Sketch of His Life and Work*, this second pamphlet was published anonymously. Polak began by speaking of Gandhi's 'extraordinary love of truth', his 'proverbial' generosity, his 'sense of public duty'. The 'majestic personality of Mohandas Gandhi', wrote this friend and follower, 'overshadows his comparatively insignficant physique. One feels oneself in the presence of a moral giant, whose pellucid soul is a clear, still lake, in which one sees Truth clearly mirrored.'

These personal qualities were oriented towards a large cause. 'Mr Gandhi had appointed for himself one supreme task – to bring Hindus and Mussalmans together and to make them realise that they were one brotherhood and sons of the same Motherland.' Polak made the large, daring, claim that 'perhaps, in this generation, India has not produced such a noble man – saint, patriot, statesman in one.' Gandhi, said his English admirer, 'lives for God and for India'. His 'one desire is to see unity among his fellow-countrymen'. By forging unity among Hindus and Muslims in South Africa, Gandhi had demonstrated 'the possibility of Indian national unity and the lines upon which the national edifice shall be constructed'.[43]

Polak wrote to his friend that 'with your great modesty you will probably be unable to appreciate the fact that you are regarded as one of India's greatest men today. But I am afraid I shall play but a poor Boswell to your Johnson.' In another letter he was slightly less modest. 'I have revealed to the Indian leaders what sort of man *you* are,' wrote Polak to Gandhi. 'Do you know, I have not met *one* man to equal you in meekness, spirituality, devotion, and practical energy. I don't believe any other country could have given you birth.'

Through his conversations, speeches and writings in India, Polak had helped make Gandhi far better known in his own country. The admiration was manifest and genuine, and the subject was suitably grateful. When an Anglo-Indian paper dismissed Polak as a 'paid agent' of the Transvaal Indians, Gandhi wrote a spirited rejoinder, praising his commitment and sacrifice, and saying, with uncharacteristic sharpness, that 'if a son in a joint family dying in the performance of his sonship may be described as a paid agent, because he is clothed and fed out of the family funds, then Mr Polak is undoubtedly a paid agent, but not until then.'[44]

The Government of India knew how important and effective Polak's work was. He was followed everywhere by police spies, who tampered with his mail, and asked questions of those working in the homes and inns where he stayed. Polak noticed this with amusement at first, but with time also with irritation. 'The authorities must be mad,' he told Gandhi, 'to follow that damnable Russian System [of spying] which in England we affect to condemn but apparently it is all lies and hypocrisy!'[45]

When told of the spies, Gandhi told Polak that he could 'understand my letters to you being opened, but that Millie's letters to you are deliberately opened, passes my comprehension. Let us hope they are wiser for having read the letters, and also that they have learnt the meaning of wifely devotion.'[46] Polak's reply underscored the difference between the marriage of the Gandhis, based as it was on obligation and tradition, and his own, based rather on love and romance. 'You take the opening of Millie's letter more philosophically than she and I do,' he remarked. 'I see that your days of writing love-letters are over! I am sorry for you! I haven't yet authorised Millie to start classes in marital devotion!'

Polak's extended trip to India was itself an object lesson in devotion to a friend and a cause. The real nature of his sacrifice is revealed in a letter that thanked Gandhi, with sincerity and also envy, for spending so much time with his family in London. 'Don't you find Millie more lovable as time passes?' he wrote, adding, 'I do!!! (Amazing discovery, isn't it?)'[47]

From Madras, Polak took a boat to Rangoon. He was met at the wharf by Pranjivan Mehta – now back from London – and by Madanjit Vyavaharik, one of Gandhi's original collaborators on *Indian Opinion*, who was also based here, editing a journal called *United Burma*.[48] Polak stayed with Mehta, discussing, among other things, the past and future of their mutual friend. Either off his own bat, or in consultation with Polak, Mehta wrote Gopal Krishna Gokhale a remarkable letter which began:

Dear Sir,

During my last trip to Europe I saw a great deal of Mr Gandhi. From
year to year (I have known him intimately for over twenty years) I have
found him getting more and more selfless. He is now leading almost an
ascetic sort of life – not the life of an ordinary ascetic that we usually
see but that of a great Mahatma and the one idea that engrosses his
mind is his motherland.

It seems to me that any one who desires to work for his country ought
to study Gandhi and his latest institution – Phoenix Colony and Phoenix
School. The passive resistance as carried on in the Transvaal under his
Guidance can also be better studied on the spot.

Mr Polak who is now here and living with me, tells me that the
'Servants of India' are doing excellent work; it seems to me that the
study of every worker for India is not complete unless he has studied
Mr Gandhi and his Institutions.

Mehta went on to offer to fund an associate of Gokhale's to go to South
Africa 'and put himself absolutely at the disposal of Mr Gandhi'. He
even suggested a name – that of the Madras scholar and orator, V. S.
Srinivasa Sastri.[49]

This was a precocious pronouncement of Mohandas K. Gandhi's
greatness. Particularly striking is Mehta's use of the honorific 'Mahatma',
'great and holy soul', normally reserved for spiritual figures whose influence resonates down the centuries, here conferred on a mere lawyer and
activist. The conventional wisdom has it that it was the poet Rabindranath Tagore who, around 1919, first began to call Gandhi 'Mahatma',
after he had become a major figure in Indian politics. An alternate claim
has been made on behalf of the Gujarat town of Gondal, which seems
to have conferred the title on Gandhi when he visited it on his return
from South Africa in 1915. Pranjivan Mehta preceded them both –
although, of course, in a private letter rather than a public declaration.

We do not know whether Polak read Mehta's letter before it was
sent, and it appears that Gandhi never saw or knew of it at all. The
recipient of the letter, although a man of great wisdom and selflessness,
must have read it with mixed emotions. Gandhi professed Gokhale to
be his mentor; but here was Mehta telling the teacher that he could
learn a lesson from the student in South Africa, that the struggle for the

emancipation of millions in India could profit from a close study of the struggle of a few thousand migrants in Natal and the Transvaal.

After staying with Mehta in Rangoon, Polak sailed to Calcutta to carry on his campaign for the South African Indians. A large public meeting was held here on 3 December, 'to protest against the treatment of Indians in the Transvaal'. The gathering was ecumenical – it included the prominent Hindu liberals Bhupendranath Basu and Surendranath Bannerjee, leading Bengali Muslims, as well as some Marwari business-men of the city.[50]

From Calcutta, Polak proceeded to the north of the country, speak-ing at towns across the United Provinces and Punjab. In Banaras the meeting was chaired by Annie Besant, the former British socialist who was now an Indian spiritualist. Besant, said Polak, 'delivered the finest address that I have heard for many years. There was no play acting in it. What she said was from the heart and she spoke very strongly.' Mrs Besant subscribed Rs 30 for a fund for the South African Indians, which had collected Rs 1,000 by the end of the meeting. This pleased Polak, as did a 'most refreshing dip' the next day in the river Ganges, a rite of passage for a Hindu, but purely optional for this mostly lapsed Jew.[51]

Polak's talks and writings were noticed by, among other people, the brilliant Bengali radical Aurobindo Ghose (later known as Sri Auro-bindo). In April 1907, Ghose had written a series of essays on the possibilities of passive resistance in India.[52] He had not, it appears, read Gandhi at that stage; nor, it seems, had Gandhi read him. Now, Polak's visit spurred the Bengali revolutionary to write a fascinating essay on the situation in South Africa. 'The great glory of the Transvaal Indians,' wrote Ghose,

> is that while men under such circumstances have always sunk into the
> condition to which they have been condemned and needed others to help
> them out of the mire, these sons of Bharatavarsha, inheritors of an unex-
> ampled moral and spiritual tradition, have vindicated the superiority of
> the Indian people and its civilisation to all other peoples in the globe and
> all other civilisations by the spirit in which they have refused to recognise
> the dominance of brute force over the human soul. Stripped of all means
> of resistance, a helpless handful in a foreign land, unaided by India, put
> off with empty professions of sympathy by English statesmen, they, ignored

by humanity, are fighting humanity's battle in the pure strength of the spirit, with no weapon but the moral force of their voluntary sufferings and utter self-sacrifice ... The passive resistance which we had not the courage and unselfishness to carry out in India, they have carried to the utmost in the Transvaal under far more arduous circumstances, with far less right to hope for success. Whether they win or lose in the struggle, they have contributed far more than their share to the future greatness of their country.[53]

Indian politics was then divided into 'Moderate' and 'Extreme' camps, the former politely, even apologetically, asking for concessions from the British, the latter militantly, even angrily, demanding them. Aurobindo Ghose was in political terms an 'extremist', indeed, an *extreme* Extremist. He had close contacts with terrorist groups in Bengal, and in May 1908 he and his brother Barindranath were arrested in what became known as the Alipore Bomb Case. Barin was sentenced to life imprisonment; Aurobindo, however, was released after a year in prison.[54]

The party of the Ghoses had (the word is inescapable) extreme contempt for Moderates like Gandhi's mentor, Gokhale. It is a measure of Polak's success as a publicist that he could obtain, for their cause in the Transvaal, the endorsement of both Gopal Krishna Gokhale and Aurobindo Ghose.

With Gandhi in London and Polak in the subcontinent, the English pages of *Indian Opinion* were being edited by the Reverend Joseph Doke. As before, the journal carried weekly updates on the struggle. One issue noticed the death of a young Tamil named Nagappen, who had contracted pneumonia in jail. Thirty horse-driven cabs accompanied the cortège to the cemetery. There was a wreath from the British Indian Association, and another 'from Leung Quinn with deepest sympathy; he died for conscience's sake.' An editorial in *Indian Opinion* praised the contributions of Tamil women. 'They have seen their husbands and sons imprisoned, they have taken up the duties of life which do not usually fall to a woman's lot and have borne the heaviest burdens to make it possible for those they love to be true to conscience.'[55]

Gandhi's journal also wrote about a failed assassination attempt on the Viceroy of India. 'As passive resisters,' commented the paper, we have absolutely no sympathy with the employment of bombs and such like symbols of force to achieve Nationalist objects . . . We are thankful to believe that the upholders of bomb throwing are a small minority of the responsible men, who are working for the uplifting of India, and we trust that the ethics of passive resistance, which are now prominent in our Motherland through the interest which she is taking in our welfare [in South Africa], may lay hold of the judgment of our people.

This was written by the stand-in editor, Joseph Doke, who had to ventriloquize in the absence of Gandhi and speak thus of India as his 'Motherland', too.[56]

In other issues, Harilal's fourth term in prison was noticed, as also the fresh incarcerations of Parsee Rustomjee, Thambi Naidoo and others. In other places and past times, remarked *Indian Opinion*, jail-going 'brought shame, humiliation and the criminal taint with it.' In this place at this time, however, 'the glory of heroism rests like a halo upon it – and in the Transvaal the man who has not been to gaol is the questionable character.'[57]

As before, meetings were held every Sunday at the Hamidia Mosque in Johannesburg, where the latest batch of satyagrahis released were welcomed and the latest batch of satyagrahis who had courted arrest were saluted. At one meeting, in early September, Joseph Doke made a special point of praising the Chinese resisters. He told his Indian friends that they 'ought to be delighted how loyally they were standing by their Asiatic brethren, so that Mr Quinn and 74 Chinese had just been arrested, and would have to face imprisonment.'[58]

Gandhi was keeping in touch with South Africa through *Indian Opinion* and via letters from friends. One of these was Thambi Naidoo, now temporarily out of jail. When he emerged from his most recent prison sentence, *Indian Opinion* wrote that 'Mr Thambi Naidoo looks well and hardy, and he has come out a giant in purpose. His is an uncrushable spirit.'[59] In early October, Thambi wrote to Gandhi that 'all Tamil prisoners discharged from the prison during your absence are ready to go to jail again and again until the Government will grant to [*sic*] our request.' The Tamil leader travelled to Pretoria in the last week of September, receiving a batch of resisters who had recently been discharged. He found them 'thin and weak' owing to the 'insufficiency of food and the absence of ghee' in the prison diet, and yet 'they are all prepare[d] to go back to gaol.' Thambi saluted their human will, adding however that 'I depend upon no other than Bhagawan [God], he is the only one who can bring the Government down to do their duty towards [the] weak.'[60]

By October 1909 it was clear that the diplomatic method advocated by Lord Ampthill had failed. Gandhi now wrote to the Colonial Office that since a settlement was not forthcoming, he intended to address a series of public meetings before returning to South Africa. He spoke to a group of Parsis in London, where he saluted the sacrifice of their co-religionists – Parsee Rustomjee, Shapurji Sorabjee, *et al.* – in South Africa. On 24 October, he spoke to a mixed gathering of Indians, sharing a platform with V. D. Savarkar. It was Vijaya Dashami, the last day of the Dasehra festival, marking the victory on the battlefield of Ram over Ravan. The moderate and the extremist were a study in contrast. Gandhi wore a tailcoat and a dress shirt. Savarkar was dressed more casually. Gandhi wrote later that 'Mr Savarkar delivered a spirited speech on the great excellence of the Ramayana.' Savarkar had insisted that just as, in ancient times, Hindu gods had vanquished Lankan demons with the force of arms, so with the same methods would modern Hindus now put their British conquerors to flight.[61]

A young student who was present remembered – forty years later – the contrast between the two men. Savarkar was 'by far the most arresting personality' at the meeting; for 'around him had been built a flaming galaxy of violent revolutionism'. Gandhi, on the other hand, seemed shy and diffident; the students had to 'ben[d] their heads forward to hear the great Mr Gandhi speak'. His voice and speech were of a piece with his manner – 'calm, unemotional, simple, and devoid of rhetoric'.[62]

It fell to Gandhi to introduce Savarkar at the Dasehra meeting. In public he was polite, saying he did not want to stand between the speaker and his audience. His real feelings were communicated in a letter to Lord Ampthill, which noted the unmistakable 'awakening of the national consciousness' among Indians in London, tarred somewhat by an 'impatience of British rule. In some cases the hatred of the whole [white] race is virulent.' Gandhi had been in discussion with the extremists, trying to 'convince them of the errors of their ways'. One extremist (whom he does not name, but who most likely was Savarkar) spoke to Gandhi 'with a view to convince me that I was wrong in my methods and that nothing but the use of violence, covert or open or both, was likely to bring about redress of the wrongs they consider they suffer.' Gandhi answered that he wished to take his own 'humble share in national regeneration', albeit with gentler, more incremental methods.[63]

Gandhi was alarmed by the hostility of the extremists towards his mentor, Gopal Krishna Gokhale. Their house journal, *Bande Matram*, had dismissed the Poona leader as 'mean and cowardly'. In a public rejoinder, Gandhi saluted Gokhale's decades of service, remarking that 'it is the duty of both the extremists and moderates to see that they do not pull down the work of those who have been called the pillars of India; they are welcome to build further on it. Otherwise, they will be cutting off the very branch on which they are sitting.'[64]

Gandhi also wrote to Gokhale, reporting the 'extreme bitterness' against him among Savarkar and company in London. The criticism could best be answered, he thought, by Gokhale visiting the Transvaal and identifying with the movement. 'I claim that the Transvaal struggle is national in every sense of the term', wrote Gandhi. 'It deserves the greatest encouragement. I have considered it to be the greatest struggle of modern time. That it will succeed in the end I have not the slightest doubt. But an early success will break up the violence movement in India.' Gandhi wanted Gokhale to come 'to the Transvaal, publicly declaring that it was your intention to share our sorrows and, therefore, to cross the Transvaal border as a citizen of the Empire'. His coming would give the cause a 'world-wide significance, the struggle will soon end and your countrymen will know you better. The last consideration may not weigh with you. But it does with me . . . If you are arrested and imprisoned, I should be delighted. I may be wrong, but I do feel that it is a step worth taking for the sake of India.'[65] This was a letter as confidently presumptuous as that written to Tolstoy. To be sure, it was written out of concern for his mentor, and for his reputation. Gokhale's reply is unavailable. But he could scarcely have gone back on the principles and prejudices of a lifetime. His style was to reason and appeal, to draft petitions and make sonorous – if occasionally also ponderous – speeches in the Imperial Council. To court arrest was as foreign to his temperament as the firing of a gun was to Gandhi's.

*

In London, Gandhi continued to monitor, from long distance, the moral education of his son Manilal. The boy was now fifteen, and his father was determined that his passage into adulthood would be smoother – or at any rate less rocky – than his brother Harilal's. The excerpts below are revealing.

Gandhi to Manilal, 10 August 1909:

> Thinking of the state of affairs in the country, I believe very few Indians need marry at the present time . . . A person who marries in order to satisfy his carnal desire is lower than even the beast. For the married, it is considered proper to have sexual intercourse only for having progeny. The scriptures also say so . . . I want you to understand the purport of what I said above; and, understanding it, conquer your senses. Do not be scared by this and think that I want to bind you not to marry even after the age of 25. I do not want to put undue pressure on you or anyone whatever. I just want to give you advice. If you do not think of marriage even at the age of 25, I think it will be to your good.

Gandhi to Manilal, 17 September, on hearing that the boy had been nursing the ailing Albert West:

> To do good to others and serve them without any sense of egoism – this is real education.

Gandhi to Manilal, 27 September, in reply to an apparently anxious, confused letter:

> You get nervous at the question, 'What are you going to do?' If I was to answer on your behalf, I would say that you are going to do your duty. Your present duty is to serve your parents, to study as much as you can get the opportunity to do and to work in the fields . . . You must be definite on this point at least – that you are not going to practise law or medicine. We are poor and want to remain so . . . Our mission is to elevate Phoenix; for through it we can find our soul and serve our country. Be sure that I am always thinking of you. The true occupation of man is to build his character . . . He who does not leave the path of morality never starves, and is not afraid if such a contingency arises . . . While writing this I feel like meeting and embracing you; and tears come to my eyes as I am unable

to do that. Be sure that Bapu [Father] will not be cruel to you. Whatever I do, I do it because I think it will be in your interest. You will never come to grief, for you are doing service to others.

Gandhi to Manilal, 22 October:

> I see that you have again begun to be worried about your education. Can you not give an answer to the question, 'What class are you in?' Henceforward you may say that you are in Bapu's class. Why does the idea of study haunt you again and again? If you want to study for earning your livelihood, it is not proper; for God gives food to all. You can get enough to eat even by doing manual labour ... I want you to shed all fear. Do have faith in me.[66]

Manilal appears from these letters to be less truculent or questioning than his elder brother, if likewise concerned with his education and his sexuality. As for the father, he cannot but be hortatory, yet one notices an undercurrent of tenderness, absent in the often unfeeling letters to his elder son. A letter written to his third son, Ramdas, also displays a softness that is new. 'Do not be angry with me if I have not brought anything for you [from London]. There was nothing I liked. What could I do if nothing European appealed to me?' wrote Gandhi. Then he added, 'Do not be upset with me if I go to gaol; rather you should rejoice. I should be where Harilal is.'[67]

It does appear that Gandhi was, albeit slowly, growing into fatherhood.

On 3 November 1909, the Colonial Office wrote to Gandhi that 'Mr Smuts was unable to accept the claim that Asiatics should be placed in a position of equality with Europeans in respect of right of entry or otherwise'.[68] The rejection was definitive. Two days later, Gandhi and Hajee Habib released a statement to the press, summarizing their visit, their meetings with Imperial officials, the refusal of General Smuts to introduce a non-racial law. The Transvaal legislation, they said, 'cuts at the very root' of the principle of 'elementary equality' of all British subjects. Interviewed by Reuters, Gandhi said Habib and he expected to be arrested when they sought to re-enter the Transvaal. Their campaign would be 'continued most strenuously' in India, the United Kingdom and South Africa.[69]

A week later, the Nonconformist minister F. B. Meyer hosted a farewell dinner for Gandhi. In attendance were the Parsi statesman M. M.

Bhownaggree, several serving Members of Parliament and the rising Indian politician Motilal Nehru. Some who could not come sent heartfelt letters of support. Gertrude Toynbee, daughter of the reformer Arnold, wrote to Gandhi that the Indian struggle in the Transvaal 'raises one's conception of the possibilities of humanity'. A Christian from Fife wrote to the Reverend Meyer that

> although the cause they [Gandhi and colleagues] represent is passing through a dark hour, I am not dismayed. In the history of the human race it has always been darkest before dawn ... Never did the cause of the Negro seem more hopeless than during the years that preceded the abolition of slavery ... May I add with all reverence that the saviour of the world himself seemed lost in the moment that brought about our redemption? And so I join you in spirit in wishing God-Speed to Messrs Gandhi and Haji Habib.[70]

Also present at the party for Gandhi was Sir Frederick Lely, who, back in 1888 and 1889, had refused to provide the aspiring law student with a scholarship from the State of Porbandar. Twenty years later, now living in retirement in London, the once unfeeling Administrator issued a partial *mea culpa*. Remembering his years in Kathiawar, and his friendship with Kaba Gandhi, Sir Frederick told the gathering that 'he was quite sure that his old friend Mr Gandhi, had he been alive now, would have been proud of his son'.[71]

As for Gandhi himself, he spoke at this reception of how their struggle turned on a question of national honour. They had refused to meet violence with violence, and instead adopted passive resistance. He explained this method with reference to the Bible, namely the chapter where Daniel refused to accept the laws of the Medes and the Persians.[72] Afterwards, L. W. Ritch sent a report to his fellow Gandhi worshipper Henry Polak:

> Our big little chief left for S. Africa on Monday. A big crowd was at the St[atio]n to wish the little man farewell, and his going creates a gap in our circle of workers ... Gandhi's magnificent personality attracted about him the best spirits among the Indians resident here, and those Europeans who are capable of quiet solid work.[73]

The person who missed Gandhi most was Maud Polak. With his departure, she would work under L. W. Ritch on the South African

British Indian Committee. 'She is throwing herself heart and soul into the work', wrote Ritch to her brother. 'Gandhi has influenced her wonderfully and I am looking upon her as a sister.' Precisely how wonderful the chief's influence was is described in two little-known letters written by Gandhi himself to Henry Polak. On 11 November, the day before Meyer's party, he wrote that Maud was 'very seriously thinking' of coming to South Africa. 'Last evening she could not restrain herself, and told me she wanted to go to South Africa very badly and work for the cause.' Gandhi said that while Maud was 'very sweet-natured' and 'capable of great self-sacrifice', he did

> not know how far the Phoenix life would suit her . . . I have told her all I could about things. I have told her as well as I could about the jarring notes there, and I have told her, too, that there is no money in it. I have further told her how Millie herself finds it difficult to reconcile . . . to life at Phoenix . . . I have told her, too, that however much she may regard my view, and like it, I consider myself incompetent to enter into all a woman's feelings, and when she has accessible to her Millie's loving assistance and advice, she cannot do better than rely upon her judgment.[74]

Four days later, while on board ship, Gandhi wrote to Polak again about his sister's growing attachment to himself and his cause. 'She cannot tear herself away from me', he remarked:

> I was watching her closely at the station. She was on the point of breaking down. She would not shake hands with me. She wanted a kiss. That she could not have at the station, not that she or I was afraid but it would be misunderstood. So she stood right on the platform . . . If all she has shown to be genuine she may eclipse you [in devotion to me].

Maud Polak had been desperately keen to accompany Gandhi to South Africa. Her sister-in-law Millie, probably at his urgings, filled her in on the 'jarring notes': namely, 'beetles everywhere, spiders, ants in the milk, no baths, water bad, people half naked, filth too, lift a plate and you will find an insect underneath, snakes hanging from the tree, you have not only to tolerate this but love the insect life, you may not destroy any life . . .' Maud Polak was undeterred by these descriptions – she still wanted to go where Gandhi was. South Africa was to her *terra nova*. Jobless, unmarried, stuck with her parents in London, it was a land with enormous appeal, not least because Gandhi lived there. The past four months had been spent almost continuously in his company. Maud's feelings for Gandhi were intense, and probably romantic. (Years later, with his sister's attachment to his friend in mind, Polak recalled that while Gandhi 'was by no means good-looking by Indian standards ... throughout his life many notable women were greatly attracted by his personality, and he always had women friends, both British and Indian.')[75]

Maud Polak was attracted by Gandhi's personality, and perhaps also by his profile – a successful lawyer, a leader of a popular movement, an Indian who parleyed with Secretaries of State and Members of Parliament. His feelings for her, on the other hand, were paternal. Gandhi's letter to her brother Henry thus continues:

I have told her [Maud] that I consider Indian civilization to be the best in the world and therefore [what] it means for her to be more Indianized than you are. She revels in the thought. Such is the condition in which I have left her. Mrs. G[andhi] used to describe you as my first born lovingly. She would accept Maud as my first born lovingly. She I think will fill her life. Mark a father's selfishness. You are to me – Chhota Bhai – a younger brother and yet more than a brother ... Maud on the other hand can be my first born and therefore in some ways more than you are to me. She will claim more of me. Can I give it? Am I worthy of all affection? Is she worthy of it from me? Unless she is a downright impostor which she is not, she is quite capable of it. The other theory is that the whole thing is a nine days wonder due to the glamour of my personality. If so, I should be shot on sight. For if people can be so falsely enthused by me, I am useless – a power more for harm than good. However that may be, there is a huge problem for you and me to solve. May Maud go to Phoenix? If her affection is real it will be a sin for anybody to prevent that. I leave it at that.[76]

Gandhi also wrote to Millie, who, in London, had seen his friendship with her sister-in-law develop at rather close quarters. The 'intensity of affection' that Maud displayed, her insistence that she would go wherever Gandhi was – was 'all this real', he wondered, 'or is it the glamour of my presence?' Gandhi asked Millie now 'to observe Maud, analyse her, cross-examine her and find out where she is. There is no present need of anybody at Phoenix. And yet if Maud is what she says she is, she will always be wanted.'[77]

To Millie, Gandhi likewise described Maud as 'my first-born daughter'. Her devotion to him was apparently unconditional – so unlike the attitude towards him of his first-born biological son. In London, Maud could attend to Gandhi from daybreak to dusk, but in South Africa, of course, there were other claimants on his time. Henry and Millie Polak seem to have advised her to treat the friendship as a nine weeks' wonder, and not to pursue Gandhi across the oceans.

Millie Polak has left a vivid portrait of Gandhi entertaining his guests in the Westminster Palace Hotel. At lunchtime, his friends and associates would come in to discuss the progress of the negotiations. As the guests trooped in,

> the table in the centre, normally covered with a nice velvet cloth . . . would be cleared. Books and papers would get stacked upon the floor. Then newspapers would be spread over the table, and piles of oranges, apples, bananas, perhaps grapes, and a big bag of unshelled monkey- or pea-nuts, would be put ready. Mr Gandhi would ring for the waiter, and when an attendant, resplendent in white shirt and tail-coat, appeared, he would order tea and toast for those who desired it . . . Soon the silver tea-tray, beautifully appointed, would be brought in; then we would set to work, eating, drinking, talking and laughing. Some would walk about or stand, and the nut-shells would fly around the room, orange juice would run over the paper-covered table, and at the end of the meal the room looked rather as if an ill-bred party of schoolboys had been let loose in it . . . Mr Gandhi would be totally untroubled by all the mess and muddle in the room, and the waiter never lost his dignified gravity as he cleared away the rubbish.[78]

It had been an intense four and a half months in London, in which Gandhi had argued with Indian extremists, exchanged courtesies with British Baptists, and exchanged letters with the most famous Russian novelist of his time (or any other). He had developed a relationship of rare, if wholly non-sexual, intimacy with a young Englishwoman. Even so, the visit had to be reckoned a failure, for the concessions he had sought for Indians in the Transvaal were denied him. Letters written by his associates in the week of Gandhi's departure keenly capture the disappointment. Lord Ampthill, writing to Lord Curzon, lamented that it was a Liberal Government that, for the first time in the history of the Empire, had instituted 'an actual "colour" bar'. He planned to move a motion in the House of Lords, and expected Curzon to support him. The 'spirit of the Transvaal Indians has not been broken', noted Ampthill. 'Meanwhile, the question has become thoroughly understood in India and there will be irreparable mischief if the situation is not saved at once'.[79]

16

The Contest of Civilizations

On 13 November 1909, Mohandas Gandhi and Hajee Habib boarded the SS *Kildonan Castle*, bound for Cape Town. For the next week Gandhi scarcely saw his companion at all. This was by choice, for he was occupied with writing a text whose contours had become clear in his mind those months in London. He wrote it in Gujarati, by hand, and at such a fast clip that he completed a draft in nine days. He was tired – turning now to his left hand to write letters – but satisfied. In 275 pages of manuscript, only a dozen lines seem to have been scratched out and rewritten.[1]

The Gujarati edition of the book was published in January 1910, with the title, *Hind Swaraj*. The English version, dictated by Gandhi to Hermann Kallenbach, was called *Indian Home Rule*, and appeared two months later. (Both were printed on the press at Phoenix that also brought out *Indian Opinion*.) In either language it carries, a hundred years later, a singular status as the first book Gandhi published, and as the only extended, if not wholly considered, statement of his political and moral philosophy. Although many thematic collections of his writings appeared in his lifetime, Gandhi published only three books *qua* books. Since the other two were works of autobiography, *Hind Swaraj* carries even more weight as representing, so to speak, his most important political testament.[2]

Hind Swaraj was profoundly shaped by Gandhi's recent stay in the United Kingdom. What he heard, saw and said in those four months fed directly and immediately into the writing of the book. There were, in particular, two provocations. The first was the murder of Curzon Wyllie and the flurry of excitement it provoked. Dhingra's act, and its endorsement by young Indians such as Savarkar, alerted Gandhi to the appeal of violence among the young. To combat this, he needed to state – or restate – the case for non-violence.

The second provocation was more curious. In the third week of September 1909, the *Illustrated London News* published a withering attack on the idea of Indian nationalism. Its author was G. K. Chesterton, who was then writing a weekly column for the magazine. Chesterton was not especially known for his interest in Britain's colonies; indeed, this may have been his only essay on the subject.

Chesterton had been reading *Indian Sociologist*, the journal published by Shyamaji Krishnavarma, and keenly followed by Indian students in England and the Continent. He thought their ideas unoriginal; as he wrote, 'the principal weakness of Indian Nationalism seems to be that it is not very Indian and not very national'. There was a world of difference between 'a conquered people demanding its own institutions and the same people demanding the institutions of a conqueror'. The Indian nationalists Chesterton was reading (and meeting)

> simply say with ever-increasing excitability, 'Give me a ballot-box. Provide me with a Ministerial dispatch-box. Hand me over the Lord Chancellor's wig. I have a natural right to be Prime Minister. I have a heaven-born claim to introduce a Budget. My soul is starved if I am excluded from the Editorship of the *Daily Mail*', or words to that effect.

If, on the other hand, one of these men had demanded a return to a pre-British past, on the grounds that 'every system has its sins, and we prefer our own', Chesterton would have considered 'him an Indian Nationalist, or, at least, an authentic Indian'. This kind of Indian would have chosen Maharajas over civil servants, on the grounds that 'I prefer one king whom I hardly ever see to a hundred kings regulating my diet and my children.' Admitting the existence of sectarian differences in India, he would nonetheless have insisted that 'religion is more important than peace'. 'If you do not like our sort of spiritual comfort', this authentic Nationalist would have told the alien ruler, 'we never asked you to. Go and leave us with it.'[3]

Gandhi read Chesterton's article, and its message resonated with him. He sent a piece to *Indian Opinion* which contained long excerpts from this article written by one 'read by millions with great avidity'. He thought

Indians must reflect over these views of Mr Chesterton and consider what they should rightly demand. May it not be that we seek to advance our own interests in the name of the Indian people? Or, that we have been endeavouring to destroy what the Indian people have carefully nurtured through thousands of years?[4]

The views of Dhingra and Savarkar, and the gloss on them by Chesterton, persuaded Gandhi that he needed to write a manifesto for the freedom of India that was not derivative; that was based on the traditions of the subcontinent rather than on received models of European nationalism.

In late September 1909, when Chesterton's article appeared, it was clear that the Indian deputation to London would return empty-handed. Gandhi was now free to make public statements about their mission – and about other matters. Two speeches he made form an important part of the background to the writing of *Hind Swaraj*. On 5 October, some expatriates in London held a meeting in support of the third Gujarati Literary Conference, being held in Rajkot. They asked Gandhi to speak. He urged his audience to cultivate pride in their mother tongue, noting that 'one strong reason why the Boers enjoy *swarajya* [freedom] today is that they and their children mostly use their own language.' As 'the basis of my pride as an Indian', he said,

> I must have pride in myself as a Gujarati. Otherwise we will be left without any moorings . . . If only we make on Indian languages half the effort that we waste on English, thanks to certain notions of ours, the situation will change altogether . . . It is, therefore, a very good sign that Gujarati, Bengali, Urdu and Marathi conferences are beginning to be held.[5]

A week later, Gandhi spoke to the Hampstead Peace and Arbitration Society. The writer C. E. Maurice (a heterodox Christian) was in the chair. Rejecting Kipling's claim that East and West could never meet, Gandhi observed that

> there had been individual instances of English and Indian people living together under the same rule without a jarring note, and what was true of individuals could be made true of nations . . . [At the same time] to a certain extent it was true that there was no meeting place between civilisations . . . It seemed to him that the chief characteristic of modern civilisation

[was that it] worshipped the body more than the spirit, and gave everything for the glorifying of the body. Their railways, telegraphs and telephones, did they tend to help them forward to a moral elevation?

Gandhi drew for himself and his audience a contrast between the holy Hindu city 'Benares of old, before there was a mad rush of civilization' and the Banaras of today, which was an 'unholy city'. 'Unless this mad rush was changed, a calamity must come. One way would be for them to adopt modern civilization; but far be it for him to say that they should ever do so. India would then be the football of the world, and the two nations [India and Britain] would be flying at each other.'[6]

The day after his Hampstead speech Gandhi wrote to Henry Polak about it. The talk and the discussion that followed had provoked in him a series of reflections and conclusions. He had come round to the view that 'there is no impassable barrier between East and West'; rather, there was one between ancient and modern civilization. Thus 'the people of Europe, before they were touched by modern civilisation, had much in common with the people of the East.' India was now being damaged by modern artefacts such as the railway and telephones, with cities like Bombay and Calcutta becoming the 'real plague spots'. If 'British rule was replaced tomorrow by Indian rule based on modern methods', said Gandhi to Polak, 'India would be no better'; in fact, then 'Indians would only become a second or fifth edition of Europe or America.' Therefore, 'India's salvation consists in unlearning what she has learnt during the past fifty years.' Among the reforms proposed by Gandhi in this letter was that Indians should stop wearing machine-made clothing, whether manufactured in factories owned by Europeans or by Indians themselves.

Gandhi also felt that 'it was simply impertinence for any man or any body of men to begin or contemplate reform of the whole world.' Rather,

> all of us who think likewise must take the necessary step; and the rest, if we are in the right, must follow. The theory is there: our practice will have to approach it as much as possible. Living in the midst of the rush, we may not be able to shake ourselves free from all taint. Every time I get into a railway car, or use a motor-bus, I know that I am doing violence to my sense of what is right.

His time in London had convinced him that 'I was entirely off the track when I considered that I should receive a medical training.' He now felt that modern hospitals 'perpetuate vice, misery and degradation'; had there been no hospitals for the cure of venereal diseases, there would be 'less sexual vice amongst us'. So it 'would be sinful for me in any way whatsoever to take part in the abominations that go on in the hospitals'.[7]

The speeches to Gujaratis and pacifists were throat-clearing exercises, hesitant, abbreviated anticipations of the full-blown polemic that was *Hind Swaraj*. The book was written in the demotic mode, with an abundant use of metaphors. It was constructed around an imaginary conversation between a 'Reader', who was almost certainly modelled on Pranjivan Mehta, and an 'Editor', who, of course, was Gandhi himself.[8] The sanction for this device came from tradition, for it was widely used in classical Indian literature, above all the Bhagavad-Gita, where Krishna answers and clarifies the doubts and anxieties of Arjuna.

The twenty short chapters of *Hind Swaraj* dealt with such subjects as the meanings of freedom and passive resistance, and the definition of 'true civilization'. One chapter deals with 'the condition of England'; five chapters with the 'condition of India'.

The book begins by rehearsing the history of Indian nationalism since the founding of the Congress in 1885. Gandhi deplored the dismissal by young hotheads of Naoroji and Gokhale as lackeys of Empire. These moderates had prepared the way for what followed, and 'it is a mark of wisdom not to kick against the very step from which we have risen higher. The removal of a step from a staircase brings down the whole of it.' The partisanship of the radicals distressed him; it was, he remarked, 'a bad habit to say that another man's thoughts are bad and ours only are good, and that those holding different views from ours are the enemies of the country.'

The chapter on the condition of England is severe on British political institutions. 'That which you consider the mother of Parliaments,' the editor tells the reader, 'is like a sterile woman and prostitute. The Parliament has not yet of its own accord done a single good thing, hence I have compared it to a sterile woman. The natural condition of that Parliament is such that, without outside pressure, it can do nothing. It is like a prostitute because it is under the control of ministers who change from time to time.'

Still, Gandhi did not think that the rulers were beyond redemption.

The English, he said, 'rather deserve our sympathy . . . They are enterprising and industrious, and their mode of thought is not inherently immoral.'

The book's core consists of five chapters on 'the condition of India'. These condemn railways, lawyers and doctors for spreading poverty and disease, and for intensifying social conflict. The railways, claimed Gandhi, had promoted famine (by encouraging a shift to cash crops), carried plague, and in general 'accentuate[d] the evil nature of man'. Lawyers had stoked divisions, fomented quarrels from which they alone benefited (through client fees), and helped consolidate British rule by allowing law courts to act as arbiters of the destiny of Indians. For their part, doctors made patients dependent on pills, and encouraged them to take to alcohol and unhealthy foods.

Gandhi made the case for an anterior Indian nationhood, existing from long before colonial rule. The presence of Muslim conquerors did not, he thought, invalidate his claim. For 'India cannot cease to be a single nation because people belonging to different religions live in it. The introduction of foreigners does not necessarily destroy the nation, they merge in it.'

Having defended the idea of India as a nation, Gandhi now exalted the Indian way of life. He insisted that 'the civilization India has evolved is not to be beaten in the world.' For

> the tendency of Indian civilization is to elevate the moral being, that of the Western civilization to propagate immorality. The latter is godless, the former is based on a belief in God. So understanding and so believing, it behooves every lover of India to cling to the old Indian civilization even as a child clings to its mother's breast.

This love of the old was coupled with a distaste for the new. 'Machinery is the chief symbol of modern civilization', said Gandhi. 'It represents a great sin.' And, again: 'I cannot recall a single good point in connection with machinery.' Machines had impoverished India, by throwing craftsmen out of work and encouraging a division between capitalists and labourers. He thought 'it would be folly to assume that an Indian Rockefeller would be better than the American Rockefeller.'

If such passages seem a direct engagement with G. K. Chesterton, other parts of the book answered other provocations – those represented, for example, by the recently executed Madan Lal Dhingra and the still active V. D. Savarkar, who believed that freedom from colonial subjection would come about only through armed struggle. To those who lived (and died) by the gun, Gandhi said the claim that 'there is no connection between the means and the end is a great mistake'. He spoke of how the wrong means produced an escalating cycle of violence and counter-violence. He offered the example of a robber who came to one's house. If one mobilized one's neighbours, the robber would in turn call on his mates, and the two factions would fight and fight. If, on the other hand, one kept one's windows open for his next visit, the robber might be confused and repent, and stop stealing altogether.

Gandhi did not want to suggest that all robbers would act like this, but 'only to show that only fair means can produce fair results, and that, at least in the majority of cases, if not, indeed, in all, the force of love and pity is infinitely greater than the force of arms'.

For Gandhi, those who wrote history were preoccupied with wars and bloodshed. Thus, if two brothers quarrelled, their neighbours and the newspapers, and hence history, would take notice of it; but if they peaceably settled their dispute, it would remain unrecorded. Extrapolating, Gandhi said, in a striking passage, that 'hundreds of nations live in peace. History does not, and cannot, take note of this fact. History is really a record of every interruption of the even working of love or of the soul.' Contrary to what was popularly believed, non-violence had been a far more active force in human affairs than violence. The 'greatest and most unimpeachable evidence of the success of this force is to be found in the fact that, in spite of the wars of the world, it still lives on'.

Gandhi argued that non-violent resistance required greater courage than armed struggle. 'Who is the true warrior', he asked: the person 'who keeps death always as a bosom-friend or he who controls the death of others?' He insisted that 'passive resistance is an all-sided sword; it can be used anyhow; it blesses him who uses it and him against whom it is used. Without shedding a drop of blood, it produces far-reaching results.'

Hind Swaraj is also notable for its advocacy of inter-faith harmony. The British claimed there existed an 'inborn enmity between Hindus and Mahomedans'. Gandhi answered that 'the Hindus flourished under Moslem sovereigns, and Moslems under the Hindu. Each party recognised that mutual fighting was suicidal, and that neither party would abandon its religion by force of arms. Both parties, therefore, decided to live in peace. With the English advent the quarrels recommenced.' In Gandhi's view, the different religions were merely 'different roads converging to the same point. What does it matter that we take different roads, so long as we reach the same goal? Wherein is the cause of quarrelling?'

In a chapter on education, Gandhi vigorously advocated the use, within India, of languages other than English. All Indians should know their mother-tongue. Hindi could be promoted as a link language, to be read in either the Devanagari or Persian script, thus forging closer relations between Hindus and Muslims. If this were done, 'we can drive the English language out of the field in a short time'.

The book ended with a list of nineteen prescriptions for the reader, the middle-class Indian who was Gandhi's main audience. This, among other things, urged the value of suffering, deplored the tendency of blaming the British for everything, and asked lawyers, doctors and rich men in general to take to wearing and promoting cloth made with hand-looms.[9]

At the time of the publication of *Hind Swaraj*, Gandhi had been seeing his work in print for two decades. However, this was his first published book, and also, more importantly, his first considered piece of writing on *Indian* politics and society. His earlier essays, abundant though they were, were on rather specialized, specific, themes – such as vegetarian diets, racial laws in Natal and the Transvaal, the origins and outcomes of a particular satyagraha, the pleasures and pains of a particular term in jail, the greatness and relevance of Mazzini, Lincoln, Florence Nightingale, Dadabhai Naoroji, etc. *Hind Swaraj* was Gandhi's claim to a larger role for himself in the homeland to which he hoped one day to return. The book appeared at the end of a decade of intense political agitation in India. The Swadeshi movement of 1905–7 had seen the liberals in the Congress being overshadowed, and indeed overwhelmed, by the radicals. This Moderate/Extremist split was formalized in the Surat Congress of December 1907, when the fragile unity of the organization came apart amidst a barrage of shouting, sloganeering and the throwing of shoes.[10]

The Congress had previously confined itself to issuing appeals and writing petitions. Now, bonfires of foreign cloth and fiery speeches became the order of the day. And even Swadeshi was tame in comparison with the terrorist groups that had sprung up in Bengal and Maharashtra, composed of young men seeking to assassinate British officials and thereby further the glory of the Motherland.[11]

One consequence of the Swadeshi movement was the polarization of religious sentiments. In Bengal, the movement had coalesced with a struggle to undo the partition of the province, which the British had promoted to separate the Muslim-majority districts of the east from the radicalizing influence of the intellectuals of Calcutta. But, as Gandhi's mentor Gokhale noted, the 'wild talk' of the leaders of the Swadeshi movement, demanding 'Swarajya without British control', had set the rulers against the Hindus. They patronized a newly formed Muslim League, promising its grandees a greater share of public posts and government appointments. Gokhale now worried about the 'fierce antagonism between Hindus and Mahomedans'. Some Hindu organizations were 'frankly anti-Mahomedan, as the Moslem League is frankly anti-Hindu, and both are anti-national'.[12]

Another consequence of the Swadeshi movement was the marginalization of the Moderates. Young patriots were fired with the dream of freedom, to be achieved not by incremental, constitutional means, but by spectacular acts of violence against prominent officials and proconsuls. These revolutionaries thought – or hoped – that by murdering policemen or setting off bombs in government buildings they would awaken the masses, catalyzing their nascent, suppressed, anti-colonial sentiments.

The Moderates believed that, in their own struggle against the oppressive aspects of colonial rule, they had the British people and British institutions on their side. Harsh laws and punitive taxes were 'un-British', to be lifted or withdrawn when their true nature was revealed to His Majesty's distant but not necessarily unfeeling Government. The ultimate, long-term goal was Dominion Status, where India would have its own elected legislatures on the Westminster model, with the British tie kept alive by the King acting (as he did in Australia and Canada) as head of state.

The Extremists, on the other hand, rejected British rule, British institutions and British exemplars. They saw the struggle in black-and-white, akin to battles in Hindu myth between gods and demons, *devas* and *asuras*. The British were all evil. Gokhale and his ilk liked to quote Mill and Burke (approvingly). On the other side, Gokhale's great rival, Bal

Gangadhar Tilak, idolized the medieval Maratha warrior Shivaji, who had conducted a series of guerrilla battles against Muslim rulers based in Delhi. Tilak had also started an annual festival in honour of Ganapati, the god whose invocation at the start of any task (or battle) was believed to aid in its success (or victory).

Across the subcontinent, in Bengal, young radicals formed secret societies where they learned to assemble bombs and use guns. They were fired by the example of the Goddess Durga, wife of Shiva, known and revered for slaying the forces of evil. Shivaji and Durga, revenge and retribution – these were the models and methods of the Extremists in the Indian national movement. This invocation of Hindu gods and warriors inevitably disenchanted Muslims, who had recourse to their own holy texts, from which vantage point Hindus were seen as infidels and idolaters.[13]

There was a muscular, masculine edge to the patriotism of the Extremists. British rule (and Muslim rule before it) had emasculated the Hindu. He needed now to recover his vigour and his virility, to renew it through daring acts of heroism and sacrifice. Once the British had been evicted through terror, the motherland would rebuild itself along classical Hindu lines. In imagining their post-colonial future, some revolutionaries put their faith in the ancient Indian village *panchayat*; others, in a pan-Indian *Hindu Rashtra* which would unite, in one solid, strong, centralized state, Hindus currently divided by language, caste and region.

The mood in India at the time Gandhi composed and wrote *Hind Swaraj* was captured in two books by British journalists based in the subcontinent. Both noted the intensity and vigour of the new political movements, yet they had somewhat different understandings of it. The man from the pro-Establishment *Times* of London saw 'an illusory "Nationalism" which appeals to nothing in Indian history, but which is calculated and meant to appeal with dangerous force to Western sentiment and ignorance.' While professing democratic values and aspirations, this movement, claimed the *Times* man, appealed on the one hand to 'the old tyranny of caste and to the worst superstitions of Hinduism', and on the other to 'the murderous methods of Western Anarchism'.[14]

The man from the liberal *Manchester Guardian* was more sympathetic. He observed that the political upsurge was both deep and widespread. 'It is the conviction of many', he remarked, that 'India is now standing on the verge of a national renaissance – a new birth in intellect, social life, and the affairs of the state.' This renaissance was inspired by the 'example set to all Oriental nationalities by Japan', but also by a keen understanding of the political heritage of the conquerors themselves. The *Guardian* man thus wrote that

> the visits of highly educated Indians to England, the use of English as a common tongue among educated people of all races and religions, the increasing knowledge of our history and our hard-won liberties, the increasing study of our great Liberal thinkers – all these admirable advantages we have ourselves contributed to the new spirit, and it is useless for startled reactionaries to think of withdrawing them now.[15]

Gandhi, in South Africa, was keenly following political and social developments in his homeland. The pages of *Indian Opinion* were peppered with reports on Congress meetings and Swadeshi protests. Gandhi himself subscribed to a variety of English and Gujarati papers, which came to him through the post. Now, in his own little book, written with speed on the ship, he brought together his views on what ailed India and what might redeem it.

As revealed in *Hind Swaraj*, Gandhi remained in some respects close to the Moderates. He deplored the savage criticisms of Gokhale by Savarkar and company. Like his mentor, he was deeply committed to Hindu–Muslim harmony. He saw the religious divide as a product of British rule (which, for its own interests, had set one community against the other), and not as an essential or perennial part of the Indian condition.

In other respects, Gandhi appears in this book to be closer to the Extremists. His harsh words on the British Parliament distanced him from Gokhale and Naoroji. His exaltation of ancient Indian moral and civic virtues, his idealization of a past where Indians lived at peace with themselves, his insistence that education should be in the mother tongue alone – these all may have been congenial to the patriot who looked to indigenous rather than Western models of progress or redemption.

Finally, in *Hind Swaraj* Gandhi set himself apart from *both* Extremists and Moderates in his advocacy of non-violent resistance. He was opposed to both petitioning and to bomb-throwing. He saw the former as ineffective and the latter as immoral. The rulers would not concede ground unless pressed to do so. But murdering officials would not scare the British into leaving either. Besides, violence tended to beget violence – once aimed at the foreigner, it would in time be aimed at Indians of rival views or backgrounds. The Transvaal protests of 1907–9 had convinced Gandhi of the efficacy and moral superiority of satyagraha, a method for whose application India offered a larger and more inviting stage.

Hind Swaraj was a summation of Gandhi's political views, and a statement of his political ambition. The Indian national movement had thus far been dominated by Bengalis and Maharashtrians. Valuable supporting parts had been played by Tamils, Punjabis and Hindi-speakers. Now, through the writing and publication of this book, a Gujarati based in South Africa sought to clear a space for himself, and to make his voice heard. His experiences in the diaspora, uniting and mobilizing Indians, gave him (he thought) a unique vantage point from which to illuminate and intervene in debates within the motherland.

Gandhi had hoped that *Hind Swaraj* would be read and discussed in India, its parallels and departures with prevailing political trends noted and acted upon. In February 1910, a certain Chibba Prabhu arrived in Bombay from Durban with 415 copies of the original Gujarati edition of the book. However, these were seized by Customs and a copy passed on to the Oriental Translator of the Bombay Government. The book, reported this Translator, is 'of a decidedly objectionable nature, especially considering the present disturbed political condition in the country'. He then provided a summary of *Hind Swaraj*'s contents in a single extended paragraph, this constituting (so far as we know) the first written response to a text that has attracted hundreds of thousands of readers down the decades:

> It purports to be a dialogue between the 'Editor' and a 'Reader', in which the former inculcates his peculiar views regarding the present political condition and the possible future, of India. The 'Reader', representing probably the average Indian 'passive resister' of the Transvaal, is represented as holding frankly Extremist views, and indeed speaks quite frankly of 'driving out' the British from India as a principal object of political agitation in this country. The 'Editor' is no less anxious to see the rule in

India pass from the hands of the British to those of Indians. But he holds views about the evils of armed resistance of any kind, peculiar to Tolstoy, whose follower the author Mohanchand [*sic*] Karamchand Gandhi, professes to be. He ascribes all the evils from which India is suffering, plague, famine, poverty, crime, etc., to the railways, education, reforms, lawyers, doctors, in fact everything introduced by Englishmen in this country. Indeed, in places the man seems to be crazy in his passionate desire to keep India and her life and ways unpolluted by the least contact with the West. The English have no place in India, says the 'Editor', if they want to bring their harmful civilisation with them into this country. On condition that this civilisation is kept out of India, the English may be allowed to live in the land. The 'Reader' is made to express revolutionary ideas and even to approve of political assassinations. 'We will first terrorise (the British) by a few murders. Then a few of our people, who will have been trained up, will fight openly. Of course 20 or 25 lakhs of people will die in this fight. But ultimately we shall regain the country. We shall defeat the British by means of guerilla warfare'. The 'Editor' strongly condemns these ideas as borrowed from the West and says that bloodshed can never make India independent though by the way he calls Dhingra a true patriot, 'but his patriotism was mad'. 'But', says the Reader, 'you must admit that what little has been granted by Lord Morley is owing to these political murders'. 'It is quite possible', says the 'Editor', 'that what Lord Morley has granted has been granted through fear. But what has been gained through fear can be retained only so long as that fear lasts.' Therefore he advocates peaceful means, and among them 'passive resistance'.[16]

Based on this report, the Bombay Government formally 'forfeited to his Majesty' the book, *Hind Swaraj*, 'purporting to be printed at the International Press, Phoenix, Natal'. The book, said the order, contained 'words which are likely to bring into hatred and contempt the Government established by law in British India and to excite disaffection to the said Government'. The circulation of the book was banned under the Press Act, and its import prohibited under the Sea Customs Act. The Government of India endorsed the ban, noting – on the basis of materials sent it from Bombay – that from the contents of this 'clearly seditious' book 'it may be fairly concluded that Mr M. K. Gandhi is not the innocent martyr as which he poses to be'.[17]

The Oriental Translator of the Bombay Government had written what in effect was the first review of *Hind Swaraj*. Gandhi did not of course read the review, nor the glosses on it by other officials. All he knew was that copies of the Gujarati edition had been seized. He immediately wrote a letter of complaint, which is worth reproducing for its intrinsic value and because it escaped the attention of the editors of his *Collected Works*. Dated 16 April 1910, and written from Johannesburg, it was addressed to the Home Secretary of the Government of India. Enclosing the English edition of the book, then just out in Durban, Gandhi said:

> I do not know why the Gujarati copies have been confiscated. If the Government will kindly favour me with their views and their advice, I shall endeavour, so far as possible, to carry them out. In writing 'Hind Swaraj' it has not been my intention to embarrass the Government in so far as any writing of mine could do so, but entirely to assist it. This in no way means that I necessarily approve of any or all the actions of the Government or the methods on which it is based. In my humble opinion, every man has a right to hold any opinion he chooses, and to give effect to it also, so long as, in doing so, he does not use physical violence against anybody. Being connected with a newspaper which commands some influence and attention, and knowing that methods of violence among my countrymen may become popular even in South Africa, and feeling assured that the adoption of passive resistance as I have ventured to do in 'Indian Home Rule' was the surest preventative of physical violence, I did not hesitate to publish [the book] in Gujarati. The English edition has not been circulated by me in India except among officials and the leading newspapers. At the same time, I am aware that some buyers have sent it on their own account to India also.
>
> I need hardly say that the views expressed in 'Indian Home Rule' have nothing to do with the struggle that is going on in the Transvaal and in other parts of South Africa, intimately connected though I am with it; and I am not in a position to know how many of my countrymen share those views. At the same time, no matter where I am placed, I consider it my duty to popularize them to the best of my ability as being in the best interests of India and the Empire.[18]

Gandhi is here acting as both loyalist and rebel: suggesting that his advocacy of non-violence may come to the aid of the Raj, but reserving to himself the right to say what he wished about the Raj's policies and actions. The letter held out an offer of compromise; that he might consider revising passages considered excessively provocative. Gandhi was extremely keen that his book (and his ideas) be discussed and debated within India, and by Indians. He was willing to make some changes to his text to make this possible.

Meanwhile, the Government had commissioned its own English translation of *Hind Swaraj*, undertaken by the Gujarati interpreter of the Madras High Court.[19] Comparing their version with Gandhi's, the Home Department found them very similar – and equally dangerous. The distinction made by the author between words and deeds, and between passive resistance and armed violence, was characterized as 'curious' and dismissed as unsustainable. 'Preaching and disseminating sedition', remarked a senior official in the Home Department, was as offensive and dangerous to public order as actual physical violence.[20] For, as the Director of the Criminal Intelligence Branch wrote on the file, 'we must, I think, aim at destroying the open market for imported seditious publications of all kinds: we cannot afford to pick and choose very much according to the degree and quantity of the sedition.' He continued, tellingly, 'More real perversion of ideas in the direction of sedition is effected by moderate seditious publications than by those breathing violence and revolution in every line.'[21]

The Government of India's decision to ban the book was the subject of a scathing editorial in P. S. Aiyar's *African Chronicle*. 'No wonder', said the paper, that 'sedition is ripening day by day, and discontent is growing abroad.' For

> if the Viceroy and his colleagues were to be frightened at such a simple booklet as [Hind] *Swarexaj*, and if they could not tolerate the expression of opinion of even men of Mr Gandhi's stamp, we do not know what else the Indian Government would tolerate. Under the most provocating circumstances we have not seen Mr Gandhi using a single cross word to any one, and as a leader in politics, no country could find a better man than Mr Gandhi. Should his production be unfit for circulation, we believe, few men could be found in India who could give expression to the popular will in a sober and adequate language.[22]

The Government's argument was here being turned on its head. Paranoid policemen claimed that allowing moderates like Gandhi to openly criticize aspects of Government policy would provide wanton encouragement to the extremists. P. S. Aiyar argued exactly the opposite: if even moderates such as Gandhi could not be heard, then ordinary Indians would completely lose faith in the rulers, and seek redemption by the methods of the extremists.

In May 1910, some copies of the printed English edition of *Hind Swaraj* reached the shores of the Madras Presidency. An early reader was the Province's Home Secretary. He concluded that while the author 'affects to treat the English with forbearance', the argument of the book was 'calculated to lessen the esteem in which they have been held, and the writer's whole ideal is by implication at any rate, inconsistent with the continuance of British rule, or indeed of any settled administration in India'. The critic highlighted four contentious claims made by the author:

(i) English politicians are dishonest and unscrupulous, and English newspapers are imbued with a partisan spirit.

(ii) English administration in India rests upon the Courts, and then again upon lawyers, who are corrupt from top to bottom.

(iii) The members of the English nation who have settled in India are of an inferior stamp to their countrymen at home.

(iv) The continuation of the English in India depends entirely upon their adoption of Oriental languages and civilisation. If they fail to conform to this condition, India will be made too hot to hold them.

The Home Secretary in Madras recommended a ban on the English edition of the book as well. The Secretary of the Judicial Department concurred. Then, against point (i) above, he quoted Adam Smith: 'That corrupt and insidious animal called a politician.' He also expressed his 'regret that extracts from this work cannot be more widely known. The advice to lawyers to give up law and take to a handloom would, for instance, be worth communicating to the Legislative Council.'[23]

The Government of India had made sure that *Hind Swaraj* was not circulated within the subcontinent, in either its Gujarati or English versions. There were thus no printed, public reviews of the book within Gandhi's homeland. But it was reviewed by some newspapers in South Africa, where the book circulated freely. In the first week of May 1910, the *Transvaal Leader* published a critical assessment of the book by an acquaintance of Gandhi named Edward Dallow. An accountant of British stock, a Nonconformist by faith, Dallow had been sympathetic to the claims of the Indians in the Transvaal. He was a signatory to the letter written by Europeans to *The Times* in January 1909. Later that same year, he wrote to the Colonial Secretary urging him to 'receive the Indian deputation [led by Gandhi] with sympathetic regard', and to use 'the influence of your high office to procure for them the amelioration of the law which they demand.'[24]

Dallow opposed laws that discriminated on the basis of colour. However, he was a defender of Empire, and in this capacity thought the banning of *Hind Swaraj* in India both prudent and necessary. For 'under cover of a dissertation on modern civilisation this little booklet of 104 pages is in reality written in support of the political propaganda to free India from English rule, and as such the Indian Government were acting wisely in endeavouring to prevent its circulation in India.' Gandhi might have kept his argument impersonal, distinguishing between modern civilization (which he abominated) and the English people (whom he tolerated). Nonetheless, the fact

> that all his illustrations of the degrading effects of modern civilisation are taken from English government, from English life, from English Ministers, Parliament and people, makes it highly improbable that any but a cultivated man and a scholar will keep the subtle distinction in mind. To the ordinary reader . . . the effect will be to raise a hatred not only of modern civilisation, but of the English people in India as its particular exponents.

Dallow chastised Gandhi for his narrow range of reading. The lawyer had consulted the works of novelists and critics, and exalted the 'masters of Indian philosophy'. At the same time, he had overlooked 'masters of modern philosophy' such as Mill, Spencer, Goethe, Kant, Hegel and de Tocqueville. Dallow ended the review with his own vision of the past and possible future of the author's homeland:

> India is not so immovable as Mr Gandhi would have us believe; the caste system, which is the basis – the evil basis – of her civilisation is showing signs of weakening under the influence of modern thought and experience acquired by Indians visiting other lands. The discoveries of modern science,

which show the plant to be as truly alive as the animal, have undermined one of the chief dogmas of their religion. Under the guidance of English rule, India is gradually adopting representative institutions, and her rulers look forward to the time, as yet still far distant, when India will take upon her own shoulders the burden of government as an independent and loyal appanage of the Imperial Crown.[25]

The review stung Gandhi, who immediately sent a reply. He began by saying that he too was a 'lover of the Empire to which Mr Dallow and I belong'. This love, he clarified,

> proceeds from my faith in the individuals who compose it, whether they be European, Kaffir, or Indian, but I decline to bow in idolatrous homage to the term. To me it simply means this: Whether the English and the Indians intend it or not, they have been thrown together by the Divine will for their mutual good; but, as free agents, they may turn the connection to evil. This latter activity of ours I call Satanic. In common with many Englishmen, after eighteen years' close observation and, shall I say, practical life, I have come to believe that for the English people to Anglicise India, even if they could do so, would be a tragedy.

Dallow had condemned the caste system; in Gandhi's view, however, it had 'saved India from the ruinous and brutal effect of the competitive system which has been exalted to the dignity of a science by modern civilisation'. To the charge that he was poorly read in modern philosophy, Gandhi answered that he was acquainted with the works of Mill and Spencer, but saw no reason to read more glosses of modern civilisation when he saw the thing itself unfold before his eyes. 'Must I read a critique of "Hamlet",' he said with some asperity, 'when I have only to pay a shilling and see the play?'

Gandhi said that his tract was aimed at two different audiences: the party of violence within India, to whom he said that 'whatever evils India is suffering from are mainly to our own defects and to our having worshipped the golden calf'; and to the English, to whom his appeal was 'not necessarily to discard modern civilisation themselves, but to help India to retain her own civilisation'. On both parties he pressed the immorality of violence. To the British he said that 'methods of repression . . . are absolutely useless'. To the revolutionaries he said that 'violence cannot be rooted out of India or anywhere else by violence'.

It was thus that he had 'commended in all humility passive resistance, that is, soul force, both to the Governors and to the Governed. It is not necessary that both the sides should take it up. Either may adopt it to the advantage of both.'[26]

Meanwhile, Gandhi was carrying on a private, if equally instructive, debate with his friend W. J. Wybergh. As Transvaal's Commissioner of Mines in the early 1900s, and later as a Member of the Legislative Assembly, Wybergh had vigorously promoted the segregation of Asians.[27] But he made an exception for Gandhi, the English-educated lawyer. The two met regularly at meetings of Johannesburg's Theosophical Society. Sent *Hind Swaraj* by Gandhi, Wybergh commented that he did not think that 'on the whole your argument is coherent or that the various statements and opinions you express have any real dependence upon one another'. He was not surprised that the pamphlet was seen as disloyal, since (and he seems to have been reading Dallow here)

> the average plain ignorant man without intellectual subtlety would suppose that you were preaching against British rule in India. On the far more important general principle underlying your book, I must say definitely that I think you are going wrong. European civilisation has many defects and I agree with many of your criticisms, but I do not believe that it is 'the Kingdom of Satan' or that it should be abolished. It appears to me a necessary step in the evolution of mankind, especially manifested in and suitable for Western nations. While I recognise that the highest ideals of India (and Europe too) are in advance of this civilisation, yet I think also, with all modesty, that the bulk of the Indian population require to be roused by the lash of competition and the other material and sensuous as well as intellectual stimuli which 'civilisation' supplies.

Wybergh conceded that not

> all *forms* of Western civilisation are suitable for India, and I don't doubt that we British have erred (in all good faith) in trying to introduce British institutions indiscriminately. But Western *ideals* are necessary to India, not to supersede but to modify and develop her own. India ought, I think, to be governed on Indian lines, (whether by Indians or Englishmen is another question) but 'civilisation' is both necessary and useful, if it grows naturally and is not forced and it cannot be avoided.

The critic turned next to the question of passive resistance. One might have no objection to its adoption by an individual saint, but

> as a practical political principle suitable for adoption by ordinary men living the ordinary life of citizens, it seems to be altogether pernicious, and utterly disastrous to the public welfare. It is mere anarchy, and I have always regarded Tolstoy, its principal apostle, as very likely a saint personally, but when he preaches his doctrines as political propaganda and recommends them for indiscriminate adoption, as the most dangerous enemy of humanity. I have no manner of doubt that Governments and laws and police and physical force are absolutely essential to average humanity, and are as truly 'natural' in their stage of development and as truly moral as eating and drinking and propagating the species . . . When all humanity has reached sainthood Governments will become unnecessary but not until then. Meanwhile civilisation must be mended, not ended.

Gandhi, characteristically, printed Wybergh's critical assessment in full in *Indian Opinion* and then sought courteously to answer it. He was, he said, 'painfully conscious of the imperfections and defects' in presentation that Wybergh pointed to. These might make a superficial reader conclude that the book was 'a disloyal production'. However, he had 'the position of a publicist practically forced upon me by circumstances'. Both the tone and content of the pamphlet had their genesis in the fact that it was written with a view to drawing Indians away from 'the insane violence that is now going on in India.'

As for modern civilization, Gandhi argued those who were outside its ambit and

> have a well-tried civilisation to guide them, should be helped to remain where they are, if only as a measure of prudence . . . I cannot help most strongly contesting the idea that the Indian population requires to be roused by 'the lash of competition and the other material and sensuous as well as intellectual stimuli'; I cannot admit that these will add a single inch to its moral stature.

Finally, he said that his own reading of Tolstoy's works

> has never led me to consider that, in spite of his merciless analysis of institutions organised and based upon force, that is governments, he in

any way anticipates or contemplates that the whole world will be able to live in a state of philosophical anarchy. What he has preached, as, in my opinion, have all world-teachers, is that every man has to obey the voice of his own conscience, and be his own master, and seek the Kingdom of God from within. For him there is no government that can control him without his sanction.[28]

Some of Gandhi's British friends had profound reservations about *Hind Swaraj*. There are hints that even some Indians in South Africa did not entirely identify with the book's contents. Maganlal Gandhi wrote his uncle a letter asking why he had so sharply attacked railways, doctors and elected Parliaments. Meanwhile, Gandhi wrote to Gokhale (who would certainly have taken even stronger exception to the dismissal of modern professions and modern institutions) clarifying that the book represented his personal views. He hoped his mentor would 'be able, should any prejudice arise against me personally or the pamphlet, to keep the merits of the struggle [in the Transvaal] entirely separate from me.'[29]

There were, of course, responses to *Hind Swaraj* that required no answer at all. One such came from Isabella Fyvie Mayo, a Scottish writer and disciple of Tolstoy who worked (in her own words) for 'the brotherhood of all races of men, the cause of international peace, and the recognition of the rights of animals'.[30] In a letter to Hermann Kallenbach, Miss Mayo said she was 'lost in admiration of Mr Gandhi's "Home Rule for India"'. When she heard it had been banned in India, her first reaction was that the Bible itself might be proscribed, since 'Mr Gandhi only makes practical application of the precepts of the "Sermon on the Mount".' The central thesis of the book Miss Mayo unreservedly endorsed. For

> as long as Indians delight in being Britonised, so long as 'Swadeshi' means only more 'factories', so long as Indian ambitions point to entering Government service, so long will India be enslaved. Her freedom is absolutely in her own hands, and the proscription of Mr Gandhi's book shows that the authorities know this – for not only does he oppose all revolutionary violence and bloodshed but he would give an entirely new, irresistible and peaceable character to all progressive movements everywhere.[31]

Reading *Hind Swaraj* today, one finds some portions of the book enormously appealing, other parts disconcerting and even bizarre. The polemic is powerful, but also crude. The linguistic infelicities may be because it was both written and translated in a hurry. The English version was, as noted, dictated to Hermann Kallenbach. Gandhi sent a typescript to the Baptist pastor Joseph Doke, with the request that he 'correct and criticize' it. 'Some of the similes', said Gandhi, 'read very crude in English.' He was 'painfully aware of the fact' that the book 'was not a "finished product". I have simply jotted down my thoughts as they have come to me.' The minister, taking this judgement at face value, sent what seems to have been a long list of criticisms. But Gandhi was keen to see the book in print at once, and chose not to rewrite it on the lines suggested by Doke.[32]

One striking feature of the book is its extraordinarily positive portrait of ancient Indian culture and civilization. This was perhaps not unrelated to the fact that Gandhi had lived for so many years out of India. For diasporic nationalism tends to be uncritical, eulogizing the faraway homeland, its hallowed and mostly unsullied past, and its pristine and ageless culture.

The celebration of Indian civilization went hand-in-hand with a thoroughgoing condemnation of Western civilization. Ironically, this was based mostly on Western authorities. The Appendix lists twenty books or pamphlets consulted by Gandhi in writing the book, of which as many as six are by the Russian, Leo Tolstoy. Other works are by the Italian, Mazzini; the American, Thoreau; and the Englishmen, Carpenter, Ruskin and Maine. Only two of the twenty books are by Gandhi's fellow countrymen, these being Dadabhai Naoroji's and Romesh Chunder Dutt's studies of the economic exploitation of the subcontinent under British rule.

Gandhi wrote *Hind Swaraj* in 1909, at a time he scarcely knew India at all. By 1888, when he departed for London at the age of nineteen, he had lived only in towns in his native Kathiawar. There is no evidence that he had travelled in the countryside, and he knew no other part of India. Later, in 1892 and again in 1902, he came to spend several months in the city of Bombay. In 1896 he visited Calcutta and Madras to lobby for the rights of Indians in South Africa. However, at the time of the writing of *Hind Swaraj*, Gandhi may never have spoken to a single Indian peasant or worker (or landlord or moneylender) living or working in India itself. Hence, perhaps, the romantic (and to a modern eye hopelessly unreal) representation of indigenous Indian culture in the book.

It may be worth pointing out that while *Hind Swaraj* was the first book that Gandhi published, it was not the first book he had written. This was his 'Guide to London', drafted during those solitary evenings in Pretoria during his first year in South Africa, when he hoped still to make a career as an Anglicized barrister in Bombay. This first, unpublished, book was a paean to English education and English manners, written, appropriately, in English. The book that Gandhi wrote some sixteen years later was conceived and penned in his native Gujarati, in which language he vigorously upheld the virtues of his own civilization while diminishing that of the conqueror.

17

Seeking a Settlement

Just before he left London, Gandhi heard that the funds in his Phoenix settlement were running dangerously low. The satyagraha of 1908 and 1909 had severely tested the community's will to give. Much money had been collected, and spent, on sustaining the families of passive resisters. Now the main organ of the struggle was in danger of going under. On 27 November 1909 – shortly after he had completed the first draft of *Hind Swaraj* – Gandhi wrote to his nephew Maganlal that they must somehow keep their weekly magazine afloat. Whatever happened, they would 'bring out at least a one-page issue of *Indian Opinion* and distribute it among the people as long as there is even one person in Phoenix'.[1]

The SS *Kildonan Castle* arrived in Cape Town on 30 November. On disembarking, Gandhi heard that the philanthrophist Ratan Tata had sent a cheque for Rs 25,000 to aid the struggle in South Africa. *Indian Opinion* had been saved; so too, perhaps, the struggle itself.

Ratan Tata was the son of Jamshedji Tata, the pioneering Parsi entrepreneur who had started India's first steel mill and endowed the Indian Institute of Science. The younger Tata spent a great deal of time on the Continent and in England – he had a home in Twickenham – but maintained an interest in Indian politics. Naturally, he preferred the Moderates to the Extremists. Gokhale in particular was a friend. In 1905, Gokhale had started a 'Servants of India Society', whose members were required to 'work for the advancement of all [Indians], regardless of caste and creed'. The objectives of the society included the promotion of education and communal harmony, and the advancement of women and low castes.[2] Tata was an early supporter of the Servants of India Society, which he sent Rs 6,000 a year because he saw it as 'a constitutional and rational alternative to the violent methods which some people adopt for the progress of our people and our country'.[3]

Tata followed developments in the Transvaal closely. He was disappointed that Gandhi's trip to London had ended in failure. He noted the public meetings held in India, but felt that the time had come 'when our appreciation . . . must take the form, not merely of expressions of sympathy but also of substantial money help'. In the last week of November, he sent Gokhale a cheque for Rs 25,000 (equivalent, roughly, to £1,650 then, and to £131,000 today), asking him to forward it to Gandhi 'to be spent in relieving destitution, and in aid of the struggle generally.' Explaining his gesture, Tata said he had

> watched with unfeigned admiration the undaunted and determined stand which our countrymen in the Transvaal – a mere handful in numbers – have made and are making against heavy odds and in the face of monstrous injustice and oppression, to assert their rights as citizens of the Empire and as freemen, and to vindicate the honour and dignity of our motherland . . . The ruinous sacrifices which men mostly of very modest means are cheerfully making in this unequal struggle, the fortitude with which men of education and refinement are ungrudgingly submitting to treatment ordinarily accorded to hardened convicts and criminals, the calm resignation of men devotedly attached to their homes to cruel disruption of family ties, and the perfectly legitimate and constitutional character of the resistance which is being offered and which is in such striking contrast to the occasional acts of violence which we deplore nearer home – all these to my mind, present a spectacle of great nobility of aim, resoluteness of purpose and strength of moral fibre with which we Indians are not usually credited.[4]

This was a striking passage, which (among other things) strongly suggests that Ratan Tata had been reading *Indian Opinion*. It displays an acute understanding of the larger issues at stake, relating to the status of British subjects across the Empire, to the prestige and honour of India, and not least, to rival methods of obtaining justice and redress. On receiving the news, Gokhale sent Gandhi a telegram urging him to write directly to Tata thanking him for his 'munificent [and] timely help'. He also issued a public statement asking other patrons to follow Mr Tata's lead. The industrialist's gesture would 'put fresh heart and hope' into Gandhi and his colleagues, who were 'determined to win in this struggle or perish'. Should not the mother country, for whose sake all this suffering is being 'undergone', asked Gokhale, now 'recognise her responsibilities in the matter and come to their assistance? Mr Tata's example needs to be widely followed and that without delay.'[5]

It was. Inspired by Ratan Tata, his fellow Parsi grandee J. B. Petit sent £750 from Bombay, and Gandhi's friend Pranjivan Mehta raised a similar sum in Rangoon. Other sections of the Indian diaspora also chipped in: £135 came from London, £61 from Mozambique and £59 from Zanzibar.[6]

Disembarking at Cape Town on their return from London, Gandhi and Hajee Habib took a train north-east to Johannesburg. At the city's Park Station they were met by a large crowd, mostly of Indians, with a sprinkling of Chinese and European supporters. The next day, Gandhi spoke at a meeting of Tamil ladies, thanking them for supporting their brothers and husbands who had been to jail. On the 5th, he addressed an audience of 1,500 at the Hamidia Mosque, where he spoke of the larger importance of their struggle and thanked Ratan Tata for his gift (a product, in Gandhi's view, of 'the magnificent efforts that were being made [in India] by the self-sacrificing Mr Polak').

The struggle was now to be renewed. Gandhi sent a letter to *Indian Opinion* announcing this, saying, 'I hope I shall find myself lodged in gaol before this letter appears.' His second son, Manilal, who had turned seventeen in October, would also court arrest, in pursuit of his father's belief that 'to go to gaol or suffer similar hardships with a pure motive for the motherland is the truest kind of education.'[7]

In the third week of December, Gandhi went to Natal. He arrived at Umgeni station at night and walked three hours in the dark to Phoenix through the grass, nervous that he might 'tread upon a snake or scorpion'. Kasturba was pleased to see him. 'Mrs G. has considerably improved', he wrote to Kallenbach, 'she is sweet. She has been working regularly at the Press for one hour. She folds Tolstoy's letter. What a privilege for her!'[8]

On Sunday, 19 December, Gandhi was due to speak at a meeting in Durban. A crowd of more than 1,000 had gathered at the Victoria Street Indian Market, but the main speaker did not come. That was no fault of his, however. The journalist P. S. Aiyar had gone in a car to pick up Gandhi from his settlement. That mode of transport was very new in

South Africa. En route to Phoenix, the car got stuck in a stream (whether it was the vehicle's or the driver's fault the sources do not say). No one was injured, but by the time word of the mishap got to Phoenix, it was too late for Gandhi to come to Durban.

The next day, Gandhi went to Durban by the safer route, that of the railway. The meeting this time was held in the Albert Street Hall. After being garlanded 'amid rousing cheers', he announced that some young men, among them his son Manilal and the Cambridge-educated barrister Joseph Royeppen, would 'accompany him to the Transvaal and [were] expected with him to go to gaol.'[9]

Gandhi crossed back into the Transvaal with six companions. He hoped they would be arrested; when they were not, he sent Royeppen and Manilal back to Natal, asking them to travel afresh to Johannesburg and hawk without a licence, to simultaneously break the law and demonstrate that selling fruits and vegetables was as honourable a trade as being a clerk or lawyer. This time the young men were detained, and sentenced to ten days with hard labour.[10]

In this new phase of the campaign, the Tamils were, as before, in the vanguard. Gandhi wrote to Gokhale that Thambi Naidoo was 'perhaps the bravest and staunchest' of the passive resisters.

> I do not know of any Indian who knows the spirit of the struggle so well as he does. He was born in Mauritius, but is more Indian than most of us. He has sacrificed himself entirely, and has sent me a defiant message, saying that, even though I may yield . . . he alone will offer resistance and die in the Transvaal gaols.

The Tamil women were not far behind. In a spectacular affirmation of solidarity, Mrs Amacanoo and Mrs Packirsamy – whose husbands were in jail – came to Gandhi's office in Rissik Street, removed their earrings, nose-rings, bangles and necklaces, and said they would not wear them again until the end of the struggle.[11]

The most steadfast woman supporter of the satyagraha, however, was Gandhi's secretary, Sonja Schlesin. In times of peace, she dealt patiently – not to say heroically – with her employer's indecipherable scrawl, his eccentric work and eating habits, and his many and various clients. In times of strife she was called upon to urge and mobilize the women. On their behalf she drafted and sent many petitions to government. The formal historical record has few traces of Miss Schlesin's contributions. Henry and Millie Polak spoke of their involvement in books, essays and letters. Kallenbach's correspondence with Gandhi and others is very extensive. But since Miss Schlesin was with Gandhi all day, most days, there are few letters between them. From stray reports in *Indian Opinion*, however, we get a sense of how much Sonja Schlesin did for the struggle. Passive resisters in jail were allowed a weekly visit. Sometimes relatives made the trip; when these were unavailable, or in jail themselves, Miss Schlesin rushed about on her bicycle from prison to prison, carrying food and messages. With the main Indian leaders going in and out of jail, Gandhi's secretary also handled the 'Passive Resistance Fund': monitoring and recording the inflow of donations, and directing the money to individuals and families in need.

A rare letter from Sonja Schlesin in the archives gives glimpes both of her competence and her independence of mind. Gandhi was spending several weeks outside Johannesburg; in his absence, Miss Schlesin was keeping the office going. Her letter begins with the question of some scholarships Pranjivan Mehta had endowed for Indian students. Applications had begun coming in, and Miss Schlesin was deciding which young man seemed 'clever' and which not. She moves next to dues owed by the office to other lawyers, then to the renewal of Gandhi's and Polak's subscriptions to the Law Society. News of the Gujarati merchant and activist A. M. Cachalia follows. The last paragraph turns to her own self-education. Here she tells Gandhi that she has been

> just reading a book recently issued called 'The Truth about Women'. I don't agree with the conclusion of the writer, but she has gathered together much material which is interesting and instructive. Amongst other things, she says that chastity is not a moral evolution, but that the origination of the idea is connected with the question of property.[12]

In this letter, Miss Schlesin addresses her employer as 'Bapu', or Father. She was, in age, between Harilal and Manilal, yet far more willing to stand up to Gandhi than they were. This last line of her letter was surely a tease, which suggested, to her friend, employer and fictive father, that the *brahmacharya* he so exalted had its basis in the desire to keep large estates from being broken up. Miss Schlesin thus implied that younger brothers became monks to keep the economic status of the family intact, rather than (as Gandhi may have fancifully imagined) for elevated spiritual reasons alone.

For all her cheekiness, Sonja Schlesin was devoted to Gandhi and his cause. Hers was a double or perhaps triple transgression: a white, Jewish woman expressing her solidarity with persecuted Indian males. Much later, her employer gratefully recalled what his struggle owed her. This 'young girl', he wrote, 'soon constituted herself the watchman and warder of the morality not only of my office but of the whole movement'. Thus

> Pathans, Patels, ex-indentured men, Indians of all classes and ages surrounded her, sought her advice and followed it. Europeans in South Africa would generally never travel in the same railway compartment as Indians, and in the Transvaal they are even prohibited from doing so. Yet Miss Schlesin would deliberately sit in the third class compartment for Indians like other Satyagrahis and even resist the guards who interfered with her.[13]

In February 1910, Parsee Rustomjee was released after a year in jail. He told the press of the difficulties he had faced. He was asked to break stones; when he complained, the prison doctor told him that 'I would be all right when I had thrown off superfluous fat.' The flying chips affected his eyesight; when he complained about that too, the doctor flippantly remarked that 'I should, on being discharged, spend from £10 to £20, and be operated upon.' Rustomjee believed that the passive resisters had been sent to Diepkloof, a notoriously harsh prison, 'in order to break their spirit and resolution'. After his release he had come back to Natal to restore his business and his health, both in ruins. He remained defiant, telling the Johannesburg press, and by extension the Transvaal Government, that 'there are some Indians left, including myself, who will not be broken, no matter what hardships they are subjected to, and I shall soon have the privilege of affording the Government an opportunity of sending me to Diepkloof or any other place they choose.'[14]

On 18 February the passive resisters of the Transvaal hosted a banquet for Joseph Doke, who was departing on a tour of the United States. There were three hundred guests, among them sixty Europeans.

Kallenbach and Thambi Naidoo supervised the kitchen, while Gandhi helped serve the dishes. The menu was wholly vegetarian: soup, macaroni and cheese, fruits, coffee and mineral water. The main speaker was Doke's fellow Nonconformist minister, Charles Phillips. His Congregational Church had, from very early on, been sympathetic to Gandhi's cause. When the Asiatic Ordinance was first proposed, Phillips had written that 'Indians are just as amenable to sanitary regulations' as Europeans, adding that 'in morals they are in no way inferior; in matters of temperance they are decidedly superior'.[15] Now the minister recalled the 'grand old passive resister John Bunyan', also a Baptist minister, who had spent twelve years in prison for following his conscience. Rev. Phillips said Thambi Naidoo 'showed something of the spirit of John Bunyan'. There was now a window in Westminster Abbey in honour of Bunyan; the minister hoped 'that in the future they would be able to erect a monument in remembrance of Indians and Chinese in the Transvaal, who had suffered so bravely and splendidly'.[16]

As ever, Gandhi left open the possibility of a compromise. Two English friends, the lawyer J. C. Gibson and the minister Charles Phillips, had offered to talk to the Government. Gandhi told them that if the existing legislation was repealed, so that all *bona fide* Indian residents of Transvaal were allowed to enter, live and practise their trade, and the laws so modified 'as to enable any Asiatic immigrants of culture to enter the Colony on precisely the same terms as Europeans', then 'the granting of these two concessions will finally close the struggle, and remove the question from the arena of Indian politics.'[17]

In India, Gopal Krishna Gokhale introduced a bill in the Viceroy's Legislative Council seeking to stop the export of indentured labour to Natal. The bill was tabled on 25 February 1910, with Gokhale speaking eloquently on the handicaps of Indians in different provinces of South Africa. Indenture was the original sin; had it not been introduced there 'would have been no Indian problem in that sub-continent today'. The system was akin to slavery; it ferried 'helpless men and women to a distant land' to labour under harsh conditions and under employers whose language, customs and traditions were so alien to their own. When freed, the labourers were subject to a savage and punitive tax. The traders who serviced their needs were, in turn, subject to manifold restrictions.

Such was the situation in Natal; the whites in the Transvaal, meanwhile, had inflicted on their Indian co-subjects 'galling and degrading indignities and humiliations' of a kind unprecedented in the history of the Empire. These cumulative insults meant that 'no single question of our time has evoked more bitter feelings throughout India – feelings in the presence of which the best friends of British rule have had to remain helpless – than the continued ill-treatment of Indians in South Africa.'[18]

Gokhale's motion was resoundingly endorsed by other members. The gifted Bombay lawyer M. A. Jinnah said the treatment of Indians in South Africa had 'roused the feelings of all classes in this country to the highest pitch'. Yet, because of the indifference of the Government of India, 'we are not a wee bit better than we were at the commencement of 1907 when the struggle reached its very height'. A Mr Mudholkar affirmed that on this question there was 'a singular unanimity of opinion among men of all the races, creeds, castes and sections who inhabit this vast continent'. Mazharul Haque, a member from Bihar, compared the £3 tax in Natal to the *jeziya*, the fee levied on non-believers in Islamic states about which European historians had written so harshly. Its application was both ironic and shameful, since 'Buddha, Christ and Mohammed were [all] Asiatics.'[19]

Gokhale was followed by more than a dozen speakers, with the debate covering sixty closely printed pages of the legislative record. The motion passed unanimously: with effect from 1 July 1911, no more Indians would be sent to work on the sugar plantations or in the coal mines of Natal. Following the proceedings through the newspapers that came to him by post, Gandhi thought this would lead to an 'immediate improvement' in the status of Indians in Natal. In the Transvaal, the struggle for just treatment would continue, but now perhaps with a greater chance of success.[20]

The hopes were illusory. From March, the Transvaal Government instituted harsh measures to break the resistance. Many prisoners (among them Manilal Gandhi) were put in solitary confinement. Other resisters were sent overland to the Portuguese-controlled port of Delagoa Bay and back by ship to India. They arrived in Bombay and Madras, in near destitution. The stories of the deportees were circulated in the Indian press and passed on to the Colonial Office by L. W. Ritch. From Ritch's account, it appeared the authorities had picked on the poorest and most vulnerable. Those deported included Gulam Maho-med, a mine worker who had served with the British in the Anglo-Boer War; Kathia, a washerman who had originally come to Natal under indenture; Narajana Apanna, a bottle-seller who had lost an arm during the war; and Ramsamy Moodlai, a hawker who had lived in the Trans-vaal since 1888.[21]

On 1 June 1910, the four Colonies of Natal, Transvaal, the Cape and the Orange Free State – previously autonomous if not independent – became constituents of a larger entity, known officially as the Union of South Africa. There would be a new, whites-only parliament, with a Prime Minister and cabinet working under the (nominal) supervision of a Governor-General sent out from London.

Superficially, the Union in South Africa followed the pattern laid down by other British dominions. In 1867 the different provinces of Canada came together and formed a central parliament. In 1900 the Australian colonies did likewise. The South African case, however, dif-fered in one crucial respect from its predecessors. At the time of the Union, the white settlers were very far from being a majority in a land they claimed as their own.

On 2 June, Gandhi issued a letter to the press, noting that for his people the day of Union was marked by fresh arrests. Those in jail included 'Mr Joseph Royeppen, the Barrister and Cambridge Graduate' and 'a cultured Indian and representative Parsee, Mr Sorabji'. The Indian leader pointedly and poignantly asked:

> What can a Union under which the above state of things is continued mean to Asiatics, except that it is a combination of hostile forces arrayed against them? The Empire is supposed to have become stronger for the Union. Is it to crush by its weight and importance Asiatic subjects of the Crown? It was no doubt right and proper that the birth of Union should have been signalised for the Natives of South Africa by the clemency of the Crown towards [the Zulu chief] Dinizulu. Dinizulu's discharge will naturally fire the imagination of the South African Natives. Will it not be equally proper to enable the Asiatics in South Africa to feel that there is a new and benig-nant spirit abroad in South Africa by conceding their demands, which are held, I make bold to say, to be intrinsically just by nine out of every ten intelligent people in this Continent?[22]

The Union of Europeans in South Africa was hostile to the Asians who lived in the country. However, individual Europeans were sympathetic, none more so than Hermann Kallenbach. On 30 May, the architect had donated a farm outside Johannesburg to the Indians. So long as the struggle lasted, 'passive resisters and their indigent families' could live on the farm 'free of any rent or charge'.[23] The farm was large – more than 1,000 acres – and had many fruit trees, two wells and a small spring. The ground was mostly level, but a small hillock rose at one edge of the property. The property was twenty-two miles from the city, yet close to a railway station named Lawley. Gandhi, with Kallenbach's endorsement, chose to name the farm after Tolstoy.

As a vegetarian himself, Kallenbach prohibited shooting on the farm. He also eschewed, as far as possible, the use of machinery and hired labour. A reporter who visited shortly after the gift described Tolstoy Farm as 'an earnest attempt to bring East and West nearer along (shall I say) right lines and by easy though slow stages.'[24]

Tolstoy Farm had further consolidated the friendship between the European Jew, Hermann Kallenbach and the Indian Bania, Mohandas Gandhi. Yet some other Western friends of Gandhi were not equally enamoured of the experiment. Henry Polak had presented Ruskin's *Unto This Last* to Gandhi, thinking it would appeal to his friend's romantic ruralism. It did, and the founding of Phoenix followed. But the Polaks themselves did not spend much time at the settlement. They were anti-racist egalitarians without being anti-industrial polemicists. Millie especially had found the facilities at Phoenix primitive, and the company confining. The Polaks were all city people, and quite happy (and proud) to be so.[25]

Likewise, some of Gandhi's closest Indian companions were not ascetic in their disposition. He himself was very aware that not all protesters were seekers. He knew that few satyagrahis would become *sevak*s, servants of society in the deeper sense. He knew that Gujarati merchants, whether Hindu or Muslim, did not like working with their hands. So, for this new venture, he asked them merely to contribute money and materials. The work of settling and improving Tolstoy Farm would be done by the Gandhi family, by Indians from castes and communities more accustomed to hard labour and by the owner and patron himself.

The first residents of the new settlement were Gandhi, his son Mani-lal and Kallenbach. They were soon joined by a group of Tamils, among them Thambi Naidoo and his family. The Indians worked with African labourers on constructing new buildings, carrying stones from the hill to the site. Friends and supporters in Johannesburg sent mattresses, blankets, towels, utensils, fruits and vegetables. The donors were not all Indian; thus the wife of a Nonconformist minister sent forty pounds of home-made marmalade, while the Cantonese Club of Johannesburg gave rice, sugar, monkey-nuts and paraffin.[26]

By the end of June, a school was functioning on the farm. It had five pupils, including Manilal and Ramdas Gandhi. Their father was the main teacher. In late July, Kasturba Gandhi arrived to join her husband. The family unit had been restored, after a five-year period in which the father had been mostly in Johannesburg, the mother wholly at Phoenix, and the sons shuttling in between.

Since Kasturba had the company of other women, she was not lonely. And the experience for her boys was transformative. Cooking, cleaning, digging the land – his sons, Gandhi told his nephew Maganlal, were no longer

> engrossed in thought as [they] used to be in Phoenix. This is the result of manual labour. In pampering the corpulent body that has been given to us and pretending that we earn [our living] by our intellect, we have become sinners and are tempted to fall into a thousand and one evil ways. I regard the Kaffirs, with whom I constantly work these days, as superior to us. What they do in their ignorance we have to do knowingly. In outward appearance we should look just like the Kaffirs.[27]

Working alongside the Africans, Gandhi came to a clearer realization of their predicament. 'The negroes alone are the original inhabitants of this land', he wrote in *Indian Opinion*. 'We have not seized the land from them by force; we live here with their goodwill. The whites, on the other hand, have occupied the country forcibly and appropriated it to themselves'. The formulation was striking, as well as new – once accustomed to praising British values and British institutions, Gandhi now pointed instead to the illegitimacy of their presence and rule in Africa.[28] Clearly, he had progressed considerably from the unsympathetic and hostile attitude towards Africans he had displayed in his first years in

Natal. When the annual high school examinations for 1910 were held in Pretoria, *Indian Opinion* asked why Africans were not allowed to sit with their white peers. In previous years, all students had taken the examination together. This time, the management of the Town Hall – where the exams were held – passed a resolution that no African or any other person of colour would be allowed to enter the building.[29] Gandhi thought this provocation enough for passive resistance. 'In a country like this', he remarked,

> the Coloured people are placed in an extremely difficult situation. We think there is no way out of this except satyagraha. Such instances are a natural consequence of the whites' refusal to treat the Coloured people as their equals. It is in order to put an end to this state of affairs that we have been fighting in the Transvaal, and it is not surprising that the fight against a people with deep prejudice should take a long time.[30]

Shortly afterwards, Gandhi received a letter from two friends in Natal, who felt that his having recently travelled third-class was demeaning to the leader and to the prestige of the community he represented. Gandhi answered that he wished to live like a poor man; besides, he 'shuddered to read the account of the hardships the Kaffirs had to suffer in the third-class carriages in the Cape and I wanted to experience the same hardships myself.'[31]

At Tolstoy Farm, the Gandhi family and the African labourers both worked under the direction of Hermann Kallenbach, who was both a trained architect and a superbly skilled mason and carpenter. The benefactor found rich fulfilment in his gift and his work. 'I have given up meat-eating, smoking and drinking, and practise asceticism,' he wrote to his brother Simon. 'What Tolstoy wants and what I too strive for, is to recognise the correct thing without disturbing my fellow man.'[32]

Gandhi, meanwhile, had written to Tolstoy, telling him about the farm named after him and worked according to his principles. The seer wrote back, saying, 'your work in Transvaal, which seems to be far away from the centre of our world, is yet the most fundamental and the most important to us [in] supplying the most weighty practical proof in which the world can now share and with which must participate not only the Christians but all the peoples of the world.' He compared the work of the Indians to men in Russia refusing to serve in the military.

The two struggles were joined, in Tolstoy's mind, in a common, heroic endeavour. Thus, 'however small may be the number of your participants in non-resistance and the number of those in Russia who refuse military service, both the one and the other may assert with audacity that "God is with us" and "God is more powerful than men".'

Two months later Tolstoy died. *Indian Opinion* printed a commemorative issue, with a large portrait and several appreciations. Gandhi noted, not without pride, that 'in his last days' Tolstoy had extended 'encouragement to the [Transvaal] satyagrahis', assuring them 'justice from God, if not from the rulers'.[33]

The Transvaal Government's attempts to break the movement continued. In April–May 1910, several hundred satyagrahis, Indians and Chinese, were placed on ships bound for Madras and Bombay. The deportation intensified the resolve of the resisters, and also consolidated support for them within India. Henry Polak was at hand to receive the deportees as they disembarked in Madras and Bombay, sending some of them straight back to South Africa, while organizing receptions for those who chose to stay behind.[34]

Polak was aided by the liberal reformer G. A. Natesan, editor and publisher of the Madras-based *Indian Review*. Natesan was a Tamil, and hence well placed to look after the Tamil-speaking satyagrahis who arrived in Madras. The *Indian Review* published representative accounts of the deportees' suffering. One Subramanya Asari had gone to Natal in about 1900 to join his father, who was a jeweller. Joining the satyagraha out of solidarity with the Transvaal Indians, he was arrested, deported to Delagoa Bay, and then put with fifty-nine other resisters on a ship to India. They travelled in great discomfort on deck, with meagre rations. A satyagrahi named Narayanaswamy fell sick and died on board. The spirit of his compatriots was undaunted; a few days after the steamer carrying them landed in Madras, twenty-six of the sixty deportees, themselves born or domiciled in Natal, boarded a ship back to Durban.[35]

The reports in the *Indian Review* often spoke of the veneration in which satyagrahis from South India held their Gujarati leader. Consider the case of P. K. Naidoo. A barber in Johannesburg, he was an autodidact who had taught himself to speak French, Zulu and Hindi in addition to his native Telugu. Arrested in January 1908 for not possessing a registration certificate, he was tried and convicted along with Gandhi. When he arrived at the jail a few hours later, Naidoo was 'struck with horror to see my leader attired in the native criminal convict's garb. My wish, in the present instance, was to make a noise, but Mr Gandhi, who was acquainted with my deportment, at once, told me in a mild tone: "Simply do what you are told, Naidoo."' The barber was put in prison garb and taken to his cell. Next morning, he was appalled to find that the meal consisted of mealie porridge. 'None of us, excluding Mr Gandhi, who wished to show that it was good food, relished it as [we did] our breakfast at home.'

Naidoo was released, but rearrested a second time, and then a third. At this point he had not seen Gandhi for eight months. 'When I was out he was in, and when I was out I was in, and on this occasion he was gone to London.' In May 1910, on release from his fifth term, P. K. Naidoo was met at the prison gate by a large contingent, including Cachalia and Kallenbach. Of his reception committee Naidoo remarked that 'Mr Gandhi, whom I had not met for 17 months, was naturally the most attractive.'[36]

Among those deported to Madras was the Chinese leader Leung Quinn. In an essay for Natesan's journal he explained why he and his compatriots had joined Gandhi's struggle. The laws in the Transvaal, 'erected by reason of racial antipathies and jealousies', were such that even Chinese ambassadors welcomed in the courts of Europe would not be allowed into the colony. It was, said Quinn, 'not possible for us, who belong to an ancient and dignified civilisation to sit silent under such a flagrant insult'. Judging that the 'honour of Asia was at stake', the Chinese joined the Indian resisters. Quinn told his Indian audience that 'the Transvaal colonists have foolishly thrown down the gauntlet to the whole of Asia. Neither they nor other Europeans should be surprised if Asiatics, as a body, take it up.'[37]

The presence of the deportees and the sympathies they aroused worried officials of the Raj, who thought they might inflame nationalist sentiments in India. The Madras Government found their presence 'very embarrassing'. The deportees were being treated as martyrs. Their troubles in South Africa evoked feelings that were 'rapidly becoming more bitter and more widespread'.[38] In Bombay, the arrival of shiploads of satyagrahis from the Transvaal attracted the attentions of the

Commissioner of Police. He went to meet the deportees, finding them in 'fairly good spirits and quite ready to converse amicably'. The Commissioner nonetheless wished the process of deportation would stop, 'in view of the capital which the local agitator can make of it if he chooses.'[39]

The Transvaal Government had hoped the deportations would demoralize the satyagrahis and demolish the satyagraha. As it happened, the adverse publicity in India helped infuse it with, among other things, a new source of funds. When the deportations began, in April 1910, the balance in the 'Passive Resistance Fund Account' of the Natal Bank in Johannesburg stood at slightly over £3,000. This, Gandhi told Gokhale, would only last them till the end of the year. He noted that he had himself given the bulk of his earnings to the cause, as had 'a European friend' (Kallenbach).[40] Hearing of the deportations, Ratan Tata wrote to Gokhale in July 1910 that he wished to make a further donation of Rs 25,000. He asked that the matter be kept private for the moment, in reserve

> for the psychological moment when the publication of it in a similar sensational manner to my last donation, might again touch the emotions of some people, and goad them into making a second effort to keep alive this struggle of our cause in South Africa, which is getting so painfully feeble day by day owing to the want of financial support.[41]

Gokhale wrote back that the atmosphere in India was not very encouraging. He did not think that a public announcement of Tata's bequest would stimulate other donations. The philanthrophist found it hard to accept that 'the finer feelings are dead amongst *all* our countrymen', but deferred to the judgement of the man on the spot. In that case, he would send the money directly to Gandhi. As he saw it,

> once the struggle in South Africa is given up, the whites will see that Indians have not grit enough to fight to a finish and that wherever Indians are not wanted, the whites have only to persist long enough, to drive them out of any country. It is pitiful to see a handful of Indians suffering and fighting for the rights of a whole nation, whilst that nation sits inertly and watches the struggle with absolute indifference.[42]

Ratan Tata had asked Gokhale to 'embody my views in a letter to Mr Ghandi [sic]'.[43] What Gokhale wrote to Gandhi is unrecorded. We do know however that on 18 November 1910, Ratan Tata sent Gandhi a cheque for Rs 25,000, with a brief note saying that 'the admiration and good wishes of all true Indians are with you in your noble work.'[44]

Meanwhile, on his tour across India, by his enthusiasm and his eloquence Polak had proved Tata right and Gokhale wrong. In nine months on the road he had raised over Rs 50,000, with contributions, big and small, coming from Hindu Maharajas, Muslim nawabs, Parsi millionaires, Christian clergymen and secularized members of a growing middle class.[45]

In the last week of August 1910, after nearly a year in his friend's homeland, Henry Polak returned to South Africa. At a farewell meeting in Madras, Annie Besant paid tribute to his work for the Indians of the Transvaal. 'Himself of a persecuted race, whose blood has been shed in every country in Europe,' Polak had not 'allowed himself to be soured and embittered by the suffering of his kinsfolk. He has shown himself to possess a heart softened, and . . . he finds in the suffering of others a reason for taking the cause of the other.'[46]

From Madras Polak took a train to Bombay, where he boarded a ship for South Africa. He arrived in Durban at daybreak on 28 September. Gandhi was there to receive him, along with some 400 other Indians. A few at least had been inspired to go there by Sheikh Mehtab, Gandhi's once-estranged friend who was now a vigorous cheerleader for his movement. In a poem in *Indian Opinion* Mehtab told his compatriots to come to the Point to greet their English friend. For

> Polak awakened India
> He declared that no indentured labourers will come
> He has conquered a citadel [of power]
> Honour him, putting flower garlands on his back.

Their welcome, continued the poet, should confirm the spirit of inter-religious solidarity. When Polak came ashore, the Indians must

> Sing the songs of Vande Matram and Allah Akbar
> Shower him with basketfuls of pearls
> Indians with shawls or Turkish caps
> Pick up the arrow of unity and
> Shoot disunity down.[47]

After a few days at Phoenix, the friends returned together to the city. On the morning of 4 October, Gandhi and Polak went down to the Point to welcome a shipload of Natal Indians previously deported to Madras and Bombay for illegally entering the Transvaal. Here Polak told a reporter that 'our programme will remain, as it has always been, not one of violence or attempts to disturb, but one of suffering on the part of our people, who intend to go on enduring these hardships until they make the authorities ashamed of themselves.'[48]

That same evening, the Indians of Natal threw a large reception for Polak. A little Tamil girl presented him with a rose buttonhole 'amid continuous cheering'. An address was read out on behalf of the hosts: this saluted Polak's 'noble and self-sacrificing work' in India, by which, he was told, 'you have identified yourself with our troubles and sorrows in a manner in which very few Europeans or Indians have.'[49]

Among the Indians, Henry Polak was known as 'Keshavlal', since he had long, uncut locks like Lord Krishna himself. But the name also suited him in other respects, since he was likewise playful, mischievous, a romantic at heart, and yet possessed of a sharp political intelligence. Gandhi's other great European friend, Kallenbach, was known as 'Hanuman', to denote his unquestioning devotion to his Lord (here Gandhi rather than Ram) and his willingness to put his muscles (in this case, financial as well as physical) at his master's service.[50]

The reception for Henry Polak in Durban was followed by a meeting to discuss the current state of the movement. When Gandhi began speaking, in English, the crowd shouted: 'Tamil! Tamil!' Gandhi answered that if General Smuts sent him to jail again he would have the time, and leisure, to learn their language. Meanwhile, he passed on the responsibility to his nephew Maganlal, who was now managing Phoenix and *Indian Opinion* on Gandhi's behalf. Since his elder brother Chhagan was in London (on a scholarship funded by Pranjivan Mehta), Magan, in Natal, would study Tamil seriously, and thus become a bridge between his uncle and the most committed of his supporters. Gandhi wrote regularly to Magan asking about his progress. 'Do not give up your study of Tamil', began one letter. 'I have a constant feeling that you alone and none else will be able to master Tamil', said another.[51]

Gandhi was now very keen to be arrested. Every month, he would visit Natal and cross back into the Transvaal without registration papers. The authorities stayed their hand, but when, in early November, he brought with him some other Indians, they detained a woman named Mrs Sodha, whose husband was already in prison. The police declared her to be an illegal alien. Gandhi was able to get the case adjourned, and to proceed with Mrs Sodha and her children to Tolstoy Farm. He wired the Minister of the Interior, General Smuts, seeking permission to keep them on the farm till Mr Sodha had served out his term. He pointed out that 'hitherto Indian women have been left unmolested.' When Smuts answered that the law would take its course, Gandhi told the press that while the 'Government are at war with Indian males', the 'community was, however, unprepared for an unchivalrous attack on its womanhood'. Mrs Sodha was not a competitor in trade; indeed, 'a meeker woman' could not perhaps be found anywhere in South Africa. 'Whatever may be their views on Asiatic immigration or on the question of general passive resistance', asked Gandhi, 'will not the Christian men and women of this Union rise in unanimous protest against this latest parody of administration on the part of the Government?'[52]

The invocation of the rulers' faith was in character. Gandhi was calling on them to recognize the divine rather than devilish aspects of Christianity, and to have empathy for the suffering of all religions (and nationalities). To show them the Path, Gandhi organized an inter-faith picnic on Christmas Day, turning Tolstoy Farm, otherwise a place of work and contemplation, into a theatre of joy and celebration. Three hundred guests from Johannesburg joined the fifty-odd settlers for the festivities. The children 'were let loose on Mr Kallenbach's fruit trees, which ... they did not treat with any very great consideration. They plucked both ripe and unripe fruit, and what they could not eat they took for future consumption in their kerchiefs.' At noon, lunch was served, *khichri* and vegetables followed by plum pudding. Afterwards a series of running and jumping competitions were held. The eating and playing was supervised by two Jewish ladies, Sonja Schlesin and Mrs William Vogt.[53]

Five days after this party, the case of Mrs Ramabhai Sodha came up for hearing in Johannesburg. The accused had with her two small children, aged eight months and three years respectively. Gandhi served as her lawyer and interpreter. The proceedings were watched by a full house, mostly of Indians, but also including Gandhi's European friends (and followers) Joseph Doke, Hermann Kallenbach, Mrs Vogt and Sonja Schlesin.

The prosecution claimed that Mrs Sodha was brought to Transvaal 'for the purpose of agitating against the Asiatic Act'. Gandhi said this was 'entirely wrong'. In Natal, 'Mrs Sodha was living in a lonely place. And she could be best protected at Tolstoy Farm.' The judge sentenced Mrs. Sodha to a £10 fine and one month's imprisonment, but she was released on bail pending an appeal.[54]

The echoes of the Sodha case reached London, where the Colonial Office received a petition of protest from the All India Muslim League. Gandhi was said to have rescued Mrs Sodha and her children from 'a state of destitution'. Her prosecution was thus 'particularly harsh, if not actually cruel'. Sent this petition by London, the Transvaal Ministers answered that Gandhi had crossed the border with Mrs Sodha 'with the deliberate purpose of embarrassing the Government'. In view of the fact that 'many thousands of pounds sterling have recently been collected in India and elsewhere by the emissaries of the Transvaal British Indian Association in support of resistance to the laws and the Government', said the Ministers, 'it is difficult to understand why Mrs Sodha should be in the destitute condition alleged, or why the cost of her removal from Johannesburg should have been undertaken unless there existed an ulterior motive.'[55]

The claims were in conflict, but not, in fact, irreconcilable. Gandhi may have had both objectives in mind. By providing succour to the Sodha family, he was issuing a fresh challenge to the authorities as well.

In the first weeks of 1911, the government gazette printed a proposed new Immigration Bill. This would repeal the existing legislation, but did not explicitly protect the wives and children of domiciled Asiatics. It specified a language test for new entrants to the Transvaal, but was ambiguous about whether Indians who passed the test would be allowed in. Polak wrote to Gokhale that the last clause was crucial; on its interpretation would depend the Indians' response. 'Gandhi is fairly optimistic,' he remarked. 'I am not so satisfied.'[56]

Gandhi asked a senior European lawyer in Johannesburg to analyse the bill on his behalf. He also wrote to the Minister of the Interior, who answered that, yes, educated Asiatics admitted under the new bill would

not be made to register. Gandhi now said that if the Government clarified the position of women and children, he would 'advise the community
in the Transvaal to send a formal acquiescence [to the bill], and passive
resistance will then naturally end.'⁵⁷

On 3 March, Gandhi wrote to Maganlal that 'it appears that the
struggle will definitely come to an end.' In that case, most Indians would
leave Tolstoy Farm, but Gandhi and Kasturba, and their sons, would
stay on. 'How can I leave Mr Kallenbach immediately after the struggle
is over?' he said. His friend had spent £600 on the building, and Gandhi
and his sons would try 'and make good as much of the loss as possible
by physical labour'.

Preoccupied with the negotiations, Gandhi had neglected Kasturba.
She was suffering from bleeding and acute pain, and may have been
passing through menopause. One day Gandhi found her in tears. He
joked that if she died, there was plenty of wood on the Farm to cremate
her. That got her laughing, and 'half the pain disappeared with the
laugh'. Thereafter the two of them decided to go on a salt-free diet, and
her health improved. 'The bleeding stopped immediately', he told
Maganlal.⁵⁸

Gandhi could now return to the negotiations, which had turned difficult again. As the Immigration Bill passed through its second and
third reading, General Smuts met with stiff opposition from MPs
belonging to the Orange Free State. Any law now framed had to be relevant to the Union as a whole. But the Free Staters insisted that whatever
the concessions in other provinces, no Asians would be permitted to
enter their territory. Gandhi sent Smuts' secretary a series of telegrams
in protest. They were not concerned, he said, with 'individual material
gain', or with 'whether a single Asiatic actually enters [the] Free State',
but they must, on a matter of principle, oppose a racial bar in any legislation intended to replace the Transvaal laws against which their
struggle had been aimed. He pointed out that the 'absence of any substantial Indian population' in the Free State 'effectively bar [the] entrance
of educated Indians'. However, if the Union Parliament ratified the Free
State policy, they were then 'saying to the world [that] no Indian even
though a potentate can legally enter and reside in a Province of the
Union'.

Smuts replied that this was an 'absolutely new contention' on the
part of the Indians, which would 'exasperate the European community

and complicate the position even further'. Glossing this letter to Joseph Doke, Gandhi said that the General's remark 'reminds me of what the demonstrators did to inflame the crowd in the December of 1896 and the January of 1897. The European community is certainly not exasperated, but General Smuts is, and he wants to impart his own exasperation to the community.'[59]

Gandhi was not far wrong. In a conversation with the Governor-General's Private Secretary, Smuts outlined his views on the question. 'If South Africa were to be a white man's country', said the General, then more Europeans had to be brought in. At present white immigration was mostly Jewish. Jews (in his view) were 'apt to take up activities of a parasitical nature'; 'although ethnically and socially they remained a distinct entity', they were at least white. Smuts was 'not prepared to face the alternative of the whole retail trade of the country falling into Asiatic hands. As between the two evils of the undesirable business methods of white traders on the one hand and the unlimited extension of Asiatic trading on the other, he did not hesitate to choose the former.'[60]

Meanwhile, the Prime Minister, Louis Botha, had received a petition asking that all Asiatics be deported from South Africa. Botha answered that he would personally like the Indians to be sent away, but operating as they did under the British flag they had to be more careful. The matter continued to vex his Government; as he joked in a speech to his constituents, 'General Smuts had wasted away to a shadow (laughter) when as a result of his incessant efforts to settle the question, the gaols were filled.'[61]

L. W. Ritch was now in Cape Town, from where he sent a report on the mood in the Union Parliament. 'The feeling against the admission of any more of our people is overwhelming', he remarked:

> There was only one chorus [in Parliament]. Different representatives of different interests opposed the Bill because it appeared to threaten the particular interests of their class, but there was undoubted unanimity about exclusion. We have, I think, been wise to restrict our demands to existing rights of persons already domiciled.[62]

The last sentence is crucial – it differentiated the position of Gandhi and company from radicals who wished there to be no bar to immigration at all. Among these radicals was P. S. Aiyar, the Durban journalist and editor of the Tamil-oriented *African Chronicle*, who by now had begun to move away from the incremental moderation of Gandhi. In March 1911, Aiyar complained to Gokhale that 'Gandhi and Polak do not wish to press forward our claims for freedom of movement throughout the Union.' If provincial barriers were not removed, argued Aiyar, then 'the last four years of terrific suffering and the great sacrifice made by our Motherland towards their cause would result in no practical material benefits'.[63]

Aiyar's proposal implied a wholesale redistribution of the Indian population throughout South Africa. But would the white residents (and rulers) of Transvaal, the Cape and the Free State have permitted thousands of Indian traders and craftsmen from Natal to come to their states seeking 'practical material benefits'? Gandhi understood the impossibility of such a demand and hence set his sights lower, on securing the rights of individuals and their families in the provinces *in which they already lived*, and on opening the door for a small, incremental immigration of a few educated Indians a year. However, the extreme demands of the radicals prejudiced even the modest claims of the moderates. 'Asiatic demands,' wrote an influential white paper in Johannesburg, 'often display a tendency to grow bigger whenever any part of them is conceded.' This was 'one of the dangers of the new policy. There is no finality about it. Once you begin to allow a certain number to enter, you invite an application for increasing the number.' The paper was in 'no doubt [that] if the figure was fixed at one hundred and twenty tomorrow, they would be asking for twelve hundred next week.'[64]

Gandhi and Polak were actually asking only for six new entrants a year. Even this many MPs were unwilling to concede. Seeking to break the deadlock, Gandhi met General Smuts in Cape Town on 27 March, and immediately afterwards set down a record of the meeting. It opened with the General saying that to ask for (theoretical) entry to the Free State was both 'very unreasonable' and 'absolutely new'. Gandhi said what existed was a racial bar, and they had always opposed that. As he put it, 'the combined effect of the Free State Law and the New Bill will be to shut out the Nizam of Hyderabad [the richest Indian potentate], and I assure you the passive resisters will fight against it.' Smuts answered that 'the Free Staters will never consent' to the change proposed by the Indians. Gandhi responded that 'it is your duty to persuade them'. Smuts said that he would talk again to Free State MPs.

As the meeting came to a close, Smuts asked Gandhi what he was doing in Johannesburg. Gandhi answered that he was looking after the families of passive resisters. Smuts said that 'it has hurt me more than you to imprison these people. It has been the unpleasantest episode of my life to imprison men who suffer for their conscience.' To this Gandhi riposted, 'And yet you are persecuting Mrs. Sodha.' The notes end here, with the note-writer having the last word. There does not appear to be another version in the Smuts papers.[65]

In April 1911, Gandhi went again to Cape Town. This time he stayed four weeks, furiously lobbying MPs to make the changes he desired in the Immigration Law. In the absence of Sonja Schlesin – who had stayed behind in Johannesburg to keep the office going – Gandhi had to type his correspondence himself. And there was plenty of this: letters seeking appointments, letters seeking clarifications, letters stating his own point of view. His fingers were so tired that he used his left hand to write to his family.

In Cape Town, Gandhi met MPs of different parties and provinces. Two weeks into his stay, General Smuts granted him a further appointment. They met at 11.30 a.m. on 19 April, and spoke for forty minutes. Once more, Gandhi wrote down, by hand, his recollections of the meeting. Smuts said the Free Staters were still opposed to admitting Asiatics. He could defeat them in the Assembly but not in the Senate, so thought it best to postpone the bill to the next session of Parliament. Meanwhile, he wanted Gandhi to withdraw his agitation. 'I want time', said the General. 'I shall yet beat the Free Staters. But you should not be aggressive.'

In the course of the conversation, Smuts said that 'this country is the Kaffirs'. We whites are a handful. We do not want Asia to come in.' Then he paused, and continued: 'I do not know how your people spread. They go everywhere. I have now more petitions against [Indian] dealers. My difficulty of the future will be regarding them.' He then changed the subject, and the following conversation ensued:

S. Gandhi, what are you doing for a living?

G. I am not practising at present.

S. But how then are you living? Have you plenty of money?

G. No. I am living like a pauper, the same as other passive resisters on Tolstoy Farm.

S. Whose is it?

G. It is Mr Kallenbach's. He is a German.

S. (Laughing) Oh, old Kallenbach! He is your admirer, eh? I know.

G. I do not know that he is my admirer. We are certainly very great friends.

S. I must come and see the Farm – where is it?

G. Near Lawley.

S. I know – on the Vereeniging line. What is the distance from the station?

G. About twenty minutes. We shall be pleased to see you there.

S. Yes, I must come one day.

The same evening, Gandhi wrote to Smuts confirming that, to use

> military terms, our conversation implies a truce for a year or longer, i.e., until the Parliament meets again ... I am sincerely anxious to help you, but I do not know how I could promise inactivity on the part of the passive resisters. What you, the Imperial Government and I want to avoid is the ferment. I fear that, in the nature of things, it is well nigh impossible to avoid it if the matter is not closed during this season.

Gandhi was suggesting that he did not have full control over his sometimes militant followers. By way of calming tempers, he asked Smuts to make three assurances: that in the next session the existing legislation would be repealed, that passive resisters who had the right do so could now freely register in Transvaal and that, pending legislation, up to six educated passive resisters in Transvaal would be allowed to remain as 'educated immigrants'. If this were done, he did 'not anticipate any difficulty in persuading my countrymen to suspend passive resistance'.

The General's secretary wrote back, agreeing to these conditions, and conveying Smuts's hope that this temporary settlement 'will leave all concerned free to devote their energies to securing a more lasting one'.

On 24 April, with the truce in place, Gandhi left Cape Town to return to Johannesburg. On the way back, he remembered that he had forgotten one crucial concession. The provisional settlement envisaged the release from prison of all passive resisters. But he had omitted to specify that these should be Chinese as well as Indian. He rang up Smuts's secretary, E. F. C. Lane, to make this clear, and then set it down in writing. 'There are now,' he said, 'more Chinese than Indian passive resisters in gaol. I am quite sure that General Smuts will not expect Indian passive resisters to desert their Chinese fellow sufferers. They naturally ask for the same protection for the Chinese passive resisters as for themselves' – namely, that they be released from jail, be allowed to voluntarily register, and to secure their own rights of domicile and livelihood in Transvaal. With Leung Quinn away in India, Gandhi had taken it upon himself to represent the interests of the Chinese, too.[66]

On 27 April 1911 a meeting of Indians was held in Johannesburg's Hamidia Hall to discuss the correspondence between Gandhi and Smuts. Coovadia, Thambi Naidoo, Joseph Royeppen, Imran Kadir, Sodha, Adajania and Gandhi himself spoke in favour of accepting the settlement. However, 'the greatest difficulty that the Indian leaders had to face [was] the almost ineradicable suspicion the rank and file entertain regarding the Government's motives.' There was 'a very heated controversy', but 'calmness ultimately prevailed', with the meeting deciding to accept the provisional settlement, only five members (of an estimated 500 present) dissenting.[67] This, Gandhi told a reporter, 'would simply mean that the British Indians, as also the Chinese, would cease to court arrest and imprisonment pending the forthcoming legislation'.[68]

Gandhi was hopeful that Smuts would see suitable legislation through the next session of Parliament. The *Star* of Johannesburg had likewise concluded that the Indian question in the Transvaal was now closed. The day after the meeting in the Hamidia Hall, it ran a long article rehearsing the history of the conflict. The rights of domicile of the Indians were, it recalled, rejected by 'practically the whole white community'. In deference to their wishes, the Government passed Act 2 of 1907. Then

> Mr Gandhi appeared on the scene. He took up a hostile attitude to this law, and his personality was so marked that from the start he secured practically the undivided support of the entire Indian community of the Transvaal, and material assurances of his countrymen in India and elsewhere. The controversy has gone through many phases since then, and through them all the authorities were confronted with an unflinching resoluteness and implacable passivity on the part of Gandhi and his followers. Rather small in stature and frail in constitution, Gandhi has bound the Indians together by his earnestness and his belief in the justice of his cause.

There was no rigorous pledge or blind obedience demanded, and the appeal to conscience has been sufficient to enable him to carry his campaign from the Commons to the Lords to the very foot of the Throne. The cry that a colour bar was enacted by the force of law in a British Colony against the people of the great Dependency of the East which acknowledges the King Emperor was sufficient to rouse deep feelings of animosity. The Indians in the Transvaal played their part in a remarkable manner. Like the religious valiants of Huguenot times, they embraced the hardships and tasks that were in the power of the authorities to enforce. Some three thousand five hundred have been imprisoned. Gandhi himself has been in jail three times, his son eight times, and most of the prominent Indian merchants have experienced the rigours of confinement.

The *Star* went on to say that 'both parties to the struggle believed that they were in the right, and if the two central figures, General Smuts and Mr Gandhi, can now close an unpleasant chapter the relief that will be experienced will extend far beyond the limits of the Transvaal and South Africa.'

The Johannesburg *Star* was, by South African standards, a liberal paper. Still, its appreciation of Gandhi's character and leadership was noteworthy. Gandhi would certainly have read the article, and may especially have liked the phrase 'implacable passivity', perhaps an unintended pun, but which finely captured the distinctive moral force of his practice of non-violent resistance.

Having offered its assessment of the present and the past, the *Star* then let Gandhi speak on how he saw the future. He told the newspaper that he was handing over his legal practice in Johannesburg to L. W. Ritch. He said 'his immediate intention' now was

to provide for the care and education of the children whose parents are now in necessitous circumstances, and then he intends to retire to his farm in Natal, and in the spells of leisure no doubt to come in closer touch with the philosophic musings of Tolstoy and to reap inspiration from the savants of his beloved India.[69]

Within a few weeks Gandhi was not so certain about his retirement. On 27 May – exactly a month after the meeting in the Hamidia Hall – *Indian Opinion* carried an editorial on the settlement, which had put Smuts 'upon his honour' to have the necessary laws passed in the next session of Parliament. If he did not, then 'the same stubborn, calm and dignified resistance that was offered to General Smuts could next year with equal certainty of success be offered, if need be, to the mighty Union Parliament.'[70]

The dilution of Gandhi's optimism may have been a consequence of the pressure of the rank-and-file, who naturally and instinctively distrusted the Government. One supposes that he had also been talking to the ever-sceptical Henry Polak.

With the settlement between Gandhi and Smuts, the workload of Henry Polak was now lightened, and he left to see his family in England. He took with him three boxes of grapes given by the Indians of Johannesburg to sustain him during the voyage.[71]

By leaving for London, Polak missed a banquet held at the Masonic Lodge in honour of the whites who had crossed racial boundaries. There had been, since 1908, an active committee of Europeans who raised funds for the struggle. Its chairman was William Hosken, who had abandoned his initial scepticism to take up an 'open, consistent and persistent advocacy of the cause of passive resistance'. This advocacy lost Hosken his parliamentary seat in the elections of 1910. Yet his support continued. So did that of other white dissenters. The party at the Masonic Lodge was a collective tribute to them all. There were some sixty Europeans present, among them the Dokes (father, mother and children), Kallenbach, Ritch, Sonja Schlesin, Hosken, the jeweller Gabriel Isaac, the draper William Vogl and his wife, David Pollock and the critic of *Hind Swaraj* Edward Dallow. The cooking of the meal (vegetarian, naturally) was supervised by Gandhi.

Reporting the event, *Indian Opinion* said the committee chaired by Hosken represented

> the effective individual support that hundreds of Europeans on the Rand gave to the passive resistance hawkers; the few warders and other gaol officials who, out of sympathy, made the lives of passive resisters in the Transvaal prisons as free from difficulty as possible, whilst the hand of perhaps the majority of them was against these prisoners. It represents Miss Schlesin, at the mention of whose name at the banquet an enthusiastic applause rang through the hall and who has been working for the cause as no other man or woman, European or Asiatic, has worked. It represents

an unknown railway refreshment waitress who was glad to serve bread and cheese for a passive resister, who was being taken under custody to Volksrust, for which she would not accept payment. It represents Mrs. Vogl who, as a direct result of the struggle, has, as a labour of love, established a sewing class for Indian women and girls.[72]

These words do not appear in the *Collected Works*, but they must surely have been written by Gandhi. The language is his, as are the sentiments, nurtured through twenty and more years of friendship with Europeans (from the vegetarians of London onwards), friendships that survived his social objections to their laws and his moral objections to their civilization.

18

A Son Departs, a Mentor Arrives

In the last months of 1910, Gandhi's relationship with his eldest son had once more come under strain. Harilal was now twenty-two, and had a daughter of his own. His wife Chanchi and their child were due to visit India, and Harilal wanted to accompany them, but Gandhi refused to give permission, saying, 'We are poor and cannot spend money like that. Moreover, a man who has joined the struggle cannot go away like that for three months.' Someone else would escort Chanchi home instead.[1] Harilal stayed behind and courted arrest, but his resentment would not go away. In March 1911 he accused Gandhi of shifting Kasturba to Tolstoy Farm against her will. His mother, he claimed, wished to stay on at Phoenix. With the provisional settlement in place, Harilal wanted to return to India and take the matriculation examination. He keenly felt his lack of proficiency in mathematics and literature; besides, he wished to join his wife, who had just given birth to a baby boy.[2]

Harilal was at Phoenix, so Gandhi asked his nephew Maganlal to take the boy in hand. 'The more defects you discover in Harilal, the more love you should have for him. One requires a great deal of water to put out a big fire. To overcome the baser elements in Harilal's nature, you have to develop in yourself and pit against it a more powerful force of goodness.'[3]

Maganlal failed, as Gandhi had failed before him. In the first week of May, Harilal came to Johannesburg to attend a function in honour of his fellow satyagrahis. Then he collected his belongings – and apparently also a photograph of his father – and took a train to Delagoa Bay, from where he planned to take a ship to India. Before he left, he told Joseph Royeppen that when back in India he wished to live in the Punjab rather than in Ahmedabad. This may have been because the Punjab

413

was then the epicentre of Indian nationalism, or because his father knew no one in that province and could not monitor his movements or suppress his ambitions.[4]

When Harilal left home, two friends were deputed to find him. They scoured all of Johannesburg, in vain. A Parsi friend told Gandhi that Harilal had recently borrowed twenty pounds from him (presumably for the journey). As news of the boy's disappearance spread, friends and clients rushed to Gandhi's office in Rissik Street. Some Muslim merchants remonstrated with Gandhi: had he only told them of his son's desires, they would have paid for Harilal to study law in London. That evening, a group including Gandhi left for Tolstoy Farm. On the train, Gandhi told the others not to tell Kasturba what had happened. He would wait till they were alone, and then tell her 'in my own way'.[5]

Harilal had left behind a long letter explaining to his parents why he had left. To Gandhi he said,

> I have done what my heart dictated. I have done nothing with evil motives. Please do not consider that I have fled away. I am still the same obedient Harilal. You may not think so, but you have and will always remain the same for me to respect. Please rest assured that I shall endeavour to follow your teachings and copy your actions ... Please tell mother that I have gone for the sake of earning. I shall feel the separation from her but I have done this considering it to be my duty. There was no help for me but to do this without delay.

There was also a message for Kallenbach, to whom all the Gandhi boys were deeply attached, as an affectionate uncle or 'Kaka' (father's brother) who indulged them with love and presents. 'Please tell Mr Kallenbach', said Harilal, 'that I hope he will not harbour any anger against me for not having returned to the farm, and that he will bless me. I shall never forget the obligation that I am under to him.'

Harilal told Gandhi that when he reached India, 'for the moment I intend only to study. I shall certainly need money, and if you can send it please send. After I am settled, if I am [to] succeed in my ambition, I shall write to you.' He added a telling, and moving, postscript: 'Although I am leaving, if the struggle is to be revived, no matter in what part of the world I may be I shall present myself there and seek imprisonment.'[6]

The letter was deeply felt, its text and subtext swirling with contradictory emotions – affection, anger, anguish, ambition. Harilal's feelings towards his father were confusing and complicated; so, too, his reasons for leaving South Africa. He wished to break free of Gandhi, yet remained dependent on him. Not satisfied with the schooling he had received in India, Harilal had asked his father to send him to London to qualify as a barrister. Gandhi said it was not necessary to qualify as a barrister or doctor to serve the people. The saint Ramakrishna, the reformer Dayananda Saraswati, the warriors Shivaji and Rana Pratap – none had the benefit of English education, and yet admirably served the motherland. Harilal countered with the names of Ranade, Gokhale, Tilak and Lajpat Rai, well-educated men who had served India nobly as well.[7]

The arguments were renewed when Pranjivan Mehta endowed two scholarships for Phoenix boys to study in London. Rather than nominate his son, Gandhi had first chosen Chhaganlal, and then a Parsi student named Sorabji Adajania. Mehta now agreed to fund a third scholarship, but Harilal's pride would not allow him to accept.[8] His desire to educate himself remained; this he now wished to fulfil in India, with his wife by his side, and with a subsidy from an overbearing yet indispensable father.

When he reached Delagoa Bay from Johannesburg, Harilal walked into the British Consulate and said he was a poor Indian in need of a free passage to Bombay. The officials recognized him and sent word to Gandhi, who wired Harilal asking him to come back to Johannesburg.[9] Harilal returned to the city on 15 May. Father and son talked through the night, eventually agreeing that he could continue with his plans and return to India. Gandhi's account of their conversation is contained in a letter written immediately afterwards to Maganlal:

> It is just as well that Harilal has left. He was much unsettled in mind . . . He bears no ill-will towards any of you. He was angry with me, really. He gave vent to all his pent-up feelings on Monday evening [the 15th]. He feels that I have kept all the four boys very much suppressed, that I did not respect their wishes at any time, that I have treated them as of no account, and that I have often been hard-hearted. He made this charge against me with the utmost courtesy and seemed very hesitant as he did so . . . Unlike other fathers, I have not admired my sons or done anything specially for them, but always put them and [Kastur]Ba last; such was the charge. He seemed to have calmed down after this outburst. I pointed out

his error in believing what he did. He saw it partly. What remains, he will correct only when he thinks further. He has now left with a calm mind. He is resolved to learn more about those things on account of which I was displeased [with him]. He is strongly inclined to study Sanskrit. Thinking that, since Gujarati is our language, his education should for the most part be in Gujarat, I have advised Harilal to stay in Ahmedabad. I believe that is what he will do. However, I have left him free. I feel it will all turn out well.[10]

Harilal's version of the conversation is shorter, and written some years after the event. It diverges on some crucial points of detail and interpretation. 'I was delayed at Delagoa Bay', recalled the son,

> you came to know of my whereabouts and caught up with me. Obeying your orders I returned. I remained steadfast in my views. Therefore, instead of giving me a patient hearing you mutilated my thoughts and clipped my wings. You made me give up the idea of going to Lahore and instead made me stay in Ahmedabad. You promised to give me thirty rupees for monthly expenditure. You did not allow me to measure my capabilities; you measured them for me.[11]

'You did not allow me to measure my capabilities; you measured them for me.' This is a harsh but accurate judgement, confirmed – albeit in gentler and more euphemistic language – by a close observer of the Gandhi household, Millie Polak. At Phoenix and at Tolstoy Farm, Gandhi was often found cradling a baby while talking politics with an adult. Juxtaposing this with his treatment of Harilal, Millie concluded that it was easier for Gandhi

> to deal with the needs of young children than those of adolescence, with its warring emotions, its struggle for liberty and self-expression, and its developing mind. During that period in the life of the developing individual, he did not so easily realise the strength of the storms that can sweep reason aside.[12]

The clash between father and son was intensified by their closeness in age. Harilal was born when Gandhi was only eighteen. His adolescent crisis thus coincided with his father's midlife crisis. As Harilal sought a career and education path of his own, Gandhi was moving away from the law towards social service and political activism. The desires of the one clashed with the convictions of the other. Gandhi would not, could not, recognize that there were two sides to the story. He blamed Harilal's rebellion on his recent reading of *Sarasvatichandra*, a Gujarati novel by Govardhanram Tripathi whose hero, disenchanted with his father, leaves the parental home to discover himself.[13]

There is little question that Gandhi bore down heavily on his eldest son. He did not recognize his good fortune in being allowed to follow his own path independent of his parents' wishes. Had his father Kaba Gandhi been alive when Mohandas finished his Matriculation, he might never have allowed the boy to proceed across the *kala pani* to London. Had his mother been alive in 1893, she might not have permitted him to make another perilous overseas journey to South Africa. Once in the diaspora, Gandhi was able to carve out a professional and activist career of his choice, without interference from family elders.

With his children, Gandhi was the traditional overbearing Hindu patriarch – making them do what he intended for them. Because he had now become disenchanted with modern professions, his sons must not be permitted a modern education. Because he had himself embraced *brahmacharya* they must do likewise. Harilal and Manilal, as the two elder boys, were expected to be perfect and exemplary satyagrahis, courting arrest or labouring on the land as per their father's whims and desires.

When the Hindu priest Ram Sundar Pandit had abandoned the struggle, Gandhi dryly dismissed him as a 'bad coin'. That detachment was not possible as regards his sons. The more they disagreed with him, the more intense and impatient he became with them. Those who secretly signed permits or failed to court arrest were not worthy of redemption. But his own sons could never be permitted to become 'bad coins'. That what was bad in terms of their conduct and what good was a matter of opinion, bias and prejudice, rather than parental fiat, was something that Gandhi – in common, it must be said, with most or all Indian fathers of his generation – did not or could not understand.

Gandhi's harsh response to Harilal may have had a deeper basis – the fact that, in South Africa, he was accustomed to enmity and suppression, but not, really, to rebellion or disagreement. The white reactionaries of Durban and the militant Pathans of Johannesburg had both physically attacked him. The regime of the Boers had several times put him in jail. But among his own flock and his own friends he was accustomed to being the leader. The mentors he recognized – Gokhale, Raychandbhai, Tolstoy – had all lived in other continents.

Gandhi had a real gift for friendship – for making connections and conveying affection across racial, linguistic, religious and gender boundaries. The love he had for, and the intimacy he shared with, Henry and Millie Polak, Kallenbach, Sonja Schlesin, Ritch, the Dokes, Leung Quinn, Thambi Naidoo, A. M. Cachalia and Parsee Rustomjee was visible proof of this. But all these friends (and others like them) were ultimately in a position of deference to him. Their love for Gandhi had strong elements of reverence and adoration. Only the Polaks had the intellectual independence to argue with Gandhi on major or minor matters – and even they, in the end, recognized him as their leader.

Here lay the deeper significance of Harilal's self-assertion ('defiance' would be too strong a word). His cardinal mistake was in not going all the way down the road marked out for him by his father. Harilal had, several times, bravely and unselfishly courted arrest. But the desire to study, to make a career of his own, remained with him. Gandhi was, by now, accustomed to the loyal, unquestioning support of many Indians in South Africa. (And of more than a few Europeans too.) That one of his own sons would choose to rebel was both unexpected and, for him, inexplicable.

Harilal knew this, which is why he had left in the first place without telling his father directly. He was too frightened to face Gandhi. He was brought back to Johannesburg, but remained truculent. When Gandhi failed, in that all-night conversation, to persuade Harilal to abandon his plans to return to India, he reluctantly agreed not to stand in his way. But he was never really reconciled to his son's going.

When Harilal finally left, on 16 May, some students from Tolstoy Farm accompanied Gandhi to Johannesburg Station to wish the boy good-bye. One student recalled that 'when the train was about to start, Bapu kissed Harilal, gave a gentle slap on his cheek, and said: "Forgive your father, if you think he has done you wrong".'[14]

Ten days after Harilal left for India, Gandhi wrote urging him to read *Indian Opinion* 'carefully'. He was sent a list of Gujarati books to study – among them the works of Narmadashanker and Raychandbhai. He was advised to 'make it a regular practice to read Tulsidas's Ramayana'. Gandhi added that 'most of the books I have listed at the end of

Indian Home Rule are worth going through', and ended by saying, 'please write to me in detail and regularly'.[15]

Harilal was going back to India to break free of his father. Following him by the next boat was this letter of instruction and command. The barrage continued: in the first months of his return, Harilal was dissuaded by his father from learning French, told to give up his 'infatuation' with the matriculation exam, and chastised for having 'again succumbed to passion in regard to [his wife] Chanchal'.[16]

Through the middle months of 1911, Gandhi was based at Tolstoy Farm. The day began with several hours of physical labour. He taught at the school from ten-thirty to four. The students, like their master, did not eat salt, vegetables and pulses between Monday and Saturday. They lived on fruits (especially apples and bananas), bread with olive oil, and rice and sago porridge. The community had dinner early, at five-thirty, and Gandhi attended to his correspondence before going to bed. He went into Johannesburg only once a week. L. W. Ritch was taking care of his clients, to Gandhi's relief; he 'fervently' hoped he never had to practise law again.[17]

Gandhi was now increasingly thinking of returning to India. That country presented a far wider canvas for the kind of work he was doing. He was keen to go back; even keener to see him return was his friend Pranjivan Mehta. Gandhi, thought Mehta, was the 'Mahatma' their country so desperately needed. Mehta was Gandhi's oldest and – Polak and Kallenbach notwithstanding – closest friend. They had become intimate as students in London. Mehta spent several weeks with Gandhi in Durban in 1898; some years later, Gandhi had visited the doctor-turned-jeweller in Rangoon, where he was a leading light of the Indian community.

In 1908, Pranjivan Mehta started the Burma Provincial Congress Committee, as a branch of the Indian National Congress. This was the first political organization in that territory, bringing together Indian migrants of all classes under one umbrella, and encouraging the native Burmese to found their own representative associations.[18] However, the jeweller's political ambitions were not so much for himself as for his friend Gandhi, and for their country. In the autumn of 1909 he spent several weeks in London, arguing with Gandhi late into the night as to the most plausible route to self-government for India. Those conversations were to find their way into *Hind Swaraj*, written as a dialogue between the oracular Editor (Gandhi) and the questioning Reader (Mehta).

Pranjivan Mehta was to Mohandas Gandhi what Friedrich Engels was to Karl Marx: at once a disciple and a patron, who saw, very early, that the friend of his youth had the makings of the heroic, world-transforming figure he was to later become. Their friendship was consolidated by a shared language and culture – it mattered that Engels and Marx were both Germans, and that Mehta and Gandhi were both Gujaratis. There were differences: Engels believed Marx would redeem a class (the proletariat); Mehta believed Gandhi would save a nation, India. Both, however, had a deep, almost unquestioning faith in their compatriot's genius. Both were prepared to reach deep into their pockets to activate and enable it.[19]

Mehta venerated Gandhi. His veneration was communicated in private letters to mutual friends, and in public through a series of articles he published in 1911 in the *Indian Review* of Madras, later published as a book. Here Mehta reprised the main outlines of the struggle in the Transvaal. Gandhi, he argued, had endowed his comrades with the three cardinal virtues of 'Truthfulness, Fearlessness, and Poverty'. The sacrifices of the satyagrahis were 'a good augury for the high destiny' of India itself. 'No Indian in modern times', he pointed out, 'has succeeded so well in bringing the Hindus and Mahomedans together on a common platform as Mr Gandhi.'

Of more interest to us are Mehta's observations on Gandhi the person. 'The one virtue which distinguishes Mr Gandhi from all others', he remarked, 'is that he never puts forward an idea or extols an action, which he himself would not be prepared to act upon when circumstances required him to do so. In fact, he practises himself first what he desires to preach to others.' Once Gandhi had decided upon a particular line of conduct, wrote his friend, 'no risk, nothing, will deter him from going on, on that path without in the least caring whether anyone else believes in it at all, or is prepared to follow him in his footsteps.'

'No earthly temptations,' continued Mehta, were 'too strong' for Gandhi, and 'none of them can make him swerve from the noble path that he has chalked out for himself. It is no exaggeration to say that in this age of materialism it is not possible to come across another man who lives the Ideal life he preaches.'[20]

Gandhi and Pranjivan Mehta corresponded regularly, and while we mostly have one side of the correspondence, it is revealing enough. Gandhi thus wrote to Mehta on 1 July 1911 that 'it would be a mistake if you imagined that we would get the young men we wanted the moment I got to India. As I understand it, we shall have the same difficulties we had to face in this country. It will do us credit if we leave for India only after the work we have begun here has been put on a firm footing.'[21]

In August 1911 Mehta was in London, and so was Henry Polak. The two had an acrimonious argument, an account of which was passed on by Mehta. Gandhi answered that 'I do not think Polak will become an Anglo-Indian out and out' (Mehta must have implied he would). Mehta had called Polak 'hot-tempered'; Gandhi agreed, but added that 'his heart is absolutely frank and he is unswerving in his duty'. Mehta had suggested that Polak was developing a swollen head; Gandhi answered that 'praise is everyone's enemy; how, then, can it be otherwise with him? But I do not so much as suspect that he would be corrupted by praise. He is as honest as he is frank.'[22]

Among the things Mehta and Polak had argued about was Gandhi's future. The doctor wanted his friend and hero to return to India soon – very soon – to revive and lead the nationalist movement there. Polak thought Gandhi still had much work to do in South Africa. Mehta answered that Polak himself could take on the responsibility of representing the Indians in Natal and the Transvaal. He seems to have accused Polak of shirking his duties. Polak replied angrily that no one could keep Gandhi from doing what he wanted; Gandhi's conscience was his own, and for the moment it told him that he was to remain in South Africa rather than return to India.[23]

As it happens, Hermann Kallenbach was also in Europe at this time. Before he left, Gandhi made him take a vow that while he was away, he would not get married, would not 'look lustfully upon any woman', would not 'spend any money beyond necessaries befitting the position of a simple-living poor farmer', and would only travel third class by land or on sea. Kallenbach was enjoined not to eat meat either. The vow was uncannily similar to that extracted by his mother from young Mohandas when he left for London in 1888. To soften the blow, Gandhi and Kasturba baked their friend several tins' worth of biscuits and cake for the journey.[24]

In Europe Kallenbach met Dr Mehta, and spent a day walking with him in the Ardennes.[25] They got along well enough, but when he returned to England, Kallenbach, like Mehta, seems to have quarrelled with Henry Polak. He wrote to Gandhi giving his version of the disagreement. Gandhi replied that 'your analysis of Polak is in the main true. I would only add that his virtues far outbalance his weaknesses and that not one of us is without weaknesses. I know that you know this. Still it bears repetition in order to enable us to exercise the virtue of charity.'[26]

Mehta, Polak and Kallenbach were all competing for Gandhi's friendship – and benediction. That they would be rivalrous was not surprising. Mehta was congenitally suspicious of white men, perhaps because he lived in Rangoon, where a small group of Britons controlled the natives with an iron hand. Characteristically, after criticizing Polak, Mehta then commented adversely on L. W. Ritch. He thought Gandhi excessive in his praise of his European associates. Gandhi agreed that

it is likely that whites entertain more hatred towards us than we do towards them. If, however, we make a great show of love in return for the little that they show us, there is another reason. It is that we fear them. Otherwise, so far as my experience goes, many Indians do not even distinguish between good and bad and take all whites to be bad. On the one hand, this needless fear must go; on the other, one must learn to distinguish between good and bad . . .

I do not look upon Ritch, Polak or anyone else as my disciples. They will all work with us as long as they think fit. There is no reason to believe that, after my death, people would imagine that their actions would necessarily have my approval. Those who have come in contact with me know that differences of opinion do exist among us on subjects other than satyagraha. However, I shall not dismiss your suggestions from my mind.

He concluded by asking Mehta to read Tolstoy's 'Ivan the Fool'.[27]

In October Gandhi wrote to Mehta, 'I know you are very keen that I should leave for India at an early date, and stay there for good. The idea appeals to me and I shall go the moment I can become free here.' Mehta seems to have complained that, by staying on for the time being in South Africa, his friend was neglecting their homeland. 'Please do not think,' answered Gandhi, 'that I shall incur the sin of falling into the delusion that I should serve the entire world. I well realize that my work can only be in India.'[28]

Mehta, meanwhile, had sent a journalist named Manilal Doctor to work with Gandhi. Doctor had once run a newspaper in Mauritius; the hope was that he would take over *Indian Opinion* when Gandhi returned to India. He was also Mehta's son-in-law, married to his daughter Jayakunwar (Jeki). Gandhi thought the young man 'pleasant and good-natured', but complained that he shirked physical labour. Jeki, who followed some months later, was more useful; she was, wrote Gandhi to his daughter-in-law Chanchi, 'a great help to me in teaching the children'.[29]

Gandhi's verdict was endorsed by Kallenbach, who wrote to Pranjivan Mehta that 'your daughter has indeed been a very desirable addition at the farm. We all feel that she has fallen in with our ideas and ways, as if she had been one of us for years.' The architect now hoped that her father, his fellow Gandhi worshipper, would come visit them soon. Mehta visited Europe almost every year, and it was not, as Kallenbach reminded him, 'much of a detour' to go there via South Africa. 'We are all very anxious to see you here, and so many matters which we all have in common, could then be thoroughly thrashed out'.[30]

With Gandhi based in the Transvaal, the Durban journalist P. S. Aiyar offered himself as a stand-in leader for the Indians of Natal. His ambitions were, at first, delicately worded. 'Since Mr Gandhi left Natal', wrote the *African Chronicle* in June 1910, 'the Indian public work in this colony has not been conducted in that steady manner which predominates in him as one of the excellent qualities.'[31]

Slowly, however, the language became more bold. Gandhi was still praised, but his policies questioned. In March 1911, Aiyar called Gandhi 'our great leader', 'that noble soul', the 'originator and architect' of the Indian struggle, yet wondered why he asked only for the form rather than the substance of theoretical equality. The fight, thought Aiyar, should be for the free movement of all Indians throughout the Union, not merely for the entry of a few educated professionals into the Transvaal. Gandhi was urged to 'fight for our birthright of British citizenship to a finish in honour and glory of our motherland.'[32]

In September 1911 Aiyar got entangled in a bitter fight with Gandhi's former clerk and long-time devotee, Joseph Royeppen. Now back with a law degree from London, Royeppen thought that if anyone should be Gandhi's second-in-command in Natal, it was he. P. S. Aiyar naturally disagreed. Royeppen taunted Aiyar that he was unwilling to go to jail for the cause; the journalist accused him of seeking funds from the Durban merchants for a trip to India. Aiyar and Albert West also clashed; *African Chronicle* had carried reports of ill-treatment of indentured labourers that West believed were untrue. Aiyar now sneeringly asked, 'Has the glory departed from Phoenix? Has the sword grown rusty in the scabbard and is the strenuous fight against injustice to be hampered by tedious rivalry?' *Indian Opinion* itself he dismissed as 'apparently the vehicle of expression for Mr Royeppen and his confrères'.[33]

While Royeppen was concerned with the entry of educated men like himself into the Transvaal, Aiyar focused more on the abolition of the £3 tax. Here he had support from, among other bodies, the Natal Indian Congress, which had termed the cess 'oppressive, unjust and immoral'.[34] In December 1911 Aiyar wrote a long pamphlet giving flesh to these accusatory adjectives. He estimated that the tax constituted 25 per cent of the average annual income of an Indian in Natal. Levied on boys when they turned sixteen, and on girls older than thirteen, the tax had 'been the ruin of many a home, and it has blighted the future career of many girls and youths by driving them to destruction and immorality'. Addressed to white voters (and legislators), the pamphlet characterized the tax as manifestly unchristian. 'It seems to me', wrote Aiyar,

> that whatever opinion one may hold regarding the colour and Asiatic questions, the disabilities of the people referred to in this pamphlet do not become the subject of party or colour controversy. Thousands of poor, illiterate, voiceless, creatures, ground down by a heavy tax, cry aloud for relief.[35]

The Indians sent this pamphlet and other materials to the Colonial Office. They, in turn, asked the South African Government to consider the request sympathetically. The Prime Minister, Louis Botha, wrote back that 'in view of the state of [white] public feeling in South Africa on the Indian question', legislation repealing the £3 tax was not possible at 'the present juncture'.[36]

Despite their professional (and/or personal) rivalry, the Phoenix crowd in fact agreed with P. S. Aiyar on the question of the tax. In late 1911, A. E. West wrote to Gandhi proposing an immediate satyagraha asking for its abolition. Gandhi, in reply, advocated a more incrementalist approach. 'With reference to the £3 tax', he told West, the first step to take is not to advise the men to refuse to pay the tax, but for the [Natal Indian] Congress to send a petition to the Prime Minister, signed by all the Indians in Natal – say 15,000 signatures. There should be a mass meeting held. The Congress should then ask the Indians in the other Provinces to support. We must then await the reply from the Prime Minister. Then there should be a petition to Parliament next year, and, if Parliament rejects the petition, there should be an appeal to the Imperial Government by the Congress aided by the other Associations in South Africa. Finally the refusal to pay the tax! Then, undoubtedly, the Congress should undertake to feed the wives and families of those who may be imprisoned. The men would undoubtedly go to gaol, if there is a body of earnest workers. For this purpose, either you will have to be in Durban continuously, or someone else will. The thing cannot be taken up haphazard. If the men were asked to go to gaol today, I do not think you would find anybody taking up the suggestion, but if the preliminary steps as described above, are taken, by the time a final reply is received the men will have been thoroughly prepared to face the music. I know, too, that the thing is quite capable of being done, but one man at least must be prepared to devote the whole of his time to the matter.[37]

The letter concisely captures Gandhi's philosophy of non-violent resistance to unjust laws. He was a strategist of slow reform, of protesting by stages, of systematically preparing himself and his colleagues rather than spontaneously (or, as he would have it, haphazardly) rushing into confrontation.

In April 1912, Gandhi wrote to Ratan Tata, giving an account of the struggle he had so generously supported. He described the teaching methods, the regime of labour and the student profile at Tolstoy Farm. There were currently eighteen Gujaratis, six Tamils and one North Indian in the school. These students were taught that 'they are first Indians and everything else after that, and that, while they must remain absolutely true to their own faiths, they should regard with equal respect those of their fellow-pupils.'

With his letter, Gandhi enclosed a statement of accounts. They had received £8,509 (equivalent to about £680,000 today). £6,723 came from India (about half of this from Tata himself), £972 from Rangoon, £59 from Zanzibar, £61 from Mozambique, £18 from Mombasa and

£159 from London. Turning to their expenses, £2,335 was spent on relief for passive resisters and families, £1,490 on the London committee, £1,200 on *Indian Opinion*, £530 on salaries and lesser amounts on rent, legal expenses, travel, stamps and stationery.[38]

The account – and accounts – pleased Ratan Tata, so much so that he pledged a third gift of Rs 25,000. This was announced at a public meeting held in Bombay on 31 July 1912. The Parsi magnate Sir Jamshetjee Jeejebhoy presided over the meeting, which discussed the handicaps faced by Indians in different parts of the Empire. A memorial forwarded by Sir Jamshetjee urged the Imperial Government to put an end to discriminatory statutes and practices. 'South Africa has long been the worst offender against Indian national sentiment', it declared; it was 'hardly to be expected that the people of this country will acquiesce in the treatment of Indians as an inferior race in order that the rights of self-government accorded to the Colonies may remain intact'.[39]

In the last week of July 1911, *Indian Opinion* had written about a proposal to unite the various native associations in South Africa. Its prime mover was a young Zulu attorney in Johannesburg named Pixley Seme. Seme took a first degree at Columbia University in New York and later studied law in London. Now, asked by a reporter about the aims of the new initiative,

> Seme was at pains to remove any suspicion that force in any degree would be countenanced, but it is clear that the lessons of the Indian agitation have not been lost on the natives, and though nothing definite was said to indicate reliance on passive resistance, it is not improbable that in certain eventualities recourse will be had to it.[40]

These links between the Indian struggle and the new African initiative were also personal. In an unpublished memoir that has recently come to light – written by a lady of Russian extraction living in Johannesburg – it seems that Pixley Seme visited Tolstoy Farm sometime in 1911. Here, 'Mr Gandhi told Dr Seme about his passive resistance movement and how he had settled the women and children on the farm. He remarked on how satisfactorily it had all worked out.'[41]

In the last week of October 1911, Seme published an article advocating the formation of a South African native congress. 'The demons of racialism,' he wrote, 'the aberrations of the Xhosa–Fingo feud, the animosity that exists between the Zulus and the Tongas, between the Basutos and every other Native must be buried and forgotten . . . We are one people. These divisions, these jealousies, are the cause of all our woes and of all our backwardness and ignorance today.'[42]

On his visit to Tolstoy Farm, Pixley Seme may have noticed that its residents included, by ethnicity, Gujaratis, Tamils, North Indians and Europeans – and, by faith, Parsis, Muslims, Christians, Jews and Hindus. It is hard to decisively establish a chain of influence. Still, there is no doubt that there was a family resemblance between what Seme sought to do with the Africans and what Gandhi had already done with the Indians – that is to help them overcome distinctions of sect and tribe, and present a united front to the rulers.

As a result of Pixley Seme's efforts, some sixty Africans met in Bloemfontein in the second week of January 1912. They included chiefs, journalists and community lawyers. The meeting led to the formation of a body called the South African Native National Congress. The veteran Zulu reformer John Dube was elected its first president, *in absentia*, since previous commitments prevented him from attending the meeting.

The new Congress was a response to the white Union of South Africa, in which Africans had no voice in administration or law-making. Their Congress, said Seme, would 'together devise ways and means of forming our national union for the purpose of creating national unity and defending our rights and privileges.' The attorney noted that this was 'the first time that so many elements representing different tongues and tribes ever attempted to co-operate under one umbrella in one great house.'[43]

John Dube, the first president of the Native National Congress, was a neighbour and acquaintance of Gandhi's in Natal. The two men had written appreciatively about one another. Congratulating him on his elevation, *Indian Opinion* now reproduced two paragraphs of the 'excellent' manifesto he had issued 'to his countrymen'. Although the natives were 'the first-born sons of this great and beautiful continent', remarked Dube, 'as citizens of the glorious British Empire, we are the last-born children, just awakening into political life' – after the whites, the Indians and the Cape Coloureds. They had therefore to tread 'softly, ploddingly, along the bright path illuminated by righteousness and reason . . . that will surely and safely lead us to our goal, the attainment of our rightful inheritance as sons of Africa and citizens of the South African Commonwealth.'

Dube understood that this would be an 'uphill fight', with 'enemies without' and 'dangers within'. Yet he insisted that 'by dint of our patience, our reasonableness, our law-abiding methods and the justice of our demands, all these obstacles shall be removed and enemies overcome.' By 'the nobility of our character', he said, 'shall we break down the adamantine wall of colour prejudice and force even our enemies to be our admirers and friends.'[44]

Despite the proximity of Ilanga and Phoenix, Dube and Gandhi met rarely, in part because in these years Gandhi was based mostly in the Transvaal. The resemblances in their political views are striking. The African reformer and the Indian reformer both practised – and preached – a principled incrementalism. Their opposition to racial prejudice was unswerving, yet they thought – or hoped – that a combination of patience and courtesy would make their adversaries see reason and finally dispense justice.

Gandhi's law practice was now in the hands of L. W. Ritch. His visits to the city were mostly to take advantage of the skills of his secretary Sonja Schlesin. Through the first half of 1912, Gandhi was in correspondence with the Ministry of Interior with regard to a new Immigration Bill. The issues he raised included the rights of domicile of women and minor children, the arbitrary powers of immigration officers, the right of appeal to courts, and the right of inter-provincial migration for educated Indians.[45]

In May 1912, General Smuts introduced a fresh 'Immigrants Restrictions Bill' in Parliament. The General said that to work out a satisfactory immigration law was like a 'Chinese puzzle'. For, 'whilst, on one hand, they were most anxious to foster immigration of white people, they were most anxious to keep Asiatics out of the country. (Hear! Hear!).' The Government was thinking of applying an education test on the Australian model, since that test 'admitted of being applied with rigour in the one case and treated with some laxity in the other. The white people would thus be encouraged to come into the country and the Asiatics kept out.' In the debate that followed, a member from Bechuanaland said the exclusion of Asiatics 'was the one question upon which Dutch and English agreed'. He claimed that since the coming of the Indians, hundreds, he might say thousands, of white people who used to do a respectable business had been entirely ousted. The competition of the Asiatic was such that no European could stand up against him, and he would like it to be laid down clearly that in future no Asiatic should be allowed to come into the country.[46]

The signs were unmistakable, and this time too the bill failed to pass through the Senate. The Interior Ministry wrote to Gandhi saying they hoped still to pass an amended Bill in the next session.[47]

In late June, Gandhi spent a week in Durban. The Natal Indians were now divided down the middle. One K. D. Naidoo was canvassing signatures of people who opposed Gandhi; he alleged the lawyer represented the interests only of Gujarati merchants, of those 'Banyans in South Africa who make money and make cheap living'. On the other side, Gandhi's old friend Parsee Rustomjee charged K. D. Naidoo and his colleagues of 'assuming titles of leadership and undertaking public work without the public mandate'.[48]

Some Indians in Natal were unhappy with Gandhi's wait-and-see policy. He had not, they thought, campaigned hard enough for the abolition of the £3 tax on Indians in the province. The hostility of this faction worried Gandhi's friends, who had seen him attacked for his views before. On 27 June, Kallenbach wrote to Chhaganlal Gandhi asking him and his brother Maganlal 'to be on the look-out and observe matters' during Gandhi's stay in Natal. 'One of you', said Kallenbach,

> *should always accompany him to Durban and not lose sight of him.* At the present moment the feeling runs rather high at Durban and therefore be on your guard . . . [L]et us keep our eyes open. We all know Mr Gandhi dislikes and refuses bodyguards, but under one or another pretext, you and Maganlal will, I hope, be able, without attracting Mr Gandhi's attention, to accomplish the above. May we jointly be able to guide him from some fanatic in this country.[49]

Gandhi returned to the Transvaal unscathed. Meanwhile, he had asked Gokhale to visit South Africa. To have an established 'Imperial' statesman lobby for the Indians might finally get them the concessions they desired. Gandhi must also have hoped that the arrival of Gokhale would tame and shame his critics in Durban.

Gokhale had in fact planned to come to South Africa the previous year, on his way back from the United Kingdom, but his doctors had advised against it. So had Gandhi's friend Pranjivan Mehta. Meeting him in London in August 1911, Mehta reported that 'Mr Gokhale's body looks like a paper bag'. A chronic diabetic, he had recently been diagnosed with an excess of albumin, and he was also overweight. Mehta told Gandhi that while Gokhale was indeed very keen to visit South Africa, he worried that the myriad public functions he would have to attend (and speak at) would strain him further. As things stood, it was 'necessary for his health that he gets as much rest as possible'.[50]

The trip was aborted, but a year later Gokhale was in somewhat better shape. In London for the summer (as usual), he booked a passage to Cape Town for October. He asked for one of two berths in a first-class cabin; the shipping company answered that if he paid £10 extra he could have the cabin to himself. Gokhale answered that he had made nine voyages between India and the United Kingdom by ship,

> and never has such an insult been offered to me . . . I feel it is grossly unjust that I should be penalised and compelled to pay more than my fare because some Europeans have a prejudice against travelling with Indians. I think the Company should give me one berth and then leave it to those who come after me to take the second or not as they like.[51]

Gokhale had made many voyages between India and England; but none, before this, to South Africa. The experience with the shipping company prepared him for the sort of racism that Indians in that country experienced on a daily basis. Before making the booking, he had suggested to Gandhi that Maud Polak also come to South Africa. He had been impressed by the work she was doing for the South African British Indian Committee, and thought some first-hand experience would enable her to lobby even more effectively. Gandhi was lukewarm about the proposal, perhaps because he knew what Gokhale did not – namely, that Maud Polak's interest was principally in one Indian in Johannesburg rather than in Indians in South Africa in general.[52]

When the news of Gokhale's trip became public, a liberal editor in Cape Town wrote to the South African Prime Minister, General Botha, urging that the visitor be treated with courtesy. The editor had met Gokhale in India, and thus knew that he was not 'a coolie or a mere agitator', but 'a man of the highest birth, character and intellect, a member of the Council of the Viceroy of India, and perhaps the strongest individual force in Indian politics at the present time.' Botha agreed that the guest should be treated well. Nonetheless, the risks associated with Gokhale's visit were 'considerable'. For instance, the municipal authorities in Johannesburg, Cape Town and other cities did not allow coloured people to travel in trams. 'What would Mr Gokhale say', asked Botha, 'if he were to enter a tram and be asked to get out!'[53]

In the last week of August 1912, Pranjivan Mehta wrote to Gokhale about what he might expect to see in South Africa. Mehta worried that 'too much strain' would be put on Gokhale's 'mind and body by the gatherings and ceremonies that may have to be unavoidably held in your honour'. He then continued:

> So, you will soon have an opportunity of meeting and discussing things with him. From what little conversation we have had about him, I was led to believe that you had not studied G[andhi] quite well. In my humble opinion, men like him are born on very rare occasions and then in India alone. As far as I can see, it seems to me that India has not produced an equally far-seeing prophet like him, during the last five or six centuries and that [if] he was born in the eighteenth century, India would have been a far different land from what it is now and its history would have been altogether differently written. I shall be anxiously waiting to hear from you that your present view of his capacity has altered considerably since coming in greater personal contact with him and that you see in him one of those rare men who are occasionally born to elevate humanity in the land of their birth.[54]

Gandhi was being placed by his friend in very elevated company. Although Mehta mentioned no names, it is clear that he was comparing Gandhi to the medieval saints Nanak and Kabir, and, going further back, to Mahavira and Gautama Buddha, founders of Jainism and Buddhism respectively. He suggested that had Gandhi been born in the eighteenth century, India would not have been colonized by the British.

To place a mere lawyer and diasporic leader in this pantheon was an act of faith, and friendship. Gokhale's answer is unavailable. How might he have reacted to Mehta's letter? He was a generous man, and had praised Gandhi in private and in public. He probably considered Gandhi his most able protégé. He hoped that Gandhi would come back to India and take over the Servants of India Society. But surely he must have been puzzled, if not offended, by this implicit reversal of their roles and place in Indian history. Gokhale was widely acknowledged to be the 'strongest individual force in Indian politics'; it was in that capacity that he had been asked by Gandhi to visit South Africa. But here was Pranjivan Mehta telling him that a man he considered his follower was actually far greater than himself.

In September 1912 Gandhi executed a deed transferring ownership of Phoenix Farm to five trustees, these being the Durban merchant Omar Hajee Amod Johari, Parsee Rustomjee, Kallenbach, Ritch and Pranjivan Mehta – a Muslim, a Parsi, two Jews and a Hindu respectively. The document transferred to these five others Gandhi's right, title and interest in the land and machinery of Phoenix, and listed eight aims by which the farm would be run: namely, to earn a livelihood as far as possible by one's own labour; to promote better relations between Indians and Europeans; to 'follow and promote the ideas' set forth by Tolstoy and Ruskin; to promote 'purity of private life in individuals by living pure lives themselves'; to start a school to educate children mainly in their own vernaculars; to establish a sanitation and hygiene institute; to 'train themselves generally for the service of humanity'; and to publish *Indian Opinion* for the advancement of these ideals.

Gandhi was to be manager of the trust during his lifetime, and have two acres and a building for the use of his family. He would draw the same allowance as other settlers, which was £5 a month. If he died, or left the settlement, the trustees would appoint a manager from among themselves.[55]

At the same time, Gandhi announced that *Indian Opinion* would no longer carry any advertisements. He had come round to the view that 'the system of advertisement is bad in itself, in that it sets up insidious competition, to which we are opposed, and often lends itself to misrepresentation on a large scale'. In the past, the journal had 'always used our discrimination and rejected many advertisements which we could not conscientiously take'. Now it would stop taking ads altogether.[56]

The affairs of Phoenix sorted, Gandhi turned his attention to welcoming Gokhale. He had not seen the older man for ten years, but they had been in regular correspondence. More recently, Gandhi's nephew Chhaganlal had visited Poona. While studying law in London, Chhagan had fallen ill with tuberculosis, and had to abort his studies and return to India to recover, before rejoining his uncle in South Africa. While in Poona he had written of Gokhale's work in less-than-flattering terms. Writing to Maganlal, Gandhi said,

> I felt sad when I read Chi. Chhaganlal's description of the Servants of India Society. It is a matter of regret that a great man like Prof. Gokhale is engrossed in it. I believe he will come out of it, for he is honest. It is simply an indifferent imitation of the West. Is it proper for the servants to have servants? And who are the servants? Why was it necessary to engage them? Why do they have others cook for them? Why should there be large buildings in India? Why should not huts be enough? . . . What a superstition that only an M. A. or B. A. could become a 'servant'? . . . I do feel that the aims of Phoenix as well as the way of life there surpass those of the [Servants of India] Society.[57]

There is a clear sense here that, as a person, social worker and political activist, Gandhi had equalled, if not surpassed, Gokhale. But respect was due to the latter's status in Indian politics and his early encouragement of the then unknown Gandhi. So when Gokhale came to South Africa, his one-time disciple made sure he would get a stirring reception. He knew his mentor to have a fetish about etiquette and attire; so, to humour and honour him, he would, for the first time in years, wear a formal Kathiawari turban when meeting him off the ship in Cape Town.[58]

The ship carrying Gokhale, the RMS *Saxon*, landed at Cape Town on Tuesday, 22 October 1912. A large crowd of Indians had gathered at the quayside, making what Kallenbach (who was present) called 'peculiar scenes', a reference to the raising of flags and the shouting of slogans.[59] Gandhi and a senior Muslim cleric, Imam Bawazeer, boarded the ship to escort the visitor ashore. They then took Gokhale to the home of his local hosts, the Gools, in a procession of fifty carriages.

Gokhale was presented an address on behalf of the local Indians. This was suitably ecumenical, with Hindus, Muslims and Parsis, and Gujaratis, Tamils and Hindi-speakers all signing on. Later, at a public meeeting, he was welcomed by the leading white liberal of the city, Senator W. P. Schreiner. In his speech, Schreiner praised Gandhi for his unselfishness of spirit; Gandhi, speaking next, doffed his hat in turn to the visitor, his 'political teacher', whose name was sacred to all Indians.

It was left to Gokhale to deal with the substantive issues. He reminded the Europeans that since 'everything in India was open to all', they 'could not hope to shut the Indian out of their territory altogether without inflicting a very serious blow on the prestige of the Empire'. He had not come to South Africa 'to light a flame'; he had come in a 'spirit of compromise', with the desire to 'aid the cause of justice'. He noted however that

> India is now watching what is being done to her sons. There is a new awakening throughout the East, not merely in India, but all through Eastern lands. You feel a new life throbbing, a new national consciousness everywhere; and however indifferent India may have been in the past to the sufferings of her children and to her own humiliations, there will be more and more self-respect in the future in her dealings with such matters.[60]

Gokhale also met the leading Cape politician J. X. Merriman at Cape Town. Unlike Schreiner, Merriman had been too timid to attend the public reception in Gokhale's honour. But he met him privately, later writing to Smuts that the Indian had 'impressed me very favourably – an educated gentleman who speaks English as well as we do, is not a Baboo but a High Caste Mahratta, who were, as you know, a fighting race who gave us many a twister'. In Gokhale, Merriman saw 'the new spirit that has arisen in the East of disgust at Western domination'. He urged Smuts to 'do away with all the odious and illiberal machinery of repression' against the Indians, to recognize that 'there are other and surely greater interests at stake [in South Africa] than the conveniences of [white] traders and the prejudices of the [white] community'.[61]

For the next four weeks, as Gokhale travelled through South Africa, Gandhi was at his side. Everywhere, mentor and disciple made similar speeches, with Gandhi professing his admiration for Gokhale, and Gokhale asking the Europeans to look at the question not from their narrow communal interest but from the standpoint of Justice and Empire. Everywhere, Indians turned out in numbers to receive him, and to pass on messages from community groups to which they belonged – which included the Madras Indians, the United Hindu Association, the Hamidia Islamia Society, the Patidar Association, the Transvaal Indian Women's Association, the Brahman Mandal, the Zoroastrian Anjuman, even the Ottoman Cricket Club.

From Cape Town, Gokhale carried on to Kimberley, where among those who received him was the novelist Olive Schreiner.[62] Indians and

Europeans sat down together for a meal for the first time in the history of the mining town. Here, Gandhi praised Gokhale for, among other things, having 'brought with him the much-needed rain which the parched land of Kimberley required so badly'.[63]

Gokhale and Gandhi carried on northwards, halting at the small towns of the Rand – Bloemhof, Klerksdorf, Potchefstroom, Krugersdorp, etc. – to allow the local Indians to pay their respects. At Krugersdorp the mayor turned up at the station to receive Gokhale, earning the ire of his fellow whites, who demanded why he had gone to meet the 'Coolie Gentleman' who had 'evidently come here with the express purpose of stirring up strife'. Just because the mayor of Cape Town had met Gokhale, 'it was not necessary that the Mayors of the Transvaal towns should follow suit.' A meeting of whites affirmed that 'they in Krugersdorp would do their share to help to keep this a white man's country.'[64]

On 28 October, Gokhale's party arrived at Johannesburg's Park Station, whose 'sombre grey of corrugated iron and girders' had been 'transformed for the time at least into a brilliant blaze of colours'. Gokhale exited the station through a giant arch of flowers, designed by Kallenbach, which had 'Hearty Welcome' written in Gujarati, and twin domes shaped in the form of the Muslim crescent and the Hindu trident.

Among the speakers at the Johannesburg meeting were two Europeans. William Hosken said that the recent incarceration of 2,700 out of 9,000 Indians in the Transvaal was 'a horrible disgrace to our Christianity and our civilisation'. Joseph Doke asked that under the British flag 'there should be justice for every man as a man, whether he was an Indian or a Chinese, or whatever his nationality'.

In his speech, Gokhale praised Gandhi in terms that might not have displeased Pranjivan Mehta. The Indians in South Africa, he said, 'had self-reliance and they had a great leader'. Gandhi, 'his friend, their friend, the friend of everyone in the room', was 'a great and illustrious son of whom she [India] was proud beyond words, and he was sure that men of all races and creeds would recognise in him one of the most remarkable personalities of their time'.[65]

On 30 October, Gandhi was interviewed by the *Transvaal Leader* on the progress of Gokhale's visit. His mentor, he said, had 'come to the general conclusion that the Indians resident here are entitled to civic equality. That is to say, their movement within the Union should not be hampered and, under restrictions of a general character applying to the community at large, they should be allowed freedom of trade.' The caveat was crucial: *civic*, not *social* or *political* equality: the freedom to practise one's trade and to live where one wished, not the right to vote or be treated as equal in all respects with the ruling race.

Gandhi was also asked about the attitude of the Orange Free State. In his view, it was 'part of the compromise that under the new Act the few fresh immigrants that will be allowed to come in will be free to move in any part of the Union'. In other words, Indians would or should be allowed to enter the Free State, but not perhaps to trade or farm in it. 'But some day or other', added Gandhi, 'the Free State barrier [to holding property or trading] must entirely disappear. Otherwise the Union will be a farce.'[66]

On 1 November, Gokhale was hosted for breakfast by the Chinese Association of Johannesburg. He was welcomed by Leung Quinn, now back in the Transvaal. Quinn spoke of how the Chinese 'stood shoulder to shoulder with their brother Asiatics'. Theirs was 'a fraternity larger than that of common religion and race ... They hoped for the passing of British antagonism, and looked forward to the reign of sweet reason instead of stupid prejudice.' Gokhale, in reply, spoke of the two communities having much in common, 'both being old peoples and India having given China one of her oldest religions'.[67]

Gokhale then spent a few days resting at Tolstoy Farm. On the 6th Gandhi and he left for Natal. They stopped at the smaller mining and plantation towns, such as Newcastle and Dundee, before arriving in Durban on the morning of the 8th. A crowded meeting was attended by very many Indians, 'who, at least for that night, felt that the Town Hall really belonged to them and that they enjoyed the rights of citizenship'. Among those who spoke was F. A. Laughton, KC, he who had bravely stood by Gandhi when the white mob attacked him in 1897.

The next day, Gokhale presented the prizes at a sports meeting and then heard grievances against the £3 tax. Some sixty individuals filed up, one by one, and spoke of how their inability to pay the tax had led to their imprisonment. They were heard by a crowd of several thousand, who had come from the outlying districts by train, cycle, cart, wagon or on foot. The testimonies were offered in Tamil and Gujarati, and then translated for Gokhale's benefit, the narration often interrupted by cries of 'Shame! Shame!'[68]

On Sunday, 10 November Gokhale and Gandhi visited the Ohlange Industrial School and 'spent some time discussing the Native question with the Rev. John Dube'. The students sang Zulu songs for the visitors.[69] Later that week Gokhale returned to the Transvaal. On Thursday 14 November he travelled to Pretoria to meet the Prime Minister and the Minister of the Interior. General Botha had followed Gokhale's progress through the country with dismay. He was offended that the Indian leader had not come to see him soon after landing. That Gokhale was warmly received in most places did not please him either. Gokhale's statements, grumbled Prime Minister Botha to the Governor-General, had raised 'false hopes among our Indian population'. They had 'put up the backs of our European population – Dutch as well as English-speaking, and made them more than ever opposed to any kind of concession'. But, said Botha to the Governor-General, he would still 'meet him in the most reasonable spirit'.[70]

Gokhale had asked that Gandhi be allowed to come with him, but the request was refused.[71] Meeting the ministers, he urged the abolition of the £3 tax and the admission of a select number of educated Indians to the Transvaal.

The next day Gokhale and the Prime Minister independently met the Governor-General, Lord Gladstone (a son of the great Liberal Prime Minister, who had served as home secretary before coming out to South Africa). Later, Gladstone sent London this report: 'As regards the £3 tax, the Prime Minister told me that he thought it would be possible to meet Mr Gokhale's views, though there might be strong opposition in Natal. From what Mr Gokhale said I gathered that the Prime Minister had given him a satisfactory assurance.' The Governor-General was also hopeful that the Immigration Bill would finally be passed in an acceptable form. He was 'convinced that the Prime Minister and General Smuts are sincerely anxious to put it through'.[72]

Gokhale came away from these meetings convinced that the Indians' demands would be met. 'You must return to India in a year', he told Gandhi. 'Everything has been settled. The Black Act will be repealed. The racial bar will be removed from the immigration law. The £3 tax will be abolished.'[73]

In a farewell speech in Pretoria, Gokhale appealed to 'the better mind of the two communities, European and Indian'. To the former he said, 'the Government must exist for promoting the prosperity not of the European community only, but of all its subjects.' To the latter he said, 'your future is largely in your own hands.' He hoped that a struggle of the kind waged in the Transvaal between 1907 and 1910 would not have to be fought again. But 'if it has to be resumed', said Gokhale, 'or if you have to enter on other struggles of a like nature for justice denied or injustice forced on you, remember that the issue will largely turn on the character you show, on your capacity for combined action, on your readiness to suffer and sacrifice in a just cause.'[74]

Overlapping with Gokhale's trip to South Africa was the visit of a rather more obscure friend of Gandhi's. This was Maud Polak, who had managed to travel to South Africa after all. She had come to study the Indian situation at first-hand – the better to aid her lobbying work in London – and perhaps also to spend time with Mohandas Gandhi. She succeeded in the first endeavour but not in the second. *Indian Opinion* reported her movements – a tea party for her in Johannesburg on 14 October, another on the 19th, both hosted and attended by women, Europeans as well as Indians. Then she crossed over to Natal, where she spent two weeks, speaking to labourers and merchants, and attending at least two parties in her honour.[75] Her arrival and stay in South Africa was drowned out by the visit of Gopal Krishna Gokhale. Gandhi himself was criss-crossing the country with his mentor, and appears to have hardly seen Maud at all. Whether this was by accident or design the sources do not say.

In London, Gokhale had been impressed by Maud Polak's commitment; now, in South Africa, he was even more impressed by Sonja Schlesin, a young woman who worked for Gandhi without having a romantic interest in him. In his travels through Natal and the Transvaal he met many among Gandhi's friends and associates – those who ran his journal and his ashrams, those who went to jail with him, those who raised money for him. Having seen them all, and seen some admirable social workers in India and England too, Gokhale told Gandhi, 'I have rarely met with the sacrifice, the purity and the fearlessness I have seen in Miss [Sonja] Schlesin. Amongst your co-workers, she takes the first place in my estimation.'[76]

*

Gokhale spent his last weekend in South Africa at Tolstoy Farm. On the evening of 17 November, he left Johannesburg by train for the Portuguese port of Lourenço Marques. Gandhi and Kallenbach accompanied him. At a reception in the town hall, Gandhi used the chance to flog his ideas on diet, health and religious pluralism. He said he

> remembered Lourenço Marques when it had the reputation of being a malarious place, but it was almost superfluous to drink the health of the European guests in a town so admittedly healthy as the town was to-day. They also had partaken of a vegetarian, non-alcoholic repast – these things were also considered consistent with good health. He considered the gathering unique; they had with them Christians, Jews, Hindus, Mahomedans, and Parsees.

The British Consul General, speaking next, 'referred to the trouble this same Mr Gandhi had given to the Consulate in days past [with regard to permits, etc.], but he remembered that the proposer of the toast had also done good service to the Empire during the [Boer] War, and after all loyalty was the chief thing'.[77]

Gokhale now proceeded, his disciples in tow, to Dar-es-Salaam by ship. On board, Gandhi promised Gokhale that he 'would not leave for I[ndia] without making arrangements for the work in S[outh] A[frica] to be carried on in my absence. Most probably the management of affairs will be left in Polak's hands.'[78]

En route, they stopped at Zanzibar. The island had an active Indian community, who, it turned out, knew all about the satyagraha in South Africa, and its leader, whose struggle deeply resonated with them. 'Remarkable how the men's faces light up when they hear the name "Gandhi"', wrote Kallenbach in his diary, 'and how eager they are to shake hands.'[79]

There was one last public meeting in Africa, this 'the largest gathering Indians at Dar-es-Salam have ever had',[80] before Gokhale took leave of his companions and headed east to Bombay. The next day, Gandhi wrote to Gokhale that 'I want to be a worthy pupil of yours. This is not mock humility but Indian seriousness. I want to realize in myself the conception I have of an Eastern pupil. We have many differences of opinion, but you shall still be my pattern in political life.' After this expression of qualified devotion, he continued:

One word from the quack physician. Ample fasting, strict adherence to two meals, entire absence of condiments of all kinds from your food, omission of pulses, tea, coffee, etc., regular taking of Kuhne baths, regular and brisk walking in the country (not the pacing up and down for stimulating thought), ample allowance of olive oil and acid fruit and gradual elimination of cooked food – and you will get rid of your diabetes and add a few more years than you think to your life of service in your present body.[81]

In a month spent in each other's company, Gokhale and Gandhi must have made manifest their many differences of opinion – with regard to the respective merits of petitioning versus protest, modern versus traditional civilization, allopathic versus naturopathic systems of medicine. Speaking to Gandhi, watching him at work among his compatriots, Gokhale nonetheless came away with a distinctly elevated view of his protégé's personality and achievements. In a public meeting on his return to Bombay – held on 13 December – Gokhale said Gandhi was 'without doubt made of the stuff of which heroes and martyrs are made. Nay, more. He has in him the marvellous spiritual power to turn ordinary men around him into heroes and martyrs.' He told the assembled Indians of Gandhi's sacrifices, of how he built up the movement in South Africa, and how he inspired others to follow him. Some among the several thousand satyagrahis who went to jail at his behest were established traders and professionals, but the bulk, observed Gokhale,

> were poor humble individuals, hawkers, working men and so forth, men without education, men not accustomed in their life to think or talk of their country. And yet these men braved the horrors of gaol-life in the Transvaal and some of them braved them again and again rather than submit to degrading legislation directed against their country . . . [T]hey were touched by Gandhi's spirit and that had wrought the transformation, thus illustrating the great power which the spirit of man can exercise over human minds and even over physical surroundings.

Gokhale defended Gandhi against his critics at home and abroad. Some radicals thought Gandhi should have argued for an 'open door' policy, whereby Indians could freely migrate to South Africa. But, said Gokhale, it was precisely 'the fear of an indiscriminate influx which haunted the European mind'. The demand for free migration would have made 'the Europeans more implacable in their determination to get rid of the Indians at all costs and the eventual expulsion of the Indians from the [South African] sub-continent would only have been hastened by such a move'. He claimed that the 'theoretical rights' that Gandhi had so valiantly fought for 'would no doubt steadily grow more and more into rights actually enjoyed in practice, but that was a matter of slow growth and it depended on a large measure upon the improvement of their position in India itself.'[82]

Saints, it appears, could or should be pragmatists as well. Thus argued Gokhale, in whose view Gandhi's distinctive combination of personal saintliness and social meliorism was necessary to safeguard the position of Indians in South Africa.

Gokhale's visit, important in itself, also helped consolidate Gandhi's position within the community. That the great Indian leader placed himself entirely in Gandhi's hands, that Gandhi accompanied him wherever he went, that Gandhi's public words of praise for Gokhale were often answered by Gokhale's public words of praise for Gandhi – none of this was lost on the varied audiences in Natal, Transvaal and the Cape.

Gokhale's endorsement of Gandhi irritated and angered the Durban journalist P. S. Aiyar. For some time now, Aiyar had pressed for a more prominent place for himself. In his call for attention he had attacked Gandhi's followers, but not, as yet, Gandhi himself. As late as June 1912 he was writing that while Swami Shankeranand was 'the leader of the reactionary group' among Indians, 'Mr Gandhi is and has been recognised as the leader of the progressive party'.[83]

When Gokhale arrived in South Africa later in the year, and Gandhi was always at his side, Aiyar was not pleased, although he was not yet willing to confront Gandhi directly. An essay of November 1912 started by expressing 'the highest admiration and respect for Mr Gandhi', while claiming there was nonetheless 'a considerable body of opinion outside the Transvaal which do not apparently fall in line with all his views and conclusions'.

Aiyar then set out his own view of the Indian predicament in South Africa. As inheritors of an ancient civilization, they could not allow themselves to be submerged by 'materialistic western civilization'; nor, however, could they identify with the 'savagery' of the Africans. The way forward was to 'improve themselves on their traditional lines of civilisation. For doing so, they must have social and commercial intercourse with the country of their origin'. This continuous intercourse was what the proposed Asiatic Act forbade.[84]

Aiyar's position was not dissimilar to that held by Gandhi before the Anglo-Boer War, when he had likewise argued for equal rights for all British subjects, which implied the free movement of Indians into (and across) South Africa. As white attitudes hardened, however, Gandhi modified his stand, now asking only for guaranteed rights of residence and work for Indians *already* in South Africa. That was what he asked Lord Milner for in 1904, and what he had asked General Smuts for between 1906 and 1911.

Aiyar also grumbled that Gokhale's itinerary in South Africa was dictated by Gandhi and company. The journalist was able to get only a half-hour appointment with the visitor, which left him deeply dissatisfied. Gokhale told him that the demand for free immigration and free movement was impractical, and the further demand for an Indian franchise highly premature. Aiyar wrote bitterly that 'instead of endeavouring to find a remedy to put our countrymen on our legs he [Gokhale] simply evaded to tackle the real and lectured on the maintenance of European civilisation and praised Mr Gandhi as a wonderful personage and all ended there.'[85]

Gokhale departed for India, with Aiyar's complaints following him across the ocean. Aiyar now wanted a deputation to proceed to the motherland and stir up the Indian public. 'Of course', he wrote, 'such a deputation must be absolutely free from the influence of Messrs Gandhi, Polak, Rustomjee and Co.' When Gokhale praised Gandhi in a public meeting in Bombay, Aiyar erupted again. It 'is a national misfortune', said the angry journalist,

> that a man of Gokhale's intellectual calibre should have been hypnotised by Messrs Gandhi and Pollock [sic] who are notoriously lacking in those ingredients [necessary] for political work, and but for the regrettable influence that these two men possess over Mr Gokhale, he would have been able to do more solid work for the Indians of South Africa.[86]

P. S. Aiyar's animus was in part born out of jealousy. He would have liked Gandhi to consult him, to work with him, to substitute Polak with him as his second-in-command. While Aiyar himself had marginal influence, for the biographer he merits attention as the only *articulate* opponent of Gandhi within the Indian community. From 1895 or there-abouts the whites of Natal had poured a steady stream of abuse at Gandhi. From 1907 or thereabouts they had been joined by their col-leagues in the Transvaal. Polak, Kallenbach, Doke and Sonja Schlesin notwithstanding, Gandhi was an object of hate and ridicule to the majority of Europeans. Conversely, he was the acknowledged popular leader of the Indians in Natal and the Transvaal. To be sure, the respect he commanded among his people was not universal: some Pathans had attacked him physically when he sought to compromise with the rulers, some merchants had refused to follow him into jail when he resumed the struggle. P. S. Aiyar, however, was *sui generis* – the only Indian in South Africa who expressed his disagreements with Gandhi in print and in sometimes splendidly vituperative prose.

19

A Physician at Phoenix

With the Union of South Africa in place, there was no reason for Gandhi to remain in the Transvaal any more. Immigration laws were no longer colony-specific: any settlement General Smuts and he arrived at would apply to South Africa as a whole. And so, at the beginning of 1913, Gandhi moved to Natal, to live with his family and his disciples on the farm he had founded eight years previously.

When he was based in Johannesburg, Gandhi had still considered Phoenix his home. It was where his family lived, where his journal was produced, where his ideas for moral regeneration were enacted. The settlers looked forward to his visits with keen anticipation. The children prepared welcome arches for him; or, if he arrived at night, lighted the path to his hut with candles. The affection was reciprocated; so long as they were not his own, and not yet teenagers, Gandhi delighted in the company of children. Chhaganlal's son recalled how the patriarch carried them across his shoulder, rolled them down a sloping garden plot, showed them his teeth fillings and – not least – cured their ailments by, in this case, prescribing raw tomatoes for boils. 'Another thing that attracted me', remembered the boy, 'was that he laughed more often than anyone in Phoenix in spite of being such an important person.'[1]

When Gandhi moved to Phoenix in January 1913, the school had thirty children. Teachers and students worked on the farm from 6 to 8 a.m. After breakfast Gandhi took the boys to the classroom, while the men went off to the press. In the afternoons, while someone else took class, Gandhi worked at the press himself. Dinner, at 5.30, was followed by songs and prayer. From 7.30 to 9 p.m. Gandhi supervised Manilal's lessons, in a belated recognition of the special obligations of biological parenthood.

In the nine years since the settlement was founded, it had made steady progress. The hedges were trim and neat, marking out fields that produced an array of vegetables and fruits, among them succulent pineapples. The homes were furnished; some even had (as Millie Polak noted appreciatively) 'attractive curtains at the windows'. The common areas included the river, open grounds, shrubs and trees, and a large one-room structure that served as a school in the day and as a meeting-place in the evening.

Every Sunday the residents of Phoenix gathered for an inter-faith prayer meeting. Passages from the Gita and the New Testament (among other texts) were read, and hymns in Gujarati and English sung. The founder's own favourites included 'Lead, Kindly Light' and 'The Hymn of Consecration'. An admittedly partisan observer wrote that 'perhaps in no place in the world' were these hymns 'sung with greater fervour and meaning than in that little lamp-lit corrugated-iron room, where Mr Gandhi was the centre of the life of an assembled congregation of about twenty people, from East and West'.[2]

With *Indian Opinion*'s first issue for 1913, Gandhi began a weekly series in Gujarati called 'General Knowledge about Health'. This drew on wide reading and, even more, on his own experiments and experiences. This 'quack physician' (to use Gandhi's self-description) was critical of the modern dependence on drugs. 'Once the [medicine] bottle enters a house', he complained, 'it never leaves.' He thought bad air to be the cause of most diseases. Dirty latrines and open-air urination fouled the atmosphere, as did the casual dumping of food peelings and garbage, and spitting – all practices common to Indians. He spoke of the dangers of drinking contaminated water, and explained how water could be cleaned and purified in homes.

The self-taught physician turned next to substances to be eschewed or encouraged. 'Drink, tobacco, hemp, etc., not only damage physical health', he said, 'but also impair mental fitness and entail wasteful expenditure. We lose all our moral sense and become slaves to our weakness.' Chillies, spices and salt were also to be avoided. Gandhi outlined a hierarchy of ideal and preferred diets. A purely fruit diet was the best, then fruit and vegetables with no salt or spices, then a mix of vegetables and meat. Last, and most deplorable, was a purely carnivorous diet. 'Those who . . . subsist exclusively on flesh', remarked Gandhi, 'need not detain us here. Their state is so vile that the very thought of them should be enough to put us off meat-eating. They are not healthy in any sense of the term.'[3]

In the last week of January 1913, Gandhi wrote to his son Harilal saying that he hoped to return to India quite soon. With him would come some of the boys he was schooling at Phoenix. 'I should certainly be able to go if a law satisfying to our demands is passed', he remarked, 'so it appears. I have therefore settled in Phoenix. I don't wish to stir out from here for five months.'[4]

As before, Gandhi's optimism was misplaced. In February, he complained to Gokhale that the assurances given him by the ministers were not being honoured. 'The Immigration Acts are being administered with an ever-growing severity. Wives of lawfully resident Indians are being put to great trouble and expense.'[5]

In the third week of March, a judgement in a Cape Town court called into question the validity of Indian marriages. One Hassan Esop, a barber working in Port Elizabeth, had, while on holiday in India, married a lady named Bal Mariam. After his return, he applied for a permit for his wife to join him. Although Bal Mariam was his only wife, the court refused to allow her to join her husband, on the grounds that Islam permitted polygamy. 'The courts of this country,' said the judge, a Justice Searle, 'have always set their faces against recognition of these so-called Mahommedan marriages as legal unions', since a woman admitted as a wife could 'be repudiated the next day after the arrival by the husband'. To the argument that at least one wife should be admitted, the judge said sarcastically, 'I do not know whether it is to be the first that comes, or the first that is married.'[6]

Hindu law did not ban polygamy either. Did this mean that only Christian marriages would be recognized as valid in South Africa? The judgement alarmed the Indians, whose concerns were forcefully articulated by Gandhi in an editorial in *Indian Opinion*:

> This decision means as from today all Hindu or Muslim wives living in South Africa lose their right to live there . . . a Hindu, Muslim or Parsi wife can live in this country only by the grace of the Government. It is quite on the cards that the Government will not permit any more wives to come in or that, if it does, it will entirely be a matter of favour . . . The remedy is

entirely in our hands. Every Anjuman, every Dharma Sabha and every one of the [community] associations must respectfully submit to the Government that the law should be amended and that marriages solemnized under the rites of Indian religions should be recognized as legal. Any nation that fails to protect the honour of its women, any individual who fails to protect the honour of his wife is considered lower in level than a brute.[7]

Gandhi's own marriage had its good periods and bad. His children and his wife had to bear the brunt of his social and ethical experiments. But of his commitment to marriage as a social institution there could be no doubt. The Searle judgement, if interpreted literally and implemented vigorously, threatened to sunder husband from wife, mother from children. This would seriously damage the life of the Indian community in South Africa. Gandhi may also have worried that, in the absence of their wives, Indian men would patronize prostitutes. Hence his call to community organizations to mobilize in protest against the Searle judgement. He was heeded, and quickly. The judgement was delivered on 21 March; eight days later, a mass meeting of Indians was held at the Hamidia Hall in Johannesburg. The meeting expressed 'deep distress and disappointment' at the court verdict, which was calculated 'to disturb Indian domestic relations, to break up established homes, to put husband and wife asunder, to deprive lawful children of their inheritance . . .' The Indians wanted remedial legislation that recognized as valid any marriage solemnized under the rites of 'the great religions of India'. If this was not forthcoming, then it became 'the bounden duty of the community, for the protection of its womanhood and its honour, to adopt passive resistance'.[8]

This meeting was attended only by men, but the women were likewise outraged by the Searle judgement. Kasturba asked Gandhi whether this meant 'that I am not your wife according to the laws of this country'. When he answered in the affirmative, she suggested that they should perhaps return to India. Gandhi said that would be cowardly, whereupon Kasturba asked, 'Could I not, then, join the struggle and be imprisoned myself?'

Kasturba's offer was a mark of her deep loyalty to her husband, and of her acquired understanding of his cause. Despite their very different temperaments, Gandhi and Kasturba had, over thirty years of marriage, developed a relationship of understanding and companionship, to which the word 'love' may also be applied. Back in 1901, Kasturba had resisted Gandhi giving back jewels presented to him for his work. Now, twelve years later, she was herself volunteering to go to jail. Thus she underlined her commitment to a marriage the new law chose to regard as 'invalid'; thus also she showed her solidarity with the Indian community as a whole.

Reporting their conversation to Gokhale, Gandhi said, 'this time the struggle, if it comes, will involve more sufferings than before.' He did not want to ask the public in India for support; rather, 'the plan would be to beg in S[outh] A[frica] from door to door.' He thought 'most of the settlers [at Phoenix] including the womenfolk will join the struggle. The latter feel they can no longer refrain from facing the gaol no matter what it may mean in a place like this. Mrs. Gandhi made the offer on her own initiative and I do not want to debar her.'[9]

The resentment against the Searle judgement was felt equally in Natal and the Transvaal. In recent years, the Indians in these two provinces had tended to conduct their affairs separately. The marriage question bound them together once more. The Natalians were also very exercised by the continuance of the £3 tax. The Durban journalist P. S. Aiyar had convened several meetings asking for its removal. Aiyar wrote to the Prime Minister, General Botha, that a repeal of the tax would be 'hailed with unbounded joy' and 'have a far-reaching influence on the consolidation and stability of the Empire'.[10]

The request, or plea, was disregarded. In April 1913 the Government released the draft of a new Immigration Bill. This had distinctly, and perhaps deliberately, failed to take the sentiments of Indians into account. It retained the £3 tax, while making the qualifications for domicile more stringent and inter-provincial migration for Indians more difficult. It did not allow appeals to courts, and rendered the status of wives and children uncertain and insecure. The Bill gave wide discretionary powers to officials, allowing them to keep out 'any person or class of persons deemed ... on economic grounds or on account of standard or habits of life to be unsuited to the requirements of the Union or any particular Province thereof'.[11]

In the third week of April, the Natal Indian Congress wired the Governor-General in protest. Unless the amendments it asked for were made, it said, the 'Indian community will be obliged strenuously to oppose [the] Bill with all [the] resources in its power'.[12] The same week,

Gandhi travelled from Phoenix to Johannesburg, to attend a meeting at the Hamidia Hall. A large and excited crowd heard him say that since the Union Bill incorporated the worst features of provincial legislation, this time 'the struggle might be prolonged and fierce'. L. W. Ritch, speaking after him, said that 'if he as an Englishman were settled in any country and found himself treated as his Indian brothers were, he would fight unto death'.[13]

The Interior Minister now was Abraham Fischer, a Free Stater who, on the Indian question, was even more hardline than General Smuts. Fischer defended the harshness of the Bill in Parliament. For the 'self-preservation of the white man', he said, it 'was considered undesirable that this country should be encroached upon by Asiatics'. His predecessor, Smuts, had once complained to Gandhi about the intransigent attitude of the MPs from the Orange Free State. Fischer now praised them for having 'shown from the start what was good for the country'. As for the contentious question of Indian marriages, the Minister told Parliament that 'a man was entitled to have only one wife, which some people maintained was quite sufficient. (Laughter.) A European was not allowed the privilege of having more than one wife, and surely we were not going to give that privilege to non-Europeans? (Laughter.)'[14]

A few liberal politicians opposed the Bill in Parliament. The Cape lawyer Morris Alexander called it a 'serious infringement' of the rights of Asiatics. W. P. Schreiner thought this was really an 'Immigrants Restriction [rather than Regulation] Bill'; its provisions were contrary to the assurances given to Gokhale, whom Schreiner described as 'one of the greatest men of the time'. The majority opinion, however, was solidly behind the Minister and his Bill, which was necessary for 'the self-preservation of the white race in South Africa'. As one Boer MP put it, apart from 'a few cranks' the 'unanimous opinion of [white] South Africa was against the importation of Asiatics'. Some of them wanted to go further, and deport the Asiatics already in the country.[15]

As Interior Minister, Smuts had at least been prepared to talk to Gandhi. His successor, however, treated Gandhi as an interloper. The lawyer, said Abraham Fischer, was 'representing only that section of the Indian community in the Transvaal, which was known some three or four years back as the "Passive Resisters".' His secretary told Gandhi that the Minister did not accept that he was 'acting on behalf of the entire Asiatic population of the Transvaal'. Later, when Gandhi asked for the

Searle judgement to be overturned, the Minister answered that 'from the earliest times, following the introduction of European civilization into South Africa, the law of the land has only recognised as a valid union the marriage, by a recognised marriage officer, of one man to one woman, to the exclusion, while it lasted, of any other.'[16]

The implications were enormous, and ominous. Marriages between Hindus and Muslims were solemnized in private ceremonies conducted by priests and imams, not before a registrar or marriage official appointed or recognized by the state. The Minister's interpretation would make thousands of Indian marriages in South Africa illegal – among them Gandhi and Kasturba's.[17]

In late April, Gandhi travelled from Phoenix to Johannesburg for a meeting of the Transvaal Indians. He asked whether they were 'ready to undergo the ordeal' of passive resistance. He trusted that, 'as self-respecting men, they could not shirk it. They must be prepared to risk all for the honour of their womanhood, for the sake of their religions and for the good name of the country of their birth.' The same week, he wrote in his newspaper asking Indians in the Cape and Natal to 'wake up'. They too should come forward and be prepared to go to jail.[18]

Meanwhile, Henry Polak was peppering the Government of India and the Colonial Office with letters asking them to intervene. He outlined the Bill's flaws, and suggested how they could be overcome. Gandhi would go down to Cape Town if required to talk with the ministers. But if negotiations failed, then a revival of passive resistance was 'certain', and Gandhi himself would 'not hesitate to put personal inclination on one side in order to take his part in the struggle.'[19]

Polak's intervention angered the Interior Minister, who asserted that he had in the past carried out an 'active campaign of mis-statement' against the Government. Fischer had hoped 'that by this time the Colonial Office would have formed a correct estimate of communications written by Polak; but apparently his highly coloured and sensational communications still find credence, or at least more consideration than they ought to have in that quarter.'[20]

Two weeks later, the Interior Minister received a letter forwarded by another European supporter of the Indians. Sent by Sonja Schlesin on behalf of 'over forty Indian ladies of Johannesburg professing the Hindu, the Mahomedan and the Christian faiths', this said that if the law was not amended to recognize Indian marriages, the women would offer passive resistance along with their menfolk. Schlesin was here acting, and writing, as the Honorary Secretary of the Transvaal Indian Women's Association. Reproducing her lettter, *Indian Opinion* commented that Miss Schlesin held that office because of the knowledge of English and of South African politics that her 'Indian sisters' lacked. 'Miss Schlesin, like the male European workers in South Africa for the Indian cause, demonstrates the unity of human nature, whether residing in a brown-skinned or a white-skinned body.'[21]

The tribute to the white-skinned Sonja Schlesin was written by the brown-skinned Gandhi. To underscore the unity of human nature, Polak returned the compliment in another section of the newspaper, by praising Indian women for daring 'to fight the Government rather than submit to the insult offered by the Searle judgment'. Polak hoped now that the men would rise as quickly to the challenge, since, as he put it, '"the larger the number of passive resisters the quicker the termination of the struggle" is a mathematical formula.'[22]

Unlike Polak and Sonja Schlesin, Hermann Kallenbach was too mild and not political enough to lobby the Government on behalf of the Indians. However, in a series of private letters written at this time, he laid bare his own understanding of the character and personality of their leader. He also revealed his own plans, which were to accompany Gandhi to India as and when his friend moved there for good. The letters were addressed to British followers of Tolstoy, whom Kallenbach had befriended on his visit to that country in 1911. Here, in part, is what the architect told them about their fellow Tolstoyan.[23]

Hermann Kallenbach to George Ferdinand, 3 March 1913:

> I cannot describe the man's character to you by letter, but I can only say that the more I have had the privilege of being with, and near him, the clearer I have recognized the utter unselfishness of his character. True, it is sometimes hard – very hard – to live near and with him, but it is also true that he cannot serve God and Mammon . . .
>
> My wishing to go to India is not really a pilgrimage in the right sense of the word. It is more that I clearly recognize how very deficient my character is in many respects, and that I am hoping that the life there will give me more energy to throw off this defectiveness.

Hermann Kallenbach to Isabella Fyvie Mayo, 3 March 1913:

> As long as I know Mr G[andhi] he has always loaded upon himself work
> and responsibilities, which no ordinary ten men would undertake ... I
> believe that on account of this desire to be of such great service to all, he
> can not in my opinion pay sufficient attention to his family and his nearer
> friends, and in still doing so he has to curtail his meals, do with less sleep
> and to make time here and there when necessity arises.

Hermann Kallenbach to Isabella Fyvie Mayo, 10 March 1913:

> If you would know him better you would also recognise that it is indeed
> somewhat difficult to be near him and with him, unless one covers the
> whole distance with him ... [H]e is so severe with himself that he simply
> goes ahead, and it is a question of either being with him, or not being able
> to be near him.

Hermann Kallenbach to Isabella Fyvie Mayo, 21 April 1913:

> Your judgement about Mr G[andhi] placing him next [to] Ruskin and
> Tolstoy is a true one, and if he lives, posterity will once recognize it.

The devotion was intensely personal. Like Pranjivan Mehta, Kallenbach
was clear that his friend would one day be recognized as a moral exemplar to his country and the world. But where Mehta saw in Gandhi's
qualities and personality the redemption of India, Kallenbach saw in
them the route to the improvement of his own anguished, flawed self.

Even as his European friend (or devotee) was praising Gandhi in private, Gandhi was being attacked in public by his Indian rival, the
Durban journalist P. S. Aiyar. *African Chronicle*'s issue of 19 April
1913 carried an essay with the bald title: 'Why Mr Gandhi Is a Failure'.
The lawyer's politics, claimed the critic, have 'resulted in no tangible
good to anyone'. On the other hand, they had caused 'endless misery,
loss of wealth, and deprivation of existing rights'.

Aiyar accused Gandhi of thinking 'that he is an immutable, omnipo-
tent Czar', and Polak of seeing himself as a 'white Dinizulu [the Zulu
chief] for the Indians'. He charged both men with 'rank arrogance and
inordinate ambition'. He urged Gandhi now 'to climb down from his
high pedestal', and to 'make some sacrifice of his personal antipathies
and prejudices'. Instead of 'sulking in the tent at Phoenix', and being 'as
shy to face an audience as an Indian bride', Gandhi should 'come to

Durban and convene a caucus meeting of the leaders, and . . . have a free and frank exchange of ideas with the people'.

The screed reeked of animosity, but also of ambition – Aiyar was pleading, rather desperately, to be heard. The challenge to Gandhi was followed by a meaningful remark about his chief lieutenant: 'As for Mr Polak, a large body of Indians do not seem to care much to be led by this gentleman.'[24]

Did Gandhi read Aiyar's challenge? Did he read it as what – the bile that covered it notwithstanding – it really seems to be, a cry for attention, an appeal to be considered worthier than the Englishman Polak in being the second-in-command of the Indian leader? The name of P. S. Aiyar does not figure in Gandhi's memoirs of his South African days. We do know, from stray reports in *Indian Opinion*, that the two men knew each other, and had shared a common platform several times in Durban. But at least in print Gandhi steadfastly disregarded the taunts, the complaints, the challenges and the abusive remarks that came his way from the editor of the *African Chronicle*.

This was Aiyar's most strongly worded attack yet; and although Gandhi ignored it his admirers were compelled to respond. Some forty Tamils wrote to the *African Chronicle* declaring that 'whatever your attacks may be upon Mr Gandhi, it will not deter us from being his faithful and staunch followers'. The editor printed their letter, appending a comment of his own, which urged the Tamils not to 'subject themselves to be led by cattle, not knowing where the leader leads them whether to Heaven or to Hell'.[25]

As the private praise and public invective poured in, Gandhi carried on with his series on health. Part XIV paid attention to what leaves the body. 'From the appearance of our faeces', remarked the author, 'we can make out if we have eaten too much.' The faeces of one who had eaten 'only as much as he can comfortably digest' would tend to be 'small, well formed, darkish, sticky, dry and free from bad odour'.

Part XVII, entitled 'An Intimate Chapter', was on *brahmacharya*, here deemed 'the most important' thing to promote good health. It implied not 'merely refraining from contact with each other with such enjoyment in view, but also keeping the mind free from the very thought of it – one must not even dream about it'. In Gandhi's view, the violation of *brahmacharya* was 'the basic cause of pleasure-hunting, envy, ostentation, hypocrisy, anger, impatience, violent hatred and other such evils'. Once a couple had children, they must desist from sexual relations. 'I, who was married in childhood', recalled this converted celibate, 'was blinded [by lust] in childhood and had children while a mere child, awoke after many years and seem to have realized on awakening that I had been pursuing a disastrous course. If anyone learns from my mistakes and my experience and saves himself, I shall be happy to have written this chapter.'[26]

Kallenbach may, among other things, have had this paragraph in mind when he wrote that Gandhi 'is so severe upon himself that he simply goes ahead, and it is a question of either being with him, or not being able to be near him.'

In May 1913, the Immigration Bill passed its second reading. Gandhi wrote to MPs and the Minister of the Interior, asking that the £3 tax be withdrawn and the marriage question satisfactorily settled. The Minister answered that the tax would be removed for women but not for men, and that marriages would be recognized if they were registered. The concessions were meagre and, unsurprisingly, rejected, with Gandhi pointing out that Gokhale had been assured that the tax would be removed for men as well, and that virtually no Indian marriages were registered.[27]

The Bill passed through the Senate, and received Royal Assent on 14 June. Lord Gladstone complained to London of 'the truculent and minatory attitude of the Indian community generally, and of Mr Gandhi in particular'. He was confident the resistance would dissipate, telling the Colonial Office in London that 'attempt on the part of the Indians in this country to extort concessions by threats and charges of bad faith' was 'foredoomed to failure'.[28]

The breakdown of negotiations was reported to Gokhale by Henry Polak via a series of melancholy missives. In early June he wrote that 'the relations between the Government and the Indian community are almost as seriously strained as ever they have been.' In late June, after the passage of the Bill, he remarked, 'the betrayal has been complete.' Polak felt 'thoroughly ashamed to have to call myself an Englishman today'.[29]

Gokhale, who was then in London, wrote to the Government of India, warning that 'unless the compromise agreed to between the two sides is scrupulously carried out there is sure to be renewal of a bitter struggle.' He complained that 'the Union Government, under pressure from Boer Extremists, has again broken faith with the Indians.' If passive resistance broke out once more, Gokhale would return to India and move a resolution supporting it in the Imperial Council.[30]

Also making the case for Gandhi was his old English patron Lord Ampthill. Ampthill had been briefed by Maud Polak, who prepared for his scrutiny a 78-page document listing the handicaps under which Indians in South Africa still suffered. Speaking in the House of Lords, Ampthill launched a wide-ranging attack on the new Immigration Bill. It did not maintain existing rights of entry and re-entry; it did not recognize Hindu and Muslim marriages; it did not honour the South Africans ministers' promise to Gokhale that they would abolish the £3 tax.

Lord Ampthill recalled how, between 1907 and 1910, under the leadership of the 'devoted patriot' Gandhi, the Indians in South Africa 'were obliged to resort to passive resistance and to voluntarily undergo untold sacrifices'. 'My Lords', asked Ampthill of his fellow peers, 'how are you going to meet the untold scandal which will be created if there shall be a renewal of passive resistance?'[31]

In the third week of June 1913, Gandhi wrote to Gokhale that 'the Bill is so bad that passive resistance is a necessity. By the time this is in your hands, some of us may already be in gaol.' He listed the defects in the bill: namely, the persistence of the racial bar in the Orange Free State, the merely partial relief in the tax and marriage questions, the taking away of the right of Indians in other provinces to enter the Cape. He thought passive resistance might begin as early as July, with educated and uneducated Indians alike entering provinces and refusing to show any papers. 'So far as I can judge at present', he wrote, '100 men and 13 women will start the struggle. As time goes, we may have more.' Food and clothing would be collected by begging. 'If we all go to gaol, Kallenbach has undertaken to do the begging himself. He can be thoroughly relied upon to see that no family is starved so long as he has life in him.' He added: 'Some of my private burdens are being found by Dr. Mehta.' Gandhi expected the 'struggle ... to last a year but if we have more men than I anticipate, it may close during the next session of the Union Parliament. We are making provisions for an indefinite prolongation.'[32]

The imminent revival of passive resistance worried Gokhale's close friend William Wedderburn. A former member of the Indian Civil Service, Wedderburn had played a key role in starting the Indian National Congress. After serving two terms as Congress president, he had returned to England, where he became a Liberal Member of Parliament. Gokhale spent much time with Wedderburn on his visits to England, discussing imperial policies and India. When Gokhale arrived in London in May 1913, he was suffering from diabetes and its complications. His ears were painful and he could not sleep. The doctors had advised three months' rest. Wedderburn wrote to Gandhi that 'unfortunately the sad crisis in S. Africa ... has got upon his nerves.' Gokhale now planned to return to India in August, place the South African question before the Imperial Council, and raise money for the cause, but his friends felt that his health would not stand the strain of the sea journey – the Red Sea would be boiling in August – or the burden of organizing a campaign in India in the heat and humidity of September and October.

Given the 'vital importance to India of [Gokhale's] life and health', Gandhi was asked to request him to delay his journey. And perhaps the struggle itself could be postponed. 'My (private) suggestion', wrote Wedderburn to Gandhi,

> is that if passive resistance is resolved on, it should not commence before the end of the year, the interval being employed in negotiations, with an ultimatum that it will begin on the 1st of January. Passive resistance, including women and children, is a serious matter, and should not be undertaken hastily, nor until all means of compromise have been tried.[33]

Gandhi was sensible of the importance of Gokhale's health. He recognized the enormous suffering that a fresh bout of satyagraha would entail. And so he explored the last remaining avenues for a settlement. Having failed with the new Interior Minister, he tried his luck with General Smuts. Smuts was now Defence Minister, but had a long connection with Indian affairs, and with Gandhi himself. In the last week of June, Gandhi went down from Natal to Transvaal and sought an interview with the General. The changes that would satisfy them, he said, would be those permitting Indians born in South Africa to enter the Cape as before; allowing ex-indentures who had lived three years in Natal as free men to re-enter the province even if they had gone back to India;

legalizing all monogamous Indian marriages celebrated within the Union; and allowing in one wife of an Indian 'so long as she is the only one in South Africa, irrespective of the number of wives he might have in India'. He was waiting for the summons in Kallenbach's home in Johannesburg. 'If you require me at the telephone', Gandhi told the Minister, 'you have only to ring up 1635, and I shall be at the telephone from wherever I may be.'[34]

At the same time, Gandhi deputed Polak to London for a last-ditch effort to lobby the Imperial Government. Gokhale was already in the United Kingdom. They both – the one courteously, the other insistently – wrote to and met various officials of the Colonial and India Offices.[35] The South African Interior Minister, Abraham Fischer, was in London too, and met Gokhale. He said 'further legislation was out of the question'; however, he was prepared to see that the law would not be implemented harshly. Gokhale pointed out that 'Indian sentiment attached great importance' to the marriage question. The Minister answered that 'South Africa could not alter her marriage law'; Indians would have to register their marriages if they wished them to be legal.[36]

While in London, Henry Polak gave an interview to the *Jewish Chronicle*, in which he said Indians in South Africa had been 'fighting the Jewish fight'. For 'not a single argument that was advanced against Indians but had already been urged against Jews in one or other European country'. They were accused of unfair competition, of being an insanitary nuisance, of being strange, different, an inferior race. Out of an 'unworthy fear' of being classed with dark-skinned Indians, many Jews in South Africa had taken the British side. But some would not – Polak here singled out Ritch, Kallenbach and the Cape politician Morris Alexander. Honourable Jews everywhere had to stand with Gandhi and company, insisted Polak, for 'the Indian problem in South Africa is, at bottom, neither political nor economic. It is ethical, and I feel justified in asking for the hearty co-operation of our coreligionists in endeavouring to seek an ethical solution of it.'[37]

In early July, there was a major strike in the mines around Johannesburg, provoked by managers extracting extra work for the same pay. Militants went from mine to mine, asking men to stop work. Some 20,000 white workers laid down tools, and when the owners called in the police, turned violent. They burnt the offices of the *Star* newspaper, looted shops and attacked railway stations, pulling staff off trains. They then marched on the Rand Club, the watering-hole of the mine managers and owners. They were met by armed police; in the ensuing battle, a dozen miners died. They were buried the next day after a funeral procession in which more than 30,000 people participated.[38]

On the day of the Rand Club affray, Gandhi and Kallenbach were in downtown Johannesburg. The Indian wanted to help nurse the wounded, but his friend said they'd better stay out of the trouble. They then walked the five miles to Kallenbach's home in Mountain View. On the way, Gandhi 'proposed that we should in the face of so much suffering, which we had just witnessed, have only one meal [a day]'. Kallenbach dissuaded him, saying that they should stick to the diet that was the norm at Phoenix. That was austere enough: two scant meals with no rice, no bread, no salt, no spices and no sweets.[39]

As Defence Minister, General Smuts was in the thick of the battle between the Government and the miners. Gandhi recognized this, but still pressed his case for an appointment. 'It is cruel to worry General Smuts whilst his attention is engrossed in the all-important strike matter', he wrote to the Minister's secretary on 11 July. 'But politics are a cruel game, and I am afraid I must be a party to it so long as I must to obtain all I want through that channel, rather than Passive Resistance.' He still hoped for a compromise which would satisfy the concerns of the Government as well as the honour and prestige of the Indians.[40]

Smuts's secretary wired back to say that owing to the crisis caused by the miners' strike he had no time to go into the settlement proposed by Gandhi. As it turned out, Gandhi's own attentions now emphatically turned from the political to the personal. On 12 July – the day after he wrote to Smuts – a letter arrived from Phoenix which has not survived, but whose explosive contents are hinted at in Kallenbach's diary:

> Rose at 6.45 a.m. Got letter from Manilal with enclosed for Mr G[andhi] in which he makes serious confession. Mr G. came to my office and [I] broke the news to him and gave him the letter. He felt it most keenly. We both wired to Manilal. I decided to accompany Mr Gandhi to Phoenix.[41]

Manilal's 'confession' was with regard to his affair with a girl at Phoenix. But this was no ordinary girl; she was Jeki, daughter of Pranjivan Mehta. In any event, his son's violation of *brahmacharya* before marriage would have angered Gandhi; that he had done so with the married daughter of his closest friend and oldest patron made the transgression even harder to forgive.

The only traces of this incident in Gandhi's *Collected Works* are a brief reference in the *Autobiography* to 'the moral fall of two of the inmates of the ashram'. The fallen folk are not named, nor is their sin specified.[42] The details of the incident have however been painstakingly pieced together by Manilal's biographer, Uma Meshtrie.[43] There is also an account in the memoir of Millie Polak, who was a witness, if not to the actual event, to its painful aftermath. Millie does not refer to the couple by name: Jeki is called 'Lila' and Manilal referred to, equally misleadingly, as 'N.', and without his relationship to Gandhi being mentioned. Since Jeki was both married and older than Manilal, Millie thought it was 'a case of deliberate seduction on her part'.[44]

This may have been unfair. Phoenix was unusual in that it brought under one roof boys and girls who were not related together. This would not have happened in an Indian home in Gujarat (or Durban, or Johannesburg). Although Gandhi does not seem to have realized it, the risk of sexual attraction was inherent in this experiment in communal living. Manilal had seen, at first hand, the loving and even passionate relationship between his brother Harilal and his wife Chanchal. At the age of twenty it was entirely natural that he would be open to such a relationship himself. At Phoenix, he and Jeki were thrown together in the house, in the fields, in the school, on trips to the city.

On Jeki's side, she had stayed on at Phoenix to be mentored by her father's friend. Living apart from her husband Manilal Doctor (who was now back in Mauritius), she probably welcomed the attentions and company of Gandhi's son Manilal. That they developed a mutual attraction does not, in retrospect, appear to be so surprising or shocking. In fact, from an essay written by Manilal forty years later – by which time he was a father of grown-up children himself – it appears that Gandhi had for some time harboured suspicions about his son's feelings for Jeki. In this recollection, Manilal wrote cryptically that

> I must confess to my utter shame that I was the cause of father having to undergo a fast for seven days in 1912 [*sic*]. I had tried to deceive him. He wanted an admission from me but I persisted in denying until at last I received a letter from him which was signed 'Blessings from your father in Agony'. I could no longer bear it. I wanted to confess but I had not the

courage to approach him direct. I, therefore, enclosed the letter in a letter to Mr Kallenbach who was to us like a member of a family. I asked father to forgive me in the letter. I received a telegram from him: 'I forgive you. Ask God to forgive you.'[45]

On receiving Manilal's letter (via Kallenbach) Gandhi rushed back to Phoenix. He spoke to the boys in the settlement, who – to shield their comrades – told first one story, then another. After evening prayers, Gandhi told the gathering that he was upset with them for 'keeping the truth from me'. From Manilal, Gandhi 'extracted a solemn vow that he should not marry for some years and that he would live a strictly celibate life, until such time as he, Mr Gandhi, should release him from his vow'. Jeki, apparently of her own volition, chose to repent by cutting her beautiful long hair, dressing in white (traditionally widow's garb) and taking to a saltless diet.[46]

For several years now, Gandhi had sensed that his eldest son, Harilal, was taking a path somewhat different to that marked out for him by his father. Disenchanted with one son, Gandhi had pinned his hopes on the others. He had great expectations of Manilal especially, training him to be a *brahmachari*, to work with his hands, to turn his back on the rewards and comforts of a conventional career. His exhortations had had, it now appeared, limited effect. Although Manilal worked hard on the farm and at the press, although he had come forward to court arrest, he had failed the true and ultimate test by succumbing to 'basal' passions and having an affair with Jeki.

Manilal's transgression was in some ways even harder to take than his brother's rebellion. Gandhi's response was to fast for a whole week; after it ended, he would have only one meal a day for a year. That latter vow he had wanted to take after witnessing the violence against the miners; dissuaded by Kallenbach, he now took it as a mark of his pain at being let down by his son and his ward, and also as atonement for what he felt was his inadequate and incomplete supervision.

Against this backdrop of political turmoil and personal strife, the series on health published by Gandhi in *Indian Opinion* continued serenely on. Later parts dealt with water treatments and earth cures, with fruits that could cure constipation and with 'the husband's duty not to agitate the wife by starting quarrels with her' during pregnancy. The thirty-fourth instalment carried the definitive title 'Conclusion'. Gandhi once more clarified that he was not a trained doctor; yet, he thought, he had written this guide 'from a worthy motive. The intention is not to recommend what medicines to take after the onset of a disease. The more immediate purpose, rather, has been to show how sickness may be averted.'[47]

Even as he wrote this, Gandhi was augmenting his already considerable experience of nature cures and naturopathy. Living at Phoenix was a young Gujarati who suffered from acute rheumatism, to control which he took 'large doses of oral medication'. Gandhi took him off the tablets and put him on a diet of fruit and tomatoes. The patient was given a series of steam-baths, one every other day. He sat, covered with blankets, on a chair beneath which was a pot of boiling water. When the water had boiled over, his sweating body was wiped clean. After several weeks of this treatment, recalled Gandhi's young patient, 'the pain got reduced but became mobile and began circulating in my system – one day in the knees, the other day in the wrists, and the next day either the back or the finger joints would be stiff.' With the pain having 'lessened comparatively', he could now participate in the activities of the ashram.[48]

The last two instalments of the series on health had appeared in the same issue of *Indian Opinion*: that dated 16 August 1913. Gandhi wrote that if he got time later, he would tell readers of the 'qualities and uses of a number of simple materials'.[49] For now, the author, and his periodical, would have to focus on other, though not necessarily more important questions. A fresh satyagraha loomed, and the leader had to prepare for it.

Among the letters of solidarity received by Gandhi at this time, the most curious (and perhaps also the most charming) came from John Cordes, his somewhat errant disciple who was still in thrall to Theosophy. Cordes had recently been in India, where he met both Annie Besant and the boy she had chosen as the Representative of God on Earth, Jiddu Krishnamurti. 'I have not met your equal regarding outward virtues', wrote Cordes to Gandhi. 'You are a mystic. But in neatness J. Krishnamurti surpasses you.'[50] From India, Cordes proceeded to Vienna, to see his mother. He now hoped Gandhi would 'find money to carry on [your] next campaign'. The Theosophist had been 'mentally arguing with friend Smuts imagining myself in possession of £100,000 which I tendered him as bribe to try to be honest for once but he said it was foreign to his nature and quite impossible, so I handed this fund to you for P[assive] R[esistance].'[51]

In the middle of August, the Baptist minister Joseph Doke died. Gandhi wrote tributes to him in both English and Gujarati, and also travelled to Johannesburg to speak at a memorial service. The minister was 'a great and altruistic man' with no trace of class or colour prejudice, in whose house 'every Indian, whether rich or poor, was given the same consideration'. Gandhi remembered Doke's efforts to convert him to his faith. The Indian had answered that the 'fullness of Christianity could only be found in its interpretation of the light and by the aid of Hinduism. But Mr Doke was not satisfied. He missed no occasion to bring home to him (the speaker) the truth as he (Mr Doke) knew it and which brought him and his so much inward peace.'[52]

The memorial service for Joseph Doke was held in Johannesburg's Baptist Church on 24 August. Two weeks later, Gandhi informed the Government that due to the continuance of the £3 tax, the racial bar in the Immigration Law, and the uncertain status of their married women, the Indians had 'most reluctantly and with the utmost regret decided to revive passive resistance'.[53] They had waited long enough in any case.

20

Breaking Boundaries

In 1913, it was twenty years since Mohandas Gandhi had first come out to South Africa. In that time the Indian community had become larger and more varied in its composition. The population in Natal had tripled, from just over 40,000 in the early 1890s to about 135,000 now. A large number were indentured labourers, working in sugar plantations and coal mines. In the year 1911 the import of labour was stopped; well before that, Indians had moved out of the fields into other trades and professions. They were a visible component of the population of Natal, present in the tens of thousands in the main city, Durban, streets and sections of which were dominated by them. Indian families were also scattered through the countryside, working as farmers and traders in the towns and villages of the province.

There were roughly 10,000 Indians in the Transvaal. These included some prosperous merchants, a larger number of petty traders and hawkers, and a significant sector of clerks, hotel workers and other members of the salariat. The Cape had about 6,500 Indians, among them some successful traders and professionals. There were, according to the 1911 census, a mere 106 Indians in the Orange Free State. Of the main provinces of South Africa, only the Free State had no real 'Indian problem' at all.[1]

A key difference from the time of Gandhi's first arrival was that many more Indians were now born and raised in South Africa. There was even a 'Colonial-Born' Indian Association in Natal. This was their home and, increasingly, their homeland. Their connections to the Indian subcontinent now were more sentimental than substantial. It was in South Africa that they would raise families and make their future. Younger Indians especially were keen to move out of the working class into more secure and highly regarded professions such as medicine, the law and government service.

Despite his own extended stay in South Africa, Gandhi still considered himself Indian. Yet he recognized the profound change in the orientation of the community he worked with. He would return to India, but the others would stay on, to live and labour under a government – and ruling race – that was often strongly prejudiced against their interests. This is why Gandhi was so keen to arrive at a settlement with General Smuts, whereby the rights to work and residence of Indians in all provinces of the Union were safeguarded, existing policies that bore down unfairly on them (such as the £3 tax in Natal) removed, and proposed policies that threatened the integrity of the community (such as the marriage restrictions implied by the Searle judgement) withdrawn.

Ever the incrementalist, Gandhi had appealed to Smuts and his colleagues to have these changes in the laws made. Through 1912 and much of 1913 he had written hundreds of letters, printed dozens of appeals, sought audiences with Smuts and lobbied MPs. By September 1913, this series of preliminary steps had got nowhere. With the government still disinclined to concede their claims, the Indians now prepared, under Gandhi's leadership, to use their final recourse and reserve weapon, that of satyagraha.

On Monday, 15 September 1913, a party of sixteen Indians left the settlement at Phoenix to illegally enter the Transvaal. Such transgressions of provincial boundaries had been commonly practised during past satyagrahas. What was novel, this time, was that some of the protesters were women. They were breaking a boundary far more rigid or sacrosanct than that dividing one province of South Africa from another.

While in London in 1906 and 1909, Gandhi had seen the suffragettes at work – and admired them. Their courage and suffering, he thought, could inspire Indians facing discrimination in South Africa. Apart from the suffragettes, Gandhi had also been influenced by his friendship with Millie Polak. Millie believed that 'all the questions relating to life really belong to women'. She argued that for 'thousands of years, men have used women and the greatest beauties in their nature rather to their detriment than her glory'. She insisted that 'only when the finer forces of life are realised can woman come into her own.'[2]

In India itself, the idea that women could participate in popular social movements was out of the question. Middle-class women, whether Hindu or Muslim, were not expected to mix socially with members of the other sex. The only men they spoke to were family members, or servants, or itinerant traders who came knocking at their door. They were not supposed to leave the house unescorted.

The Swadeshi movement in Bengal and Maharashtra had been an all-male affair. The terrorists who assassinated British officials were all men. By the 1910s, a sprinkling of upper-class women had begun attending the meetings of the Indian National Congress. But none had gone to jail. The possibility did not, could not, enter their heads – not least because it would have appalled their husbands. However much they disliked colonial rule, Indian patriots (both Hindu and Muslim) saw struggle and sacrifice in exclusively male terms. The most progressive nationalist in India, *c.* 1913, could scarcely have countenanced his wife being fed and ordered about by male jailors not of her kin or caste.

In this respect, the Tamil women in the diaspora were ahead of their sisters at home. In the summer of 1909, the wives of satyagrahis in prison held a meeting in a temple in Germiston, which passed the following resolution: 'As our religion teaches us that a wife may not be separated from her husband, we pray the Government to send us to gaol with our husbands, and to confiscate our property, if that be justice.' The resolution was moved by one Thayee Ammall, and seconded by a Mrs Marriam and a Mrs Chengalaraya Moodaley.[3]

The Tamil ladies were dissuaded from courting arrest. Four years later, with the struggle reaching its climax, Gandhi's wife, Kasturba, offered to go to jail. This was a spontaneous reaction, an outraged response to a judge and a judgement that called into question the validity of her own marriage. That Gandhi agreed to let his wife court imprisonment may have been a result of his encounters with suffragettes in England and Tamil women in Transvaal. There was also the example of African women in the Orange Free State, who had recently turned in their passes to the authorities, pledging never to carry them again.[4]

As for Kasturba, without diminishing in any way the radical and unprecedented nature of her gesture, perhaps she had been prepared for it by the years spent living in proximity to that energetic feminist Millie Polak.

Three days before the first batch of satyagrahis were to leave Phoenix, Gandhi wrote to Kallenbach asking him to come down from Johannesburg to the Transvaal border to meet them. 'I shall send the resisters from here on Monday', wrote Gandhi:

> They will reach Volksrust on Tuesday. You should leave Monday night by the mail train so that you are at the station when the Kaffir Mail reaches Volksrust on Tuesday evening. You should simply watch as a spectator. They are not to speak in English. One of them only will speak in that tongue, interpret for the others. They will not give finger-prints. If the police arrest them, they must ask for shelter at the police station. If the police do not arrest them, you should, there and then, buy tickets for them and proceed to Johannesburg. I then suggest their being housed at Mountain View . . . No more than Boer meal and a little *dholl* and rice will be required and fruits and nuts of course. If they are arrested, you should attend court, send full wire to me from Volksrust as also full letter. If they are imprisoned you should immediately see the gaol doctor and the jailor and tell them of religious and health foods they may take and not take. But you should also say that they will not complain if they do not get what they want. Mrs. Gandhi will be purely fruitarian. Jeki and others will not touch bread. Some of them will be able to take only one meal. The names and further details later. It is well that you will be free from your business even if passive resistance is to start. Your whole time will be wanted for the struggle.[5]

This is a striking letter, demonstrating that Gandhi was at once a theorist and moralist of non-violent resistance, and its strategist and tactician too. Essays in *Indian Opinion* from 1907 onwards had outlined the philosophy and relevance of satyagraha – within South Africa, and to the world. Now, as a fresh satyagraha was about to commence, Gandhi was providing detailed instructions to each of its main participants and patrons.

The first batch of resisters left Phoenix Farm on 15 September. Work in the fields, the press and the school was suspended for the day. The children helped the women pack their bags and carry them to the station. Before they left the settlement, the satyagrahis gathered for one last meeting, where Gandhi told the departing mothers that their children were safe in the hands of God. Some hymns were sung, but (as a boy staying back recalled) 'nobody's voice was clear. Everyone was overwhelmed.'[6]

Gandhi wrote to Manilal – who was in Johannesburg – that 'Ba and others boarded the train with great courage on Monday.' The 'others' included their son Ramdas, Parsee Rustomjee, Jeki Mehta, and the wives of Chhaganlal and Maganlal (named Kashi and Santok respectively), the last two offering to go out of solidarity with their aunt. The party – numbering sixteen in all, four women and twelve men – crossed the border, and were detained at Volksrust. Kasturba and company were tried on 23 September, and pleaded guilty to the charge of violating the immigration acts. They refused to offer further testimony, and waived their right to ask questions of the prosecutor or judge. A reporter noted that 'the case created great commotion among the local [Indian] community, most of whom were present in court.'[7]

The satyagrahis were all sentenced to three months in prison. They were at first taken to a jail at Volksrust, and later shifted to Maritzburg. The women were housed in the same cell as African women convicts; the boys put to work in the prison orchards.[8]

Gandhi, meanwhile, wrote two strong, stirring articles in *Indian Opinion*. The first called for Indians in every town to join the fight and court arrest. The second said that removing the £3 'blood tax' was 'the central point of this struggle'. Recalling the promise made by the leading whites to Gokhale, he said the removal of the tax 'is a simple, primary duty every Indian in South Africa owes to his country, to Mr Gokhale and to the poor men who are the victims of gold hunger'.[9]

This, too – the foregrounding of the poorest Indians in South Africa – was a departure. Indentured labourers had been among Gandhi's clients, and he had campaigned for better working conditions for them. However, in past satyagrahas in Transvaal, hawkers, merchants and professionals had been in the vanguard. Now, the 'central point' was the abolition of a discriminatory tax that hit the poor most.

On the morning of 25 September, Gandhi left Phoenix for the Transvaal. His hope was that he would be arrested and follow Kasturba into jail. He was under great stress, as a growing number of Indians in Natal now resented his leadership. During the last struggle, he had found it increasingly hard to get volunteers from the merchant class. Now, as the struggle recommenced, Gandhi was confronted with questions to which the answers seemed unclear. How would the satyagraha turn out? How readily would the Indians in either province court arrest? His nerves were on edge. On the 25th, in a hurry to catch the train, he lost his temper with the children at Phoenix while eating breakfast. Later, from his carriage, he wrote Maganlal an abashed, apologetic letter that revealed 'the awful state' he was in. As he 'ran for the train', remembered Gandhi,

> I gave no end of trouble to the boys. Everyone was delayed because of me ... Thinking of this, I felt extremely miserable. Even those of my actions which I believed to be for a spiritual purpose have a big flaw in them ... It is never the mark of a spiritual aspirant to be in too great a hurry and make himself a nuisance to others. He may, of course, not overtax himself – ought not to. What an ignoble state to be in! All this is the consequence of initial mistakes. I also realized that if I had skipped the meal, I could have worked with an unruffled mind, with plenty of time on hand, and would have been no trouble to any of you ... I felt ashamed within myself even as I was on the way. I reproached myself. I, who used to believe that I had perhaps something in me, find myself today in a humiliating state. I tell you all this because you attribute so many excellences to me. You should see the faults in me in order that you may save yourself from like faults. Plunged as I have been in the affairs of South Africa, I think I can be entirely free only in India. But please warn me whenever I take upon myself too heavy a burden. You will be with me, no doubt, even in India. If I am imprisoned, it will be all peace and nothing but peace for me. If not, I may return there [to India]. But please warn me if ever in future, even in South Africa, you find today's story being repeated. We could have done without bread for Mr Kallenbach and without groundnut jam for me. We need not have been particular about feeding the children. Or rather, we might have pleased ourselves in all these ways and yet things would have been all right if I had not insisted on having my meal. But I would ride all the horses and that is why God ordained my fall. Surely, this is not the first occasion when such a thing has happened to me. This time, however, the lesson has been brought home to me. I will now change myself a little.[10]

The self-scrutiny, the self-criticism, was in character. The key phrase perhaps is 'I would ride *all* the horses'. Seeking simultaneously to be a conscientious (by his lights) teacher, father, editor, opponent of racial injustice (whether suffered by hawkers, merchants, professionals or labourers) and multi-purpose reformer (of diet, health, sexual attitudes, relations between religions), Gandhi would, from time to time, find the obligations of one calling competing with the demands of another, the clash leading to a loss of temper or loss of direction, this then recognized and, if possible, rectified.

Gandhi crossed into Transvaal without being detained. He proceeded to Johannesburg, where he addressed two meetings on 28 September, speaking once to an audience of men, the other time to women who had decided to court arrest.[11] Two days later, the *Transvaal Leader* wrote that 'the Indian passive resistance movement is threatened with collapse.' The story's headlines ran: 'No Money for Martyrs / Passive Resisters in a Pickle / Indian Merchants against the Campaign / Support Very Scanty'.

The newspaper claimed that while Gandhi and his colleague A. M. Cachalia – chairman of the British Indian Association – were 'proclaiming the opening of hostilities, and urging their compatriots to fill the gaols, there are growls and curses from the rank and file, open defiance, and frank avowals of contentment with the present order of things'. Last time, there were more than 3,000 convictions; but 'on this occasion', it was being said that 'Mr Gandhi himself does not expect that more than 150 persons will go to prison in the cause.' Even this was thought to be an over-estimate, since 'a leading Indian merchant' interviewed by the paper thought that at most fifty people in Johannesburg would 'risk their liberty'. That the arrests so far had been of people from Natal showed, to the newspaper, that 'whatever measure of success Mr Gandhi achieves amongst the poorer and more ignorant of his countrymen, the wealthy Indian traders [of the Transvaal] . . . are making no secret of their antagonism to the passive resistance campaign.'[12]

The same day, Gandhi wrote to the *Transvaal Leader* disputing this story. The meeting of 28 September had, he pointed out, been attended by many merchants. He called the paper's claim that passive resisters were 'demand[ing] payment for their penance' an 'atrocious libel, and a cruel wrong to the men and women who have suffered during the last campaign, and who will suffer now'.[13]

The protests continued. On 1 October, Manilal Gandhi was detained in Johannesburg for hawking without a licence. Like the other resisters, he chose to go to jail rather than pay a fine.[14] Two of the Gandhi boys were now in prison; perhaps the eldest, an experienced jailbird, could be summoned to join them. Gandhi thus wrote to Harilal saying 'both of you may come over here [from India] and get arrested. Chanchi may come while the fight is on only if she has the courage to go to gaol.'[15]

In the second week of October, General Smuts – who had now resumed charge of the Interior Ministry – spoke to the Governor-General's secretary about the developing situation. Smuts said 'Gandhi was suffering from one of his periodic attacks of mental derangement, and was, for the time being, attracted by the role of prophet and martyr.' The General 'doubted whether there was much real enthusiasm or financial support behind it [the passive resistance movement], and he rather expected that it would soon collapse.' Asked about specific grievances he said, with regard to the marriage question, that it was impossible to give 'legal recognition to a polygamous system'. He was personally opposed to the £3 tax and was keen to repeal it, 'but the narrow-minded folly of the [white] Natalians had been, and still was, an insuperable obstacle'. The planters wanted the tax as a means to get the workers to re-indenture; the non-planters wanted it to induce them to return to India.[16]

On 12 October, the first Muslim woman joined the satyagraha movement. This was the wife of Gandhi's old classmate Sheikh Mehtab. Mrs Mehtab left Durban with her mother, son and servant, aiming to cross the border and court arrest. She was seen off at the station by a large crowd, who presented her with bouquets and parcels of food for the journey.[17]

The same day, Gandhi journeyed in the reverse direction, from the Transvaal to Natal. At a meeting in Durban's Union Theatre, he was asked why Henry Polak had recently been sent to England. Did the Indians need to have 'paid European workers'? Gandhi answered that Polak had been deputed at Gokhale's request.[18]

Gandhi now left for the coal-mining town of Newcastle. A meeting held here on the evening of the 13th ended 'with cheers to the brave son of India, Mr M. K. Gandhi'. Thambi Naidoo also spoke, in Tamil, after which the mineworkers endorsed both Gandhi and passive resistance; they were particularly exercised by the £3 tax.[19]

Gandhi returned to Durban, where there had recently been sharp criticism of his methods. He had spent much of the past decade in the Transvaal; in his absence, other leaders had emerged, who did not always endorse his views. In July 1913, Gandhi's old adversary P. S. Aiyar had claimed that passive resistance had outlived its usefulness. Instead of fighting for their rights in South Africa, said Aiyar, the Indians should depart *en masse* for the motherland. The South African Government should be made to buy their properties at market price, and pay for their passage back to India.[20]

Now, in October, at a well-attended meeting of the Natal Indian Congress, Gandhi was attacked for his 'provocative and inefficient leadership'. A Gujarati merchant named M. C. Anglia said that Gandhi's methods had not made their position more secure or elevated their standing among the whites. Why should they support him now? So long as the Indians 'have a professional and political agitator at the head of political affairs', said Anglia, 'we are doomed to failure with the Government and the European public of South Africa.'[21] Some people rose to defend Gandhi, and since 'passions were rising on either side' the chairman closed the meeting, upon which his supporters 'carried Mr Gandhi shoulder high through the Victoria, Albert, Queen and Field Streets'.[22]

In the days after the contentious meeting, Gandhi's leadership was endorsed by the Hindustani Association of Durban and by a group of Muslim merchants.[23] Among his newer admirers were the workers in mines and plantations, whose endorsement turned out to be definitive. By now, some 2,000 Indians working in the Natal collieries were on strike. The districts of Dundee and Newcastle were said to be 'in a feverish state of excitement'. The striking miners assembled in the grounds of Dundee's Hindu Temple, where they 'expressed confidence in the leadership of Mr Gandhi'. They had been mobilized by eleven Tamil-speaking women, among them Mrs Thambi Naidoo. As Gandhi admiringly noted, 'the presence of these brave women who had never suffered hardship and had never spoken at public meetings acted like electricity, and the men left their work'.[24] For speaking at these meetings and urging the workers to strike, Mrs Thambi Naidoo and her colleagues were sentenced to three months in prison with hard labour.[25]

In the second and third weeks of October, Gandhi addressed crowds of striking workers in Durban, Newcastle, Hatting Spruit and other towns in Natal. Contemporary photographs show people listening to him in all variety of dress, Indian and Western, and in all manner of headgear – caps, hats, *topis* and turbans. The gatherings were large and densely packed, with several thousand Indians come to support their leader.[26]

On 24 October, Gandhi wrote to Maganlal that 'great things are happening in Newcastle. There is a move to lead a march of 2,000 men to Transvaal.' The next day he told mine and plantation owners that their workers were on strike because of the Government's failure to honour their promise to Gokhale to abolish the £3 tax.[27] A Tamil poster circulated in the plantations quoted Gandhi as saying: 'I have no grievances against the employers . . . I ask [them] to assist in getting the tax repealed. I am quite aware of the loss and hardship my unfortunate brethren have to suffer, and I trust even if you have to beg you would not return to work until the tax is repealed.'[28]

Reading these reports in Pretoria, General Smuts was provoked to deny them. In a speech on the 26th, he said the £3 tax was part of the contract signed by labourers in India before coming out to Natal. The Government had not promised Gokhale that the tax would be repealed; merely that they would consider the question afresh. Smuts wired the mineowners' association that to repeal the tax now, under the pressure of Gandhi and company, 'would be [a] public disaster'. He claimed that 'with Gandhi repeal of tax is an afterthought, and is intended to influence Natal Indians to whom the real grounds on which he has started passive resistance and which never included this tax, do not appeal.'[29]

The evidence on this question supports Gandhi rather than Smuts. Gokhale was clearly given the impression the tax would be repealed; for that is what he told the Governor-General on 15 November 1912, immediately after he had met the Prime Minister, Louis Botha. In March 1913, when the South African Immigration Bill came up for debate, Gokhale again told a senior official of the Government of India that 'Ministers have promised him, and quite publicly, that the Natal £3 licence tax will be revoked.'[30]

The repeal of the tax was manifestly one of the 'real grounds' on which the current satyagraha was begun. Truth was on Gandhi's side, and so, as it happens, were the workers. A news report dated Wednesday, 29 October, tells this part of the story: 'The [coal-mine] managers assembled the Indians on the mines this morning, but the Indians declined to listen, insulting the managers, and intimating that they were only prepared to receive instructions and advice from Mr Gandhi.'

Back in July 1913, the Durban journalist P. S. Aiyar had written off passive resistance as a method of assering one's rights. Two months later the first batch of satyagrahis, led by Kasturba Gandhi, courted arrest. Hundreds more followed them into jail. The Indian workers in the coal mines and sugar plantations downed tools. The editor of the *African Chronicle* was now obliged to do his professional duty, which was to report the news. The bravery of Kasturba's pioneering band of resisters was praised. Two pages of the journal were devoted to the 'Progress of Passive Resistance', reporting arrests, speeches and strikes in different parts of Natal. But the editor could not suppress his prejudices entirely, calling upon the Indians to 'keep in view the cause, not the man' (namely, Gandhi).

In challenging Gandhi's claims to lead the Indians, P. S. Aiyar was always fighting an uphill battle. The surge of support for the satyagraha now made his a pretty hopeless task. A report in his own newspaper conveyed the comprehensiveness of his defeat. In November 1913 the *Chronicle* was compelled to reduce its pages from sixteen to eight, noting that 'the compositors, employed in our office, having joined the ranks of the strikers, we regret, we are unable to publish our paper in its usual form.'[31]

The Indians on strike moved out of the collieries and plantations to the towns of Dundee and Newcastle, so that they could not be coerced back to work. When agents of the owners reached these towns nevertheless, it was decided to shift the striking workers to Charlestown, thirty-five miles away, closer to the border with the Transvaal. 'To provide railway fare for thousands was out of the question', so they walked, with Gandhi leading the first batch. The workers shouted '*Vande Matram!*' and '*Ramchandra ki jai!*', the first slogan a salute to the motherland, the second a homage to the mythical just and good king, Ram. They carried their own rice and *dal*. The marchers slept the first night in the open, reaching Charlestown the next day. But keeping so many people close together was deemed a risk – what if plague broke out?[32]

Gandhi liked walking. In the 1880s, he walked the streets of London in the company of his vegetarian comrade Josiah Oldfield. In the 1890s, he walked to the Bombay High Court from his home in Santa Cruz. In the 1900s, he walked a lot with Kallenbach in Johannesburg. He liked walking so much that when Henry Polak wrote a profile of his friend, he placed him not in the law court or his office, not in the Phoenix or

Tolstoy settlements, not even in a vegetarian restaurant, but on the road. 'Here he is', wrote Polak of Gandhi,

> a slim-built man of middle height, the tanned cheeks a little sunken, bare-headed, somewhat close-cropped and grizzled, with a small moustache. You see him walking along the road in profound meditation or animatedly conversing with a companion, the shoulders bent, the head thrown slightly forward, his arms behind his back, the left wrist grasped in the right hand, the sandaled feet outspread – a not too gainly walk, rather rapid, for he is an accomplished pedestrian from long practice, preference, and force of circumstance.[33]

Gandhi liked walking, but this was a very long march, even by his standards. For the satyagrahis under his command had now decided to walk on to the Transvaal. If not detained at the border, they would proceed onwards, all the way to Johannesburg, several hundred miles into the interior. A rich Hindu offered a 600-acre farm to host them; to this was added the 1,100 acres of Tolstoy Farm. Kallenbach was excited by the prospect. 'We will have "common" tables and ordinary family life will not exist for the time being', the architect told a reporter. 'This system was properly tested during the last campaign, and it can be carried on indefinitely . . . Passive Resistance does not mean idleness. There will be no lack of funds. Merchants everywhere are giving freely, and Professor Gokhale is with us heart and soul.'

Proof of the last statement was provided in an accompanying report, which quoted Gokhale in Bombay as saying that the Indian public would send £2,000 a month for the next six months to sustain the passive resisters.[34]

On 29 October, a large public meeting was held at Johannesburg's West End Bioscope Hall, to coincide with the Hindu festival of Dasehra. The Indians turned out in force, as did their European sympathizers, W. Hosken, L. W. Ritch, Sonja Schlesin, *et al.* The Gujarati S. K. Patel, in the chair, said this Dasehra day, which should be 'one of rejoicing and festivity', had instead been turned by the Government into one 'of sadness and mourning'. He was followed by L. W. Ritch, whose message was more hopeful. The resisters, said Ritch, should be congratulated for 'using the weapons of the soul and not the weapons of the mob' (these being the 'bludgeon and the bomb').

The audience was then asked to stand as a mark of respect for the women resisters. A photograph of the Johannesburg ladies in jail (Mrs Thambi Naidoo and company) was flashed on the screen. Collections were then called for,

> and a scene of great enthusiasm followed. Rings, pocket-knives, caps, watches, etc., were offered up by their owners, and were put up for auction, fetching extraordinary prices. An umbrella was sold for five guineas, a ring for seventeen guineas, pocket knives for 10s. 6d., a bottle of sweets for £1 10s. A large amount was contributed both in cash and provisions. On the termination of the proceedings, those present formed in procession and quietly marched along Fox and Commissioner Streets, then up Rissik Street and through Pritchard Street to the house of the Chairman [of the British Indian Association] in Diagonal Street. The procession was preceded by two men carrying black flags and all wore rosettes to mark the present sufferings of the community.[35]

The same day, Gandhi set out for the Transvaal border with some 200 men, women and children.[36] Other batches followed. 'We may any hour get the news of G[andhi]'s arrest', wired Polak to Gokhale on the 30th.[37]

By 3 November, 1,500 passive resisters had reached Charlestown. 'All were in sole charge of Mr Gandhi', reported the *Natal Mercury*. The marchers were fed in the grounds of the local mosque, with the food provided, for free, by local merchants. Also in attendance was Sonja Schlesin, who had come down especially from Johannesburg to look after the women in the gathering.[38]

A journalist from the *Natal Advertiser*, visiting Charlestown on 5 November, reported that 'the whole appearance of the town resembled nothing but an Indian bazaar.' He found Gandhi 'at the back of an Indian store, in the yard, serving out curry and rice to his followers, who marched up, and each man received his quota. One baker sold 500 loaves to the Indians in one day.'[39]

On the morning of the 6th, the resisters left Charlestown, walking towards Volksrust, the town just the other side of the border. They halted there for refreshments, and then proceeded deeper into the Transvaal. Till they reached the border, Gandhi was at the rear, but once they entered Volksrust he led from the front. He told a reporter that they would march to their final destination, Tolstoy Farm, in eight stages, covering twenty-four miles every day.[40]

On Monday the 3rd, while the marchers were camped in Charlestown, the Governor-General summoned General Smuts for a meeting. Smuts said he intended, for the moment, to adopt a policy of *laissez-faire*. He thought 'Mr Gandhi appeared to be in a position of much difficulty. Like Frankenstein, he found his monster an uncomfortable creation, and he would be glad to be relieved of further responsibility for its support.' If the Government arrested Gandhi, argued Smuts, then 'he would be able to disclaim responsibility for the maintenance of his array of strikers.' The longer the march continued, the more difficult it would be to feed them, at which point the strikers would themselves 'ask to be sent back to their work in Natal'.[41]

The police, however, were pressing Smuts to arrest Gandhi. They were worried about the adverse publicity, and perhaps also that the marchers might turn violent. On the evening of the 6th, when the march had reached the town of Palmford, Gandhi was taken into custody. The next morning, he appeared in court in Volksrust and was charged with breaching the law regarding the movement of people across provinces. Gandhi appealed for bail, which 'was strongly opposed by the Public Prosecutor'. The judge, however, granted the application, asking for a deposit of £50, a sum 'promptly found by the local Indian merchants'.[42]

Kallenbach had attended the court proceedings at Volksrust. No sooner was Gandhi granted bail than the two of them jumped into a car to rejoin the marchers. A reporter climbed in too, and they drove 'through beautiful grassy country'. They caught up with their fellows some thirty miles from Volksrust. 'All along the road,' noted the accompanying journalist, 'the car passed stragglers, who lined up and saluted Mr Gandhi, calling him "Bapoo", or father.'[43]

On 7 November, with their leader back to lead them, the strikers continued on their journey. That night they camped at Krorndraai, by the river. The next morning they carried on towards Vaal. At Standerton they were stopped, and Gandhi was detained once more. He was taken to court, where he was released on bail and returned to the march.[44] His antagonist Montford Chamney then came down from Johannesburg to stop Gandhi, accompanied by a posse of police. For General Smuts had finally come round to the view that the Indians who had illegally entered the Transvaal must be sent back across the border.

Chamney and his companions met the Indians west of Standerton. Years later, he recalled his first sight of the march and the marchers, the memory made more colourful by the passage of time:

> Three determined men marching abreast with single purpose at steady, rhythmic pace, Ghandi, Polak, and another, followed closely by a great company that stretched far back like a moving ribbon until lost beyond the next rise of the ground. Many of these wore the gay colours of the East, a few were clad in cheap European garb while others had little beyond the Oriental loin-cloth and mantle. Ready-made boots had been supplied to the poorer classes, but this unfamiliar form of Western footgear only proved an impediment that was soon removed, the owners carrying the boots strung by the laces from their necks. But every class of marcher seemed to carry something – a babe, a basket or perhaps a few household chattels.[45]

The police halted the column, and a warrant for Gandhi's arrest was executed. He was taken to the town of Dundee, where he was charged with inducing the strike and inciting the strikers. This time his request for bail was rejected and he was sent off to prison. From there he wrote a remarkable letter to the magistrate, which, among other things, gives the lie to Smuts's charge that Gandhi was keen to wash his hands of the strikers:

> Sir,
>
> I have the honour to request you to lay before the Government by telegram the following facts:
>
> Whilst I was marching from Charlestown with nearly 2,000 men women and children to Tolstoy Farm Lawley, nearly 150 men women and children were footsore and otherwise disabled had to be left at Paarsdekop at the store of Mr M. C. Desai. These people have to be attended to and I suggest that the Government take charge of them.
>
> Yesterday at Val there were eight or nine men footsore and otherwise ill. One or two men were even seriously ill. I had hoped to be able to make complete arrangements about them today. They were left in charge of Mr Patel an Indian storekeeper at Val. These men should in my humble opinion receive medical attention without delay.

Probably 150 Indians entered the Transvaal without a leader on Thursday last. They were last heard of at Standerton and rations were supplied to them. I could have, during my march, traced them and fed them. These men should be traced and fed.

Eight men who were not seriously ill but were too fatigued to walk entrained at Val for Balfour where they were to join the main body. These too should be traced and provisioned.

If my information is correct I understand that the Government intend to put back the main body of the Indians who marched with me on the Natal Border in a helpless condition. In that event the men will attempt, I feel, to reenter. I venture to suggest that they should be dealt with under the Indentured Indians Immigration Law of Natal or otherwise taken charge of and fed.

I have the
Honour to be
Sir
Your obedient servant
M. K. Gandhi.[46]

After their leader was taken away, the marchers were escorted by the police to the town of Balfour, from where they were sent back to Natal in three trains. 'The men appear in no way dispirited after their fruitless tramp', reported one observer, 'and expressed their intention to further the passive resistance movement again when Mr Gandhi is at liberty.'[47]

On 11 November Gandhi was tried at Dundee, charged with inducing indentured labour to leave Natal. His lawyer said 'he was under an obligation to the defendant not to plead in mitigation in any way whatsoever'. In his statement, Gandhi referred to himself as an old resident of Natal and a member of its Bar, who 'was in honour bound, in view of the position of things between Mr Smuts and Professor Gokhale, to produce a striking demonstration'. He pleaded guilty, and was sentenced to nine months in prison with hard labour.[48]

Three days later Gandhi was tried at Volksrust, charged this time with bringing prohibited immigrants into Transvaal. He pleaded guilty once more, noting however that 'throughout the march into the Transvaal, I endeavoured to keep the men under control and to prevent them from dispersing, and I claim that not a single Indian left the column if it may be so called.' In his defence, he called upon a miner named Poldat. Asked why he had entered the Transvaal, Poldat answered that he had done so in protest against the £3 tax. Asked if he would have gone back to work if the tax had been repealed, Poldat said yes, he would have.

The point made, Gandhi added that he was aware that

> the steps he had taken were fraught with the greatest risks and intense personal suffering by those who had accepted his advice, but after very mature consideration, based on twenty years experience in South Africa, he had come to the conclusion that nothing short of such suffering would move the conscience of the Government, as also of the [white] inhabitants of the Union, of which, in spite of the so-called breach of the statutory laws, he claimed to be a sane and law-abiding citizen.

He was sentenced to an additional three months in prison.[49]

As the march swelled and its leader was arrested, released, arrested again, released again, Polak and Kallenbach supervised it in the periodic, enforced absences of Gandhi. The architect was accustomed to simple living, but the journalist – husband of the aesthete Millie, and a man who stayed away from the Tolstoy and Phoenix settlements himself – had to strive strenuously to put cause before body. Later, he wrote with some feeling about trying to get to sleep under the sky and the stars:

> I shall not easily forget that night! Our small campfires gradually flickered out as we lay down to rest and sleep after a very frugal meal that had been cooked in the early morning. The clouds rolled up heavily and a thunder-storm played in the distance. A light rain fell at intervals during the night and a cool wind blew in gusts, increasing the general discomfort. I had not slept in the open for years, and the blanket that I carried with me was little protection against the roughness and inequalities of the ground upon which we lay. On either side of me was a poor wretched striker in the early stages, apparently, of consumption, and they coughed continually throughout the night. It was, therefore, with considerable relief that I rose with the dawn, and we struck camp after a hurried wash and without eating for we were due at the township of Balfour, where we understood arrangements had been made for the next meal.

Characteristically, after laying bare his own squeamishness, Polak then praised the resolution of his Indian comrades. The morning's march, he wrote, 'was one that would have done credit to a well-drilled army since we did the distance to Balfour at the rate of three and a half miles an hour. These mine coolies were splendid fellows, full of courage and strong of purpose.'[50]

Polak and Kallenbach were themselves arrested on 10 November, and took their punishment gladly. Polak wrote to Lord Ampthill that 'in view of the fact that I, as an outsider, had so often counselled Indian passive resisters to challenge arrest, I felt that it would be highly dishonourable for me – an Englishman – to draw back before a risk, and I did not hesitate to join [the Indians].'[51] Kallenbach explained – or justified – his jail-going in a long letter to his sister, where he detailed the discriminations against the Indians and argued that satyagraha – 'the teaching not to meet force and violence in a likewise manner, but to meet them with passive suffering' – was consistent with the teachings of 'almost all religions', Judaism among them.[52]

Kallenbach and Polak were both tried before a judge named Jooste. In his testimony, the architect began by describing himself as 'an intimate friend of Mr Gandhi for many years'. The 'voiceless and voteless' Indians had drawn attention to their grievances through petitions and representations. Having tried and failed with these methods, their leader, Gandhi, then introduced what Kallenbach considered 'the only effective means of securing redress, viz., passive resistance, a means in which I, for many years a disciple of Tolstoy, thoroughly believe.'

Polak spoke of his long association with the Indians of South Africa, and his work as editor of their weekly newspaper. He supported their passive resistance movement as an Englishman, a Jew and a member of the legal profession. As an Englishman, he said,

> it is impossible for me to sit silent whilst the Government of the Union, claiming to speak in my name, repudiate, as they have done twice this year, their solemn pledges towards my fellow-British subject of Indian nationality, in defiance of what is best in British public opinion, and regardless of Imperial obligations and responsibilities towards the people of India . . .
>
> As a Jew, it is impossible for me to associate myself, even passively, with the persecution of any race or nationality. My co-religionists to-day, in certain parts of Europe, are undergoing suffering and persecution on racial grounds, and, finding the same spirit of persecution in this country, directed

against the Indian people, I have felt impelled to protest against it with every fibre of my being.

As a member of the legal profession, I have made a declaration of loyalty to the Crown and to do my duty as an Attorney of this honourable court. In taking the part of the Indian passive resisters, loyal subjects of the Crown, in their demand for justice, I claim to have proved my loyalty in the most practical possible manner, and, as an Attorney, I claim to have given the only advice to them possible to me as an honourable man who places justice before loyalty and moral law before human law.

Polak then added a fourth reason – that he was a friend of Gokhale's, a man revered by millions of Indians, who had been promised by the South African Government that the £3 tax would be repealed. Polak called the tax 'a relic of barbarism', whose 'direct effect is to drive the tax-payers back to conditions of servitude, dishonourable to British traditions of freedom, or to expel them from this country, which has reaped the fruits of their labour for a period of years.'

These statements of Gandhi's closest colleagues were both deeply moving. Yet they were very differently articulated. Kallenbach's was spontaneous and heart-felt, drawing attention to the friend who was leading the struggle. Polak's was more closely crafted. The work of a writer and polemicist, it stressed rather the principles by which one who was not an Indian himself would choose to support their movement.[53]

Kallenbach was unattached, but Polak had a wife and children. When Millie Graham came out to South Africa in 1905 to join him, she was prepared for a life of service. But surely she would not have anticipated that this would land her husband in prison. Now, she was consoled and cheered by a lovely letter from her husband's best friend, which read:

My Dear Millie,

You are brave. So I know you will consider yourself a proud and happy wife in having a husband who has dared to go to gaol for a cause he believes in. The £3 tax is the cause of the helpless and the dumb. And I ask you to work away in the shape of begging, advising and doing all you can. Do not wait for their call but call the workers. Seek them out even though they should insult you. Miss S[chlesin] knows the struggle almost like Henry. Assist her. I have asked her to move forward and backward and assume full control. Draw upon West and Maganbhai for your needs. May you have strength of mind and body to go through the fire.

With love,
Yours
Bhai.[54]

A third Jewish supporter of the satyagraha, L. W. Ritch, could not seek arrest, since he had to run Gandhi's law practice. But he showed his solidarity in other ways, peppering the press with letters defending the Indian cause. When General Smuts claimed that the new marriage laws were necessary because Muslim men had only to utter 'talaq' three times to secure a divorce, Ritch answered that the practice was in fact so rare that when it occurred, it was regarded as a 'scandal of communal importance'. He estimated that there had not been more than fifty cases of *talaq* in the past thirty years among the Indian community in South Africa. On the other hand, divorce was rampant among Europeans in Natal and the Transvaal. 'South African lawyers cannot complain of lack of practice in this branch of our profession', said Ritch sarcastically. 'A husband absents himself from his wife for a few months, ignores the ensuing order of court, and the divorce is granted. Almost as simple as saying [*talaq*], don't you think?'[55]

Then, when a Johannesburg paper claimed that the Indians wanted an 'open door to immigration', Ritch answered that what they actually asked for was fair treatment for those resident in South Africa. In his view, the policy of the Union Government

> resembles nothing as much as the conduct of Holy Russia towards Russia's Jewish population. All the same elements are present – repression, segregation, studied insult and neglect. And the same excuses are advanced by way of justification: economic danger, unassimilability, alien race, incompatibility of ideas – and all the rest of it. That Russia's attitude is one of criminal folly nobody doubts; that the future will prove us to have similarly erred is to my mind no less certain.[56]

No less tireless was a fourth Jewish friend of the Indians, Gandhi's secretary Sonja Schlesin. She came down to Natal, shuttling between Phoenix and the prisons, nourishing the morale and the stomachs of first-time satyagrahis. She sent Gokhale, in India, a series of telegrams, updating him on the struggle. The duties assigned to her were substantial, and she sometimes took upon other tasks voluntarily. When a white planter, angry with the strike, assaulted and injured two of his workers, Miss Schlesin had their wounds attended to. She also photographed their bruises, sending the prints to the press and to the Government.[57]

Gandhi and his friends were sent to Volksrust Prison, before the authorities decided to separate them. Polak was shifted to Boksburg, and Kallenbach to Krugersdorp. Gandhi himself was transferred first to Pietermaritzburg and then to Bloemfontein.

The leader was away, yet the protests continued. On 13 November, 2,000 Indians working in sugar fields and sugar mills in southern Natal went on strike. At one major estate, Mount Edgecombe, the managers 'enrolled a corps of special police, and drew a cordon around the estate, with the idea of keeping out the agitators and apostles of Gandhi, and of protecting loyal Indians from intimidation.' The coercion failed, with an estimated 1,500 out of the 2,700 labourers at Mount Edgecombe downing tools and going off to join their fellows.[58]

In the fifty years that they had worked on the sugar plantations and coal mines, Indian labourers had occasionally protested against harsh working conditions or brutal supervisors and managers. When provoked or humiliated, they had deserted their work, marched in a body to their manager's office, petitioned government authorities, and sometimes even assaulted their employers.[59] Still, the strikes in 1913 were unprecedented in their scale and scope. In the sugar plantations of the south these were wholly self-organized. Indian workers had heard of the protests among the mines in the north; and of the leaders who had organized them. They were disturbed and moved by Gandhi's arrest. But Gandhi had not ever worked with or mobilized sugar workers. These now came out on their own, in a remarkable display of solidarity with their compatriots. By the middle of November, some 15,000 sugar workers were on strike. A rumour spread that Gokhale was coming out again from India to have the £3 tax abolished. Many workers believed that Gandhi had sent a message urging them to down tools. Some strikers left the plantations and moved into towns nearby; others converged on the settlement founded by Gandhi at Phoenix.[60]

While Gandhi's name was invoked, the methods of protest were not always 'Gandhian'. Angry strikers burned cane fields, and attacked policemen with sticks and stones (and even cane knives). In clashes between constables with guns and Indians with swords, there were many casualties, some fatal. European planters, unnerved, sent their wives and children to the comparative safety of Durban.[61]

As the strike spread through the colony, the army was called in. Several hundred mounted riflemen under the command of a brigadier-general were sent to the sugar country. The navy was also put on alert, in case troops had to be sent from the Cape to Durban.[62]

The show of force failed once more. The strike now spread to the brick kilns and to Durban, where Indians employed by the City Corporation and in the port stopped work. At a well-attended meeting, the strikers were 'unanimous in their decision, which was a refusal to work until the £3 tax had been repealed, and until Gandhi was released.'[63]

On Saturday, 15 November, 1,200 Indians gathered in Pietermaritzburg to discuss the state of their movement. A certain T. R. Naidoo said that while 'he was not against the passive resistance movement as a matter of principle, he was against the Maritzburg Indians doing anything which would be likely to jeopardize the trade or interests of the Indians by adopting an antagonistic attitude towards the Europeans'. Other speakers vigorously disagreed. One Ramsingh pointed out that 'Mr Gandhi had gone to prison for them all, and he wanted to know whether they were going to leave him to face the trouble alone, or whether they were going to join forces with him.' A priest named Dhonduram Maharaj praised Gandhi for bringing Hindus and Muslims together. Under his leadership, they had made 'common [cause] in the passive resistance movement'. The mood of the meeting was very clearly pro-satyagraha and pro-Gandhi.[64] On the crucial issue of the £3 tax, it accused the Government of betrayal. Thus when one speaker 'asked whether his confrères placed reliance on General Smuts or on Mr Gokhale, there was a loud cry of Mr Gokhale'.[65]

On Sunday, 16 November, a meeting of Indians in Johannesburg asked the Government to release Gandhi and begin talks.[66] Meanwhile, Natal's largest town, Durban, 'was seething with the strike spirit'. On the afternoon of the 16th, 3,000 Indians gathered for a meeting, where 'cheers were given for Mr Gandhi and the strikers.' One speaker asked hospital and sanitary workers to return to duty as an act of courtesy to their fellow citizens. Otherwise, the strike embraced all trades and professions. It was 'practically universal amongst the Indians in the Borough'.

The chief magistrate of Durban toured the city, urging the strikers to return to work. At each place he was informed that 'they had been told by their "Rajah" or "King", Mr Gandhi, that they were to strike until the £3 Licence was repealed.' Then he toured the plantations outside the town, to be told there too that 'Gandhi had ordered them to strike'. The magistrate thought that beyond the specific grievance of the £3 tax, the protestors also wanted the franchise and 'equal rights'.[67]

Across Natal, Indians had stopped working in sugar plantations, coal mines, railways, ships, shops and hotels. The authorities sought to compel them back to work. The police arrested 120 'ringleaders' in Durban. In the country districts, riflemen marched up and down the plantations in a show of strength, sometimes provoking clashes with angry Indians. In a scuffle at Avoica several indentured labourers were injured. At the Beneva sugar estate, 'the coolies came out in strength and a volley was fired'. Two Indians were killed by bullets, and ten seriously wounded. At Mount Edgecombe, soldiers with revolvers battled coolies with sticks and stones. Five Europeans were injured, as against four Indians killed and twenty-four wounded.[68]

One eyewitness to the conflict was the Zulu reformer John Dube. He saw Indian strikers congregate on a piece of open ground, and refuse to move despite being beaten by the police. Constables mounted on horses ran through them, and yet they did not disperse. Dube was impressed by their courage and endurance, telling a friend that while he had once thought plantation coolies crude and uncivilized, now he had 'acquired a sense of respect for all the Indians'.[69]

The Indian satyagraha also came in for praise from the leader of the Cape Coloureds, Dr Abdurahman. In the last week of November, he told the annual conference of the African Political Organization that

if a handful of Indians, in a matter of conscience, can so firmly resist what they consider injustice, what could the coloured races not do if they were to adopt this practice of passive resistance? We must all admire what these

485

British Indians have shown, and are showing, in their determination to maintain what they deem to be their right.[70]

In response to the Indian upsurge, the Europeans in Natal reinforced their own solidarities of race and class. Angry letters to the papers singled out Gandhi as the chief trouble-maker. One spoke of 'the rebellion on the part of Indians at the bidding of Gandhi and Co.'; another spoke sarcastically of agitators 'elevating Gokhale and Gandhi to the level of little gods'. A third asked the South African Government to 'deport to India and permanently banish Gandhi, Polak, Kallenbach, [Thambi] Naidoo, and all Indians convicted of agitation in the "strike"'. A fourth said the best answer to the strike was to demonstrate that 'we can do without the Indian.' The whites should sweep their own backyards and blacken their own boots. They could then 'do away with 50 per cent of these Indians and coincidentally smash up the backbone of this Young India menace'.[71]

On 26 November the *Natal Mercury* carried an interview with a local legislator, J. T. Henderson. Henderson noted that in 1874 there were a mere 6,000 Indians in Natal; now they were in excess of 130,000. If the £3 tax on free Indians was abolished, the numbers would increase even more, and 'the outlook for the white population here [would be] a very dark one indeed.' The ambition of the Indians was worrying; they tended to look 'for a higher plane of employment' than labouring in fields and mines, and were 'exceedingly keen' on education. The tax was necessary to discourage them from challenging the whites even more directly than they presently did.[72]

The legislator was refuted by F. A. Laughton, in whose opinion the £3 tax was illegal. Since wages on plantations were much below market rates, Indians were 'under no obligation either to leave Natal after the expiration of their indentures or to take out a licence if they remain'. This opinion from a 'jurist of standing' led to 'jubilation among local Indians and considerable astonishment amongst Europeans'.[73]

Meanwhile, back in the Transvaal, the Boer party, Het Volk, renewed its call to deport the Indians *en masse*. The party paper *Die Transvaler* complained that the Indians 'have increased their demands, become more obstreperous than they have ever been, caused more trouble than ever before, and evidently they are never going to be satisfied until every article of the Immigration Act has been repealed'. 'South Africa has had enough of these Indians', said the Boer organ. 'We want no more of them from India or elsewhere.'[74]

In the last week of November, the Government renewed its efforts to break the strike in Natal by force. Contingents of police were dispatched to get labourers back to work. Fleeing the police, many workers swarmed on to the farm at Phoenix. They were taken in hand by Albert West and Maganlal Gandhi, who fed them and allowed them to sleep over at the settlement. The workers 'repeatedly stated that they would rather die than go back to their work, and they seemed to be really afraid'. West wired the Government, suggesting that it 'allow people [to] remain quietly here until disturbance is over, or Government supply food and take charge [of the] camp'.[75]

The upsurge in Natal, and the arrest of Gandhi and company, provoked a wave of sympathy and support in the protesters' homeland. 'India thrilling with indignation', wired Gokhale to Millie Polak. 'Protests pouring upon [Indian] Government for forwarding Imperial Government.' A public subscription had already collected £5,000; Gokhale wanted to know where to send it. He also asked who was leading the movement in the absence of Gandhi. 'Full information present position prospects necessary', he said.[76]

The range and depth of the Indian interest in Gandhi's movement is manifest in a series of wires sent by the Viceroy on to London. Here are two samples:

Viceroy to India Office, 26 November 1913:

> My telegram dated 22nd November S. Africa. 23 further telegrams received, two from private individuals, twenty are from Chairmen of meetings held at Ahmedabad, Ongole, Amalapuram, Bezwada, Tanuku, Yeotmal, two meetings Bombay, Coonoor, Lucknow, Narsapur, Rajkot, Bapatla, Poona, Guntur, Nasik, Kovur, Ellore, Rampurhat, Gudiwada, and Bhimavaram. Contents similar to that of previous telegrams reported to you protesting against treatment of Indians in Natal and urging government intervention.

Viceroy to India Office, 8 December 1913:

> Thirteen further telegrams received from women of Bombay and citizens of Rangoon, Hyderabad, Sind, Cawnpore, Hardoi, from All India Muslim

League Lucknow; Chairmen public meetings Calicut, Yeotmal, Ajmer, Bombay mill-hands, Sanghsabha Shanghai, Chandra Chairman Political Association Kimberley, public of Kotdwara, and letter from Chairmen of public meetings Nellore, Raipur, and Coimbatore, and from Joint Secretary Godavari District Association Cocanada praying for adoption of measures for the prevention of sufferings of Indians in S. Africa.[77]

The interest in the South African struggle was particularly keen in South India, the region from where the majority of the satyagrahis came. A Tamil paper published out of Madras praised the 'wonderful determination' of 'Mr Gandhi and his followers'; they had 'glorif[ied] the good name of India by means of their noble and courageous conduct, risking even their lives'. A Kannada paper printed in Bangalore saluted 'the leadership of that zealous servant of India, that generous and heroic personage, Mr Gandhi'. A Telugu weekly in Guntur reached for mythic parallels – Gandhi, the leader of the resistance, was like Arjuna, brave and fearless, while Gokhale was like Krishna, providing sage advice from behind the scenes.[78]

To raise money for the struggle, G. A. Natesan reprinted Polak's booklet on Gandhi. In December 1913, a rival publisher in Madras, Ganesh and Company, commissioned its own capsule biography of 'the hero of the Passive Resistance Movement', its proceeds to go 'in relief of our brethren in South Africa in their present struggle'.[79] And a rising lawyer in Salem, C. Rajagopalachari, reprinted Gandhi's account of his jail experiences for the same purpose. Rajagopalachari said Gandhi 'must be ranked with the Avatars', while his followers, 'even in these degenerate days, act[ed] like real heroes in the cause of the Nation'. The booklet sold rapidly, so quickly in fact that the lawyer was able to send a cheque for Rs 1,500 to aid the struggle in South Africa.[80]

The massively enhanced stature of Gandhi in his homeland was most strikingly underlined by a Telugu play in five acts, performed at this time in the Andhra country. The first four acts detail the handicaps of the Indians in South Africa. In the final act Gandhi appears in the flesh and embarks on an extended soliloquy. He reflects on the condition of his compatriots, and on the degradation and humiliation they suffer in the workplace and away from it. The cruelties of the poll-tax and the marriage laws are dwelt upon. The (prosperous) lawyer then asks himself: 'Am I to live in this mansion while my fellow-brothers and sisters are suffering from untold miseries?', and provides this answer:

> O, Gandhi; O mind of mine! Have no desire for wealth or fame. No more happiness so long as the children of Bharata [India] are in slavery. You shall have no peace until you put an end to the racial hatred that has converted these South Africans into brutes. To achieve this you do not require the strength of the sword . . . Truth is your existence. Your colour is justice, your name is liberty . . . Throughout the length and breadth of this sacred land of Bharata one determination is blazing forth in one flame and resounding in one voice. The Lord has sent his message. It is resounding from the craggy Cape Comorin to the snow-peaked Himalayas. No gaols can oppose our determination. The whips cannot cow down our spirits. Even the cannon balls cannot keep our country behind.
>
> Victory to our motherland.

This play was originally published in Telugu in a journal called the *Kistna Patrika*, and then translated into English and printed afresh in Dublin, from where copies were posted to school and college teachers across South India, to be staged in public. Copies were intercepted by the police; but one copy reached an archive in London, providing the basis of this account. That Gandhi's struggle could prompt such a passionate rendering in Telugu is remarkable; for in 1913 Gandhi had not been in India for a decade, and he had never visited the Andhra country at all.[81]

Across the subcontinent, in the holy city of Banaras, protesters burned effigies of Generals Botha and Smuts. In a meeting chaired by the celebrated nationalist leader Madan Mohan Malaviya, a Hindi poet named Pratap read out verses urging patriots to hear the 'far cry from distant Africa', where 'heroes like Gandhi in jail' were 'showing the bravery of India to the world'.[82]

Back in 1910, Gandhi had published *Hind Swaraj* as a direct response to, and a passionate intervention in, debates on Indian nationalist politics. The book was banned in both its Gujarati and English versions. Even had it been available in India, one wonders how widely it would have been read. It bore the marks of its hasty production; and in a society with such low levels of literacy, there wasn't much of a market for books in any case. Nonetheless, by 1913 many parts of India were familiar with Gandhi's name. More Indians read newspapers than books; more still attended or heard of meetings organized in solidarity with the South African protests. That so many of their countrymen had so heroically resisted racial oppression in that faraway land was now known in towns across the subcontinent. Their leader was saluted and celebrated in talks, editorials, reports, poems and at least one play. This was testimony not so much to the originality of his political ideas as to the vigour of his political practice. Mohandas Gandhi had made a definite impact on the popular consciousness of the motherland; not, however, as the author of an obscure text named *Hind Swaraj*, but as the chief inspirer of the collective defiance of discriminatory laws and the collective courting of imprisonment by Indians in South Africa.

One of the many 'indignation meetings' was held in Gandhi's place of birth, Porbandar. The princely states had thus far kept out of the national movement. They were insulated from British India, whose political ferment did not affect them. The princes themselves were resolutely loyal to the Raj. But now the residents of Porbandar were moved to act, because some of the satyagrahis in South Africa came from the Kathiawar coast, and because their leader was born and raised in the town. The resolutions passed at this meeting included one praising 'the inspiring leadership' of the native son, M. K. Gandhi, and another thanking 'Major F. de Hancock, our popular administrator for the liberal and munificent State contribution of Rs 1,000 towards the fund [for Indians in South Africa] and for allowing the use of the Victoria Memorial Hall for convening their meeting.'[83]

In 1888, the British Administrator in Porbandar had refused to pay for Gandhi's studies in London; now, twenty-five years later, his successor was funding the lawyer-turned-activist's campaign chest. In this respect, Porbandar was no exception; at other meetings, too, large sums of money were raised and dispatched to Gokhale in Poona. On 28 November, Sonja Schlesin passed on a message from Gandhi to his mentor: 'He says that you are not to *worry* yourself about funds. If they did not come, we should manage here somehow.' Gokhale's response was to wire £5,000 two days later. On 3 December, a further instalment of £5,000 was sent to Maganlal Gandhi at Phoenix.[84]

All kinds of people chipped in, some famous, some obscure. In the first category fell the poet Rabindranath Tagore, who had recently been awarded the Nobel Prize for literature. In November, Tagore sent Gokhale Rs 100 as his 'humble contribution' to the South African Indian Fund.[85] Three weeks later he sent another cheque, apologizing for its niggardly contents. 'I am ashamed to own that the response has been feeble in Bengal to the call of our countrymen in trouble in South Africa', wrote the poet. 'But I can assure you that my boys' hearts were moved to genuine sympathy when appealed to and little though these children were able to raise for the fund it was not the less valuable in its moral worth.'[86]

More surprising than Tagore's endorsement was that of the Bishop of Madras, a pillar of the Establishment and, of course, an Englishman. 'I frankly confess', remarked the Bishop in December 1913, 'though it pains me to say it, that I see in Mr Gandhi, the patient sufferer for the cause of righteousness and mercy, a truer representative of the Crucified Saviour, than the men who have thrown him into prison and yet call themselves by the name of Christ.'[87]

More surprising still was the support for Gandhi and company expressed by the most powerful individual in India, the Viceroy, Lord Hardinge. Also speaking in Madras, he said the passive resisters in South Africa had 'the deep and burning sympathy of India and also of those who like myself, without being Indian, sympathise with the people of this country'. The Viceroy argued that 'if the South African Government desires to justify itself in the eyes of India and the world, the only course open to it is to appoint a strong impartial committee, whereon Indian interests will be represented, to conduct the most searching enquiry.'[88]

There were some less well-known supporters of the struggle too. One A. K. Hariharan sent Rs 250 to Gokhale from Kuala Lumpur, on behalf of 'the Indians who are employed in Railways and other petty positions in the town'. The 'Heroes of South Africa', said this representative of the Indian diaspora, 'are superior to our adversaries in courage, in devotion, and in knowledge of the wants of the people'. A certain A. E. Lall, manager of a motor agency in the northern town of Peshawar, wrote to Gokhale offering his services. He had previously lived in South Africa, claimed to have 'known Mr Gandhi intimately', counting him 'the best man I have met in any part of the world'.[89]

Kasturba Gandhi also came in for her share of praise. In early

December, while speaking at a meeting in the Bombay Town Hall, Sir Pherozeshah Mehta recalled the 'touching episode' wherein Kasturba told Gandhi that if the court claimed her marriage was illegal, then she would insist on joining the satyagraha. Mehta said that

> Mr Gandhi must have known what it was to expose tender women to the hardship of the campaign, but in spite of his pleading, that brave lady decided to cast in her lot with those men who were fighting for the cause. History records the deeds of many heroines and I feel Mrs Gandhi will stand as one of the foremost heroines in the whole world.[90]

By the end of November 1913, more than 1,000 Indians were in jail. A majority were workers from Natal, punished for going on strike. The others included merchants and hawkers from the Transvaal, and followers, friends and family members of M. K. Gandhi.

Only one letter written by Gandhi from jail has survived. Written to Albert West's sister, Devi, this asked about the routine of the boys at Phoenix, and told her to 'remind Dev[a]das of the promises he has made me at various times'. 'Much of my spare time is being devoted to Tamil study', added Gandhi. In this latest satyagraha the Tamils had shone more brightly still, and their leader was, it seems, suitably grateful.

Gandhi's letter had specific instructions for one resident of Phoenix. This was Jeki Mehta, who had just been released from jail after the expiry of her sentence. Gandhi now wrote to Devi West that

> Jekiben should adhere to the promises made by her to me. Please tell her that hardly a day passes when I do not give much thought to her. As to her diet, I do not bind her to any promises or resolutions she may have made. She may take whatever suits her constitution. But she must not only keep good health but be robust. She must grow her hair unless she has definitely heard otherwise from Dr. Mehta.[91]

Meanwhile, unknown to Gandhi, Jeki Mehta was the subject of angry letters written to the Government of South Africa by her estranged husband, Manilal Doctor. This other Manilal was now in Fiji, having shifted there from Mauritius. He had set up practice as a barrister in Suva, servicing the town's Indian residents. When rumours of what his wife had been up to with his namesake Manilal Gandhi reached him,

Doctor wrote to the Governor-General, Lord Gladstone, asking that he arrange for Jeki to be sent to Fiji. The message was passed on, but Jeki declined to go. She wanted to remain with the satyagraha in South Africa.

His wife's refusal to join him infuriated Manilal Doctor. He wrote once more to Lord Gladstone, suggesting that if Jeki courted arrest again, the sentence should be deportation, 'in which case there would be greater chances of her cure from Mr Gandhi's influences and therefore of settling down to a stable life with me here'. He was willing to pay the expenses of his wife's travel to Fiji.

Since Gandhi was in jail, Manilal Doctor could not communicate with him directly. So he asked the Governor-General to tell him that

> my wife's father and I myself desire her to leave his place and that he would spare me the painful necessity of taking legal steps against himself and his son Manilal Gandhi for intercepting the smooth flow of my married life in the way they have in fact done. Allow me to add that my wife is a minor, I am legally her guardian, and that Mr Gandhi is no relation at all to us.[92]

Manilal Doctor certainly spoke for himself. But did he also speak for Pranjivan Mehta, who was his father-in-law, but also Gandhi's closest and oldest friend? Alas, the archives are silent on the matter. Dr Mehta could not have been pleased with Jeki's affair with Gandhi's son Manilal – but would he have laid the blame for this at Gandhi's own door? That seems unlikely. Jeki herself seems to have been unwilling to rejoin her husband. She was focused on staying in South Africa – but whether out of admiration for Gandhi's politics or love for Gandhi's son we cannot say.

In the second week of December, the South African Government announced that it would set up an 'Indian Enquiry Commission' to report on the recent disturbances and their causes. In his speech in Madras in late November, the Viceroy of India had called for such a commission. The Viceroy's idea had now been taken forward by Lord Gladstone, the Governor-General of South Africa. For the protests by the Indians had been unprecedented in scope and scale. They had breached the boundaries of province, class and gender. They had fully stretched the forces of law and order, and had seriously endangered the economy of Natal. Despite brave talk in the newspapers, whites were not really prepared to labour in mines, plantations, hotels or shops. Gladstone thus suggested to General Smuts that the Commission should go into the marriage and tax questions that had so exercised the Indians.[93]

Smuts agreed. A three-member Commission was appointed, to be chaired by the jurist Sir William Solomon. As a gesture to the Indians, Gandhi was released from jail on the morning of 18 December. Polak and Kallenbach were set free the same day. At a public meeting in Johannesburg, Gandhi said he was not satisfied with the constitution of the Enquiry Commission. Sir William Solomon was fine, but the other two members, Lt.-Col. Wylie and Edward Esselen, were known to have anti-Indian views. Gandhi said that 'rather than have a weighted or packed Commission, which would militate against the welfare of the Indian community in South Africa, he would prefer to go back to prison and allow the Indian case to stand upon its own merits.' In response, William Hosken 'begged' Gandhi to retain his 'self-control', and 'to do nothing that would bring discredit on their cause'.[94]

The next day, Gandhi proceeded by train to Durban. As he stepped on to the platform on arrival, 'flowers were thrown round him, and the Indians clambered around him'. He was conveyed from the station into an open carriage, which was pulled by young men 'through the streets with every manifestation of enthusiasm'.[95]

It was a triumphant return to his first home in South Africa, but also a sombre one. In jail, Gandhi had shaved his head and chosen to wear white. His feet were bare. Speaking to a crowd of 5,000 assembled at the Durban racecourse, Gandhi said he had changed his dress when he heard of the police firing on Indian strikers. The bullets that shot his countrymen shot him through the heart as well. Henceforth, he would dress like an indentured labourer. Then he spoke of the Commission just appointed. He complained that Indians had no voice, while two of its three members were known for their hostility to them. Unless 'the Commission is supplemented by responsible South African members of known standing, who are not prejudiced against Asiatics generally', he said, 'we shall certainly be against it'.[96]

On 21 December, Gandhi wrote to Smuts suggesting the addition of two members to the Commission. W. P. Schreiner and Sir James-Innes were both known for their liberal views. Smuts rejected the suggestion, insisting that the Commission as it stood was 'impartial and judicious'. Gandhi now said the Indians would boycott the Commission.

The composition of the Enquiry Commission angered the rank-and-file even more. 'The Government have treated us in such a rascally manner in the appointment of this Commission', wrote Henry Polak to his family in England, adding, 'I fear that it will be impossible to avoid a revival of the struggle in its most bitter form.' In that case Polak would court arrest once more, for which he asked in advance for the 'sympathy and understanding' of his parents. The senior Polaks admired and liked Gandhi, but as loyalist, assimilationist Jews, they were naturally not very keen for their son to follow him all the way into jail. 'Whatever the consequences may be both personally and publicly', wrote Henry Polak to his parents, 'I feel I am bound to support Mr Gandhi in his present attitude, of which I wholly approve. It may not be customary politics, but the Passive Resistance struggle has never been based upon politics but upon principles.'[97]

Speaking to reporters on 21 December, L. W. Ritch claimed that if their demands were not conceded, the Indians would once more go on strike. 'Mr Gandhi will collect all the Indians who follow him', said Ritch, 'and will march to Pretoria', the march to commence on 1 January. Ritch predicted that Gandhi 'would leave Durban with a thousand Indians, and by the time he reached the border, if he does so, his "army" will increase to at least 20,000'.[98]

The next day Kasturba Gandhi was released from prison. Gandhi had come up from Durban to Maritzburg to meet her. The Indians of the town had preceded him. They met Kasturba and her fellow prisoners outside the jail and pulled them in a flower-strewn carriage through the streets. At the meeting that followed, the speakers included Gandhi, Kallenbach and Millie Polak. Millie said that

> this was essentially a women's movement, and there was no question that had it not been for the women taking the lead, there would have been no strike. When women once realized the enormous power they had they would rise up and make their own lives and the world what they wished (loud applause).[99]

Kasturba and her comrades had spent eight weeks in jail. Unfortunately, whereas Gandhi wrote in much detail of his various prison terms, his wife left no record of her ordeal. How did she cope with this radically new experience? Since her fellow satyagrahis included her nephews' wives, at least she had some people to speak Gujarati with. In other respects life would have been altogether different, and much harder, than what she had been accustomed to in Porbandar, Rajkot, Johannesburg and Phoenix. The food in South African jails was uniformly bad. As a vegetarian, Kasturba had to make do with the terrible mealie pap. Her sentence also included 'hard labour', which took the form of washing clothes in the prison courtyard.[100]

Millie Polak saluted Kasturba's spirit; her husband, meanwhile, was shocked at the state of her health. 'Mrs Gandhi discharged prison almost irrecognisably altered owing refusal special diet', Polak wired Gokhale. 'Reduced skeleton tottering appearance old woman heart breaking sight.'[101]

Between 21 and 28 December, Gandhi and Gokhale wired each other once or twice a day. Gokhale said the boycott of the Commission would be a 'grave mistake', alienating friends and sympathisers, and forgoing the chance to present evidence of cruelty to Indians. Gandhi answered that he was 'besieged by people all day' protesting against the Commission and calling for a march on Pretoria. Gokhale said both boycott and march would constitute a 'great personal humiliation' to the Viceroy. Gokhale had persuaded Lord Hardinge to depute a senior civil servant named Sir Benjamin Robertson as the representative of the Government of India to the Commission. Even if Gandhi persisted with a boycott, Sir Benjamin would convey his concerns to the body.[102]

Gokhale's counsel prevailed. Speaking to reporters on the 29th, Gandhi said that 'at the request of friends' he had postponed the march to Pretoria. They would 'wait until we know that we have left no stone unturned to arrive at a honourable settlement'.[103]

Gokhale had asked Gandhi to be restrained; on the other side, Smuts was urged to be magnanimous by the British social reformer Emily Hobhouse. A Quaker by religious conviction, Hobhouse had endeared herself to the General during the Anglo-Boer War. In the first half of 1901 she travelled through South Africa, documenting the harsh treatment of Boer prisoners of war. She returned to England to present her findings before the British public, before taking a ship back to continue her investigations. Her criticisms had so angered British colonists, that – in a striking reprise of Gandhi's own experience in Durban in 1896–7 – she had not been allowed to land in Cape Town.[104]

In the latter part of 1913 Emily Hobhouse was back in South Africa, where she contacted Gandhi. They were introduced by a common friend, Elizabeth Molteno. The daughter of the first Prime Minister of the Cape Colony, Betty Molteno had left South Africa in disgust following the Anglo-Boer War. She had met Gandhi in London in 1909, returning from exile soon afterwards.

In December 1913, after Gandhi and Kasturba were released from prison, Betty Molteno travelled from Cape Town to Natal to meet them. She was moved by their stories of jail life, and by the cross-class support for the satyagraha. She passed on her impressions to Emily Hobhouse, urging her to press the Indian case on Smuts. Miss Hobhouse was sympathetic, not least because several members of her family had served in India, and back home in England she had friends from the subcontinent.

From Millie Polak on through Sonja Schlesin, Maud Polak and beyond, Gandhi got along with independent-minded Western women. Betty Molteno and he had hit it off from their first meeting, and so now did he and Emily Hobhouse. They discussed the Indian question, of course, but also other matters such as the tactics of the suffragettes and the respective merits of city life versus rural living. Miss Hobhouse had been unwell, so Gandhi wrote inviting her to Phoenix, where 'the scenery around is certainly very charming', where 'there is no bustle or noise', and where she would 'find loving hands to administer to your wants'. Nothing, said Gandhi to Miss Hobhouse, 'would give me personally greater pleasure than, if I were free, to be able to wait upon you and nurse you'.[105]

On 29 December, Miss Hobhouse wrote to Smuts as someone who was not 'South African or Indian but in fullest sympathy with both'. While recognizing that white South Africa already 'has as many Indians as it can digest', she hoped the General would find 'a *modus vivendi* to suit their *amour propre*'. To begin with, he could, she suggested, 'readjust the marriage question and abolish that stupid £3 tax'.

There was now talk in Gandhi's circle of starting the march to Pretoria on 15 January. Before then, said Hobhouse to Smuts, 'some way should be found [of] giving private assurance to the leaders that satisfaction is coming to them.' The grievance of the Indians, she continued,

> is really moral not material and so, having all the power of the spiritual behind him, he [Gandhi] and you are like [the British suffragette] Mrs Pankhurst and [the British Home Secretary Reginald] McKenna and never never will governmental physical force prevail against a great moral and spiritual upheaval.[106]

Like that other English friend of Smuts, the Cambridge don H. J. Wolstenholme, Emily Hobhouse was far in advance of white opinion in South Africa. More representative was an article published in the *Natal Advertiser* on 30 December, entitled 'The Political Creed of Mr Gandhi'. The paper 'deemed it well to enlighten the South African public, from Mr Gandhi's own mouth, as to what manner of man this is, and what his ultimate political creed is as to the relations between the British and the Indian people'. A string of quotations from Gandhi's book *Hind Swaraj* followed, damning modern civilization and British rule in India. 'And it is an Indian capable of this farago of incoherent, inconsequent and hysterical nonsense', commented the newspaper,

> whom our Union Government is negotiating with as a representative of the concrete demands of the South African Indian community! . . . This is the language of acute hypocrisy! If Western civilisation be so immoral as Mr Gandhi says, a British Dominion should be the last place he would wish his compatriots to enter . . . And it is a man capable of using this language to the British of India who is posing as a martyr here in South Africa because denied the privileges of a European British citizen![107]

That was one view of Gandhi, expressed in public by whites angry and humiliated by the consequences of the recent uprising. Another view was expressed in private by Gopal Krishna Gokhale, in a letter written to Sir Benjamin Robertson on 31 December. 'I do not think you have met Mr Gandhi', said Gokhale to the Viceroy's emissary to the Enquiry Commission:

> He is a thoroughly straightforward, honourable and high-minded man and though he may at times appear obstinate and even fanatical, he is really open to conviction . . . The bulk of the community there is devoted to Mr Gandhi and any confidence that you may repose in him will not

only be amply justified by him by his conduct, but will be repaid tenfold by the gratitude which it will inspire in the community.[108]

Gandhi himself stressed what he owed the Indian community in South Africa, not what they owed him. On 31 December 1913, *Indian Opinion* printed its last issue for the year. This noted that the last satyagraha campaign 'has hardly a parallel in history. The real credit for this goes to the Hindi and Tamil speaking brothers and sisters living in this country.' To mark their sacrifice, and the memory of those killed by soldiers' bullets, the periodical would now resume the publication of sections in Tamil and Hindi.[109]

21

Farewell to Africa

On 2 January 1914, two English clergymen arrived in Durban to meet Gandhi. Their names were C. F. Andrews and W. W. Pearson. Both taught at St Stephen's College in Delhi; both were associates and admirers of Rabindranath Tagore. Andrews in particular had identified strongly with the people of India. Like an Indian *sadhu* he was celibate, lived simply and cultivated friendships with a wide cross-section of society.[1]

C. F. Andrews was an old acquaintance of Gokhale's. After they met at a Congress session in 1906, he wrote to Gokhale that 'if at any time there is any way you can suggest in which I can help the national cause you know how glad I shall be to do so if it is within my power.'[2] Gokhale remembered this promise, and some years later decided to redeem it. In December 1913, when Gandhi and company were still in jail, he asked Andrews and Pearson to go out to South Africa to mediate between the Indians and the Government. Introducing them to Albert West of the Phoenix Settlement, Gokhale described them as 'both great friends of India'.[3]

Andrews was a 'non-official' mediator. His official counterpart was Sir Benjamin Robertson, the civil servant deputed by the Viceroy to represent the Government of India. Robertson was briefed by Gokhale, who sent him copies of *Indian Opinion* for the middle months of 1913, which showed 'that every possible effort was made by Mr Gandhi to arrive at a settlement before resuming the struggle'. Gokhale then listed, for Robertson's benefit, the five major demands of the Indians in South Africa, namely, the removal of racial handicaps in the immigration law; the restoration of the right of South Africa born Indians to enter Cape

Province; the abolition of the £3 tax; the recognition of monogamous marriages performed under the rites of Indian religions; and, finally, a more generous and sympathetic administration of all laws concerning Indians. Gokhale recalled the assurance given him in 1912 that the £3 tax would be repealed, and said that without a recognition of Hindu and Muslim marriages, 'the position of Indian women in South Africa cannot be honourable.'[4]

When C. F. Andrews and W. W. Pearson arrived in Durban, the local Indians hosted a reception in their honour. Here Andrews spoke with 'deep feeling' about the widespread sympathy in India with their sufferings. A 'profound impression was caused when Mr Andrews recited, with beautiful accent and effect, a Sanskrit mantra, which was given to him as a message to South African Indians by the poet Tagore.'[5] So reported the *Natal Mercury*, whereas *Indian Opinion* highlighted the songs sung in the visitor's honour by Gandhi's old schoolmate Sheikh Mehtab. The two were now quite reconciled, with the erstwhile sportsman, meat-eater and brothel visitor having become a singer and passive resister. The songs rendered at this Durban reception, reported *Indian Opinion*, had 'been specially composed by Mr Shaikh Mehtab as a tribute to the devotion of Messrs. Andrews and Pearson to the Indian cause'.[6]

Also present at the meeting was Gandhi's friend from Cape Town, Betty Molteno. At this Indian welcome for their English visitors, she spoke of a deeper humanity that would overcome divisions of race and gender. 'After the Boer War', said Miss Molteno,

> I saw that Boer and Briton would have to unite, but would they try to do it at the cost of their dark brothers? Broken-hearted I went to England. For eight long years I remained away from Africa – in body – never in soul and spirit. And England and Europe have sent me back with this message to white South Africa: 'Open your hearts – your souls – to your brethren of colour'. We are in the 20th century. Rise to the heights of this glorious century. Try to comprehend the words of Du Bois – that grand and sympathetic soul: 'The 20th century will be the century of colour.' And I say it is also the century of the woman. She, too, is divine and supreme. She, too, must play her God-appointed part – and in this 20th century her part will be a great one.[7]

The morning after the Durban meeting, the clergymen went off with Gandhi to Phoenix. Despite Andrews's arrival, Gandhi was not hopeful of a settlement. He had yielded to Gokhale's plea and called off the march to Pretoria; now, given the character of the Enquiry Commission, he wanted satyagraha to resume. Among the volunteers who would have to court arrest was his eldest son. 'Subject your sanction feel Hari-lal should come,' Gandhi wired Gokhale. 'He vowed see struggle through as resister. Should be permitted fulfil obligation. My opinion gaol other experiences substantial education.'[8]

This wire, sent on 3 January, is best read in juxtaposition with a letter sent the next day to his second son. Manilal was serving a sentence of three months in prison; he awaited release pending a formal amnesty. His father said that on his discharge he must come straight to Phoenix to see Kasturba and himself. 'Ramdas is looking well and has done well', wrote Gandhi. 'Dev[a]das has proved a hero. He has developed a sense of responsibility which was unexpected.'[9] There is a note here of quiet pride with regard to the growing closeness of the family during the campaign. The father as leader; the mother as a pioneering woman resister; the second and third sons as satyagrahis themselves; the young-est son, only twelve, who could not go to jail but played his part in keeping Phoenix going – all had acquitted themselves honourably. Only Harilal was in India and out of it altogether.

Gandhi had for some time wanted Harilal back in South Africa. In late December he had cabled his son to take a ship to Durban. That cable is lost, but its contents can be guessed at from one sent by Gokhale to Gandhi, which read: 'Your son Harilal saw me Bombay, told me you had asked him return South Africa immediately rejoin struggle. I have taken on myself responsibility asking him remain India and continue studies. Forgive my intervention.'[10]

The intervention was disregarded. Thus Gandhi's cable of 3 January, which Gokhale passed on to Harilal himself. Harilal wrote back from the family home in Rajkot, where he then was. He asked about Gokha-le's health – reported to be indifferent – offering his own prayer 'that you may soon be out of bed and be working again'. 'Before reading the news of your health', wrote Harilal,

> my friends and me all here in our house used always to chat away with
> much éclat about you and the S[outh] A[frican] struggle . . . I notice my

father's reply to your cable. I admit I promised my father and others to return to rejoin the struggle if necessary. I will not refuse to keep it. I shall go if I must, though I certainly feel that my education is being hampered. As it is, it is after a long interruption of six years that I have again come to India for University education. However I shall leave for S[outh] A[frica] in about a fortnight.[11]

Harilal's letter was written in a firm, clear hand, and in direct and eco-nomical prose. The form barely masked the contents, which are of a young man deeply torn between the expectations of his father and his own hopes and desires. Gokhale was moved by Harilal's predicament in person; and must surely have been moved by his letter, whose apparent willingness to catch a ship to Durban is hedged and qualified in such telling ways. As it happens, Harilal did not return to South Africa. We do not know why – whether Gokhale wrote again to Gandhi pleading on behalf of the boy, whether Gandhi himself chose not to press the point, whether Harilal decided to follow his own instincts rather than his father's command.

The clergyman visiting from India, C. F. Andrews, was one of nature's reconcilers. At Phoenix he prevailed upon Gandhi to meet Smuts to seek a compromise. The always complicated, fraught relations between the two had recently gone through a very bitter phase. Through the mass march across the border, Gandhi had mounted an open challenge to Smuts. The General had responded by putting his tormentor in jail. Pressed by the Imperial and Indian Governments, Smuts released him. Then they exchanged sharp letters about the constitution of the Enquiry Committee.

Now, Gandhi was persuaded by Andrews (acting on Gokhale's behalf) that it was time to talk to Smuts again. On 6 January, 'much to his surprise', the General received a letter from Gandhi asking for an appointment.[12]

Smuts said he could meet Gandhi on either Friday the 9th or Saturday the 10th. Gandhi and Andrews reached Pretoria on the 8th, to be met first by a reporter, who was struck by the Indian's 'extraordinary appear-ance, with his shaven head, his mourning suit of unbleached calico and his bare feet'.[13] Meanwhile, a nationwide strike of white workers had broken out, forcing the General's attention in that direction. Andrews was impressed by Gandhi's 'gentlemanly conduct', as he waited patiently while Smuts 'put him off again and again on account of the General Strike'. They had a brief meeting on the 13th, when, as Andrews reported, Gandhi 'was so kindly and courteous that the old relation of respect between them gradually came back again'.[14]

On the 14th, in a conversation of seconds as it were, C. F. Andrews met the Governor-General, Lord Gladstone. The clergyman 'impressed me favourably', reported Gladstone, not least because he seemed to 'have an exceptionally intimate acquaintance with the working of Mr Gandhi's mind'. Andrews said the two main demands that must be met were the abolition of the £3 tax and the recognition of Indian marriages. These had been promised by the leader to his increasingly militant followers, and were non-negotiable. 'Nothing could shake Mr Gandhi on matters of conscience', remarked Andrews. He reminded the Governor-General of how, in Johannesburg in 1908, Gandhi had been assaulted and nearly killed 'because after taking a vow he had come to an agreement' with the Government. A capitulation on those two points would make Gandhi vulnerable to another attempt on his life.[15]

Gandhi met Smuts for a longer conversation on the 16th. He asked, in addition to the repeal of the tax and the recognition of marriages, for the entry of South African Indians into the Cape, and for the removal of an overt racial bar in the laws of the Free State. (The logic of allowing free entry into the Cape was that, like Natal, it was originally a British colony, with greater and older obligations to British imperial subjects than Transvaal or the Orange Free State.) Smuts was sympathetic, but requested Gandhi to state these issues in front of the Enquiry Commission, who, in turn, could then formally recommend these changes to the Government. Gandhi answered that they could not go back now on their boycott of the Commission.

Reporting this interview to the Colonial Office, Lord Gladstone said:

General Smuts has shown a most patient and conciliatory temper. In spite of a series of conflicts extending over many years, he retains a sympathetic interest in Mr Gandhi as an unusual type of humanity, whose peculiarities, however inconvenient they may be to the Minister, are not devoid of attraction to the student . . . It is no easy task for a European to conduct negotiations with Mr Gandhi. The workings of his conscience are inscrutable to the occidental mind and produce complications in wholly unexpected places. His ethical and intellectual attitude, based as it appears to be on a curious compound of mysticism and astuteness, baffles the ordinary processes of thought. Nevertheless, a tolerably practical understanding has been reached.[16]

Gandhi and Andrews returned to Durban. Letters and phone calls passed between Phoenix and Pretoria, with Smuts assuring Gandhi that he need feel

> no serious apprehensions as to the probable nature of the Commission's recommendations on his four points and as to the Government's intentions, but he should promise not to revive passive resistance until the Commission had reported and the Government had been given an opportunity of acting on the report.[17]

Gandhi also had several long meetings with Sir Benjamin Robertson, which focused on the marriage question. He said the Commission, and the law, should recognize as valid all *de facto* monogamous marriages celebrated anywhere in the past. Monogamous marriages contracted in the future could be solemnized before a priest and, if required, registered. This anterior recognition, said Gandhi, was crucial; otherwise the children of such unions were in danger of being stigmatized as 'illegitimate'.

Gandhi further asked that wives who were *de facto* monogamous be admitted into South Africa; and that existing plural wives of Indians who had rights of residence in South Africa be registered. The Government was especially worried about the legitimacy accorded by Indian faiths to polygamy. Gandhi argued that an acceptance of his proposals 'as to legal recognition of *de facto* monogamous unions enables the State to popularise monogamy to an extent hitherto unknown' in South Africa.[18]

The course of the negotiations with Smuts and others were reported to Gokhale in a long and intensely felt letter written to him by C. F. Andrews. This stressed Gandhi's goodness of character, but also the fragility of his nerves, on edge as a consequence of the crises he had faced these past few months. As he was negotiating with Smuts, Kasturba again fell ill, while his old rivals P. S. Aiyar and M. C. Anglia had decided to renege on the boycott and testify to the Commission. When the General's letter outlining the settlement came, Gandhi was 'terribly excited and said that from first to last the letter was a studied insult'. Andrews was now 'in despair'. Gandhi had expected a personal letter, corresponding with the friendliness of the interviews. What he got was a missive in neutral, even officious language. Going over the communication sentence by sentence, Andrews 'saw at last where the one omission lay. It lay in General Smuts not recognizing the honourableness of Mr Gandhi's motives.' The priest went up to meet Smuts once more, and had a clause inserted that satisfied Gandhi's honour.

It had been a close-run thing, wrote Andrews to Gokhale, which he had recounted in detail as it bore on Gandhi's own future and the future of the Indians in South Africa. In a magisterial analysis of Gandhi's personality, Andrews observed,

> His work in S. Africa is *done* – and nobly done: and this time it was very near to a collapse. Everyone here says he is 'played out'. Polak, Kallenbach, Ritch, etc. – All say the same. He must go, both for his own sake and for the community's. Yes! For the community's: for if he stays on he will dwarf everyone else and there will be no leaders here for at least another generation. It is painfully, palpably evident already: and it will be more evident still in a year's time, if he does not go. Let this honourable settlement be reached and then immediately without a moment's delay let him go to India and be with you or at one of the Servant of India Houses. It is pitiful to see him here at work. He does everything – he *will* do everything: and people simply get to lean on him more and more and the selfish ones take advantage of his goodness. He gets into the way of giving hasty orders without careful thinking (having to settle so many affairs) and when it comes to the *big* things on which the whole issue is staked again and again lately he has acted or thought hastily . . . He is one of the best men in the world! . . . He has made the noblest fight that has been made for years, and I cannot bear to think that it should all end in some great and huge mistake made in haste . . . but persisted in because of a mind distracted or outworn.[19]

This is a perceptive letter, showing (*pace* Lord Gladstone) that at least one European understood the mind and methods of (the mystical) Mr Gandhi. These past months had been incredibly intense for Gandhi. Planning for the satyagraha without knowing where the volunteers or funds would come from; courting arrest and the spell in jail; the illness

FAREWELL TO AFRICA

of his wife and the still problematic relationship with his eldest son; the difficult and still unresolved negotiations with his old adversary; indeed the whole question of whether or not he should even remain in South Africa – all these issues agonized and troubled him. And he would yet ride all the horses – 'he does everything – he *will* do everything', as Andrews put it, the accumlated stress making his friends fearful that he might be headed for a breakdown.

Throughout January, batches of passive resisters were released from prison. They were met at the jail gates by their comrades, and then conveyed to receptions in Durban. When Mrs Sheikh Mehtab and her mother were released on 12 January, Maganlal Gandhi and his wife were at hand to receive them. Eight days later it was the turn of Mrs Thambi Naidoo and her fellow Tamils to be freed. The ladies were taken from the Durban prison to Parsee Rustomjee's store on Field Street, where they were garlanded and fed with home-cooked food. Their stoicism and sacrifice was saluted in speeches made by, among others, Henry and Millie Polak, and Sonja Schlesin. Songs of praise were sung by Sheikh Mehtab and his pupils in Hindustani, and by the Moodley sisters, in Tamil.[20]

In the second week of February Gandhi came down to Cape Town with Kasturba and C. F. Andrews. The Hindu couple and their Christian friend stayed with a Muslim family, the Gools. On the 14th, Andrews gave a lecture on the life and work of Rabindranath Tagore at the Town Hall. The Governor-General, Lord Gladstone, presided. Among the 'large [and] distinguished audience' were some Members of Parliament. The point of Andrews's talk was to demonstrate that India was not merely a land of 'coolies' but also of 'noble ideals'. He expressed the 'warmest appreciation of higher Indian life and thought', as represented particularly by Tagore.[21]

The conflict in South Africa was not mentioned, but Andrews clearly had it in mind when stressing Tagore's universalism, his capacity to rise above parochial identities of language and race. The poet's work, he argued, offered the hope that

> in the higher phases of life and thought East and West may become wholly
> and intimately one ... [Where] the disruptive forces and jealous rivalries

of race and colour and intolerant creeds, of commerce and trade and party politics, are so seemingly strong and outwardly powerful, it is indeed no small blessing to mankind, if even a single voice can be heard above their discordant tumult, speaking a message which East and West alike acknowledge to be true and great . . . [The] sovereignty of the poet is no shadowy thing. It is already heralding the downfall of ancient tyrannies and the coming in of new world forces which make for peace.[22]

On 19 February, the Indians of Cape Town threw a farewell party for C. F. Andrews. The guest of honour was the liberal MP W. P. Schreiner, who saluted the priest as a representative of 'the entire brotherhood of humanity'. So, of course, was the speaker himself. Andrews's blindness to matters of race was rare enough among white men in British India, but truly exceptional in Schreiner's South Africa.

Andrews himself spoke both in Hindustani and English. He had penned a last message for the newspapers, which thanked South Africans for their hospitality, and observed that the atmosphere regarding the Indian question had 'wonderfully changed' in recent weeks. The credit for this change he gave to 'Mr Gandhi's chivalrous attitude' and 'General Smuts' great considerateness'. He modestly omitted to mention his own reconciling role.[23]

Andrews left by the SS *Briton* on 21 February. Five days later, he sent Gandhi a letter suffused with love and regard. When 'I saw you on the wharf standing with hands raised in prayer and benediction', he wrote, 'I knew, as I had not known, even in Pretoria, how very, very dear you had become to me and I gazed and gazed and the sadness grew upon me and even the thought that I was on my way to India could not overcome it.' Later, when he felt seasick, he was consoled by the memory of his friend, of

> this new gift in my life which God had given me; and it made me so happy, Mohan, even while I was in utter physical misery, – just to think of it and remember it! . . . Somehow I didn't quite know how much you had learnt to love me till that morning when you put your hand on my shoulder and spoke of the loneliness that there would be to you when I was gone.

In the six weeks that Gandhi and Andrews had spent in each other's company, they had come to be soulmates. The word, or cliché, is inescapable, and apposite. These were both seekers after truth and God, men of sentiment and conscience who sought heroically to reconcile East and West, white and brown, colonizer and colonized, and, not least, Hinduism and Christianity. More than the £3 tax and the marriage question and the personality of General Smuts, the duo had discussed – at Phoenix, Pretoria, Johannesburg, Cape Town – the multiple paths to God. Thus, after its intimate and emotionally charged prologue, Andrews's letter moved on to matters of faith. His month with Gandhi had inspired him to write a book on the comparative history of religion, on how the 'persistent voice of conscience' had 'become marvellously developed and expressed in the two great races which possessed religious *genius*, – the Semitic and the Indo-Aryan'. The writing of this book would mean 'a lonely pilgrimage', because – no doubt under the influence of his new Hindu friend – it would mean 'giving up claims for the Christian position which everyone in the West whom I know and love ... could not conceive of doing'.[24]

Shortly after his new friend had left, a letter arrived for Gandhi from his oldest friend, Pranjivan Mehta. This asked for a receipt for Mehta's contributions in 1913 – amounting to the considerable sum of Rs 32,000 – and added: 'I hope the [proposed] new Bill [embodying the agreement between Gandhi and Smuts] has mitigated your hardships.'[25] Left unspoken was the other (and greater) hope, so long and so passionately held by Mehta, that his friend would now move back to India and prepare to take charge of the political movement there.

There had been several occasions in the past when Gandhi had been on the verge of returning home. In October 1901 he left Durban with his family, in his eyes for good. A little over a year later, he was brought back to negotiate the rights of South African Indians in the post-War settlement. He came, hoping however to return as soon as he possibly could. In September 1904 he offered a compromise solution to Lord Milner, a halfway house between the extreme demands of the White Leaguers and those of the more radical Indians. Had this been accepted, Gandhi would have rejoined Kasturba and the children, and had a third try at establishing himself in the Bombay High Court.

When Milner rebuffed him, Gandhi asked the family to join him in Johannesburg instead. In 1906 and 1909 he visited London to lobby for the rights of the Indian community; on either occasion, had their demands been met he would have returned to India. In the summer of

1911 he once more had strong hopes that Smuts would acquiesce to their main demands. That, too, was not to be – so a fresh round of satyagraha was launched. Now, finally, an honourable settlement was about to be inked into law – and the Gandhis could fulfil Pranjivan Mehta's deepest desire and go back to their homeland.

Back in 1911, preparing for his eventual departure from South Africa, Gandhi had handed over his practice in Johannesburg to L. W. Ritch. Then in May 1913, Henry Polak moved to Durban, opening an office on Smith Street, where he met clients as well as subscribers to *Indian Opinion*.[26] Gandhi's hope now was that since he had arranged for experienced hands to represent the community, he – who had come to South Africa to settle a single dispute, staying on, with interruptions, for two decades – could finally return to India himself.

In the last week of February 1914, Gandhi wrote to Gokhale that he planned to depart in April with his family, and with some boys from the Phoenix School. His mentor had bound him to a vow of silence on political matters, operative for a full year after his return to India. That vow he would 'scrupulously observe'. His 'present ambition', he told Gokhale, was to 'be by your side as your nurse and attendant. I want to have the real discipline of obeying someone whom I love and look up to. I know I made a bad secretary in South Africa. I hope to do better in the Motherland if I am accepted.'[27]

Gandhi was still in Cape Town, in part because he wished to be at hand while the report of the Enquiry Commission was finalized, and in part because Kasturba was very ill. She could not sit without support, and could not eat solid food either. Grapes and orange juice were her main sustenance. Gandhi was anxious about the settlement, and anxious about his wife's health. She had developed 'ominous swellings' whose cause the doctor, their friend and host Dr Gool, could not yet locate.[28] Kasturba lay 'hanging between life and death'. She was claiming Gandhi's 'undivided attention'; she wanted him 'by her side the whole day'. In one twenty-four hour period, all she consumed was the juice of two tomatoes and a teaspoonful of oil. 'It seems to me,' wrote Gandhi to Kallenbach, that 'she is gradually sinking.'[29]

These factors explain, but do not excuse, the extraordinary harshness of a letter Gandhi wrote his son Harilal on 2 March. 'I have your letter', he began. 'You apologize in every letter of yours and put up a defence as well. It all seems to me sheer hypocrisy now. For years, you have been slack in writing letters, and then come forward with apologies. Will this go on until death, I forgiving every time.'

Gandhi went on to compare Harilal with his brothers. 'You violate all the conditions I had made and you promised to fulfil', he complained:

> You were never asked to go in for studies at the cost of your health. You have failed to take care of it. No wonder that Ramdas and Manilal have outdone you. And Ramdas has put in a fine effort, indeed, and grown in size as well. Manilal, too, has plenty of strength and would have been stronger yet if he had not taken to the evil ways of pleasure [with Jeki Mehta]. Even their studies I take to be sounder than yours.

Harilal had expressed a desire to go to Bombay to continue his studies. In that case, said Gandhi, he must leave his wife Chanchi and children in Gujarat. 'Weighing my advice against that of others', concluded Gandhi, 'do what you think best. I am a father who is prejudiced against you. I do not approve of your ways at all. I doubt whether you have any love for us. This statement sounds very harsh, but I see extreme insincerity in your letters.'[30]

Gandhi sent Harilal's letter to Manilal. 'Think over the wretched state he has been reduced to', he remarked. 'The fault is not his, but mine. During his childhood, I followed a way of life none too strict in its rule and he is still under its influence. Tear off the letter after reading it.' The prejudiced father hoped that the second son would make up for the deficencies of his brother. Once they returned, said Gandhi to Manilal, 'It is my desire to see you esteemed in India as a *brahmachari* of a high order, your conduct so naturally well-disciplined that it cannot but produce an impression on others. This will require hard work, study and purity in you.'[31]

By the second week of March, Kasturba's health had improved. Gandhi attributed the recovery to his own methods of healing. There was speculation that the swelling in her stomach might be cancerous. Gandhi believed that cancer 'never yields to medical treatment but it must yield to fasting treatment if the patient has stamina'.[32] He put his wife on an extended fast, feeding her only with *neem* leaves in water. The pain in her stomach eased. She could now sit up, and eat. 'If she survives', he told his nephew Maganlal, 'take it for certain that our [nature-cure] remedies and faith in God have saved her. She has come to realize that the doctor's medicine was the cause of her breakdown.'[33]

Kasturba's life was no longer in danger, but now her husband's life was. Word that the Enquiry Commission would only recognize monogamous marriages had reached the Muslim merchants in the Transvaal. These merchants had brought Gandhi to South Africa; they had funded his early campaigns; many of them had gone to jail under his leadership. But recognition of the right of a man to have multiple wives was a central article of their faith. Now they accused Gandhi of betraying their interests, and, more crucially, their religion.

In early March, Gandhi heard that his brother Laxmidas had passed away in Porbandar. He had been sick for some time. Although they had not met for more than a decade, in recent years they had become somewhat reconciled. Gandhi had forgiven or forgotten the intrigue that got the family into trouble in Porbandar in 1891. Laxmidas had gloried in the popular acclaim his younger brother was receiving in India for the work he was doing in South Africa.[34] Gandhi's other brother, Karsandas, had died the previous June. Preoccupied with the satyagraha, he did not comment in public on either death; but he knew now that he would go back to a India bereft of his parents and his brothers too. Only his sister Raliat, herself a widow, still survived.

On 11 March, Gandhi wrote to his nephew Chhaganlal that he had heard that 'they are plotting again in Johannesburg to take my life. That would indeed be welcome and a fit end to my work.' In case he was killed, Gandhi left instructions on what the family must do. They should live like farmers on the land, simply. Gandhi had to provide for five widows, these being his sister, the wives of his two dead brothers, and two other family members. If Gandhi was now murdered by his enemies, the money for this could be taken from Pranjivan Mehta. Over the course of time, however, sons should assume responsibility for their widowed mothers, including Harilal for Kasturba.[35]

It was a young man named Medh who had written to Gandhi about the plot to murder him. We do not know who the plotters were. The Pathans who had assaulted and nearly killed him in 1908? And were they to act on their own or as mercenaries of the merchants? How active was the plot in any case? Had Medh drawn hasty conclusions from words spoken in anger? What we do know is there were increasing concerns in Johannesburg about what the Commission would say on the marriage question. In the last week of March, a 'largely attended meeting representing all sections of Mohammedans in the Transvaal' took place in the Hamidia Hall. Gandhi had often spoken here to appreciative and even admiring crowds. But this time he was, so to speak, an absent presence. The meeting resolved that 'the recommendation of recognising one wife only and her children ... if carried out, will molest and violate the principle of our sacred religion.' The meeting further made 'it known to whom it may concern that Messrs Gandhi, Polak and their associates have no right or authority whatsoever to represent the Moslem community or any matters concerning them.'[36]

In the last week of March, the report of the Enquiry Commission was published. It was ambivalent about Gandhi, acknowledging that he was 'the recognised leader of the Indian community', but regretting that he and his followers chose 'entirely to ignore the Commission', so that no witnesses came forward to substantiate the allegations of the excessive use of force against the strikers. Compelled to rely on the evidence of the police, the Commission concluded that in the places where men in uniform had shot bullets into crowds, 'the use of firearms was fully justified'.

Other recommendations of the Commission were more comforting to the Indians. It asked the Government to pass legislation that would, among other things, allow Indian residents in South Africa to bring in one wife and minor children by her; permit the appointment of Indian priests of different denominations to solemnize marriages in South Africa; register *de facto* monogamous marriages already in existence; repeal the £3 tax applied annually on Indians in Natal; issue identification certificates for three years at a time (rather than for one year, the existing practice); and to provide interpreters to assist Indians in making applications to register marriages, obtain certificates, etc.[37]

Gandhi was pleased with the report, whose promptness justified his boycott. Had the Indians given evidence, he argued, then the Europeans would have insisted on doing likewise, and the report would have been delayed by months. Indians and whites would have exchanged bitter words in public, and it would 'not have been possible for Mr Andrews to do what he did, sowing the seeds of conciliation so silently and with such deep love and humility'. In any case, the Commission's recommendations on the £3 tax and marriage question 'could not possibly have been better even if we had tendered voluminous evidence'. He now hoped that the Government would meet Indian demands in the Cape and the Free State.[38]

The favourable recommendations of the Enquiry Commission were noted in the press in India, which gave the credit to the passive resisters. *Sadhva*, a Kannada weekly published in Mysore, published a striking paean to the distinctiveness of Gandhi's political method. Thus

> not a sword was drawn, not a gun fired . . . Mr Gandhi merely defied the unjust laws of the South African Government, agitated for their removal, even went to jail, and renewed his campaign of passive resistance the moment he was released. In this manner he raised an uproar against their iniquities and finally forced them to the right path. He performed, so to speak, the obsequies of unrighteousness. History has its heroes in men of the type of Alexander the Great whose fame is measured by the havoc and devastation they caused, but heroism of the type displayed by Mr Gandhi in making iniquity's defeat its own end is without a parallel.[39]

In early May the Gandhis were back at Phoenix, where Kasturba's health continued to improve. 'If her progress continues', wrote her husband to Gokhale, 'in a month's time she should regain most of her former health. In that case and in any case I could come to London taking her with me. And after consultation with you, we may both proceed to India directly and the rest of the party may leave here after we have left.'[40]

Gokhale was spending the summer in London, as was C. F. Andrews. They had long talks, the gist of which were passed on to Gandhi in Durban. Unlike the priest and the ascetic, Gokhale was not a seeker for or after God. He told Andrews that 'his love for the Motherland, his vision, his absorption in its life and future was to him religion itself and made the Divine real to him.' Patriotism was Gokhale's religion; a patriotism that did not rule out partnership with the foreign rulers as long as they remained on Indian soil. Gokhale told Andrews that 'there was the need of three kinds of national work – that in connection with the foreign Government, that in independence of it, and that in opposition to it. And all were needed.' He worried that Gandhi's insistence on the 'independence' of Indians from Government 'would be a stumbling block' in his working for, and in, the Servants of India Society.[41]

Meanwhile, back at Phoenix, Gandhi's attentions were again diverted to rumours of sexual transgression at the ashram. In mid April Kasturba told Gandhi that she suspected Jeki Mehta of still harbouring romantic feelings for Manilal. Gandhi dismissed the speculation. Kasturba, he thought, was excessively prejudiced against Pranjivan Mehta's daughter; she tended to 'spit fire' on Jeki at every opportunity.

Kasturba then accused Gandhi of shielding Jeki. He answered that she was paranoid. The disagreement spiralled into a fearful row, by all accounts the most intense the Gandhis had had in the thirty years of their marriage. The husband's version, outlined in a letter to Kallenbach, ran:

> Immediately she began to howl. I had made her leave all the good food in order to kill her. I was tired of her, I wished her to die, I was a hooded snake . . . The more I spoke the more vicious she became . . . She is quite normal today. But yesterday's was one of the richest lessons of my life. All the charges she brought against me she undoubtedly means. She has contrary emotions. I have nursed her as a son would nurse his mother. But my love has not been sufficiently intense and selfless to make her change her nature . . . Yes, a man who wishes to work with detachment must not marry. I cannot complain of her being a particularly bad wife . . . On the other hand no other woman would probably have stood the changes in her husband's life as she has. On the whole she has not thwarted me and has been most exemplary . . . My point is that you cannot attach yourself to a particular woman and yet live for humanity. The two do not harmonise. That is the real cause of the devil waking in her now and again. Otherwise he might have remained in her asleep and unnoticed.[42]

As with Harilal, Gandhi's relations with his wife were tested again and again by his tendency to place career and cause above family and marriage. In this case, Kasturba was protective about her second son, and thus inclined to blame Jeki for her romance with Manilal. Gandhi was more even-handed, seeing the son as equally responsible for the transgression.

This particular dispute brought to the fore other disagreements the couple had over the years. In his reflections on their relationship, Gandhi is detached and (to a degree) balanced. With Harilal he tended to be more one-sided. The boy was blamed, and blamed again, for not living up to the ideals of the father. On the other hand, this letter to Kallenbach, while unable to conceal a sense of impatience with Kasturba, sees her discontent as having its origins in choices made by him, that she (and he) were unaware of when they got married in their teens in Porbandar.

Two weeks after Kasturba and Gandhi quarrelled, Jeki Mehta was found making sexual overtures to another man, not Manilal. Gandhi was hurt and angry. Jeki was a 'finished hypocrite', a pathological liar who had betrayed him, her father and the community. He decided to send her back to join her husband Manilal Doctor in Fiji.[43]

To atone for Jeki's new lapse, and his own inadequate supervision, Gandhi decided to go on a two-week fast. Kasturba asked him to desist; she feared for his health. Her husband went ahead anyway. After it ended, he wrote to Kallenbach that

> this fast has brought me as near death's door. I can still hardly crawl, can eat very little, restless nights, mouth bad . . . The fast was a necessity. I was so grossly deceived. I owed it to Manilal of Fiji, to Dr. Mehta, and to myself. It was one of the severest lessons of my life. The discipline was very great. Everyone around me was most charming. Mrs. Gandhi was divine. Immediately she realized that there was no turning me back, she set about making my path smooth. She forgot her own sorrows and became my ministering angel.[44]

In the last week of May, a bill embodying the Enquiry Commission's recommendations was published. This provided for the recognition of past monogamous marriages conducted under the tenets of any Indian religion the parties professed; recognized the rights of children such unions produced; mandated the appointment of priests of any Indian religion to be marriage officers; abolished the £3 tax and waived the right of the state to collect past arrears against it; and permitted the Government to provide free passage to anyone in South Africa who wished to go back permanently to India.[45]

Gandhi spent the whole of June in Cape Town, lobbying MPs and meeting ministers. The bill passed through Parliament in stages, meeting opposition which was skilfully negotiated and eventually overcome by General Smuts and the Prime Minister, General Botha. The Governor-General wrote to the Colonial Office praising the duo 'for their courage in forcing a thoroughly distasteful policy upon their followers'. For 'the strength of the anti-Indian prejudice among our Dutch legislators and the extraordinary cussedness of some of our British

Natalians [were] really amazing'. The former were loth to recognize any Indian marriages; the latter loth to give up the punitive £3 tax. To tame the opposition, Botha and Smuts had to use all their 'powers of persuasion'; in fact, 'but for party loyalty all the Dutch back-benchers would have voted against the Bill.'[46]

On 27 June, there was a meeting of Europeans and Indians in Cape Town to celebrate the passage of the Indians' Relief Bill. Here Gandhi thanked 'the many European friends whose help had most materially contributed to the success now realized'. He said that

potent, however, though passive resistance was as an instrument for winning reforms – perhaps the mightiest instrument on earth – it could not have achieved success had the Indian community not moderated their demands to what was reasonable and practical. This, again, was not possible until some of them were able to see the question of Indian rights from the European standpoint . . . The Indians knew perfectly well which was the dominant and governing race. They aspired to no social equality with Europeans. They felt that the path of their development was separate. They did not even aspire to the franchise, or, if the aspiration existed, it was with no idea of its having present effect. Ultimately – in the future – he believed his people would get the franchise if they deserved to get it, but the matter did not belong to practical politics. All he would ask for the Indian community was that, on the basis of the rights now conceded to them, they should be suffered to live with dignity and honour on the soil of South Africa.[47]

As the bill was making its progress through Parliament, Gandhi wrote to Gokhale that Kallenbach would accompany Kasturba and him to London. The architect had long wished to visit India; to this wish was now added the desire not to be separated from his friend. After Gandhi had consulted with Gokhale in London, and Kallenbach said good-bye to his family in Europe, they would carry on to India. With the bill now gazetted, their bookings were made for 18 July. 'My one desire', wrote Gandhi to Gokhale, 'is now to meet you and see you, take my orders from you and leave at once for India.'[48]

On 1 July, Gandhi left Cape Town. He travelled via Kimberley and Johannesburg, reaching Durban on the 4th. Two weeks were left for his departure; two weeks to bid good-bye to the friends, followers, associations and places that he had known and experienced in twenty years in South Africa.

On 8 July, there was a farewell meeting for the Gandhis in the Durban Town Hall. Back in 1897, this had been the venue for the meetings of the mob that wanted to lynch him. Now, Indians and Europeans gathered in friendship, to hear Gandhi say that 'he did not deserve all the praise bestowed on him. Nor did his wife claim to deserve all that had been said of her. Many an Indian woman had done greater service during the struggle than Mrs. Gandhi.' He thanked all the Europeans who had helped him and the struggle, from the lawyer F. A. Laughton, who 'stood by him against the mob' in 1897, to Mrs Alexander, the policeman's wife who 'protected him with her umbrella from the missiles thrown by the excited crowd', to his long-time comrades Kallenbach and Polak. He would go away with 'no ill-will against a single European. I have received many hard knocks in my life, but here I admit that I have received those most precious gifts from Europeans – love and sympathy.'[49]

The Town Hall meeting was ecumenical. The next day, the Gandhis were congratulated by their own community, the Gujaratis of Durban. Gandhi asked the audience to 'learn their mother-tongue and study the history and traditions of their Motherland, where he hoped to see them one day'. He urged them to treat members of other communities like guests in their house. Gandhi himself had 'always shown the same respect for Muslims as for Hindus . . . If every Indian lived thus in amity with others, there is not the slightest doubt that we shall make great advance in South Africa.'

The same day, the 9th, Gandhi spoke at a sports day for children, held in the Albert Park. He was pleased that the trophy had been presented by Parsee Rustomjee, of whom he said the Indians

> had no better, no more constant leader to work with in South Africa. Mr Rustomjee knew no distinction of race or religion. He was a Parsee among Parsees, but also a Mahomedan among Mahomedans in that he would do for them, die for them, live for them. He was a Hindu among Hindus and would do for them likewise.

Also on the 9th, Gandhi attended a reception hosted by the Dheds, a caste of untouchables charged with sanitary duties. The reformer saw them as 'our own brethren', and said that 'to regard them with the slightest disrespect not only argues our own unworthiness but is morally wrong, for it is contrary to the teaching of the Bhagavad Gita.'[50]

Two days later, Gandhi spoke at a banquet hosted by the Europeans of Durban. The value of the recent settlement, he said here, 'lay in the struggle which preceded it – a struggle which quickened the conscience of South Africa – and the fact that there was a different tone prevailing today'. However, while the Commission and the Act had sorted out some difficulties, 'it was not a full settlement. It was not a charter of full liberties.' He especially urged a 'sense of justice' in administering and granting licences, on which many Indians who were traders depended.

The hosts had presented an address to Gandhi, and a set of books to Sonja Schlesin. The latter was not present, so Gandhi accepted the books on her behalf, noting that 'Miss Schlesin had played a great part in the passive resistance movement. She had worked night and day and thrown herself into the work. She had not hesitated to court imprisonment but that was denied her.'

In Durban, Gandhi also called on his friend-turned-rival M. C. Anglia. Anglia had recently started a newspaper that regularly ran articles critical of Gandhi, complaining in particular that the settlement with the Government prohibited polygamy.[51] Notably, while Gandhi sought to mend fences with Anglia he did not do the same with P. S. Aiyar, judging perhaps that *this* critic was too far gone to be reconciled.

Gandhi then travelled to Phoenix where, on 11 July, there was a farewell party for him and Kasturba hosted by the settlers. There were two short speeches: one by Gandhi, the other by Albert West, who, 'in a few brief sentences, referred to the ever-growing friendship, commenced eleven years ago, between Mr Gandhi and himself and its influence upon their lives and the history of the Phoenix Settlement. The singing of some favourite hymns in English and Gujarati brought the proceedings to a close.' West had played a vital role in sustaining Phoenix and sustaining the struggle. He was one of Gandhi's two greatest supporters in Natal; the other, equally self-effacing, was Parsee Rustomjee, who on this occasion too chipped in by providing the food.[52]

Gandhi now moved deeper into the countryside. He spoke to a large audience of indentured labourers in Verulam. This, to him, was

> like going on a pilgrimage, for the Indian friends here played a great part
> in the recent strike; and in what wonderful a manner! When all the so-called

leaders [in Durban] were resting in their private rooms or were busy making money, the indentured brethren of this place, the moment they happened
to hear that a strike was on in Charlestown and elsewhere about the £3 tax,
struck work too. They looked for no leaders.

With the settlement in place, said Gandhi to the labourers, they could
stay on in South Africa as free men, without paying tax or re-indenturing.
Although he was leaving for India, they could approach those who
remained at Phoenix for advice and help. And wherever he was, said
Gandhi, 'I shall, of course, continue to work for you. You are under
indenture for one person for five years, but I am under indenture with
300 millions [of Indians] for a life-time. I shall go on with that service
and never displace you from my heart.'

There was a sprinkling of white managers in the crowd. Addressing
them directly, Gandhi said that

> sometimes the European employer was inclined to be selfish, and he asked
> them to bear in mind that the indentured Indians were human beings, with
> the same sentiments as themselves. They were not cattle, but had all the
> weaknesses of themselves, and all the virtues if only they were brought
> out. He made a plea for sanitary housing, and asked that the Europeans
> would look upon their indentured Indians as fellow-beings, and not as
> Asiatics who had nothing in common with them. The indentured Indian
> was a moral being.[53]

Everywhere he went, Gandhi was presented with addresses and
sometimes with a purse, which he said he would use for public work
only. His speeches at these farewells were artful but also sincere, addressing the specific concerns and anxieties of the audience, while underlining
his own special connection to them.

Europeans, Indians, labourers, merchants, high-castes, low-castes,
Hindus, Muslims, Christians, Parsis – all had worked with Gandhi at
various points in his years in Natal. His links with these groups were
varied – political, personal, professional; social, spiritual, sentimental.
One group however is absent from this otherwise capacious list – the
Africans. To them alone were Gandhi's connections too slight to merit a
formal and public farewell. This was a sign in part of his own orientation, and a sign, perhaps in greater part, of the times.

*

On 12 July, Gandhi and Kasturba left for Johannesburg. This city he had come to later than Durban, but had come to know more intimately. It was where he had befriended Polak, Kallenbach, L. W. Ritch, A. M. Cachalia, Sonja Schlesin, Joseph Doke and Thambi Naidoo; where he had first formulated the theory of satyagraha; and where, with the aid of Gujarati merchants and later of Tamils, he had put this theory to the test.

On the 13th, Gandhi was interviewed by a representative of the *Transvaal Leader*. Asked to recall 'the more remarkable incidents in his career', he selected some from the recent march across the border. He spoke of how he had convinced the striking miners 'that they would win, not by putting their sticks over the shoulders of others, but over their own'. He praised their doggedness, their ability to march days and days on meagre rations. Then he praised the Europeans who had helped them, such as the station-master who had offered the marchers milk, the woman shopkeeper who invited them to take what they wanted, the hotel-owner who said they would be warmer spending the night inside his premises – gestures made spontaneously and without asking for payment, proof of the 'old British sense of sympathy' present in some whites in South Africa.

Gandhi told the newspaper that he was leaving for good, 'with the intention of never returning'. If 'I ever have to return to South Africa or leave India', he said, 'it will be owing to circumstances beyond my control, and at present beyond my conception'. The definitiveness of this departure prompted an elegy for the man and what he represented. 'So it is humanly certain', remarked the *Leader*,

> that the most arresting figure in the Indian community in South Africa to-day is to say good-bye to a country in which he has spent many years, crowded with experience and exertion, his work on behalf of his countrymen at last crowned with success. When a man has been imprisoned so often that were his offences not merely political he would have qualified as a 'habitual', when he has time without number endured fatigue, and fasted with a smile, when he has moved steadily on over obstacles that might daunt the bravest, to the goal to which his eye has been fixed, you might picture him physically as an Apollo, and imagine his heart made of the fibre that belongs to martyrs. In the qualities of the heart and of the soul you may believe the best of Gandhi, but you would wonder,

did you see him, that so frail a figure could house so vigorous a character.[54]

Gandhi would surely have read this tribute. Swept along by its eloquence, did he recall that this was the same paper that, a bare nine months previously, had written off his leadership and his movement? In September 1913 the *Leader* had spoken of an 'astonishing apathy' among the Indians, of an 'absolute distrust' in Gandhi. It had suggested that the satyagraha campaign was 'threatened with collapse'. Now, after the march and the mass strike, the arrest of hundreds of Indians (including women and children) and the acceptance of their demands by the Enquiry Commission, the supposedly failed leader had become a 'most arresting figure', his exertions 'crowned with success'.

The *Leader* was, as some newspapers tend to do, bowing and bending with the wind. The day after its reporter met Gandhi, a meeting in honour of the Indian hero was held at Johannesburg's Masonic Lodge. Addresses were presented on behalf of the British Indian Association, the Cantonese Club, the Tamil Benefit Society, the Transvaal Indian Women's Association, the European Committee, and the Gujarati, Mahomedan and Parsee communities of the city. In a dramatic gesture, Thambi Naidoo offered his four sons to Gandhi, to become under his guidance, 'servants of India'.

The details of some of these tributes have come down to us. That presented by the British Indian Association had as its first signatories A. M. Cachalia and Thambi Naidoo, respectively the foremost Gujarati and Tamil colleague of Gandhi in the satyagraha. It praised the leader's 'nobility, steadfastness, self-sacrifice, and indomitable courage'. It also offered salutations to 'the dignified and silent devotion, to the cause of Indian Womanhood, of the Gracious Lady who shares your joys and sorrows'. Kasturba's 'wonderful self-surrender', the tribute noted, had played a key role in mobilizing the Indians against the marriage laws, now amended in light of their struggle. For their part, the Cantonese Club of Johannesburg offered thanks for Gandhi's 'wise counsel' and the 'remarkable example' of his 'character and conduct'. Through the campaigns of which he was the 'shining exemplar', he had 'raised the prestige of the Asiatic name not only throughout the Union of South Africa, but in the whole civilised world'.[55]

Responding to the tributes, Gandhi gave a speech whose contents were noted by a reporter who was present. He lovingly marked his own memories of, and debts to, this city of gold, greed, conflict and conscience:

> Johannesburg was not a new place to him. He saw many friendly faces there, many who had worked with him in many struggles in Johannesburg. He had gone through much in life. A great deal of depression and sorrow had been his lot, but he had also learnt during all those years to love Johannesburg even though it was a Mining Camp. It was in Johannesburg that he had found his most precious friends. It was in Johannesburg that the foundation for the great struggle of Passive Resistance was laid in the September of 1906. It was in Johannesburg that he had found a friend, a guide, and a biographer in the late Mr Doke. It was in Johannesburg that he had found in Mrs. Doke a loving sister, who had nursed him back to life when he had been assaulted by a countryman who had misunderstood his mission and who misunderstood what he had done. It was in Johannesburg that he had found a Kallenbach, a Polak, a Miss Schlesin, and many another who had always helped him, and had always cheered him and his countrymen . . . It was in Johannesburg again that the European Committee had been formed, when Indians were going through the darkest stage in their history, presided over then, as it still was, by Mr Hosken.

Having praised his European friends, Gandhi now turned to the Indians of the city who had given their lives in and for the satyagraha campaign. He singled out three names: all Tamil, all young; two men, one woman; two who had died in prison and one who had died while being deported to India. It was, said Gandhi,

> Johannesburg that had given Valiamma, that young girl, whose picture rose before him even as he spoke, who had died in the cause of truth . . . [I]t was Johannesburg again that had produced a Nagappen and Narayansamy, two lovely youths hardly out of their teens, who also died. But both Mrs Gandhi and he stood living before them. He and Mrs Gandhi had worked in the lime-light; those others had worked behind the scenes, not knowing where they were going, except this, that what they were doing was right and proper, and, if any praise was due anywhere at all, it was due to the three who died.[56]

The meeting was followed by a dinner, the invitation for which has survived. It was advertised as a farewell to 'Mr and Mrs. M. K. Gandhi and Mr H. Kallenbach'. The union of brown and white was symbolized by a portrait of a handshake. The chairman's name was also printed: he was the Hon. H. A. Wyndham, M.L.A. The other side of the card contained the menu, this divided into hors d'oeuvres ('various'), soups (milk and celery, tomato), main dishes (seven in all, including mashed potatoes, aubergine cutlets, macaroni with cheese, stuffed tomatoes, asparagus à la vinaigrette) and sweets (among them apple pie and custard, blancmange, plum tart and pastries). In deference to the chief guests, no alcohol was served (the drinks on offer being coffee and mineral water), and the food was wholly vegetarian. Still, the spread was substantial, and one wonders whether Gandhi and Kallenbach did anything other than pick at what was put in front of them. Perhaps, as was their custom, they feasted chiefly on two items also printed on the menu, namely, 'fruits' and 'nuts'.[57]

The next day, the 15th, Gandhi attended four meetings in Johannesburg. In the morning, he unveiled tablets at Bramfontein Cemetery in memory of Nagappen, who had died in 1909 and Valiamma, the young woman resister who had died in February 1914. Gandhi recalled the harsh conditions in which they perished, in jail, with 'no feather mattress . . . simply the wooden floor'. He moved next to a meeting of the Transvaal Indian Women's Association, where he asked for the blessings of his sisters for his work in India. A third meeting was of Tamils, whom Gandhi praised for having 'borne the brunt of the struggle'. The majority of the deportees, passive resisters and women in jail were Tamil. The Tamils, said their grateful leader, 'had shown so much pluck, so much faith, so much devotion to duty and such noble simplicity, and yet had been so self-effacing'. Gandhi turned to the terms of the settlement, stressing that 'the £3 tax was now a matter of the past', and that 'all those dear sisters who had gone to gaol could now be called the wives of their husbands, whilst but yesterday they might have been called so out of courtesy by a friend but were not so in the eyes of the law.' Despite his debts to the Tamils, Gandhi still had some advice for them. For 'he had known something of Madras, and how sharp caste distinctions were there. He felt that they would have come to South Africa in vain if they were to carry those caste prejudices with them . . . They should remember that they were not high caste or low caste, but all Indians, all Tamils.'

The most important meeting attended by Gandhi on this day, 15 July 1914, was held at that once familiar venue, the Hamidia Hall. Here, he heard a long harangue from his one-time comrade Essop Mia, who had worked shoulder-to-shoulder with him during their first satyagrahas, who had been with him when he was nearly beaten to death in 1908, and then suffered an assassination attempt himself. Now, six years later, Mia charged Gandhi with having obtained only one and a half of the four points they had asked for. He had now 'left them with the battle to be fought all over again'. Replying to these criticisms, Gandhi said the settlement had abolished the £3 tax, recognized wives and children and clarified the Cape and Free State questions. Then he added, tellingly:

> The merchants had gained everything that the community had gained, and had gained probably most of all. The Indian community had raised its status in the estimation of Europeans throughout South Africa. They could no longer be classed as coolies by General Botha and others. The term had been removed as a term of reproach, silently but effectively. If they had not fought for the past eight years, no trace would have been left here of Indians as a self-respecting community.

The 'half' point Essop Mia mentioned related to the absence of the explicit recognition of polygamy, a practice sacred to Islam. Another speaker, H. O. Ally – he who had accompanied the lawyer to London in 1906 – said he had told Gandhi 'not to bind the Mussulmans with regard to one man one wife', since 'it was impossible for Mussulmans to break one syllable out of their holy *Koran*.' Gandhi answered that the settlement had legalized monogamous marriages, and 'all he expected the South African Government to do was to become tolerant of polygamy, but not to legalise it.'[58]

The meetings with the Tamils and the Gujaratis were a study in contrast, one marked by a mutual respect and affection between the speaker and his audience, the other by mutual reserve, and even antagonism. The Gandhi of 1906 was supported morally and financially by Gujarati merchants; the Gandhi of 1914 was a leader largely of working-class Tamils. The contrast, implied and implicit, was made manifest in his last engagement in Johannesburg. Speaking to a group mostly of Gujarati Hindus on the 16th, he observed that 'my Gujarati brethren have done a great deal for me and Mrs. Gandhi but they did not, I must say, render as much service in the cause of the struggle as the Tamil community did. I wish the Gujaratis to learn a lesson from the Tamils. Though I do not know their language, they have given me the greatest help in the fight.'[59]

On 16 July, Gandhi made a hurried trip to Pretoria, where the merchant Hajee Habib – who had accompanied Gandhi to London in 1909 – organized a party for him. In attendance was Montford Chamney, the long-time Protector-cum-Persecutor of the Indians. Gandhi recalled that

> he had certainly stood up against Mr Chamney and the management of his office, but there had been no personal ill-will on the speaker's part, and he had always received the utmost courtesy at Mr Chamney's hands. He appreciated the compliment Mr Chamney paid him by coming out to arrest him with only one man to assist, when the speaker was at the head of 2,000 men and women. It showed the confidence Mr Chamney had in him as a passive resister.[60]

The same night, Gandhi, Kasturba and Kallenbach took a train to Cape Town. They arrived on the morning of the 18th, to be met at Monument Station by friends with garlands, who took them in carriages into the city. The procession was headed by a band playing music, marching under a banner wishing 'Bon voyage to the great Indian patriot, M. K. Gandhi, and family, also Mr Kallenbach. God be with you until we meet again.'

The Gandhis spent their last night in South Africa at the home of a Jewish couple who were friends of Hermann Kallenbach. Morris Alexander was a liberal lawyer and MP; his wife Ruth was a fiery radical from a family of learned rabbis.[61] Gandhi 'spoke long and earnestly of his mission for his fellow men, and begged that his small band of supporters [in South Africa] should continue to defend their interests'. What struck Morris Alexander was his guest's simplicity – refusing the use of the master bedroom, he slept instead on the floor. His wife Ruth was moved by Gandhi's patience with his hosts, by 'how uncondemning' he was of things (such as the ostentatious furniture) of which he must have disapproved. The Indian, she concluded, was one of the 'three great souls' she had known (the others being her father and Olive Schreiner).[62]

The next day, the Gandhis and Kallenbach proceeded to the docks. Here addresses were presented to Gandhi on behalf of, among others, the Tamils of Cape Town and Port Elizabeth. He was also presented with a gold watch, while Kallenbach was given a pair of binoculars, presents that Gandhi politely yet publicly rejected as 'inconsistent with his life here and with the life he had marked out for himself in India'.

He disavowed the gifts but not the praise, here offered by Dr Gool on behalf of the Indian community, and Dr Abdurahman on behalf of the coloured people of the Cape. In his own speech, Gandhi articulated the hope that with the settlement in place, the 'Europeans of South Africa [would] take a humanitarian and Imperial view of the Indian question'. He was optimistic, for Cape Town itself had produced such people as the liberal MPs W. P. Schreiner and J. X. Merriman, and the great writer Olive Schreiner. Striking a personal note, he 'expressed warm gratitude for what had been done for him by the Europeans of South Africa, and, turning to Mr Kallenbach, placed his hand on the latter's shoulder and said that South Africa had done this for him – it had given him a brother.'

After the speeches, the Gandhis and Kallenbach boarded the SS *Kinfaus Castle*, bound for London. A crowd of friends and admirers walked with them up to the ship, before – as a journalist on the spot reported – 'coming down the gangway wiping the tears from their eyes'.[63]

One person was conspicuously missing from that round of farewells for Mohandas and Kasturba Gandhi – their old friend and one-time housemate Henry Polak. Polak had gone to England to spend time with his family. He sailed back to South Africa in July, and on board wrote an emotional letter to Gandhi, saying he was feeeling 'miserable' because of

> the probability that I shall not see you again for some years at least ... There must be some peculiar bond between us that keeps us near each other in spite of these prolonged absences ... I suppose that your Indian relation of elder and younger brother most nearly approaches it, and possibly I realise it more intimately because of my Oriental trend of thought. It is strange, this persistent turning to the East with me, and Millie's equally persistent turning to the West. I suppose that it is this union of East and West that makes for the best of all human understandings.

In case he returned after Gandhi had left, he asked him to spend an evening at their house and have 'a heart to heart talk with Millie, so that she may know, and I may know, what you hope for, and what you propose to do'.[64]

The letter was written on 14 July; since the Gandhis left four days later, they didn't get to see it. They, and Kallenbach, were booked third class on the *Kinfaus Castle*. Gandhi himself had travelled in the lowest class often on trains, but never before on a ship. They mostly ate fruits and boiled peanuts, a diet to which Gandhi attributed his lack of sea-sickness.[65]

Following the Gandhis from South Africa were a torrent of telegrams, sent from different people representing different interests in different parts of South Africa. These 132 telegrams of farewell lie in the National Archives of India. They came from Natal, Transvaal and the Cape, from Hindus, Muslims and Parsis. Sorabjee Rustomjee of Durban, son of the brave and generous Parsee Rustomjee, said 'we younger Indians who are colonial born look to your self sacrificing life as an inspiration to work in a similar spirit for the sake of motherland may almighty shower richest blessings upon your labours and grant long life health and strength to continue labour love for beloved motherland goodbye'. Sorabjee spoke for a particular generation (the young); others offered their wishes and admiration on behalf of groups such as the Catholic Indians, the Natal Zoroastrian Anjuman, the Anjuman-i-Islam, the Tamil Benefit Society of Johannesburg, the Gujarati Hindus of the same city and the Kathiawar Arya Mandal of Durban. From outside the community, there was a wire from a certain 'Mulder', secretary of the African Political Organization, who wrote that 'members of Doornfontein branch wish you a hearty farewell and bon voyage to your motherland.'

Among the wires sent by and on behalf of individuals were several sent by Muslims. 'May Allah take you and Mrs. Gandhi', said Abdurawoof Thangay of Vereeniging – a Tamil Muslim from the sound of his name – 'to our holy fatherland and wishing you every success in future please express my thanks to Kallenbach goodbye'. Abdul Gaffar Fajandar from Johannesburg wrote that 'your departure from this country has been a great grief to the Indian community who will never cease to remember your trojan like heroic and [sic] self sacrifice your personality will be ever idolised'. Other wires were sent by lovers of the Hindu epics. The Ramayan Sabha of Lugenberthy wired: 'Our loss our mothers gain her care of us our comfort.'

Perhaps the most emotional message came from Bughwan from Durban, who 'was exited station could not therefore wish goodbye as my heart desired forgive our weaknesses pray for us'. The most evocative came from the 'Farewell Committee' of the same city, which observed that the light of their communal existence disappears with your departure their consolation being that it may be a lighthouse to them from the heights of Mount Everest shining near and far may god in his plenitude bestow the spirit to burn for the good of humanity to you and your compatriots.[66]

These wishes and felicitations provide a conspectus of the social and geographical range of Gandhi's influence in the large, complex and conflicted land that, for two decades, was his home.

It may be apposite, however, to juxtapose to these endorsements a comment on Gandhi's departure from someone who was not sorry to see him go. This was General Jan Christian Smuts. In May 1914 Smuts received a letter from Emily Hobhouse, who was now back in London. This conveyed news about mutual friends, and went on to discuss a man whom the Quaker now considered a friend but whom the Afrikaner still could not. 'I have been reading Gandhi's *Home Rule for India – Hind Swaraj*', wrote Hobhouse to Smuts. 'Have you read it? I like it *very much*, all about India and the harm English Civilization is doing there ... It is a book you would have enjoyed at one period of your life.'[67]

Smuts's reply is unrecorded. Whatever he might have thought of the English on the battlefield, after the war ended he had been first in the ranks of those seeking to unite the white people against the coloured. Hobhouse's endorsement of Gandhi's attack on Western civilization could scarcely have pleased him. In recent years he had read and seen too much of the man in any case. His feelings are contained in a letter he wrote to Sir Benjamin Robertson, where he said that after the Viceroy's representative had returned to India, 'Gandhi approached me on a number of small administrative points, some of which I could meet him on, and as a result, the saint has left our shores – I sincerely hope for ever.'[68]

22

How the Mahatma Was Made

*Often there is justice in the working of history. India had given
to South Africa one of the most difficult of its problems; South
Africa in turn gave to India the idea of civil disobedience.*
                    —The Afrikaner politician Jan H. Hofmeyr,
                                                  writing in 1931

You gave us a lawyer; we gave you back a Mahatma.
                              —A South African friend to this writer,
                                                  Cape Town, 2002

This book has reconstructed Mohandas K. Gandhi's less known and
sometimes forgotten years in Porbandar, Rajkot, Bombay, London,
Durban and Johannesburg, on the basis of contemporary records rather
than retrospective accounts. Now, however, with my subject having
finally sailed from South Africa, it may be time to bring in questions I
have kept at a distance all this while. In what ways did the first forty-five
years of Gandhi's life shape him as a social reformer, religious thinker
and political actor? What is the significance of his South African years
in particular for those who know Gandhi as the leader of the Indian
freedom struggle, as an icon and inspiration for non-violent movements
the world over, as a prophet of inter-faith harmony, and more?

Let's start at the beginning, with how a Bania from Kathiawar out-
grew the conventions of his caste. As a schoolboy, Gandhi befriended a
Muslim classmate in Rajkot. As a law student, he shared a home with a
Christian vegetarian in London. However, it was in South Africa that
he more fully elaborated his unique spirit of ecumenism. This was
religious – originally employed by Muslim merchants, Gandhi came to

count Jews, Christians and Parsis among his closest friends. It was social – a middle-class man himself, Gandhi was to identify closely with hawkers and labourers. As the poorer Indians in South Africa were largely Tamil-speaking, he came to understand the diversity of language as well.

Gandhi was born and raised a Hindu, and he avowed that denominational label all his life. Yet no Hindu before or since has had such a close, intense engagement with the great Abrahamic religions. He understood Judaism through a highly personal lens – through his friendships with Polak, Kallenbach and Sonja Schlesin especially. His interest in Christianity was both personal and theological – he liked Doke and loved Andrews, but whereas he was not really influenced by Jewish thought he was profoundly shaped by heterodox Christian texts – above all Tolstoy's *The Kingdom of God Is Within You*. His relations with Islam were partly personal, but largely pragmatic and political. He had read the Koran (probably more than once), but was never really moved by it in the same way as he was moved by the Gita or the Sermon on the Mount. He had some Muslim friends, but what concerned him more – much more – was the forging of a compact between Hindus and Muslims: the major communities in the Indian diaspora in South Africa, as they were in India itself.

Perhaps even more striking than his religious inclusiveness was Gandhi's complete lack of bitterness towards the ruling race. The roots of this lay in those years in London, and his friendly interactions with vegetarians and others. In May 1891, just before he left England for India, he expressed the hope that 'in the future we shall tend towards unity of custom, and also unity of hearts'. Some years later, when set upon by a white mob in Durban, Gandhi chose to remember not his persecutors but the whites who stood by him. Still later, when faced with the rigorous racial exclusivism of the Transvaal, Gandhi sought 'points of agreement' with the oppressors, with whom he hoped to live in 'perfect peace'. Years of harassment and vilification at the hands of Boers and Britons did not deter him from seeking 'the unity of human nature, whether residing in a brown-skinned or a white-skinned body'.[1]

To be sure, it was harder, and perhaps more admirable, for Europeans to befriend Gandhi. In 1904, when Boer and Briton alike were being driven to a frenzy by the prospect of Asian immigration, a meeting in Volksrust resolved that 'any white person who aids, abets, assists or in any way connives, directly or indirectly, to the establishing of the Indian trader within our gates is an enemy to the advancement of the white races of the country'.[2] Ritch, the Polaks, the Dokes, Kallenbach and Sonja Schlesin were all happy enough to be counted as enemies by the herd – and the mob.

Gandhi's ability to disregard differences of race and faith was exceptional in any time and place, not least the South Africa of the 1890s and 1900s. His first encounter with Winston Churchill, which took place in London in 1906, at a time when they were both relatively obscure, is instructive here. Gandhi, as secretary of the British Indian Association of the Transvaal, had gone to call on Churchill, who was Under-Secretary of State for the Colonies. They were discussing the fate and future of the Johannesburg locality of Vrededorp, where Dutch burghers and Indian immigrants traded side by side – an arrangement that Churchill considered violated tradition, custom and human nature itself.

Churchill's perceptions – and prejudices – in this regard had been consolidated by his experiences in South Africa during the Anglo-Boer War. Thus, to the plea that Indians be allowed to live and trade in Vrededorp, Churchill answered that 'the practice of allowing European, Asiatic and native families to live side by side in [a] mixed community is fraught with many evils.' It was an argument which could not resonate with Gandhi, who, in the same city of Johannesburg, already had as housemates a European couple – one Christian, the other Jewish.[3]

Gandhi's broadmindedness was most forcefully stressed in an unpublished memoir by one of these housemates. Henry Polak wrote of his friend and leader that while he was

> a Vaishnava Bania by birth, he is by nature a Brahmin, the . . . teacher of his fellow-men, not by the preaching of virtue, but by its practice; by impulse a Kshatriya, in his chivalrous defence of those who had placed their trust in him and look to him for protection; by choice a Sudra, servant of the humblest and most despised of his fellow-men. It is said of [the seer] Ramkrishna that he once swept out the foul hut of a pariah with his own hair, to prove his freedom from arrogance towards and contempt for the untouchable outcast. The twice-born [i.e., upper-caste] Prime Minister's son has been seen . . . with his own hands to purify the sanitary convenience of his own house and of the gaols in which he has been interned.

Having spoken of Gandhi's ability to be of all castes and of no caste at all, Polak then stressed his ecumenism of faith:

> Religion implies, for him, a mighty and all-embracing tolerance, and a large charity is the first of the virtues. Hindu by birth, he regards all men – Mahomedans, Christians, Zoroastrians, Jews, Buddhists, Confucians – as spiritual brothers. He makes no differences amongst them, recognising that all faiths lead to salvation, that all are ways of viewing God, and that, in their relation to each other, men are fellow-human beings first, and followers of creeds afterwards. Hence it is that men of all faiths and even of none, are his devoted friends, admirers, and helpers.[4]

Many years later, reflecting on his South African experience, Gandhi remembered that the residents of Phoenix and Tolstoy farms were, in religious terms, Hindus of different castes, Sunnis and Shias, Protestants and Catholics, Parsis and Jews. The careers they had previously practised included architecture, journalism, the law and trade. They now submerged their faiths and their qualifications in the common work of printing, gardening, carpentry and house-building. And so, as Gandhi recalled, the 'practice of truth and non-violence melted religious differences, and we learnt to see beauty in each religion. I do not remember a single religious quarrel in the two colonies I founded in South Africa ... Labour was no drudgery, it was a joy.'[5]

The settlements at Phoenix and Tolstoy were a meeting place, a melting pot, where, as the settlers lived and laboured together, social and religious distinctions were made insubstantial and even irrelevant.

Gandhi's ability to transcend his class, religious and ethnic background was greatly in advance of his contemporaries within India. The Indian National Congress was set up in 1885 as a sort of 'Noah's ark of nationalism', seeking to represent all sects and tribes.[6] The practice fell far short of the ideal. For the first thirty years of its existence the Congress was essentially middle-class and city-bound. Doctors, lawyers, editors and teachers turned out in numbers for its annual meetings. Peasants and proletarians were absent and remained unrepresented. Muslim leaders also drifted away, as did intellectuals and reformers from the lower castes. And of course the Congress remained a solidly male body.

Gandhi's political mentors, Dadabhai Naoroji and Gopal Krishna Gokhale, were conspicuously free of sectarian bias. Both were Indian rather than Parsi and Gujarati, or Hindu and Maharashtrian respectively. Gokhale was one of the first Congress leaders to call for an end to caste discrimination. However, in their everyday life, both Naoroji and Gokhale remained confined to the urban, professional, privileged, male mileu in which they were born and educated. Neither counted labourers (or even traders) as their friends or co-workers.

In a speech delivered in 1897, Gokhale's mentor, Mahadev Govind Ranade, had urged on his largely Brahmin audience a 'new mode of thought . . . cast on the lines of fraternity, a capacity to expand outwards, and to make more cohesive inwards the bonds of fellowship'. He asked high-born Hindus to 'increase the circle of your friends and associates, slowly and cautiously if you will, but the tendency must be towards a general recognition of the essential equality between man and man'.[7]

Gandhi was then in South Africa and never heard the speech, and probably never read it either. But in his practice and his conduct he fulfilled Ranade's injunction more fully (and nobly) than any other high-born Hindu. By the time he was in his mid thirties – by the time of the epic Empire Theatre meeting of September 1906 (if not earlier) – Gandhi had exceeded his own mentor, Gokhale, in the breadth of his social vision and (especially) his personal practice. He had successfully reached out to compatriots of other religions and linguistic communities, and of disadvantaged social backgrounds.

The involvement of women in the struggles led by Gandhi was also impressive – as supporters and cheerleaders in the first satyagrahas, and as resisters and jailbirds in the last. Speaking to a group of women students in Lahore in July 1934, Gandhi remarked, 'When I was in South Africa, I had realized that if I did not serve the cause of women, all my work would remain unfinished.'[8] How did this realization come about? In terms of his upbringing, Gandhi was a typical Hindu patriarch. He first began to shed some of his prejudices while living with the Polaks in Johannesburg in 1906. Kasturba was brought up to revere and follow her husband; but Millie was under no such constraints. She argued with her husband Henry, and she would argue with their housemate as well. The word of men, to her, had always to be tested against both reason and justice.

Only just behind Millie in making Gandhi more open-minded in this regard was his secretary, Sonja Schlesin. Her indomitable spirit comes through in a letter she wrote to him not long after he had left South

Africa. Municipal elections had just been held in the Transvaal – while the voters and candidates were all white, for the first time women were allowed to stand for election. Miss Schlesin reported that as many as eleven women had won their seats and become councillors. Conveying further news of 'the nobler sex', she told Gandhi of a woman doctor being appointed a medical inspector of schools. If the 'civilisation of a country is measured by the position it accords to women,' she said proudly, 'you see how high the Transvaal stands in the scale of nations!' After the results were in, Miss Schlesin phoned a prominent male politician and advised him 'that so long as he allowed himself to be guided by the woman councillors it would be alright.'[9]

Like Millie Polak, Sonja Schlesin greatly admired Gandhi; yet she too would not follow him always or all the way. Her independence of mind and her physical courage made Gandhi see more clearly the ways in which women could and must take charge of their lives. Then, on visits to England in 1906 and 1909, he was struck by the commitment of the suffragettes.

The influence of these European women was consolidated by the Tamil women of Johannesburg, who were absolutely selfless in their support of the first satyagrahas and absolutely fearless in joining the final struggle of 1913–14. Henry Polak, husband of the feminist Millie, wrote of these Tamil ladies that 'when the women could show such courage ... the men dared not prove themselves weaker than the women.' Their example animated and challenged their Tamil husbands and sons, but it inspired and moved the Gujarati lawyer Gandhi too.[10]

Indian men, in India, did not at this time cultivate friendships with women. They knew women as wives, sisters, daughters; but as friends, no. Once more, it was context as much as character that explains Gandhi's departure from the norm. Had he not lived in South Africa, he might never have outgrown the conventional, confined, views of Indian men of his class and his generation.[11]

Gandhi's ability to reach out to different classes and communities was admired among Indians in South Africa. But it also became known among Indians in India. Not the least of the many surprises in researching this book was the depth of contemporary interest that I found, within the subcontinent, in the satyagrahas led by Gandhi in Transvaal in 1907–11 and in Natal in 1913. That in an age before television and the internet, a man who lived across the oceans and who had not been in the motherland for a full decade was so widely and appreciatively spoken of, was a striking revelation indeed.

The interest in those early satyagrahas was manifest across British India, and in some princely states too. Newspapers in languages Gandhi did not speak, indeed at this stage had barely even heard, carried long reports on the sacrifices made by him and his fellow satyagrahis. Meetings in solidarity with them were held in towns Gandhi could not place accurately on the map. This support cut across linguistic and geographic lines, and – what may be even more notable – across religious lines as well. The All India Muslim League and the Bishop of Madras were among the institutions and individuals who recognized the moral force and political salience of Gandhi's campaigns in South Africa. And, as speakers in several meetings feelingly observed, Gandhi's campaigns had broken new ground in not being led or staffed by men alone. At a time when Indian women of all castes and creeds were confined to the home, or in purdah, that Kasturba and her colleagues went to jail in protest against discriminatory laws was a fact – or achievement – noted with not a little admiration.

Gandhi's capaciousness was not complete, however. It was constrained in one fundamental sense. While he had Indian and European friends of all castes, classes and faiths, he forged no real friendships with Africans. He knew and respected the educationist John Dube. He met, and possibly influenced, the political pioneer Pixley Seme. And he laboured alongside some Africans at Tolstoy Farm. That was the extent of his personal and professional relations with the original inhabitants and majority community of South Africa.

That said, over the twenty and more years he lived in the land, Gandhi's understanding of the African predicament steadily widened. At first, he adhered to the then common idea of a hierarchy of civilizations – the Europeans on top, the Indians just below them, the Africans at the very bottom. Everyday life in Durban and Johannesburg alerted him to the real and structured discrimination that Africans were subject to. In 1904 and 1905 *Indian Opinion* carried reports of laws and practices that bore down heavily on them. In a speech of 1908 he looked forward to a 'commingling' of the races in a future South Africa. By this time he was prescribing satyagraha as a cure for the predicament of Africans, too.

*

From his days as a student, Gandhi was curious about other faiths, other ways of living and relating to the world. This tendency was further deepened by the experience of living in countries other than his own. London, Durban, Johannesburg – these were cities much larger and more varied than Rajkot or Porbandar. Gandhi was free to explore their pluralism and their cosmopolitanism, not least because he lived for such long periods away from his family.

Of these different cities, perhaps it was Johannesburg that shaped Gandhi most decisively. In the early 1900s this was a city being made in a society (and country) being formed. There was a churning abroad, as migrants from all parts of the world came seeking not just a share of the mining boom but also a liberation from social orthodoxies. On the one side, the rulers sought to impose a new, stable, racial order; on the other side, individuals sought to fashion their lives in accordance with their own inner urges, experimenting with new forms of diet, health-care and inter-cultural and inter-religious dialogue. It was among these amiably eccentric (and distinctly non-violent) dissenters that Gandhi found his own cohort – Polak, Kallenbach, Ritch, Joseph Doke, Sonja Schlesin, *et al.*

Had Gandhi always lived or worked in India, he would never have met dissident Jews or Nonconformist Christians. Life in the diaspora also exposed him more keenly to the hetereogeneity of his own homeland. Had he followed the family tradition and worked in a princely state in Kathiawar he would never have met Tamils or North Indians. Had he practised law in Bombay he could not have counted plantation workers or roadside hawkers among his clients.

For most people, South Africa in the early 1900s was a crucible of social inequality, where individuals of one race or class learned very quickly to separate themselves from people of other races and classes. For this Indian, however, South Africa became a crucible of human togetherness, allowing him to forge bonds of affiliation with compatriots with whom, had he remained at home, he would have had absolutely no contact whatsoever.

In this dissolving of social distinctions so prevalent (and so confining) at home, Gandhi subsumed and embodied the experience of Indians in South Africa more generally. The lives of Indians in India were circumscribed by caste, kin and religion. Even in cities such as Bombay and Calcutta, migrants tended to live with those with whom they shared a language or caste. But here in South Africa, inspired by Gandhi, the

Indians came together in an inclusive social movement. This happened over a twenty-year period: first in Natal, then in the Transvaal, and finally in the massive strikes and epic march of 1913. During these satyagrahas, and in between them, Tamils, Gujaratis, Hindi-speakers; Parsis, Hindus, Muslims, Christians; high, middle and low castes; labourers, merchants, priests ate together, talked together and struggled together.

An intriguing manifestation of Gandhi's cosmopolitanism was his relations with the Chinese in the Transvaal. Now, in the twenty-first century, China and India have begun increasingly to be coupled together. Both were ancient civilizations that are now assertive new nations, both have experienced a sharp spurt in economic growth. Their rise has been made more noteworthy by their size and population – together, they account for a little less than 40 per cent of all human beings on earth.

In the context of this rise – variously viewed as alarming, admirable and premature – these previously obscure connections between the greatest of Indian nationalists and his Chinese comrades in South Africa acquire a curious contemporary resonance. That some Chinese men were among the audience in that epochal meeting in the Empire Theatre on 11 September 1906; that these Chinese men willingly courted arrest when the satyagraha actually started; that in prison Gandhi discussed the multiple paths to God with his Chinese comrades; that the Chinese (as Gandhi acknowledged) surpassed the Indians in generosity towards their European supporters – these facts, interesting in their own right, acquire perhaps a fresh relevance now.

When, in January 1908, the passive resisters signed a pact with the Transvaal Government, there were three signatories from their side: a Gujarati, Gandhi; a Tamil, Thambi Naidoo; and a Chinese, Leung Quinn. This implied a certain parity, each man speaking for his own particular community. Over time, Gandhi emerged as the main leader of the Asians in the Transvaal. But the support of the Tamils, and the Chinese, remained crucial to him, and his movement.

In these years, Gandhi himself did not speak specifically of a pan-Asian solidarity. But Leung Quinn did, saying in a speech in Madras (after he was deported there) that the satyagraha in the Transvaal was for 'the honour of Asia'. In the same manner, Smuts's English friend H. J. Wolstenholme thought that Gandhi's movement reflected an 'epoch-making' change between East and West, whereby Indians and

Chinese were 'developing rapidly a sense of nationality' with which to challenge their European rulers.

After he came back to India in 1915, Gandhi lost touch with his Chinese colleagues. Now, as he applied his techniques of satyagraha to win political freedom for India, nationalists in China were fighting Western (and Japanese) imperialism by other methods, namely, armed struggle. In the 1930s, the American journalist Edgar Snow went to meet Mao Zedong after the latter's Long March. Snow was coming from India, where he had met and come to admire Gandhi. The Mahatma was by this time a figure of great world renown, especially in America, where he figured often in the *New York Times* and had been chosen by *Time Magazine* as their Man of the Year (in 1930, after his own Long March to break the salt laws). The Chinese revolutionary and the American journalist discussed the Indian path to political freedom. Mao was dismissive, since, unlike the Chinese Communists, Gandhi had not undertaken an agrarian revolution by forcibly dispossessing large landlords.[12]

In the 1930s and 1940s there were few takers for Gandhian methods in China. In the China of today, however, there is an increasing interest in Gandhi and what he stood for. A prominent Chinese blogger has a portrait of Gandhi on his profile. Another admirer is the Nobel Laureate Liu Xiabao. A recent collection of his essays has many references to Mao, all hostile or pejorative, and several references to Gandhi, all appreciative. In January 2000 he wrote:

> Compared to people in other nations that have lived under the dreary pall of Communism, we resisters in China have not measured up very well. Even after so many years of tremendous tragedies, we still don't have a moral leader like Václav Havel. It seems ironic that in order to win the right of ordinary people to pursue self-interest, a society needs a moral giant to make a selfless sacrifice. In order to secure 'passive freedom' – freedom from state oppression – there needs to be a will to do active resistance. History is not fated. The appearance of a single martyr can fundamentally turn the spirit of a nation and strengthen its moral fibre. Gandhi was such a figure.[13]

What Liu Xiabao did not know – but we may hope one day will know – is that the 'moral giant' and 'martyr' Gandhi was supported, at an early and crucial stage of his political career, by Chinese activists such as Leung Quinn.

*

The relationships that Gandhi pursued were at once personal and instrumental. He had enormous affection for his sons (or at least three of them), for his nephews and for his Indian and European friends. But that they aided him in his social and political work was of more than incidental importance. They assisted him with his journal and his law practice; they canvassed support for his cause among the community and among the ruling race; they helped, if they had the means, to fund his public and social activities; they went, if they had the will, to jail with him.

These 'secondary' characters were considerable figures in their own right. They were men and women of intelligence and commitment. And it is through them that we get to know Gandhi more fully as an individual and as an historical actor. It is through his relations with Henry Polak, Thambi Naidoo, A. M. Cachalia, Sonja Schlesin and Parsee Rustomjee that we can more properly appreciate Gandhi's political campaigns; through his experiments with Hermann Kallenbach that we get a deeper insight into his interactions with Tolstoy and Tolstoyans and his intense desire for self-improvement (and also self-abasement); through his conversations with Raychandbhai, Joseph Doke and C. F. Andrews that we see how he arrived at his own brand of religious pluralism; through his lifelong friendship and correspondence with Pranjivan Mehta that we understand his larger ambitions for himself and his homeland; through his relations with (and misrecognitions of) Kasturba, Harilal and Manilal that we arrive at a more nuanced understanding of the man, juxtaposing his familial failures with his social and spiritual successes.

As it happens, we can come to know Gandhi better through his South African adversaries as well. The parochial Montford Chamney, the proud General Smuts, the paranoid East Rand Vigilantes and the perfervid white mob in Natal – they shaped Gandhi's world and world-view too. So did the militant Pathans and the jealous Durban editor P. S. Aiyar. As much as his friends and followers, his critics and enemies helped convert the earnest, naïve lawyer who arrived in Durban in 1893 into the smart, sagacious and focused thinker-activist who sailed from Cape Town in 1914.

The two most powerful of these adversaries were the imperial proconsul Alfred Milner and the scholar-warrior Jan Christian Smuts. History has already placed Gandhi substantially above Smuts and massively above

Milner. But in the South Africa of Gandhi's day they were far more sub-stantial figures than he. It was this perceived aysmmetry of status that led both men to treat the lawyer's modest demands with contempt. Had either bent slightly, and taken some account of the Indian point of view, who knows what history's verdict on Gandhi now would be? If, in 1904, Milner had agreed to legalize the existing rights of Indian traders in the Transvaal, Gandhi would have returned home without ever hav-ing thought of civil disobedience. If, three years later, Smuts had repealed the Asiatic Act and agreed to the return of about a thousand Indians who claimed pre–Boer War rights of residence, Gandhi would have returned home with no knowledge of how long he could sustain the morale of his followers.

In 1903, the Johannesburg correspondent of the *Daily Telegraph* said of Lord Milner's sanctioning of 'locations' that 'the controversy it will arouse will not be confined to the Transvaal, but will extend to England and India.' In 1907, the *Natal Mercury* wrote of General Smuts's intran-sigence that it would 'produce quite unforeseen results, both here and in India'. Both statements were prescient. Had either Milner or Smuts compromised early with Gandhi, he might never have had the chance to develop the technique of satyagraha, nor the confidence to think it might work in a country so large and so divided as India. In the event, the arrogance of British imperialist and Boer racist gave Gandhi the opportunity to emerge as a mass leader in South Africa and, in time, in his homeland as well.

It was in South Africa that Gandhi achieved proficiency as a writer and editor. To be sure, he got a start in England, where his fellow vegetarians allowed him a free run of their journal. In his early years in Natal, a stream of letters to newspapers and petitions to Government poured from his pen. In 1903 he chose to start his own periodical, *Indian Opin-ion*. Its purpose was at once documentary and political: it was a journal meant to advance not Gandhi's interests, but the interests of Indians in Natal and the Transvaal. Gandhi wrote many essays for it, in Gujarati and in English. He also supervised its production from week to week, and was chiefly responsible for its financing.

Gandhi's skills as writer and editor were considerable. He was, how-ever, an indifferent, if not disastrous, public speaker. His friend and admirer Joseph Doke noted that, in Johannesburg itself, there were 'several of his countrymen whose elocution, natural and unaffected, is far superior to his'. Gandhi spoke in a low voice, and in a monotonous tone. He 'never waves his arms', remarked Doke, 'seldom move[s] a finger'.[14]

And yet the Indians who heard him listened, because even if the tone was unvaried the words carried conviction. Gandhi inspired devotion not so much by his articles or speeches as by the exemplary nature of his life and conduct. His austerity, his hard work, his courage, were impressive enough to attract followers from very different backgrounds – be they Muslims or Jews or Christians or Tamils, merchants or hawkers or priests or indentured labourers. By influencing individuals of different backgrounds, he created a moral and in time political community, whose members were willing, under his leadership and direction, to embrace poverty and court imprisonment.

The commitment of his friends to Gandhi was striking indeed. To L. W. Ritch he was always the 'big little chief'. Henry Polak chose to travel for months in a strange land, to separate himself from his beloved wife and children, out of regard for Gandhi and his cause. Thambi Naidoo was happy to court arrest time and again, and to risk his own life to save Gandhi's. For another serial satyagrahi, P. K. Naidoo, every time he was released the one person he 'naturally' most wanted to meet was Gandhi. The spirited Sonja Schlesin worked all day to keep Gandhi's office going, while finding the time – and energy – to comfort Tamil women and carry food to their husbands in jail. And then there was Hermann Kallenbach, whose devotion was the most complete and unquestioning of them all.

The reverence for Gandhi of his inner circle is manifest in a letter Kallenbach wrote to Chhaganlal in July 1911. The architect was leaving to see his family in Europe; in his absence, he asked Chhagan 'to remain and continue to be the right hand of the man, whose life has given us all such a wonderful life, that we all wish to cling closer to him'. As Gandhi 'dauntlessly pushes ahead', remarked Kallenbach, his disciples were sometimes unable to keep pace. Yet 'in our sane and quiet moments, we all cannot help but rejoice about the brilliant fire burning in him, in order to re-light again and again the candle which so often loses his lustre. May we all fully recognize our good fortune to be with him and work with him.'[15]

Those who spent less time with Gandhi were stirred by his example too. Among the most striking of Gandhi's achievements is the fact that during the satyagrahas in the Transvaal in 1907–10, some 3,000 Indians courted arrest. They constituted an astonishing 35 per cent of the Indians in the colony. In September 1906, Gandhi's friend, the Pretoria lawyer R. Gregorowski, had advised against passive resistance, as 'not a great number of people are made of the stuff that seek martyrdom and Asiatics are no exception to the rule.' As it turned out, however, thousands of Indians were inspired by Gandhi's call to defy the law and go to jail.

Notably, many of these satyagrahis were merchants. Merchants are known to be the most cautious, conservative of men – perhaps Indian merchants especially so (some would say – and Gujarati merchants most especially so). Singly or collectively, merchants are loth to take political risks or confront established authority.[16]

Gandhi was mobilizing merchants in a colonial context who were living away from their homeland, in circumstances where one would expect them to be even more timid. And yet they followed their leader into prison. As did, in time, the hawkers, workers and professionals whose diasporic status would likewise have made them reluctant to throw away their livelihood by embracing a struggle so uncertain of success.

In acting as they did, the Indians knew that their leader was not just prepared to court arrest for the cause, but to be killed for it as well. After Gandhi was attacked and nearly murdered in Durban in January 1897, he received a stirring letter of support from a Gujarati fish curer in Cape Town. This praised his 'single-hearted efforts and fearless representations of grievances under which the unfortunate Indians suffer'. His correspondent, 'deeply grieved' that Gandhi 'should have been subjected to the cruel treatments reported in the papers here ... at the hands of a mad mob', assured him 'that the eyes of thousands [of Indians in the Cape] are on you and are watching with sympathetic appreciation on all you have done'.[17]

Those who set upon Gandhi in Durban in 1897 were working-class whites. Eleven years later, he was attacked once more, this time in Johannesburg, and by a group of Pathans. Once more, his calmness and determination brought around Indians otherwise unimpressed by him and his movement. These two attempts on Gandhi's life, and his resolution in the face of both, confirmed his standing in the community.

Gandhi met later threats with equanimity. Thus, when stories spread in 1909 that some Pathans in Johannesburg were planning to attack him once more, he told his nephew Maganlal that he did not fear, and even welcomed, the prospect of death at the hands of his countrymen, since it would 'unite the Hindus and Mussalmans'.[18]

Gandhi, his fellow Indians knew, was 'so frail a figure [but] so vigorous a character', in the description of a meat-eating and whisky-guzzling Johannesburg journalist who marvelled at the unexpected or at any rate counter-intutitive courage shown by a teetotal vegetarian. Relevant here is a remark of the Gujarati headmaster who, in the 1960s, found the young Mohandas's school records in Rajkot, which brought to light the erratic attendance and indifferent academic performance of a now most venerated figure. 'Gandhiji, it has been well said', wrote this teacher-archivist, 'could fashion heroes out of common clay. His first and, undoubtedly, his most successful experiment was with himself.'[19]

In his years outside India, Gandhi came gradually, and in time decisively, to turn his back on his profession. Had he not found it hard to get briefs in Rajkot and Bombay he might never have left for Durban. In South Africa he met with considerable professional success. Slowly, however, his legal work was conducted less for monetary gain and more to aid his fellow Indians. Moving further away from the career for which he had been trained, he eventually handed over his practice to his colleagues L. W. Ritch and Henry Polak. At the same time, he began simplifying his life and his needs, exchanging a home in the city for a place on the land. Over the years, he elaborated an ascetic, workaholic regime, disregarding pleasure and leisure: no alcohol or meat, of course; no sugar or spices: and – lest it be forgotten – no sports or pastimes either.

Gandhi's abiding interest in the simple life in general, and in a vegetarian diet, natural methods of healing, and celibacy, in particular, are to the modern eye difficult to appreciate. Why be so fussy about what to eat and what not to eat? Why not be rational and scientific, and embrace the allopathic regimen of pills and surgeries, rather than treat illnesses with natural methods learnt from untrained quacks or of one's own concoction? And why the obsession with *brahmacharya*? Is not sex one of the joys and pleasures of life? And is not sex with one's wife in particular the very enactment and embodiment of true, enduring love?

In truth, these concerns were not always appreciated by Gandhi's contemporaries, nor even by some of his friends. In her book *Mr Gandhi: The Man*, an always affectionate, often insightful and absolutely indispensable account of their life together in South Africa, Millie Polak could not conceal her puzzlement with her friend's sometimes strange ways. Her husband Henry, while deeply devoted to his Bada Bhai's political programme, was not particularly enchanted by his social or natural philosophy either. Neither Millie nor Henry spent much time at Phoenix or Tolstoy Farms; neither subjected themselves to steam baths and mud packs; neither ever remotely contemplated the practice of celibacy.

To some people then (and now), Gandhi's ascetic, austere regimen, his idiosyncratic diet, his refusal to take pills when sick, his sexual abstinence, were hard to take and harder to understand. If one admired Gandhi's political philosophy, then – like the Polaks – one treated these as amiable eccentricities, as fads. If one disagreed with Gandhi's political philosophy, then one saw in these obsessions confirmation of how irrelevant his entire world-view was to the modern era. The prominent Indian Communist E. M. S. Namboodiripad, writing of Gandhi's membership of the Vegetarian Society of London as a law student, thought it an early illustration of the 'extremely reactionary social outlook which guided Gandhi throughout his activities'. Namboodiripad continued:

> While Gandhi, the young barrister, was writing articles for the *Vegetarian*, Lenin, also a young lawyer, was translating Marx, Sydney Webb, etc., and himself writing *The Development of Capitalism in Russia*. Lenin combined the militant mass movement of the working class with the most advanced ideology. Gandhi combined it with the most reactionary and obscurantist of ideologies that was current in the contemporary world.[20]

In the first half of the twentieth century, Marxism had an enormous appeal. Well-read young men all over the world saw it as the way, and wave, of the future. (The French sociologist Raymond Aron, a precocious dissenter himself, termed it the 'opium of the intellectuals'.) These same men, if they knew or knew of Gandhi, saw him as 'reactionary and obscurantist' because he used a religious idiom rather than a secular-scientific one, because he preached a moderation of material wants rather than welcoming the cornucopian promises of modernity, because he advocated the (to them) tame, timid, effeminate alternative of satyagraha to the militant, masculine route of armed struggle.

Namboodiripad's emphatic dismissal of Gandhi (and Gandhism) was first published in the winter of 1955–6. The next year, Khrushchev's speech to the 20th Congress of the Communist Party of the Soviet Union confirmed the murderous outcomes of the 'most advanced ideology' of Lenin and his successor Stalin. The image of Marxism took a battering in subsequent decades. News of the Gulag, the purges, the brutal suppression of minorities, and the mass famines induced by Communist regimes, have made it less easy to hail Marxism as 'progressive' while dismissing Gandhism as 'reactionary'.

But let us not win the argument between these rival philosophies through hindsight, but rather try and see Gandhi's own experiments as he saw them, as steps to a purer, more meaningful life. To simplify his diet, to reduce his dependence on medicines and doctors, to embrace *brahmacharya*, were all for him ways of strengthening his will and his resolve. By conquering the need to be stimulated by sex or rich food – the 'basal passions' according to his teacher Tolstoy – Gandhi was preparing himself for a life lived for other people and for higher values. If he ate little, and that merely fruits and vegetables, without salt, sugar and spices; if he didn't care how often (or if at all) he had sex with his wife (or with others); if he dressed simply and didn't own property or jewellery, he could more easily embrace the rigours of prison life, more fully and whole-heartedly devote his being and his body to the oppressed Indians of Natal and the Transvaal.

His religious quest, his individual and social relationships, his work as writer and editor, his legal career, his lifestyle choices – these were all subordinated, in lesser or greater degree, to Gandhi's work for the rights of the Indians in South Africa. This subordination of individual choice to social commitment happened incrementally, over the twenty-odd years that Gandhi spent there.

This gradualism may have had its roots in the time he spent as a student in London. As his old flatmate Josiah Oldfield once noted, the vegetarians provided 'a fine training ground in which Gandhi learnt [that] by quiet persistence he could do far more to change men's minds than by any oratory or loud trumpeting'.[21]

Henry Salt, who was, properly speaking, Gandhi's first mentor (since he met him even before he met Raychandbhai) had said that 'to insist on an all-or-nothing policy would be fatal to any reform whatsoever.

Improvements never come in the mass, but always by instalment.' Likewise, Gandhi's policy for personal improvement as well as his agenda for social reform was that of one step at a time. However, even if he recognized that the individual self was not, ultimately, perfectible, he never lost sight of the ultimate social goal of racial and national equality.

Someone who understood the pragmatic roots of Gandhi's gradualism was his friend L. W. Ritch. When asked why Indians did not immediately demand the franchise, Ritch answered that 'the whole tone and temper of white South Africa was such that any claim of that kind was absolutely outside the range of practical politics.' Then he continued, 'Still, the ideals of the one day become the practical politics of another, and the children of a later generation will in all likelihood look with amazement upon what they will doubtless consider the narrow-mindedness of their predecessors.'[22]

While fighting for the repeal of an unjust law or tax, or for more freedom of movement or of trade, Gandhi did not go so far as to press for equal citizenship or for voting rights for Indians. To speak of comprehensive equality for coloured people was premature in early twentieth-century South Africa. Nonetheless, Gandhi believed that in time such equality would come, that (as he put it in a speech of May 1908) the rulers would one day recognize the need to raise subject peoples 'to equality with themselves, to give them absolutely free institutions and make them absolutely free men'. Six years later, in his farewell speech to the Europeans of Durban, he told them that they could not forever postpone the day when coloured peoples would enjoy 'a charter of full liberties' in South Africa.

As his political thought evolved, so also did Gandhi's confidence in himself as a leader and maker of men. His letters to Lord Milner in 1903 and 1904 were extremely deferential in tone. Within a few years this had changed. Gandhi's letters to General Smuts were courteously worded, yet far more assured. He spoke to him as the leader of one community to another. To be sure, equivalence did not imply equality, since the whites were the dominant race in a political as well as economic sense. Still, the confidence conveyed in Gandhi's exchanges with Smuts is unmistakable, a product of the fact that so many Indians had followed his call and courted arrest.

This political and personal evolution was also accompanied by shifts in how Gandhi viewed rival cultures and civilizations. When he first went to South Africa, Gandhi was both an Empire loyalist and a believer in the superiority of British justice and British institutions. He was, in dress and orientation of mind, a *Westernized* Oriental Gentleman, a modern man who admired and was comfortable with (European) modernity. Reading Tolstoy and Ruskin, and re-reading Raychandbhai, led him to reconsider his position. He began to exalt the rural against the urban, the agrarian against the industrial and, eventually the Indic versus the European. As this London-trained barrister began to think more like an Indian, he began to look more like an Indian too. His adoption of the home-spun dress of a peasant after the satyagraha of 1913 was the analogue, in apparel, of the intellectual indigenism contained within the pages of *Hind Swaraj*.

Gandhi's experiences in South Africa were astonishingly varied and always intense. Life in Durban and Johannesburg, at Phoenix and Tolstoy farms, in court and in jail, on the road and on the train, gave him a deeper understanding of what divided (or united) human beings in general and Indians in particular. Two decades in the diaspora gave him the eyes to see and the tools to use when he came back home. As writer, editor, leader, bridge-builder, social reformer, moral exemplar, political organizer and political theorist, Gandhi returned to India in 1915 fully formed and fully primed to carry out these callings over a far wider spatial, social and – not least – historical scale.

The South African years were crucial to Gandhi, and to the distinctive form of political protest that is his most enduring legacy to India and the world. From 1894, when the Natal Indian Congress was founded, until 1906, Gandhi and his colleagues relied on letters, articles, petitions and deputations to make their case. On 11 September 1906, the Indians of the Transvaal made a radical departure, when, in that mass meeting at Johannesburg's Empire Theatre, they resolved to seek imprisonment if their demands were not met. Gandhi now travelled to London to give the older methods a last chance. He returned empty-handed. The following year he led hundreds of Indians (and some Chinese) in courting arrest by breaking the law.

In subsequent years, satyagraha took various forms: hawking without a licence, crossing colonial boundaries without a permit, refusing to provide thumb impressions when asked to do so, burning registration certificates that the law obliged one to possess and carry at all times.

The actions were individual and collective – first conducted by a person acting alone, then by a few people acting together, then, in the march across the border in November 1913, by thousands of people at once. These methods of civil disobedience lay in between the older method of petitioning the authorities and the rival method – then gathering ground in India – of bombing public places and assassinating public officials.

Gandhi was both a practitioner and a theorist of satyagraha. He planned his campaigns meticulously. Which law was to be broken when, by whom, in which place and in what manner – to these matters he gave careful attention and issued precise instructions. Before and after these campaigns he explained the wider moral and political significance of satyagraha. In letters, speeches, articles, editorials and in his book *Hind Swaraj*, he explained why non-violence was more effective as well as more noble than the armed struggle to which some brilliant and courageous young Indians were more immediately attracted.

In August 1911, a time we may describe in retrospect as a lull between two storms, after one major satyagraha and before another, *The Times* of London carried a leader on 'The Asiatic Problem in South Africa'. This summarized the campaigns of Indians in South Africa, conducted 'under the guidance of Mr M. K. Gandhi, an able and tenacious leader'.[23] The description was not inaccurate. For Gandhi was in 1911 essentially a *community* leader, who represented the interests of about 100,000 Indians in South Africa.

To be sure, given what we now know of the man and his impact on his country and the world, we may think the praise parsimonious. So, had they read *The Times* at the time, would some of Gandhi's closest friends. The people of Porbandar, writing to Lord Morley in 1908, insisted that in the struggle led by their native son 'the fate and future of India is involved'. Kallenbach, writing a few years later, thought history would place Gandhi alongside Tolstoy and Ruskin. Pranjivan Mehta went even further – he called his fellow Gujarati a 'Mahatma', the sort of spiritual leader born every few hundred years to rescue and redeem the motherland.

Kallenbach was Gandhi's most devoted European friend; Mehta, Gandhi's oldest and most steadfast Indian admirer. They would have followed their leader wherever he went, even down the path of armed struggle had he chosen that route instead. The moral force of Gandhi's political method, however, was better appreciated by two men, one

Indian, the other European, whose personal affection for the man was matched by a sharp understanding of his political technique. In a speech in Johannesburg in November 1908, the trader A. M. Cachalia observed that 'the passive resister is higher in the moral scale, and in that of human development than the active resister ... Passive resistance is a matter of heart, of conscience, of trained understanding.' Speaking to a reporter in Durban in September 1910, Henry Polak observed that 'our programme will remain, as it has always been, not one of violence or attempts to disturb, but one of suffering on the part of our people, who intend to go on enduring these hardships until they make the authorities ashamed of themselves.'

Gandhi's own belief in the power and relevance of non-violent resistance was enormous, and unshakeable. As early as November 1907 – when the first protests against permits were taking shape in the Transvaal, and when he had not yet been jailed himself – he said of passive resistance that it 'may well be adopted by every oppressed people [and] by every oppressed individual, as being a more reliable and more honourable instrument for securing the redress of wrongs than any which has heretofore been adopted'. Two years later, writing to Tolstoy from London, he went so far as to claim that 'the struggle of the Indians in the Transvaal is the greatest of modern times, inasmuch as it has been idealised both as to the goal as also the methods adoped to reach the goal.' Then, in June 1914 – on the eve of his departure from South Africa – he described satyagraha as 'perhaps the mightiest instrument on earth'.

As I write this in August 2012, sixty-five years after Indian independence, forty-four years after the passage of the Civil Rights Act in the United States, twenty-three years after the fall of the Berlin Wall, eighteen years after the ending of apartheid, and in the midst of ongoing non-violent struggles for democracy and dignity in Burma, Tibet, Yemen, Egypt and other places, Gandhi's words (and claims) appear less immodest than they might have seemed when he first articulated them.

Acknowledgements

In 1998 I made my first visit to South Africa. I have been back four times. My greatest debts in that country are to three outstanding historians: Surenda Bhana, Uma Dhupelia-Mesthrie and Goolam Vahed. They have given generously of their time and their scholarship. I have raided their published works, of course, but also gained much from letters and conversations over the years.

Three other South Africans took me on journeys through places Gandhi lived or worked in. Sudeshan Reddy drove me through Johannesburg, ending up at the Hamidia Mosque, around which so much of the action described in this book takes place. The novelist Aziz Hassim took me on a wonderful walking tour of central Durban. Ela Gandhi, daughter of Manilal and an admired South African democrat herself, took me on a guided tour of the now reconstructed Phoenix Settlement.

As the 'Note on Sources' indicates, the research for this book was done in archives spread across five countries. In the National Archives of India and the Nehru Memorial Museum and Library, both in New Delhi; at the old India Office collections in London, now housed in a wing of the British Library; at the British Library Newspaper Library at Colindale; at Rhodes House in Oxford and at the New York Public Library; at the National Archives of the United Kingdom at Kew; at the Maharashtra State Archives in Mumbai and the Tamil Nadu State Archives in Chennai; and at the University of South Africa and the South African National Archives, both in Pretoria – in all these places, I was assisted by kindly and competent record-keepers.

I do, however, owe special thanks to four very special archivists. Jenni Mackenzie went through the Baptist archive in Johannesburg, digging out every scrap relevant in any way to Gandhi. At the Sabarmati Ashram in Ahmedabad, Kinnari Bhatt guided me to (and through) the news clippings and diaries of the South African years, rarely used and yet (or thus) staggeringly valuable. Kinnari *ben* also answered many queries about Gandhi's Gujarati background, and helped select the photographs for this book. At the National Gandhi Museum in New Delhi, the vastly experienced S. K. Bhatnagar guided me through the many volumes of letters to Gandhi.

Jenni, Kinnari and Bhatnagar *Saab* are all thorough professionals. A fourth benefactor, Isa Sarid, was acting out of an intensely personal interest. In her home, in the Israeli port town of Haifa, lay the papers of Gandhi's friend and patron Hermann Kallenbach. I spent a most rewarding week among these papers, with dear Isa (then a sprightly and ever-smiling eighty-seven) at hand to provide clues and – when my hand tired from note-taking – a vegetarian lunch of the kind her uncle and Gandhi sometimes ate. I regret that Isa Sarid did not live long enough to see this book in print. Fortunately, before she died, she was able, as she had long wished, to supervise the transfer of her beloved uncle's papers to the National Archives of India.

I should also mention four fine bookshops, where I obtained many old and out-of-print books and pamphlets that proved enormously helpful in my research. These are Clarke's Bookshop in Cape Town; Ike's Bookshop and Collectables in Durban; the Collectors Treasury in Johannesburg; and Prabhu Book Service in Gurgaon (the old town, not the new city).

The first full draft of this book was written while I held the Philippe Roman Chair in History and International Affairs at the London School of Economics. A few furlongs to the south of my office (in Columbia House, on the corner of Houghton Street and the Aldwych) lies the Inner Temple, where Gandhi studied. A few furlongs to the north runs High Holborn, the street on which there was once a vegetarian restaurant where Gandhi ate.

As I thought and wrote about Gandhi (writing, among other things, the three chapters set in London) I was fortunate to have at hand the extraordinarily capable staff at LSE IDEAS, where the Roman Chair is housed. I wish especially to thank Arne Westad, Emilia Knight and Tiha Franulovic for their friendship and their generosity. This, along with the friendship and generosity of Emmanuel (Manny) Roman, made my year in London the most enjoyable and productive of all my spells outside India.

A host of other friends contributed ideas, suggested sources, translated letters from languages I do not know, and in other ways helped in the making of this book. They include N. Balakrishnan, Rakesh Basant, William Beinart, Deepa Bhatnagar, Sharad Chari, Rajesh Chopra, Varsha Das, V. N. Datta, Ashwin Desai, Keshav Desiraju, Richard Duguid, Patrick French, Supriya Gandhi, Stephen Gelb, Amitav Ghosh, Peter Heehs, Isabel Hofmeyr, Nasreen Munni Kabir, Prashant Kidambi, Shimon Low, John McLeod, Ashish Mitter, Rajendraprasad Narla, Anil Nauriya, Zac O'Yeah, Dina Patel, Dinyar Patel, Achal Prabala, Achintya Prasad, Tirthankar Roy, Usha Sahay, Navtej and Avina Sarna, Ornit Shahni, Hemali Sodhi, Neelima Shukla-Bhatt, Tridip Suhrud, Akhila Yechury, Geoffrey Ward and my parents Visalakshi and (the late) Dr S. R. D. Guha. A special *salaam* to my friends Jagadev Gajare, M. V. Ravishankar and R. Ullagadi, all of Ray+Keshavan Design Associates, who lovingly restored and sequenced the photos for this book.

I would like to thank three individuals who read the entire manuscript in draft: Katherine Boo, Saul Dubow and David Gilmour. Distinguished writers all, they brought different but complementary perspectives, correcting errors, smoothing out my prose, alerting me to new lines of enquiry. David and Kate are old friends, whose assistance may in this case be (somewhat) taken for granted. Saul Dubow, on the other hand, I know only through email. That he agreed to read a book by a stranger, on short notice, and did so with such acuity and thoroughness, speaks of a collegiality absent among historians of many countries but not, it seems, among those of South Africa.

I also owe a large debt to two Indian scholars. The publisher and literary historian Rukun Advani read some early chapters and advised on how they might be improved; this book also draws on dozens of conversations we have had over the years on the technique(s) of biographical writing. Meanwhile, the veteran political historian S. R. Mehrotra alerted me to the crucial importance to the Gandhi story of Pranjivan Mehta. He selflessly guided me to the key sources, despite working on a life of Mehta himself. Professor Mehrotra's zest and zeal (in his eighties, he thinks nothing of taking a night train from Shimla to Delhi, checking some documents in the archives and taking a night train back home) provided nourishment and example when my own energies flagged.

As always, this book could not have been written without the solidarity and support of my family. My wife and son read some chapters and commented most helpfully on them. My daughter accompanied me on a magical tour of Gandhi's Kathiawar. But merely the fact of being with them is enough to keep me going.

It was my agent Gill Coleridge who first convinced me that I should write a biography of Gandhi. When I had accumulated too many materials to do this in one go, she suggested I make it two volumes instead. Meanwhile, Gill's colleague, Melanie Jackson, has been quite superb at working out the North American end of things. I am also grateful to all Gill's colleagues at Rogers, Coleridge and White for their assistance over the years, and particularly to the indispensable Cara Jones and to my old mentor Peter Straus.

Gill and Melanie helped place this book in the hands of some fantastic editors. My year in London was thus further enriched by many stimulating conversations with Simon Winder at Penguin Press. Simon read my drafts very closely, and was particularly helpful in making me think through the links between biography and history. Also at Penguin UK, Jane Birdsell has been an expert and extremely understanding copy-editor.

I carry warm memories of long lunches in New York with Sonny Mehta, the conversation mostly around Gandhi but not excluding the game of cricket. Sonny read several drafts, encouraging me especially to flesh out the secondary characters. His Knopf colleague Dan Frank also provided excellent comments. At Random House Canada, Anne Collins commented most valuably on an early draft, and was always available as a sounding board on matters of structure and style.

At Penguin India, my dear friend Nandini Mehta has been a solid source of support. She has worked with me through more drafts of this book than I (or she) care to remember. Like Sonny, Nandini insisted that I pay more attention to Gandhi's friends and family. I am also grateful to Chiki Sarkar for her insightful comments on a late draft, and for her enthusiasm for all things connected with publishing, which makes her authors work harder than they might otherwise tend to do.

The person with whom I have discussed my subject longest is Gopalkrishna Gandhi. In the twenty (and more) years of our friendship, Gopal Gandhi has taught me much about Mohandas Gandhi, about Gujarati culture and about Indian history. In the context of this particular book, however, his greatest gift was that he sent me to meet Enuga S. Reddy in New York in or around the year 1992. It was a cold and dark winter evening, and Mr Reddy then worked out of a small (and dark) room somewhere near the UN headquarters in midtown Manhattan. Ever since, Mr Reddy has illuminated my path to Gandhi. All through the research and writing of this book, I have drawn regularly and repeatedly on his phenomenal knowledge of Gandhi and of South Africa. He has directed me to rare materials in archives around the world. He has provided many materials from his own collection. And, in between various hospital stints and family commitments (among them celebrating the birth of a great-grandchild), he has read and corrected my drafts. The dedication to *Gandhi Before India* inadequately expresses what I (and numerous other Gandhi scholars) owe this shy, gentle, greatly learned and truly heroic man.

A Note on Sources

The first twelve volumes of the *Collected Works of Mahatma Gandhi* run to some 5,000 pages in print. They cover his years in Kathiawar, London, Bombay and South Africa. Two scholars played a critical role in putting together these volumes. They were K. Swaminathan, chief editor of the project; and his deputy, C. N. Patel. Swaminathan was previously a professor of English in Madras; he had also briefly edited a Sunday newspaper. Patel had also been an English teacher (in a college in Ahmedabad); and he was a native Gujarati speaker.

Swaminathan supervised the project as a whole, setting the texts in context by providing footnotes, cross-references and appendices. Much of the translation of Gandhi's Gujarati letters and articles was done by Patel. The duo were helped, in these early volumes, by two others – Gandhi's nephew Chhaganlal and his one-time *alter ego* Henry Polak. Chhagan passed on his large stock of Gandhi letters; with Polak, he also helped identify the authors of the usually unsigned articles in *Indian Opinion*. Both had been intimately involved in the production of this journal in South Africa; now, fifty years later, they assessed, as accurately as they could, which pieces could reliably be attributed to Gandhi himself.

The first twelve volumes of the *Collected Works of Mahatma Gandhi* have naturally been raided for this book. So has a supplementary volume of the *Collected Works*, which reproduces some letters written by Gandhi to Hermann Kallenbach, Henry and Millie Polak, and Albert West. However, almost as important to this biography have been the letters written by *other people to* Gandhi, a source strangely neglected in the past. In the library of the National Gandhi Museum in New Delhi, which is located across the road from his memorial in Rajghat, lie a series of large black-bound volumes containing Gandhi's correspondence.

They run chronologically, with the first ten volumes covering the period of this book. Here one finds the letters written to Gandhi by the closest associates of his South African years – Pranjivan Mehta, Henry Polak, Joseph Doke, G. K. Gokhale, C. F. Andrews, *et al*. These letters throw much light on Gandhi's personality, familial relationships, religious beliefs and social and political views.

In the library of the Gandhi Museum, these volumes are housed in the bottom shelves of bookcases, behind sliding doors, so that they are not immediately visible, which may be one reason why they have been neglected. The letters are copies; the originals are housed in the National Archives, with copies and some additional materials also available in the Sabarmati Ashram in Ahmedabad, where Gandhi lived from 1917 to 1930. Each carries a number, prefaced by the initials 'S. N.', for 'Serial Number'.

A third set of sources crucial to this work were the papers of Gandhi's friends and associates. These contain letters about Gandhi, and reflections about Gandhi, that provide rich details and often striking insights about his multiple careers. This book has thus drawn extensively on the papers of Gopal Krishna Gokhale, housed at the National Archives of India in New Delhi; the papers of Henry Polak, split between the Rhodes House Library in Oxford and the Asian and African Collections of the British Library in London; the papers of Hermann Kallenbach, at the time this book was being researched in the Israeli town of Haifa (but at the time it is being finished in the process of being transferred to a public archive in India); and the papers of Joseph Doke, held in part in the South African Baptist Union archives in Johannesburg and in part in the papers of his son C. M. Doke, which are kept in the library of the University of South Africa (UNISA) in Pretoria. Among the other manuscript collections that have been helpful in my research are the Louis Fischer Papers, held at the New York Public Library; a diary of Kallenbach's for 1912–13 that is in the Sabarmati Ashram in Ahmedabad; and the papers of the Servants of India Society, which are housed at the Nehru Memorial Museum and Library in New Delhi (NMML). The NMML also has a vast cache of Gandhi papers; while these deal principally with the 1930s and 1940s, there is some material on South Africa, including a file of news clippings on the 1913–14 satyagraha apparently maintained by Henry Polak. I have also drawn abundantly on Gandhi-related materials collected over the years by E. S. Reddy. Some of Mr Reddy's papers are housed at the Sterling Library in Yale University; some at the NMML; and some are retained by him in New York.

A fourth major source were the archival records of the Indian, South African and British Governments. The racial policies of the South African state, and the reactions to them in London and India, are often best reconstructed through these records. They are particularly valuable in understanding how Gandhi's political adversaries – from the lowly Protector of Asiatics to elevated Ministers, Prime Ministers and Governor Generals – wrote about and responded to him.

Records pertaining to Gandhi's years in Natal were photocopied at the public archives in Pietermaritzburg by E. S. Reddy; these copies now rest in the Nehru Memorial Museum and Library in New Delhi. Even more valuable are a series of eight microfilms of records from Natal Government House. These are held at the NMML, which obtained them in the 1970s, when the Indian Government had no dealings with the apartheid regime. A visionary archivist persuaded an American scholar with a large budget to film these records and pass on a copy to New Delhi. Running to some 10,000 pages, these microfilms are an invaluable window into the lives and labours of Indians in South Africa, and of the role played therein by a certain M. K. Gandhi.

The records of the Transvaal Government, and of the Union of South Africa itself, are kept in the National Archives of South Africa. These are housed in what may be the most unattractive building in Pretoria. However, the richness of the materials within compensate for the horror without. More attractive, at least from the outside, is the National Archives in New Delhi, where I consulted the records of the Foreign and Political Department (for Kathiawar), the Emigration Branch of the Department of Commerce and Industry (dealing with the Indian diaspora) and the Home Department (regarding the ban on Gandhi's book, *Hind Swaraj*). Supplementary material was also located in the Maharashtra State Archives in Mumbai and the Tamil Nadu State archives in Chennai.

A third set of state records are held in London, which, *c.* 1869–1914, was the capital of an Empire whose territories included all of India and most of South Africa. Particularly helpful to this project were the Colonial Office records, kept in the National Archives of the United Kingdom, at Kew; and the records of the old India Office, held by the British Library in St Pancras, both of which contain much valuable material on Gandhi and his struggles.

Also useful were the papers of the proconsuls themselves. I consulted the papers of Lord Selborne at the Bodleian Library in Oxford, and of Lord Ripon and Lord Gladstone in the British Library in London.

Letters, manuscripts and government records are generally classified as 'unpublished primary sources'. Turning next to 'primary printed sources', I have drawn on the rich series of Parliamentary Papers on South Africa (which reproduce many letters from the archives); on the published volumes of the Jan Christian Smuts correspondence, edited by Keith Hancock and Jean Van Der Poel; and on various government reports published between (roughly) 1890 and 1910.

An absolutely critical source for this book – oddly overlooked by previous biographers – have been newspapers printed in the three countries Gandhi lived in and had dealings with. I have thus drawn extensively on relevant reports in the British press, and on newspaper comments on Gandhi and his activities published in Indian newspapers and, most importantly, in South Africa.

Twelve bound volumes of news clippings are kept in a Godrej almi-rah in the Sabarmati Ashram in Ahmedabad. They cover the period 1894 to 1901, and deal principally with attitudes to Indians and Gandhi in Natal. While kept separately, in the ashram's catalogue they are indexed chronologically with the letters by and to Gandhi. I have therefore cited them too by their 'S. N.', or 'Serial Number'.

Who maintained these clippings? I think it very likely that it was Gandhi himself. How did they get to Sabarmati? The veteran Gandhian activist Narayan Desai thinks that they were brought back from South Africa by Chhaganlal Gandhi. In that case, it may be that when Gandhi left for India in 1901, the clippings were left behind in Natal in the keeping of a friend (Parsee Rustomjee?), and later salvaged by Chhaganlal. This, of course, is speculation – what is hard fact is that the clippings are now at Sabarmati. They provide a fascinating perspective on how the young Gandhi was viewed by the white public of Natal.

In 1903, on his return to South Africa, Gandhi started *Indian Opinion*. The newspaper regularly excerpted reports and commentary from other periodicals, which I have drawn upon in my narrative. *Indian Opinion* itself is indispensable for a fuller understanding of Gandhi, his community, his struggles and his time. The volumes from 1903 to 1914 (inclusive) have been put on CD-ROM by the National Gandhi Museum. I read these 500-odd issues on a large computer, consistently absorbed and fascinated by their content and tone, taking notes on a split screen as I read. (My notes ran to 40,000 words, only a fraction of which have found their way into the preceding pages).

The news clippings at Sabarmati and the material in *Indian Opinion* (whether original to that journal or reproduced from elsewhere) were very revealing indeed. So were copies of *African Chronicle*, the newspaper of Gandhi's rival P. S. Aiyar, microfilms of which are held in the British Library's newspaper section, in the north London suburb of Collindale. For key incidents in Gandhi's life and the satyagrahas he led, I also consulted copies of *The Times* of London; the *Transvaal Leader*; the *Rand Daily Mail*; the *Star* of Johannesburg; the *Natal Advertiser*; and the *Madras Mail*. Particularly valuable were the microfilms of the *Natal Mercury* for the period 1893–1914 housed at the NMML, and presumably brought there by a route as devious (and creative) as the microfilms of Natal Government House.

The last set of sources consist of printed books and essays. I have, where necessary and relevant, used secondary works by specialists published in recent decades. However, I have also read many books and pamphlets published in the last decade of the nineteenth century and the first decade of the twentieth, to get a direct, unmediated flavour of how the debates in which Gandhi figured were understood and articulated at the time.

As explained in the prologue, this book sought in the first instance to go beyond the *Collected Works*, and thus to provide an account that did not rely exclusively or even largely on what Gandhi said and wrote. The sources described above, which were consulted over many years in many different collections, have allowed me to paint what I trust is a portrait, from all angles, of Gandhi's life before his departure from South Africa in July 1914. During the course of my research I also found many letters written by Gandhi that, for one reason or another, had not been published or known of before. These previously unknown or uncollected letters lie in the National Archives of India and of South Africa, in the British Library, in the C. M. Doke papers in Pretoria, in the Kallenbach Papers in Haifa and in the papers of E. S. Reddy in New York and New Delhi. They reveal unexpected details of Gandhi's motivations, of how, at various critical moments, he behaved towards the Natal, Transvaal and Indian Governments; towards his fellow passive resisters; and towards his eldest son.

Notes

ABBREVIATIONS USED IN THE NOTES

AC   *African Chronicle*
APAC/BL   Asia, Pacific and Africa Collections, British Library,
                            London
BL   British Library, London
C. M. Doke Papers   C. M. Doke Collection, Documentation Centre for
                            African Studies, UNISA Library, Pretoria
CO   Colonial Office
CWMG   *Collected Works of Mahatma Gandhi* (New Delhi:
                            Government of India, 1958 onwards).
Gandhi, *An Autobiography* M. K. Gandhi, *An Autobiography, or the Story of
                            My Experiments with Truth*, translated from the
                            Gujarati by Mahadev Desai (first published in 1927;
                            2nd edn, 1940; reprint Ahmedabad: Navajivan
                            Publishing House, 1995). There are many print
                            editions of Gandhi's autobiography in English,
                            published in India, the United Kingdom, the United
                            States and other countries. And there will be more.
                            The book has also been translated into many lan-
                            guages. The pagination of these editions varies
                            enormously. Therefore in my references to it I have
                            cited Part and Chapter rather than page numbers.
                            However, since the book originated in a series of
                            newspaper articles, each chapter is merely a few
                            pages long, so my citations will be relatively easy
                            to track down by those who have editions other
                            than mine, or in languages other than English.
ILN   *Illustrated London News*
IO   *Indian Opinion*
IR   *Indian Review*

J. J. Doke Papers	J. J. Doke Papers, South African Baptist Union Archives, Johannesburg
KP	Hermann Kallenbach papers, in the possession of Isa Sarid, Haifa, Israel
Memorial	*Memorial to The Right Honourable Joseph Chamberlain, Her Majesty's Principal Secretary for the Colonies, by the British Indians in Natal, re Anti-Indian Demonstration*
MSA	Maharashtra State Archives, Mumbai
NA	*Natal Advertiser*
NAI	National Archives of India, New Delhi
NAUK	National Archives of the United Kingdom, Kew
NASA	National Archives of South Africa, Pretoria
NGM	National Gandhi Museum, Delhi
NM	*Natal Mercury*
NMML	Nehru Memorial Museum and Library, New Delhi
NYPL	New York Public Library, New York
S.N.	Serial Number(s)
SAAA	Sabarmati Ashram Archives, Ahmedabad

PROLOGUE: GANDHI FROM ALL ANGLES

1. http://freedomhouse.org/template.cfm?page=70&release=275 (accessed 26 July 2011).

2. Cf. reports in *New York Times*, 16 February 2011; and in *New Yorker*, 11 April 2011. These various affirmations, personal and political, have provoked vigorous denunciations from left-wing critics disenchanted – or even disgusted – by how widely Gandhi is admired across the world. In the *London Review of Books*, the political theorist Perry Anderson launched a three-part attack on Gandhi and his legacy, calling him an 'autocrat' and 'Hindu revivalist' whose thought contained 'a battery of archaisms', and whose 'conception of himself as a vessel of divine intention allowed him to escape the trammels of human logic or coherence'. Anderson went on to suggest that Gandhi's intellectual weaknesses were substantially responsible for the flawed nature of Indian democracy today. See *London Review of Books*, 5 July, 19 July and 2 August 2012. The length (the series ran to some 50,000 words in all), the (harsh, often angry) tone, and the fact that Anderson had never (in a five decade long career) previously written anything on Gandhi (or India) lends credence to the speculation that the series was provoked by Gandhi's (to the Marxist) inexplicable popularity so long after his death.

3. On Gandhi's Gujarati and English prose styles, see, respectively, C. N. Patel, *Mahatma Gandhi in His Gujarati Writings* (New Delhi: Sahitya Akademi,

1981); Sunil Khilnani, 'Gandhi and Nehru: The Uses of English', in Arvind Krishna Mehrotra, ed., *An Illustrated History of English Literature in English* (New Delhi: Permanent Black, 2003).

4. The project of compiling all of Gandhi's writings was launched in February 1956, eight years after his death. The first volume in the series was published in 1958; the ninetieth and last, in 1984. Seven supplementary volumes were then published, consisting of letters collected too late to include in the chronological volumes. A 'subject index' and an 'index of persons' followed. That made it ninety-nine; whereupon, to satisfy the Indian's incurable love of symmetry, a book of 'prefaces' to the individual volumes was also brought out. The *Collected Works* have been published in three languages – English, Gujarati and Hindi.

5. Two older books on Gandhi that deal specifically with his South African experience are Robert A. Huttenback, *Gandhi in South Africa* (Ithaca, NY: Cornell University Press, 1971); Maureen Swan, *Gandhi: The South African Experience* (Johannesburg: Ravan Press, 1985). Written by scholars rather than journalists, both works were important and necessary – at the time at which they appeared. Focusing on Gandhi's public career, neither dealt with his personal, familial or religious life. Neither scholar did any serious research on Indian sources; and of course many important sources outside India have come to light in the decades since their books were published.

6. H. S. L. Polak, 'Passive Resistance Movement in South Africa', typescript composed *c.*1908–12, Mss. Afr. R. 125, Rhodes House Library, Oxford, p. 103.

7. Bhawani Dayal, *Dakshin Africa ké Satyagraha ka Itihas* (Indore: Saraswati Sadan, 1916), p. 1 (my translation).

I   MIDDLE CASTE, MIDDLE RANK

1. The classical or scriptural name for this category of Hindus is 'Vaishya'. However, the Vaishyas are more often referred to in everyday conversation as 'Bania' (or, in the plural, as 'Banias'). The name is subject to regional variations and alternate spellings, among them 'Vaniya', 'Baniya' and even 'Bunyan'.

2. A lexicon in Gandhi's mother tongue, Gujarati, says of them that *Vaniyani mochchh nichi* ('the Bania is always ready to compromise'; literally, 'the Bania's moustache is ready to droop downwards'); *Vaniya Vaniya fervi tol* ('the Bania always changes according to circumstance'); *Vaniya mugnu naam pade nahi* ('the Bania will not commit himself to anything'). To this a Gujarati–English dictionary adds, *Jaate Vaniyabhai, etle todjod karvaman kushal* ('Being born a merchant, he was possessed of tact and was good in settling quarrels'). See Achyut Yagnik and Suchitra Sheth, *The Shaping of Modern Gujarat: Plurality, Hinduism, and Beyond* (New Delhi: Penguin Books, 2005), p. 34.

3. See David Hardiman, *Feeding the Baniya: Peasants and Usurers in Western India* (Delhi: Oxford University Press, 1996), especially Chapter 4 (quotes from pp. 68–9, 71, 75).

4. Harald Tambs-Lyche, *Power, Profit and Poetry: Traditional Society in Kathiawar, Western India* (Delhi: Manohar, 1997), Chapter IX ('The Banias: The Merchant Estate').

5. Cf. Howard Spodek, *Urban–Rural Integration in Regional Development: A Case Study of Saurashtra, India, 1800–1960* (University of Chicago Geography Research Papers, 1976), p. 11.

6. Ibid., pp. 2–3.

7. Cf. Harald Tambs-Lyche, 'Reflections on Caste in Gujarat', in Edward Simpson and Aparna Kapadia, *The Idea of Gujarat: History, Ethnography and Text* (Hyderabad: Orient BlackSwan, 2010), pp. 101–2, 104, 108.

8. C. F. Andrews, 'Mahatma Gandhi's Birthplace', *The Centenary Review* (January 1938), pp. 35f.

9. *The Imperial Gazetteer of India* (Oxford: Clarendon Press, 1908), XX: *Pardi to Pusad*, pp. 188–91.

10. Chandran D. S. Devanesan, *The Making of the Mahatma* (Bombay: Orient Longman, 1969), pp. 100–5.

11. Cf. Satish C. Misra, *Muslim Communities in Gujarat: Preliminary Studies in Their History and Social Organization* (2nd edn, New Delhi: Munshiram Manoharlal, 1985).

12. Devanesan, *Making of the Mahatma*, Chapter 2 ('Whirlwinds of Change: Kathiawar in the Nineteenth Century'); Howard Spodek, 'Urban Politics in the Local Kingdoms of India: A View from the Princely States of Saurashtra under British Rule', *Modern Asian Studies*, 7:2 (1973).

13. This incident has been narrated, based on primary sources, in Krishnalal Mohanlal Jhaveri, *The Gujaratis: The People, Their History, and Culture*, 4: *Gujarati Social Organization* (New Delhi: Indigo Books, 2002), p. 141.

14. Pyarelal, *Mahatma Gandhi*, I: *The Early Phase* (Ahmedabad: Navajivan Press, 1965), pp. 173–8.

15. Anon., *Heroes of the Hour: Mahatma Gandhi, Tilak Maharaj, Sir Subramanya Iyer* (Madras: Ganesh and Co., 1918), p. 5.

16. See compilation no. 190, vol. 48 of 1950, Political Department, MSA.

17. Pyarelal, *Mahatma Gandhi*, I, pp. 186–7.

18. This account is based on the correspondence in A Proceedings 130–147 (Political), December 1869, Foreign Department, NAI.

19. Prabhudas Gandhi, *My Childhood with Gandhiji* (Ahmedabad: Navajivan Publishing House, 1957), pp. 4–5.

20. M. N. Buch, 'Answers to Louis Fischer's questions regarding Porbandar and Rajkot', dated 9 March 1949, in Box 1, Louis Fischer Papers, NYPL.

21. Quoted in Pyarelal, *Mahatma Gandhi*, I, p. 194.

22. Stephen Hay, 'Digging up Gandhi's Psychological Roots', *Biography*, 6:3 (1983), pp. 211–12.

23. Henry Yule and Arthur Coke Burnell, *Hobson-Jobson: Being a Glossary of Anglo-Indian Colloquial Words and Phrases, and of Kindred Terms, Etymological, Historical, Geographical, and Discursive* (London: John Murray, 1886), p. 48.

24. Hardiman, *Feeding the Baniya*, p. 65.

25. For more details, see K. T. Achaya, *Indian Food: A Historical Companion* (New Delhi: Oxford University Press, 1994), pp. 133ff. I do not know of a stand-alone work in English on the culinary arts of Gujarat, but a sampling of this superb cuisine may be had in restaurants such as Chetna, in the Kala Ghoda area of Mumbai, and Swati Snacks, near Law College in Ahmedabad.

26. Gandhi, *An Autobiography*, Part I, Chapter I. A footnote (added most likely by Mahadev Desai) explains that *Chaturmas* was 'literally a period of four months. A vow of fasting and semi-fasting during the four months of the rains. The period is a sort of long Lent'.

27. Yagnik and Sheth, *Shaping of Gujarat*, pp. 159–60; Devanesan, *Making of the Mahatma*, p. 34.

28. See Narayan Desai, *My Life Is My Message*, I: *Sadhana (1869–1915)* (Hyderabad: Orient BlackSwan, 2009), pp. 10–11.

29. Cf. Pyarelal, *Mahatma Gandhi*, I, Appendix E, pp. 737–8.

30. *Imperial Gazetteer of India*, XXI: *Pushkar to Salween*, pp. 73–5.

31. See J. M. Upadhyaya, ed., *Mahatma Gandhi as a Student* (New Delhi: Publications Division, 1965) and *Mahatma Gandhi: A Teacher's Discovery* (Vallabh Vidyanagar: Sardar Patel University, 1969). Unless otherwise stated, the rest of this section is based on these two books. Remarkably, the material reproduced in these books has never before been used by a Gandhi biographer.

32. The school is referred to as 'Alfred High School' in some recent biographies of Gandhi. However, it acquired that name only in 1907, long after Mohandas had left it. 'Kattywar' is the way the British then spelt 'Kathiawar'. In 1969, on the centenary of Gandhi's birth, the school was renamed 'Mahatma Gandhi Memorial High School'.

33. Notes of an interview with Raliatbehn, 14 December 1948, in Box 1, Louis Fischer Papers, NYPL. (The questions were framed by Fischer, but asked of Raliat by an Indian friend on his behalf.)

34. See Stephen Hay, 'Between Two Worlds: Gandhi's First Impressions of British Culture', *Modern Asian Studies*, 3:4 (1969), pp. 308–9; Gandhi, *An Autobiography*, Part I, Chapter X. The preacher's name was H. R. Scott; years later, he identified himself in a letter to Gandhi, but disputed the Indian's recollection that he had 'poured abuse' on Hindu gods. See correspondence in Mss. Eur. C. 487, APAC/BL.

35. Upadhyaya, *Mahatma Gandhi as a Student*, pp. 14–15, 32, 35.

36. See J. M. Upadhyaya, *Gandhiji's Early Contemporaries and Companions* (Ahmedabad: Navajivan Publishing House, 1971), photo opposite p. 23.

37. Gandhi, *An Autobiography*, Part I, Chapters VII and VIII.

38. Cf. Stephen Hay, 'Gandhi's First Five Years', in Donald Capps, Walter H. Capps and M. Gerald Bradford, eds, *Encounter with Erikson: Historical Interpretation in Religious Biography* (Missoula, Montana: Scholars Press, 1977), fn. 5.

39. Gandhi, *An Autobiography*, Part I, Chapter III.

40. Arun and Sunanda Gandhi, *The Untold Story of Kasturba: Wife of Mahatma Gandhi* (Mumbai: Jaico Publishing House, 2000), p. 5.

41. Anon., *Smt. Kasturba's House at Porbandar* (Ahmedabad: Directorate of Archaeology, 1973). These wall-paintings would have been of religious themes, perhaps of the lives (and legends) of Krishna and Ram.

42. Gandhi, *An Autobiography*, Part I, Chapter IV.

43. Ibid., Part I, Chapter IX.

44. These paragraphs are based on Upadhyaya, *Mahatma Gandhi as a Student*, passim.

45. See Sitamshu Yashaschandra, 'From Hemacandra to *Hind Svaraj*: Region and Power in Gujarati Literary Culture', in Sheldon Pollock, ed., *Literary Cultures in History: Reconstructions from South Asia* (Berkeley: University of Calfornia Press, 2003).

46. For more details, see Tridip Suhurd, *Writing Life: Three Gujarati Thinkers* (Hyderabad: Orient BlackSwan, 2009), Chapters 2 and 4.

47. Based on an analysis of the names in a photocopied page of the class register in Subject File no. 1, Gandhi Papers, NMML.

48. This account of Gandhi's time in Samaldas College is based on Upadhyaya, *Mahatma Gandhi: A Teacher's Discovery*, pp. 95–102.

49. Gandhi, *An Autobiography*, Part I, Chapter XI.

50. Cf. Yashaschandra, 'Hemacandra to *Hind Svaraj*', p. 596.

51. Political Agent of Kathiawar, quoted in *Gazetteer of the Bombay Presidency*, VII: *Kathiawar* (Bombay: Government Central Press, 1884), p. 343.

52. Gandhi, *An Autobiography*, Part I, Chapter XI.

53. See File no. R/1/1/740, APAC/BL.

54. Extract from the *Kathiawar Times*, 12 August 1888, reproduced in Upadhyaya, *Mahatma Gandhi as a Student*, p. 83.

55. On the likely date of Harilal's birth, see Chandulal Bhagubhai Dalal, *Harilal Gandhi: A Life*, edited and translated from the Gujarati by Tridip Suhrud (Chennai: Orient Longman, 2007), p. 1.

56. Gandhi, 'London Diary', *CWMG*, I, p. 45.

57. Ibid., pp. 45–6; Gandhi, *An Autobiography*, Part I, Chapter XII.

2 AMONG THE VEGETARIANS

1. Unless otherwise stated, this section is based on M. K. Gandhi, 'London Diary', *CWMG*, I, pp. 2–16.
2. Gandhi, 'Guide to London' (Appendix), in *CWMG*, I, p. 117.
3. James D. Hunt, *Gandhi in London* (revised edn, New Delhi: Promilla and Co, 1993), pp. 7–8.
4. Cover of *ILN*, 13 July 1889.
5. See *ILN*, 7 September 1889.
6. Jonathan Schneer, *London in 1900: The Imperial Metropolis* (New Haven: Yale University Press, 1999), pp. 7–8.
7. Rozina Visram, *Asians in Britain: 400 Years of History* (London: Pluto Press, 2002), pp. 45–6, 125–6.
8. This paragraph is based on issues of the *Illustrated London News* for the period.
9. Gandhi, *An Autobiography*, Part I, Chapter XIII.
10. Hunt, *Gandhi in London*, pp. 220–22; Gandhi, 'Guide to London', *CWMG*, I, pp. 94, 117, 119.
11. Hunt, *Gandhi in London*, p. 14.
12. *CWMG*, I, pp. 2, 16–18.
13. Gilchrist Alexander, *The Temple of the Nineties* (London: William Hodge and Company, 1938), p. 78.
14. Ibid., p. 269.
15. Thomas Leaming, *A Philadelphia Lawyer in the London Courts* (New York: Henry Holt and Company, 1911), p. 137.
16. Gandhi, *An Autobiography*, Part I, Chapter XXIV.
17. *The Recollections of Sir Henry Dickens, K. C.* (London: William Heinemann, 1934), p. 296. The author was a son of Charles Dickens.
18. Sachindananda Sinha, 'Gandhiji's Earlier Career as I Knew It' (11-page typescript written *c.*1949), in Box 3, Louis Fischer Papers, NYPL.
19. Gandhi, *An Autobiography*, Part I, Chapters XVII and XVIII.
20. See Tristram Stuart, *The Bloodless Revolution: Radical Vegetarians and the Discovery of India* (London: Harper Press, 2006), pp. 40, 43, 49, 50, 53, 57, 62–3, 69, 280f., 284–5, 342–3, 422–3, etc.
21. Stephen Winsten, *Salt and His Circle* (London: Hutchinson and Co., 1951); George Hendrick, *Henry Salt: Humanitarian Reformer and Man of Letters* (Urbana: University of Illinois Press, 1977).
22. George Hendrick and Willene Hendrick, eds, *The Savour of Salt: A Henry Salt Anthology* (Fontwell, Sussex: Centaur Press, 1999), pp. 25–8.
23. Henry S. Salt, *Animals' Rights: Considered in Relation to Social Progress* (New York: Macmillan and Co., 1894), pp. 51–2, 89–90, 94.
24. Grant Richards, *Memories of a Misspent Youth, 1872–1896* (London: William Heinemann, 1932), p. 106.

25. In his 'Guide to London', Gandhi does not mention sport at all, and says of the theatre that to visit it 'once a month on the average is quite sufficient' (an average one suspects he had difficulty in meeting). See *CWMG*, I, pp. 110–11.

26. See Stephen Hay, 'The Making of a Late-Victorian Hindu: M. K. Gandhi in London, 1888–1891', *Victorian Studies* (Autumn 1989), esp. pp. 89–90. The large (and still expanding) world of Gandhi scholarship owes a great debt to Stephen Hay and James D. Hunt. These American scholars, both now deceased, have contributed immensely to our understanding of Gandhi's early years, through archival research that has variously clarified, disputed, contextualized or supplemented the recollections in the *Autobiography*.

27. Hunt, *Gandhi in London*, p. 221.

28. As recalled in Josiah Oldfield, 'My Friend Gandhi', in Chandrashanker Shukla, ed., *Reminiscences of Gandhiji* (Bombay: Vora and Co., 1951), pp. 187–8.

29. Hunt, *Gandhi in London*, pp. 28–30; Gandhi, *An Autobiography*, Part I, Chapter XX.

30. Gandhi, *An Autobiography*, Part I, Chapter XX.

31. Ibid., Part I, Chapter XVI.

32. Hunt, *Gandhi in London*, pp. 16–18.

33. Gandhi, 'Guide to London', *CWMG*, I, pp. 83–4, 120.

34. Gandhi, *An Autobiography*, Part I, Chapters XXI to XXIII.

35. G. Parameswaran Pillai, *London and Paris Through Indian Spectacles* (1897, reprint, New Delhi: Sahitya Akademi, 2006), pp. 83–5.

36. See notice on 'Inns of Court', *The Times*, 16 April 1890. (I am grateful to Zac O'Yeah for this reference.)

37. Hunt, *Gandhi in London*, pp. 17–18.

38. M. K. Gandhi, 'Indian Vegetarians', *CWMG*, I, pp. 19–29.

39. See Compilation no. 140, vol. 108 of 1892, Political Department, MSA.

40. See, among other works, Raymond Williams, *The Country and the City* (London: Chatto and Windus, 1973); Jan March, *Back to the Land: The Pastoral Impulse in England, from 1800 to 1914* (London: Quartet Books, 1982).

41. M. K. Gandhi, 'Some Indian Festivals', three-part series originally published in *The Vegetarian*, 28 March, 4 and 25 April 1891, *CWMG*, I, pp. 29–34.

42. M. K. Gandhi, 'The Foods of India', originally published in *The Vegetarian Messenger*, 1 May 1891, *CWMG*, I, pp. 36–41.

43. See Jerry White, *London in the Nineteenth Century* (London: Jonathan Cape, 2007), pp. 3, 29–30, 289–90.

44. Hunt, *Gandhi in London*, p. 10.

45. Hay, 'Making of a Late-Victorian Hindu', pp. 82–3, 88.

46. Cf. Schneer, *London in 1900*, pp. 184–9.

47. Obituary notice, *ILN*, 7 February 1891.

48. Gandhi, *An Autobiography*, Part I, Chapter XX.

49. Anon., 'The First Mosque in England', *ILN*, 9 November 1889.
50. See Gandhi, 'Guide to London', *CWMG*, I, pp. 76–87, 96–7, 117–18.
51. *CWMG*, I, pp. 41, 49.
52. M. K. Gandhi, 'On [the] Way Home to India', *The Vegetarian*, 9 and 16 April 1892, *CWMG*, I, pp. 50–55.

3   FROM COAST TO COAST

1. The house, Mani Bhavan, still exists. It now houses a Gandhi museum and library.
2. Gandhi, *An Autobiography*, Part II, Chapter I.
3. See, for biographical details, Satish Sharma, *Gandhi's Teachers: Rajchandra Ravjibhai Mehta* (Ahmedabad: Gujarat Vidyapith, 2005), Chapter 2.
4. See James Laidlaw, *Riches and Renunciation: Religion, Economy, and Society among the Jains* (Oxford: Clarendon Press, 1995), pp. 235–7.
5. Gandhi, 'A Great Seer', *CWMG*, XLIII, p. 98.
6. Gandhi, 'Preface to "Srimad Rajchandra"', 5 November 1926, *CWMG*, XXXII, pp. 5–7.
7. Arun and Sunanda Gandhi, *The Untold Story of Kasturba: Wife of Mahatma Gandhi* (Mumbai: Jaico Publishing House, 2000), pp. 49–50.
8. Gandhi, *An Autobiography*, Part II, Chapter II.
9. Ibid., Part II, Chapter IV.
10. Administrator, Porbandar State, to Political Agent, Kathiawar, 9 September 1891, in R/2/720/49, APAC/BL.
11. Gandhi, *An Autobiography*, Part II, Chapter II.
12. Letter, dated *c.* June 1891, by J. B. Benson, State Engineer, Porbandar State; Administrator to Political Agent, Kathiawar, 15 August 1891, both in R/2/720/49, APAC/BL.
13. Bhavsinghji to Political Agent, Kathiawar, 5 September 1891; Administrator, Porbandar State, to Political Agent, Kathiawar, 9 September 1891, ibid.
14. 'Testimony of Kalidas [Laxmidas] Gandhi, 8 August 1891', in ibid. Laxmidas Gandhi's pet name was 'Kalidas': that is how he was known to his friends and family in Porbandar.
15. Political Agent, Kathiawar, to Home Secretary, Bombay Government, 12 September 1891, ibid.
16. Gandhi, *An Autobiography*, Part II, Chapter IV.
17. Cf. Stephen Hay, 'Gandhi's Reasons for Leaving Rajkot for South Africa in 1893' (unpublished paper in the possession of E. S. Reddy).
18. Cf. *CWMG*, I, item 21, p. 50.
19. G. W. Stevens, 'All India in Miniature', in R. P. Karkaria, *The Charm of Bombay: An Anthology of Writings in Praise of the First City in India* (Bombay: D. B. Taraporavala and Sons, 1915), pp. 81–4.

20. Prashant Kidambi, *The Making of an Indian Metropolis: Colonial Governance and Public Culture in Bombay, 1890–1920* (Aldershot: Ashgate, 2007), Chapter I, 'The Rise of Bombay'.
21. S. M. Edwardes, *The Rise of Bombay* (Bombay: The Times of India Press, 1902), p. 327.
22. See Rahul Mehrotra and Sharada Dwivedi, *The Bombay High Court: The Story of the Building, 1878–2003* (Bombay: Eminence Designs, 2004).
23. Gandhi, *An Autobiography*, Part II, Chapter III.
24. M. K. Gandhi to Ranchhodlal Patwari, 5 September 1892, *CWMG*, I, pp. 56–7. The letter was apparently written in English.
25. Gandhi, 'Preface to "Srimad Rajchandra"', p. 6; 'Speech on Birth Anniversary of Rajchandra' (Ahmedabad, 16 November 1921), *CWMG*, XXI, pp. 432–4.
26. Gandhi, *An Autobiography*, Part II, Chapter IV. For an example of a petition drafted by Gandhi while in Rajkot, see Pyarelal, *Mahatma Gandhi*, I: *The Early Phase* (Ahmedabad: Navajivan Press, 1965), Appendix H, pp. 739–44.
27. See Goolam Vahed, 'Passengers, Partnerships, and Promissory Notes: Gujarati Traders in Colonial Natal, 1870–1920', *International Journal of African Historical Studies*, 38:3, p. 459 and passim.
28. Gandhi, *An Autobiography*, pp. 84–5.
29. *NM*, 22 November 1860, quoted in C. G. Henning, *The Indentured Indian in Natal (1860–1917)* (New Delhi: Promilla and Co., 1993), pp. 30–1.
30. This account of the immigration of Indians into Natal and their life there is based on, among other works, Surendra Bhana and Joy Brain, *Settling Down Roots: Indian Migrants in South Africa, 1860–1911* (Johannesburg: Witwatersrand University Press, 1990); Mabel Palmer, *The History of the Indians in Natal* (1957; reprint, Westport, Conn.: Greenwood Press, 1977); Surendra Bhana, *Indentured Indian Emigrants to Natal, 1860–1902: A Study Based on Ships' Lists* (New Delhi: Promilla and Co., 1991); G. H. Calpin, *Indians in South Africa* (Pietermaritzburg: Shuter and Shooter, 1949); C. J. Ferguson-Davie, *The Early History of Indians in Natal* (Johannesburg: South African Institute of Race Relations, 1952); Surendra Bhana, ed., *Essays on Indentured Indians in Natal* (Leeds: Peepal Tree Press, 1990); Nile Green, *Bombay Islam: The Religious Economy of the West Indian Ocean, 1840–1915* (Cambridge: Cambridge University Press, 2011); Ashwin Desai and Goolam Vahed, *Inside Indenture: A South African Story, 1860–1914* (Durban: Madiba Publishers, 2007); Robert A. Huttenback, 'Indians in South Africa, 1860–1914: The British Imperial Philosophy on Trial', *English Historical Review*, 319 (April 1966); Jo Beall, 'Women under Indenture in Colonial Natal, 1860–1911', in Colin Clarke, Ceri Peach and Steven Vertovec, eds, *South Asians Overseas: Migration and Ethnicity* (Cambridge: Cambridge University Press, 1990); Joy Brain, 'Natal's Indians: From Co-operation, through Competition, to Conflict', in Andrew Duminy

and Bill Guest, eds, *Natal and Zululand: From Earliest Times to 1910: A New History* (Pietermaritzburg: University of Natal Press, 1989); Thomas R. Metcalf, '"Hard Hands and Sound Healthy Bodies": Recruiting "Coolies" for Natal, 1860–1911', *Journal of Imperial and Commonwealth History*, 30:3 (2002); Goolam Vahed, '"A Man of Keen Perceptive Faculties": Aboobaker Amod Jhaveri, an "Arab" in Colonial Natal, circa 1872–1887', *Historia*, 50:1 (2005).

31. 'Report of the Protector of Immigrants for the year ending June 30, 1893', in Natal Government House Documents, on microfilm, Reel 6, Accession no. 2179, NMML.

32. This paragraph is based on a walking tour of Durban in October 2009, in the company (and under the guidance) of the novelist Aziz Hassim.

33. *NM*, 24 May 1893.

34. Letter in *NA*, 29 May 1893, reproduced in *CWMG*, I, pp. 57–8.

35. See Gandhi, *An Autobiography*, Part II, Chapters VIII and IX. I return to the significance of the train incident in Chapter 5 below.

36. Gandhi, *An Autobiography*, Part II, Chapters X, XI and XIV.

37. Bengt Sundkler and Christopher Steed, *A History of the Church in Africa* (Cambridge: Cambridge University Press, 2000), pp. 417–18.

38. A. W. Baker, *Grace Triumphant: The Life Story of a Carpenter, Lawyer, and Missionary, in South Africa from 1856 to 1939* (London: Pickering and Inglis, 1939), pp. 84–6.

39. Gandhi, *An Autobiography*, Part II, Chapter XIV.

40. Cf. Surendra Bhana and Bridglal Pachai, eds, *A Documentary History of Indian South Africans* (Cape Town: David Philip, 1984), pp. 33–4.

41. *NA*, 19 September 1893, in *CWMG*, I, pp. 59–61.

42. *NA*, clippings dated 19 and 28 September 1893, S. N. 37 and S. N. 40, SAAA.

43. *NA*, 29 September 1893, in *CWMG*, I, pp. 63–4.

44. 'Guide to London', *CWMG*, I, pp. 66–120.

45. Gandhi, *An Autobiography*, Part II, Chapters XVI and XVII.

46. See Burnett Britton, *Gandhi Arrives in South Africa* (Canton, Maine: Greenleaf Books, 1999), pp. 75–6, 80–83, 88; Swan, *Gandhi*, p. 38f.

47. See CO 179/185, NAUK.

48. As quoted in E. H. Brookes and C. de B. Webb, *A History of Natal* (2nd edn, Pietermaritzburg: University of Natal Press, 1987), pp. 172.

49. John Robinson, *A Life Time in South Africa: Being the Recollections of the First Premier of Natal* (London: Smith, Elder, and Co., 1900), pp. 76–7.

50. *NA*, 3 September 1894; *Natal Witness*, of the same date, respectively S. N. 107 and S. N. 99, SAAA.

51. Quoted in Maynard W. Swanson, '"The Asiatic Menace": Creating Segregation in Durban, 1870–1900', *International Journal of African Historical Studies*, 16:3, p. 411.

52. Petition dated 28 June 1894, in *CWMG*, I, pp. 128–32.

53. *NM*, 29 June 1894.

54. Cf. Laughlin to Gandhi, 18 May 1896, S. N. 964, NGM.

55. In CWMG, this petition to Ripon is said to have been signed by 'Hajee Mohamed Hajee Dada and Sixteen Others'; however, the original petition, which I have seen on microfilm, says it was signed by 'Hajee Mohamed Hajee Dada and 8,888 others'.

56. This account of the petitions and letters written by Gandhi is based on the documents in *CWMG*, I, pp. 128–91.

57. Minute dated 27 July 1894, in Natal Government House Documents, on microfilm, Reel 6, Accession No. 2179, NMML.

58. Sir Hercules Robinson to Lord Ripon, 11 July 1894, in Ms. 43563, Ripon Papers, BL.

59. See correspondence in Ms. 43563, Ripon Papers, BL.

60. See *CWMG*, I, pp. 162–5.

61. Gandhi, *An Autobiography*, Part II, Chapter XVIII; *NM*, 6 September 1894; *NA*, 20 September 1894, S. N. 149 and 159 respectively, SAAA.

62. *Natal Witness*, 6 September 1894, S. N. 150, SAAA.

63. *Star*, 26 December 1894, S. N. 204, SAAA.

64. *Natal Witness*, 29 December 1894; *NM*, 7 January 1895, S.N 208 and 212 respectively, SAAA.

65. *NA*, 7 January 1895.

66. *Times of Natal*, 22 and 27 October 1894, S. N. 171 and 173 respectively, SAAA. Gandhi's letter is reprinted in *CWMG*, I, pp. 166–7.

4   A BARRISTER IN DURBAN

1. *CWMG*, Supplementary Volume I *(1894–1928)*, p. 14.

2. Gandhi, *An Autobiography*, Part II, Chapter XXII.

3. This incident is recounted, based on 'personal information', in E. H. Brookes and C. de B. Webb, *A History of Natal* (2nd edn, Pietermaritzburg: University of Natal Press, 1987), p. 185.

4. See A. N. Wilson, *God's Funeral: The Decline of Faith in Western Civilization* (New York: W. W. Norton, 1999); J. T. F. Jordens, *Dayananda Saraswati: His Life and Ideas* (Delhi: Oxford University Press, 1978).

5. Anna Kingsford, *The Perfect Way in Diet: A Treatise Advocating a Return to the Natural and Ancient Food of Our Race* (6th edn, London: Kegan Paul, Trench, Trübner and Co., 1895), pp. 19, 76ff, 114.

6. *The Perfect Way, Or the Finding of Christ*, was first published by Adams and Co. in London in 1882. Maitland published enlarged and revised editions in 1887 and 1890. I have here used an excerpt published in Kessinger Publishing's Rare Reprints series.

7. See Rene Fueloep-Miller, 'Tolstoy: The Apostolic Crusader', *Russian Review*, 19:2 (1960); Rosamund Bartlett, *Tolstoy: A Russian Life* (London: Profile Books, 2010), Chapters 11 and 12.

8. Leo Tolstoy, *The Kingdom of God Is Within You* (1893) reprinted in *The Kingdom of God and Peace Essays*, translated by Aylmer Maude (reprint New Delhi: Rupa Publications India Pvt. Ltd., 2001).

9. Gandhi, *An Autobiography*, Part II, Chapter XV.

10. Cf. J. T. F. Jordens, *Gandhi's Religion: A Homespun Shawl* (first published in 1998; 2nd edn, New Delhi: Oxford University Press, 2012), Chapter 2 and *passim*.

11. *NM*, 28 November and 19 December 1894, S. N. 184 and 202, SAAA.

12. This account of the correspondence between Gandhi and Raychandbhai is based on *Mahatma Gandhi and Kavi Rajchandraji: Questions Answered* (3rd edn, Ahmedabad: Shrimad Rajchandra Gyan Pracharak Trust, 1991 – translated from the Gujarati by Brahmachari Sri Goverdhandas). A different and apparently less reliable translation is published in *CWMG*, XXXII, pp. 593–602.

13. 'A Band of Vegetarian Missionaries', *CWMG*, I, pp. 222–8.

14. *CWMG*, I, pp. 229–44.

15. These paragraphs are based on the correspondence between the Secretary of State for the Colonies and the Natal Government in Natal Government House Documents, on microfilm, Reel 6, Accession No. 2179, NMML.

16. S. N. 890 and 958, SAAA.

17. *Natal Witness*, 9 February 1896, S. N. 753, SAAA.

18. Undated editorial from a Natal newspaper, entitled 'Durban Doings', *c*. August/September 1895, S. N. 529, SAAA.

19. *CWMG*, II, pp. 16–8.

20. Gandhi's legal career in Durban, *c*.1895–6, is covered in depth in Burnett Britton, *Gandhi Arrives in South Africa* (Canton, Maine: Greenleaf Books, 1999). This is a little-known privately published work, but immensely valuable nonetheless.

21. Charles DiSalvio, *The Man Before the Mahatma: M. K. Gandhi, Attorney-at-Law* (NOIDA, UP: Random House India, 2012), pp. 65, 80–82.

22. Report from the *Natal Mercury*, cited in Britton, *Gandhi Arrives in South Africa*, notes section, p. xviii.

23. Ian Morrison, *Durban: A Pictorial History* (Cape Town: C. Struik, 1987); Monica Fairall, *When in Durban* (Cape Town; C. Struik, 1983).

24. The term 'neo-Europe' was coined by Alfred Crosby in his *Ecological Imperialism: The Biological Expansion of Europe, 900–1900* (Cambridge: Cambridge University Press, 1986).

25. Walter Hely Hutchinson, 'Natal: Its Resources and Capabilities' (address to the London Chamber of Commerce, 8 June 1898), copy in File 2399, L/P&J/6/497, APAC/BL.

26. Cf. the biographical information provided in David Dick, *Who Was Who in Durban Street Names* (Durban: Clerkington Publishing Co., 1998).

27. See table dated 13 April 1904, prepared by the Town Clerk, Durban, in Natal Government House Records, on microfilm, Reel 6, Accession No. 2174, NMML. In the decade of the 1890s, the proportion of Indians in trade increased from 0.8 per cent to 5 per cent. *c.* 1900, the per capita income of Indians in Natal was roughly six times that of Africans, but still one-sixth that of Europeans. See Zbigniew A. Konczacki, *Public Finance and Economic Development in Natal, 1893–1910* (Durham, NC: Duke University Press, 1967), pp. 5, 27.

28. Robert A. Huttenback, *Gandhi in South Africa* (Ithaca, NY: Cornell University Press, 1971), pp. 38–9.

29. Letter dated 7 March 1891, in *Correspondence Relating to the Proposal to Establish Responsible Government in Natal* (London: HMSO, 1891 – C. 4687), pp. 40–41.

30. *CWMG*, I, pp. 245–51.

31. Gillian Berning, ed., *Gandhi Letters: From Upper House to Lower House, 1906–1914* (Durban: Local History Museum, 1994), p. 44; interview with Azim Hassan, Durban, October 2009.

32. Quoted in Britton, *Gandhi Arrives in South Africa*, pp. 256–7.

33. See ibid., pp. 296–300.

34. Cf. André Odendaal, *Black Protest Politics in South Africa to 1912* (Towota, NJ: Barnes and Noble Books, 1984), Chapter 1, 'African Politics from the Earliest Years to 1899'.

35. *NM*, 18 and 25 October 1895, S. N. 572 and 595, SAAA.

36. Cf. S. N. 606, 611, 628, 629, 639 and 650, SAAA.

37. 'The Indians in the Transvaal', editorial in *NA*, 19 November 1895, S. N. 640, SAAA.

38. Clipping dated 4 November 1895, S. N. 612, SAAA.

39. Cf. 'Sixty Years Memoir of Vincent Lawrence of 67 Gale Street, Durban, Natal', typescript in E. S. Reddy Papers, NMML.

40. Paul Tichman, *Gandhi Sites in Durban* (Durban: Old Court House Museum, n.d.), pp. 17–8; Gandhi, *An Autobiography*, Part II, chapters XXIII and XXIV; Pyarelal, *Mahatma Gandhi*, I: *The Early Phase* (Ahmedabad: Navajivan Press, 1965), pp. 491–3. So as not to embarrass Mehtab's family, Gandhi did not name him in his text, referring merely to a 'friend'.

41. 'The Indian Franchise', *CWMG*, I, pp. 266–90.

42. W. W. Hunter to M. K. Gandhi, 13 May 1896, S. N. 948, SAAA.

43. H. K. Khare to M. K. Gandhi, 11 July 1896, S. N. 743, SAAA.

44. *Natal Witness*, 25 December 1895; *South African Times*, 25 December 1895, respectively S. N. 699 and 703, SAAA.

45. *NA*, 11 January 1896, S. N. 715, SAAA.

46. Gandhi, *An Autobiography*, Part II, Chapter XXIV.

5 TRAVELLING ACTIVIST

1. *NA*, 5 June 1896, S. N. 1004, SAAA.
2. See S. N. 1005, SAAA.
3. See S. N. 1006, SAAA.
4. Gandhi, *An Autobiography*, Part II, Chapter XXIV.
5. 'The Grievances of the British Indians in South Africa', *CWMG*, II, pp. 2–50.
6. Gandhi, *An Autobiography*, Part II, Chapters XXV and XXVI.
7. 'Out of pocket expenses in connection with the movement in India with regard to the grievances of the British Indian in South Africa', S. N. 1310, SAAA; also in *CWMG*, II, pp. 104–15.
8. *Times of India*, 2 September 1896, quoted in Burnett Britton, *Gandhi Arrives in South Africa* (Canton, Maine: Greenleaf Books, 1999), pp. 442–3.
9. 'Speech at Public Meeting', Bombay, 26 September 1896, *CWMG*, II, pp. 50–60.
10. See 'The Elevation of the Depressed Classes', in *Speeches of Gopal Krishna Gokhale* (2nd edn, Madras: G. A. Natesan, 1916), pp. 1055–6. This is Gokhale's recollection of Ranade's talk – an original text of which does not exist. Ranade was a precocious critic of caste hierarchies and caste exclusivism. Throughout the 1890s, in his annual addresses to the Indian Social Conference, he promoted inter-dining, intermarriage, the emancipation of women and other such measures. See *The Miscellaneous Writings of the Late Hon'ble Mr Justice M. G. Ranade* (Bombay: The Manoranjan Press, 1915), *passim*.
11. For a still valuable dual biography, see Stanley Wolpert's *Tilak and Gokhale: Revolution and Reform in the Making of Modern India* (1961, reprint, New Delhi: Oxford University Press, 1989).
12. Gandhi, *An Autobiography*, Part II, Chapter XXVIII.
13. Gandhi to F. S. Taleyarkhan, 18 October 1896, *CWMG*, II, pp. 67–8.
14. 'Out of pocket expenses', S. N. 1310, SAAA.
15. Gandhi to G. K. Gokhale, 18 October 1896, *CMWG*, II, p. 66.
16. Based on an analysis of the surnames in the notice, a copy of which is in the SAAA (S. N. 1213).
17. 'Speech at Meeting, Madras', *CWMG*, II, pp. 71–2.
18. *Madras Mail*, 27 October 1896.
19. 'Preface to the Second Edition of the Green Pamphlet', *CWMG*, II, p. 93.
20. Gandhi, *An Autobiography*, Part II, Chapter XXIX.
21. Gopalkrishna Gandhi, ed., *A Frank Friendship: Gandhi and Bengal* (Calcutta: Seagull Books, 2007), p. 4.
22. *CWMG*, II, p. 94; Gandhi, *An Autobiography*, Part III, Chapter I.
23. See letters and clippings in File No. 138, CO 179/195, NAUK.

24. *NM*, 19 September 1896.

25. *NM*, 21 September 1896.

26. *Natal Witness*, 6 January 1897, clipping in CO 179/197, NAUK.

27. *NA*, 17 September 1896, S. N. 1112, SAAA.

28. See J. T. Henderson, ed., *Speeches of the Late Right Honourable Harry Escombe, P.C., M.L.A., Q.C., L.L.D* (Maritzburg: Davis and Sons, 1904), p. 324.

29. *NM*, 27 November 1896.

30. *NA*, 7 December 1896, S. N. 1366, SAAA.

31. See David Arnold, 'Touching the Body: Perspectives on the Indian Plague, 1896–1900', in Ranajit Guha, ed., *Subaltern Studies V* (New Delhi: Oxford University Press, 1987).

32. See Annie Besant, ed., *How India Wrought for Freedom: The Story of the National Congress Told from Official Records* (Madras: Theosophical Publishing House, 1915), pp. 246, 236–7.

33. Quoted in Britton, *Gandhi Arrives in South Africa*, pp. 513–14.

34. *NA*, 30 December 1896, S. N. 1508, SAAA.

35. See Britton, *Gandhi Arrives in South Africa*, pp. 526–7.

36. *NM*, 30 December 1897.

37. *NM*, 5 January 1897.

38. *Times of Natal*, 6 January 1897, clipping in CO 179/197, NAUK; *NA*, 5 January 1897, quoted in *Memorial*, *CWMG*, II, p. 151.

39. *NM*, 8 January 1897.

40. See *Memorial*, Appendix Aa, *CWMG*, II, p. 198.

41. See S. N. 3638, NGM.

42. *Natal Witness*, 11 January 1897; *NA*, 11 and 12 January 1897, clippings in CO 179/197, NAUK.

43. 'Interview to "The Natal Advertiser"', *CWMG*, II, pp. 118–26.

44. Ian Morrison, *Durban: A Pictorial History* (Cape Town: C. Struik, 1987), pp. 76ff.

45. Cf. correspondence in Natal Government House Documents, on microfilm, Reel 6, Accession no. 2179, NMML.

46. *Memorial*, *CWMG*, II, pp. 159–60.

47. See reports in *NM*, 14 January 1897.

48. See Gandhi, *An Autobiography*, Part III, Chapter III.

49. This account of the assault on Gandhi is largely based on the extensive reports – covering several pages of the newspaper – printed in *NM*, 14 January 1897. Cf. also 'How Gandhi Got Away Disguised as a Servant', *Natal Witness*, 16 January 1897, S. N. 1894, SAAA. When R. C. Alexander died, ten years later, an obituarist wrote that the police chief 'had more influence over a mob, through the medium of his commanding personality, than the whole of the police force combined, and many are the instances on record where, by the display of surprising ingenuity, he hoodwinked the

gatherings of angered men'. (*NM*, 21 October 1907). The writer here may perhaps have had Alexander's ingenious hoodwinking of Gandhi's persecutors foremost in mind.

50. *NM*, 15 January 1897.
51. *NM*, 16 January 1897.
52. R. C. Alexander and Jane Alexander to M. K. Gandhi, both letters dated 22 January 1897, respectively S. N. 1938 and 1939, NGM. Ironically, in February 1896, before Gandhi left for India, he had clashed with the police superintendent in court, when Alexander insinuated that two Indian Christians the lawyer was defending had changed their faith merely to ingratiate them with the ruling race. See Charles DiSalvio, *The Man Before the Mahatma: M. K. Gandhi, Attorney-at-Law* (NOIDA, UP: Random House India, 2012), pp. 92–4.

On behalf of the Indian community in Natal, a gold watch was presented to Alexander for being 'instrumental in saving the life of one whom we delight to love'. In addition, £10 was sent 'for distribution among those of your Force who assisted on the occasion'. See *CWMG*, II, pp. 229–30.
53. I found this previously unknown essay in a file in the records of the old India Office, where it had been marked for attention by the reforming civil servant Sir Alfred Lyall. See 'D. B.', 'East Indians in South Africa', *The Nation*, 6 May 1897, clipping in File 2536, L/P&J/6/467, APAC/BL.
54. Quoted in *NM*, 16 January 1897.
55. *NM*, 18 February 1897, S. N. 2046, SAAA.
56. Louis Fischer, *The Life of Mahatma Gandhi* (first published in 1951; reprint, Mumbai: Bharatiya Vidya Bhavan, 1998), pp. 50–51.

6 LAWYER-LOYALIST

1. David Dick, *Who Was Who in Durban Street Names* (Durban: Clerkington Publishing Co., 1998), pp. 62–3.
2. J. T. Henderson, ed., *Speeches of the Late Right Honourable Harry Escombe, P.C., M.L.A., Q.C., L.L.D* (Maritzburg: Davis and Sons, 1904), pp. 154–5, 291–4.
3. The text of these Acts is reproduced in *CWMG*, II, pp. 272–8.
4. *Speeches of Harry Escombe*, p. 340.
5. *CWMG*, II, p. 241.
6. *CWMG*, II, pp. 246f.
7. Petition dated 26 March 1897, *CWMG*, II, pp. 231–5.
8. Petition dated 2 July 1897, *CWMG*, II, pp. 260–72.
9. Letter written 'before September 18, 1897', in *CWMG*, II, pp. 284–7.
10. Naoroji to Chamberlain, 11 October 1897, copy in S. N. 2568, NGM.
11. http://en.wikisource.org/wiki/Queen_Victoria%27s_Proclamation.

12. Harry Escombe to M. K. Gandhi, 20 September 1897, S. N. 2549, SAAA.

13. Paul Tichman, *Gandhi Sites in Durban* (Durban: Old Court House Museum, n.d.), p. 21.

14. The editors of the *Collected Works of Mahatma Gandhi* did not have access to these files, for during the apartheid years it was forbidden for Indians to have any dealings with the Government or people of South Africa. The files were photocopied from the Pietermaritzburg Archives by the Gandhi scholar E. S. Reddy, who then generously made them available to me. This and the next two paragraphs are based on this material.

15. Cf. S. N. 3856, SAAA.

16. The logbook, running to thirty-one pages in all, is filed as S. N. 2711, SAAA.

17. News clipping dated 27 February 1898, S. N. 2700, SAAA.

18. Francis Younghusband, *South Africa of To-day* (London: Macmillan and Co., 1899), pp. 228–31.

19. P. J. Mehta, *M. K. Gandhi and the South African Indian Problem* (Madras: G. A. Natesan and Co., 1912), p. 80. The title-page of this booklet wrongly spells the author's name as 'Metha'.

20. Text of speech in Gujarati by Pranjivan Mehta, Durban, 17 October 1898, S. N. 2825, SAAA.

21. Cf. Vernon February, *The Afrikaners of South Africa* (London: Kegan Paul International, 1991), Chapters 1 and 2. The British annexed the Transvaal in 1877, but restored it to the Boers in 1881, on condition that Britain retained control over its foreign relations.

22. See J. Emrys Evans, 'Report on Indian Immigration into the Transvaal', 2 March 1898, in L/P&J/6/478, File 789, APAC/BL.

23. See, for an excellent overview, Bala Pillay, *British Indians in the Transvaal: Trade, Politics and Imperial Relations, 1885–1906* (London: Longman, 1976), Chapters 1 and 2. Cf. also Iqbal Narain, *The Politics of Racialism: A Study of the Indian Minority in South Africa Down to the Gandhi–Smuts Agreement* (Delhi: Shiva Lal Agarwal and Co., 1962), Chapters 6 and 7.

24. I have borrowed this story from Edward Roux, *Time Longer Than Rope: The Black Man's Struggle for Freedom in South Africa* (first published 1948; 2nd edn, Madison: University of Wisconsin Press, 1964), p. 102.

25. The judgement is reproduced in *Papers Relating to the Grievances of Her Majesty's Indian Subjects in the South African Republic* (London: HMSO, 1895 [C. 7911]), p. 24. This assertion of the right of 'every European nation' to 'exclude alien elements which it considers to be dangerous', seems strikingly contemporary, with the rise of right-wing nativist parties across Western Europe whose platform rests on such sentiments (or prejudices).

26. Petition dated 31 December 1898, signed by 'Tayob Hajee Khan Mohammed, Hajee Habib Hajee Dadee Hajee Cassim, H. Joosw, Mohammed H. Joosw, and 27 others', in Natal Government House Records, on microfilm, Reel 2, Accession No. 2175, NMML. This petition is not in the *Collected*

Works, but a document in the archives confirms that it was Gandhi's handiwork. Forwarding it to his boss in Cape Town, the British Agent in Pretoria said that 'they [the traders] informed me that the petition had been drawn up by Mr Gandhi' (Edmund Fraser, Her Majesty's Agent in Pretoria, to High Commissioner, Cape Town, 31 December 1898, in Natal Government House Records, on microfilm, Reel 2, Accession No. 2175, NMML.)

27. For the Uitlander point of view, see Alfred Hillier, *South African Studies* (London: Macmillan and Co., 1900) and J. P. Fitzpatrick, *The Transvaal from Within: A Private Record of Public Affairs* (New York: Frederick A. Stokes, 1899); for accounts sympathetic to the Boer perspective, F. Reginald Statham, *South Africa As It Is* (London: T. Fisher Unwin, 1897) and F. V. Engelenburge, 'The South African Question from the Transvaal Point of View', in John Clark Ridpath and Edward S. Ellis, eds., *The Story of South Africa: An Account of the Transformation of the Dark Continent by the European Powers and the Culminating Contest between Great Britain and the South African Republic in the Transvaal War* (London: C. B. Burrows, 1899). Cf. also Murat Halstead, *Briton and Boer in South Africa* (Philadelphia: The Bell Publishing Co., 1900) and C. E. Vulliamy, *Outlanders: A Study of Imperial Expansion in South Africa, 1877–1902* (London: Jonathan Cape, 1938), Chapters 10 and 11.

    Two useful recent summaries of the background to the conflict are James Barber, *South Africa in the Twentieth Century* (Oxford: Basil Blackwell, 1999), Chapter I, 'Prelude to War: Afrikaner and British Imperial Nationalism' and Hermann Gilimore, *The Afrikaners: Biography of a People* (Charlottesville, VA: University of Virginia Press, 2003), Chapter VIII, 'The Crucible of War'. The definitive history remains Thomas Pakenham, *The Boer War* (first published in 1979; reprint, London: Abacus, 2007).

28. Milner, quoted in John Marlowe, *Milner: Apostle of Empire* (London: Hamish Hamilton, 1976), p. 47; Chamberlain, quoted in Ronald Robinson and John Gallagher, *Africa and the Victorians: The Climax of Imperialism in the Dark Continent* (New York: St. Martins Press, 1961), p. 455.

29. M. K. Gandhi, *Satyagraha in South Africa*, translated from the Gujarati by Valji Govindji Desai (2nd edn, 1950; reprint, Ahmedabad: Navjivan Press, 1972), pp. 65–6.

30. Letter of 19 October 1899, *CWMG*, III, pp. 134–5.

31. See S. N. 3302, NGM.

32. See M. K. Gandhi, 'Indian Ambulance Corps in Natal' and 'Indian Ambulance Corps', in *CWMG*, III, pp. 163–9, 174–6.

33. Vere Stent, 'On the Battle-field' (originally published in 1911), reprinted in Chandrashanker Shukla, ed., *Gandhiji as We Know Him: By Seventeen Contributors* (Bombay: Vora and Co., 1945), pp. 18–19.

34. Herbert Kitchin to M. K. Gandhi, 20 April 1900, S. N. 3444, NGM.

35. News clipping dated 16 March 1900, S. N. 3412, SAAA.

36. See *Indian Opinion*, 12 November 1903.

37. *CWMG*, I, pp. 188, 199, 233; *CWMG*, III, pp. 4, 44, 108, 137.

38. Gokhale, quoted in David Omissi, 'India: Some Perceptions of Race and Empire', in David Omissi and Andrew S. Thompson, eds, *The Impact of the South African War* (Basingstoke: Palgrave, 2002), p. 224.

39. Gandhi, *An Autobiography*, Part III, Chapter X.

40. Peter Warwick, *Black People and the South African War, 1899–1902* (Cambridge: Cambridge University Press, 1983), pp. 110–11. See also Hulme T. Siwundhia, 'White Ideologies and Non-European Participation in the Anglo-Boer War, 1899–1902', *Journal of Black Studies*, 15:2 (1984).

41. Gandhi, *An Autobiography*, Part III, Chapter V.

42. See 'Report on the James Godfrey Case', in Natal Government House Records, on microfilm, Reel 1, Accession No. 2174, NMML.

43. Gandhi, *An Autobiography*, Part III, Chapter V.

44. Gandhi, *An Autobiography*, Part IV, Chapter X.

45. M. K. Gandhi to Revashankar Zaveri, 21 May 1901, in *CWMG*, III, pp. 230–31.

46. *CWMG*, XIII, p. 143.

47. Gandhi, 'Preface to "Srimad Rajchandra"', *CWMG*, XXXII, pp. 9–13.

48. Gandhi, *An Autobiography*, Part III, Chapter XII.

49. Charles DiSalvio, *The Man Before the Mahatma: M. K. Gandhi, Attorney-at-Law* (NOIDA, UP: Random House India, 2012), p. 147.

50. See S. N. 3920, SAAA.

51. *NA*, 16 October 1901, S. N. 3919, SAAA.

52. M. K. Gandhi to Parsee Rustomjee, 18 October 1901, *CWMG*, III, pp. 246–7.

53. Gandhi, *An Autobiography*, Part III, Chapter XII. Kasturba's chastisement is here rendered in Mahadev Desai's English translation of her husband's recollections; it would, of course, originally have been offered in Gujarati.

54. Parsee Rustomjee to M. K. Gandhi, 19 October 1901, S. N. 3924, SAAA.

55. This account of Gandhi's visit to Mauritius is largely based on the news reports (in French and English) reproduced in Pahlad Ramsurrun, *Mahatma Gandhi and His Impact on Mauritius* (New Delhi: Sterling Publishers, 1995), pp. 120–31; supplemented by U. Bissoondoyal, *Gandhi and Mauritius and Other Essays* (Moka: Mahatma Gandhi Institute, 1988), pp. 6–12.

56. Annie Besant, ed., *How India Wrought for Freedom: The Story of the National Congress Told from Official Records* (Madras: Theosophical Publishing House, 1915), pp. 333–40.

57. *CWMG*, III, pp. 252–5.

58. The standard biography, on which these paragraphs draw, remains B. R. Nanda, *Gokhale: The Indian Moderates and the British Raj* (Princeton: Princeton University Press, 1977). Also useful is Govind Talwalkar's *Gopal Krishna Gokhale: His Life and Times* (New Delhi: Rupa and Co., 2006).

59. Gandhi, *An Autobiography*, Part III, Chapter XVII.
60. *Indian Mirror*, 26 January 1902, quoted in Gopalkrishna Gandhi, ed., *A Frank Friendship: Gandhi and Bengal* (Calcutta: Seagull Books, 2007), pp. 26–9.
61. *CWMG*, III, pp. 255–7, 260–66.
62. Gandhi to Gokhale, 30 January 1902, *CWMG*, III, pp. 266–7.
63. Gandhi to Chhaganlal Gandhi, 23 January 1902, *CWMG*, II, p. 257.
64. Chandulal Bhagubhai Dalal, *Harilal Gandhi: A Life*, edited and translated from the Gujarati by Tridip Suhrud (Hyderabad: Orient Longman, 2007), pp. 4–5.
65. Pyarelal, *Mahatma Gandhi*, II: *The Discovery of Satyagraha – On the Threshold* (first published in 1980; reprint, Ahmedabad: Navajivan Publishing House, 1997), pp. 399–403; *CWMG*, III, pp. 274–306.
66. See Arthur Percival Newton, ed., *Select Documents Relating to the Unification of South Africa* (1924; reprint, London: Frank Cass, 1968), vol. I, pp. 205–8.
67. A. P. Thornton, *The Imperial Idea and Its Enemies: A Study in British Power* (first published in 1959; 2nd edn, London: Macmillan, 1985), p. 137.
68. Gandhi to D. B. Shukla, 8 November 1902, *CWMG*, III, pp. 315–6.
69. See Uma Dhupelia-Mesthrie, *Gandhi's Prisoner? The Life of Gandhi's Son Manilal* (Cape Town: Kwela Books, 2004), p. 50.
70. Gandhi, *An Autobiography*, Part III, Chapter XXIII.
71. Gandh to Devchand Parekh, 6 August 1902, *CWMG*, III, pp. 312–13.

7 WHITE AGAINST BROWN

1. *CWMG*, III, p. 316.
2. W. H. Moor, Assistant Colonial Secretary, to Tayob Hadji Khan Mohomed, 6 January 1903, in Natal Government Records (on microfilm), Reel 2, Accession No. 2175, NMML.
3. *CWMG*, III, pp. 325–32.
4. Gandhi to Chhaganlal, 5 February 1903, *CWMG*, III, p. 337.
5. See Application 252, vol. 8/654, ZTPD, NASA.
6. Eric Itzkin, *Gandhi's Johannesburg: Birthplace of Satyagraha* (Johannesburg: Witwatersrand University Press, 2000), pp. 12–3.
7. Quoted in Geoffrey Wheatcroft, *The Randlords* (London: Weidenfeld and Nicolson, 1985), p. 4.
8. 'Johannesburg: A City of Unrest', originally published in the *Pall Mall Gazette*, reproduced in *Indian Opinion*, 12 May 1906.
9. Jonathan Hyslop, 'Gandhi, Mandela, and the African Modern', in Sarah Nuttall and Achille Mbembe, eds, *Johannesburg: The Elusive Metropolis* (Durham, North Carolina: Duke University Press, 2008), pp. 121–2. Cf. also

Nechama Brodie, ed., *The Joburg Book: A Guide to the City's History, People and Places* (Johannesburg: Pan Macmillan South Africa, 2008), Chapter 3, 'Foundations of the City'.

10. Hannes Meiring, with G-M van der Waal and Wilhelm Grütter, *Early Johannesburg: Its Building and Its People* (Cape Town: Human and Rousseau, 1985), pp. 36–8; Diary of the Town Clerk of Johannesburg for 1904, Reel 34, Lionel Curtis Papers (on microfilm), Bodleian Library, Oxford.

11. John Buchan, *The African Colony: Studies in the Reconstuction* (Edinburgh: William Blackwood and Sons, 1903), Chapter 15, 'Johannesburg'.

12. See for instance, File 8593, vol. 367, CS; File 9199, vol. 377, CS; File 8491, vol. 365, CS; all in NASA.

13. Milner to Joseph Chamberlain (Secretary of State for the Colonies), 11 May 1903, in *Despatch from the Governor of the Transvaal Respecting the Position of British Indians in That Colony* (London: HMSO, 1903 – Cd. 1684).

14. Milner to Joseph Chamberlain, 12 May 1903, in *Correspondence Relating to a Proposal to Employ Indian Coolies Under Indenture on Railways in the Transvaal and the Orange River Colony* (London: HMSO, 1903 – Cd. 1683). On Milner's attitude to Indians, see also Cecil Headlam, ed., *The Milner Papers: South Africa, 1899–1905*, vol. II (London: Cassell and Company, Ltd., 1933), pp. 429–30.

15. *CWMG*, III, pp. 364–71.

16. *Rand Daily Mail*, 6 June 1903, clipping in Natal Government Records (on microfilm), Reel 3, Accession No. 2176, NMML.

17. 'Indians in the Transvaal: The Johannesburg Meeting', *IO*, 4 June 1903.

18. Cf. advertisement in *IO*, 4 June 1903.

19. Burnett Britton, *Gandhi Arrives in South Africa* (Canton, Maine: Greenleaf Books, 1999), pp. 232, 303: *CWMG*, II, p. 251 and footnote.

20. Uma Dhupelia-Mesthrie, 'From Advocacy to Mobilisation: *Indian Opinion, 1903–1914*', in L. Switzer, ed., *South Africa's Alternative Press: Voices of Protest and Resistance, 1850–1960* (Cambridge: Cambridge University Press, 1987).

21. Isabel Hofmeyr, 'Gandhi's Printing Press: Print Cultures of the Indian Ocean', in Kris Manjapra and Sugata Bose, eds, *Cosmopolitan Thought Zones* (London: Palgrave Macmillan, 2010).

22. *CWMG*, III, pp. 376–7, 380.

23. *IO*, 3 June 1903.

24. Cf. Vijaya Ramaswamy, '*Indian Opinion*: Voice of the Tamil Diaspora', in *The Editor Gandhi and* Indian Opinion: *Seminar Papers* (New Delhi: National Gandhi Museum, 2007).

25. See Surendra Bhana and James D. Hunt, eds, *Gandhi's Editor: The Letters of M. H. Nazar, 1902–1903* (New Delhi: Promilla and Co., 1989), pp. 94–5, 99–100, 107–8, etc; Pyarelal, *Mahatma Gandhi*, III: *The Birth of Satyagraha –*

from Petitioning to Passive Resistance (Ahmedabad: Navajivan Publishing House, 1986), pp. 74–7.

26. *CWMG*, III, pp. 424–7.

27. *IO*, 9 July 1903.

28. *IO*, 10 September 1903.

29. See *IO*, 13 August 1903.

30. To this dispassionate summary, we might juxtapose the rather more fevered language of the common or garden variety of colonist. In 1902, a Uitlander published a book defending the Boer treatment of Indians. This rejected the idea that as 'British subjects' they deserved a sympathetic hearing. Indian traders and hawkers constituted a 'frightful danger to public health'. Their removal to locations out of sight of whites was 'a most necessary sanitary reform'. Warming to his theme, the colonist claimed that it was 'quite a common thing to find the coolies – the majority of them fruit and vegetable hawkers – not only huddled together, men, women, and children, to the number of eight or ten, or even more, in a tin shanty of perhaps less than ten feet square, with their stock-in-trade in the same room, as often as not packed under the bed, if indeed there was a bed at all, but in some cases actually sleeping on the vegetables which the following day they would be hawking around the town.'

   See Edward B. Rose, *The Truth about the Transvaal: A Record of Facts Based upon Twelve Years Residence in the Country* (London: published by the author, 1902), pp. 142–4.

31. *IO*, 25 June 1903, in *CWMG*, III, pp. 417–19.

32. See letter from L. W. Ritch, published in *The Theosophist*, April 1897. (I am grateful to Shimon Low for this reference.)

33. Albert West, 'In the Early Days with Gandhi – 1', *Illustrated Weekly of India*, 3 October 1965.

34. These biographical details are drawn from H. S. L. Polak, 'Who's Who? An Essay in World Consciousness', typescript written probably in the 1940s, in Mss. Eur. D. 1238/1, APAC/BL. Cf. also 'Mr and Mrs. Polak', *IO*, 13 January 1906.

35. H. S. L. Polak, 'Mahatma Gandhi: Some Early Reminiscences', typescript probably from the early 1930s, in Mss. Eur. D. 1238/1, APAC/BL.

36. Cf. Gustav Saron and Louis Hotz, eds, *The Jews in South Africa: A History* (Cape Town: Oxford University Press, 1955), pp. 85–6, 89.

37. See Shimon Low, 'Mahatma Gandhi and Hermann Kallenbach in South Africa, 1904–1914', MA dissertation (Faculty of Humanities, The Hebrew University of Jerusalem, April 2010), pp. 26–9, 35–40, etc. As this book goes to press, Mr Low's dissertation has been published as *Soulmates: The Story of Mahatma Gandhi and Hermann Kallenbach* (Hyderabad: Orient Black-Swan, 2012).

38. In 1895, when the first attempts to consign Asians to locations were made, a group of forty European merchants wrote to the government saying the

Indians in Johannesburg kept 'their business places, as well as their places of residence, in a clean and proper sanitary state – in fact, as good as the Europeans'. The names appended to this letter were mostly Jewish – Schneider, Fogelman, Behrens, Friedman, etc. See correspondence in File 3681, L/P&J/6/783, APAC/BL.

39. Cf. File 402, L/P&J/6/628, APAC/BL.

40. The letters of Bhownaggree, Lyttelton, Lawley and Milner are printed in *Correspondence Relating to the Position of British Indians in the Transvaal (in Continuation of Cd. 1684)* (London: HMSO, 1904). Despite his manifest prejudice against Indians, Alfred Lawley was, shortly afterwards, appointed Governor of the Madras Presidency.

41. For details, see John Mcleod, '"Indian Tory": A Biography of Sir Mancherjee Merwanjee Bhownaggree' (book manuscript in preparation), Chapter 12.

42. See *Daily Graphic*, 5 August 1904, S. N. 4201, SAAA. Bhownaggree was answered in the same columns by the president of the Amalgamated Chambers of Commerce of the Transvaal, who accused Indian merchants of 'unfair competition', claiming 'the encroachments' they had made were already so large that, if left unchecked, they 'could only ultimately result in South Africa becoming an Asiatic country'. The white trader was answered in turn by an Indian student from London University, who noted that in Bombay, Europeans and Indians lived and traded side by side, because 'the English traders do not want their 25 to 30 per cent on their capital, as the traders and capitalists in South Africa do.' See letters by H. R. Abercrombie and S. B. Gadgil, *Daily Graphic*, 16 and 24 September 1904, clippings in Mss. Eur. F. 111/258, APAC/BL.

43. *CWMG*, IV, pp. 49–50, 112–13.

44. *CWMG*, IV, pp. 149–51.

45. West, 'In the Early Days with Gandhi – 1'; *IO*, 30 April 1904.

46. Keith Brown, *Johannesburg: The Making and Shaping of the City* (Pretoria: University of South Africa Press, 2004), pp. 75–8.

47. *CWMG*, IV, pp. 183–4, 203–5.

48. Note of a meeting held on 26 February 1904, in Natal Government Records (on microfilm), Reel 3, Accession No. 2176, NMML.

49. See *IO*, 27 May 1905.

50. Reports in *IO*, 28 May, 4 June and 13 August 1904.

51. 'National Convention re Asiatic Question Held at the Opera House, Pretoria, Thursday, 10 November 1904: Verbatim Record of Proceedings', in Natal Government Records (on microfilm), Reel 3, Accession No. 2176, NMML.

52. Governor of the Transvaal to Secretary of State for the Colonies, letters of 13 May and 13 July 1904, in ibid.

53. M. K. Gandhi to Private Secretary to Lord Milner, High Commissioner and Governor of the Transvaal, 3 September 1904, in Natal Government Records (on microfilm), Reel 3, Accession No. 2176, NMML. (This letter is not in *CWMG*.)

54. Cf. Arthur Percival Newton, ed., *Select Documents Relating to the Unification of South Africa* (1924; reprint, London: Frank Cass, 1968), vol. II, pp. 1–2.
55. Letter of 3 October 1904, *CWMG*, IV, pp. 272–3.
56. Emily Hobhouse, quoted in Adam Hochschild, *To End All Wars: A Story of Loyalty and Rebellion, 1914–1918* (Boston: Houghton Mifflin Harcourt, 2011), p. 34.
57. Saul Dubow, 'How British Was the British World? The Case of South Africa', *Journal of Imperial and Commonwealth History*, 37:1 (2009), p. 13.
58. John Ruskin, *'Unto This Last': Four Essays on the First Principles of Political Economy*, edited and introduced by Lloyd J. Hubenka (first published 1860; this edition, Lincoln: University of Nebraska Press, 1967).
59. Gandhi, *An Autobiography*, Part IV, Chapter XVIII. Cf. also M. L. Dantwala, 'Gandhiji and Ruskin's *Unto This Last*', *Economic and Political Weekly*, 4 November 1995.
60. *CWMG*, IV, pp. 319–21.
61. West, 'In the Early Days with Gandhi – 1'.
62. Letter of 13 January 1905, *CWMG*, IV, pp. 332–3.
63. Sir William Wedderburn to Colonial Office, 13 January 1899, in Natal Government House Records, Reel 2 (Accession No. 2175), NMML.
64. 'Notes taken at interview with Sir Denzil Ibbetson on the 5 February 1903', in Natal Government House Records, Reel 1 (Accession No. 2174), NMML.
65. Note dated 23 May 1904, in Mss. Eur. F. 111/258, APAC/BL.

8 PLURALIST AND PURITAN

1. Eric Itzkin, *Gandhi's Johannesburg: Birthplace of Satyagraha* (Johannesburg: Witwatersrand University Press, 2000), pp. 61–3.
2. H. S. L. Polak, 'Early Years (1869–1914)', in H. S. L. Polak, H. N. Brailsford and Lord Pethick-Lawrence, *Mahatma Gandhi* (London: Oldhams Press Limited, 1949), p. 49.
3. Ramadas Gandhi, *Sansmaran*, translated from Gujarati to Hindi by Shankar Joshi (Ahmedabad: Navajivan Press, 1970), pp. 12–13, 47–8.
4. See *IO*, 7 January and 13 May 1905.
5. Reports in *IO*, 22 and 29 April 1905.
6. Reports in *IO*, 7 January and 18 February 1905.
7. Reports in *IO*, 27 May, 3 June, 5 August and 2 September 1905.
8. *CWMG*, V, pp. 5, 27–8, 50–52, 56–7, 61–2.
9. *CWMG*, IV, p. 441; V, pp. 65–8.
10. *CWMG*, V, p. 55; IV, p. 347.
11. This account of Gandhi's lectures and their aftermath draws on *CWMG*, IV, pp. 368–70, 375–7, 405–9, 430–1, 454, 458–9, 468–9; V, pp. 42, 49–50;

and on letters in the Gujarati section of *Indian Opinion*, issues of 20 May, 3 and 17 June 1905.

12. *IO*, issues of 4 and 11 November 1905, *CWMG*, V, pp. 121–2, 131–2.

13. Gandhi to Revashankar Jhaveri, 18 July 1905, in *CWMG*, V, p. 21.

14. See Chandulal Bhagubhai Dalal, *Harilal Gandhi: A Life*, edited and translated from the Gujarati by Tridip Suhrud (Hyderabad: Orient Longman, 2007), pp. 6–7.

15. Gandhi to Chhaganlal, 27 September 1905, *CWMG*, V, p. 78.

16. Millie Graham Polak, *Mr Gandhi: The Man* (London: George Allen and Unwin, 1931), pp. 17–18.

17. Gandhi to Millie Graham, 3 July 1905, *CWMG*, XCVI, pp. 1–2.

18. Gandhi, *An Autobiography*, Part IV, Chapter XXII.

19. Millie Polak, *Mr Gandhi*, pp. 21–7, 29–35, 43–5, 62–3.

20. H. S. L. Polak, 'Mahatma Gandhi: Some Early Reminscences', typescript probably from the early 1930s, in Mss. Eur. D. 1238/1, APAC/BL.

21. Millie Polak, *Mr Gandhi*, pp. 25–6.

22. Report in *IO*, 27 January 1906.

23. Editorial in *IO*, 16 June 1906.

24. Cf. Isaac Deutscher, 'The Non-Jewish Jew' (based on a lecture to the World Jewish Congress, February 1958), in Deutscher, *The Non-Jewish Jew and Other Essays* (1968; reprint, London: Merlin Press, 1981).

25. See Richard Mendelsohn, *Sammy Marks: 'The Uncrowned King of the Transvaal'* (Cape Town: David Philip, 1991), especially Chapter 11.

26. Gandhi to Kallenbach, undated, *c*.1904–5, handwritten, in KP. This letter is not in *CWMG*.

27. See Prabhudas Gandhi, *My Childhood with Gandhiji* (Ahmedabad: Navajivan Publishing House, 1957), pp. 59–60.

28. *IO*, 24 March 1906, *CWMG*, V, p 243. On Gandhi's friendship with Dr Abdurahman, see also Gavin Lewis, *Between the Wire and the Wall: A History of South African 'Coloured' Politics* (New York: St. Martin's Press, 1987), pp. 54, 63, 78, etc.; and James D. Hunt, 'Gandhi and the Black People of South Africa', *Gandhi Marg*, April–June 1989.

29. Joseph J. Doke, *M. K. Gandhi: An Indian Patriot in South Africa* (London: The London Indian Chronicle, 1909), pp. 1–2. For more on Doke, see Chapters 11 to 14 below.

30. J. H. Balfour Browne, *South Africa: A Glance at Current Conditions and Politics* (London: Longmans, Green and Co., 1905), pp. 200–202.

31. See Saul Dubow, 'Colonial Nationalism, the Milner Kindergarten, and the Rise of "South Africanism", 1902–10, *History Workshop Journal*, 43 (Spring 1997).

32. Letter of 21 September 1905, A Proceedings, no. 11, April 1906, Department of Commerce and Industry (Emigration), NAI.

33. Letter of 21 May 1906, ibid., no. 3, May 1906.

34. *CWMG*, V, pp. 142–52, 236–8.

35. See reports in *IO*, 3 March, 17 March, 26 May and 9 June 1906; Charles DiSalvio, *The Man Before the Mahatma: M. K. Gandhi, Attorney-at-Law* (NOIDA, UP: Random House India, 2012), pp. 209–13.

36. Montford Chamney, 'Mahatma Ghandi [*sic*] in the Transvaal', typescript dated *c.*1935, Mss. Eur. C. 859, APAC/BL, pp. 6, 16–17.

37. Gandhi to M. Chamney, letters of 9 March, 9 April and 19 May 1906 (not in *CWMG*); Chamney to Assistant Colonial Secretary, 9 April 1906, all in Natal Government Records (on microfilm), Reel 3, Accession No. 2176, NMML.

38. See Shula Marks, *Reluctant Rebellion: The 1906–8 Disturbances in Natal* (Oxford: Clarendon Press, 1970), Part IV.

39. *IO*, 28 April 1906.

40. *IO*, 16 and 23 June 1906.

41. *CWMG*, V, pp. 281–2, 348, 368–74.

42. Edward Roux, *Time Longer Than Rope: The Black Man's Struggle for Freedom in South Africa* (first published 1948; 2nd edn, Madison: University of Wisconsin Press, 1964), pp. 96, 104.

43. Padmanabh S. Jaini, *The Jaina Path of Purification* (Berkeley: University of California Press, 1979), pp. 175–6, 183.

44. Quoted in James Laidlaw, *Riches and Renunciation: Religion, Economy, and Society among the Jains* (Oxford: Clarendon Press, 1995), p. 237.

45. Gandhi, 'Preface to "Srimad Rajchandra"', *CWMG*, XXXII, p. 6.

46. Cf. Gail Hinich Sutherland, *Nonviolence, Consumption and Community among Ancient Indian Ascetics* (Shimla: Indian Institute of Advanced Study, 1997), pp. 6–7 and passim.

47. Gandhi, *An Autobiography*, Part III, Chapters VII and VIII.

48. 'The First Step', in *The Complete Works of Count Tolstoy*, vol. XIX, translated and edited by Leo Wiener (Boston: Dana Estes and Company, 1905), pp. 391–2 and passim.

9   TROUBLE IN THE TRANSVAAL

1. Eric Itzkin, *Gandhi's Johannesburg: Birthplace of Satyagraha* (Johannesburg: Witwatersrand University Press, 2000), pp. 68–9.

2. Millie Graham Polak, 'My South African Days with Gandhiji', *Indian Review*, October 1964.

3. Unlike in early modern Europe, wealthy Indian merchants were not often patrons of the arts or of artists. The patronage of art and music was more characteristic of Kshatriya and Muslim nobles; besides, Banias did not want to draw attention to great wealth if they had it.

A third, enduring, Gandhi characteristic may also be a residue of his Bania upbringing – an indifference to, and a lack of ability in, modern sports such as cricket, football and tennis.

4. These paragraphs on Gandhi's life with the Polaks in Johannesburg in 1906 are based on Millie Graham Polak, *Mr Gandhi: The Man* (London: George Allen and Unwin, 1931), pp. 70–87.

5. The letter is reproduced in Chandulal Bhagubhai Dalal, *Harilal Gandhi: A Life*, edited and translated from the Gujarati by Tridip Suhrud (Hyderabad: Orient Longman, 2007), pp. 225–6.

6. Chanchal was also known as 'Gulab'. Many girls in Saurashtra carried two names, one given by the mother's family, the other by the father's family. In this book however I have referred to her as 'Chanchal' throughout, or by its diminutive, 'Chanchi', by which she was also known.

7. Gandhi to Laxmidas, 27 May 1906, *CWMG*, V, p. 334–5.

8. Gandhi to Chamney, 13 August 1906, in File E 26/8, vol. 215, 'ND', NASA. This letter is not in *CWMG*.

9. Chamney to Gandhi, 15 September 1906; Gandhi to Chamney, 17 September 1906 (not in *CWMG*), both in File E 26/8, vol. 215, 'ND', NASA.

10. Letter of 27 September, in *CWMG*, V, pp. 408–9.

11. Bala Pillay, *British Indians in the Transvaal: Trade, Politics and Imperial Relations, 1885–1906* (London: Longman, 1976), pp. 210–12.

12. Statement to the press, 4 August 1906, in Natal Government Records (on microfilm), Reel 2, Accession No. 2175, NMML.

13. See Deborah Lavin, *From Empire to Commonwealth: A Biography of Lionel Curtis* (Oxford: Clarendon Press, 1995), pp. 59–60.

14. Lionel Curtis, quoted in Keith Breckenridge, 'Gandhi's Progressive Disillusionment: Thumbs, Fingers, and the Rejection of Scientific Modernism in *Hind Swaraj*', *Public Culture*, 23:2 (2011), p. 339.

15. See Lionel Curtis, *With Milner in South Africa* (Oxford: Basil Blackwell, 1951), p. 348. Curtis probably meant Trinidad or Guyana rather than Jamaica. In a book published in 1908, he outlined his larger vision for South Africa:

The present population of white to coloured is one to six; and how far the future population is to be drawn from the higher and how far from the lower races of mankind is the issue which hangs on the native problem of to-day. The answer depends upon whether South Africa accommodates her industrial system to the habits of the whites or to those of the coloured races. If the system is one in which the lower races thrive better than the higher, the coloured element will grow at the expense of the European. South Africa will then sink to the level of States such as those of central and southern America – republics in name and not seldom tyrannies in fact, unequal to the task of their own internal government and too weak to exert an influence on the world's affairs. If, on the other hand, the scheme of society offers the white population, instead of the coloured population, to be built up from outside as well as from its own natural increase, so that in the course of years the one gains upon the other, this country will gradually assume its place beside England, the United States, Canada, or Australia, as one of the powers of the world and share in the direction of its future.

To achieve this ideal, said Curtis, the 'promotion and control of immigration is a matter of supreme importance'. The Asiatic Ordinance was therefore a natural outcome of this view of the world – and of South Africa in particular. See Anon., *The Government of South Africa* (2 vols) (South Africa: Central News Agency, Ltd., 1908), vol. 1, pp. 156–8. Although without an author (or place of publication), the All Souls copy of this book has 'by L. G. Curtis' written on it in pencil on the title page. It appears the book was compiled and edited by Curtis on the basis of reports on different subjects written by others, which he then wove into a single, coherent narrative.

16. *CWMG*, V, pp. 400–405, 409–12.

17. Gregorowski to Gandhi 6 September 1906, quoted in Pyarelal, *Mahatma Gandhi*, III: *The Birth of Satyagraha – from Petitioning to Passive Resistance* (Ahmedabad: Navajivan Publishing House, 1986), pp. 492–3.

18. Quoted in *IO*, 22 September 1906.

19. This account of the 11 September meeting is based on reports in *IO*, 15 and 22 September 1906; in *CWMG*, V, pp. 419–23, 439–43; and in *NM*, 12 September 1906.

20. Charles DiSalvio has pointed out that the first time Gandhi advocated the courting of arrest was in fact in January 1904, when, in an editorial in *Indian Opinion*, he wrote that merchants seeking permanent licences 'must make respectful representations to the Government', but if these failed, should trade without a licence, refuse to pay a fine for doing so, and go to jail. See Charles DiSalvio, *The Man Before the Mahatma: M. K. Gandhi, Attorney-at-Law* (NOIDA, UP: Random House India, 2012), pp. 195–6. That early suggestion was then set aside for more than two years, in which time many respectful representations were made to Government. The proposal hesitantly offered in print in January 1904 was now, in September 1906, ringingly endorsed in a mass meeeting of several thousand Indians.

21. James D. Hunt, *Gandhi and the Non-Conformists: Encounters in South Africa* (New Delhi: Promilla and Co., 1986), Chapters 3 and 4.

22. Cf. J. G. James, 'The Ethics of Passive Resistance', *International Journal of Ethics*, 14:3 (1904).

23. *IO*, 6 October 1906, *CWMG*, V, p. 461.

24. See Howard Spodek, 'On the Origins of Gandhi's Political Methodology: The Heritage of Kathiawar and Gujarat', *Journal of Asian Studies*, 30:2 (1971). It was not merely in Kathiawar that these methods of protest were used. In the early nineteenth century, when the British took over the holy city of Banaras, they imposed a new house tax on its residents. This led to a popular outcry, with petitions being sent to Government urging that

there were too many taxes already, and that with the stagnation in trade the residents of Benares could not bear another one. A magistrate reported that 'the people are extremely clamorous; they have shut up their shops, abandoned their usual occupations, and assemble in multitudes with a view to extort from me an immediate compliance with their demands, and to prevail with me to direct the Collector to withdraw the assessors.'

The resisters in Banaras called a mass assembly, sending emissaries to hamlets and localities for volunteers. In the event, some 20,000 people sat on protest, demanding that the tax be withdrawn. 'At present open violence does not seem their aim', wrote the Collector of Benares to his superior, 'they seem rather to vaunt their security in being unarmed in that a military force would not use deadly weapons against such inoffensive foes. And in this confidence they collect and increase, knowing that the civil power can not disperse them, and thinking that the military will not.' See Dharampal, *Civil Disobedience and Indian Tradition: With Some Early Nineteenth Century Documents* (Varanasi: Sarva Seva Sangh Prakashan, 1971). Other pre-modern forms of customary rebellion that in some ways anticipate Gandhian satyagraha are also discussed in Ramachandra Guha, *The Unquiet Woods: Ecological Change and Peasant Resistance in the Himalaya* (first published in 1989; 3rd edn, Ranikhet: Permanent Black, 2010), Chapter IV.

25. Chinese Consul-General to Governor of the Transvaal, 13 September 1906, in Natal Government Records (on microfilm), Reel 3, Accession No. 2176, NMML.

26. Letter of 17 September 1906, copy in Natal Government Records (on microfilm), Reel 2, Accession No. 2175, NMML.

IO A LOBBYIST IN LONDON

1. 'Hajee Ojeer Ally', *IO*, 6 October 1906, in *CWMG*, V, pp. 459–60.

2. H. S. L. Polak, 'Passive Resistance Movement in South Africa', typescript composed *c.*1908–12, Mss. Afr. R. 125, Rhodes House Library, Oxford, pp. 221–4.

3. *CWMG*, VI, pp. 1–3.

4. Letter of 26 October 1906, in *CWMG*, VI, pp. 17–20.

5. Letter of 26 October 1906, in *CWMG*, VI, pp. 21–2.

6. Cf. James D. Hunt, *Gandhi in London* (revised edn, New Delhi: Promilla and Co, 1993), p. 62.

7. Letter of 21 September 1906, in Natal Government Records (on microfilm), Reel 3, Accession No. 2176, NMML.

8. 'Petition of British Subjects, Natives of India, resident in the Transvaal and elsewhere', in Natal Government Records (on microfilm), Reel 3, Accession No. 2176, NMML.

9. Letter in the *Rand Daily Mail*, 28 March 1904, reproduced in *Correspondence Relating to the Position of British Indians in the Transvaal (in Continuation of Cd. 1684)* (London: HMSO, 1904).

10. See correspondence in File 15/12/1906, vol. 951, GOV, NASA.

11. See correspondence in File GEN 1031/06, vol. 203, GOV, NASA.

12. Telegram dated 21 November 1906, in *Correspondence Relating to Legislation Affecting Asiatics in the Transvaal (Cd. 3308 – in Continuation of Cd. 3251)* (London: HMSO, 1907).

13. See 'Lost Hospitals of London: Lady Margaret Hospital', http://ezitis.myzen.co.uk/ladymargaret.html (accessed 12 October 2011).

14. Letters to Dr J. Oldfield, 26 and 27 October 1906; letters to H. O. Ally, 26 and 27 October 1906, in *CWMG*, VI, pp. 23, 26, 32–3, 33–4.

15. See Indulal Yajnik, *Shyamaji Krishnavarma: Life and Times of an Indian Revolutionary* (Bombay: Lakshmi Publications, 1950); Harald Fischer-Tiné, 'Indian Nationalism and the "World Forces": Transnational and Diasporic Dimensions of the Indian Freedom Movement on the Eve of the First World War', *Journal of Global History*, 2:3 (2007).

16. Letter to J. H. L. Polak, 30 October 1906, *CWMG*, VI, pp. 40–41.

17. *IO*, 1 December 1906, *CWMG*, VI, pp. 83–4.

18. Letter of 3 November 1906, *CWMG*, VI, pp. 78–80.

19. Sir Lepel may have been influenced by M. M. Bhownaggree's view (as expressed in the House of Commons in June 1905) that 'the real opposition' to Indians in South Africa 'did not proceed from British colonists from the better class, but was mainly led by a low class of aliens, Polish Jews and such like, who were permitted rights and liberties denied to the Indian subjects of the Crown'. In quoting this speech, John Mcleod (in his forthcoming book *Indian Tory*) notes that the Parsee politician saw world history as a great struggle between Aryans (among whom he included Indians) and Semites (especially Jews), hence this interpretation, certainly a mistaken one, with no credence in fact or in any materials Gandhi might have sent Bhownaggree from South Africa.

20. The proceedings of the meeting, from which this account draws, are reproduced in *CWMG*, VI, pp. 113–26.

21. Letter of 9 November 1906, *CWMG*, VI, p. 133.

22. Secretary of State for the Colonies to the Governor of the Transvaal, 29 November 1906, in *Correspondence Relating to Legislation Affecting Asiatics*.

23. *The Times*, 10 November 1906.

24. Letter of 16 November 1906, in *CWMG*, VI, pp. 168–9.

25. George Birdwood to M. K. Gandhi, 3 November 1906, S. N. 449, SAAA.

26. See File 827, L/P&J/6/752, APAC/BL.

27. *CWMG*, VI, pp. 224–6.

28. As reported in *IO*, 29 December 1906, *CWMG*, VI, pp. 257–60.

29. Letter of 27 November 1906, *CWMG*, VI, p. 237.

30. See report of meeting in *IO*, 29 December 1906.

31. *CWMG*, VI, pp. 244–6.

32. Letter dated 3 December 1906, A Progs No. 4, May 1907, in Department of Commerce and Industry (Emigration), NAI.

33. Governor of Transvaal to Secretary of State for the Colonies, 14 January 1907, in *Correspondence Relating to Legislation Affecting Asiatics*.

34. See L. E. Neame, *The Asiatic Danger to the Colonies* (London: George Routledge and Sons, 1907), pp. 4–6, 31–3, 53–4, 89–90, etc. Neame's book drew on a series of articles previously published by him in the *Rand Daily Mail*, here revised and rewritten for a British audience.

35. 'A Book – and Its Misnomer: A Review', *IO*, 11, 18, 25 May and 1 June 1907.

11   FROM CONCILIATION TO CONFRONTATION

1. *IO*, 29 December 1906.

2. *IO*, 5 January 1907.

3. See A Proceedings, no. 14, December 1907, in Department of Commerce and Industry (Emigration), NAI; *CWMG*, VI, pp. 253f.

4. Memorandum by Ministers of the Natal Government, dated 19 February 1907, in Natal Government Records (on microfilm), Reel 1, Accession No. 2174, NMML.

5. See File 2726, L/P&J/883, APAC/BL; Vishnu Padayachee and Robert Morrell, 'Indian Merchants and Dukawallahs in the Natal Economy, c. 1875–1914', *Journal of Southern African Studies*, 17:1 (1991).

6. *Cape Times*, 6 November 1907, File 4238, L/P&J/6/839, APAC/BL.

7. *Report of the Select Committee on Asiatic Grievances* (Cape Town: Government Printers, 1908), in File 4490, L/P&J/6/907, APAC/BL.

8. *IO*, issues of 26 January and 2 February 1907, *CWMG*, VI, pp. 291–5, 308–9.

9. Letter of 28 January 1907, *CWMG*, VI, pp. 301–2.

10. *CWMG*, VI, pp. 320–21.

11. Gandhi to Chhaganlal, 24 April 1907, copy in Gandhi–Polak Papers, vol. I, Manuscript Section, NAI.

12. Harold Spender, *General Botha: The Career and the Man* (London: Constable and Company, 1916), pp. 22, 166–7, 178–80, etc.

13. Letter of 1 April, in *Further Correspondence Relating to Legislation Affecting Asiatics in the Transvaal (Cd. 3887 – in continuation of Cd. 3308)* (London: HMSO, 1908).

14. *CWMG*, VI, pp. 381–2, 394–408.

15. *IO*, 20 April 1907. Cf. also Karen L. Harris, 'Gandhi, the Chinese and Passive Resistance', in Judith M. Brown and Martin Prozesky, eds, *Gandhi and South Africa* (Pietermaritzburg: University of Natal Press, 1996).

16. See File 2659, L/P&J/6/823, APAC/BL.

17. See petitions to Colonial Office and India Office by Joseph Royeppen, 24 April 1907, in File 1338/L/P&J/6/809, APAC/BL.

18. The paragraphs that follow draw largely on the standard (and still unsurpassed) biography by W. K. Hancock: *Smuts*, I: *The Sanguine Years, 1870–1919* (Cambridge: Cambridge University Press, 1962).

19. Emily Hobhouse to Smuts, 29 May 1904, in W. K. Hancock and Jean van der Poel, eds, *Selections from the Smuts Papers*, II: *June 1902–May 1910* (Cambridge: Cambridge University Press, 1966), p. 253 (emphasis in original).

20. See ibid., pp. 25–6, 64–5, 116, 125–6.

21. *CWMG*, VI, pp. 416–17, 423–7.

22. Letter written 'about April 20, 1907', *CWMG*, VI, pp. 423–7.

23. *IO*, 27 April 1907, *CWMG*, pp. 439–43.

24. *IO*, 11 May 1907.

25. *CWMG*, VI, pp. 480–81, 486; VII, pp. 6–7, 121–3.

26. See *IO*, issues of 18 and 25 May, 1 June 1907.

27. Letter of 5 May 1907, in *Further Correspondence Relating to Legislation Affecting Asiatics*.

28. *CWMG*, VII, p. 56.

29. *Rand Daily Mail*, 2 July 1907, *CWMG*, VII, p. 67.

30. *Rand Daily Mail*, 9 July 1907, *CWMG*, VII, p. 87.

31. *Rand Daily Mail*, quoted in *IO*, 6 July 1907.

32. *IO*, 6 July 1907.

33. *CWMG*, VII, pp. 89, 97, 98, 117.

34. 'A Serio-Comedy', *IO*, 20 July 1907.

35. *CWMG*, VII, pp. 113–44.

36. *IO*, 27 July 1907, *CWMG*, VII, pp. 128f.

37. *IO*, 3 August 1907, *CWMG*, VII, pp. 134–6.

38. *IO*, 27 July 1907, *CWMG*, pp. 123–4.

39. Reports in *IO*, 3 and 10 August 1907.

40. Cf. correspondence in *CWMG*, VII, pp. 147–9, 162.

41. Reports from the *Star* and the *Rand Daily Mail* in *IO*, 17 September 1907.

42. *CWMG*, VII, pp. 152, 154, 164.

43. Quoted in *IO*, 24 August 1907.

44. *CWMG*, VII, pp. 170–71, 180–84, 492–6.

45. See *IO*, 8 June 1906.

46. 'Johannesburg Jottings', *IO*, 17 August 1908.

47. *IO*, 7 and 21 September 1907.

48. I am grateful to the Gandhi scholar Anil Nauriya for working out the origins of this penname. If Polak's initials, 'HSL', are said very fast, they sound like 'A. Chessell', while *'piquet'* is French for 'pole'.

49. *IO*, 24 September 1907.

50. *CWMG*, pp. 211, 217–18, 228–30.

51. Polak to P. Kodanda Rao, 9 April 1948, in Kodanda Rao Papers, NMML.

52. John Cordes to M. K. Gandhi, 3 June 1907, KP.
53. This description of Phoenix, *c.* 1906–7, draws on Millie Graham Polak, *Mr Gandhi: The Man* (London: George Allen and Unwin, 1931), pp. 47–50, 56–7; and Prabhudas Gandhi, *My Childhood with Gandhiji* (Ahmedabad: Navajivan Publishing House, 1957), pp. 37–9.
54. Cordes to Gandhi, 9 July 1907, KP.
55. Gandhi to Cordes, 12 July 1907, KP.
56. Gandhi to Cordes, letters of 12 and 13 July 1907, KP. None of the Gandhi letters quoted in this section are in *CWMG*.
57. Gandhi to Cordes, letters of 17 July and 16 August 1907, KP.
58. Gandhi to Cordes, 12 October 1907, KP.
59. Polak to Cordes, 20 November 1907, KP. Ibsen was of course the great Norwegian playwright. I am unable to trace who Dr Staubman was.

12 TO JAIL

1. 'Pickets's Duty', *IO*, *CWMG*, VII, pp. 255, 258.
2. *IO*, 12 October 1907, *CWMG*, VII, p. 285.
3. *IO*, 19 October 1907, *CWMG*, VII, pp. 295–6, 316.
4. See *CWMG*, VII, pp. 320–21.
5. *IO*, 9 November 1907.
6. Cf. Monica Barlow, 'The Clouded Face of Truth: A Review of the South African Newspaper Press Approaching Union', unpublished Ph.D. thesis (Department of History, Bristol University, 1988), p. 172.
7. See Indulal Yajnik, *Shyamaji Krishnavarma: Life and Times of an Indian Revolutionary* (Bombay: Lakshmi Publications, 1950), pp. 241f.
8. Essop Mia (M. K. Gandhi) to Rash Behari Ghosh, 4 November 1907, *CWMG*, VII, pp. 332–4.
9. This account of the Ram Sundar Pundit case is based on newspaper clippings in Natal Government Records (on microfilm), Reel 4, Accession No. 2177, NMML; *CWMG*, VII, pp. 33–6, 365–8, 380–81.
10. Letter of 22 November, *CWMG*, VII, p. 376.
11. Letter of 11 November 1907, in *Further Correspondence Relating to Legislation Affecting Asiatics in the Transvaal (Cd. 3887 – in continuation of Cd. 3308)* (London: HMSO, 1908).
12. See *CWMG*, VII, pp. 409–11, 422, 446.
13. *CWMG*, VII, pp. 416–18.
14. Selborne to Smuts, 30 November 1907; Smuts to Selborne, 6 December 1907, in Box 62, Selborne Papers, Bodleian Library, Oxford.
15. Smuts to J. X. Merriman, 8 January 1908, in W. K. Hancock and Jean van der Poel, eds, *Selections from the Smuts Papers*, II: *June 1902–May 1910* (Cambridge: Cambridge University Press, 1966), p. 373.

16. Report in *NM*, 3 December 1907.
17. Gandhi to Cordes, 3 December 1907, KP. (This letter is not in *CWMG*.)
18. *The Friend*, excerpted in *IO*, 23 November 1907.
19. See *IO*, 7 December 1907.
20. *CWMG*, VII, pp. 429–30, 439–40, 443.
21. *CWMG*, VII, p. 449.
22. News reports in *CWMG*, VII, pp. 463–8.
23. *IO*, 4 January 1908, *CWMG*, VII, p. 473.
24. *NM*, 31 December 1907.
25. Telegrams dated 27 December 1907 and 7 January 1908, in Natal Government Records (on microfilm), Reel 4, Accession No. 2177, NMML.
26. William Cursons, *Joseph Doke: The Missionary-Hearted* (Johannesburg: The Christian Literature Depot, 1929), pp. 35–6, 141, etc.
27. This sketch, signed 'J. J. D.', is in the J. J. Doke Papers.
28. See George Paxton, *Gandhi's South African Secretary: Sonja Schlesin* (Glasgow: Pax Books, 2006), pp. 3–4.
29. Gandhi to Richard B. Gregg, 29 May 1927, *CWMG*, XXXIII, p. 396.
30. Joseph J. Doke, *M. K. Gandhi: An Indian Patriot in South Africa* (London: The London Indian Chronicle, 1909), pp. 5–6, 9.
31. See *CWMG*, VIII, pp. 24–5.
32. *CWMG*, VIII, pp. 8–9, 13–17, 19.
33. *IO*, 11 January 1908, *CWMG*, pp. 22–3.
34. *CWMG*, VIII, pp. 33–8.
35. Cf. Eric Itzkin, *Gandhi's Johannesburg: Birthplace of Satyagraha* (Johannesburg: Witwatersrand University Press, 2000), pp. 30–33.
36. Letter to editor from 'Pro Bono Publico', *NM*, 20 November 1907.
37. *NM*, 7 January 1908.
38. See *NM*, 7 and 14 January 1908; *IO*, 28 September 1907.
39. *NM*, 13 January 1908, *IO*, 18 January 1908.
40. *IO*, 18 January 1908.
41. Excerpts from an article entitled 'Courage' in *Ilanga lase Natal*, reproduced in *NM*, 13 January 1908.

13   A TOLSTOYAN IN JOHANNESBURG

1. This account is based on six articles on his jail experiences that Gandhi later published in *Indian Opinion*, reproduced in *CWMG*, VIII, pp. 119–20, 134–6, 139–43, 145–7, 152–6, 158–62.
2. As reported in the *Transvaal Leader*, 13 and 15 January 1908.
3. Letter to the editor, dated 14 January, *Transvaal Leader*, 16 January 1908.
4. 'Passive Resistance and the Native Mind: A Remarkable Article', *Transvaal Leader*, 28 January 1908.

5. 'General Smuts' Apologia', *IO*, 15 February 1908.

6. Viceroy to Secretary of State for India, 30 January 1908, in *Further Correspondence Relating to Legislation Affecting Asiatics in the Transvaal* (Cd. 4327 – *in continuation of Cd. 3892*) (London: HMSO, 1908).

7. Telegram dated 26 January 1908, copy in File No. 5, Servants of India Society Papers, NMML.

8. Merriman to Smuts, 13 January 1908, in W. K. Hancock and Jean van der Poel, eds, *Selections from the Smuts Papers*, II: *June 1902–May 1910* (Cambridge: Cambridge University Press, 1966), pp. 394–6.

9. *CWMG*, VIII, pp. 40–42, 161, 517.

10. Gandhi to John Cordes, 7 February 1908, in KP. (This letter is not in *CWMG*.)

11. *Rand Daily Mail*, 31 January 1908, in *CWMG*, VIII, pp. 42–3.

12. Undated news clipping entitled 'At Mr Gandhi's Office', in J. J. Doke Papers.

13. Letter of 31 January 1908, *CWMG*, VIII, pp. 49–51.

14. *IO*, 8 February 1908, *CWMG*, VIII, 59–60.

15. *NM*, 4 February 1908.

16. *NM*, 11 February 1908.

17. Cf. report in *IO*, 15 February 1908.

18. Olive C. Doke, 'Mr Gandhi in South Africa', C. M. Doke Papers.

19. See 'My Reward', *IO*, 22 February 1908, in *CWMG*, VIII, pp. 93–7.

20. *IO*, 22 February 1908.

21. Cf. Gandhi to Olive Doke, 3 April 1908, C. M. Doke Papers, UNISA (this letter is not in the *CWMG*).

22. 'Letter to Friends', dated 10 February 1908, *CWMG*, VIII, pp. 75–6.

23. 'Meeting of Punjabis', undated news clipping in J. J. Doke Papers.

24. 'A Denial', letter in the *Transvaal Leader*, 15 February 1908, signed by Emam A. K. Bawazeer, M. P. Fancy, Essop Ismail Mia, Syed Mustafa, Allibhai Akooji and M. E. Nagdee.

25. *Star*, 13 February 1908.

26. Reports in *NM*, 13 February 1908.

27. *CWMG*, VIII, pp. 76–86.

28. See reports in *IO*, 22 and 29 February 1908.

29. 'A Disorderly Meeting', *IO*, 7 March 1908.

30. *CWMG*, VIII, p. 132.

31. *CWMG*, VIII, pp. 148–50, 162–3.

32. See *IO*, 18 April 1908.

33. Gandhi to Chamney, letters of 12 and 13 March 1908, in File E 8979, vol. 480, IND, NASA (these letters are not in *CWMG*).

34. *NM*, 6 May 1908. On the other hand, the more hardline *Natal Advertiser* (in its issue of the same date) supported the Bills, arguing that the interests of the ruling race required the 'elimination, or restriction to the narrowest possible limits, of the Asiatic, on the simple and sufficient ground that there is no room for him'.

35. *CWMG*, VIII, pp. 214–15, 221–2.
36. Gandhi to E. F. C. Lane, 14 May 1908, in *CWMG*, VIII, p. 231. (Lane was a senior official in the Colonial Department, working closely with Smuts.)
37. Gandhi to Smuts, 21 May 1908, *CWMG*, VIII, pp. 253–4.
38. E. F. C. Lane to Gandhi, letters of 15 and 22 May 1908, in Natal Government Records (on microfilm), Reel 4, Accession No. 2177, NMML; *IO*, 30 May 1908.
39. *CWMG*, VIII, pp. 261–7.
40. For details on the Smuts–Gandhi meetings in June 1908, see *CWMG*, VIII, pp. 277–9, 290–92, 306–9, 316–17.
41. Smuts to William Hosken, letters of 24 March and 6 June 1908, S. N. 4802 and S. N. 4823, SAAA.
42. Cf. 'Mass Meeting of British Indians', *IO*, 27 June 1908.
43. *CWMG*, VIII, pp. 319–24.
44. Johannesburg correspondent of the *Daily Telegraph*, quoted in *IO*, 27 August 1908.
45. These paragraphs draw on the translated reports of native newspapers in the Madras and Bombay Presidencies for 1907–9, contained in the series L/P&J/R/5, File nos. 113, 114, 162 and 163, APAC/BL.
46. The previous paragraphs are based on the letters and telegrams in File 598, L/P&J/6/849; and in File 516, L/P&J/6/848, both in APAC/BL; and on reports in *IO*, 18 and 25 January, 14 and 21 March 1908.
47. See news clippings in CID Reports for November 1908, Tamil Nadu State Archives, Chennai.
48. Cf. *CWMG*, XI, p. 136, footnote.
49. As reported in *The Evening Post*, 18 May 1912, in http://hpaperspast.natlib .govt.nz/cgibin (accessed 24 September 2010). F. B. Meyer was a prolific author of books and pamphlets with titles such as 'The Soul's Wrestle with Doubt', 'The Duty of the Free Churches in an Age of Reaction' and 'Open Air Services: Hints and Suggestions'.
50. F. B. Meyer, *A Winter in South Africa* (London: National Council of Evangelical Free Churches, 1908), pp. 71–3.
51. Eric Itzkin, *Gandhi's Johannesburg: Birthplace of Satyagraha* (Johannesburg: Witwatersrand University Press, 2000), pp. 70–72.
52. See Gandhi to Harilal, undated letter *c.* 1909 (not in *CWMG*), reproduced in Nilam Parikh, *Gandhiji's Lost Jewel: Harilal Gandhi* (New Delhi: National Gandhi Museum, 2001), pp. 121–2; Gandhi to Cordes, letter quoted in Shimon Low, 'Mahatma Gandhi and Hermann Kallenbach in South Africa, 1904–1914', MA dissertation (Faculty of Humanities, The Hebrew University of Jerusalem, April 2010).
53. Cf. 'Tolstoy and the Nonviolent Imperative', Chapter IV of Steven G. Marks, *How Russia Shaped the Modern World: From Art to Anti-Semitism, from Ballet to Bolshevism* (Princeton: Princeton University Press, 2003). Also

useful is Martin Green's comparative study, *The Origins of Nonviolence: Tolstoy and Gandhi in Their Historical Settings* (1986; reprint, New Delhi: HarperCollins Publishers India, 1998).

54. Charlotte Alston, 'Tolstoy's Guiding Light', *History Today*, 60:10 (2010).

55. As related in Uma Dhupelia-Mesthrie, *Gandhi's Prisoner? The Life of Gandhi's Son Manilal* (Cape Town: Kwela Books, 2004), p. 118.

56. Letter to Charles Turner, *c.* July 1892, in Rosamund Bartlett, *Tolstoy: A Russian Life* (London: Profile Books, 2010), pp. 342–3.

57. The Gandhi–Kallenbach joint experiment in celibacy was subject to a series of spectacular misreadings following the publication of Joseph Lelyveld's book *Great Soul: Mahatma Gandhi's Struggle with India* (New York: Alfred A. Knopf, 2008). Basing his analysis on the published letters between the two men, Lelyveld concluded that the relationship was 'homoerotic'; but his interpretation was wrong-headed, and his research incomplete. He had not consulted the Kallenbach Papers in Haifa, which would have set him right as to the depth of the architect's commitment to celibacy, *c.*1908–13, and to his heterosexual instincts before and after. (Kallenbach was attracted only to women: years later, after Gandhi had returned to India, he abandoned *brahmacharya* to have affairs with women.) Lelyveld found support for his claim in casual gossip that he picked up decades after Gandhi left South Africa. He thus claimed that among 'South Africa's small Indian community', it 'was no secret then, or later, that Gandhi, leaving his wife behind, had gone to live with a man.' (p. 88). No references were provided for this attribution; who said this, to whom, and when? Such talk is entirely absent from the archival record. The hard historical evidence, on the other hand, is very clear that Gandhi was based in the Transvaal in these years because the Indians in that province were faced with the threat of eviction and deportation. That is to say, Gandhi was living in Johannesburg out of social obligation, not sexual desire.

While Lelyveld's research was suspect, his prose is understated, and his conclusion cautious – Gandhi and Kallenbach were, he suggested, in a 'homoerotic' relationship. He did not explicitly rule out sexual relations, but did not claim these existed either. This restraint was not echoed by his reviewers. One described Gandhi as a 'sexual weirdo' (also as a 'political incompetent' and 'fanatical faddist'), whose 'organ probably only rarely became aroused with his naked young ladies, because the love of his life was a German-Jewish architect and bodybuilder, for whom Gandhi left his wife in 1908'. (Andrew Roberts, 'Among the Hagiographers', *Wall Street Journal*, 26 March 2011.) Roberts's screed in turn prompted a story in a British tabloid with the headline 'Gandhi "Left His Wife to Live with a Male Lover" New Book Claims' (*Daily Mail*, 28 March 2011). This article concluded – on the basis of Roberts's misreading of Lelyveld's misreading of the friendship – that Gandhi was 'bisexual' and, further, that 'after four children together [with Kasturba] they split up so he could be with Kallenbach.' The reproduction of these reports in India prompted the country's Law Minister to propose a ban on the book, a threat fortunately not carried out (in part because two of Gandhi's distinguished grandsons, the historian Rajmohan and the civil servant and diplomat Gopalkrishna, came out strongly against it).

The speculation that Gandhi and Kallenbach were (real or suppressed) lovers is perhaps not unrelated to the fact that three great Western moral traditions – the Jewish, the Protestant and the atheistic – are all antipathetic to celibacy. And so the most widely read and cosmopolitan people tend to assume that two men living together, who wrote affectionate letters to one another, must be in a homosexual relationship. That so many Catholic priests bound in theory to celibacy have been exposed for sexually abusing young boys makes the post-modern mind even less likely to understand that other people in other times may have been deeply and honestly committed to sexual abstinence.

A celebrated Irish historian, on hearing I was working on this book, hoped that I would write at length on 'Gandhi's gay lover'. Would that I could. Alas, the relationship between Gandhi and Kallenbach was that between brothers. And, as the later chapters of this book show, Gandhi continued to have a close, continuous and deeply intimate (if also occasionally contentious) relationship with his wife Kasturba.

58. Hermann Kallenbach to Simon Kallenbach, 10/14 June 1908, KP (the letter was originally written in German; the translation is by Kallenbach's niece Hannah Lazar).
59. Meyer, *A Winter in South Africa*, p. 72.
60. There is a useful and (so far as I can tell) reliable discussion in http://en.wikipedia.org/wiki/Hydrotherapy.
61. *CWMG*, VIII, pp. 328–30.
62. Gandhi to Albert Cartwright, 14 July 1908, *CWMG*, VIII, pp. 361–3.
63. Speech of 18 May 1908, in *CWMG*, VIII, pp. 242–6.
64. *CWMG*, VIII, pp. 379, 382, 384–6.
65. These paragraphs are based on a forthcoming pamphlet by E. S. Reddy entitled *Thambi Naidoo and His Family: The Story of Thambi Naidoo, a Lieutenant of Gandhi in the Satyagraha in South Africa, and of His Family Which Sacrificed for Five Generations in the Struggle for a Free South Africa.*
66. Report in *IO*, 1 August 1908.
67. 'No Quarter', *IO*, 15 August 1908.
68. Reports in the Johannesburg *Star* of 8, 9, 10 and 20 July 1908, in *Further Correspondence Relating to Legislation Affecting Asiatics.*
69. Gandhi to Chamney, 4 August 1908, in File No. E 26/8, vol. 215, 'ND', NASA (this letter is not in *CWMG*).
70. Jail form, dated 23 June 1910, ibid.

71. 'Resolutions Passed by the Hamidia Islamia Society, Johannesburg, 28 July 1908', in Natal Government Records (on microfilm), Reel 4, Accession No. 2177, NMML.
72. Letter in *IO*, 8 August 1908, in *CWMG*, VIII, pp. 432–3.

14 PRISONER OF CONSCIENCE

1. See press reports in *CWMG*, VIII, pp. 443, 447.
2. Cf. illustrations in *CWMG*, VIII, opposite pp. 32, 33, 81, etc.
3. *CWMG*, VIII, p. 451.
4. 'Joh'burg Mass Meeting', *IO*, 22 August 1908.
5. *CWMG*, VIII, pp. 457–60.
6. *Transvaal Leader*, quoted in *CWMG*, VIII, p. 463
7. See the report on this meeting of 18 August 1908 in *Further Correspondence Relating to Legislation Affecting Asiatics in the Transvaal (Cd. 4327 – in continuation of Cd. 3892)* (London: HMSO, 1908).
8. See report in File 3722, L/P&J/6/894, APAC/BL.
9. Excerpt from *Transvaal Leader*, 22 August 1908, ibid.
10. Excerpt of debate in Transvaal Parliament, in File 3722, L/P&J/6/894, APAC/BL.
11. Governor of the Transvaal to Secretary of State for the Colonies, 5 September 1908, in *Further Correspondence Relating to Legislation Affecting Asiatics*.
12. To invoke, I hope not too anachronistically, the title of a book by the Anglo-American philosopher Alasdair Macintyre.
13. *CWMG*, VIII, pp. 473–7.
14. *CWMG*, VIII, pp. 481: IX, pp. 3, 8, 13, 29, etc.
15. *CWMG*, IX, p. 4; Bhawani Dayal, *Dakshin Africa ké Satyagraha ka Itihas* (Indore: Saraswati Sadan, 1916), p. 24.
16. Interview in the *Star*, 9 September 1908, *CWMG*, IX, pp. 30–31.
17. Extract from *Transvaal Weekly Illustrated*, 12 September 1908, in Natal Government Records (on microfilm), Reel 4, Accession No. 2177, NMML.
18. Doke to Gandhi, 11 September 1908, S. N. 4874, NGM (emphases in original).
19. *CWMG*, VIII, pp. 16, 41.
20. On Gandhi's ideas for the Phoenix School, see *CWMG*, VIII, p. 85; IX, pp. 135–9.
21. Interview in *Natal Mercury*, in *CWMG*, IX, pp. 77–9.
22. Doke to Gandhi, 30 September 1908, *CWMG*, IX, Appendix VI, pp. 556–7.
23. Message dated 13 October 1908, *CWMG*, IX, pp. 96–7.
24. See Deputy Governor of the Transvaal to the Secretary of State for the Colonies, 30 September 1908, in Natal Government Records (on microfilm),

Reel 4, Accession No. 2177, NMML; 'Volksrust Again: Mr Gandhi Sentenced', *IO*, 17 October 1908.

25. See reports in *IO*, 24 October and 21 November 1908. British friends of Gandhi also rallied to his defence. Three days after his arrest, the Rev. F. B. Meyer sent a stirring letter to the *Daily News* (quoted in *IO*, 21 November 1908). Meyer wrote that he could:

> hardly believe the evidence of my senses, when I read the announcement that my friend, Mr Gandhi, has been sentenced to two months' hard labour and to breaking stones and doing scavenger work. But I wish I were in Johannesburg that I might help him! I would count it an honour to suffer with this pure and holy soul, whom I hope to introduce to my choicest friends when he comes to this country. He is not a Christian in one sense of the word, but the face of Christ hangs over his desk, and we have talked together for hours of the deepest themes that can engage the human heart. He contends only for what he holds to be the rights of the Indians who have been settled in Johannesburg, many of them from before the war. His contention is retrospective for those who have entered the Transvaal and been its subjects and citizens for years.
>
> Even if he contravened the law there was no need to expose him to degrading labour. Yet what can degrade a pure soul? Christ made the Cross the honoured symbol of Christendom. Truth is still on the scaffold, while prejudice, fear, and selfish interests are on the throne, but there is One that keepeth watch.

26. 'The Mass Meeting', *IO*, 24 October 1908.
27. Quoted in *IO*, 24 October 1908.
28. See Doke to Albert Cartwright, 26 October 1908, in J. J. Doke Papers.
29. Cf. M. K. Gandhi, 'My Second Experience in Gaol', five-part series in *IO*, *CWMG*, IX, pp. 120–22, 140–42, 145–9, 161–6, 179–80. Quotes not sourced in the rest of this section are based on this series. A *maund* is an Indian unit of weight, roughly equivalent to 37 kilos.
30. As recalled in H. S. L. Polak, 'M. K. Gandhi: A Sketch', in *Speeches and Writings of M. K. Gandhi, with an Introduction by Mr C. F. Andrews, a Tribute by Mr G. A. Natesan, and a Biographical Sketch by Mr H. S. L. Polak* (Madras: G. A. Natesan and Co., 1918), pp. i–iii.
31. *CWMG*, IX, Appendix VIII, pp. 560–61.
32. Secretary of State for the Colonies to Governor of Transvaal, 29 October 1908; Deputy Governor of Transvaal to Secretary of State for the Colonies, 3 November 1908; both in *Further Correspondence Relating to Legislation Affecting Asiatics in the Transvaal (Cd. 4584 – in continuation of Cd. 4327)* (London: HMSO, 1909).
33. Gandhi to West, 9 September 1908, *CWMG*, IX, pp. 105–6.
34. *CWMG*, IX, pp. 108–9, 111, 115.
35. 'Mr Gandhi's Arrival', *IO*, 26 December 1908.

36. Report in *Transvaal Leader*, 30 November 1908.

37. *AC*, 4 July, 11 July, 25 July, 15 August and 17 October 1908, 18 December 1909.

38. Quoted in John Marlowe, *Milner: Apostle of Empire* (London: Hamish Hamilton, 1976), p. 146.

39. See Sir Edgar Walton, *The Inner History of the National Convention of South Africa* (1912; reprint, Westport, Connecticut: Negro Universities Press, 1970), pp. 117ff; L. M. Thompson, *The Unification of South Africa, 1902–1910* (Oxford: Clarendon Press, 1960), pp. 212–26.

40. Selbourne's scheme is reproduced in Arthur Percival Newton, ed., *Select Documents Relating to the Unification of South Africa* (1924; reprint, London: Frank Cass, 1968), vol. II, pp. 250–51.

41. Schreiner to Smuts, 2 August 1908, in W. K. Hancock and Jean van der Poel, eds, *Selections from the Smuts Papers, II: June 1902–May 1910* (Cambridge: Cambridge University Press, 1966), vol. II, p. 450 (emphasis in original).

42. See Thompson, *Unification of South Africa*, pp. 341, 35, 404, etc.

43. The standard life is Ruth First and Ann Smith, *Olive Schreiner* (New York: Schocken Books, 1980).

44. 'Olive Schreiner on Colour', *IO*, 2 January 1909.

45. Editorial in *IO*, 2 January 1909.

46. *CWMG*, IX, pp. 112–13.

47. *CWMG*, IX, pp. 130, 159–60, 180, 184, 187, 193–4.

48. Gandhi to Olive Doke, dated 'Tuesday' (almost certainly 5 January 1909), in C. M. Doke Papers (this letter is not in *CWMG*).

49. Devadas Gandhi, 'My Brother Harilal', *Hindustan Times*, 23 July 1948.

50. Gandhi to Chanchalbehn Gandhi, letters of 16 and 28 January 1909; Gandhi to Harilal, 27 January 1909, *CWMG*, IX, pp. 150, 173–5.

51. *The Times*, 6 January 1909.

52. See Pyarelal, *Mahatma Gandhi*, III: *The Birth of Satyagraha – from Petitioning to Passive Resistance* (Ahmedabad: Navajivan Publishing House, 1986), pp. 182–3.

53. Curzon to Gandhi, 26 January 1909, S. N. 4915, SAAA.

54. *CWMG*, IX, p. 175.

55. Gandhi, *An Autobiography*, Part IV, Chapter XXVIII.

56. Gandhi to Kallenbach, 5 February 1909, in Gillian Berning, ed., *Gandhi Letters: From Upper House to Lower House, 1906–1914* (Durban: Local History Museum, 1994), pp. 12–13. (This letter is not in *CWMG*.) Millie Polak, who was at Phoenix at the time, was both surprised and impressed by how well Kasturba responded to her husband's unorthodox treatment. For pernicious anaemia was then 'still looked upon as one of the fatal diseases, and very few cases indeed of recovery were on record'. And certainly no previous case had been successfully 'treated by lemon-juice, aided by what we to-day call mental healing. It was a great puzzle to the few medical men who

knew or heard of it.' (*Mr Gandhi the Man*, London: George Allen and Unwin, 1931, pp. 132–3.)

57. Curzon to Honorary Secretary, British Indian Association, Johannesburg (i. e., Gandhi), 2 February 1909, S. N. 4920, SAAA.
58. *Sunday Times* (Johannesburg) quoted in *IO*, 13 February 1909.
59. *CWMG*, IX, pp. 197–9.
60. Gandhi to Chanchalbehn Gandhi, 26 February 1909, *CWMG*, IX, pp. 200–201.
61. Gandhi wrote about his third jail term in two articles, and in a letter to the press issued afterwards: see *CWMG*, IX, pp. 221–4, 228–34, 238–43.
62. Gandhi to West, 4 March 1909, *CWMG*, IX, pp. 202–3.
63. H. S. L. Polak to David Pollock, dated Johannesburg, 27 March 1909, in Natal Government Records (on microfilm), Reel 4, Accession No. 2177, NMML. Polak says here that Gandhi had refused the Chief Justiceship of Porbandar – there is no independent confirmation of when and how that happened. The only evidence that may tangentially bear on this claim is an entry in Gandhi's office logbook for the 1890s, noting the receipt of a letter from the Chief Judge of Porbandar (see S. N. 2711, SAAA).
64. David Pollock to Lord Selborne, 29 March 1909; D. C. Malcolm, Government House, Pretoria, to David Pollock, 31 March 1909, both in Natal Government Records (on microfilm), Reel 4, Accession No. 2177, NMML.
65. Minute dated 28 April 1909, ibid.
66. *CWMG*, IX, pp. 238–9. Unfortunately, we do not know the titles or authors of the books given to Gandhi by Smuts.
67. J. C. Smuts, *Jan Christian Smuts* (London: Cassell and Company, 1952), p. 107.
68. Speech of 24 March 1909, in *Fourth Session of the Twenty-Eighth Parliament of the United Kingdom of Great Britain and Ireland*, I; *16 February 1909 to 26 May 1909* (London: HMSO, 1909).
69. W. K. Hancock: *Smuts, I: The Sanguine Years, 1870–1919* (Cambridge: Cambridge University Press, 1962), p. 44.
70. Wolstenholme to Smuts, 14 May 1909, in Hancock and van der Poel, *Smuts Papers*, vol. II, pp. 568–73.
71. These poems are available in Gujarati and in English translations in Surendra Bhana and Neelima Shukla-Bhatt, *A Fire That Blazed in the Ocean: Gandhi and the Poems of Satyagraha in South Africa, 1909–1911* (New Delhi: Promilla and Co., 2011), pp. 18–19, 26, 71–3, 87–8, 112–13, etc.
72. Letter dated 28 December 1908, *CWMG*, IX, p. 118.
73. *AC*, 17 July 1909. On Shankeranand, see also Ashwin Desai and Goolam Vahed, *Inside Indenture: A South African Story, 1860–1914* (Durban: Madiba Publishers, 2007), pp. 240–48.
74. Gandhi to Manilal, 25 March 1909, *CWMG*, IX, pp. 205–9.
75. Gandhi to Polak, 26 April 1909, *CWMG*, IX, pp. 205–9, 212–13.

76. Gandhi, *An Autobiography*, Part IV, Chapter XII.

77. George Paxton, *Gandhi's South African Secretary: Sonja Schlesin* (Glasgow: Pax Books, 2006), pp. 14–15, 100–101.

78. See *IO*, 29 May 1909.

79. *CWMG*, IX, pp. 215–19.

80. *CWMG*, IX, pp. 243–4.

81. Cf. S. N. 4938, SAAA.

82. Clipping, *c.* June 1909, from *Springfield Daily Republican*, S. N. 5022, SAAA. It is appropriate (cf. Chapter 5 above) that *The Nation* ran what seems to have been the first article on Gandhi in the American press; and that another newspaper active in the movement against slavery, the *Springfield Daily Republican*, carried what most likely was the first account of Gandhian satyagraha to appear in America.

83. Gandhi to Polak, dated 'Monday' and 'Tuesday' (i.e. 21 and 22 June 1909), in Mss. Eur. B. 272, APAC/BL. These handwritten letters, which lie in the British Library, are not in *CWMG*; this writer may be the first to have read them since Polak himself.

84. *CWMG*, IX, pp. 267–8.

85. *CWMG*, IX, pp. 270, 286–7.

86. See 'A Suggestive Letter', *IO*, 10 July 1909.

15 BIG LITTLE CHIEF

1. Letter to Olive Doke dated 5 July 1909 (not in *CWMG*), Doke Papers, UNISA.

2. *CWMG*, IX, pp. 269–74, 276–9, 281–3.

3. *CWMG*, IX, pp. 284–8.

4. Memorandum dated Brixton Prison, 22 July 1909, by S. R. Dyer, Medical Officer, in CRIM/1/113/5, NAUK.

5. Statement by Madan Lal Dhingra dated 10 July 1909, ibid.

6. David Garnett, quoted in Lesley Chamberlain, 'Bloomsbury's Teenage Terrorist', *Standpoint*, July/August 2011.

7. Cf. V. N. Datta, *Madan Lal Dhingra and the Revolutionary Movement* (New Delhi: Vikas Publishing House, 1978), pp. 38–41. The references to Rama, Krishna and Mother India do not appear in the archival record of the trial.

8. Cited in James D. Hunt, *Gandhi in London* (revised edn, New Delhi: Promilla and Co, 1993), pp. 106–7.

9. *IO*, 14 August 1909, *CWMG*, IX, pp. 302–3.

10. Gandhi to Polak, letters of 20 August, 26 August, 2 September and 29 September 1909, *CWMG*, IX, pp. 363, 368–9, 382–3, 438–40.

11. Letter of 8 September, *CWMG*, IX, p. 395.

12. Gandhi to Kallenbach, letters of 21 June, 3 July, 20 August, 30 August and 10 September 1909, *CWMG*, XCVI, pp. 9–10, 13, 23, 25. In one letter, Gandhi wrote that he had kept a bottle of Vaseline on his mantelpiece in London to remind him of Kallenbach. This prompted a speculative paragraph by Joseph Lelyveld on what the Vaseline was for (*Great Soul: Mahatma Gandhi's Struggle with India*, New York: Alfred A. Knopf, 2008, p. 89). He concluded that it was mostly likely for enemas. One of his reviewers, however, felt that 'there could be less generous explanations', meaning that it was to remind Gandhi of the (homo)sexual intercourse he was presumed (by the reviewer) to practise with Kallenbach. (Andrew Roberts, 'Among the Hagiographers', *Wall Street Journal*, 26 March 2011.) In fact, Lelyveld had missed a reference in the letter to Gandhi suffering from corns. That was what the Vaseline was for; to treat the blisters under his feet caused by long walks in London. The walks that Gandhi undertook in Johannesburg were often in the company of Kallenbach; hence the reference to corns and Vaseline.

13. Gandhi to Olive Doke, 18 August 1909 (not in *CWMG*), C. M. Doke Papers, UNISA.

14. See www.oxforddnb.com/view/printable/35874 (accessed 17 February 2012).

15. See Ampthill to L. W. Ritch, 28 July 1909, S. N. 4964, SAAA.

16. *CWMG*, IX, pp. 318–21, 576–8.

17. Gandhi to Merriman, letters of 15 and 16 July 1909, copies in E. S. Reddy Papers, New York. (These letters were sourced by Mr Reddy from the Merriman papers in Cape Town and are not in *CWMG*.)

18. General Smuts to Lord Crewe, 26 August 1909, in *Further Correspondence Relating to Legislation Affecting Asiatics in the Transvaal* (*Cd. 5363 – in continuation of Cd. 4854*; London: HMSO, 1910).

19. Ampthill to Smuts, 10 August 1909; Ampthill to Gandhi, 31 August 1909, *CWMG*, IX, pp. 583–4, 587–8.

20. Doke to Kallenbach, 12 August 1909, in KP.

21. *IO*, 21 August 1909, *CWMG*, IX, p. 313.

22. Cf. Florence Winterbottom to M. K. Gandhi, 16 August 1909, S. N. 4945, NGM.

23. *CWMG*, IX, pp. 368–9, 502.

24. See 'Gandhi, Tolstoy, and the Tolstoyans', in James D. Hunt, *An American Looks at Gandhi: Essays in Satyagraha, Civil Rights and Peace* (New Delhi: Promilla and Co., 2005).

25. On Tolstoy's correspondence with Indians other than Gandhi, see Alexander Shifman, *Tolstoy and India*, trans. A. V. Esualov (2nd edn, New Delhi: Sahtiya Akademi, 1978); D. V. Gundappa, *Tolstoy and India* (Bangalore: The Swadeshi Library, 1909). On Taraknath Das, see Tapan K. Mukherjee, *Taraknath Das: Life and Letters of a Revolutionary in Exile* (Calcutta: National Council of Education, 1997).

26. *CWMG*, XI, pp. 444–6, 448–50.

27. The 'Letter to a Hindu' and Gandhi's introduction to it are available at http://www.gutenberg.org/ebooks/7176 (accessed 14 February 2010).

28. Joseph J. Doke, *M. K. Gandhi: An Indian Patriot in South Africa* (London: The London Indian Chronicle, 1909), pp. 7, 8, 23, 84, 92–3, etc.

29. In a letter written at about the same time to the Madras editor G. A. Natesan, Gandhi said the forthcoming meeting of the Indian National Congress should concentrate its attention on the South African struggle, for it might then 'perchance find out that for the many ills we suffer from in India it is an infallible panacea'. He was 'sure it will be found that it is the only weapon suited to the genius of our people and our land'. See *CWMG*, IX, pp. 506–7.

To the Indian patriot, Gandhi wrote that passive resistance would solve their country's problems; to the great Russian writer, he argued that the method was actually of universal significance.

30. This discussion of the correspondence between Tolstoy and Gandhi is based on *CWMG*, IX, pp. 444–6, 448–50, 483, 528–9, 593.

31. Mehta to Gandhi, 29 September 1909, S. N. 5101, SAAA.

32. Mehta to Gandhi, 27 September 1909, S. N. 5097, SAAA.

33. *CWMG*, IX, pp. 406–11.

34. Polak to Gandhi, letters of 14 and 21 August 1909, S. N. 5011 and 5021, SAAA.

35. Polak to Gandhi, 9 September 1909, S. N. 5061, SAAA. Lord Curzon had been a controversial Viceroy, whose decision to partition Bengal had provoked widespread popular protest.

36. See reports and clippings in File No. 242, Part I, G. K. Gokhale Papers, NAI; and in L/P&J/6/1000, APAC/BL.

37. Polak to Gandhi, 19 October 1909, S. N. 5138, SAAA.

38. See reports in File 184, L/P&J/6/917, APAC/BL.

39. Gandhi to Polak, 14 October 1909, *CWMG*, IX, p. 478.

40. Polak to Gandhi, letters of 7 and 14 October 1909, S. N. 5116 and 5126, SAAA.

41. H. S. L. Polak, *The Indians of South Africa: Helots Within the Empire and How They Are Treated* (Madras: G. A. Natesan and Co., 1909), Part I, pp. 4, 21, 70ff; Part II, pp. 16–17, 22–3, 41, 43–4.

42. See *Report of the Protector of Indian Immigrants for the Year ending 31 December, 1909*, in Natal Government Records (on microfilm), Reel No. 6., Accession No. 2179, NMML.

43. Anon., *M. K. Gandhi: A Sketch of His Life and Work* (Madras: G. A. Natesan and Co., 1910).

44. See *CWMG*, IX, pp. 436–7.

45. Polak to Gandhi, 7 October 1909, S. N. 5116, SAAA.

46. Letter of 23 September, 1909, *CWMG*, IX, pp. 429f.

47. Polak to Gandhi, 7 October 1909, S. N. 5116, SAAA.

48. 'Mr Polak's Visit to Rangoon', *IO*, 22 January 1910.

49. Pranjivan Mehta to G. K. Gokhale, dated Rangoon, 8 November 1909, File No. 4, Servants of India Society Papers, NMML.

50. Cf. the names appended to the notice of the meeting in the Town Hall, Calcutta, 3 December 1909, copy in E. S. Reddy Papers, NMML.

51. H. S. L. Polak to G. K. Gokhale, 10 January 1910, File No. 242, Part I, Gokhale Papers, NAI; report on Banaras meeting in *IO*, 12 February 1910.

52. First published in *Bande Matram*, 11 to 23 April 1907, reprinted in Sri Aurobindo, *Bande Matram: Early Political Writings* (Pondicherry: Sri Aurobindo Ashram, 1972; fourth impression 1995), pp. 90–123.

53. 'The Transvaal Indians', first published in *Karmayogin*, 11 December 1909, reprinted in Sri Aurobindo, *Karmayogin: Political Writings and Speeches, 1909–1910* (Pondicherry: Sri Aurobindo Ashram Trust, 1997), pp. 347–9. I am grateful to Peter Heehs for this reference.

54. See Peter Heehs, *The Lives of Sri Aurobindo* (New York: Columbia University Press, 2009).

55. Reports in *IO*, 10 July and 25 September 1909.

56. Editorial in *IO*, 20 November 1909.

57. See *IO*, 6 and 13 November 1909.

58. *IO*, 9 September 1909.

59. *IO*, 3 April 1909.

60. C. K. T. Naidoo to Gandhi, 4 October 1909, S. N. 5107, SAAA.

61. *CWMG*, IX, p. 499; Dhananjay Keer, *Veer Savarkar* (1950; 3rd edn, Bombay: Popular Prakashan, 1988), pp. 62–4.

62. Asaf Ali, 'Gandhiji: 1909–1920', in Chandrashanker Shukla, ed., *Reminiscences of Gandhiji* (Bombay: Vora and Co., 1951), p. 17.

63. Letter of 30 October 1909, *CWMG*, IX, pp. 508–9.

64. *CWMG*, IX, pp. 450–51.

65. *CWMG*, IX, pp. 531–2.

66. *CWMG*, IX, pp. 352–3, 417, 435–6, 495.

67. Gandhi to Ramdas, 27 November 1909, *CWMG*, XI, pp. 81–2.

68. Francis Hopwood, Under-Secretary of State for the Colonies, to M. K. Gandhi, 3 November 1909, in *Further Correspondence Relating to Legislation Affecting Asiatics (Cd. 5363)*.

69. *CWMG*, IX, pp. 514–17, 527.

70. S. N. 5156, SAAA.

71. 'Notes of a meeting held at the Westminster Palace Hotel on November 12th 1909 to bid farewell to the Transvaal British Indian Association', in File No. 242, Part I, Gokhale Papers, NAI.

72. See *CWMG*, IX, pp. 539–43.

73. Ritch to Polak, 19 November 1909, in File No. 242, Part I, Gokhale Papers, NAI.

74. *CWMG*, IX, pp. 533–4.

75. H. S. L. Polak, 'Early Years (1869–1914)', in H. S. L. Polak, H. N. Brailsford and Lord Pethick-Lawrence, *Mahatma Gandhi* (London: Oldhams Press Limited, 1949), p. 17.

76. Gandhi to Polak, 15 November 1909, *CWMG*, XCVI (Supplementary Volume – Six), pp. 34–6.

77. Gandhi to Millie Polak, 14 November 1909, *CWMG*, XCVI (Supplementary Volume – Six), pp. 32–3.

78. Millie Graham Polak, *Mr Gandhi: The Man* (London: George Allen and Unwin, 1931), pp. 124–5.

79. Ampthill to Curzon, 14 November 1909, Mss. Eur. F. 112/79, APAC/BL.

16   THE CONTEST OF CIVILIZATIONS

1. M. K. Gandhi, *Hind Swaraj and Other Writings*, ed. Anthony Parel (Cambridge: Cambridge University Press, 1997), editor's introduction, p. xiv.

2. In writing about *Hind Swaraj*, it is hard to keep out of one's mind the continuing debates about what the book means to us now. But this is a biography, not a work of political or literary criticism. In what follows, I write about the book in terms of what it meant to Gandhi and his readers, *at the time it was published and circulated*. For recent writings on or around *Hind Swaraj*, see Varsha Das, ed., *Gandhiji on* Hind Swaraj *and Select Views of Others* (New Delhi: National Gandhi Museum, 2009); M. K. Gandhi, *Indian Home Rule (*Hind Swaraj*)*, a centenary edition introduced by S. R. Mehrotra (New Delhi: Rajendra Prasad Academy, 2010); Suresh Sharma and Tridip Suhrud, eds and trans, *M. K. Gandhi's* Hind Swaraj: *A Critical Edition* (Hyderabad: Orient BlackSwan, 2010). The journal *Aryan Path*, in its issue of September 1938, published a fascinating and still readable symposium on *Hind Swaraj*, with contributions from (among others) the Nobel prize–winning chemist Frederick Soddy, the economist G. D. H. Cole and the critic John Middleton Murry.

3. G. K. Chesterton, 'Our Notebook', *Illustrated London News*, 18 September 1909.

4. *IO*, 8 January 1910, *CWMG*, IX, p. 425 (the article was written by Gandhi in the last week of October 1909).

5. *CWMG*, IX, pp. 457–60.

6. *CWMG*, IX, pp. 475–6.

7. *CWMG*, IX, pp. 477–82.

8. The case that Pranjivan Mehta was the 'Reader' of *Hind Swaraj* has been convincingly made by S. R. Mehrotra. See his *Gandhiji ké Aajivan Ananya Mitra* [Gandhi's Intimate Lifelong Friend] (Allahabad: Etawah Hindi Seva Nidhi, 2008); and his introduction to the centenary edition of *Indian Home Rule*.

9. Gandhi, *Hind Swaraj* (ed. Parel) pp. 14–16, 17, 31, 38, 47, 52, 58, 61, 63–4, 71, 89–90, 93–5, 105–6, 112–19, etc.

10. Cf. the eyewitness accounts of the Surat Congress reproduced in Govind Talwalkar, *Gopal Krishna Gokhale: His Life and Times* (New Delhi: Rupa and Co., 2006), pp. 381–6.

11. The standard work on the Swadeshi movement remains Sumit Sarkar, *The Swadeshi Movement in Bengal, 1905–7* (first published 1973; new edn, Ranikhet: Permanent Black, 2010).

12. Gokhale to William Wedderburn, letters of 24 May 1907 and 24 September 1909, in B. N. Pandey, ed., *The Indian Nationalist Movement, 1885–1947: Select Documents* (London: Macmillan, 1979), pp. 7–8, 10–11.

13. These paragraphs draw on Amales Tripathi, *The Extremist Challenge: India between 1890 and 1910* (Bombay: Orient Longmans, 1967) and Peter Heehs, *The Bomb in Bengal: The Rise of Revolutionary Terrorism in India, 1900–1910* (Delhi: Oxford University Press, 1993). Tripathi (p. 134) notes that the Bhagavad Gita was a constant companion of the revolutionaries of Bengal. 'In their hands, it was a more terrible weapon than the bomb. It steeled them for the killing, which was God's will and ordained decree, and it assured them of salvation through death in God's service. The Gita provided a better philosophy of tyrannicide than Bakunin.' Heehs, for his part, gives us such revealing chapter titles as 'Militancy in a Vanquished Land' and 'Mother Kali's Bomb'.

14. Valentine Chirol, *Indian Unrest* (London: Macmillan and Co., 1910), pp. 324, 321–2. This book was based on reports published in *The Times*, some of which Gandhi must have read.

15. Henry W. Nevinson, *The New Spirit in India* (London: Harper and Brothers, 1908), pp. 321–2.

16. Syed Shamsuddin Kadri, Oriental Translator, Government of Bombay, to Commissioner of Police, 16 February 1910, in B Proceedings nos. 4–5, Home (Political), NAI.

17. Bombay Government notification dated 17 March 1910; Home Department note dated 12 April, both ibid.

18. M. K. Gandhi to Home Secretary, Government of India, 16 April 1910, in A Proceedings nos. 96–103, Home (Political), NAI. This letter is not in *CWMG*; it was discovered in the National Archives of India by Professor S. R. Mehrotra, who generously shared it with me.

19. This is reproduced, with a brief preface by Anthony Parel, in *Gandhi Marg*, issue of July–September 1993, pp. 240–54.

20. Note signed 'A. L.', dated 27 May 1910, in A Proceedings nos. 96–103, Home (Political), NAI.

21. Note by C. R. Cleveland, dated 24 June 1910, ibid.

22. 'Anglo-Indian Funk', *AC*, 19 March 1910.

23. Note by S. H. Slater, dated 13 May 1910; note by A. G. Cardew, dated 19 May 1910, both in G. O. No. 753, 21 May 1910, Judicial Department, Tamil Nadu State Archives, Chennai.

24. Edward Dallow to Lord Crewe, 7 June 1909, in File 2757, L/P&J/6/954, APAC/BL.

25. I have here used a clipping of the printed review in the Doke Papers, UNISA, which has 'Transvaal Leader, May 1910' written on it by hand. It seems to have been published on 2 May, since it is mentioned by Gandhi to Gokhale in a letter of that date (cf. CWMG, X, pp. 239-40).

26. Typescript dated 4 May 1910, marked 'unsigned reply by M. K. G. to E. Dallow's Review of "Indian Home Rule"', in C. M. Doke Papers, UNISA. This rejoinder is not in CWMG; nor, apparently, was it published in the *Transvaal Leader*.

27. Cf. Bala Pillay, *British Indians in the Transvaal: Trade, Politics and Imperial Relations, 1885-1906* (London: Longman, 1976), pp. 75-6.

28. See CWMG, X, pp. 507-10, 246-50.

29. See CWMG, XI, pp. 203-7, 249-50.

30. Cf. Lindy Moore, 'The Reputation of Isabella Fyvie Mayo', *Women's History Review*, 19:1 (2010).

31. Isabella Fyvie Mayo to Hermann Kallenbach, 3 February 1911, in KP.

32. Cf. Gandhi to Doke, letters of 21 January and 5 February 1910 (not in CWMG), C. M. Doke Papers.

17   SEEKING A SETTLEMENT

1. CWMG, XI, pp. 81-2.

2. See B. R. Nanda, *Gokhale: The Indian Moderates and the British Raj* (Princeton: Princeton University Press, 1977), Chapter 16.

3. Ratan Tata to G. K. Gokhale, 17 December 1907, in File No. 4, Servants of India Society Papers, NMML.

4. Ratan Tata to Gokhale, 29 November 1909, File No. 242, Part I, Gokhale Papers, NAI.

5. Gokhale to Gandhi, 3 December 1909; undated press statement (c. first week of December 1909), both ibid.

6. See correspondence and reports, ibid.

7. CWMG, XI, pp. 86-7, 90-92.

8. Gandhi to Kallenbach, dated 'Monday' (c. end December 1909), in KP (this letter is not in CWMG).

9. See reports in IO, 25 December 1909.

10. IO, 22 January 1910.

11. CWMG, XI, pp. 96-8, 101, 103-4, 128-30, 140-41, 149-50, 153.

12. Sonja Schlesin to Gandhi, 31 July 1913, S. N. 5829, SAAA.

13. Gandhi, *Satyagraha in South Africa*, pp. 165–6.
14. *CWMG*, X, pp. 503–5. Much later, Diepkloof was where the liberal reformer (and novelist) Alan Paton served as a warden.
15. See piece from *The Outlook*, reproduced in *IO*, 1 April 1905. Phillips may also have been the author of an extraordinary essay written in December 1903, which chastised laws aimed at Indians as unchristian, while asking: 'And at this season, too, when thoughts of Christendom are said to be sweetly stirred by the memory of a Message and a Messenger, shall the Teacher's lessons be held so lightly that upon His very anniversary the demon of injustice shall mount triumphant, and virtue and brotherly charity be heartlessly trampled beneath the heel of mercenary greed, and callous indifference to sufferings about to be inflicted?' See 'The Excommunication of a People', *IO*, 3 December 1903.
16. Report in *IO*, 26 February 1910.
17. *CWMG*, X, pp. 117–19.
18. The speech is reproduced in full in R. P. Patwardhan and D. V. Ambekar, eds, *Speeches and Writings of Gopal Krishna Gokhale*, I: *Economic* (Poona: The Deccan Sabha, 1966), pp. 284–94.
19. Proceedings of the Council of the Governor-General of India, 25 February 1910, in Natal Government House Records, Reel 4, Accession No. 2177, NMML.
20. *CWMG*, X, p. 201.
21. L. W. Ritch to Colonial Office, letters of 16 April, 9 May and 7 June 1910, in *Further Correspondence Relating to Legislation Affecting Asiatics in the Transvaal (Cd. 5363 – in continuation of Cd. 4854)* (London: HMSO, 1910).
22. *CWMG*, X, p. 263.
23. Kallenbach to Gandhi, 30 May 1910, in KP.
24. See 'The Passive Resistance Farm', *IO*, 18 June 1910.
25. Polak once wrote to Gokhale that 'you have an ally against Gandhi and myself regarding the simple life in Mrs Polak' (letter of 10 January 1910, File No. 242, Part I, Gokhale Papers, NAI). Polak's support for the simple life was in any case largely theoretical; over time, Millie's views in this regard became his, too.
26. *CWMG*, X, pp. 262, 272, 288–90, 297, etc; reports in *IO*, 13 August and 15 October 1910, 4 January 1911, etc.
27. Gandhi to Maganlal, 21 August 1910, *CWMG*, X, pp. 307–8. Years later, Ramdas Gandhi recalled the rigid regimen by reproducing the Farm's daily timetable in his memoirs:

    5.30: Wake-up
    5.30 to 7: Cleaning and Prayer
    7 to 8: Work in the fields
    8 to 9: Breakfast

9 to 11: Work in the fields, in the kitchen, and in the printing press

11 to 1: Bath, lunch, washing dishes and rest

1 to 4.30: School

4.30 to 5.30: Work in the fields and collect firewood

5.30 to 6.30: Sports and Games (football, cricket, kabaddi, etc)

6.30 to 7: Supper, cleaning of kitchen

7 to 8: Prayer and reading of religious texts

8 to 10: Relaxation

10 to 5.30: Sleep

See Ramadas Gandhi, *Sansmaran,* translated from Gujarati to Hindi by Shankar Joshi (Ahmedabad: Navajivan Press, 1970), p. 36. (The translation from the Hindi is mine.)

28. *IO*, 22 October 1910, *CWMG*, X, p. 340.

29. One supposes an exception was made for African peons and cleaners.

30. *CWMG*, X, pp. 113, 176–7. In apartheid-era terminology 'Coloured people' referred to those of mixed race; Gandhi, however, was using the term to denote those who were not white, who included blacks, Indians, Chinese, and those of mixed race.

31. *CWMG*, X, pp. 182–4.

32. Letter dated 27 August 1910 (translated from the German probably by Christian Bartolf), in KP.

33. These paragraphs are based on *CWMG*, X, pp. 369–70, 512–4.

34. See reports in *IO*, 23 April, 21 and 28 May, etc.

35. Report in *IR*, May 1910.

36. P. K. Naidu, 'Five Times to the Transvaal Jail', *IR*, September 1910. P. K. Naidu was not related to Thambi Naidoo.

37. Leung Quinn, 'A Chinese View of the Transvaal Trouble', *IR*, June 1910.

38. Chief Secretary, Madras Government, to Commerce and Industry Secrerary, Government of India, 13 August 1910, in File 3604, L/P&J/6/1037, APAC/BL.

39. Commissioner of Police to Bombay Government, 24 May 1910, in File 3200, L/P&J/6/1031, APAC/BL.

40. See Gandhi to Gokhale, 25 April 1910, *CWMG*, X, pp. 229–33.

41. Ratan Tata to G. K. Gokhale, 8 July 1910, File No. 242, Part I, Gokhale Papers, NAI.

42. Ratan Tata to G. K. Gokhale, 22 September 1910, File No. 242, Part I, Gokhale Papers, NAI; emphasis in original.

43. 'Ghandi' and 'Ghandy' are both variant spellings of Gandhi, especially common among Parsis.

44. See S. N. 5192 and 5193, SAAA.

45. Reports in *IO*, 3 September and 5 November 1910.

46. See report in *IR*, August 1910. Mrs Besant was speaking as an Irishwoman who had embraced the cause of Indian freedom herself.

47. The poem is reproduced in Surendra Bhana and Neelima Shukla-Bhatt, *A Fire That Blazed in the Ocean: Gandhi and the Poems of Satyagraha in South Africa, 1909–1911* (New Delhi: Promilla and Co., 2011), pp. 164–5.
48. See *NM*, 5 October 1910.
49. See reports in *IO*, 1 and 8 October 1910; *NM*, 5 October 1910.
50. Prabhudas Gandhi, *My Childhood with Gandhiji* (Ahmedabad: Navajivan Publishing House, 1957), pp. 56, 135.
51. Cf. *CWMG*, X, pp. 336–7, 355, 375, 446, 476.
52. *CWMG*, X, pp. 350–53.
53. 'A Great Day at Tolstoy Farm', *IO*, 31 December 1910.
54. *CWMG*, X, pp. 392–5.
55. All-India Moslem League, London, to Colonial Office, 17 January 1911; Governor-General of South Africa to Secretary of State for the Colonies, 15 March 1911, both in CO 879/108/1, NAUK.
56. Letter dated 3 March 1911, in File No. 427, Gokhale Papers, NAI.
57. *CWMG*, XI, pp. 412–14, 424–6.
58. *CWMG*, XI, pp. 446–7.
59. *CWMG*, X, pp. 477–8, 487–8, 491–2, 530, 531–2.
60. Memorandum dated 26 November 1911 by H. J. Stanley, Add Mss. 46004, BL.
61. Extract from the *Transvaal Leader*, 27 September 1911, File 4625, L/P&J/6/1125, APAC/BL.
62. Ritch to Gandhi, 15 March 1911, S. N. 5294, SAAA.
63. Aiyar to Gokhale, 18 March 1911, in File No. 242, Part I, Gokhale Papers, NAI.
64. Editorial in *Rand Daily Mail*, 28 March 1911, clipping in C. M. Doke Papers, UNISA.
65. *CWMG*, X, pp. 494–6.
66. This discussion of the provisional settlement is based on *CWMG*, XI, pp. 5–39, 49, 515–16, 519–20.
67. *CWMG*, XI, pp. 45, 56–7.
68. Extract from the *Rand Daily Mail*, 28 April 1911, in Natal Government House Records, Reel 7, Accession No. 2180, NMML.
69. *Star*, 28 April 1911, clipping in C. M. Doke Papers.
70. *CWMG*, XI, pp. 90–92.
71. *IO*, 6 May 1911.
72. 'Successful Banquet in Johannesburg', *IO*, 17 June 1911.

18 A SON DEPARTS, A MENTOR ARRIVES

1. Gandhi to Maganlal, 21 August 1910, *CWMG*, X, p. 273.
2. Gandhi to Harilal, 5 March 1911, *CWMG*, X, pp. 428–9.

3. Gandhi to Maganlal, 19 March 1911, *CWMG*, X, p. 476.

4. Chandulal Bhagubhai Dalal, *Harilal Gandhi: A Life*, edited and translated from the Gujarati by Tridip Suhrud (Chennai: Orient Longman, 2007), pp. 28–9.

5. Pragji Desai, 'Satyagraha in South Africa', in Chandrashanker Shukla, ed., *Reminiscences of Gandhiji* (Bombay: Vora and Co., 1951), p. 83. Desai was a resident of Phoenix, who had been arrested several times during the satyagraha campaigns.

6. Harilal to Gandhi, *c.* 8 May 1911, copy in E. S. Reddy Papers, NMML. This letter was not available to Harilal's biographer C. B. Dalal. The original is lost, but a copy was retrieved by E. S. Reddy from the library of the University of Cape Town.

7. As recalled in Pragji Desai, 'Satyagraha in South Africa', pp. 82–3.

8. Cf. Gandhi to Pranjivan Mehta, 8 May 1911, *CWMG*, XI, p. 65.

9. Dalal, *Harilal Gandhi*, pp. 29–30.

10. Gandhi to Maganlal, 18 May 1911, *CWMG*, XI, pp. 77–8.

11. Dalal, *Harilal Gandhi*, Appendix I, p. 134 (from a letter written in 1915 or 1916).

12. Cf. appreciation by Millie Graham Polak, originally published in the *Indian Review*, reprinted in *Mahatma Gandhi: An Enlarged and Up-to-Date Edition of His Life and Teaching with an Account of His Activities in South Africa and India Down to His Great March, in Connection with 'Salt Satyagraha'* (Madras: G. A. Natesan and Co., 1930), pp. 13f.

13. Cf. Tridip Suhrud, *Reading Gandhi in Two Tongues and Other Essays* (Shimla: Indian Institute of Advanced Study, 2012), pp. 24–5; Pragji Desai, 'Satyagraha in South Africa', in Chandrashanker Shukla, ed., *Reminiscences of Gandhiji* (Bombay: Vora and Co., 1951), pp. 82–3.

14. Desai, 'Satyagraha in South Africa', p. 84.

15. Gandhi to Harilal, 27 May 1911, *CWMG*, XI, pp. 94–5.

16. See *CWMG*, XI, pp. 165–7, 312–13, 315–16, 333–4.

17. *CWMG*, XI, pp. 129–31, 149–50, 154, 157.

18. Nalini Ranjan Chakravarti, *The Indian Minority in Burma: The Rise and Decline of an Immigrant Community* (London: Oxford University Press, 1971), pp. 98–9.

19. Regrettably, while no biography of Marx can be written without taking full account of Engels's contribution, and while there have been several excellent biographies of Engels himself, this may be the first book on Gandhi to attempt to give Pranjivan Mehta something like his due. The historian S. R. Mehrotra is now completing a biography of Mehta.

20. P. J. Mehta, *M. K. Gandhi and the South African Indian Problem* (Madras: G. A. Natesan and Co., 1912), pp. 21–2, 26–32, 74, 87, 96.

21. *CWMG*, XI, pp. 138–9.

22. Gandhi to Mehta, 25 August 1911, *CWMG*, XI, pp. 130–33.

23. Cf. Polak to Mehta, 22 August 1911, copy in E. S. Reddy Papers, NMML.

24. *CWMG*, XCVI (Supplementary Volume Six: Gandhi–Kallenbach Correspondence), pp. 62–3; Ramadas Gandhi, *Sansmaran*, translated from Gujarati to Hindi by Shankar Joshi (Ahmedabad: Navajivan Press, 1970), p. 48.

25. See entry for 11 September 1911, Kallenbach Diary, KP.

26. Gandhi to Kallenbach, 7 October 1911, KP (not in *CWMG*).

27. Gandhi to Mehta, 24 September 1911, *CWMG*, XI, pp. 160–61. 'Ivan the Fool' is a fable of three brothers, one brilliant and warlike, the second smart and acquisitive, the third foolish yet upright, in which the honesty and hard work of the last is rewarded by the love of his family and his community. See 'The Story of Ivan the Fool' in *More Tales from Tolstoi*, trans. R. Nisbet Bain (1902; reprint, New York: Core Collection Books, 1979).

28. Gandhi to Mehta, 10 October 1911, *CWMG*, XI, pp. 165–7.

29. *CWMG*, XI, pp. 168–71, 296–7. Gandhi and Manilal Doctor first met in London in 1906, when the young man was qualifying to be a barrister. At Gandhi's suggestion, he went to Mauritius to work with the Indians there. It may, or may not, have been Gandhi who suggested to Pranjivan Mehta that Doctor would be a suitable husband for his daughter Jeki.

30. Kallenbach to Mehta, 18 October 1912, copy in KP.

31. *AC*, 23 June 1910.

32. *AC*, 11 March 1911.

33. *AC*, issues of 23 September, 7 and 14 October 1911.

34. See L/P&J/6/1017, APAC/BL.

35. P. Subramania Aiyar, *An Unjust Tax on Indian Immigrants: Appeal to the Empire* (Durban: African Chronicle Printing Works, 1911), in File 3810, L/P&J/1113, APAC/BL.

36. Minute dated 6 February 1912, ibid.

37. Gandhi to West, 27 November 1911, *CWMG*, XCVI, pp. 93–4.

38. Gandhi to Tata, 1 April 1912, *CWMG*, XI, pp. 248–53.

39. Memorial dated 1 August 1912, in L/P&J/6/1226, APAC/BL.

40. 'A Native Union: The Lessons of the Passive Resistance Movement', *IO*, 29 July 1911.

41. I am grateful to the Gandhi scholar Anil Nauriya for sharing this information with me. The memoirist, a Russian Jew named Pauline Podlashuk, may incidentally have helped in translating Tolstoy's letter to Gandhi.

42. Quoted in Edward Roux, *Time Longer Than Rope: The Black Man's Struggle for Freedom in South Africa* (first published 1948; 2nd edn, Madison: University of Wisconsin Press, 1964), p. 110.

43. See André Odendaal, *Black Protest Politics in South Africa to 1912* (Totowa, NJ: Barnes and Noble Books, 1984), Chapter 11.

44. 'The Awakening of the Natives: Mr Dube's Address', *IO*, 10 February 1912. Cf. also A. P. Walshe, 'The Origins of African Political Consciousness in South Africa', *Journal of Modern African Studies*, 7:4 (1969), pp. 595f.

45. *CWMG*, XI, pp. 213–17, 227–8, 231, 241, 254, 264, 275, 556–8.

46. Assembly Debates of the Union of South Africa, 30 May and 14 June 1912, in Natal Government House Records, Reel 7, Accession No. 2180, NMML.

47. See S. N. 5662, SAAA.

48. Cf. enclosures in Governor-General of South Africa to Secretary of State for the Colonies, 13 April 1912, in CD 879/111/2, NAUK.

49. S. N. 5658, SAAA (emphasis in original).

50. Mehta to Gandhi, *c.* September 1911 (written from Hotel Genève, Marseille), S. N. 5588, SAAA.

51. Gokhale to Union Castle Company, letters dated 24 and 29 July 1912, copies in File No. 242, Part I, Gokhale Papers, NAI.

52. See Gokhale to Gandhi, 7 July 1912, S. N. 5672, SAAA. There are two letters extant from this period by Maud Polak to Gandhi. At his suggestion – or command – she had begun to call him *Bapu*, 'Father'. Still, it appears that her love for him remained deep, and even obsessive. One letter begs him to allow her to continue lobbying for the Indians in London; it goes on to claim that her work was as important as Gokhale's in stopping the export of indentured labour from India. A second letter, fourteen handwritten pages in length, presents a rambling, somewhat incoherent account of what she had got from Gandhi's book *Hind Swaraj*. See Maud Polak to Gandhi, letters of 6 December 1911 and 23 December 1912, S. N. 5594 and 5600, SAAA. There are no replies by Gandhi on record. Perhaps there were none, since her own brother told Gandhi that 'Maud is quite unbalanced. She much disappoints me. I shall not reply to her letter.' (Henry Polak to Gandhi, 19 January 1911, S. N. 5204, SAAA.)

53. Dr Maitland Park, editor *Cape Times*, to General Louis Botha, 13 August 1912; Botha to Park, 23 August 1912, both in Natal Government House Records, Reel 5, Accession No. 2178, NMML. Another Cape liberal, the politician J. X. Merriman, wrote to Smuts on similar liness, urging that the Government treat him with respect, and not 'as a mere *kleurling* [coloured person]'. Merriman to Smuts, 3 October 1912, in W. K. Hancock and Jean van der Poel, *Selections from the Smuts Papers*, III: *June 1910 – November 1918* (Cambridge: Cambridge University Press, 1966), pp. 115–16.

54. Mehta to Gokhale, 28 August 1912, in File No. 242, Part II, Gokhale Papers, NAI.

55. *CWMG*, XI, pp. 320–25.

56. *IO*, 14 September 1912.

57. Gandhi to Maganlal, 27 January 1910, *CWMG*, X, pp. 138–9.

58. Kasturba was commanded to find a turban from one of the boxes at Phoenix, iron it and send it by post to Johannesburg. See Prabhudas Gandhi, *My Childhood with Gandhiji* (Ahmedabad: Navajivan Publishing House, 1957), pp. 95–6.

59. Entry for 22 October 1912, in Kallenbach Diary, SAAA.

60. Anon., *Hon. Mr G. K. Gokhale's Visit to South Africa, 1912* (Durban: Indian Opinion, 1912), pp. 4–7.

61. Merriman to Smuts, 25 October 1912, in Hancock and van der Poel, *Selections from the Smuts Papers*, vol. III, p. 119. In other letters written at around the same time, Merriman compared Gokhale to John Dube. Both were 'moderate and civilized', both 'spoke extraordinary good English', both had an intense sense of 'national feeling'. Quoted in Shula Marks, 'The Ambiguities of Dependence: John L. Dube of Natal', *Journal of Southern African Studies*, 1:2 (1975), p. 164.

62. Entry for 25 October 1912, in Kallenbach Diary, SAAA.

63. Anon., *Mr Gokhale's Visit*, pp. 8–9.

64. See report in *IO*, 23 November 1912.

65. Anon., *Mr Gokhale's Visit*, pp. 13, 16–17, 201.

66. *CWMG*, XI, pp. 343–4.

67. *IO*, 9 November 1912.

68. Anon., *Mr Gokhale's Visit*, pp. 34–5.

69. *IO*, 23 November 1912.

70. Letter dated 11 November 1912, in Add Mss. 46006, BL.

71. Cf. Secretary of Interior to G. K. Gokhale, 11 November 1912, in File No. 242, Part I, Gokhale Papers, NAI.

72. Governor-General of South Africa to Secretary of State for the Colonies, 16 November 1912, in CD 879/111/2, NAUK.

73. As recalled in H. S. L. Polak, 'Early Years (1869–1914)', in H. S. L. Polak, H. N. Brailsford and Lord Pethick-Lawrence, *Mahatma Gandhi* (London: Oldhams Press Limited, 1949), pp. 81–2.

74. Anon., *Mr Gokhale's Visit*, p. 4.

75. See reports in *IO*, 19 October, 2 and 30 November, and 28 December 1912.

76. Quoted in Gandhi, *An Autobiography*, Part IV, Chapter XII.

77. Clipping from the *Lourenço Marques Guardian*, 21 November 1912, in File 1398, L/P&J/6/1235, APAC/BL.

78. *CWMG*, XI, p. 414.

79. Entry for 27 November 1912, in Kallenbach Diary, SAAA.

80. Entry for 3 December 1912, ibid.

81. Gandhi to Gokhale, 4 December 1912, *CWMG*, XI, pp. 351–2.

82. This account of Gokhale's speech in Bombay is based on two news reports: that in the *Times of India* (mail edition), 21 December 1912, in Natal Government House Records, Reel 5, Accession No. 2178, NMML; and that in *The Leader*, 19 December 1912, in File No. 242, Part I, Gokhale Papers, NAI.

83. *AC*, 15 June 1912.

84. 'A Puzzling Problem', *AC*, 30 November 1912.

85. *AC*, 28 December 1912.

86. *AC*, 28 December 1912 and 8 February 1913.

19 A PHYSICIAN AT PHOENIX

1. Prabhudas Gandhi, *My Childhood with Gandhiji* (Ahmedabad: Navajivan Publishing House, 1957), pp. 44–5.
2. Millie Graham Polak, *Mr Gandhi: The Man* (London: George Allen and Unwin, 1931), pp. 137–41.
3. *CWMG*, XI, pp. 428–30, 434–6, 441–3, 447–9, 453–5, etc.
4. See Gandhi to Harilal, 26 January 1913, *CWMG*, XI, pp. 449–50.
5. Gandhi to Gokhale, 14 February 1914, *CWMG*, 14 February 1913.
6. Clipping from *Cape Times*, 21 March 1913, in A Proceedings 25–49 for September 1913, Department of Commerce and Industry (Emigration Branch), NAI; *CWMG*, XI, pp. 568–9.
7. *Indian Opinion*, 22 March 1913, *CWMG*, XI, pp. 497.
8. See copies of resolutions enclosed with A. M. Cachalia, Chairman, British Indian Association, to Governor-General of South Africa, 10 April 1913, in A Proceedings 25–49 for September 1913, Department of Commerce and Industry (Emigration Branch), NAI. Cf. also 'Mass Meeting in Johannesburg', *IO*, 5 April 1913.
9. *Indian Opinion*, 19 April 1913; Gandhi to Gokhale, 19 April 1913, *CWMG*, XII, pp. 31, 41.
10. Cf. *IO*, 10 November and 9 December 1911.
11. Cf. *Further Correspondence Relating to a Bill to Regulate Immigration into the Union of South Africa: With Special Reference to Asiatics (In continuation of Cd. 6283)* (London: HMSO, 1913).
12. Telegram dated Durban, 22 April 1913, in Natal Government House Records, Reel 7, Accession No. 2180, NMML.
13. Report in *Rand Daily Mail*, 23 April 1913.
14. Speech of 30 April 1913, ibid.
15. See Union of South Africa: *House of Assembly: Debates of the Third Session of the First Parliament* (Cape Town: Union Parliament of South Africa, 1913), cols. 2050ff, 2235f; Union of South Africa, *Debates of the Senate: Third Session of the First Parliament* (Cape Town: Union Parliament of South Africa, 1913), col. 336.
16. Secretary for the Interior to Gandhi, letters of 4 and 10 April 1913, S. N. 5750 and 5761, SAAA.
17. Back in 1910, Lord Selborne had proposed that Indian women in South Africa be given a cash inducement to return to their homeland. 'It need not require a very large sum to be an inducement to the coolie woman to earn a dowry in this way', he wrote to the Prime Minister, General Botha, adding, 'And of course once in India, I take it, she would have no right to return.' Selborne thought that with these bribes to women 'the [Indian] question would in time resolve itself.' (Lord Selborne to General Louis Botha, 3 May

1910, in Box 60, Selborne Papers, Bodleian Library, Oxford.) Selborne's suggestion was not acted upon; three years later, the Searle judgement outlined another way of reducing the numbers of Indians in South Africa – by not allowing their women to come in from India, rather than bribing those already in South Africa to go back.

18. Extract from *Rand Daily Mail*, 28 April 1914, in File No. 242, Part I, Gokhale Papers, NAI; *CWMG*, XII, pp. 52–3, 59.

19. Cf. H. S. L. Polak to W. Clark, Member, Commerce and Industry, Government of India, letter of 17 April and telegram of 23 April 1913, in A Proceedings nos. 25–49 for September 1913, Department of Commerce and Industry (Emigration Branch), NAI. Copies of these communications were also sent to the Colonial Office in London.

20. A. Fischer, Interior Minister, to Lord Gladstone, Governor-General, 22 April 1913, in File 15/388, vol. 895, GG, NASA.

21. 'Indian Women as Passive Resisters', *IO*, 10 May 1913; also *CWMG*, XII, p. 65.

22. 'From the Editor's Chair', *IO*, 10 May 1913.

23. The letters that follow are all from the Kallenbach Papers in the possession of Isa Sarid, Haifa, Israel.

24. 'Why Mr Gandhi Is a Failure', *AC*, 19 April 1913.

25. *AC*, 24 May 1913. While working-class Tamils in Natal were largely on Gandhi's side, among educated members of the community Aiyar was not alone in having reservations about his leadership. In June 1913 one Leo R. Gopaul wrote to Kallenbach complaining that despite applying several times, he had not been chosen as one of the six educated Indians allowed into the Transvaal as a result of the provisional settlement of 1911. He thought it was because he had once criticized Gandhi's *Hind Swaraj*. Kallenbach wrote back that while Gandhi played no part in the decision, preference would naturally be given to those who had courted arrest in past satyagrahas. This Gopaul (like Aiyar) had conspicuously failed to do. Kallenbach told the complainant that a revival of the struggle was imminent, and he might consider courting arrest this time around. Gopaul to Kallenbach, 10 June 1913; Kallenbach to Gopaul, 19 June 1913, both in KP.

26. *CWMG*, XII, pp. 4–7, 45–52.

27. See *CWMG*, XII, pp. 87–8, 90–91, 101, 574–5.

28. Governor-General to Secretary of State for the Colonies, 16 June 1913, in CO 879/112/4, NAUK.

29. Polak to Gokhale, 1 and 22 June, in File No. 242, Part I, Gokhale Papers, NAI.

30. Gokhale to Legislative Secretary, Government of India, letters of 13 June and 11 July 1913, File 4104, L/P&J/6/1278, APAC/BL.

31. See Maud Polak to Under Secretary of State, Colonial Office, 27 February 1913 (with enclosures); Official report of debate in House of Lords, 30 July, 1913, both in File 1398, L/P&J/6/1235, APAC/BL.

32. Gandhi to Gokhale, 20 June 1913, *CWMG*, XII, pp. 113–15.

33. Wedderburn to Gandhi, letters of 19 and 26 June 1913, S. N. 5813 and 5817a, SAAA.

34. Letter of 2 July 1913, *CWMG*, XII, pp. 122–4.

35. See the correspondence in CO 879/112/4, NAUK.

36. See File 15/462, vol. 896, GG, NASA.

37. 'A South African Problem', *Jewish Chronicle*, 5 September 1913.

38. See *IO*, 12 July 1913; Jack and Ray Simons, *Class and Colour in South Africa, 1850–1950* (Lusaka: International Defence and Aid Fund for Southern Africa, 1983), pp. 156–9.

39. Kallenbach to Isabella Fyvie Mayo, 18 August 1913, KP.

40. Gandhi to E. F. C. Lane, 11 July 1913, copy in KP.

41. Entry for 12 July 1913, in Hermann Kallenbach's Diary for 1912–13, S. N. 33996, SAAA.

42. Gandhi, *An Autobiography*, Part IV, Chapter XXVI.

43. Uma Dhupelia-Mesthrie, *Gandhi's Prisoner? The Life of Gandhi's Son Manilal* (Cape Town: Kwela Books, 2004), pp. 106–11.

44. Millie Polak, *Mr Gandhi: The Man*, pp. 142–8.

45. See Manilal Gandhi, 'Memories of Gandhiji', *Indian Review*, March 1952. Manilal had – understandably – got the year slightly wrong. It was 1913, not 1912.

46. Prabhudas Gandhi, *My Childhood with Gandhiji*, pp. 116–17; Millie Polak, *Mr Gandhi: The Man*, p. 148; Dhupelia-Mesthrie, *Gandhi's Prisoner?*, p. 110.

47. *CWMG*, XII, pp. 79–81, 102–4, 137, 164–5, etc.

48. See Ravjibhai Patel, *The Making of the Mahatma*, trans. Abid Shamshi (Ahmedabad: Ravindra R. Patel, 1990), Chapter IX ('The Affectionate Healer').

49. *CWMG*, XII, p. 164.

50. Cordes to Gandhi, 11 December 1911, S. N. 5592, SAAA.

51. Cordes to Gandhi, *c.* July or August 1913, S. N. 5819, SAAA.

52. *CWMG*, XII, pp. 167–75.

53. Cf. *CWMG*, XII, pp. 183–6, 192–5.

20 BREAKING BOUNDARIES

1. The detailed figures are available in Surendra Bhana and Joy Brain, *Settling Down Roots: Indian Migrants in South Africa, 1860–1911* (Johannesburg: Witwatersrand University Press, 1990).

2. Millie G. Polak to V. S. Srinivasa Sastri, 22 July 1912, in V. S. Srinivasa Sastri Papers, 2nd instalment, NMML.

3. Undated news clipping (*c.* May 1909), entitled 'A Fresh Development / Indian Women's Meeting / Desire to be Imprisoned', in J. J. Doke Papers.

4. Cf. 'Native Women's Brave Stand', *IO*, 2 August 1913.

5. Gandhi to Kallenbach, 12 September 1913, *CWMG*, XCVI, p. 142.

6. Prabhudas Gandhi, *My Childhood with Gandhiji* (Ahmedabad: Navajivan Publishing House, 1957), p. 129.

7. Report in *NM*, 24 September 1913.

8. *CWMG*, XII, pp. 188–91; Ramadas Gandhi, *Sansmaran*, translated from Gujarati to Hindi by Shankar Joshi (Ahmedabad: Navajivan Press, 1970), pp. 59–62.

9. *CWMG*, XII, pp. 196–8, 204–6.

10. See *CWMG*, XII, pp. 209–10.

11. *CWMG*, XII, p. 215.

12. *Transvaal Leader*, 30 September 1913.

13. *Transvaal Leader*, 1 October 1913. The paper printed three letters alongside Gandhi's. L. W. Ritch archly noted that 'the concern of us Europeans should be not with whether their [the Indians'] campaign will succeed or fail, but rather, whether right is or is not on their side.' Kallenbach, like Gandhi, refuted the slur that the satyagrahis were mercenaries. It was 'an absolute falsehood that any monetary consideration has been received by them . . . beyond the mere maintenance for themselves and their families'. The third letter came from some forty merchants 'throughout the principal towns of the Transvaal', who stated 'that we are in full sympathy with the [satyagraha] movement, and that the merchants along with the others are contributing both men and money to the movement.'

14. *NM*, 2 October 1913.

15. Letter of 17 October 1913, *CWMG*, XII, p. 242.

16. The conversation took place on Smuts's farm, on 10 or 11 October, and is reported in H. J. Stanley to H. C. M. Lambert of the Colonial Office, 12 October 1913, in File 15/486A, vol. 897, GG, NASA.

17. *IO*, 15 October 1913.

18. As reported in *NM*, 13 October 1913.

19. Reports in *NM*, 17 and 18 October 1913.

20. *AC*, 5 July 1913.

21. Report in *Transvaal Leader*, 21 October 1913.

22. See *NM*, issues of 20, 21 and 23 October 1913; *CWMG*, XII, pp. 245–6.

23. Cf. reports in *NM*, 20 October 1913.

24. Gandhi, quoted in *Rand Daily Mail*, 23 October 1913.

25. See *NM*, 24 and 25 October 1913.

26. See Gillian Berning, ed., *Gandhi Letters: From Upper House to Lower House, 1906–1914* (Durban: Local History Museum, 1994), photos on pp. 34–6.

27. *CWMG*, XII, pp. 251–3.

28. Report in File 1389, L/P&J/6/1306, APAC/BL.

29. See Governor-General of South Africa to Secretary of State for the Colonies, 30 October 1913; clipping from the *Transvaal Leader*, 29 October 1913, both in L/PJ/6/1283, APAC/BL.

30. Note by W. H. Clark, Member, Commerce and Industry, Government of India, dated 20 March 1913, in File 1398, L/P&J/6/1235, APAC/BL.

31. Clipping from the *Transvaal Leader*, 30 October 1913, ibid. See also *AC*, issues of 27 September, 8, 15 and 22 November 1913, etc.

32. M. K. Gandhi, 'The Last Satyagraha Campaign: My Experience', *CWMG*, XII, pp. 508–19.

33. H. S. L. Polak, 'Passive Resistance Movement in South Africa', typescript composed *c*.1908–12, Mss. Afr. R. 125, Rhodes House Library, Oxford, p. 103.

34. *NM*, 27 October 1913.

35. Reports in *Rand Daily Mail*, 30 October 1910; *IO*, 5 November 1913.

36. Reports in *NM*, 30 and 31 October 1913.

37. Telegram dated 30 October 1913, in File No. 427, Gokhale Papers, NAI.

38. *NM*, 1 and 4 November 1913.

39. *NA*, 10 November 1913.

40. *Times of Natal*, 7 November 1913.

41. Governor-General of South Africa to Secretary of State for the Colonies, 6 November 1913, in CO 879/112/4, NAUK.

42. *NM*, 8 November 1913.

43. *Transvaal Leader*, 8 November 1913.

44. *NA*, 9 November 1911.

45. Montford Chamney, 'Mahatma Ghandi [*sic*] in the Transvaal', typescript dated *c*.1935, Mss. Eur. C. 859, APAC/BL.

46. M. K. Gandhi to the Resident Magistrate, Heidelburg, 10 November 1913, in File 4/572/13, vol. 181, JUS, NASA (this letter is not in *CWMG*).

47. *NA*, 12 and 14 November 1913.

48. *CWMG*, XII, pp. 263–4.

49. *CWMG*, XII, pp. 266–8; File 15/228, vol. 897, GG, NASA.

50. See H. S. L. Polak, 'A South African Reminiscence', *Indian Review*, October 1926.

51. Polak to Ampthill, 12 November 1913, written from Volksrust Prison, in CO 879/112/4, NAUK.

52. The letter is reproduced in its entirety in Isa Sarid and Christian Bartolf, *Hermann Kallenbach: Mahatma Gandhi's Friend in South Africa* (Berlin: Gandhi Informations Zentrum, 1997), pp. 34–61 (quote from p. 37).

53. 'The Leaders Sentenced', *IO*, 26 November 1913.

54. Gandhi to Millie Polak, 12 November 1913, *CWMG*, XCVI, p. 155.

55. Letter from Ritch in *Rand Daily Mail*, 21 October 1913.

56. Letter from Ritch in *Transvaal Leader*, 31 December 1913.

57. See Percy Binns, Magistrate's Office, Durban, to E. Gorges, Department of the Interior, 1 December 1913, in Natal Government Records (on microfilm), Reel 5 (Accession No. 2178), NMML.

58. Cf. press reports quoted in *IO*, 19 November 1913.

59. See Ashwin Desai and Goolam Vahed, *Inside Indenture: A South African Story, 1860–1914* (Durban: Madiba Publishers, 2007), pp. 147–57.

60. Maureen Swan, 'The 1913 Natal Indian Strike', *Journal of Southern African Studies*, 10:2 (1984).

61. Desai and Vahed, *Inside Indenture*, pp. 376–85.

62. Cf. correspondence in File 15/516, vol. 897, GG, NASA.

63. Reports in *NA*, 14, 15 and 16 November 1913; in *NM*, 14 November 1913.

64. *NM*, 17 November 1913.

65. See enclosure no. 8 to Governor-General of South Africa to Secretary of State for the Colonies, 20 November 1913, in CO 879/112/4, NAUK.

66. Reports in *NM*, 18 November 1913.

67. 'Report on the Indian Strike in the Division of Durban', dated 3 December 1913, in File 4/572/13, vol. 203, JUS, NASA.

68. Telegrams from General Lukin to 'Defence, Pretoria', dated 21, 25 and 27 November, ibid.

69. See Heather Hughes, *First President: A Life of John L. Dube, Founding President of the ANC* (Auckland Park, South Africa: Jacana, 2011), pp. 178–9.

70. 'Dr. Abdurahman and Passive Resistance', *IO*, 3 December 1913.

71. *NA*, 20 November, 2 and 8 December 1913.

72. 'The Indian Menace: Question of Natal's Future', *NM*, 26 November 1913. Henderson was a protégé of Harry Escombe, whose speeches he edited for publication.

73. *Transvaal Leader*, 22 November 1913, clipping in CO 879/112/4, NAUK. A more emotional defence was sent by Millie Graham Polak to the *Natal Advertiser*, which declined to publish it, on the grounds that among the matters she had mentioned were some (presumably the cases against her husband, Kallenbach and Gandhi) which were *sub judice*. See *NA*, 22 November 1913.

74. Quoted in *Transvaal Leader*, 8 December 1913, clipping in Add. Mss. 46001, BL.

75. See A. H. West to G. K. Gokhale, undated, *c.* 24 November 1913, in File No. 242, Part I, Gokhale Papers, NAI.

76. Gokhale to Mrs Polak, 17 November 1913, ibid.

77. See File 202, L/P&J/6/1295, APAC/BL.

78. Cf. reports in L/P&J/R/5/118, APAC/BL.

79. Anon., *M. K. Gandhi: A Study* (Madras: Ganesh and Co., 1913).

80. C. Rajagopalachari, ed., *Mr Gandhi's Jail Experiences: Told by Himself* (Salem: T. Adinarayana Cetti, 1913). Rajagolachari was to become a close companion of Gandhi in the freedom movement in India.

81. A copy of the play is in File 1041, L/P&J/6/1302, APAC/BL. The playwright (whose name, alas, has not come down to posterity) may have attended some of Henry Polak's talks in South India. He seems to have been reading the journals *Indian Review* and *Indian Opinion*; and perhaps various

biographies of Gandhi as well, thus to extol the patriotism, the principled non-violence and the spirit of sacrifice of a successful lawyer who had embraced poverty and public service.

82. Bhawani Dayal, *Dakshin Africa ké Satyagraha ka Itihas* (Indore: Saraswati Sadan, 1916), pp. 53–7.

83. For more details on these meetings, see documents and clippings in L/PJ/6/1284, APAC/BL; *NA*, 21 November 1913; B Proceedings No. 29 for December 1913, Department of Commerce and Industry (Emigration Branch), NAI.

84. Cf. correspondence in File No. 242, Part II, Gokhale Papers, NAI (emphasis in original).

85. Tagore to Gokhale, 18 November 1913, in File No. 242, Part I, Gokhale Papers, NAI.

86. Tagore to Gokhale, 9 December 1913, in File No. 547, Gokhale Papers, NAI.

87. The Bishop of Madras, quoted in *Speeches and Writings of M. K. Gandhi: With an Introduction by Mr C. F. Andrews, a Tribute by Mr G. A. Natesan, a Biographical Sketch by Mr H. S. L. Polak* (2nd edn: Madras: G. A. Natesan and Co., 1918), Appendix III, p. x.

88. *CWMG*, XII, pp. 602–3; Robert A. Huttenback, *Gandhi in South Africa* (Ithaca, NY: Cornell University Press, 1971), pp. 319–21.

89. K. Hariharan to Gokhale, 11 December 1913; A. E. Lall to Gokhale, 29 November 1913, both in File No. 242, Part II, Gokhale Papers, NAI.

90. Mehta, quoted in *Speeches and Writings of M. K. Gandhi*, Appendix III, p. xiv.

91. Gandhi to Devi West, 14 December 1913, *CWMG*, XII, pp. 269–71.

92. D. M. Manilal [Manilal Doctor], Barrister-at-Law, Suva, Fiji, to Lord Gladstone, 30 December 1913, in File 15/652, vol. 899, GG, NASA.

93. See correspondence in File 15/543, vol. 897, GG, NASA.

94. *NA*, 19 December 1913.

95. *NA*, 20 December 1913; *NM*, 22 December 1913.

96. *CWMG*, XII, pp. 274–7.

97. Henry Polak to his family in England (addressed as 'Dear Folks'), Durban, 31 December 1913, Mss. Brit. Emp. S 372/2, Rhodes House Library, Oxford.

98. *NM*, 22 December 1913.

99. *NM*, 23 December 1913.

100. Cf. M. K. Gandhi, *Satyagraha in South Africa*, translated from the Gujarati by Valji Govindji Desai (2nd edn, 1950; reprint, Ahmedabad: Navjivan Press, 1972), p. 258.

101. Telegram dated 23 December 1913, in File No. 242, Part II, Gokhale Papers, NAI.

102. See correspondence in *CWMG*, XII, pp. 277–81, 599, 283–4, 286, 289, 295–6, 301–5; and in File No. 242, Parts I and II, Gokhale Papers, NAI.

103. *NM*, 30 December 1913.

104. See Hope Hay Hewison, *Hedge of Wild Almonds: South Africa, the Pro-Boers and the Quaker Conscience, 1890–1910* (London: James Curry, 1989), pp. 187–95.

105. Gandhi to Emily Hobhouse, 5 January 1914, copy in E. S. Reddy Papers, NMML (this letter is not in *CWMG*).

106. Emily Hobhouse to Smuts, 29 December 1913, in W. K. Hancock and Jean van der Poel, *Selections from the Smuts Papers*, III: *June 1910 – November 1918* (Cambridge: Cambridge University Press, 1966), pp. 152–6. On the Hobhouse–Smuts friendship, see W. K. Hancock: *Smuts*, I: *The Sanguine Years, 1870–1919* (Cambridge: Cambridge University Press, 1962), especially pp. 179–88, 282–6.

107. *NA*, 30 December 1913.

108. Gokhale to Robertson, 31 December 1913, in File No. 242, Part II, Gokhale Papers, NAI.

109. *CWMG*, XII, p. 311.

21   FAREWELL TO AFRICA

1. Unlike some other figures in Indian history, C. F. Andrews has been well served by his biographers. There are three excellent studies, each focusing on a different aspect of his life, work and friendships: Benarsidas Chaturvedi and Marjorie Sykes, *Charles Freer Andrews: A Narrative* (London: George Allen and Unwin, 1949); Hugh Tinker, *The Ordeal of Love: C. F. Andrews and India* (Delhi: Oxford University Press, 1979); and Daniel O'Connor, *Gospel, Raj, and Swaraj: The Missionary Years of C. F. Andrews (1904–14)* (Frankfurt: Peter Lang, 1990).

2. Andrews to Gokhale, 24 January 1906, File No. 11, Gokhale Papers, NAI.

3. Gokhale to West, 12 December 1913, File No. 242, Part II, Gokhale Papers, NAI.

4. Gokhale to Robertson, 31 December 1913, in File No. 242, Part I, Gokhale Papers, NAI.

5. *NM*, 5 January 1914.

6. 'Arrival of Mr Andrews and Mr Pearson', *IO*, 7 January 1914.

7. Ibid.

8. *CWMG*, XII, p. 316.

9. *CWMG*, XII, pp. 317–18.

10. Gokhale to Gandhi, 26 December 1913, File No. 242, Part II, Gokhale Papers, NAI.

11. Harilal to Gokhale, 13 January 1914, File No. 242, Part II, Gokhale Papers, NAI.

12. J. C. Smuts to Lord Gladstone, 6 January 1914, in File 15/622, vol. 899, GG, NASA.

13. Clipping from the *Pretoria News*, in File 15/640, vol. 899, GG, NASA.

14. As recalled in Andrews to Gokhale, 30 January 1914, in File No. 242, Part I, Gokhale Papers, NAI.

15. Lord Gladstone, Governor-General of South Africa, to Lewis Harcourt, Secretary of State for the Colonies, 14 January 1914, in File 15/640, vol. 899, GG, NASA.

16. *CWMG*, XII, pp. 324–6,

17. *CWMG*, XII, pp. 609–10.

18. See File 15/647A, vol. 899, GG, NASA.

19. Andrews to Gokhale, 30 January 1914, in File No. 242, Part I, Gokhale Papers, NAI, emphasis in original.

20. *IO*, issues of 14, 21 and 28 January 1914.

21. As reported in Gandhi to Gokhale, 18 February 1914, *CWMG*, XII, pp. 353–4.

22. *Rabindranath Tagore: A Lecture by the Rev. C. F. Andrews of Delhi* (Cape Town: Cape Times Limited, 1914), copy in Mss. Eur. D. 1238/5, APAC/BL.

23. Clippings from *Cape Times*, dated 23 February 1914, in File 15/658, vol. 899, GG, NASA.

24. Andrews to Gandhi, 26 February 1914, S. N. 5943, NGM.

25. Mehta to Gandhi, 14 February 1914, S. N. 6034, SAAA. Posted from Burma, the letter would have arrived in Durban towards the end of February or in early March.

26. See *IO*, 5 April 1913.

27. Letter dated 27 February 1914, *CWMG*, XII, pp. 360–61.

28. Gandhi to Kallenbach, 25 March 1914, *CWMG*, XCVI, p. 165.

29. See Gandhi to Kallenbach, 6 March 1914 (not in the *CWMG*), KP.

30. *CWMG*, XII, pp. 367–9.

31. Letter dated 22 March 1914, *CWMG*, XII, p. 395.

32. Gandhi to Kallenbach, 15 March 1914, *CWMG*, XCVI, p. 175.

33. *CWMG*, XII, pp. 378–80.

34. In late February, Gandhi wrote to Kallenbach that 'my eldest brother who used always to go strongly against me has now completely changed and repents of his past letters and thinks I have not discredited the family after all as he used to think before. His one wish is to see me before he dies'. Now, when the news of Laxmidas's death came, Gandhi wrote again, saying: 'What a passionate wish it was on his part to meet me! And for me I was hurrying everything on so that I could go to India with the quickest despatch and fall down at his feet and nurse him. But it was not to be'. Letters of 25 February and 10 March, *CWMG*, XCVI, pp. 165, 173.

35. *CWMG*, XII, pp. 380–83.

36. News clipping dated 25 March 1914, S. N. 5949, SAAA.

37. See *Report of the Indian Enquiry Commission* (Cape Town: Government Printers, 1914).

38. *IO*, 25 March 1914, in *CWMG*, XII, pp. 396-9.

39. *Sadhva*, 24 July 1914, translated excerpt in L/R/5/119, APAC/BL.

40. Gandhi to Gokhale, 6 May 1914, *CWMG*, XII, p. 414.

41. Andrews to Gandhi, 5 April 1914, S. N. 5956, NGM.

42. Gandhi to Kallenbach, 12 April 1914, *CWMG*, XCVI, pp. 181-2.

43. Gandhi to Kallenbach, 5 May 1914, *CWMG*, XCVI, p. 186.

44. Gandhi to Kallenbach, 18 May 1914, *CWMG*, XCVI, p. 190.

45. See 'Correspondence Relating to the Indian Relief Act, 1914', copy in E. S. Reddy Papers, NMML.

46. See correspondence in File 15/708, vol. 900, GG, NASA.

47. *CWMG*, XII, pp. 436-7.

48. Gandhi to Gokhale, letters of 5 June and 1 July 1914, *CWMG*, XII, pp. 422, 440.

49. *CWMG*, XII, pp. 445-7.

50. *CWMG*, XII, pp. 454-9.

51. See File 1305, L/P&J/6/1305, APAC/BL.

52. *IO*, 22 July 1914.

53. *CWMG*, XII, pp. 463-72.

54. *Transvaal Leader*, 15 July 1914.

55. This paragraph is based on materials supplied by the Gandhi scholar Ian Desai, who found these addresses in the basement of the M. J. Library in Ahmedabad.

56. *CWMG*, XII, pp. 472-5.

57. A copy of the invitation is in the Kallenbach Papers, Haifa.

58. *CWMG*, XII, pp. 486-95.

59. *CWMG*, XII, p. 497.

60. *CWMG*, XII, pp. 459-60. Gandhi's memory may have been at fault here. Other sources say Chamney was accompanied by a 'posse' of police – at least several, not one, constable; but still a small number when confronting more than 2,000 strikers. The date of the Pretoria meeting is wrongly given as 10 July in *CWMG* – it was in fact held on the 16th.

61. Her father, Solomon Schechter, had rescued a huge cache of old Hebrew documents from the attic of a Cairo synagogue – known as the 'Geniza' documents, these were then passed on by him to Cambridge University.

62. Baruch Hirson, *The Cape Town Intellectuals: Ruth Schechter and Her Circle, 1907-1954* (Johannesburg: Witwatersrand University Press, 2001), pp. 3, 13, 15, 37-8; Enid Alexander, *Morris Alexander: A Biography* (Cape Town: Juta and Co., 1953), p. 118.

63. The account of the Cape Town farewell is based on clippings in File 15/730, vol. 900, GG, NASA.

64. Polak to Gandhi, 14 July 1914, S. N. 6006, NGM.

65. *CWMG*, XII, p. 507.

66. The telegrams are all in 'Gandhi–Kallenbach Correspondence', vol. IV, NAI. (The first three volumes of this correspondence, mostly letters to Gandhi by Kallenbach, are published in *CWMG*, XCVI. The fourth volume, on which these paragraphs are based, consists of these unpublished telegrams, lying in the NAI.)

67. Hobhouse to Smuts, 23 April 1914, in W. K. Hancock and Jean van der Poel, *Selections from the Smuts Papers*, III: *June 1910–November 1918* (Cambridge: Cambridge University Press, 1966), pp. 173–4 (emphasis in original). Posted in the last week of April, the letter would have reached Smuts sometime in the middle of May.

68. Smuts to Robertson, 21 August 1914, ibid., pp. 190–91.

22 HOW THE MAHATMA WAS MADE

1. Source notes have not been provided in this concluding chapter for remarks by Gandhi (and others) that have also been quoted earlier in the book.

2. *IO*, 4 June 1906.

3. This encounter presaged the events of the 1930s and 1940s, when Gandhi led the movement for Indian independence, and Churchill, both in and out of office, campaigned vigorously for India to remain in the Empire and for Indians to be for ever subject to British rule.

4. H. S. L. Polak, 'Passive Resistance Movement in South Africa', typescript composed *c.*1908–12, Mss. Afr. R. 125, Rhodes House Library, Oxford, pp. 105, 109–10.

5. *Harijan*, 27 January 1940, in *CWMG*, LXXI, p. 131.

6. The resonant phrase in quotes is that of Mukul Kesavan. See his *Secular Common Sense* (Delhi: Penguin India, 2001).

7. *The Miscellaneous Writings of the Late Hon'ble Mr Justice M. G. Ranade* (Bombay: The Manoranjan Press, 1915), p. 193.

8. *CWMG*, LVIII, pp. 188–9.

9. Sonja Schlesin to Gandhi, 25 December 1915, S. N. 6250, SAAA. In this letter, Miss Schlesin also wrote that 'I think, if I took up Law seriously, I should want to be a Consulting Barrister – a Specialist in some special branch of law'. Sadly, she wasn't able to fulfil that long-standing ambition, instead becoming headmistress of a girls' school in the Transvaal.

10. A. Chessel Piquet, 'Indian Women and the Struggle', *IO*, 1 February 1908.

11. Writing in 1931, by which time Gandhi was an acknowledged 'Mahatma' and had just been chosen *Time Magazine*'s 'Man of the Year', Millie Polak called him a 'great and loving man, who had shown to me and mine an affection that transcended race and sex and time'. (*Mr Gandhi the Man*,

London: George Allen and Unwin, 1931, p. 14). She modestly omitted to add the part she had played in the broadening of Gandhi's world-view.

12. See Edgar Snow, *Red Star Over China* (New York: Grove Press, 1968), p. 94.

13. Liu Xiabao, *No Enemies, No Hatred: Selected Essays and Poems*, ed. Perry Link, Tienchi Martin-Liao and Liu Xia (Cambridge, Mass.: Harvard University Press, 2012), p. 288.

14. Joseph J. Doke, *M. K. Gandhi: An Indian Patriot in South Africa* (London: The London Indian Chronicle, 1909), pp. 41f.

15. Kallenbach to Chhaganlal, 29 July 1911, S. N. 5582, SAAA.

16. A latter-day Gujarati reformer writes that 'for traders, freedom means nothing; what matters is that they should be able to carry on with their trade peacefully. They prefer to buy their way to peace rather than fight for any principle, much less the principle of freedom.' Asghar Ali Engineer, *A Living Faith: My Quest for Peace, Harmony and Social Change* (Hyderabad: Orient BlackSwan 2011), p. 44.

17. J. H. M. Gool to Gandhi, 23 January 1897, quoted in Baruch Hirson, *The Cape Town Intellectuals: Ruth Schechter and her Circle, 1907–1954* (Johannesburg: Witwatersrand University Press, 2001), p. 42.

18. These words were prophetic. The Partition riots of 1946–8 caused several million deaths in the Indian subcontinent, the result of unspeakable brutalities by Hindu, Muslim and Sikh rioters. It took Gandhi's martyrdom in January 1948 for the rioters to realize the extent of the barbarism they had unleashed. The revulsion against Gandhi's death led to an immediate cessation of hostilities, prompting a period of communal peace in India that lasted a decade and a half.

19. J. M. Upadhyaya, ed., *Mahatma Gandhi as a Student* (New Delhi: Publications Division, 1965), Introduction.

20. E. M. S. Namboodiripad, *The Mahatma and the Ism* (first published 1958; 2nd edn, Calcutta, National Book Agency, 1981), pp. 11–12. The book was based on articles published in the Communist Party's journal *New Age* in 1955–6.

21. Josiah Oldfield, 'My Friend Gandhi', in Chandrashanker Shukla, ed., *Reminiscences of Gandhiji* (Bombay: Vora and Co., 1951), p. 188.

22. Letter to the editor from L. W. Ritch, in the *Transvaal Leader*, 5 December 1912.

23. *The Times*, 14 August 1911.

Index

A NOTE ABOUT THE AUTHOR

Ramachandra Guha has previously taught at Yale and Stanford Universities, the University of Oslo, the Indian Institute of Science and the London School of Economics. His books include a pioneering environmental history, an award-winning social history of cricket and the award-winning *India After Gandhi*. He writes regularly on social and political issues for the British and Indian press, including columns in *The Telegraph* and the *Hindustan Times,* and his work has also appeared in *The New York Times*.